ORGANIZATION AND PEOPLE

Readings, Cases, and Exercises
in Organizational Behavior

THE WEST SERIES IN MANAGEMENT

Consulting Editors

Don Hellreigel — Texas A & M
John W. Slocum, Jr. — Southern Methodist University

Aldag and Brief	*Managing Organizational Behavior*
Burback	*Personnel Management: Cases and Exercises*
Costley and Todd	*Human Relations in Organizations, 2d Ed.*
Daft	*Organization Theory and Design*
Daft and Dahlen	*Organization Theory: Cases and Applications*
Downey, Hellriegel, and Slocum	*Organizational Behavior: A Reader*
Hellriegel, Slocum, and Woodman	*Organizational Behavior: 3rd Ed.*
Hitt, Middlemist, and Mathis	*Management: Concepts and Effective Practices*
Hrebiniak	*Complex Organizations*
Huse	*Organization Development and Change, 2d Ed.*
Huse	*Management, 2d Ed.*
Kelley and Whatley	*Personnel Management in Action: Skill Building Experiences, 3rd Ed.*
Matthis and Jackson	*Personnel: Contemporary Perspectives and Applications, 3d Ed.*
Morris and Sashkin	*Organization Behavior in Action: Skill and Building Experiences*
Newport	*Supervisory Management: Tools and Techniques*
Ritchie and Thompson	*Organizations and People, 3rd Ed.*
Schuler	*Effective Personnel Management*
Schuler	*Personnel and Human Resource Management, 2d Ed.*
Schuler, Dalton, and Huse	*Case Problems in Management, 2d Ed.*
Schuler and Youngblood	*Readings in Personnel and Human Resource Management, 2d Ed.*
Veiga and Yanouzas	*The Dynamics of Organization Theory: Gaining a Macro Perspective, 2d Ed.*

ORGANIZATION AND PEOPLE

Readings, Cases, and Exercises in Organizational Behavior

THIRD EDITION

J. B. Ritchie and Paul Thompson

Brigham Young University

WEST PUBLISHING COMPANY

St. Paul ☐ *New York* ☐ *Los Angeles* ☐ *San Francisco*

Photo Credits:
George Gardner   163
Jeffrey Grosscup   164, 165 and 166

CARTOONS by MALCOLM HANCOCK

Library of Congress Cataloging in Publication Data
Main entry under title:

Organizations and people.

   Includes index.
   1. Organizational behavior — Addresses, essays,
lectures. 2. Management — Addresses, essays, lectures.
I. Ritchie, J. B. II. Thompson, Paul, 1938 —
HD58.7.0747 1984   658.4   83-25969
ISBN: 0-314-77785-7

ACKNOWLEDGMENTS

(In numerical Table of Contents order)

Selection No.

1   Corporate culture: The hard-to-choose values that spell success or failure. Reprinted from the October 27, 1980 issue of *Business Week by special permission,* © 1980 by McGraw-Hill, Inc., New York, NY 10020. All rights reserved.

2   We need a nation of scholar-leaders (J.B. Ritchie) Reprinted courtesy of *Exchange,* a publication of the Brigham Young University School of Management, Fall 1980.

3   The first job dilemma: An appraisal of why college graduates change jobs and what can be done about it (Edgar H. Schein) Reprinted from *Psychology Today* Magazine, Copyright © 1968, Ziff-Davis Publishing Company.

4   A conversation with Peter F. Drucker: Or the psychology of managing management (Mary Harrington Hall) Reprinted from *Psychology Today* Magazine, Copyright © 1968, Ziff-Davis Publishing Company.

6   Washington Elementary School This case was prepared by Hal B. Gregersen and Judyth Peterson under the direction of Paul H Thompson, Brigham Young University.

8   Phantoms fill Boy Scout rolls (David Young) Reprinted, courtesy of the *Chicago Tribune,* Sunday, June 9, 1974.

9   Scouting motto forgotten in signup drive Reprinted, courtesy of the *Chicago Tribune,* Monday, June 10, 1974.

13   On the folly of rewarding A, while hoping for B (Steven Kerr) Reprinted with the permission of the publisher and author from the *Academy of Management Journal,* Volume 18, No. 4 (1975), pp. 769-783.

14   That urge to achieve (David C. McClelland) Reprinted by permission from *Think* magazine, published by IBM copyright 1966 by International Business Machines Corporation.

15   Behavior modification on the bottom line (W. Clay Hamner and Ellen P. Hamner) Reprinted, by permission of the publisher, from *Organizational Dynamics,* Spring 1976, © 1976 by AMACOM, a division of American Management Associations. All rights reserved.

16   Motivation and Performance — A diagnostic approach (J. Richard Hackman, Edward E. Lawler III). Reprinted by permissions of the authors from ''Perspectives on Behavior in Organizations'', Second Edition, 1983.

17   A new strategy for job enrichment (J.

Richard Hackman, Greg Oldham, Robert Jansen, and Kenneth Purdy) © 1975 by the Regents of the University of California. reprinted/adapted/condensed from *California Management Review,* Volume 17, No. 4, pp. 57-71 by permission of the Regents.

18   Tear down the pyramids (Paul H. Thompson) Reprinted from *Exchange,* a publication of the Brigham Young University School of Management, 730 TNRB, Provo, Utah 84602.

19   New light on adult life cycles (*Time*) Copyright 1975 Time Inc. All rights reserved. Reprinted by permission from Time.

20   On wasting time (James Michener) Reprinted by permission of William Morris Agency, Inc. on behalf of the author. Copyright by James A. Michener.

21   Motivators — America's new glamour figures (Jeannye Thornton) Reprinted from *U.S. News & World Report,* Copyright, 1982, U.S. News & World Report, Inc.

22   How to make an intelligent decision (Robert Heilbroner) Reprinted from *Think* magazine, copyright © 1960. Reproduced by permission of Robert L. Heilbroner.

23   Working connections (Reba L. Keele and Christine Russell) This article appeared in the April 1982 *Network* magazine and is reprinted with permission of Network Publications.

25   The slab yard slowdown This case was prepared by Hal B. Gregersen under the direction of Paul H. Thompson, Brigham Young University.

28   Motivational style exercise Copyright © 1969 by McBer and Company, 137 Newbury St., Boston, Mass. This Questionnaire is not to be reproduced or copied without the express written permission of McBer and Company and is available from McBer and Company.

32   Suppose we took groups seriously... (Harold Leavitt). Selection from "Man and Work in Society" Edited by Eugene L.

Cass and Frederick G. Zimmer. Copyright © 1975 by Van Nostrand Reinhold Company Inc. Reprinted by permission of publisher.

33   Assets and liabilities in group problem solving: The need for an integrative function (Norman R.F. Maier) From *Psychological Review,* 1967, pp. 239-249. Copyright 1967 by the American Psychological Association. Reprinted by permission.

*The research reported in the following reading was supported by Grant No. MH-02704 from the United States Public Health Service. Grateful acknowledgment is made for the constructive criticism of Melba Colgrove, Junie Janzen, Mara Julius, and James Thurber.

34   The Abilene Paradox: The management of agreement (Jerry B. Harvey) Excerpted, by permission of the publisher, from "The Abilene Paradox: The management of agreement" by Harvey, pp 63-80, *Organizational Dynamics,* Summer 1974 © 1974 by AMACOM, a division of American Management Associations, New York. All rights reserved.

35   Intergroup problems in organizations (Edgar H. Schein) Schein, *Organizational Psychology,* 2d ed., © 1970, Englewood Cliffs, New Jersey.

36   Defensive communication (Jack R. Gibb) Reprinted from the *Journal of Communication,* Vol. 11, No. 3 (1961), pp. 141-148, Reproduced with permission of the *Journal of Communication* and the International Communication Association.

37   Why should my conscience bother me? (Kermit Vandivier) "Why Should My Conscience Bother Me? by Vandivier, from *In The Name of Profit* by Heilbroner, copyright © 1972 by Doubleday & Company, Inc. Used by permission of the publisher.

38   Group observer instructions Written by Hal B. Gregersen, University of California, Irvine.

39   Eight tips on holding a staff meeting (Gary Blake) Reprint permission *Pace*

magazine, the inflight magazine for Piedmont Airlines.

48 Workingman and management (Eric Hoffer) "Workingman and Management" from *The Ordeal of Change* (1963) by Hoffer. Copyright 1954 by Eric Hoffer. By permission of Harper & Row, Publishers, Inc.

49 The manager's job: Folklore and fact (Henry Mintzberg) Reprinted by permission of *Harvard Business Review,* "The manager's job: folklore and fact" by Mintzberg (July-August 1975). Copyright © 1975 by the President and Fellows of Harvard College; all rights reserved.

50 Power, dependence, and effective management (John P. Kotter) Reprinted by permission of *Harvard Business Review,* "Power, dependence, and effective management" by Kotter (*HBR* July-August 1977). Copyright © 1977 by the President and Fellows of Harvard College: all rights reserved.

51 Participative management: Quality vs. quantity (Raymond E. Miles and J.B. Ritchie) © 1971 by The Regents of the University of California. Reprinted from *California Management Review,* Vol. 13, No. 4, pp. 48-56, by permission of the Regents.

52 How to choose a leadership pattern (Robert Tannenbaum and Warren H. Schmidt) Reprinted from the *Harvard Business Review,* May-June 1973. © 1973 by the President and Fellows of Harvard College; all rights reserved.

53 Managing your manager: The effective subordinate (Norman C. Hill and Paul H. Thompson) Reprinted from Fall/Winter 1978 *Exchange,* a publication of the Brigham Young University School of Management, 730 TNRB, Provo, Utah 84602.

57 How Iacocca won the big one Reprinted from the December 19, 1970 issue of *Business Week* by special permission, © 1970 by McGraw-Hill, Inc. All rights reserved.

58 Upheaval in the House of Ford Copyright 1978 Time Inc. All rights reserved. Reprinted by permission from *Time.*

60 Fables for management: The ill-informed walrus Reprinted by permission of the publisher from *Management Review,* October 1961. © 1961 by American Management Associations, Inc.

62 Leadership exercise Reprinted from: J. William Pfeiffer and John E. Jones, (Eds), *A Handbook of Structured Experiences for Human Relations Training,* Vol. I (Rev.), San Diego, CA: University Associates, Inc., 1974. Used with permission.

64 New era for management (*Business Week*). "Reprinted from the April 25, 1983 issue of *Business Week* by special permission, © 1983 by McGraw-Hill, Inc."

65 Planned change (William Dyer) From Dyer, W.G., *Insight to Impact,* pp. 71-76. Copyright 1972 by Brigham Young University Press. Reprinted by permission.

66 Choosing strategies for change (John P. Kotter and Leonard A. Schlesinger) Reprinted by permission of *Harvard Business Review,* "Choosing strategies for change" by Kotter and Schlesinger (*HBR,* March-April 1979). Copyright © 1979 by the President and Fellows of Harvard College; all rights reserved.

67 An introduction to organization development (John J. Sherwood) Copyright © 1971 by the American Psychological Association, Inc. Reprinted by permission. Washington, D.C. All rights reserved. The Experimental Publication System, Issue No. 11.

68 Hard hats in the boardroom: New trends in workers' participation (Warner Woodworth) Copyright © 1983 by Woodworth. Reprinted by permission.

69 A Billion Levi's later (Ed Cray). Reprinted from Politics Today. Reprinted by permission of author.

70 Beyond tokenism: Women as true corporate peers (Eleanor Brantley Schwartz and James J. Rago, Jr.) Reprinted by

PREFACE

Organizational behavior is both a very old and a very new field. It is old in the sense that people have been behaving in organizations for a very long time. In fact, we suspect that some of the earliest debates in primitive society had to do with the advantages and disadvantages of different types of organizations. But organizational behavior is a *new* field of study. In spite of the traditional and pervasive nature of organizations, the formal development of an area of study entitled *organizational behavior* is still in its infancy. Sociology, psychology, industrial relations, and various programs in administration (business, education, public, hospital) have probed facets of the behavior of people in organizations, but only recently have we attempted to bring it all together in a single field of study.

The synthesis is important. In most societies, but especially in those in an advanced state of industrialization, people are members of many different organizations — family, social, political, religious, athletic, military, educational, service, economic. And they must relate to even more, all of them competing for time, money, loyalty — perhaps even people's fundamental values. But, although some memberships are mutually advantageous, others produce severe role conflicts, and coping with these multiple, and often conflicting, roles occupies increasing amounts of each person's energy. More and more, individual well-being is affected by the quality of organizational relationships, and that quality depends largely on the degree of understanding of increasingly complex organizations.

Students are taught these relationships in several ways. Some books in the field present a large number of readings, primarily from academic journals. Others contain many case studies and a few theoretical articles. Still others include numerous exercises designed to increase student involvement. As the title indicates, this book contains all three: readings, cases, and exercises. We recognize that for a given group of students (and instructors) one approach may be more useful than another in understanding a given concept. Furthermore, for most students a combination of approaches is better that one exclusive technique. We have followed the maxim that "a change of medium reduces the tedium." We feel that a textbook in organizational behavior need not be boring or extremely complex for students to learn a great deal from it. A course should not only promote optimum learning, but it should also be interesting and fun. Our personal experience with the material has convinced us that it really does help students enjoy the course as well as understand the subject.

The readings are intended to provide the students with a wide variety of perspectives regarding the day-to-day operations of organizations. They were selected from such diverse sources as *Time, Black Enterprise, Psychology Today, Harvard Business Review,* and *Organizational Dynamics.* This affords flexibility. The instructor can explore and develop a variety of concepts from articles written on different levels of complexity. The theoretical models can be used in analysis of organizational phenomena, and the empirical evidence can be analyzed, debated, and extended. Interviews offer provoking shotgun comments on issues; other readings contain prescriptions for specific problems. Finally, some contributions are fun, or frightening, depending on your viewpoint. Breadth, rather that depth, is clearly our intent.

The cases also represent a spectrum of situations from which students or instructors can choose a setting appropriate for analysis or application of various organizational concepts. Some cases are simply undisguised accounts of reports appearing in newspapers or magazines. These incidents, often poignant and familiar, pose problems of ethics and strategy and are therefore fuel for lively discussions. Other cases focus more carefully on an organizational issue. Although the issues are real, the organizations' identities are disguised.

Our experience with cases in introductory courses suggests that students learn more if they can move back and forth between a theory in an article and a problem in a case. They need both teaching tools if they are going to develop skill in identification and analysis of problems, as well as in development of plans for dealing with those problems.

The exercises add still another dimension. For example, students will experience some of the frustrations and competitive feelings that commonly arise in group decision making. Since people often find it easier to discuss concepts and theories than to apply them, involvement in exercises and role plays can help them to achieve certain introspective and applied skill objectives as well as various theoretical insights. There seems to be a trend toward designing courses that use such activities almost exclusively. But, while such exercises can be very useful tools, we advocate a more balanced approach, using a variety of vehicles rather than the singular approach.

In recent years students have expressed an increasing interest in acquiring behavioral skills that will help them to function as supervisors or managers. In the third edition we have responded by adding materials that focus specifically on the development of management skills, including: meeting management, networking, decision making, and performance appraisal. The new materials have been very popular with our students and we're confident that they are an important addition to the book.

The book is organized into five sections with introductory comments for each section. We have intended that these comments be used in the transition between sections of a course. The materials in the book which come from other sources are referenced in the Acknowledgement section on page 000. The first section, an introduction to the book, raises issues that are explored more thoroughly in what follows. The second section focuses on individuals and on issues such as motivation, development, and decision making. Section 3 presents material on people in groups of two or more: interpersonal, group, and intergroup. Leadership is the focus in Section 4. Section 5 turns to the future and some of the environmental forces pressing for change in organizations.

Our focus is not on a single type of organization, but, because business organizations are dominant in society, they are the subject in a majority of the discussions. Also, while our primary goal is a broad understanding of organizations in general, a corollary effect is the preparation of individuals for management and leadership roles.

A major issue in this collection is the confrontation between organizational pressures and human values. Current journals are replete with evidence of immoral and unethical use of organizations by members at the top and the bottom of the hierarchy. We feel that at all levels in all types of organizations there is an urgent need for increased honesty and integrity and, most important, increased development of the individual.

Our assumption is that this material will be used to augment an introductory course at either a graduate or an undergraduate level. We feel that the variety of perspectives raised and issues discussed will enrich any introductory course dealing with the phenomena of organizations and people.

Although it is difficult to mention each person who has contributed to this collection, we want to acknowledge the efforts of the following graduate students: Ross Davidson, Maureen Fisher, Hal Gregersen, Mike Linford, Gordon Meyer, Kerry Patterson, Lois Ritchie, Mary Delamar-Schaefer, Tim Shurtleff, Mike Silva, and Randy Stott. In a more general sense, however, the most significant contribution has come from the thousands of students in our introductory courses in organizational behavior at Harvard, Berkeley, Michigan, Stanford, and Brigham Young.

J.B. Ritchie
Paul H. Thompson

CONTENTS

3 Differing viewpoints on the impact of groups 173

4 Some Comments on the challenge of leadership 61

CROSS-REFERENCE GUIDE

The primary purpose of this Cross-Reference Guide is to provide a link between a variety of topical areas in organizational behavior and the material in this book. An additional purpose is to suggest the breadth of the field by referencing additional material. The items mentioned, of course, are only illustrative (an extensive list would defy reproduction), but they indicate the diverse avenues which might be used in better understanding organizational behavior. Fiction, non-fiction, and films all provide a useful vehicle for exploring topics which are illuminated by the artist's sensitivity in addition to the researcher's measurements.

*(M) Instructional Movie   (A) Article
(MH) Hollywood movie   (P) Play
(B) Book   (SS) Short story
(N) Novel

Topic	Articles	Page	Skills/Cases/Exercises	Page	Related materials outside book
Ethics	A conversation with Peter F. Drucker	26	Phantoms fill Boy Scout rolls	48	(A) Blowing the Whistle on Corporate Misconduct, D. Clutterbuck, *International Management*, Jan. 1980; (A) Corporate Responsibility, B. Moskal, *Industry Week*, July 26, 1982. (M) The Lottery; (M) Obedience; (M) Moral Development; (M) Whether to Tell the Truth; (N) *All the President's Men*, C. Bernstein and B. Woodward; (A) "Stimulus/Response: Social Scientists Ought to Stop Lying," D. Warwick, *Psychology Today*, Feb. 75.
	"Why should my conscience bother me?"	215	An ancient tale	56	
	A billion Levi's later	413	Hural Corporation	348	
Groups	Suppose we took groups seriously. . . .	176	The Tinkertoy exercise	56	(M) Social Animal; (M) Group Dynamics: "Groupthing"; (M) Group Pressure; (MH) Cool Hand Luke; (MH-N) *Lord of the Flies*, W. Golding; (A) "Productivity and Group Success: Team Spirit Vs. the Individual," A. Zander, *Psychology Today*, Nov. 74.
	The Abilene Paradox	194	Group observers instructions	213	
	"Why should my conscience bother me?"[11]	215	8 tips on holding a staff meeting	235	
			Claremont Instrument Company	247	
			Giant Food Company	267	
			Hovey and Beard Company	467	
Intergroup	Intergroup problems in organizations	204	The Tinkertoy exercise	56	(B) *Groups in Harmony and Tension*, M. and C. Sherif; (A) "Organization and Conflict," K. Boulding, *Journal of Conflict Resolution*, 1957, 1; (B) *Managing Intergroup Problems in Organizations*, R. Blake, H. Shepard, J. Mouton.
	"Why should my conscience bother me?"	215	Northwest Industries	254	
	Workingman and management	274	Intergroup exercise	266	
			Hovey and Beard Company	467	

Topic	Articles	Page	Skills/Cases/Exercises	Page	Related materials outside book
Perception	On the folly of rewarding A, while hoping for B	65	The reluctant operator	170	(M) Powers of Ten; (M) The Eye of the Beholder; (M) Is It Always Right to be Right?; (M) In the Name of the Law; (M) Meanings Are In People; (M) The Way I See It; (A) "Perception: Implications for Administration," S. Zalkind and T. Costello, ASQ, Sept. 62.
	Defensive communication	210	Ranch Supplies Company	241	
	Planned change	384	Giant Food Company	267	
			Who's in charge around here?	371	
			Universal Bank	456	
			DMG Corporation	460	
Power	That urge to achieve	76	Phantoms fill Boy Scout rolls	48	(MH-N) A Man For All Seasons, R.Bolt; (B) The Sovereign State of I.T.T., A Sampson; (B) Management and Machiavelli, A. Jay; (B) In the Name of Profit, B. Heilbroner et. al.; (A) "Two Faces of Power," D. McClelland, Journal of International Affairs, Vol. 24, # 1.
	"Why should my conscience bother me?"	215	Supervision, hair, and all that	58	
	Workingman and management	274	Intergroup exercise	266	
	Power, dependence and effective management	293	How Iacocca won the big one	349	
			L.J. Summers Company	358	
			Who's in charge around here?	371	
			Hovey and Beard Company	467	
Reinforce-ment	On the folly of rewarding A, while hoping for B	65	Denver Department Stores	148	(M) Business, Behaviorism and the Bottom Line; (B) Walden Two, B.F. Skinner; (B) Contingency Management in Education and Other Equally Exciting Places, R. Mallott; (A) "Performance Audit, Feedback and Positive Reinforcement," E. Feeney, Training and Development Journal, Nov. 72.
	Behavior modification on the bottom line	84	The reluctant operator	170	
			Some thoughts on appraisal interview	344	

Topic	Articles	Page	Skills/Cases/Exercises	Page	Related materials outside book
Systems	"Why should my conscience bother me?"	215	Framework for organizational analysis	40	(M) The Factory; (B) *Systems Analysis and Organizational Behavior,* J. Seiler; (B) *The Systems Approach,* C. Churchman; (A) "A Structural Approach to Organizational Change," V. Averch, *JABS,* Sept.-Oct. 73; (A) "Understanding Your Organization's Characteristics," R. Harrison, *HBR,* May-June 72.
	The manager's job . . .	276	City National Bank	46	
	Choosing strategies for change	388	The Tinkertoy exercise	56	
			Denver Department Stores	148	
			Ranch Supplies Company	241	
			DMG Corporation	460	

ORGANIZATION AND PEOPLE
Readings, Cases, and Exercises
in Organizational Behavior

Different people have different reasons for joining organizations

"Isn't there any other reason you would like a job with this organization other than 'Want to work within the system to destroy it'?"

1

In search of organizational behavior

If visitors from another planet were to travel to Earth during the 1980s, it would not take them long to recognize one of the more poignant debates of our time, that is, the significance, dominance, and controversial nature of contemporary organizations. They would hear of monumental achievements and colossal failures, humanitarian causes and deceptive exploitation, optimistic forecasts and doomsday predictions, the promise and the threat of multinational organizations, the fear of big organizations, and the impotence of small ones, the advent of exciting new concepts of administration and the bankruptcy of modern theories.

Through all these judgments, however, runs a theme by no means unique to the contemporary setting, namely, how to better utilize organizational resources for achieving worthwhile goals. *Worthwhile*, of course, can be defined in terms of a global objective (eliminating smallpox or gaining military supremacy), a more limited activity (winning a ball game or increasing production by 10 percent), or an individual goal (achieving a position or finding meaningful work). In each case, an organization is a means to pursue an end *someone* thinks is important. And there lies the essential problem of organizations — individuals define organizational goals, values, and success from their own perspective. We need to understand the impact of these individual perspectives. To understand their impact means to remember that organizations do not behave; rather, *people* behave in organizations. Similarly, organizations do not have goals; *people* have goals in organizations. Of course, people articulate the goals they want the organization to achieve, but such statements may or may not determine the direction of behavior. The sum of the behavior of all the individual members adds up to the dynamic phenomenon we call *organization*.

1

Each person occupies a unique combination of roles in different organizations, and each, therefore, has unique needs and objectives in any one of those organizations. An individual may be a manager of a large work force attempting to achieve a complex task. If so, she may find that problems of motivation, control, and coordination are the most important. However, an individual may also find himself as the president of a union negotiating for ten cents in a collective bargaining session with a firm. Another individual may be a student in a university who is struggling with a variety of communication and power techniques to convince a committee that she really does deserve a staff parking sticker or that he should not be dismissed from school. Such issues are included in the study of organizational behavior.

Another set of important considerations for students of contemporary organizations comes from the changing nature of the society in which we live. Our affluent society has created the imperative for justice, equality, and the ``good life'' in addition to the conventional measures of success. Demands from women, minorities, and special interest groups for an equitable share of opportunities and rewards have added a new dimension to the challenge of dealing with organizations.

In a very general sense we define organizational behavior as the *analysis of factors that influence and are influenced by the behavior of people in organizations.* This means that an organizational behavior course can turn into an applied management class, a course in individual development, a theoretical review of research findings, or one of many other variations. Regardless of the orientation, however, we always return to the issue of how an individual identifies his or her organizational role.

This section is intended to suggest different perceptions of an individual's role in an organization. Our intent is to confront students with many different dimensions of involvement in contemporary organizations. For example, the article on corporate culture suggests that organizations develop very different cultures that are supportive of some employees' values but are in conflict with other people's basic beliefs about their roles in organizations. The Ritchie article maintains that organizations may not be very effective and we cannot expect them to meet our needs for self-development. He suggests that people need to become scholar-leaders who are well-informed, active members of organizations. They need to develop analytical tools to understand what organizations in our societies are doing.

Schein's article focuses on the expectations and frustrations surrounding the first job. Entry into organizations is an important phase of each person's total organizational history. Concepts reinforced or rejected at this point may be crucial in later success or failure. Peter Drucker, a leading management writer and consultant, then probes some philosophical and pragmatic approaches to organizations. Looking at organizations from the perspective of an individual member, he raises questions regarding issues of loyalty and conformity.

The framework for organizational analysis provides the reader with one approach to conducting an analysis of organizations. This is a skill that is very important if one is going to be effective in such settings. The cases and exercises in this section provide an opportunity for students to practice using the analytical framework as well as define issues central to this course of study. Strategy and ethics conflict in a variety of contexts; being sensitive to these conflicts may not eliminate them, but it should help students to consider some alternative ways of responding to them when they arise. The description of activities in the Boy Scouts shows what can happen when good intentions are subordinated to organizational realities. Noble purposes do not prevent individual needs from dictating organizational behavior.

We are all part of many organizations with a variety of forces continually pushing or pulling at us. This leaves us with three alternatives: to be victimized by the system without ever knowing what happened, to understand the process and try to protect ourselves, or to attempt to change the organization. If we fail, we should at least have a better understanding of the reasons why (although it may afford small consolation).

READINGS

Corporate Culture: the hard-to-change values that spell success or failure

Five years ago the chief executive of two major oil companies determined that they would have to diversify out of oil because their current business could not support long-term growth and it faced serious political threats. Not only did they announce their new long-range strategies to employees and the public, but they established elaborate plans to implement them. Today, after several years of floundering in attempts to acquire and build new businesses, both companies are firmly back in oil, and the two CEOs have been replaced

Each of the CEOs had been unable to implement his strategy, not because it was theoretically wrong or bad but because neither had understood that his company's culture was so entrenched in the traditions and values of doing business as oilmen that employees resisted — and sabotaged — the radical changes that the CEOs tried to impose. Oil operations require long-term investments for long-term rewards; but the new businesses needed short-term views and an emphasis on current returns. Successes had come from hitting it big in wild-

catting, but the new success was to be based on such abstractions as market share or numbers growth — all seemingly nebulous concepts to them. Too late did the CEOs realize that strategies can only be implemented with the wholehearted effort and belief of everyone involved. If implementing them violates employees' basic beliefs about their roles in the company, or the traditions that underlie the corporation's culture, they are doomed to fail.

Culture implies values, such as aggressiveness, defensiveness, or nimbleness, that set a pattern for a company's activities, opinions, and actions. The pattern is instilled in employees by managers' example and passed down to succeeding generations of workers. The CEO's words alone do not produce culture; rather, his actions and those of his managers do.

A corporation's culture can be its major strength when it is consistent with its strategies. Some of the most successful companies have clearly demonstrated that fact, including:

• International Business Machines Corp.,

where marketing drives a service philosophy that is almost unparalleled. The company keeps a hot line open 24 hours a day, seven days a week, to service IBM products.

• International Telephone & Telegraph Corp., where financial discipline demands total dedication. To beat out the competition in a merger, an executive once called former Chairman Harold S. Geneen at 3 a.m. to get his approval.

• Digital Equipment Corp., where an emphasis on innovation creates freedom with responsibility. Employees can set their own hours and working style, but they are expected to articulate and support their activities with evidence of progress.

• Delta Air Lines Inc., where a focus on customer service produces a high degree of teamwork. Employees will substitute in other jobs to keep planes flying and baggage moving.

• Atlantic Richfield Co., where an emphasis on entrepreneurship encourages action. Operating men have the autonomy to bid on promising fields without hierarchial approval.

But a culture that prevents a company from meeting competitive threats, or from adapting to changing economic or social environments, can lead to the company's stagnation and ultimate demise unless it makes a conscious effort to change. One that did make this effort is PepsiCo Inc., where the cultural emphasis has been systematically changed over the past two decades from passivity to aggressiveness.

Once the company was content in its No. 2 spot, offering Pepsi as a cheaper alternative to Coca-Cola. But today, a new employee at PepsiCo quickly learns that beating the competition, whether outside or inside the company, is the surest path to success. In its soft-drink operation, for example, Pepsi's marketers now take on Coke directly, asking consumers to compare the taste of the two colas. That direct confrontation is reflected inside the company as well. Managers are pitted against each other to grab more market share, to work harder, and to wring more profits out of their businesses. Because winning is the key value at Pepsi, losing has its penalties. Consistent runners-up find their jobs gone. Employees know they must win merely to stay in place — and must devastate the competition to get ahead.

But the aggressive competitor who succeeds at Pepsi would be sorely out of place at J. C. Penney Co., where a quick victory is far less important than building long-term loyalty. Indeed, a Penney store manager once was severely rebuked by the company's president for making too much profit. That was considered unfair to customers, whose trust Penney seeks to win. The business style set by the company's founder — which one competitor describes as avoiding "taking unfair advantage of anyone the company did business with" — still prevails today. Customers know they can return merchandise with no questions asked; suppliers know that Penney will not haggle over terms; and employees are comfortable in their jobs, knowing that Penney will avoid layoffs at all costs and will find easier jobs for those who cannot handle more demanding ones. Not surprisingly, Penney's average executive tenure is 33 years while Pepsi's is 10.

These vastly different methods of doing business are but two examples of corporate culture. People who work at Pepsi and Penney sense that the corporate values are the yardstick by which they will be measured. Just as tribal cultures have totems and taboos that dictate how each member will act toward fellow members and outsiders, so does a corporation's culture influence employees' actions toward customers, competitors, suppliers, and one another. Sometimes the rules are written out. More often they are tacit. Most often, they are laid down by a strong founder and hardened by success into custom.

"Culture gives people a sense of how to behave and what they ought to be doing," explains Howard M. Schwartz, vice-president of Management Analysis Center Inc., a Cambridge (Mass.) consulting firm that just completed a study of corporate culture. Indeed, so firmly are certain values entrenched in a company's behavior that predictable responses can be counted on not only by its employees but by its competitors. "How will our competitors behave?" is a stock question that strategic planners ask when contemplating a new move. The answers come from assessing competitors' time-honored priorities, their reactions to competition, and their ability to change course.

Because a company's culture is so pervasive, changing it becomes one of the most difficult tasks that any chief executive can undertake. Just as a primitive tribe's survival depended on its ability to react to danger, and to alter its way of life when necessary, so must corporations, faced with changing economic, social, and political climates, sometimes radically change their methods of operating. What stands in the way is not only the "relative immutability of culture," as the MAC study points out, but also the fact that few executives consciously recognize what their company's culture is and how it manifests itself. The concept of culture, says Stanley M. Davis, professor of organization behavior at Boston University and a coauthor of the MAC study, is hard to understand. "It's like putting your

hand in a cloud," he says.

Thomas J. Peters, a principal in McKinsey & Co., cites a client who believed it was imperitave to his company's survival to add a marketing effort to his manufacturing-oriented organization. Because the company had no experts in marketing, it wanted to hire some. Consultants pointed out that this strategy would fail because all of the issues raised at company meetings concerned cost cutting and production — never competition or customers. Rewards were built into achieving efficiencies in the first category, while none were built into understanding the second. Ultimately, the CEO recognized that he had to educate himself and his staff so thoroughly in marketing that he could build his own in-house team.

Similarly, American Telephone & Telegraph Co. is now trying to alter its service-oriented operation to give equal weight to marketing. Past attempts to do so ignored the culture and failed. For example, in 1961, AT&T set up a school to teach managers to coordinate the design and manufacture of data products for customized sales. But when managers completed the course, they found that the traditional way of operating — making noncustomized mass sales — were what counted in the company. They were given neither the time to analyze individual customers' needs nor rewards commensurate with such efforts. The result was that 85 percent of the graduates quit, and AT&T disbanded the school.

AT&T prides itself on its service operation, and with good reason. It provides the most efficient and broadest telephone system in the world, and it reacts to disaster with a speed unknown anywhere else. In 1975, for example, a fire swept through a switching center in lower Manhattan, knocking out service to

170,000 telephones. AT&T rallied 4,000 employees and shipped in 3,000 tons of equipment to restore full service in just 22 days — a task that could have taken a lesser company more than a year.

But costs for AT&T's service had been readily passed to customers through rate increases granted by public service commissions. Keeping costs down was thus never a major consideration. Now, however, since the Federal Communications Commission has decided to allow other companies to sell products in AT&T's once-captive markets, AT&T must change the orientation of its 1 million employees. In numbers alone, such a change is unprecedented in corporate history. Still, to survive in its new environment, Bell must alter its plans, strategies, and employee expectations of what the company wants from them, as well as their belief in the security of their jobs and old way of doing business.

To make the changes, Bell has analyzed its new requirements in exquisite detail that fills thousands of pages. It acknowledges its lack of skills in certain crucial areas: marketing, cost control, and administrative ability to deal with change. The company had rewarded managers who administered set policies by the book; today it is promoting innovators with advanced degrees in business administration. Once it measured service representatives by the speed with which they responded to calls; today they are measured by the number of problems they solve.

AT&T's new role model

Instead of its traditional policy of promoting from within, some new role models were hired from outside the company. Archie J. McGill, a former executive of International Business Machines Corp., was made vice-president of business marketing, for example. McGill is described by associates as an innovator who is the antithesis of the traditional "Bell-shaped man" because of his "combative, adversarial style." Just as IBM's slogan, "Think," encouraged its employees to be problem solvers, McGill is hammering a new slogan, "I make the difference," into each of his marketers, encouraging them to become entrepreneurs. That idea is reinforced by incentives that pit salespeople against each other for bonuses, a system unknown at Bell before.

Even so, the changes are slow. Learning to become solution-sellers has produced "a tremendous amount of confusion" among Bell marketing people, reports one large corporate customer. For example, AT&T is "absolutely trapped" if a customer requests an extra editing part for its standard teletype system, he says. "If you want something they don't have, they tend to solve the problem by saying, 'Let's go out for a drink'."

Even McGill concedes that "anytime you have an orientation toward consulting (past practices) as opposed to being adaptive to a situation, change doesn't happen overnight." Bell's director of planning, W. Brooke Tunstall, estimates that it will take another three to five years to attain an 85 percent change in the company's orientation. Still, he insists, there has already been "a definite change in mindset at the upper levels." The arguments heard around the company now concern the pace of change rather than its scope. Says Tunstall, "I haven't run into anyone who doesn't understand why the changes are needed."

The AT&T example clearly demonstrates the need for a company to examine its existing culture in depth and to acknowledge the reasons for revolutionary change, if changes must be made. As AT&T learned from its earlier attempt to sell specialized services, change cannot be implemented merely by sending people to school. Nor can it be made by hiring new staff, by acquiring new businesses, by changing the name of the company, or by redefining its business. Even exhortations by the chief executive to operate differently will not succeed unless they are backed up by a changed structure, new role models, new incentive systems, and new rewards and punishments built into operations.

A chief executive, for example, who demands innovative new products from his staff, but who leaves in place a hierarchy that can smother a good new idea at its first airing, is unlikely to get what he wants. In contrast, an unwritten rule at 3M Co., says one manager, is, "Never be responsible for killing an idea." Similarly, if a CEO's staff knows that his first priority is consistent earnings growth, it will be unlikely to present him with any new product or service idea, no matter how great its potential, if it requires a long incubation period and a drag on earnings before it reaches fruition. At Pillsbury Co., for example, managers are afraid to suggest ideas for products that might require considerable research and development because they know that Chairman William H. Spoor is obsessed with improving short-term financial results, sources say.

The real priorities

One element is certain: Employees cannot be fooled. They understand the real priorities in the corporation. At the first inconsistency they will become confused, then reluctant to change, and fin-

ally intransigent. Indeed, consistency in every aspect of a culture is essential to its success, as PepsiCo's transformation into an archrival of Coke shows.

For decades, Coke's unchallenged position in the market was so complete that the brand name Coke became synonymous with cola drinks. It attained this distinction under Robert W. Woodruff, who served as chief executive for 32 years and is still chairman of the company's finance committee at age 90. Woodruff had an "almost messianic drive to get Coca-Cola (drunk) all over the world," says Harvey Z. Yazijian, coauthor of the forthcoming book, *The Cola Wars*. So successful was Coke in accomplishing this under Woodruff — and later, J. Paul Austin, who will retire in March as CEO — that Coca-Cola became known as "America's second State Department." Its trademark became a symbol of American life itself.

"A real problem in the past," says Yazijian, "was that they had a lot of deadwood" among employees. Nevertheless, Coke's marketing and advertising were extremely effective in expanding consumption of the product. But the lack of serious competition and the company's relative isolation in its home town of Atlanta allowed it to become "fat, dumb, and happy," according to one consultant. Coke executives are known to be extremely loyal to the company and circumspect to the point of secrecy in their dealings with the outside world.

In the mid-1950s, Pepsi, once a sleepy New York-based bottler with a lame slogan, "Twice as much for a nickel, too," began to develop into a serious threat under the leadership of Chairman Alfred N. Steele. The movement gathered momentum, and by the early 1970s the company had become a ferocious competitor under Chairman Donald M.

Kendall and President Andrall E. Pearson, a former director of McKinsey. The culture that these two executives determined to create was based on the goal of becoming the No. 1 marketer of soft drinks.

Severe pressure was put on managers to show continual improvement in market share, product volume, and profits. "Careers ride on tenths of a market share point," says John Sculley, vice-president and head of domestic beverage operations. This atmosphere pervades the company's nonbeverage units as well. "Everyone knows that if the results aren't there, you had better have your resume up to date," says a former snack food manager. To keep everyone on their toes, a "creative tension" is continually nurtured among departments at Pepsi, says another former executive. The staff is kept lean and managers are moved to new jobs constantly, which results in people working long hours and engaging in political maneuvering "just to keep their jobs from being reorganized out from under them" says a headhunter.

Kendall himself sets a constant example. He once resorted to using a snowmobile to get to work in a blizzard, demonstrating the ingenuity and dedication to work he expects from his staff. This type of pressure has pushed many managers out. But a recent company survey shows that others thrive under such conditions. "Most of our guys are having fun," Pearson insists. They are the kind of people, elaborates Sculley, who "would rather be in the Marines than in the Army."

Like Marines, Pepsi executives are expected to be physically fit as well as mentally alert: Pepsi employs four physical fitness instructors at its headquarters, and a former executive says it is an unwritten rule that to get ahead in the company a manager must stay in shape. The company encourages one-on-one sports as well as interdepartmental competition in such games as soccer and basketball. In company team contests or business dealings, says Sculley, "the more competitive it becomes, the more we enjoy it." In such a culture, less competitive managers are deliberately weeded out. Even suppliers notice a difference today. "They are smart, sharp negotiators who take advantage of all opportunities," says one.

While Pepsi steadily gained market share in the 1970s, Coke was reluctant to admit that a threat existed, Yazijian says. Pepsi now has bested Coke in the domestic take-home market, and it is mounting a challenge overseas. At the moment, the odds are in favor of Coke, which sells one-third of the world's soft drinks and has had Western Europe locked up for years. But Pepsi has been making inroads: Besides monopolizing the Soviet market, is has dominated the Arab Middle East ever since Coke was ousted in 1967, when it granted a bottling franchise in Israel. Still, Coke showed that it was not giving up. It cornered a potentially vast new market — China.

With Pepsi gaining domestic market share faster than Coke — last year it gained 7.5 percent vs. Coke's 5 percent — observers believe that Coke will turn more to foreign sales or food sales for growth. Roberto C. Goizueta, who will be Coke's next chairman, will not reveal Coke's strategy. But one tactic the company has already used is hiring away some of Pepsi's "tigers." Coke has lured Donald Breen, Jr., who played a major role in developing the "Pepsi Challenge" — the consumer taste test — as well as five other marketing and sales executives associated with Pepsi. Pepsi won its court battle to prevent Breen from revealing confidential information over the next twelve months. But the company's current culture is unlikely to build loyalty. Pepsi may well have to examine the dangers of cultivating ruthlessness in its managers, say former executives.

Quite a different problem faces J.C. Penney today. Its well-entrenched culture, laid down by founder James Cash Penney in a seven-point codification of the company's guiding principles, called "The Penney Idea," has brought it tremendous loyalty from its staff but lower profits recently. Its introduction of fashionable apparel has been only partially successful, because customers identify it with nonfashionable staples, such as children's clothes, work clothes, and hardware. It has also been outpaced in the low end of the market by agressive discounters, such as K-mart Corp., which knocked Penney out of the No. 2 retailer's spot in 1976 and which has been gaining market share at Penney's expense ever since.

Penney's is proud that two national magazines cited it as one of the ten best places to work in the nation, a claim that is borne out by employees. "Everyone is treated as an individual," notes one former executive. Another praises the company's "bona fide participative" decision-making process, and adds that Penney has "an openness in the organization that many large companies don't seem to achieve."

But Penney's paternalistic attitude toward its work force has meant that it always tries to find new jobs for marginally competent employees rather than firing them, says Stephen Temlock, manager of human resource strategy development. He concedes that some workers "expect us to be papa and mama, and aren't motivated enough to help themselves." The corollary of that, he admits, is that the company sometimes fails to reward outstanding performers enough.

Penney's entrenched culture makes any change slow, Temlock adds, but he insists that this solidity helps to maintain a balance between "an out-and-out agressive environment." Penney Chairman Donald V. Seibert believes that the company's problems have more to do with the retailing industry's endemic cyclicality than with company culture. Although he admits that he worries sometimes that the company is too inbred, he notes that it has brought in different types of people in the last several years as it entered new businesses, such as catalog sales and insurance.

Seibert adds that the company firmly believes that the principles of "The Penney Idea" will be relevant no matter how much the economic environment changes. "You can't say that there's a good way to modernize integrity," he emphasizes.

Seibert may be right. One competitor notes that the aggressive newcomers in retailing have profited from older retailers' mistakes, and thus have found shortcuts to growth. But, says this source, "the shortcuts are limited, and the newcomers' power has yet to be proven." Still, if the new threat continues, Penney's pace must speed up, and it must soon act more flexibly to protect itself; it may even have to abandon some of the customs that have grown up around its humanistic principles.

Another gentlemanly company found that it had to do just that to regain its leading position in banking. Chase Manhattan Bank had cruised along comfortably for years, leaning on the aristocratic image of its chairman, David Rockefeller. In the mid-1970s, however, Chase was jolted out of its lethargy by a sharp skid in earnings and a return on assets that plunged as low as 0.24 percent in 1976. Its real estate portfolio was loaded with questionable and sour loans, and its commercial lending department's reputation had been severely tarnished because high turnover of its lending officers and the resulting inexperience of those who replaced them made the bank less responsive to customers. Some embarrassing questions about Chase's basic management practices began to be raised.

Rockefeller and a group of top executives, including Willard C. Butcher, now chief executive and chairman-elect, decided that the fault lay with a culture that rewarded people more for appearance than performance and that produced inbreeding and a smugness that made the bank loath to grapple with competitors. The typical Chase executive in those days was a well-groomed functionary who did not drive himself hard or set high standards for his own performance, banking analysts remember.

The first step toward change, Chase executives felt, was for the bank to define what it wanted to be. Early in 1977 it drew up a three-page mission statement that outlined the company's business mix. "We will only do those things we can do extremely well and with the highest level of integrity," the statement said. For Chase, this meant taking a hard look at some unprofitable parts of its business. Subsequently, it closed some 50 low-volume domestic branches in New York, and it began to turn away questionable loan business that it had accepted before.

The mission statement also spelled out specific targets for financial goals, such as return on equity and assets and debt-to-capital ratio. At the start, employees doubted that the company could meet these goals; one, for example, was a return on assets of 0.55 percent to 0.65 percent, more than double the 1976 figure.

Chase began a major effort to step up communications between top management and the rest of the staff. This was a departure from the old days, when decisions were simply handed down from the 17th-floor executive suite, says one former manager. The participation of all employees created a sense of "ownership" of the program by all, something consultant Robert F. Allen, president of the Human Resources Institute in Morristown, N.J., believes is essential to any long-lasting change.

Like AT&T, Chase promoted new role models, such as Richard J. Boyle, now a senior vice-president, who took over the bank's troubled real estate operations at age 32. Boyle, described as a "workaholic" with strong opinions and a willingness to make hard decisions, such as writing off floundering projects rather than carrying them on the company's books, is the antithesis of the old-style Chase banker, analysts say. To run commercial lending, the bank lured back James H. Carey, who had left Chase for Hambros Bank. "They put absolutely brilliant people in problem areas," remarks John J. Mason, banking analyst at Shearson Loeb Rhoades Inc.

Rewards for performers

But tradition suffered: One-third of the bank's top executives were replaced by outsiders. Salaries and incentive payments were overhauled to provide greater rewards for top performers. And an advanced management course was started for promising young managers. The culture has been altered from its emphasis on style to a focus on performance. And now that employees' expectations of the company have changed, the new order is likely to prevail. But even Butcher, although pleased with the improvement, warns, "The danger is always that you become complacement."

Chase was able to effect the change in its culture under the aegis of its reigning leaders, Rockefeller and Butcher. But some companies find that the only way to solve problems is to bring in a new chief who can implement sweeping change. Yet even a new strongman can run up against a wall unless he understands the company's existing culture.

Dennis C. Stanfill, a corporate finance specialist, ran into just such problems when he took over as chief executive in 1971 at Twentieth Century-Fox Film Corp. Stanfill's aim was to balance the risks of the motion picture business with steady earnings from other leisure-time businesses, which he began acquiring. But he also insisted on running all of Fox's businesses, including the film operation, on an equal basis by keeping the corporate purse strings pulled tight — and in his hands.

What Stanfill overlooked was that creative people require a different kind of managing than do typical business employees. While the latter group can usually be motivated by using the carrot-and-stick approach, creative people are self-motivated. They will work as hard as needed to perform as perfectly as they can, because they identify their work not with the company but with themselves. What they want from their patron-managers, however, is applause and rewards for a good job, and protection when they bomb.

Stanfill violated those expectations when he refused to give Alan Ladd, Jr., president of the film group, control over

bonuses for his staff, which had produced such hits as *Star Wars*. From Stanfill's point of view, the decision was sound: In just three years he had erased a $125 million bank debt and brought the company into the black after it had been in default on its loans. He believed the traditional extravagances of the film company would keep the corporation on a shaky foundation. Indeed, he says, he wants "to keep the balance between show and business."

Not a 'brokerage'

But the film company's response was predictable. Ladd quit to start his own operation, taking several key people with him. "In my opinion, Stanfill doesn't understand what motivates creative people," says Ladd. "You don't run a film business like a brokerage house."

Fox's directors quickly stepped in and demanded that Stanfill find a "name" replacement for Ladd. Stanfill has since picked Alan J. Hirschfield, who had been laid off by Columbia Pictures Industries Inc. and who has been praised by the industry for adding a creative spark to Fox this past year. But Stanfill now must make financial decisions jointly with Hirschfield.

Whether Stanfill will ever be comfortable in such a high-risk business remains questionable. One film industry analyst thinks not. He says: "Stanfill has never felt comfortable running an entertainment company. He is down-side-risk-oriented on motion pictures, and didn't know why Ladd was so successful." If that is true, Stanfill could be on a collision course with Fox's implicit culture.

Stanfill may have recognized that the strategy he was imposing on Fox's film business, which produces 63 percent of the corporation's pretax operating earnings, violated its culture. But he obviously believed that it was necessary for the company's survival. He has not, however, changed Fox's culture. As more and more chief executives recognize the need for long-range strategies, they will have to consider the effects of these strategies on their companies. It may well be that CEOs must then decide whether their strategies must change to fit their companies' culture or the cultures must change to assure survival.

We need a nation of scholar-leaders

J. B. Ritchie

Personal responsibility and organizations: We need a nation of scholar-leaders

In the book, *The Once and Future King*, T. H. White retells the legend of King Arthur. In so doing, he captures an interesting dimension of growing up, learning, and accepting responsibility. When the young Arthur, affectionately referred to as "Wart" in the account, is despondent, a little confused, and sad, he goes to Ector and asks what he should do. Ector says he should go see the magician, Merlin, for some advice as to how to handle his frustrations. When he approaches the magician, Merlin responds as follows:

"The best thing for being sad," replied Merlin, beginning to puff and blow, "is to learn something. That is the only thing that never fails. You may grow old and trembling in your anatomies, you may lie awake at night listening to the disorder of your veins, you may miss your only love, you may see the world about you devastated by evil lunatics, or know your honor trampled in the sewers of baser minds. There is only one thing for it then — to learn. Learn why the world wags and what wags it. That is the only thing which the mind can never exhaust, never alienate, never be tortured by, never fear or distrust, and never dream of regretting. Learning is the thing for you. Look at what a lot of things there are to learn — pure science, the only purity there is. You can learn astronomy in a lifetime, natural history in three, literature in six. And then after you have exhausted a milliard of lifetimes in biology and medicine and theocriticism and geography and history and economics why, you can then start to make a cartwheel out of the appropriate wood, or spend fifty years learning to begin to learn to beat your adversary at fencing. After that you can start again on mathematics, until it is time to learn to plough."

Learning: A solution to life's frustrations

I subscribe to that advice. The solution to life's aggravations is to learn. And the solution to a frustrating life is to develop an attitude of learning. Each of us needs to develop an attitude toward life, toward organizations, toward the university, toward the Church, toward the state, toward the corporation, and toward each other of learning and of growing. We reduce the anxieties and confusions of life by developing a criterion for thinking that is based on analysis, interpretation, extrapolation, and extension of ideas rather than on judgment, classification, and rigid acceptance or rejection.

Student versus scholar perspective

The term *student* is a revered term to me. Although I will suggest a metaphor that may not reflect my reverence toward students, I do so only to make a point. Students are like computers. The system sits there waiting for an input to be determined by something like a professor, a textbook, or an expert source that tells the student what is appropriate or what is desirable or what is true. The information is put into the computer and, by some previously designed operational system, is classified, perhaps processed a bit, and then stored in some way for easy retrieval. That retrieval is triggered by something like a question in a classroom, an assignment to write a paper, or a question on an examination.

I wonder if our student model has corrupted us in the ability to learn and to grow. I wonder if we have simply mastered the art of taking a class. That can be pretty empty. There is life after college!

We should develop an eternal perspective rather than a semester perspective. We have different people reviewing and evaluating rather than a single teacher, and sometimes the stu-

dent model gets in the way. Sometimes the student model undercuts our capacity to cope in a complex world. What is needed today is a scholar model.

A student asks what to do, a scholar searches and proposes what to do. A student blames the system for failure, a scholar has no need to blame anyone. He or she accepts responsibility for correcting a failed system. A student listens to judge, a scholar listens to learn. A student transfers to the university, to the professor, to the boss, or to God both credit and blame that the individual should accept. In the process of so doing, we default in the most important function we have to perform: to decide what the meaning of life is.

The scholar and personal responsibility

From the scholar perspective, we do not search for the meaning of life, we define it, we develop it, we create it. We don't seek out who we are. Our identity is not found by searching across the land. Our identity is something we decide. Students expect someone else to define them; scholars accept the responsibility of defining themselves. Students expect the textbook to have the answer, and they want to know whether it is A or B.

I was intrigued recently in reading Norman Cousins's book, *Anatomy of an Illness*, where he describes how he accepted the joint responsibility with his doctor for his own health. He was told that his odds for getting better were 500-1 against, and he said when that announcement was made he decided he had to become a participant in this process in a way he had not considered previously. Norman Cousins, as the editor of the *Saturday Review*, had available to him a research staff. He sent his research staff out to do a survey of various medical findings, and he found that what his doctors were prescribing was not accurate. Norman Cousins did not blindly accept the diagnosis and prescriptions his doctor had arrived at working with incomplete data. Norman Cousins took the scholar-leader role and asked why. He found that the prescribed medication and the hospital environment were inappropriate. He determined that what he really needed was some Vitamin C, some laughter, and a pleasant environment. He moved himself out of a hospital into a nice hotel room. He started taking Vitamin C and watching Laurel and Hardy movies *and he got better.*

Cousins became part of the healing process. He applied the power of the participant, rather than to sit back and defer to the expert doctor.

Another example touches upon an uncomfortable and a difficult issue, but one that I find terribly compelling. Victor Frankl in *Man's Search for Meaning,* describes the fate of people in the concentration camps in Nazi captivity. He argues that what was needed was a fundamental change in attitude. Attitudes towards life, he said, had become too self-indulgent, too narcissistic, too self-serving, to really understand what was going on and to survive the brutality of the camp. In talking about the men in his camp, he said, "what was really needed was a fundamental change in our attitude towards life. We had to learn ourselves and furthermore we had to teach others that the issue was not what we expected from life but what life expected from us. We needed to stop asking what the meaning of life was and instead think of ourselves as those who were being questioned by life daily and hourly."

Beyond "looking out for number one"

Our answers must consist not simply in talk and meditation, but in right action and conduct. Life ultimately means accepting responsibility to define appropriate answers to each problem as it comes up. The more you look for the meaning of life, I would argue, the less you would find it. We can only be trapped by the contemporary pop psychology of "looking out for No. 1," "winning through intimidation," "pulling your own strings," "being your own best friend," and the whole raft of pop psychology books that tell you how to beat the system, take care of yourself, indulge yourself at the expense of other people, be calloused and insensitive to the needs of the world around you in order to come out on top and win that game of competition with each other. The more we become victimized by such philosophies, the less capable we are of turning each of life's events into a learning experience rather than just an historical occurrence. We have got to become an involved part of the dynamic, rather than a simple part of a static system.

This issue of self-service is not new. It is not a product of our most recent five years. I refer to John Steinbeck's comments in *Grapes of Wrath,* where he described some of the landowners of the 1930s: "Some were kind because they hated what they had to do. Some of them were angry because they hated to be cruel. Some of them were cold because they long ago found that one could not be an owner unless one were cold. And all of them were caught up in something larger than themselves. Some of them hated the mathematics that drove them and were afraid. Some worshipped the mathematics that drove them because it provided a refuge from thought and from feeling."

The student and overreliance on organizations

I think we have overdemanded our organizations to the point that we can only, ultimately, feel betrayed. Our economic, political, academic, social, and religious systems cannot answer all of the demands that we place on them. They cannot be aware enough. They cannot have an efficient enough information processing system to cope with the exponential explosion of information. They cannot acquire, digest, analyze, and resolve all of the complex and contradictory data received.

There is growing evidence of the failure of organizations just as there is growing evidence of shortcomings in the student perspective of life. Consider these examples: **Fifty percent of organizational decisions ignored**. For the past 15 years, I have been collecting observations of managers, executives, people who seemingly are in positions where others expect them to run an organization. One of the things I found interesting was that about 50 percent of the decisions these people make are never carried out in organizations. Not 50 percent of the random comments in a hall "why don't you look into this, Sue," but 50 percent of the formal decisions you can trace to board minutes, to memoranda that are distributed in an organization. Half of those decisions are not carried out! Why are they not carried out? Because no one person knows enough to account for all the variables in making those decisions. No one person nor one group — not the Soviet Politburo, not the Board of Directors of Exxon — can make all the decisions that will dictate the be-

havior of every member of that organization. "Democracy by default" may not sound elegant, but I think it comes from the inability to account for or control all the variables. The result of these decisions based on incomplete information: 50 percent of the decisions are not carried out.

When I was collecting my observations on this particular issue, I attempted to ask many people for their evaluations. When I would fly in an airplane, I would try to sit next to a person I felt was a business executive. (Sometimes I was badly mistaken, and that was an interesting experiment in itself.) I would sit next to someone that looked like an executive and I would say, "I am doing a research project, and I have been working in an organization where I find that half of the decisions made are not carried out. What do you think? It seems high to me. Can you believe that that is really true?" The responses I got were almost all confirming. In fact, one individual said, "Gee, I think that is right and maybe it is even a little low. If 50 percent of my decisions got carried out, I would be delighted."

The wrong decisions are carried out. This same respondent went on to make another point about failings in organizations. After confirming that many decisions are, in fact, ignored, he went on to say, "But I would argue that the survival and success of business depends on that 50 percent that are not carried out."

That is a telling argument, the fact that many decisions *shouldn't* be carried out. Now again, that is not comfortable to the administrator or the executive who sits back frustrated because orders are not followed. And, unfortunately, I have observed that ofttimes it is the wrong 50 percent that are not carried out. The good decisions are resented by the rebellious deviants, and the bad decisions are implemented by enthusiastic zealots. Somehow we need a nation of scholars, a nation of leaders, to discriminate as to which decisions *ought* to be carried out. But the more important point is not to sit back in judgment of which 50 percent, but to become part, in a responsible way, of that process.

There is a crisis in organizational leadership. I have been collecting other data about organizations which reveal an interesting trend. There is a crisis of leadership. There is, indeed, a crisis of confidence in our institutions: government, corporate, union, and military. I have been measuring the attitudes that people have toward those above and below them in organizations. I found it interesting that 15 years ago when I started studying this, I asked people to rate some of their character traits on seven-point scales. Consistently, these self-ratings came out about 5.7. Now there is nothing very significant about that particular point until we use it as a reference for comparison.

In the course of this research I also asked people to rate, using the same seven-point scales, their bosses and their subordinates. Fifteen years ago, they saw their bosses at about a 6.0 (three-tenths of a point above themselves) and they saw their subordinates at a 4.2 (about a point and a half below them). That was a consistent pattern regardless of organizational level. Vice-presidents saw the president at about a 6, themselves at 5.7, and the department heads at about 4.2. First-line supervisors saw themselves at about a 5.7, their foreman at about 6.0 and their subordinates at about the same point of 4.2. These people saw themselves as a lot better than their subordinates, and al-

most as good as their boss. Therefore, when they communicate with the boss, they expected the boss to have full confidence in them and to think they were almost as good as the boss. Conversely, however, they expect subordinates to be inferior clods, and they talk down to them, disregard them, and belittle them. They have little confidence in subordinates' ability to function, and, therefore, they overcontrol them and harass them.

Those indicators held for several years. But as the 1970s began, I started getting different data. People still rated themselves at 5.7 on an average, still put their subordinates at about a 4.2, but now the bosses were coming in at a 5.7 also. So now my conclusions about their relationships changed. They now saw themselves as a lot better than subordinates, and as good as their boss. Many people now felt that they could do the boss's job as well as the boss. They were losing confidence in their superiors. By the middle of the seventies the data changed again. Starting in 1975 or 1976 the data started to look this way: Individuals still rated themselves at 5.7, subordinates about 4.2 and bosses were averaging 5.3. Now my interpretation changed one more time: they now see themselves as a lot better than their subordinates and quite a bit better than the boss. They concluded that there is nobody in the world as good as themselves!

Organizational lying. One further bit of evidence of the failing organization was reflected in a recent study of organizational lying — outright misstatements of the truth. The study discussed the external pressures on organizations to misrepresent their performance. The emphasis is on the facade rather than substance. Organizational rewards come from positive external reports, valid or not, instead of the internal criterion of genuine service.

There are pressures to lie and to misrepresent in all organizations. These need to be identified.

The organization as a haven from self-responsibility

The organization has become a mechanism that many of us use to absolve ourselves of the burden of making decisions that only we can make and of accepting responsibility for thinking. Organizations will not and cannot replace the individual's need to become a scholar-leader who participates in the dynamic process of deciding. We cannot be spectators. We cannot shift the burden for self-development to others. Besides, organizations simply don't work that well.

As a "student" society, we have come to expect of organizations functions that only we as individuals can be responsible for. And when they fail to meet these expectations, our confidence in organizational leadership drops. We all need to be scholar-leaders. Our contemporary society is so complex, that it behooves each of us to become not only minimally informed, not passive members, but incredibly well-informed, active members. The burden is severe on all of us to be scholars and leaders, to develop the analytical tools to understand what organizations in our societies are doing, and to make fewer demands upon them. Not fewer demands in terms of morality or

ethics, but fewer demands in terms of the universality of organizations serving needs we must ultimately be responsible for as individuals. We must demand of leaders of essential organizations, dignity and morality. We must expect less in terms of total output.

Our civilization depends on that informed citizenry in a way we have never depended on it before. The information available is too complex, the demands and opportunities for misrepresentation are too great, and the opportunity for organizational encroachment in private lives is too great.

But the positive opportunities are also great for accepting responsibility for our own involvement in life as scholars, defining our own learning and performance objectives, evaluating ourselves, making proposals instead of simply asking questions, and listening to learn rather than to judge. I hope we can do that. I hope we can become enthused, committed, informed participants rather than ones who sit back condemning the system because it does not define things our way. And in the process, I hope that we clearly can gain an increased confidence in ourselves. I hope that we don't wait for the university or for the nation, or the state, or the corporation to change our world — but instead, accept responsibilities for being part of it. When organizations fail, don't just blame the system, but accept the opportunity to become part of a changing process of the world in which we live.

The first job dilemma:
An appraisal of why college graduates change jobs and what can be done about it

Edgar H. Schein

The new graduate comes from college to his first job in industry prepared to be a company president. He is ambitious, enthusiastic, and ready. Then come the realities of the business world. Within a year, he is very likely to suffer a serious loss of motivation, to find himself facing the thought of quitting the job that once seemed so promising as a career opportunity, or to stop trying so hard, to ease off and lapse into a kind of apathy. What is wrong?

Almost every large company admits to losing within five years more than half of the new college graduates who have been hired. In a current research study of a sample of graduates from the Massachusetts Institute of Technology master's degree management program, I found that 50 percent of the 1964 graduates already had left their first job, that 67 percent of the 1963 graduates had changed jobs, and that 73 percent of the 1962 class had moved on at least once — with some on their third or fourth job.

Why is there such a high turnover of college graduates in business and industry? One myth is that the graduate leaves merely for a higher salary. But data obtained from our M.I.T. study, in which groups of graduates were followed into early career years, have revealed that those who move on from their first job do not on the average now earn more than those who have stayed on. And, significantly, in interviews with graduates about their problems during their first few years at work, the topic of salary seldom is mentioned.

The roots of the dissatisfaction that lead to resignation are far deeper. They are embedded in the psychological conflict between the graduate's expectations and values, and the company's attempt to indoctrinate him in its values.

In one way or another, my research long has been focused on trying to understand what happens to a person when he accepts membership in an organization. My interest originally was kindled by my studies of brainwashing — or coercive persuasion, as I prefer to call it — of Western prisoners by the Communists during the Korean war. Later, I thought I could discern parallels between that kind of indoctrination and the breaking-in process a college graduate goes through when he enters an

American corporation as an employee.

To determine the impact of the organization on the attitudes and values of its new members, I undertook a longitudinal study which followed college graduates into their early career years. Sample panels were selected randomly from successive graduating classes at M.I.T.'s Alfred P. Sloan School of Management.

To measure the beliefs, attitudes, and values associated with business, I found it was necessary to design new survey instruments. Existing value tests tended to deal with very broad categories or to tap the stable parts of the person, and, therefore, were relatively insensitive to changes in values and attitudes toward business.

Our information was gathered by a combination of individual interviews, guided group discussions, and attitude and value tests. First we determined the expectations, attitudes, and values of the students before graduation and before they made any job decisions. After the student had accepted a job, he was asked to fill in the same attitude-survey questionnaires, giving the answers that he thought would be given by a typical member of the company or organization he was joining.

Six to nine months after going to work, he was visited and interviewed about his experiences. His immediate company superior and one or more of his co-workers also were interviewed and asked to fill in the same questionnaires. Then, one year after graduation, each panel of graduates was brought together for a three-day reunion and seminar, during which the entire battery of attitude-rating instruments again was administered. Subsequent developments in the careers of these graduates have been followed both in formal meetings and by regular correspondence.

A great deal of research has been conducted to identify and list the factors a student considers important in choosing his first job. However, such listings often identify only the surface characteristics of jobs, things like salary, promotion, and company benefits. In my interviews with students about their attitudes and desires, I soon noticed that they were really concerned with far deeper issues which are not easily represented as questionnaire items.

The graduating student has certain psychological needs of which he may not be aware. However, his needs may be inferred from what he says during interviews and group discussions with his peers. The graduate needs to know:

1. Will the job give me an opportunity to *test myself,* to find out if I can do anything worthwhile, and make a meaningful contribution to the company's efforts?
2. Will the job give me the the opportunity to *learn and grow,* and to make use of my present abilities and education?
3. Will I be able to retain my integrity and individuality, and not be forced to conform to a company pattern or be brainwashed into an organization-man mentality?
4. Will the company be dyanmic and exciting, receptive to new ideas, and run according to rational business principles?

The graduate's views and expectations of business are shaped to a large extent by what he has been taught in his classes. And at the university, the student is taught to look at problems from the perspective of the high-ranking executive or the technical staff expert. He thinks in terms of general concepts and rational principles. He has been trained to the overview. He is ready to solve basic, long-term problems, rather than day-to-day operating procedures.

He also has been taught an ethic of pure rationality and emotional neutrality, taught to analyze problems and to make decisions independently of his feelings about people or organizations. These are essentially professional values which universities try to impart to their students.

In most courses dealing with business problems, the student is taught approaches based on the most recent advances in mathematics, psychology, economics, operations research, statistics, and other disciplines. These approaches tend to idealize the problem, emphasizing what is possible in principle rather than the current realities and what is possible in practice. In effect, our college professors teach their students the management techniques of the future. In his first job, however, the college graduate often discovers that he is expected to put his advanced-management concepts into deep freeze and develop the sort of *ad hoc* widsom which he was taught to avoid at school Here's what some graduates in our research sample said about the value of their education:

"A good status symbol . . ."

"My education was more helpful in obtaining than in keeping a job."

"I have not had occasion to consult any of my textbooks . . . the value was in the overall program."

"Of most value is the way you learn to think . . . awareness of the big picture."

"You feel more confident . . . it buffers you from complete ignorance in areas that are not your specialty."

"Good priesthood training . . . you've been anointed."

His education has taught the college graduate management principles and how to take the corporate point of view, but his initial job experiences are aimed at teaching him how to be a good subordinate, how to be influenced, and how to be a loyal and reliable member of the organization.

Ideally, what the organization hopes for from the college graduate is ability to do a job and competence to deal with technical factors. The company needs young men who have good ideas and who can turn these ideas into practical programs, and sell those programs to others in the organization. And so senior executives and personnel recruiters may tell the graduate that they are counting on him to bring fresh points of view and new management techniques.

But the graduate soon finds that his managers and fellow workers resist change or innovation. In my interviews with graduates after they had been on the job for six months to one year, almost every one stated in one way or another that he was shocked by the degree to which his "good ideas" were rejected, the way they were undermined, sidetracked or even sabotaged. The typical sequence went like this: The new graduate was given an assignment to look into some procedure; he found some flaws in it, recommended some changes. And then nothing happened.

What else does the graduate discover during his first year on the job? Here are some representative quotes drawn from my study:

"Things are more disorganized than I expected."

"I ran into conflict with procedures . . . shaped by people far higher up . . . the informal methods of handling things, you can't buck that."

"The company has a program of planned frustration, of keeping you one step behind all the time; as soon as you master one thing, you discover so many other barriers."

"Such a tight rein is kept on you that you are not really allowed to make a mistake."

"The number of unproductive people in the corporation is simply astounding."

"They encourage deadwood to stay to get costs up to get more profits, and then have a big cost-reduction program at the same time; but top management is not really interested in cost reduction."

"All the problems boil down to communication and human relations."

"It's hard to tell when you have been promoted."

"It was quite a while before others who were below me were told my position."

"First you can't get agreement on a diagnosis and then you get resistance to change . . . you are told: Stick around for 30 years and if it is still a problem then we'll look into it."

The graduate also finds that coming up with a rational, technical solution is not enough. One graduate put it well: "I thought I could sell people with logic and was amazed at the hidden agendas people have, irrational objections; really bright people will come up with stupid excuses . . . they have their own little empires to worry about."

Not only does the graduate find his rational ideals upset, he also becomes emotionally involved in a way that he did not anticipate. After listening to a number of graduates discuss their job difficulties during the first year, I became aware that one of their most difficult problems was learning to accept emotionally the reality of the organization's human side.

With many graduates, their basic approach was not how to work in and around the human organization, but rather how to make the human organization go away. The legitimacy and reality of the human aspects of the company were being resisted at an emotional level, and the graduates were expressing a strong wish to exist in a world that by their own definition was totally rational.

The degree to which the graduate is able to accept the human organization at the emotional level may be directly related to his potential as a manager or executive. The few men who had accepted the human organization with all its foibles soon learned to apply their analytical abilities and high intelligence to getting the job done. But those who resisted accepting this reality used up their energy in denial and complaint rather than in current problem solving.

Often the same man who would view a complex technical problem as a great challenge would find the human problem unworthy of his efforts. Unlearning this attitude may well be a key factor in becoming an effective manager.

Lack of adequate feedback on their performance was another common complaint of our graduates. Of course, what fed their dissatisfaction was the underlying expectation that they should learn something on their first job and that they should get some direct reaction. This is not surprising in a group so recently out of college, where they lived a life full of feedback through examinations or grades. By failing to realize this need in the new graduate, most companies may be missing an important opportunity to train him. On the other hand, the ultimate challenge for the graduate may be to learn how to judge his own performance.

Some of the graduates also had a

problem of determining to whom in the company they owed their loyalty. One graduate presented a typical incident; "The works manager called me in and gave me a Dutch-uncle talk and defined Operations Research to me by which he meant the limitations of the use of the method; he did not really want corporate headquarters to know how bad things were in certain areas."

This put the graduate in a quandary: Should I be loyal to the department or to the overall organization? Our research shows that the first year constitutes a real and rough test of the graduates' commitment to their career plans.

Most men in our sample found their experiences full of frustrations that slowed them down. It was as though their integrity were being tested, and at the same time they were being conditioned to become compliant and to fit into the company mold. Our graduates found it very difficult to judge how much frustration was normal and how to decide whether to adapt to or leave the organization. The temptation to learn complacency is great, as illustrated by the following quote: "I can't convince people when I think that I am right; I don't know how people will react when I'm wrong; the result is that I ease off and stop pushing so hard."

While the first year provided a test of career commitment, most graduates reported they had little opportunity to *test themselves*. Often the work was totally unchallenging, and couldn't possibly make any difference to company performance no matter how well it was done. Or the graduate was hired for a specific assignment but once at work said he quit his first job because: "They were pleased with work that required only two hours per day. I wasn't."

The supervisor or manager to whom the new graduate is assigned hopes to find a man who can learn to be a good apprentice, a good staff man, a good junior problem solver, and perhaps a good low-level administrator. He expects the graduate to prove his loyalty to the company by accepting this career path gracefully.

While some managers have a highly realistic view of the needs and characteristics of new college graduates, many executives unfortunately see the college graduate as a stereotype: overambitious, unrealistic in his expectations, wanting too much money and responsibility too soon, immature, and too inexperienced for much responsibility. There is also a feeling that the recent graduate expects his education has given him some special privilege to move up fast in the organization; but that he is too theoretical and idealistic to solve practical problems; and that he is unwilling to learn the difference between having good ideas and knowing how to carry them out.

The psychological makeup of the manager is also a factor. He may well be less educated than his new subordinate, and he may have worked long, hard years to get to his present insecure position of power. He may resent the fact that the new college graduate commands a far higher starting salary than he once did — and in fact may be getting a salary uncomfortably close to his own. In addition, the manager may feel threatened by all the new management theory the graduate brings with him, much of which he, the boss, may find difficult to understand. He also knows that the new graduate well may surpass him in the next few years.

The impasse is understandable. For the graduate there seems no way to break the stereotype mold as long as he can't do meaningful work. Eager to prove himself, he oversells his education. But the boss reacts. He must put the new man in his place, and so he systematically ignores ideas which spring from the graduate's education. The graduate strives all the more for an assignment so he can prove himself. To the boss, this comes on as excessive ambition and as unwillingness to buckle down to learn. The new man, who has begun to doubt that the company can provide him with opportunities to do something worthwhile, finds his worst suspicions confirmed by his manager's behavior. And neither one understands the reactions and the needs of the other.

And so the graduate with a strong drive to do worthwhile work may move on to a new job. Occasionally a graduate succeeds in establishing a rapport with his manager that makes it possible for him to get good assignments without threatening his supervisor too much. This happens, as a rule, when a company is expanding and generating more problems than any manager can handle. In this situation, the boss is forced to give the graduate challenging work. To the manager's surprise, the graduate often does it extremely well.

The most tragic resolution is when the college graduate decides to stop trying and becomes apathetic and complacent. He adapts to the organizational realities which confront him immediately and never sees that these may change and he may be robbing himself of his future. From the company's point of view, the great loss is that the graduate may be trained *out* of the most valuable resources he brings to the job: his drive, his integrity, his desire to take on and solve difficult problems, and his high hopes.

Once apathy and complacency develop in an employee, it is probably difficult to resurrect the initial commitment. No wonder so many companies discover there is a middle management problem and a dearth of men dynamic enough for the top jobs.

The impasse is unfortunate because it is *unintended* by the company and *unanticipated* by the graduate. And, aside from the resulting high job turnover, it develops an unhealthy organization-man mentality.

Because of this failure to understand what the college graduate really wants and needs in his first job, the way he is utilized in his first years at work does not meet either his needs or the company needs. The graduate needs to be given the opportunity to test himself with work that clearly matters. He also needs adequate feedback on his performance. Yet many organizations resist giving responsible assignments to new college graduates. In doing this, the company may be unwittingly putting off a most important test — the chance for the company to evaluate the man, and for the graduate to test himself.

The college graduate may realize that he is immature and inexperienced. He is typically a postadolescent who has not yet solved all the problems of his own identity or of how to deal with authority. But he comes to his first job expecting the company to be sympathetic and to help him overcome his problems. He desperately needs to test himself in the safety of a good, secure relationship with a superior, yet often the supervisor views the idealistic expectations of the graduate as characteristics that must be promptly exorcised.

If a company takes the view that its present managers are more mature psychologically than the incoming graduate, then it would seem that the company's responsibility is to help the new man through the period of adaptation which he must go through. The company must recognize that the graduate's first supervisor exerts the strongest influence in shaping the young man's attitudes and feelings toward the organization. It is the first boss who can launch the graduate into a successful career or corporate oblivion. How paradoxical that many companies have elaborate training programs for *incoming* college graduates, but few train the men who determine how the graduate actually is utilized in his first years at work!

One obvious remedy is to select men who are mature and secure in their knowledge as supervisors of new college graduates. Special training programs and seminars should be instituted for these managers, where management men could share their problems and successes in handling college graduates, and discuss how to develop meaningful assignments for them, how to handle the high energy, the idealism, the conceit, and the underlying insecurity. College and business school faculty members could be brought in to discuss the kind of education today's student receives. College graduates who have been launched successfully in careers could tell what helped them over the first job hurdle. While such a training program is expensive, I am convinced that it would be far less costly than high employee turnover rate and the frustrations of the present system.

As for the college graduate, if he aspires to an executive position, he must come to terms with his own immaturity. He must learn to cope with the organization emotionally, as well as intellectually. He must accept some emotional unlearning and relearning must occur so he can cope with the managing of people. Most of the graduates in our research sample told us that education had prepared them very well technically but it had not given them the psychological tools for dealing and working with people. This is an area for the universities to explore. Business courses could be designed to teach a student how to translate ideas into practical programs. With our knowledge of group dynamics and organizational psychology, there is no excuse for not offering such courses.

One obvious solution to the problem of bringing the realities of organizational life to the student is to develop an apprenticeship program as part of his education — the Antioch kind of approach.

Another area in which reform is possible is the way in which college graduates are recruited for jobs in business and industry. A better dialogue is necessary between the university, the student, and the hiring organization. Many of the unrealistic expectations that the new graduate brings with him to his first job are built up by the recruiter's sales pitch. The company recruiter's task is to find the best possible men for the least amount of money. But in a tight labor market he often is forced to get bodies in the door at any cost. So he makes promises and paints glowing pictures of challenging work and opportunities for promotion that may have quite a remote connection with reality.

The graduating student has certain needs and questions, but he cannot discuss these frankly with the recruiter, partly because he is not fully aware of them and partly because the rules of the job-hunting game discourage frank discussion of personal desires. The accepted rules limit talk to salary, benefits, opportunities for promotion, and other issues which in truth have little to do with his hopes and aspirations. Both the recruiter and the graduating student, therefore, well may form false pictures of each other.

Many of the unrealistic expectations of the new graduate might be avoided if recruiters and the first managers of the graduates could coordinate their activities to some extent. In some ways this already is beginning to occur with the trend for graduates to be interviewed and hired by the line managers they will be working for rather than by professional recruiters.

The conclusions presented here are derived largely from an intensive longitudinal study of graduates selected from M.I.T.'s Sloan School of Management. The study has given us a clearer understanding of the problems facing graduates in their early careers, and we currently are planning a broad-gauge study of graduates from ten or fifteen universities, utilizing the techniques and survey instruments that we have developed.

Both universities and companies are social systems which indoctrinate or "socialize" their new members to their values, norms, and behavior patterns. As my M.I.T. colleague, Leo Moore, so aptly puts it: "Organizations like to put their fingerprints on people."

The process of socialization is so ubiquitous that it is easily overlooked. It occurs in school, where the student is socialized to value reasoning and knowledge, and again — perhaps most dramatically — when as a graduate he takes his first job. He encounters it all over again if he leaves one company to join another. The speed and effectiveness of the process in companies determine the morale, productivity, and turnover rate of its employees. The force of organizational socialization can be analyzed and controlled and we should not shrink away from social engineering to help the graduate launch his career successfully.

A conversation with Peter F. Drucker: Or the psychology of managing management

Mary Harrington Hall

Peter Drucker is perhaps the most respected management consultant in this country, and his clients include some of the nation's most respected companies. Born in Vienna, educated in Austria, England, and Germany, he received his law degree from Frankfurt University. After working as a newspaperman in Europe, he became an economist with a London international banking house. Drucker came to this country in 1937, continuing as an economist until 1942, when he began a seven-year association with Bennington College as professor of politics. In 1957, he was awarded the American Marketing Association's Parlin Award, and now is on the New York University faculty. His books include

The Practice of Management, shown by a *Harvard Business Review* survey to be read by more top executives than any other book in the field, as well as *Managing for Results,* and *The Effective Executive,* both rapidly becoming bibles for students of the business world.

Mary Harrington Hall: How can young people today know just where they might fit in this wide-open kind of world? How can they choose?

Peter Drucker: Here I am 58, and I still don't know what I am going to do when I grow up. My children and their respective spouses think I am kidding when I say that, but I am not. You know what I mean; they don't. Nobody tells them that life is not that categorized. And nobody tells them that the only way to find what you want is to create a job. Nobody worth his salt has ever moved into an existing job. That's for post office clerks.

Hall: Whether they actually are in the post office or not.

Drucker: Primarily, out of the post office. But if you told this to the 22-year-old, I don't think it would register. He doesn't understand it, and no one can make him understand. There are a few elementary things you can say.

Hall: And what are they?

Drucker: First, you know what you don't want to do, but what you *do* want to do you don't know. There is no way of finding out but by trying. Second, one doesn't marry a job. A job is your opportunity to find out — that's all it is. You owe no loyalty to your employer other than not betraying secrets. Be ruthless about finding out whether you belong; I am. Finally, looking around doesn't get you anywhere. One can always quit. Don't try to reason out those things one can learn only from experience. Do you know enough about yourself? There are things you can know, even at age 20.

Hall: When I was 20 I knew so many things. I knew that life was exciting and romantic and a great adventure. What should my career thoughts have been?

Drucker: To start out, I think one of the most important things would be to know if you like pressure or if you cannot take it at all. There may be people who can take pressure or leave it alone, but I have never met any of them. I am one who needs pressure. You are one, too, Mary. If there is no deadline staring us in the face, we have to invent one. I am sluggish, lethargic, a lizard, until the adrenaline starts pouring. A low metabolism — psychologically. People differ so. One of the men I am closest to goes to pieces under pressure. He is one of the best urologists. But he spends nights at the bedside of a critically ill patient, and it is obvious he is going to pieces before the patient dies. Mind you, he pulls a lot of them through, but he cannot take the pressure. He's a wreck — which probably makes him a good doctor.

Hall: What else should you know besides your ability to stand pressure?

Drucker: You have to know whether you belong in a big organization. In a big organization, you don't see results, you are too damn far away from them. The enjoyment is being a part of the big structure. If you tell people you work for General Electric, everyone knows what G.E. is. And I think you need to know whether you want to be in daily combat as a dragon-slayer or if you want to think things through, to analyze, prepare. Do you enjoy surmounting the daily crisis, or do you really get your satisfaction out of anticipating and preventing the crisis? These things I believe one *does* know about oneself at age 20.

Hall: What is the hardest thing to know?

Drucker: There is one great question I don't think most young people can answer: "Are you a perceptive or an analytical person?" This is terribly important. Either you start out with an insight and then think the problem through, or you start out with a train of thought and arrive at a conclusion. One really needs to be able to do both, but most people can't. I am totally unanalytical and completely perceptive. I have never in my life understood anything that I have not seen.

Hall: What about being a listener or a reader?

Drucker: That's another thing most young people don't know — are they readers or listeners? And this is something they can check easily.

Hall: It's like being right or left-handed, isn't it?

Drucker: That's right. The only ambidextrous people are trial lawyers — they both read and listen. Nobody else can. I am a listener; I can read after I listen but not before. Probably I can't even write first, but that's pathological.

Hall: But what is the most important thing about the choice of the job, apart from the personality of the person?

Drucker: Job content. The question is not, am I interested in biology. That interest may or may not change. You can't tell. This issue is: when you work, do you want to sit down to a stack of information reports and to plot figures for two weeks, or do you want to go around and pick people's brains? Do you enjoy being alone, or do you have to be a member of a team? How do you really function?

There is a fabulous amount of misinformation about jobs, because there is not one job pattern that is clear. You just can't tell by the field.

Hall: I've always thought maybe a university graduate school faculty was a more conformist bunch than a group of bankers.

Drucker: There are businesses that are quite conformist, but there is nothing as conformist as a graduate faculty. The Ph.D. program is even worse.

There are businesses that are wide open, like positions in the international divisions of some big banks — the Bank of America, Chase Manhattan, or First National City Bank of New York are examples. Their young men are really entrepreneurs. They invent new services and new branches, and no one says them nay. And there are government jobs meant for the kind of fellow who draws to an inside royal flush.

John Lindsay in New York has that kind of government job, or Richard Lee in New Haven. There are terrific opportunities in Washington in the Office of Health, Education, and Welfare. Not in the education section, though. That's dead. Another place for the creative guy is in the environmental sciences section of the Department of Commerce. You've got to be good there. They are ruthless, as they should be, if you don't come up with solid, original ideas.

Hall: Are job stereotypes changing?

Drucker: Jobs cannot be typified, cannot by classified. Ten or twenty years ago bankers were good Anglo-Saxons who parted their hair in the middle. That is no longer necessarily so. In New York a fellow with a red beard who goes barefoot to work is vice-president of a commercial bank today.

Hall: Is that *really* true, Peter Drucker?

Drucker: Yes, he can do it so long as

he stays in the data-processing department. I met him at lunch today. He's a vice-president of one of the very big banks and is very young. I don't think it's necessary for him to pretend he's 19 any longer, but that's his business.

Hall: How old is he, really?

Drucker: About 36, I would say.

Hall: What on earth has happened to banking in the past ten years?

Drucker: Nothing has happened to banking. Banks have discovered that if they have a computer that costs a million dollars a month, they had better have somebody who can make it produce. And if he goes barefoot and has a red beard and wears a blue undershirt, you just make damn sure you don't expose him to the clientele. Nobody has to see him except the computer, and the computer has no great fashion preferences. On the other hand, no university faculty would dare to hire him. And for good reasons.

Hall: Would that be the unpopularity of the image because of current student style?

Drucker: It wouldn't be his red beard, his going barefoot, or his peculiar sweatshirt that the university would mind. It would be the fact that they have to expose him. Chances are that he cannot get along with human beings. He talks so much about love that everybody hates him. The university needs somebody much more conformist than this. But the bank will set him up. I imagine the older credit officers of the bank are duly shocked, but then you know that puritans need to be shocked twice a day anyhow.

Hall: Yes, good for their livers.

Drucker: Right. Exactly.

Hall: So it's not a matter of the field, biology or education or medicine or psychology or engineering, but the specific kind of job within the field.

Drucker: Right. And there's another highly important matter. No matter what job it is, it ain't final. The first few years are trials. The probability that the first choice you make is right for you is roughly one in a million. If you decide your first choice is the right one, chances are you are just plain lazy. People believe that if they take their job for General Electric or New York University or *Psychology Today* that they have taken their vows, that the world will come to an end if it doesn't work out.

Hall: How many of us know from the very beginning what we want to be?

Drucker: There are a very few who know at, say, age 11, "This is where I want to be." They are either musicians or mathematicians or physicians. And, incidentally, the physicians all go through a horrible identity crisis when they reach the age of 28.

Hall: Why is that?

Drucker: Because medical school is unspeakably boring. They all go into medicine because they are dedicated. Then it is so Goddam scientific for seven or eight years. They are taught to be callous and to learn the bones of the body, only to forget them tomorrow. Then, when they have finished their internship or their residency, they have a terrible crisis. Only yesterday I wrote a long letter to a very sweet boy who just finished his medical training. Now he wants to go back to school and learn philosophy, because he is so terribly distraught. He doesn't realize that almost any sensitive young doctor goes through this. The medical faculties don't tell the kids. They think it's a good idea not to warn them that they will undergo a crisis. Most of them come back to medicine when they discover that once you are out of medical school, you *do* deal with people and you don't really know very much. Then they rediscover medicine. But medical school is a great place to be weaned away from being a physician.

Hall: You say that it's important to know yourself before you can know what kind of job best suits you. How early do you think this assessment can be made?

Drucker: Contrary to everything that modern psychologists tell you, I am convinced that one can acquire knowledge, one can acquire skills, but one cannot change his personality. Only the Good Lord changes personality — that's His business. I have had four great children, and I can assure you that by the time they were six months old, they were set in concrete. After six months, parents get educated, but not children.

One can take a child and try to bring him out of excessive timidity, but you won't ever make a bold one out of him. Or, one can take a bold one, a rash one, and try to teach him how to count to ten before shooting with the hope that he will count at least to three. But that is all one can do. One can take a charmer and try to get him — charmers are mostly boys — to work to catch up with what he has improvised. And one can get one of those awful, horrible, overplanners to jump once in a while. But you are not going to change the basic structure. It is much more important that in this age of psychology people tell the kids that what you *are* matters, and your values matter.

Hall: Now, what about going to graduate school? Suppose one has learned all he can about himself. Should he go on to graduate school before he tries his first job?

Drucker: As long as you go to graduate school to avoid the draft, it's rational. I don't criticize that at all. If Uncle Sam set up the draft in such a way that you are rewarded for getting out of it, don't complain if this is done. People always be-

have as they are rewarded. If the present draft system is immoral, and God help me, it is, then it is the draft that is to blame and not the kids who react to a clear incentive.

I'm not sure that it wouldn't be a smart thing for all of them to go into the Army at the age of 18. Military service is juvenile. At the age of 18, one enjoys it; at 21 or 22, one has outgrown it.

But apart from staying out of the draft, in graduate school they are going to postpone *themselves,* and they will do so with the peculiar idea that *academia* is a free environment. They soon discover that graduate school is our least vented environment. The arrogance, the petty restrictions of the learned are horrible. Nothing is more demeaning than to be forced to be conventionally unconventional.

Hall: Politics in the groves of academe fascinate and appall me. The infighting is worse than in the old Kansas City or Boston wards. And the academicians are far more shrewd and vicious.

Drucker: There's only one kind of politics that's worse. We have only 2,000 colleges, and *academia* is not so narrow here as in Europe. But look at musicians. This country has never been able to support more than 25 pianists. If you are a first-rate pianist, you take the bread out of somebody's mouth. That's not quite true of *academia,* but there is a horrible frustration if you are not Number One. In *academia* there are numerous jobs for the merely competent man, but not room for him. The kids don't understand this.

Hall: Would you say, go into the Peace Corps first, before going to graduate school?

Drucker: No! The Peace Corps is a great disappointment.

Hall: How can you say that? Why?

Drucker: I always thought the kids would get a tremendous amount out of the Peace Corps, but I have seen too many when they came back. In their personal development, they are exactly where they were when they left. The Peace Corps is just a postponement, a delay. My conclusion is that one belongs in the Peace Corps in his thirties, not in his twenties. In the twenties he belongs in the city administration of San Pedro, or out selling Gallo wine.

Hall: Out selling wine? Gallo?

Drucker: Let me tell you about one of the nicest boys I know. He took a job as a salesman for one of the large wineries. His parents were beside themselves. I asked him why he went to work as a salesman. "To find out what I can do," he answered. "But why did you go to work for a winery?" I asked. You see, he had offers from Ford and IBM and Minneapolis-Honeywell. "At the winery," he answered, "I'm the only one who can read and write."

Now he's a bright boy. I don't think he'll stay long with the winery unless he's made president within five years. That might happen. Or he might go back to law school. This boy knows exactly what he's doing. He is trying himself out. If he does a good job, he will be right at the top. If he doesn't work out, nothing has happened. Too many kids with too many opportunities are just playing around. They know only what they don't want.

Hall: I see what you mean. You think that any good young person should go out and jump in somewhere, anywhere.

Drucker: Yes, and not with the typical question the kids ask the recruiters: Is this the right place to stay for the next 25 years? Hell, the answer in all likelihood is no. There is a right question to ask the recruiter: Is this a place where I can learn something for two years and have fun for two years, and where I will have a chance if I produce?

Hall: All right. I believe you. You'd put off graduate school?

Drucker: I'd put off elementary school if I had my way. I am not a great believer in school. School is primarily an institution for perpetuation of adolescence.

Hall: If you don't believe in school how would you educate?

Drucker: That is an entirely different question. The thought that school educates is not one I have accepted yet. No, I am not joking.

Hall: I know you are not joking.

Drucker: No, Mary, I would be much happier if kids at age 17 were young adults among adults. Those who wanted to go back to school could come back later. They would be better students and much happier people. But I don't control the universe. In the university we expect everybody to sit on his butt through the full natural life span of man — which is about 25. All I can say is, thank God I am not young. I could not survive this horror. The only thing my secondary school faculty and I were in total agreement on was that I sat too long and did not belong in school. In this we were in total agreement. Otherwise, we had few points of contact. Adolescence is a man-made problem. It is not a stage of nature.

Hall: Do you think this has some bearing on the unrest and rioting on college campuses?

Drucker: I am not a bit surprised that the kids riot. I am surprised that they are so placid, because they are all so unspeakably bored. Seriously, though, I am not at all opposed to graduate school *per se.* I am opposed to graduate school as a delaying action. I am opposed to a graduate school as hibernation. And I am opposed to graduate school as education, which it is not.

Hall: Just how would you define graduate school?

Drucker: Graduate school is not focused on forming a human being but on imparting a finer set of skills. The purpose is not education, but specialization. My guess is that 20 years from now, the existing academic departments will all be gone. There is not a single one left that makes any sense.

Today knowledge exists in action, not in hard-covered books. But I am very biased. I am a doer, not a contemplator, a perceiver, not a thinker. I am one of those who has to listen to himself to know what he is thinking or saying all the time. These are all very undesirable characteristics, so I am not at all the type that graduate schools look for. There are plenty of kids to fill them up.

Hall: Did you go from the university into management consultant work, or was it the other way around?

Drucker: I have always taught on the side, because I like to teach. I started teaching at 20 when I was in law school out of sheer boredom. It was the only way to stay alive. I was working and studying and teaching too. After I finished secondary school, I went to work in England as an apprentice clerk in a woolen-export house. I was the first person to start apprenticeship as late as 18. All my bosses' sons started at 14. And I was the first who did not live over the premises — solely because a fire had destroyed the premises.

And I was the first not to start off with a goose-quill pen. That was the year they discovered they couldn't buy goose-quill pens anymore. I told all this to a friend of mine who said that only showed I didn't start off in a high-class establishment. When he began as an apprentice at a merchant bank, the banker bought a goose farm when he found out he couldn't buy goose-quill pens.

Hall: That sounds like something out of Charles Dickens. How did you get there?

Drucker: Well, I grew up in Vienna, but my family had very close ties with England.

By the way, the only connection I can claim with psychology is that my family knew Freud. My father knew him from boyhood and put him on a pedestal as a genius who could do no wrong. My mother's reaction was quite different. When she was a young medical student, she was one of Freud's favorites. (She was one of the first women to go to medical school. She had to go to Zurich to do it.) She understood why he was important but at the same time she refused to have anything to do with him. Freud loved her but she couldn't stand him.

Hall: Why couldn't she stand Freud?

Drucker: She felt that he was an evil man. She was a perceptive person. My father saw this man as a genius, and felt that geniuses should be allowed anything.

Hall: Why did your mother feel that Freud was an evil man?

Drucker: Because he was, period. He was a man who had to domineer.

Hall: Let's get back to your own life. Where did you go from your apprenticeship in the export business?

Drucker: I went to Germany. I went into investment banking there. In 1929, as you may have heard, there was a slight unpleasantness. Investment banking came to an end, and I became a newspaperman. But all the time, I was enrolled as a law student.

Hall: I didn't know that you had been a journalist.

Drucker: In a way I have never ceased being one. But for two periods in my life this was my main occupation. For a few years in the late twenties and early thirties when I worked on the Continent primarily as one of the editors of a German daily paper and then in the late thirties when I first came to the United States as American correspondent for a group of British papers. But I have really been writing all my life, and it is the only thing I claim any skill in. And in between my newspaper jobs, for four years right after the Nazis came to power, I was in London as an investment banker and economist.

Hall: You did quite a few things as a young man.

Drucker: Yes, until I was 30 I was really a drifter. I knew perfectly well all the things I didn't want to do with myself. In retrospect, I realize that I must have been a very sorry specimen and I do marvel at my parents' patience with me. It was not until I came to this country that I realized what I wanted.

Hall: But you were very successful in that interim period.

Drucker: I looked successful, but I wasn't. This is why I have such sympathy with today's young people. What saved me, they don't have. I had to have a job to pay the rent. And they, instead, have Uncle Sam with a graduate grant, which makes finding yourself a good deal harder than hard times did for my generation.

Hall: Your background and your family's is about as broad as one could ask. I know your father was an important figure in the Austrian government, an international lawyer, and a founder of the Salzburg Festival.

Drucker: Narrowness is no fun. As a writer, I think your interviews with B.F. Skinner, the father of operant conditioning, and with the humanist Rollo May, were totally marvelous.

You made so clear what Skinner has

really been talking about.

Hall: Skinner was incredibly patient in making it clear to me.

Drucker: I wish I were one-tenth as brilliant as Fred Skinner. But he is so totally a prisoner of his work that he doesn't realize what he has done.

Hall: How can you say that?

Drucker: I overstate because I worry that he may be "advertising" his work under wrong labels. He has contributed a fantastic amount, and I worry that it may get lost. God, I wish there were more of him.

Your were wonderful to Rollo May. You made him mean things he didn't know he knew.

Hall: He is an impressive thinker and a great man.

Drucker: Well, you brought out what some of us had suspected. May is a wise man. A very wise man.

I have a close friend in New York who is the diagnostician's diagnostician, and six months ago I wrote to him about a friend and he wrote back that the man didn't need a psychiatrist, he needed a friend. This is what Rollo May has been to our generation. And he doesn't know it, and you brought it out.

Hall: You came to the United States before the Second World War?

Drucker: Yes. In April, 1937. Here I also taught on the side. I taught philosophy at Bennington, then I came here to New York University. I am not a proper model for anything.

Hall: Oh, I think you are a swinging model.

Drucker: No, no, no. I am not a scholar; I am a writer. You know the difference?

Hall: Yes, there can be a vast sea between the two.

Drucker: Few people are aware of it. I am proud of not being a scholar. I am a writer, but I am not good enough to write novels. I always like to teach, because I like young people and I like the excitement of people discovering things.

Hall: When did you switch entirely to management consulting?

Drucker: I haven't. The book I am working on has nothing to do with management. It's about discontinuities — in politics, in economy. I don't have a title for it yet.

Hall: Tell me about it.

Drucker: For years and years I have been writing slowly on a book about basic American experiences, such as the separation of church and state. The only chapter I have finished is called "The Education of a Pretender." It's about Henry Adams. The title of the book probably will be *The American Political Genius* or *The American Patriot.* I am tired of management books.

Hall: You may be tired of management books, but our readers want to know about careers. Young people want to know how to find their particular round hole, or square — depending on their shape. You said the young person looking for a career should figure: "Do I fit into the large corporation?" or "Should I be on my own?" But what is the opportunity for being on one's own? Isn't the large corporation most likely?

Drucker: Even in General Electric there are places where you can be on your own, plenty of them. But let's go back to examples once again. I know two young men, each of whom decided he would like to be completely on his own. One is building a very nice business as a computer consultant on the West Coast. The other one is in the East, building his own design engineering firm. These young men are loners, they are extremes. I am one myself. But take a more typical case. Yesterday, I had a young

scientist here. He had been with a medium-sized company for eight years, was their number two man in research. He wanted a change, but refused to go into a big company. He knew he'd get better pay there, but he said that unless he was in on a whole project, from the formulation of the proposal to NASA all the way to the prototype delivery, he wasn't interested. This morning, I think I found him the job he wants.

Hall: What kind of job?

Drucker: A job as head of the field in instrumentation design at one of the country's largest hospitals. He knows nothing about biochemistry, but he can learn. He will work with the surgeons there and will head a small group of a half a dozen engineers and biochemists. Now the hospital is a hell of a big organization — 1,800 patient beds — but he won't even see the big organization.

Hall: He must be darned bright.

Drucker: On the contrary. I wouldn't send a bright boy to a hospital. It would be a great waste; they wouldn't know what to do with him.

Hall: You keep running into complaints about technology. Clark Kerr has said that we can't really make our peace with technology. How can the individual survive and function in this technology?

Drucker: There is no war; there is fear. The attitude of this generation is, what can we do for the computer? The next generation will solve the problem; their attitude will be: What will the computer do for me? It doesn't ever pay to be permissive and pleasant about mechanical gadgets. Be nasty. Throw it out if it doesn't perform.

Hall: I wonder if people were afraid of the light switch once.

Drucker: That's right. I don't know whether you know that the first advanced management training course was one that the German Post Office used in 1888. Its topic was the use of the telephone. Believe me, the next generation is going to look upon the computer the way today's teenager looks upon the telephone. At the moment you realize that you can always pull the plug, the fear is ended. Once you know what you want to do, either it can do it for you or it can't. The computer is a tool. If the tool can't do something for you, leave it in the tool box.

Hall: And careers are a tool, too.

Drucker: Precisely. The smart way to look at a career is, What does it do for me? What do I want to accomplish?

Hall: Are there any special things to look for in a company?

Drucker: Yes. You want old age at top management. You know, one question the young career seeker never asks the company recruiter is, "How old are the department heads?"

Hall: You want old ones so you can come up, right?

Drucker: Oh, my yes. You don't want the First National City Bank in the city, for instance.

Hall: They're all young?

Drucker: Oh, yes; the executive vice president is 36. Too many companies are actually lopsided. You want a company with some old and some young at the head.

Hall: Then I don't want Edgar Bronfman's Seagram's and assorted enterprises?

Drucker: Anyone would want a company run by him. He's creative. But you would prefer to have him be 90 years old if you plan to inherit his job.

Hall: People are younger longer now. How has this changed the job picture?

Drucker: The real career crisis is the extension of the working-life span. In the time of our grandparents, man's working life was over at 45. By then, few people were physically or mentally capable of working. It was a rural civilization and the preindustrial farmer was either worn out or had been killed by an accident by age 45. The Chinese or Irish who built our railroads had a five-year working life. Within five years they were gone — by liquor, or syphilis, or accident, or hard work.

Now suddenly, you have people reaching the age of 65 in the prime of physical and mental health. This is due partly to the movement of people from the farm to the city — accidents occur on the farm with about ten times the frequency of that in the most dangerous industrial employment — and partly to scientific management taking the toil out of labor. We have pushed up education to compensate for this.

Hall: What possible solution is there other than a continual increasing of lifelong education programs?

Drucker: I am absolutely convinced that one of the greatest needs is the systematic creation of second careers. At 45, after having been a market research man, or a professor of English or psychology, or an officer in the armed services for 20 years, man is spent. At least he thinks so. But he is mentally, biologically, and physically sound. His kids are grown up and the mortgage is paid off and he has plenty to contribute to society.

You know, one of the most thrilling things that has happened in the last 20 years is the new careers for the crop of military officers who are being axed by the military services at age 47. They've reached lieutenant colonel or lieutenant commander, gone as far as they can go, and they're out.

Hall: What does one do after 20 years as an officer?

Drucker: That's exactly what they want to know. They are absolutely sure there is nothing they can do. They are terribly conscious that they have been in an insulated, artificial environment.

Hall: I should think they'd be scared to death.

Drucker: They *are,* scared out of their wits. Most of them think they need a graduate degree or some kind of guidance. All they need is for someone to say: "Look, Jack, there's nothing wrong with you." They can apply to one of the big downtown law firms for a job as office manager. These have 99 people who know nothing but law, and they need someone to organize them. There are jobs as business managers of law firms or accounting firms or small colleges. All kinds of good jobs.

Hall: It would be like starting life all over again.

Drucker: Six months after these former service men have taken on their new jobs, they are 20 years younger. They have recovered enthusiasm, they are growing, they have ideas. Their wives are enchanted. They are exciting again.

Hall: Not everybody would be a success as an office manager. Are there any other jobs that are especially suited to second careers?

Drucker: Indeed there are. The older professions are best suited to become second careers. Middle age is really the best time to switch to being the lawyer, the teacher, the priest, the doctor — I shocked you — and the social worker. Twenty years from now, we'll have few young men in these fields.

Hall: However would you train a man to be a doctor as a second career?

Drucker: It is not very difficult to be a good doctor, a good physician. I am not saying these men could do good heart transplants or diagnose some obscure tropical disease, but they would know full well that this diagnosis is not right and maybe the patient ought to go see a specialist. But they could do the work the average general practitioner faces.

Hall: What has been the reaction of the medical schools to this idea?

Drucker: I've talked to them. I said: "Take men of 45, engineers, weather forecasters, career officers, how would you make doctors of them in one year?" The medical schools said it couldn't be done. I said, "What do you mean it couldn't be done? With the amount of ignorance you have, I could teach you in three weeks." They answered, "It can't be done. They have to learn the bones of the body." But they can look that up, you know. Very rarely does a bone of the throat move into the knee.

And I talked to the archdioceses about putting these men in the parishes as priests in six months. "Can't be done," I was told. But it is going to be done. Most training for these old professions consists of trying to simulate experience. Hell, these people *have* experience.

Hall: Is it being done anywhere?

Drucker: We are putting men into the classroom to teach at the University in six months.

Hall: How?

Drucker: How? By putting them into the classroom, period. Eight out of ten will swim. And, once they swim I work on polishing their style. If they sink, I jump in with a life preserver. What I can't do is to teach them how to swim.

Hall: And if they sink, you pull them out so they can do something else?

Drucker: No, I dry them off and throw them in again.

Hall: In my mind, you are the ideal management consultant. But what you have been describing to me partly is a personal employment agency. How did you ever get into this wonderful thing? I wanted to be a missionary when I was a little girl. You *are* one.

Drucker: Well, I have students, and friends who have kids. And it has gotten around that if you get thrown out of the U.S. Navy on the Eastern seaboard, there is a peculiar character around named Drucker of whom most people strongly disapprove. I'm too frivolous for them.

Hall: What's it like, being a management consultant?

Drucker: Any man who has been a consultant has dealt in the unlicensed practice of psychiatry. The great weakness of an organization is that you can't have a confidant. You are always either boss or subordinate. And people are terribly lonely, terribly lonely. Here comes an outsider, the licensed lunatic, and you just start spilling. What clients tell me is incredible. I know too much about them. Every management consultant has the same experience.

Hall: Doesn't this knowledge help you as a consultant?

Drucker: No.

Hall: It doesn't help at all?

Drucker: Oh, sometimes, But more often, one has to suppress it. I have never liked to be cruel, and as I get older, I hate cruelty more and more. But one has to force oneself to do what is right. Sometimes that means cutting off heads. Then the question is, How do we do it in a compassionate way? If the compassion enters into the initial decision, you get sentimental. In the end, you do much more harm. The real cruelty is always that of sentimental people. And so, one has to force oneself to eliminate all one knows about that poor devil and only bring it in afterwards. You say, Now that we have cut off his head, what do we do with him so that he doesn't feel it? But first, his head must be cut off.

Hall: What happens with the thousands and thousands of people who are stuck, working out their years of retirement?

Drucker: I think company managers will have to learn to sit down and say: "Look, Jack, do you want to stay here or do you really want to do something? If you stay here, you are about as far as you will ever get. Oh, maybe two more raises." Most so-called promotions are not promotions, but raises, you know. It just changes the title. And the boss should say: "You are going to remain a quality control manager. Do you want to do that for 20 more years? We are perfectly happy to have you stay around here. On the other hand, you have all the mortgages paid off. What have you always wanted to do? If you want to become a priest, well, we'll help you." Does this make any sense to you, Mary?

Hall: It makes all the sense in the world.

The perfect manager is just around the corner

"When I grow up? Well, my goal is to become the chief executive officer of a large multinational conglomerate, assume control at a time when its price-earnings ratio and earnings per share are very low, turn it around, and make it a model of economic efficiency and the talk of wall street. But first and most important, I must be a human being responsible to the needs of society."

CAMPUS MEMORANDUM

FROM: Dean, School of Business   TO: Organizational
                                                   Behavior Faculty

As a part of my interviews with a large number of our business students, I asked them about their Organizational Behavior classes. The most common response from both undergraduate and graduate students was that their OB classes were interesting, but they had some problem seeing how certain issues related to their future role as a manager. In addition, I have been talking with a variety of executives in many different organizations and many of them feel that they have a fairly clear notion as to what kinds of skills and behaviors a good manager needs to possess.

While I realize that as a professional school our primary role is to teach people the "skill" of carefully defining and analyzing problems, I feel that we may also have some responsibility to teach students some of the day-to-day behavioral skills needed to effectively function as a supervisor or manager. We have developed managerial accounting, managerial economics, and managerial communications; I wonder if we shouldn't look at the possibility of developing *Managerial Organizational Behavior*.

I would appreciate it if you would consider this issue and perhaps we can discuss it at a future faculty meeting.

Following are the major skills identified by executives which I think we might consider in constituting a skill-training module in our OB classes:

How to conduct a good meeting
How to manage your time
How to make effective decisions
How to develop an organizational support system
How to conduct a performance appraisal
How to deal with problem employees
How to communicate: listening, speaking, and writing
How to manage your career
How to motivate people

SKILLS

Framework for Organizational Analysis

Before an examination of nearly any situation, it is generally helpful to know what key areas might be analyzed. Whether you are discussing your own work setting, a news account of a government agency, or a case in this book, a "road map" can allow you to zero in quickly on central organizational issues. The tendency for many is to move rapidly to solutions, to the action stage. Failure to analyze available information restricts an individual's understanding and insights and thus limits the number of alternatives that are considered. Another pitfall is that students go to one of two extremes: Either there is only one correct answer, or there aren't any answers ("It depends on how you see it"). Avoiding these two extremes and opening up options depends upon your ability to carefully consider the task, people, social, organizational, and environmental factors that are provided in the setting. The following questions are presented as an aid in organizational analysis:

I. What is the problem?
  A. What hurts in the organization?
  B. What factors are contributing to the pain?
  C. What output of the system is not living up to the manager's expectations?

II. Analysis
  A. Task — nature of the business as defined by top management.
     1. What does the organization need to do well in order to succeed? (What are the key variables?)
     2. Important aspects of the task
        a. The amount of uncertainty in the environment
        b. The amount of inter-dependence required between subunits
        c. The time span of the performance cycle
  B. People
     1. What skills and abilities are required of them?
        a. What are their skills and abilities?
        b. How long does it take to develop those skills?
        c. How necessary is on-the-job training?
     2. What types of rewards are they

seeking from their jobs?

3. What types of rewards are they getting from their jobs?

4. How do the people in the various subunits differ from one another in —
   a. Goal orientation (e.g., a scientist vs. a production manager)
   b. Time orientation
   c. Interpersonal orientation

C. Social factors
   1. What is the nature of the existing social system?
      a. What are the norms of the group?
      b. How strong is the group's influence on individual performance?
   2. How much trust exists between management and employees?
   3. What are the management-union relationships?

D. Organization
   1. Organizational structures
      a. Division of work
      b. Span of control
      c. Management hierarchy
   2. Measurement and evaluation practices
      a. Control system
      b. Performance appraisal
   3. Compensation
   4. Recruiting and selection
   5. Training

E. Environment
   1. What boundary separates the inside and outside of the organization?
   2. How does the organization relate to other organizations within this particular industry?
   3. What is the nature of the industry?
      a. Degree of competition
      b. Degree of interdependence
      c. Types of suppliers
   4. In what ways is the government involved with the organization's activities?
   5. What outside special-interest groups are important for the organization to work with?

F. Fit
   1. Is there a fit between task, people, social, organizational, and environmental variables?
   2. Are these variables compatible with one another? (e.g., does the control system fit the structure?)

III. Action
   A. Which parts of the organization should be changed?
   B. Who is in a position to change them?
   C. How much change is necessary?
      1. Change only in the manager's behavior
      2. Change in design and implementation of a new system
      3. Change covering a large number of persons or groups
   D. What are the appropriate steps for implementing the change?

IV. Framework for organizational analysis
   A. What are the relationships among these factors?
   B. Are the task, people, social, organizational, and environmental variables compatible?
   C. Is there an adequate fit among them?

V. Environment
   A. Industry atmosphere
   B. Special-interest groups
   C. Government influence
   D. Local culture

Framework for organizational analysis

What are the relationships among these factors?
Are the task, people, social, organizational,
    and environmental variables compatible?
Is there an adequate fit among them?

Actual work performed
Physical conditions and demands
Spatial arrangements
Interdependence of work groups
Degree of structure vs. uncertainty
Performance cycle time span
    ect.

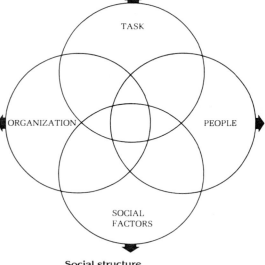

Division of work
Span of control
Management hierarchy
Rules and procedures
Performance evaluation
    and control
Rewards and compensation
Recruiting and selection
    etc.

Educational backgrounds
Age
Sex
Skill level
Ethnicity
Supply of labor
Individuals' motivation(s)
Attitudes toward work
    etc.

Social structure
Group norms
Leadership patterns, roles
Morale, climate
Influence, status
    etc.

Industry atmosphere
Special-interest groups
Government influence
Local culture

"Most people need less management than you think."

Jim Treybig, Tandem Computers
Fortune (June 28, 1982)

*"The basic philosophy, spirit, and drive of an organization
have far more to do with its relative achievement than do
technology or economic resources, organizational structure,
innovation, and timing."*

Thomas J. Watson, IBM

*"The name of the game in the 1980s is quality. We must get
back out of the wild growth of the curriculum and get back
into some core of knowledge — history, philosophy, theology,
language, literature, mathematics, science, art, and music.
Otherwise we are just graduating trained seals."*

The Reverend Theodore Hesburgh, President
Notre Dame University

Washington Elementary School

Washington Elementary School is located in an upper socio-economic area of Lincoln, Nebraska. Most parents of Washington Elementary's students are professionals and university professors. Population growth in the area has increased the number of students attending the school, but recent funding requests for an additional school in the Lincoln School District have been rejected by the voters. The result has been larger classes in most grades and a considerable drop in teacher morale.

Jack Adams, a Lincoln native and a former junior high school teacher, has been the principal at Washington for four years. In his early thirties, he is about in the middle of the faculty in age and experience. Jack is a highly regarded administrator whom the teachers perceive to be supportive, reasonable, and fair. His sense of humor is frequently exploited as the faculty plays good-natured jokes on him or on others. He is viewed as one of the team, rather than a different "animal," and he reinforces this image with activities in the teachers' organization.

Jack's classroom visits are infrequent, usually only what the district requires for twice-a-year evaluations of the staff. Teachers are assumed to be responsible and capable, and therefore not in need of his services unless something unusual happens.

The twenty-one-member faculty at Washington usually includes two or three new teachers and a majority of returning teachers, five or six of whom have been there over ten years. The older teachers are very influential in determining the activities at the school, and it is difficult to initiate any changes without their support.

Earlier administrations of Lincoln School District had conducted business in a colleaguial fashion. There was little differentiation between teachers and administrators and the loyalty was generally mutual. Several years ago, however, some teachers suggested striking over a particular issue. In response to this threat, the superintendent indicated that a strike would be just fine, as he could replace them all within twenty-four hours. Because the local supply of elementary teachers had been high, Washington's teachers were unwilling to buck the powers that be. Instead, they chose to suffer in silence.

Recently, a new superintendent was hired for the Lincoln School District. She had an intense desire to update the instructional methods and practices in the district as economically as possible. Previously, teachers had "done their own thing" and liked it that way. In spite of the district's proximity to a local university, Lincoln's teaching techniques were seen by many as very outdated. During this district curriculum transition, Sue Erickson joined the faculty of Washington Elementary. She perceived that the emphasis in the district was on teaching practices which had been used in California ten years earlier and were subsequently discarded because of their ineffectiveness.

As a result of the superintendent's desire to improve the district's educational offering, a science program was developed through the cooperation of the local teachers. The design of this program required that teachers not only cover textbook material but also develop more creative learning opportunities. The district supported the curriculum improvement effort by making an investment in materials and equipment for the teachers to use. There was some grumbling and griping about the extra effort required to implement this innovative program; however, most teachers used the ideas at least enough to make some difference in their curriculum.

On the heels of the major science changes, preparations were made for a significant overhaul of the reading program. Sue Erickson, a second-grade teacher, was assigned to the language arts curriculum committee because she had had experience using the kind of techniques which the district was going to require, as well as specific professional training in reading instruction. Most of the other teachers on the committee, she discovered, were unaware of recent developments in this area but seemed open to suggestions. One of the priorities in implementing the program was the persuasion of middle and upper-grade teachers to make significant changes in their methods, going from total group instruction to small ability groups and individualization.

From time to time, Jack Adams would ask for a report in faculty meeting from Sue on the progress of the language arts committee. Although she tried very hard to articulate the committee's action in non-threatening terms, there were two or three teachers who indicated regularly that they were content with their own teaching methods and felt no need to make any changes. Jack usually made no comment after her report.

The controversy came to a head one afternoon at a special faculty meeting to which Kathy Hadley, the district curriculum development specialist, had been invited. Washington's teachers had been informed that Kathy would be presenting the new district reading instruction guidelines for them to consider and that the district would be open to the teachers' suggestions or comments. Kathy began her presentation, and at first there were no problems; however, when she distributed a small packet of materials outlining the program, three teachers started muttering to each other, flipping through the pages, and shaking their heads. When she came to the section expressing the district's commitment to meeting individual needs of students and outlining suggestions for personalization of instruction, the tension became obvious as the faculty began voicing their opinions.

Neil Decker, a fourth-grade teacher who was considering leaving the profession because of the inadequate salary, was the first to speak. "I've got 34 children in my class. How can I handle this individual stuff? What do the other 25 kids do while I'm working with a group?"

"That's just what I'd like to know!" Jeri Wade, another fourth-grade teacher, joined in. "And another thing — what's wrong with the way we're doing it now? Our students do well on the achievement tests."

"We're not implying that your children aren't learning," Kathy said. "We just think their needs could be met more effectively. Teaching thirty children all together at the same time in the same reading skills results in a lot of wasted time for some children and pushes other children beyond what they're prepared to learn."

Neil said, "It's impossible to do. You guys come down from your ivory tower and tell us how to teach. I don't have time to do any more than I'm already doing." Several of the other teachers nodded their heads in agreement.

Kathy replied, "Of course, this isn't something we would expect you to implement all at once. We realize that you are used to your own way of teaching, and we just hope to encourage you to be moving in this direction, so that perhaps over a reasonable period of time —"

Dixie Dearden, a third-grade teacher,

broke in. "We're doing the best we can with these big classes. Why don't you spend some of that district money on relieving our class loads instead of thinking up more work for us?"

"We can't do this," Neil repeated. "It's just not possible."

"First and second-grade teachers teach this way all the time," Sue said. But no one was listening. The other first and second-grade teachers failed to comment on Sue's position, leaving her alone in her efforts. The faculty immediately broke into small, heated discussion groups. Caught off guard by the hostility to her proposal, Kathy was embarrassed about the teacher's reactions. Jack had to make some quick decisions; What should he do to restore order in the meeting, and how could he not only persuade his teachers to accept the new program in principle but also motivate them to implement it in the classroom?

City National Bank

A fter having worked two months during the previous summer for City National Bank, I returned again this summer to work while on my break from school. Though I would only be there for four months, they hired me on as a full-time staff member replacing a woman who recently terminated. They also hired a woman just out of high school to help handle the extra work load our resort town gets throughout the vacation months. These additions brought our operations division up to seven women plus the assistant manager over our di-

vision (see Exhibit 1).

The same day I started, a new woman transferred up from a larger branch to our division to take over the note department. Marilyn, the new woman, was not very well liked by most of the workers in the branch because of some negative reports which had preceded her arrival and because her family "owned" the town we worked in.

City National Bank, like any other large bank with many branches, has standardized policies, procedures, and regulations for each branch to follow. In order

Exhibit 1

City National Bank organization chart

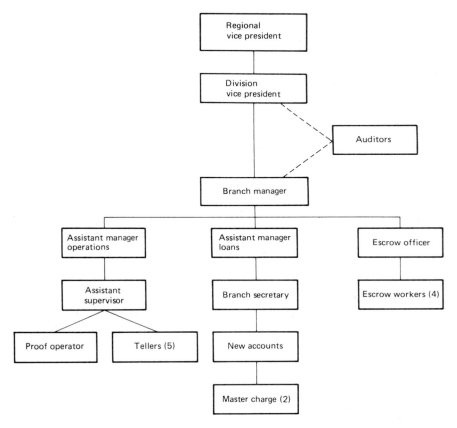

At the end of the summer the case writer left to return to school. In addition, the proof operator, the assistant supervisor, and two escrow workers quit or transferred.

to protect customers, employees, and the corporation, these procedures have to be developed and followed. The bank has auditors who come around periodically to check the books and operational procedures of the branches to assure maintenance of the high standards.

Our branch has relaxed several of the rules and has developed some policies unique to our branch. In part this stems from the informal and friendly relationships shared between customers and employees in our small town, where we know most of the customers on a first-name basis. Unlike our branch, the larger branch Marilyn previously worked in followed procedures strictly and supposedly did everything "according to the book." Marilyn let us know that we were inefficient and backward. Soon bad feelings developed and came to a head in the early part of August.

In August we were in the process of changing managers. Our assistant manager had also left on vacation, so we had a former auditor in management training and a newly promoted supervisor filling the management positions for two weeks. Their job was to sit in for people on vacations throughout our division until each was placed in his own branch. The new manager and assistant manager were upset with our lax attitude toward many rules, some of which we had never even heard of, and they set out to shape up our branch. Among the things we needed to reform were the opening and closing procedures, keeping our keys with us at *all* times, always locking our cash boxes, balancing procedures, check cashing policy, and several other regulations. Marilyn was happy with the new situation and told us "it was about time," but the rest of the branch was very defensive and uncooperative with the temporary management. During this time Marilyn changed several of her responsibilities with the temporary supervisor's permission, and when our assistant manager returned from vacation, there was a great deal of tension between them.

One afternoon while the assistant manager was out, Marilyn went around on her own and picked up three sets of keys that were lying on a table and turned them over to the other assistant manager, saying that the "women should be taught a lesson." This all occurred after the branch had closed, and there were some frantic minutes spent searching for the keys. Marilyn said nothing and we all kept looking until someone remembered seeing Marilyn in their work area. When confronted she merely told the women that Paul, the assistant manager, had the keys. When the whole story was put together, there was a lot of name-calling and derogatory comments, with Marilyn getting the silent treatment for almost a week.

Our management never took an official stand that was enforced. There was never a confrontation between the opposing sides. When Marilyn would approach them on a point, they would satisfy her by agreeing that she had a good point, and when the other side brought up complaints, they would agree with them, too. A harmony between practices and policies was never reached. As the summer ended, many problems were compounded because there was no consistent authority and so many things "had changed" according to the original employees. We never knew what was expected. By Labor Day, I left to return to school and four other women had quit or transferred out of my hometown branch of City National Bank.

Phantoms fill Boy Scout rolls

David Young

The Boy Scouts have been a tradition in America for most of this century. To the public, scouting conjures up images of camping in the woods, hikes, and troop meetings. But there is another side of scouting that is not seen, a *Tribune* reporter discovered during a four-month investigation. It includes massive cheating on the part of paid professional staff members to make their quotas. This is the first of a two-part report on the problem.

The Boy Scouts of America — that venerable institution devoted to keeping boys physically strong, mentally aware, and morally straight — is in trouble.

A $65 million national campaign to expand scouting by more than 2 million boys in 1976 is nearly two years behind schedule.

And professionals within the Scout organization claim the problem has been aggravated by extensive cheating which has inflated membership figures. Scouting officials claim to have 4.8 million boys enrolled nationwide.

Like most charitable organizations, scouting also has been plagued with the problem of finding enough adult volunteers to run programs and raising enough money to keep up with inflation, Scout officials concede.

Many officials blame scouting's problems on the inability to recruit and keep volunteers, especially in the inner cities.

But the root of the problem is scouting's Boypower 76 program — a national effort to increase the membership rolls to include one-third of all eligible boys in America — an estimated 6 million youngsters.

Dissidents within scouting's 4,600-member professional staff, which raises funds and recruits boys and volunteers, also claim that efforts to streamline the organization and use improved business techniques have encouraged cheating.

What has happened, past and present Scout professionals claim, is that many professionals under pressure continually to make increasing membership quotas have been meeting those quotas with nonexistent boys belonging to nonexistent units. The boys exist only on rosters filed away in Scout offices throughout the country.

Actually, the cheating is confined largely to the professional organization and has had little or no effect on existing Scout programs operated by adult volunteers. Once started, the troops, packs, and posts operate almost independently of the professional organization.

Thus, the 15 Cub Scouts who meet each week in a Detroit ghetto church aren't aware that their unit has 65 members on official Scout reports. And the PTA of a West Side Chicago school is not aware it is sponsoring a nonexistent, 44-member Boy Scout troop.

Scout professionals interviewed during the *Tribune's* four-month investigation revealed that sometimes they cheat with federal money. The nonexistent boys and units were paid for with poverty funds from Washington.

"This thing is national in scope," claimed one Scout executive from the national organization. He asked that his name be withheld.

"They don't know themselves how many boys they have," he said.

"As far as they are concerned, the name on a roster is a Scout until someone proves it different."

An independent report on scouting in the New York area in 1971 by the Institute of Public Affairs said that many Scout professionals believe that the pressure to meet membership goals there resulted in a "numbers game and a possible cause of paper troops." The report never was publicly released.

But nowhere is the problem more critical than in Chicago — the place where scouting started in America in 1910 and the city that gave America the Boypower 76 program.

Some Scout professionals here estimate that anywhere from 25 to 50 percent of the 87,000 Cub Scouts, Boy Scouts, and Explorers registered in the Chicago Area Council are inactive or exist only on paper.

A suppressed 1968 audit of Scout operations in Chicago shows that of the council's 2,555 units, 1,694 were substandard and 623 were phony. Though Scout officials in Chicago claimed at the time to have 75,000 boys enrolled, the actual number of Scouts was less than 40,000, the audit showed. The Scout official who ordered the audit was quietly reassigned elsewhere.

Joseph Klein, the head of scouting in Chicago, claims to have 87,000 members — making Chicago the largest council in the nation.

However, confidential membership reports obtained by the *Tribune* show that on April 12 the actual membership was about 52,000 boys — nearly 40 percent less than quoted.

Though cheating also exists in the suburbs, it is worse in the inner city, Scout professionals said. They claim that it is extremely difficult to determine the exact extent of the cheating, but said that Scout districts with widely fluctuating membership totals and few promotions indicate large numbers of phony boys and units. Nonexistent boys can't be promoted.

Though 2,321 Boy Scouts were registered in the Midwest District on the West Side last December, only 117 boys received promotions to the six ranks of scouting. Only 32 boys were promoted to Tenderfoot — an almost automatic jump.

The adjacent Fort Dearborn District listed no promotions for its 1,511 Boy Scouts, although the predominantly white Timber Trails District on the Southwest Side had 245 promotions for its 850 registered boys for the same period.

Membership in the Midwest District has fluctuated, widely since 1966, confidential Scout records show. On December 31, 1972, the district reported having 4,577 Scouts, but 2,797 of them — more than half — had evaporated in just two months. The district claimed to have recruited 3,270 new boys during its membership drive last fall, making it the largest district in the city, with 5,050 boys. But by the beginning of April 2,981 boys — nearly 60 percent of the district — had somehow disappeared.

The seven Scout districts on the West Side claim to have recruited 8,630 new Scouts during last fall's membership drive, but lost 9,000 in the following three months. The six South Side districts in the Chicago Council lost more than 8,000 scouts during the same period — nearly half of the total membership.

The worst cheating actually occurs in the federally funded programs administered through the Chicago Model Cities program, the professionals claim. The programs, collectively known as Project 13, pay the Scout dues and fees for inner city blacks and Latins, many of whom live in housing projects.

The Chicago Council has received $341,000 in federal funds for the program during the last four years, reportedly to provide a Scouting program for more than 40,000 poor youngsters, federal records show.

"It's not hard to paper your project (13) boys," bragged one Scout professional who asked to remain anonymous. "You register all the boys in December. You can put an extra 1,000 boys in a unit because they drop out in two months and there's no record of them," he said.

An official of the Lawndale Urban Progress Center, which sponsors one federally funded program on the West Side, said that not more than 500 of the 2,000 boys on the books are actually Scouts.

Scout professionals, past and present, admitted to a *Tribune* interviewer that they registered thousands of nonexistent boys to meet their quotas.

One of the most common ploys the professionals claim they used was to re-register units year after year without bothering to check to see whether the units actually exist.

"You simply change a few names so the charter looks different, then re-register it," said one former professional. "Who's going to walk through those housing projects to check you out?"

"We've got to clean the cheating up," he said. "The minute we find it (cheating) we terminate the professional."

Klein said he constantly lectures his staff on maintaining a quality scouting program, "but maybe they're not hearing me."

"I firmly believe there's a hell of a lot more good in this program than there is bad," he said.

Scouting motto forgotten in signup drive

With great fanfare the Boy Scouts of America announced in 1968 it was beginning a program to make scouting more relevant.

Boypower 76, it was called.

And its goal was to raise $65 million and to bring into scouting one-third (about 6 million) of all eligible boys 8 to 20 years old in the country by 1976.

Scouting wanted the poor black youths from the ghetto, and the Puerto Ricans from Spanish Harlem. It wanted the whites from the suburbs and the sons of steelworkers from Gary.

To make the traditional scouting program more relevant to the recruits, the Boy Scouts revised handbooks to include subjects of interest to urban dwellers, translated manuals into Spanish, and asked for federal funds to pay for programs for the poor.

But somewhere in the more than five years that Boypower 76 has been with us, something went wrong.

Professional Scout staff members have detailed to the *Tribune* widespread cheating to meet the Boypower quotas imposed on them — including cheating in the federally funded programs.

"This thing is national in scope," claimed one Scout executive assigned to the national organization.

The officials claim they were forced to cheat to make their goals. If they didn't make the goals, they were out. Scout executive Alden G. Barber conceded he is aware cheating has occurred.

"Some of our people cheat — quite frankly," Barber said.

He conceded that Boypower 76 is now two years behind schedule. The problem is economic, he said. There just isn't enough money to get the job done.

Though the national organization has raised $33 million and placed nearly 500 additional professionals on local staffs, donors who gave to the national effort apparently cut back on their contributions to local Scout councils. Many local councils were forced to cut back their staffs as a result.

"The actual net gain is close to 80 professionals," Barber said.

In Chicago, the local Scout council was faced with a $340,000 deficit and was forced to chop 10 professionals from its staff although the council was expected to increase its membership from 75,000 to 100,000. The result was cheating.

Past and present Scout professionals in Chicago estimate that from 25 to 50 percent of the 87,000 Scouts registered here exist only on paper.

The professionals also detailed how the cheating has gradually moved into the suburbs — the traditional bastions of the Boy Scout movement.

One South Suburban professional estimated that when he was transferred into his district he found about 20 percent of his Scouts existed only on paper.

A North Suburban staff member discovered one day that several hundred boys had somehow mysteriously appeared on his rolls. He was later told by a supervisor that the boys were put there to make a quota.

A Southwest Suburban volunteer told of how he held an anguished meeting with his professional late one night because the district was 200 boys short of its quota. The volunteer resigned himself to missing the quota, but early the next morning he got a call from a friend congratulating him for making it.

"I don't know where the boys came from," the volunteer said. "Our meeting ended at 11 P.M. and by 8 A.M. the next day we were on target."

But cheating in the suburbs is minor compared to the inflating of membership rolls going on in the inner city, professionals claim.

"When I left the Fort Dearborn District (West Side) in 1972, I had 3,000 Scouts on the books, but only 300 of them were real," said Andre Miller, a former professional.

"We had 850 boys registered in the Altgeld Gardens project on the South Side," said Bart Kencade, another former professional. "Realistically, there were 30 Scouts active."

A Detroit supervisor told his staff members to meet their quotas even if they had to register bodies in a cemetery to do it.

Nearly 20 charters for Cub Scout packs on the West Side in 1973 list as den mother a Mrs. Ollie Carter, 130 E. Franklin St. Mrs. Carter is in fact an employee of the Boy Scouts in their equipment store at that address. She said she wasn't sure why her named appeared on so many unit rosters.

"I haven't done anything with any units for four or five years," she said.

Edward Meier, a suburban Oak Lawn businessman, is listed on those same rosters as an official of the units.

"I haven't been in the area for years," he said. "Years ago," he claimed he allowed a professional to use his name for promotional purposes in Oak Lawn.

One professional sat in his suburban apartment one night and detailed to a *Tribune* interviewer just how the cheating is accomplished.

His favorite tactic is known in the business as "diming them in." In November and December near the end of the scouts' annual membership drive, the practice becomes common "because in those months you only have to pay a dime (dues are 10 cents a month) to register a boy for the Dec. 31 deadline. So you can sign up 100 boys for $10."

"You can go to a business for a contribution to pay the tab, you can hold back some money you raised earlier, or you can go to your field director (supervisor) for contingency funds," he said.

Some professionals admitted they paid the phony boys' dues out of their own pocket.

They claimed they got the phony names from telephone books or by visiting elementary schools to have boys fill out applications and pay their dues in advance. Once the registration cards and dues were collected, the professionals never returned to organize units, they said.

Still others claimed they reregistered entire units without checking to see whether the units still existed. In this way, units which have dissolved are carried on the books for years.

The school ploy angered the mothers at Brown Elementary School, 54 N. Hermitage Ave.

"Last September . . . a Scout representative came through the school and recruited 30 to 40 boys," one mother said. "I called them downtown (Scout headquarters) and told them we had collected the boys' money.

"They came out and picked it up but that's the last we ever saw of them."

The Scout professionals — the men who admitted cheating — blamed the problem on the Scout organization and Boypower 76.

"If you didn't make a majority of your goals, you were fired," said one 11-year veteran who was forced out after he refused to cheat.

"Membership is at one of its lowest points in the history of the district," said John P. Costello, Chicago's assistant Scout executive, in a letter to one professional last year. "Camp is 30 per cent off target," he continued.

"Failure to show dramatic progress . . . will place you in a terminal employment position with the Chicago Area Council," the letter continued.

"I couldn't send anyone to camp because paper Boy Scouts can't go to camp," said the professional. He claimed he was transferred into the district only a few months before receiving Costello's letter and discovered that 33 of his 47 registered units were nonexistent.

Another Scout professional was fired last year after he attempted to organize a union among the other professionals. The firing occurred a few days after the National Labor Relations Board refused to hear a complaint he filed against the Chicago Council charging it was threatening to fire employees trying to organize the union.

"I didn't want the union," the former professional said. "I wanted to find some way we could put an end to all these abuses."

Raymond N. Carlen, a steel company executive and president of the Chicago Area Council, has adopted a hard-nosed attitude toward the dissident professionals:

"If you don't enjoy what your are doing, look for something else to do," he said.

However, Barber believes that many of

the problems of cheating could be curbed by better training of professionals and their supervisors.

"I assumed the middle management people knew the techniques necessary to achieve the goals," he said.

Barber, who was the Scout executive in Chicago before being named national chief executive, is credited with streamlining the Scout organization, imposing the quota system, and making the professionals accountable for making the quotas. He engineered the "Years of Decision" Scout program in Chicago during the early 1960s. "Boypower 76 was an outgrowth of that program."

He also is credited with engineering the attempt by the Scout organization to reach the inner city.

"I felt that if scouting was to reach its potential, it had to be as meaningful to the boy in the inner city as to the boy in suburbia."

"And God created the organization and gave it dominion over man."

Peter Townsend, *Up the Organization*

"Why are the nations with the most developed systems of professional management education, the United States and Great Britain, performing so poorly, when two nations that provide almost no professional management training, Germany and Japan, have been the outstanding successes of the postwar period?"

David Vogel, School of Business Administration
University of California, Berkeley

"The Peter Principle: In a hierarchy every employee tends to rise to his level of incompetence."

Laurence J. Peter and Raymund Hull

"The secret of managing is to keep the five guys who hate you away from the five who are undecided."

Casey Stengel

EXERCISES

The Tinkertoy exercise

"Tinkertoy" is a registered trademark of the Questor Corporation.

To approach the field of organizational behavior it is useful to have a shared experience that students can use to define issues. This exercise provides a brief experience in which problems of organizing, planning, decision making, leadership, implementation, communication, and many others can be identified. It seems easier to appreciate organizational problems when they are experienced and discussed with actual tasks rather than abstract definitions. It also serves the purpose of bringing students together early in the term in a group activity.

Exercise objective □ To build the tallest self-support structure with the contents of one box of Tinkertoys.

Exercise rules □ The class should be divided into groups of from three to eight members. Each group is given a regular size box of Tinkertoys (120–130 pieces). The group has 20 minutes to plan their work. It is most important, however, that during the planning period there is *no* assembly of parts. The pieces can be looked at, but not even a trial assembly of any two pieces is allowed. At the end of the 20 minutes, all pieces go back in the box. Then the construction phase starts. The construction phase last *40* seconds! It is important that the instructor only start and stop the planning and construction periods. He or she should not give advice or amount of time remaining.

There are obviously many variations which can be employed with this exercise. Criteria can be stated in terms of aesthetic dimensions, number of pieces used, functional performance (how far a car will roll), etc. Monetary incentives can be used (if available), groups can be of different size, and learning can be tested with future repetitions.

An ancient tale

In attempts to understand, analyze, and improve organizations, it is imperative that we be able to think carefully through the issue of who is responsible for what activities in different organizational settings. Often we hold someone responsible who has no control over the outcome, or we fail to teach or train someone who could make the vital difference.

To explore this issue, the following exercise could be conducted with either an individual or a group. It provides an opportunity to see how different individuals assign responsibility for an event. It is also a good opportunity to discuss the concept of organizational boundaries (what is the organization, who is in or out, and so forth).

You should read the short story and respond quickly to the first three questions. Then take a little more time on questions 4 and 5. The results, criteria, and implications could then be discussed in class, in groups, or in a more formal manner, such as in a mock trial in which different individuals present an argument for or against different characters and a jury decision assigns responsibilty (or, alternately, a policy decision could be made on how to improve the environment in the kingdom).

Long ago in an ancient kingdom there lived a princess who was very young and very beautiful. The princess, recently married, lived in a large and luxurious castle with her husband, a powerful and wealthy lord. The young princess was not content, however, to sit and eat strawberries by herself while her husband took frequent and long journeys to neighboring kingdoms. She felt neglected and soon became quite unhappy. One day, while she was alone in the castle gardens, a handsome vagabond rode out of the forest bordering the castle. He spied the beautiful princess, quickly won her heart, and carried her away with him.

Following a day of dalliance, the young princess found herself ruthlessly abandoned by the vagabond. She then discovered that the only way back to the castle led through the bewitched forest of the wicked sorcerer. Fearing to venture into the forest unaccompanied, she sought out her kind and wise godfather. She explained her plight, begged forgiveness of the godfather, and asked his assistance in returning home before her husband returned. The godfather, however, surprised and shocked at her behavior, refused forgiveness and denied her any assistance.

Discouraged but still determined, the princess disguised her identity and sought the help of the most noble of all the kingdom's knights. After hearing the sad story, the knight pledged his unfailing aid — for a modest fee. But, alas, the princess had no money and the knight rode away to save other damsels.

The beautiful princess had no one else from whom she might seek help and decided to brave the great peril alone. She followed the safest path she knew, but when she was almost through the forest, the wicked sorcerer spied her and caused her to be devoured by the fire-breathing dragon.

1. Who is most responsible for the death of the beautiful princess?
2. Who is next most responsible?
3. Who is least responsible?
4. What is your criterion for the above decisions?
5. What are the implications for *organizational behavior?*

	Most responsible	Next most responsible	Least responsible
Princess			
Husband			
Vagabond			
Godfather			
Knight			
Sorcerer			

Check one character in each column.

Supervision, hair, and all that

Problems of rules and regulations seem to come up in almost every organizational setting. The process by which they are enforced can lead to many different outcomes. This exercise is an opportunity to look at the issue in terms of a situation with pressures from different sources.

Try to accept the role in terms of contemporary implications. Let your feelings develop as if you actually were that individual. Should issues develop that are not covered by the role, adapt or innovate accordingly.

To conceptualize your role, it is usually best to read it carefully two or three times; then close the book and think about it for a few minutes. Do not read the other roles; try to develop an approach in terms of the information given and your own interpretation of how a person in that position would likely behave. After you have the role in mind, do not reread it during the process of the role play.

Role for Ella James, supervisor

You are the supervisor for a work group of eighteen people on a line where cold cereal is packaged. You have been working in the plant for a long time, know your job well, and get along pretty well with your work group. There have been some problems lately, however. It seems the health department inspection team has been cracking down on rules with respect to clean uniforms, plant sanitation, and especially hair. Men are supposed to wear caps and women are supposed to wear nets whenever they are in the food processing areas. They have written you up a couple of times recently because of violations, and you must put a stop to them. It seems that your two biggest problems are a couple of young workers who always seem to be caught without their caps. One is Ed, black, 20 years old, and generally cooperative. The other is Joe, white, 19 years old, and a little surly. They seem to be friends and each of them has a thousand excuses for any problem. Ed even suggested that you buy a different cap for him because he did not like the standard issue cap. You have given them one warning. The next incident means they are laid off for three days, and the third infraction means they are through. But you do have to give them a fair hearing, and so you have called them in to try to get things straightened out. They are coming now.

Role for Ed

You are a 20-year-old black who has been working on a cold cereal packaging line for two months. When you came to work things looked pretty good. But now you and your friend, Joe, are getting all kinds of guff from Ella, your supervisor. She keeps telling you to wear that dumb cap because of some health rule. You have to wear one of the caps provided by the company, and the biggest one is too small to cover your hair. You have complained about the size of the caps several times, but it does no good. You have even offered to wear your own cap, but rules require a certain kind. Besides,

there are lots of women on the crew who have hair hanging way down below their nets, and no one says anything to them. Of course, the supervisor is a woman, and so she lets them get by. Someone suggested that you cut your hair one time so that you could keep the cap on your hair, but you and Joe play with a rock group at night, and cutting your hair would ruin your whole image.

At any rate, Ella asked you to come in to see her. You and Joe are on your way to talk to her now.

Role for Joe

You are a 19-year-old white who has been working in a cold cereal plant for two months. You and your friend, Ed, a black musician who plays in a rock group with you at night, have been receiving a lot of guff from Ella, your supervisor. At first it seemed like a pretty good job to provide a little extra cash while your rock group got going. But now you don't know. Ella keeps telling you to wear a cap because of some health rule. But your hair is too long, and it doesn't do any good anyway. She once suggested that you should cut your hair, but that would ruin your image for the rock performances. Besides, there are several women on the same line doing the same work, and most of them have long hair which hangs below the little nets they are supposed to wear. But Ella never says anything to them — probably because they are women. Anyway, you really do need the money, and there aren't any other jobs; so maybe you can put up with the problem. On the other hand, Ella has said that she wants to talk to you and Ed, and you don't know quite what to expect.

You and Ed are on your way to talk to Ella now.

People work for different reasons

"Basically people like to work. However, from time to time they need some incentive . . .

". . . so today we're firing Murphy, Gross, and Finstrap!"

2

Some perspectives on individual behavior in organizations

People spend a good part of their lives trying to understand individual behavior. Sometimes we think we're experts. ("Haven't I been dealing with people ever since I was born?") At other times, when people seem so hard to understand, we think that we know nothing about the subject. ("You have to be a psychologist to manage people.") But whether we consider ourselves expert or incompetent, most of us agree that possession of such a skill is important.

This section focuses on individual behavior within organizations. Because work organizations occupy a major part of most people's lives, the quality of the relationship between the individual and the organization is critical. When the relationship is positive, both the individual and the organization seem to benefit. When it is negative, both parties would like to terminate it. Of course, it is expected that individuals are likely to have both positive and negative experiences in their relationship with an organization.

People beginning their work life soon find that their goals do not perfectly match the goals of others in the organization, notably its supervisors or top management. And when beginners discover this discrepancy, they can adopt any of a number of approaches.

1. They can respond by trying to identify and adopt their superiors' goals. These subordinates work hard to live up to the expectations of their superiors. They are eager to get ahead and believe that this approach will help them most.
2. They can try to change the goals of their superiors. For example, they might set out to make the organization more human, to make it more conscious of pollution, or to make it less exploitative of customers. Such an approach seems to be occurring more frequently in

61

recent years.

3. They can try to avoid "selling out" to the organization. These individuals, thinking it impossible to reconcile their goals with those of management, invest as little of themselves as possible in the organization and seek fulfillment outside the job. They say, "The only thing I want from the organization is a paycheck," and in return they ask only that people in the organization not try to influence or change them. But in practice it is virtually impossible to avoid being influenced by the organization. That relationship is too much a part of their lives.

We have mentioned just a few possible responses to organizations; but, whatever the response, individuals are influenced by organizations and need to understand more about that influence.

Motivation is a theme pervading all attempts to influence people in organizations. Managers are always searching for new and more effective means of motivation. Thousands of articles and numerous conferences and workshops claim to answer the question, How do I motivate people? and those aspiring to become managers will no doubt have an interest in motivation. It is taken for granted that knowledge of some current theories of motivation and how to apply them is valuable to administrators. But it may also be worthwhile for subordinates to learn something about the topic. If they have some knowledge of motivation theory, they may be able to identify what the organization is doing to try to motivate them.

This section of the book presents several different theories of motivation. Some people are confused by all these theories. They want to know which one is the "truth" so that they can use it. Unfortunately for these people, a theory is not an all-encompassing explanation of developments in a complex world. Rather, it is just one way of looking at and trying to understand a phenomenon. We suggest that the test of a theory is its usefulness, and the usefulness of a theory depends upon the situation. This section presents several theories, so that the student might be exposed to a variety of approaches to motivation and be in a position to choose the best one at the right time.

Kerr's article notes that frequently organizations and larger social systems create motivational forces that lead to unintended consequences, rewarding behaviors that are not desired by designers but discouraging behaviors that are desired. The article describes some of the causes of "fouled-up" reward systems and presents a somewhat pessimistic view of possible strategies for the improvement of such systems. McClelland describes achievement motivation and argues that it is an essential ingredient of business success for individuals as well as for nations. He presents his techniques for teaching achievement motivation.

The article on behavior modification by Hamner and Hamner presents B. F. Skinner's theory, based on the premise that behavior is controlled by its consequences. That is, you can change a person's behavior if you change the consequences of that behavior. Drawing extensively from the experiences of several large organizations, the article presents pragmatic rules for the application of Skinner's theory to industry. Nadler and Lawler describe expectancy theory, which is an approach that is currently very popular with academics in the field. However, they also present some ideas on how managers can apply this model in dealing with people in their organizations.

In the article, "A New Strategy for Job Enrichment," the authors indicate people can be motivated by the work itself. They describe the kinds of jobs that are most likely to generate excitement and commitment about work and the kinds of employees that will be motivated by challenging work. They are proposing a new strategy for going about the redesign of work. The article, "Motivators: America's New Glamour Figures," takes a different approach. It reports on the activities of a number of celebrities on the success-motivation circuit. Speeches and seminars on motivation draw up to 10,000 people in some cities and generate fees as high as $10,000 for some speakers. Apparently many people believe that motivation is a topic that they need to learn more about.

Most people find it easier to memorize a theory than apply it. Therefore, the cases and exercises in this section are designed to provide students with an opportunity to apply some theories. The first two exercises in this section as well as the cases involving State Bank, Slab Yard Slowdown, and Denver Department Stores are motivation oriented.

Another theme in the relationship between individuals and organizations is career development. Rewards that might motivate a 22-year-old employee may be of little interest to a 52-year-old. One way to think about career development is to think about starting in an entry-level job in an organization and working hard to rise to the top. However, the dream of working up from messenger boy to president, fairly common in the first half of the twentieth century, is no longer a very realistic one for most people in our society, because organizations have grown so large and complex. As a result, we need some better ways to think about career development, ways to think about ourselves, our interests, and how those interests might change over time. We also need ways to understand the people with whom we work, including superiors, peers, and subordinates.

Thompson's article presents one way to think about careers. He argues that most organizations place too much emphasis on titles and promotions and do not adequately recognize the contributions of individual contributors. The concept of career stages is presented as an alternative to "climbing the corporate ladder" as a measure of career development. Another concept that is helpful in thinking about adult development is that of life stages. In recent years several researchers have used this concept in their studies on adult development. The article "New Light on Adult Life Cycles" presents a brief summary of that research.

In his article "On Wasting Time," Michener approaches the topic of career development from a different angle. He suggests that "fumbling one's way toward enlightenment" should not be viewed with anxiety. This short statement challenges traditional criteria for judging human beings and, implicitly, presents alternate views of motivation.

In a lifetime of work, people are required to make many important decisions, such as "Should I work for company A or company B?" "Should I quit my job and start my own business?" Most of us have difficulty making such decisions. And every day we face less important decisions: "Should I work on project X or write a report this morning?" "Should I go to lunch with the boss or with my golfing buddy?" Heilbroner's article, exploring the issue of decision making, sets out some guidelines for improving skills in this area. The career goals exercise provides an opportunity to use some of those ideas in planning one's own career.

The article by Keele and Russell focuses on the skill of building networks. They point out that the support one gains from contacts can be very helpful in advancing one's career as well as very important to health and longevity.

This section presents a number of ideas and theories designed to improve the understanding of individual behavior in organizations. It also includes several cases and exercises that provide an opportunity to apply these theories to situations so as to increase a student's understanding. It is safe to say that individual behavior is difficult to understand. However, with the help of some concepts and theories and some practice in applying these ideas, we are optimistic that students will have a better understanding of this topic after they finish this section.

On the folly of rewarding A, while hoping for B

Steven Kerr

Whether dealing with monkeys, rats, or human beings, it is hardly controversial to state that most organisms seek information concerning what activities are rewarded, and then seek to do (or at least pretend to do) those things, often to the virtual exclusion of activities not rewarded. The extent to which this occurs of course will depend on the perceived attractiveness of the rewards offered, but neither operant nor expectancy theorists would quarrel with the essence of this notion.

Nevertheless, numerous examples exist of reward systems that are fouled up in that behaviors which are rewarded are those which the rewarder is trying to *discourage*, while the behavior he desires is not being rewarded at all.

In an effort to understand and explain this phenomenon, this paper presents examples from society, from organizations in general, and from profit making firms in particular. Data from a manufacturing company and information from an insurance firm are examined to demonstrate the consequences of such reward systems for the organizations involved, and possible reasons why such reward systems continue to exist are considered.

Societal examples

Politics

Official goals are "purposely vague and general and do not indicate . . . the host of decisions that must be made among alternative ways of achieving official goals and the priority of multiple goals . . ." (Perrow 1969, 66). They usually may be relied on to offend absolutely no one, and in this sense can be considered high-acceptance, low-quality goals. An example might be "build better schools." Operative goals are higher in quality but lower in acceptance, since they specify where the money will come from, what alternative goals will be ignored, etc.

The American citizenry supposedly wants its candidates for public office to set forth operative goals, making their proposed programs "perfectly clear," specifying sources and uses of funds, etc. However, since operative goals are lower in acceptance, and since aspirants to public office need acceptance (from at least 50.1 percent of the people), most politicians prefer to speak only of official goals, at least until after the election. They of course would agree to speak at the operative level if "punished" for not doing so. The electorate could do this by refusing to support candidates who do not speak at the operative level.

Instead, however, the American voter typically punishes (withholds support from) candidates who frankly discuss where the money will come from, rewards politicians who speak only of official goals, but hopes that candidates (despite the reward system) will discuss the issues operatively. It is academic whether it was moral for Nixon, for example, to refuse to discuss his 1968 "secret plan" to end the Vietnam war, his 1972 operative goals concerning the lifting of price controls, the reshuffling of his cabinet, etc. The point is that the reward system made such refusal rational.

It seems worth mentioning that no manuscript can adequately define what is "moral" and what is not. However, examination of costs and benefits, combined with knowledge of what motivates a particular individual, often will suffice to determine what for him is "rational" (Simon 1957, 76-77). If the reward system is so designed that it is irrational to be moral, this does not necessarily mean that immorality will result. But is this not asking for trouble?

War

If some oversimplification may be permitted, let it be assumed that the primary goal of the organization (Pentagon, Luftwaffe, or whatever) is to win. Let it be assumed further that the primary goal of most individuals on the front lines is to get home alive. Then there appears to be an important conflict in goals — personally rational behavior by those at the bottom will endanger goal attainment by those at the top.

But not necessarily! It depends on how the reward system is set up. The Vietnam war was indeed a study of disobedience and rebellion, with terms such as "fragging" (killing one's own commanding officer) and "search and evade" becoming part of the military vocabulary. The difference in subordinates' acceptance of authority between World War II and Vietnam is reported to be considerable, and veterans of the Second World War often have been quoted as being outraged at the mutinous actions of many American soldiers in Vietnam.

Consider, however, some critical differences in the reward system in use during the two conflicts. What did the GI in World War II want? To go home. And when did he get to go home? When the war was won! If he disobeyed the orders to clean out the trenches and take the hills, the war would not be won and he would not go home. Furthermore, what were his chances of attaining his goal (getting home alive) if he obeyed the orders compared to his chances if he did not? What is being suggested is that the rational soldier in World War II, *whether patriotic or not*, probably found it expedient to obey.

Consider the reward system in use in Vietnam. What did the man at the bottom want? To go home. And when did he get to go home? When his tour of duty was over! This was the case *whether or not* the war was won. Furthermore, concerning the relative chance of getting home alive by obeying orders compared to the chance if they were disobeyed, it is worth noting that a mutineer in Vietnam was far more likely to be assigned rest and rehabilitation (on the assumption that fatigue was the cause) than he was

*In Simon's 1957, 76–77 terms, a decision is "subjectively rational" if it maximizes an individual's valued outcomes so far as his knowledge permits. A decison is "personally rational" if it is oriented toward the individual's goals.

to suffer any negative consequence.

In his description of the "zone of indifference," Barnard stated that "a person can and will accept a communication as authoritative only when . . . at the time of his decision, he believes it to be compatible with his personal interests as a whole" (Barnard 1964, 165). In light of the reward system used in Vietnam, would it not have been personally irrational for some orders to have been obeyed? Was not the military implementing a system which *rewarded* disobedience, while *hoping* that soldiers (despite the reward system) would obey orders?

Medicine

Theoretically, a physician can make either of two types of error, and intuitively one seems as bad as the other. A doctor can pronounce a patient sick when he is actually well, thus causing him needless anxiety and expense, curtailment of enjoyable foods and activities, and even physical danger by subjecting him to needless medication and surgery. Alternately, a doctor can label a sick person well, and thus avoid treating what might be natural to conclude that physicians seek to minimize both types of error.

Such a conclusion would be wrong (Garland 1959). It is estimated that numerous Americans are presently afflicted with iatrogenic (physician-caused) illnesses (Scheff 1965). This occurs when the doctor is approached by someone complaining of a few stray symptoms. The doctor classifies and organizes these symptoms, gives them a name, and obligingly tells the patient what further symptoms may be expected. This information often acts as a self-fulfilling prophecy, with the result that from that day on the patient for all practical purposes is sick.

Why does this happen? Why are physicians so reluctant to sustain a type 2 error (pronouncing a sick person well) that they will tolerate many type 1 errors? Again, a look at the reward system is needed. The punishments for a type 2 error are real: guilt, embarrassment, and the threat of lawsuit and scandal. On the other hand, a type 1 error (labeling a well person sick) "is sometimes seen as sound clinical practice, indicating a healthy conservative approach to medicine" (Scheff 1965, 69). Type 1 errors also are likely to generate increased income and a stream of steady customers who, being well in a limited physiological sense, will not embarrass the doctor by dying abruptly.

Fellow physicians and the general public therefore are really *rewarding* type 1 errors and at the same time *hoping* fervently that doctors will try not to make them.

General organizational examples

Rehabilitation centers and orphanages

In terms of the prime beneficiary classification (Blau and Scott, 1962, 42) organizations such as these are supposed to exist for the "public-in-contact," that is, clients. The orphanage therefore theoretically is interested in placing as many children as possible in good homes. However, often orphanages surround themselves with so many rules concerning adoption that it is nearly impossible to pry a child out of the place.

†In one study (Garland 1959, 25–38) of 14,867 films for signs of tuberculosis, 1,216 positive readings turned out to be clinically negative; only 24 negative readings proved clinically active, a ratio of 50 to 1.

Orphanages may deny adoption unless the applicants are a married couple, both of the same religion as the child, without history of emotional or vocational instability, with a specified minimum income and a private room for the child, etc.

If the primary goal is to place children in good homes, then the rules ought to constitute means toward that goal. Goal displacement results when these "means become ends in themselves that displace the original goals" (Blau and Scott 1962, 229).

To some extent these rules are required by law. But the influence of the reward system on the orphanage's management should not be ignored. Consider, for example, that the:

1. Number of children enrolled often is the most important determinant of the size of the allocated budget.
2. Number of children under the director's care also will affect the size of his staff.
3. Total organizational size will determine largely the director's prestige at the annual conventions, in the community, etc.

Therefore, to the extent that staff size, total budget, and personal prestige are valued by the orphanage's executive personnel, it becomes rational for them to make it difficult for children to be adopted. After all, who wants to be the director of the smallest orphanage in the state?

If the reward system errs in the opposite direction, paying off only for placements, extensive goal displacement again is likely to result. A common example of vocational rehabilitation in many states, for example, consists of placing someone in a job for which he has little interest and few qual-

ifications, for two months or so, and then "rehabilitating" him again in another position. Such behavior is quite consistent with the prevailing reward system, which pays off for the number of individuals placed in any position for 60 days or more. Rehabilitation counselors also confess to competing with one another to place relatively skilled clients, sometimes ignoring persons with few skills who would be harder to place. Extensively disabled clients find that counselors often prefer to work with those whose disabilities are less severe.*

Universities

Society *hopes* that teachers will not neglect their teaching responsibilities but *rewards* them almost entirely for research and publications. This is most true at the large and prestigious universities. Clichés such as "good research and good teaching go together" notwithstanding, professors often find that they must choose between teaching and research-oriented activities when allocating their time. Rewards for good teaching usually are limited to outstanding teacher awards, which are given to only a small percentage of good teachers and which usually bestow little money and fleeting prestige. Punishments for poor teaching also are rare.

Rewards for research and publications, on the other hand, and punishments for failure to accomlish these, are commonly administered by universities at which teachers are employed. Furthermore, publication-oriented resumés usually will be well received at other universities, whereas teaching credentials, harder to document and quantify, are much less transferable. Consequently it is rational for university teachers to con-

*Personal interviews conducted during 1972–1973.

centrate on research, even if to the detriment of teaching and at the expense of their students.

By the same token, it is rational for students to act based upon the goal displacement which has occurred within universities concerning what they are rewarded for. If it is assumed that a primary goal of a university is to transfer knowledge from teacher to student, then grades become identifiable as a means toward that goal, serving as motivational, control, and feedback devices to expedite the knowledge transfer. Instead, however, the grades themselves have become much more important for entrance to graduate school, successful employment, tuition refunds, parental respect, etc., than the knowledge or lack of knowledge they are supposed to signify.

It therefore should come as no surprise that information has surfaced in recent years concerning fraternity files for examinations, term paper writing services, organized cheating at the service academies, and the like. Such activities constitute a personally rational response to a reward system which pays off for grades rather than knowledge.

Business related examples

Ecology

Assume that the president of XYZ Corporation is confronted with the following alternatives:

1. Spend $11 million for antipollution equipment to keep from poisoning fish in the river adjacent to the plant; or
2. Do nothing, in violation of the law, and assume a one in ten chance of being caught, with a resultant $1 million fine plus the necessity of buying the equipment.

Under this not unrealistic set of choices it requires no linear program to determine that XYZ Corporation can maximize its probabilities by flouting the law. Add the fact that XYZ's president is probably being rewarded (by creditors, stockholders, and other salient parts of his task environment) according to criteria totally unrelated to the number of fish poisoned, and his probable course of action becomes clear.

Evaluation of training

It is axiomatic that those who care about a firm's well-being should insist that the organization get fair value for its expenditures. Yet it is commonly known that firms seldom bother to evaluate a new GRID, MBO, job enrichment program, or whatever, to see if the company is getting its money's worth. Why? Certainly it is not because people have not pointed out that this situation exists; numerous practitioner-oriented articles are written each year to just this point.

The individuals (whether in personnel, manpower planning, or wherever) who normally would be responsible for conducting such evaluations are the same ones often charged with introducing the change effort in the first place. Having convinced top management to spend the money, they usually are quite animated afterwards in collecting arigorous vignettes and anecdotes about how successful the program was. The last thing many desire is a formal, systematic, and revealing evaluation. Although members of top management may actually *hope* for such systematic evaluation, their reward systems continue to *reward* ignorance in this area. And if the personnel department abdicates its responsibility, who is to step into the breach? The change agent himself? Hardly! He is likely to be too busy collecting anecdotal "evidence" of his own, for use with his next client.

Miscellaneous

Many additional examples could be cited of systems which in fact are rewarding behaviors other than those supposedly desired by the rewarder. A few of these are described briefly below.

Most coaches disdain to discuss individual accomplishments, preferring to speak of teamwork, proper attitude, and a one-for-all spirit. Usually, however, rewards are distributed according to individual performance. The college basketball player who feeds his teammates instead of shooting will not compile impressive scoring statistics and is less likely to be drafted by the pros. The ballplayer who hits to right field to advance the runners will win neither the batting nor home run titles, and will be offered smaller raises. It therefore is rational for players to think of themselves first, and the team second.

In business organizations where rewards are dispensed for unit performance or for individual goals achieved, without regard for overall effectiveness, similar attitudes often are observed. Under most Management by Objectives (MBO) systems, goals in areas where quantification is difficult often go unspecified. The organization therefore often is in a position where it *hopes* for employee effort in the areas of team building, interpersonal relations, creativity, etc., but it formally *rewards* none of these. In cases where promotions and raises are formally tied to MBO, the system itself contains a paradox in that it "asks employees to set challenging, risky goals, only to face smaller pay-

checks and possibly damaged careers if these goals are not accomplished" (Kerr 1973a, 40).

It is *hoped* that administrators will pay attention to long run costs and opportunities and will institute programs which will bear fruit later on. However, many organizational reward systems pay off for short run sales and earnings only. Under such circumstances it is personally rational for officials to sacrifice long-term growth and profit (by selling off equipment and property, or by stifling research and development) for short-term advantages. This probably is most pertinent in the public sector, with the result that many public officials are unwilling to implement programs which will not show benefits by election time.

As a final, clear-cut example of a fouled-up reward system, consider the cost-plus contract or its next of kin, the allocation of next year's budget as a direct function of this year's expenditures. It probably is conceivable that those who award such budgets and contracts really hope for economy and prudence in spending. It is obvious, however, that adopting the proverb "to him who spends shall more be given," rewards not economy, but spending itself.

Two companies' experiences

A manufacturing organization

A midwest manufacturer of industrial goods had been troubled for some time by aspects of its organizational climate it believed dysfunctional. For research purposes, interviews were conducted with many employees and a questionnaire was administered on a company-wide basis, including plants and offices in several American and Canadian locations. The company strongly encouraged employee participation in the survey, and made available time and space during the workday for completion of the instrument. All employees in attendance during the day of the survey completed the questionnaire. All instruments were collected directly by the researcher, who personally administered each session. Since no one employed by the firm handled the questionnaires, and since respondent names were not asked for, it seems likely that the pledge of anonymity given was believed.

A modified version of the Expect Approval scale (Litwin and Stringer 1968) was included as part of the questionnaire. The instrument asked respondents to indicate the degree of approval or disapproval they could expect if they performed each of the described actions. A seven-point Likert scale was used, with one indicating that the action would probably bring strong disapproval and seven signifying likely strong approval.

Although normative data for this scale from studies of other organizations are unavailable, it is possible to examine fruitfully the data obtained from this survey in several ways. First, it may be worth

noting that the questionnaire data corresponded closely to information gathered through interviews. Furthermore, as can be seen from the results summarized in Table 1, sizable differences between various work units, and between employees at different job levels within the same work unit, were obtained. This suggests that response bias effects (social desirability in particular loomed as a potential concern) are not likely to be severe.

Most importantly, comparisons between scores obtained on the Expect Approval scale and a statement of problems which were the reason for the survey revealed that the same behaviors which managers in each division thought dysfunctional were those which lower-level employees claimed were rewarded. As compared to job levels 1 to 8 in Division B (see Table 1), those in Division A claimed a much higher acceptance by management of "conforming" activities. Between 31 and 37 percent of Division A employees at levels 1—8 stated that going along with the majority, agreeing with the boss, and staying on everyone's good side brought approval; only once (level 5—8 responses

Table 1
*Summary of two divisions data relevant to
conforming and risk-avoidance behaviors
(extent to which subjects expect approval)*

Dimension	Item	Division and sample	Total responses	Percentage of workers responding		
				1, 2, or 3 Disapproval	4	5, 6, or 7 Approval
Risk avoidance	Making a risky decision based on the best information available at the time, but which turns out wrong.	A, levels 1—4 (lowest)	127	61	25	14
		A, levels 5—8	172	46	31	23
		A, levels 9 and above	17	41	30	30
		B, levels 1—4 (lowest)	31	58	26	16
		B, levels 5—8	19	42	42	16
		B, levels 9 and above	10	50	20	30

Table 1 (continued)

Dimension	Item	Division and sample	Total responses	1, 2, or 3 Disapproval	4	5, 6, or 7 Approval
				Percentage of workers responding		
Risk avoidance (continued)	Setting extremely high and challenging standards and goals, and then narrowly failing to make them.	A, levels 1–4	122	47	28	25
		A, levels 5–8	168	33	26	41
		A, levels 9+	17	24	6	70
		B, levels 1–4	31	48	23	29
		B, levels 5–8	18	17	33	50
		B, levels 9+	10	30	0	70
	Setting goals which are extremely easy to make and then making them.	A, levels 1–4	124	35	30	35
		A, levels 5–8	171	47	27	26
		A, levels 9+	17	70	24	6
		B, levels 1–4	31	58	26	16
		B, levels 5–8	19	63	16	21
		B, levels 9+	10	80	0	20
Conformity	Being a "yes man" and always agreeing with the boss.	A, levels 1–4	126	46	17	37
		A, levels 5–8	180	54	14	31
		A, levels 9+	17	88	12	0
		B, levels 1–4	32	53	28	19
		B, levels 5–8	19	68	21	11
		B, levels 9+	10	80	10	10
	Always going along with the majority.	A, levels 1–4	125	40	25	35
		A, levels 5–8	173	47	21	32
		A, levels 9+	17	70	12	18
		B, levels 1–4	31	61	23	16
		B, levels 5–8	19	68	11	21
		B, levels 9+	10	80	10	10
	Being careful to stay on the good side of everyone, so that everyone agrees that you are a great guy.	A, levels 1–4	124	45	18	37
		A, levels 5–8	173	45	22	33
		A, levels 9+	17	64	6	30
		B, levels 1–4	31	54	23	23
		B, levels 5–8	19	73	11	16
		B, levels 9+	10	80	10	10

to one of the three items) did a majority suggest that such actions would generate disapproval.

Furthermore, responses from Division A workers at levels 1–4 indicate that behaviors geared toward risk avoidance were as likely to be rewarded as to be punished. Only at job levels 9 and above was it apparent that the reward system was positively reinforcing behaviors desired by top management. Overall, the same "tendencies toward conservatism and apple-polishing at the lower levels" which divisional management had complained about during the interviews were those claimed by subordinates to be the most rational course of action in light of the existing reward system. Management apparently was not getting the behaviors it was *hoping* for, but it certainly was getting the behaviors it was perceived by subordinates to be *rewarding*.

An insurance firm

The Group Health Claims Division of large eastern insurance company provides another rich illustration of a reward system which reinforces behaviors not desired by top management.

Attempting to measure and reward accuracy in paying surgical claims, the firm systematically keeps track of the number of returned checks and letters of complaint received from policyholders. However, underpayments are likely to provoke cries of outrage from the insured, while overpayments often are accepted in courteous silence. Since it often is impossible to tell from the physician's statement which of two surgical procedures, with different allowable benefits, was performed, and since writing for clarifications will interfere with other standards used by the firm concerning "percentage of claims paid within two days of receipt," the new hire in more than one claims section is soon acquainted with the informal norm: "When in doubt, pay it out!"

The situation would be even worse were it not for the fact that other features of the firm's reward system tend to neutralize those described. For example, annual "merit" increases are given to all employees, in one of the following three amounts:

1. If the worker is "outstanding" (a se-

lect category, into which no more than two employees per section may be placed): 5 percent.
2. If the worker is "above average" (normally all workers not "outstanding" are so rated): 4 percent.
3. If the worker commits gross acts of negligence and irresponsibility for which he might be discharged in many other companies: 3 percent.

Now, since (a) the difference between the 5 percent theoretically attainable through hard work and the 4 percent attainable merely by living until the review date is small and (b) since insurance firms seldom dispense much of a salary increase in cash (rather, the worker's insurance benefits increase, causing him to be further overinsured), many employees are rather indifferent to the possibility of obtaining the extra one percent reward and therefore tend to ignore the norm concerning indiscriminant payments.

However, most employees are not indifferent to the rule which states that, should absences or lateness total three or more in any six-month period, the entire 4 or 5 percent due at the next "merit" review must be forfeited. In this sense the firm may be described as *hoping* for performance, while *rewarding* attendance. What it gets, of course, is attendance. (If the absence-lateness rule appears to the reader to be stringent, it really is not. The company counts "times" rather than "days" absent, and a ten-day absence therefore counts the same as one lasting two days. A worker in danger of accumulating a third absence within six months merely has to remain ill (away from work) during his second absence until his first absence is more than six months old. The limiting factor is that at some point his salary ceases, and his sickness benefits take over. This usually is sufficient to get the younger workers to return, but for those with 20 or more years' service, the company provides sickness benefits of 90 percent of normal salary, tax-free! Therefore . . .)

Causes

Extremely diverse instances of systems which reward behavior A although the rewarder apparently hopes for behavior B have been given. These are useful to illustrate the breadth and magnitude of the phenomenon, but the diversity increases the difficulty of determining commonalities and establishing causes. However, four general factors may be pertinent to an explanation of why fouled-up reward systems seem to be so prevalent.

Fascination with an "objective" criterion

It has been mentioned elsewhere that:

Most "objective" measures of productivity are objective only in that their subjective elements are a) determined in advance, rather than coming into play at the time of the formal evaluation, and b) well concealed on the rating instrument itself. Thus industrial firms seeking to devise objective rating systems first decide, in an arbitrary manner, what dimensions are to be rated, . . . usually including some items having little to do with organizational effectiveness while excluding others that do. Only then does Personnel Division churn out official-looking documents on which all dimensions chosen to be rated are assigned point values, categories, or whatever (Kerr 1973b, 92).

Nonetheless, many individuals seek to establish simple, quantifiable standards against which to measure and reward performance. Such efforts may be successful in highly predictable areas within an organization, but are likely to cause goal displacement when applied anywhere else. Overconcern with attendance and lateness in the insurance firm and with number of people placed in the vocational rehabilitation division may have been largely responsible for the problems described in those organizations.

Overemphasis on highly visible behaviors

Difficulties often stem from the fact that some parts of the task are highly visible while other parts are not. For example, publications are easier to demonstrate than teaching, and scoring baskets and hitting home runs are more readily observable than feeding teammates and advancing base runners. Similarly, the adverse consequences of pronouncing a sick person well are more visible than those sustained by labeling a well person sick. Team building and creativity are other examples of behaviors which may not be rewarded simply because they are hard to observe.

Hypocrisy

In some of the instances described the rewarder may have been getting the desired behavior, notwithstanding claims that the behavior was not desired. This may be true, for example, of management's attitude toward apple-polishing in the manufacturing firm (a behavior which subordinates felt was rewarded, despite managenent's avowed dislike of the practice). This also may explain politicians' unwillingness to revise the penalties for disobedience of ecology laws, and the failure of top management to devise reward systems which would cause systematic evaluation of training and development programs.

Emphasis on morality or equity rather than efficiency

Sometimes consideration of other factors prevents the establishment of a system which rewards behaviors desired by the rewarder. The felt obligation of many Americans to vote for one candidate or another, for example, may impair their ability to withhold support from politicians who refuse to discuss the issues. Similarly, the concern for spreading the risks and costs of wartime military service may outweigh the advantage to be obtained by committing personnel to combat until the war is over.

It should be noted that only with respect to the first two causes are reward systems really paying off for other than desired behaviors. In the case of the third and fourth causes the system *is* rewarding behaviors desired by the rewarder, and the systems are fouled up only from the standpoints of those who believe the rewarder's public statements (cause 3), or those who seek to maximize efficiency rather than other outcomes (cause 4).

Conclusions

Modern organization theory requires a recognition that the members of organizations and society possess divergent goals and motives. It therefore is unlikely that managers and their subordinates will seek the same outcomes. Three possible remedies for this potential problem are suggested.

Selection

It is theoretically possible for organizations to employ only those individuals whose goals and motives are wholly consonant with those of management. In such cases the same behaviors judged by subordinates to be rational would be perceived by management as desirable. State-of-the-art reviews of selection techniques, however, provide scant grounds for hope that such an approach would be successful (for example, see Webster 1964).

Training

Another theoretical alternative is for the organization to admit those employees whose goals are not consonant with those of management and then, through training, socialization, or whatever, alter employee goals to make them consonant. However, research on the effectiveness of such training programs, though limited, provides further grounds for pessimism (for example, see Fieldler 1972).

Altering the Reward system

What would have been the result if:

1. Nixon had been assured by his advisors that he could not win reelection except by discussing the issues in detail?
2. Physicians' conduct was subjected to regular examination by review boards for type 1 errors (calling healthy people ill) and to penalties (fines, censure, etc.) for errors of either type?
3. The President of XYZ Corporation had to choose between (a) spending $11 million dollars for antipollution equipment, and (b) incurring a fifty-fifty chance of going to jail for five years?

Managers who complain that their workers are not motivated might do well to consider the possibility that they have installed reward systems which are paying off for behaviors other than those they are seeking. This, in part, is what happened in Vietnam, and this is what regularly frustrates societal efforts to bring about honest politicians, civic-minded managers, etc. This certainly is what happened in both the manufacturing and the insurance companies.

A first step for such managers might be to find out what behaviors currently are being rewarded. Perhaps an instrument similar to that used in the manufacturing firm could be useful for this purpose. Chances are excellent that these managers will be surprised by what they find — that their firms are not rewarding what they assume they are. In fact, such undesirable behavior by organizational members as they have observed may be explained largely by the reward systems in use.

This is not to say that all organizational behavior is determined by formal rewards and punishments. Certainly it is true that in the absence of formal reinforcement some soldiers will be patriotic, some president will be ecology minded, and some orphanage directors will care about children. The point, however, is that in such cases the rewarder is not *causing* the behaviors desired but is only a fortunate bystander. For an organization to *act* upon its members, the formal reward system should positively reinforce desired behaviors, not constitute an obstacle to be overcome.

It might be wise to underscore the obvious fact that there is nothing really new in what has been said. In both theory and practice these matters have been mentioned before. Thus in many states Good Samaritan laws have been installed to protect doctors who stop to assist a stricken motorist. In states without such laws it is commonplace for doctors to refuse to stop, for fear of involvement in a subsequent lawsuit. In college basketball additional penalties have been instituted against players who foul their opponents deliberately. It has long been argued by Milton Friedman and others that penalties should be altered so as to make it irrational to disobey the ecology laws, and so on.

By altering the reward system the organization escapes the necessity of selecting only desirable people or of trying to alter undesirable ones. In Skinnerian terms (as described in Swanson 1972, 704), "As for responsibility and goodness — as commonly defined — no one . . . would want or need them. They refer to a man's behaving well despite the absence of positive reinforcement that is obviously sufficient to explain it. Where such reinforcement exists, 'no one needs goodness.' "

That urge to achieve

David C. McClelland

Most people in this world, psychologically, can be divided into two broad groups. There is that minority which is challenged by opportunity and willing to work hard to achieve something, and the majority which really does not care all that much.

For nearly twenty years now, psychologists have tried to penetrate the mystery of this curious dichotomy. Is the need to achieve (or the absence of it) an accident, is it hereditary, or is it the result of environment? Is it a single, isolatable human motive, or a combination of motives — the desire to accumulate wealth, power, fame? Most important of all, is there some technique that could give this will to achieve to people, even whole societies, who do not now have it?

While we do not yet have complete answers for any of these questions, years of work have given us partial answers to most of them and insights into all of them. There is a distinct human motive, distinguishable from others. It can be found, in fact tested for, in any group.

Let me give you one example. Several years ago, a careful study was made of 450 workers who had been thrown out of work by a plant shutdown in Erie, Pennsylvania. Most of the unemployed workers stayed home for a while and then checked back with the United States Employment Service to see if their old jobs or similar ones were available. But a small minority among them behaved differently: the day they were laid off, they started job-hunting.

They checked both the United States and the Pennsylvania Employment Office; they studied the "Help Wanted" sections of the papers; they checked through their union, their church, and various fraternal organizations; they looked into training courses to learn a new skill; they even left town to look for work, while the majority when questioned said they would not under any circumstances move away from Erie to obtain a job. Obviously the members of that active minority were differently motivated. All the men were more or less in the same situation objectively: they needed work, money, food, shelter, job security. Yet only a minority showed initiative and enterprise in finding what they

needed. Why? Psychologists, after years of research, now believe they can answer that question. They have demonstrated that these men possessed in greater degree a specific type of human motivation. For the moment let us refer to this personality characteristic as "Motive A" and review some of the other characteristics of the men who have more of the motive than other men.

Suppose they are confronted by a work situation in which they can set their own goals as to how difficult a task they will undertake. In the psychological laboratory, such a situation is very simply created by asking them to throw rings over a peg from any distance they may choose. Most men throw more or less randomly, standing now close, now far away, but those with Motive A seem to calculate carefully where they are most likely to get a sense of mastery. They stand nearly always at moderate distances, not so close as to make the task ridiculously easy, nor so far away as to make it impossible. They set moderately difficult, but potentially achievable goals for themselves, where they objectively have only about a one-in-three chance of succeeding. In other words, they are always setting challenges for themselves, tasks to make them stretch themselves a little.

But they behave like this only if *they* can influence the outcome by performing the work themselves. They prefer not to gamble at all. Say they are given a choice between rolling dice with one in three chances of winning and working on a problem with a one-in-three chance of solving in the time allotted, they choose to work on the problem even though rolling the dice is obviously less work and the odds of winning are the same. They prefer to work at a problem rather than leave the outcome to chance or to others.

Obviously they are concerned with personal achievement rather than with the rewards of success *per se,* since they stand just as much chance of getting those rewards by throwing the dice. This leads to another characteristic the Motive A men show — namely, a strong preference for work situations in which they get concrete feedback on how well they are doing, as one does, say in playing golf, or in being a salesman, but as one does not in teaching, or in personnel counseling. A golfer always knows his score and can compare how well he is doing with par or with his own performance yesterday or last week. A teacher has no such concrete feedback on how well he is doing in "getting across" to his students.

The *n* Ach men

But why do certain men behave like this? At one level the reply is simple: because they habitually spend their time thinking about doing things better. In fact, psychologists typically measure the strength of Motive A by taking samples of a man's spontaneous thoughts (such as making up a story about a picture they have been shown) and counting the frequency with which he mentions doing things better. The count is objective and can even be made these days with the help of a computer program for content analysis. It yields what is referred to technically as an individual's *n* Ach score (for "need for Achievement"). It is not difficult to understand why people who think constantly about "doing better" are more apt to do better at job-hunting, to set moderate, achievable goals for themselves, to dislike gambling (because they get no achievement satisfaction from success), and to prefer work situations where they can tell easily whether they are improv-

ing or not. But why some people and not others come to think this way is another question. The evidence suggests it is not because they are born that way, but because of special training they get in the home from parents who set moderately high achievement goals but who are warm, encouraging, and non-authoritarian in helping their children reach these goals.

Such detailed knowledge about one motive helps correct a lot of common sense ideas about human motivation. For example, much public policy (and much business policy) is based on the simple minded notion that people will work harder "if they have to." As a first approximation, the idea isn't totally wrong, but it is only a half-truth. The majority of unemployed workers in Erie "had to" find work as much as those with higher *n* Ach but they certainly didn't work as hard at it. Or again, it is frequently assumed that *any* strong motive will lead to doing things better. Wouldn't it be fair to say that most of the Erie workers were just "unmotivated"? But our detailed knowledge of various human motives shows that each one leads a person to behave in *different* ways. The contrast is not between being "motivated" or "unmotivated" but between being motivated toward A or toward B or C, etc.

A simple experiment makes the point nicely: subjects were told that they could choose as a working partner either a close friend or a stranger who was known to be an expert on the problem to be solved. Those with higher *n* Ach (more "need to achieve") chose the experts over their friends, whereas those with more *n* Aff (the "need to affiliate with others") chose friends over experts. The latter were not "unmotivated"; their desire to be with someone they liked was simply a stronger motive than their desire to excel at the task. Other such needs have been studied by psychologists. For instance, the need for Achievement because both may lead to "outstanding" activities. There is a distinct difference. People with a strong need for Power want to commend attention, get recognition, and control others. They are more active in political life and tend to busy themselves primarily with controlling the channels of communication both up to the top and down to the people so that they are more "in charge." Those with high *n* Pow are not as concerned with improving their work performance daily as those with high *n* Ach.

It follows, from what we have been able to learn, that not all "great achievers" score high in *n* Ach. Many generals, outstanding politicians, great research scientists do not, for instance, because their work requires other personality characteristics, other motives. A general or a politician must be more concerned with power relationships, a research scientist must be able to go for long periods without the immediate feedback the person with high *n* Ach requires, etc. On the other hand, business executives, particularly if they are in positions of real responsibility or if they are salesmen, tend to score high in *n* Ach. This is true even in a Communist country like Poland; Apparently there, as well as in a private enterprise economy, a manager succeeds if he is concerned about improving all the time, setting moderate goals, keeping track of his or the company's performance, etc.

Motivation and half-truths

Since careful study has shown that common sense notions about motivation are at best half-truths, it also follows that you cannot trust what people tell you about their motives. After all, they often get their ideas about their own motives from common sense. Thus a general may say he is interested in achievement (because he has obviously achieved), or a businessman that he is interested only in making money (because he has made money), or one of the majority of unemployed in Erie that he desperately wants a job (because he knows he needs one); but a careful check of what each one thinks about and how he spends his time may show that each is concerned about quite different things. It requires special measurement techniques to identify the presence of *n* Ach and other such motives. Thus what people say and believe is not very closely related to these "hidden" motives which seem to affect a person's "style of life" more than his political, religious or social attitudes. Thus *n* Ach produces enterprising men among labor leaders or managers, Republicans or Democrats, Catholics or Protestants, capitalists or Communists.

Wherever people begin to think often in *n* Ach terms, things begin to move. Men with high *n* Ach get more raises and are promoted more rapidly, because they keep actively seeking ways to do a better job. Companies with many such men grow faster. In one comparison of two firms in Mexico, it was discovered that all but one of the top executives of a fast-growing firm and higher *n* Ach scores than the highest-scoring executive in an equally large but slow-growing firm. Countries with many such rapidly growing firms tend to show above average rates of national economic growth. This appears to be the reason why correlations have regularly been found between the *n* Ach content in popular literature (such as popular songs or stories in children's textbooks) and subsequent rates of national economic growth. A nation which is thinking about doing better all the time (as shown in its popular literature) actually does do better economically speaking. Careful quantitative studies have shown this to be true in Ancient Greece, in Spain in the Middle Ages, in England from 1400–1800, as well as among contemporary nations, whether capitalist or Communist, developed or underdeveloped.

Contrast these two stories for example. Which one contains more *n* Ach? Which one reflects a state of mind which ought to lead to harder striving to improve the way things are?

Excerpt from story A □ (fourth-grade reader): "Don't Ever Owe a Man — The world is an illusion. Wife, children, horses, and cows are all just ties of fate. They are ephemeral. Each after fulfiling his part in life disappears. So we should not clamour after riches which are not permanent. As long as we live it is wise not to have any attachments and just think of God. We have to spend our lives without trouble, for is it not time that there is an end to grievances? So it is better to live knowing the real state of affairs. Don't get entangled in the meshes of family life."

Excerpt from story B □ (fourth-grade reader): "How I Do Like to Learn — I was sent to an accelerated technical high school. I was so happy I cried. Learning is not very easy. In the beginning I couldn't understand what the teacher taught us. I always got a red cross mark on my papers. The boy sitting next to me was very enthusiastic and also an outstanding student. When he found I couldn't do the problems he offered to show me how he had done them. I could not copy his work. I must learn through my own reasoning. I gave his paper back and explained I had to do it myself. Sometimes I worked on a problem until midnight. If I couldn't finish, I started early in the morning. The red cross marks on my work were getting less common. I conquered my difficulties. My marks rose. I graduated and went on to college."

Most readers would agree, without any special knowledge of the *n* Ach coding system, that the second story shows more concern with improvement than the first, which comes from a contemporary reader used in Indian public schools. In fact the latter has a certain Horatio Alger quality that is reminiscent of our own McGuffey readers of several generations ago. It appears today in the textbooks of Communist China. It should not, therefore, come as a surprise if a nation like Communist China, obsessed as it is with improvement, tended in the long run to outproduce a nation like India, which appears to be more fatalistic.

The *n* Ach level is obviously important for statesmen to watch and in many instances to try to do something about, particularly if a nation's economy is lagging. Take Britain, for example. A generation ago (around 1925) it ranked fifth among 25 countries where children's readers were scored for *n* Ach — and its economy was doing well. By 1950 the *n* Ach level had dropped to 27th out of 39 countries— well below the world average — and today, its leaders are feeling the severe economic effects of this loss in the spirit of enterprise.

Economics and *n* Ach

If psychologists can detect *n* Ach levels in individuals or nations, particularly before their effects are widespread, can't the knowledge somehow be put to use to foster economic development? Obviously detection or diagnosis is not enough. What good is it to tell Britain (or India for that matter) that it needs more *n* Ach, a greater spirit of enterprise? In most such cases, informed observers of the local scene know very well that such a need exists, though they may be slower to discover it than the psychologist hovering over *n* Ach scores. What is needed is some method of developing *n* Ach in individuals or nations.

Since about 1960, psychologists in my research group at Harvard have been experimenting with techniques designed to accomplish this goal, chiefly among business executives whose work requires the action characteristics of people with high *n* Ach. Initially, we had real doubts as to whether we could succeed, partly because like most American psychologists we had been strongly influenced by the psychoanalytic view that basic motives are laid down in childhood and cannot really be changed later, and partly because many studies of intensive psychotherapy and counseling have shown minor if any long-term personality effects. On the other hand we were encouraged by the non-professionals: those enthusiasts like Dale Carnegie, the Communist ideologue or the Church missionary, who felt they could change adults and in fact seemed to be doing so. At any rate we ran some brief (7-to-10-day) "total push" training courses for businessmen, designed to increase their *n* Ach.

Four main goals

In broad outline the courses had four main goals: (1) They were designed to teach the participants how to think, talk and act like a person with high *n* Ach, based on our knowledge of such people gained through 17 years of research. For instance, men learned how to make up stories that would code high in *n* Ach (i.e., how to think in *n* Ach terms), how to set moderate goals for themselves in the ring toss game (and in life). (2) The courses stimulated the participants to set higher but carefully planned and realistic work goals for themselves over the next two years. Then we checked back with them every six months to see how well they were doing in terms of their own objectives. (3) The courses also utilized techniques for giving the participants knowledge about themselves. For instance, in playing the ring toss game, they could observe that they behaved differently from others — perhaps in refusing to adjust a goal downward after failure. This would then become a matter for group discussion and the man would have to explain what he had in mind in setting such unrealistic goals. Discussion could then lead on to what a man's ultimate goals in life were, how much he cared about actually improving performance vs. making a good impression or having many friends. In this way the participants would be freer to realize their achievement goals without being blocked by old habits and attitudes. (4) The courses also usually created a group *esprit de corps* from learning about each other's hopes and fears, successes and failures, and from going through an emotional experience together, away from everyday life, in a retreat setting. This membership in a new group helps a man achieve his goals, partly because he knows he has their sympathy and support and partly because he knows they will be watching to see how well he does. The same effect has been noted in other therapy groups like Alcoholics Anonymous. We are not sure which of these course "inputs" is really absolutely essential — that remains a research question — but we were taking no chances at the outset in view of the general pessimism about such efforts, and we wanted to include any and all techniques that were thought to change people.

The courses have been given: to executives in a large American firm, and in several Mexican firms; to underachieving high school boys; and to businessmen in India from Bombay and from a small city — Kakinada in the state of Andhra Pradesh. In every instance save one (the Mexican case), it was possible to demonstrate statistically, some two years later, that the men who took the course had done better (made more money, got promoted faster, expanded their businesses faster) than comparable men who did not take the course or who took some other management course.

Consider the Kakinada results, for example. In the two years preceding the course 9 men, 18 percent of the 52 participants, had shown "unusual" enterprise in their businesses. In the 18 months following the course 25 of the men, in other words nearly 50 percent, were unusually active. And this was not due to a general upturn of business in India. Data from a control city, some forty-five miles away, show the same base rate of "unusually active" men as in Kakinada before the course — namely, about 20 percent. Something clearly happened in Kakinada: the owner of a small radio shop started a chemical plant; a banker was so successful in making commercial loans in an enterprising way that he was promoted to a much larger branch of his bank in Calcutta; the local political leader accomplished his goal (it was set in the course) to get the federal government to deepen the harbor and make it into an all-weather port;

plans are far along for establishing a steel rolling mill, etc. All this took place without any substantial capital from the outside. In fact, the only costs were for our 10-day courses plus some brief follow-up visits every six months. The men are raising their own capital and using their own resources for getting business and industry moving in a city that had been considered stagnant and unenterprising.

The promise of such a method of developing achievement motivation seems very great. It has obvious applications in helping underdeveloped countries, or "pockets of poverty" in the United States, to move faster economically. It has great potential for businesses that need to "turn around" and take a more enterprising approach toward their growth and development. It may even be helpful in developing more n Ach among low-income groups. For instance, data show that lower-class Negro Americans have a very low level of n Ach. This is not surprising. Society has systematically discouraged and blocked their achievement striving. But as the barriers to upward mobility are broken down, it will be necessary to help stimulate the motivation that will lead them to take advantage of new opportunities opening up.

Extreme reactions

But a word of caution: Whenever I speak of this research and its great potential, audience reaction tends to go to opposite extremes. Either people remain skeptical and argue that motives can't really be changed, that all we are doing is dressing Dale Carnegie up in fancy "psychologese," or they become converts and want instant course descriptions by return mail to solve their local motivation problems. Either response is unjustified.

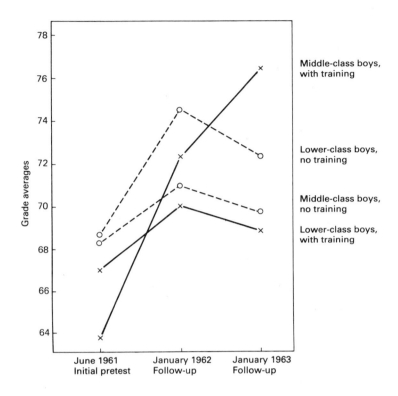

Grade averages

78

76   Middle-class boys,
      with training

74

72   Lower-class boys,
      no training

70   Middle-class boys,
      no training

68   Lower-class boys,
      with training

66

64

June 1961   January 1962   January 1963
Initial pretest   Follow-up   Follow-up

In a Harvard study, a group of underachieving 14-year-olds was given a six-week's course designed to help them do better in school. Some of the boys were also given training in achievement motivation, or n Ach (solid lines). As the graph reveals, the only boys who continued to improve after a two-year period were the middle-class boys with the special n Ach training. Psychologists suspect the lower-class boys dropped back, even with n Ach training, because they returned to an environment in which neither parents nor friends encouraged achievement.

What I have described here in a few pages has taken 20 years of patient research effort, and hundreds of thousands of dollars in basic research costs. What remains to be done will involve even larger sums and more time for development to turn a promising idea into something of wide practical utility.

Encouragement needed

To take only one example, we have not yet learned how to develop *n* Ach really well among low-income groups (see chart). In our first effort — a summer course for bright underachieving 14-year-olds — we found that boys from the middle class improved steadily in grades in school over a two-year period, but boys from the lower class showed an improvement after the first year followed by a drop back to their beginning low grade average. Why? We speculated that it was because they moved back into an environment in which neither parents nor friends encouraged achievement or upward mobility. In other words, it isn't enough to change a man's motivation if the environment in which he lives doesn't support at least to some degree his new efforts. Negroes striving to rise out of the ghetto frequently confront this problem: they are often faced by skepticism at home and suspicion on the job, so that even if their *n* Ach is raised, it can be lowered again by the heavy odds against their success. We must learn not only to raise *n* Ach but also to find methods of instructing people in how to manage it, to create a favorable environment in which it can flourish.

Many of these training techniques are now only in the pilot testing stage. It will take time and money to perfect them, but society should be willing to invest heavily in them in view of their tremendous potential for contributing to human betterment.

Behavior modification on the bottom line

W. Clay Hamner and Ellen P. Hamner

It may be easy to say *what* a manager does. Telling *how* he influences the behavior of the employee in the direction of task accomplishment is far more difficult to comprehend and describe. The purpose of this article is to describe and spell out the determinants of employee productivity or performance from a reinforcement theory point of view, and to show how managing the contingencies of positive reinforcement in organizational settings leads to successful management. We hope these descriptions will enable the manager to understand how his or her behavior affects the behavior of subordinates and to see that, in many cases, a worker's failure to perform a task properly is a direct outcome of the manager's own behavior. The employee has failed to perform because the manager has failed to motivate.

Managing the contingencies of reinforcement

The interrelationship among three components — work environment, task performance, and consequences of reinforcements — are known as the contingencies of reinforcement. The reward that is contingent upon good performance in a given work situation (environment) acts as a motivator for future performance. The manager controls the *work environment* (Where am I going? What are the goals? Is the leader supportive? Is this a pleasant place to work?), the *task assignment* (How will I get there? What behavior is desired? What is considered appropriate performance?), and the *consequences* of job performance (How will I know when I've reached the desired goal? Is the feedback relevant and timely? Is my pay based upon my performance?). By shaping these three components of behavior so that all are positive, the manager can go a long way toward creating a work climate that supports high productivity.

Arranging the contingencies of reinforcement

Someone who expects to influence behavior must be able to manipulate the consequences of behavior. Whether managers realize it or not, they constantly shape the behavior of their subordinates by the way they utilize the rewards at their disposal. Employers intuitively use rewards all the time — but their efforts often produce limited results because the methods are used improperly, inconsistently, or inefficiently. In many instances employees are given rewards that are not conditional or contingent on the behavior the manager wishes to promote. Even when they are, long delays often intervene between the occurrence of the desired behavior and its intended consequences. Special privileges, activities, and rewards are often furnished according to length of service rather than performance requirements. In many cases, positive reinforcers are inadvertently made contingent upon the wrong kind of behavior. In short, intuition provides a poor guide to motivation.

A primary reason managers fail to "motivate" workers to perform in the desired manner is their failure to understand the power of the contingencies of reinforcement over the employee. The laws or principles for arranging the con-

tingencies to condition behavior are not hard to understand; if properly applied, they constitute powerful managerial tools that can be used for increasing supervisory effectiveness.

Conditioning is the process by which behavior is modified through manipulation of the contingencies of behavior. To understand how this works, we will first look at various kinds of arrangements of the contingencies: *positive reinforcement* conditioning, *escape* conditioning, *extinction* conditioning, and *punishment* conditioning. The differences among these kinds of contingencies depend on the consequences that result from the behavioral act. Positive reinforcement and avoidance learning are methods of strengthening desired behavior, while extinction and punishment are methods of weakening undesired behavior.

Positive reinforcement

According to B. F. Skinner, a positive reinforcer or reward is a stimulus that, when added to a situation, strengthens the probability of the response in that situation. Behavior that appears to lead to a positive consequence tends to be repeated, while behavior that appears to lead to a negative consequence tends not to be repeated.

Once it has been determined that a specific consequence has reward value to a work group, we can use it to increase that group's performance. Thus the first step in the successful application of reinforcement procedures is to select reinforcers that are sufficiently powerful and durable to establish and strengthen desired behavior. These could include such things as an interesting work assignment, the chance to use one's mind, seeing the results of one's work, good pay, recognition for a job well done, promotion, freedom to decide how to do a job, and so on.

The second step is to design the contingencies in such a way that the reinforcing events are made contingent on the desired level of performance. This is the rule of reinforcement most often violated. Rewards *must* result from performance — and the better an employee's performance is, the greater his or her rewards should be.

Unless a manager is willing to discriminate among employees on the basis of their performance levels, the effectiveness of his or her power over the employee is nil. For example, Edward E. Lawler III, a leading researcher on pay and performance, has noted that one of the major reasons managers are unhappy with their salary system is that they do not perceive the relationship between how hard they work (productivity) and how much they earn. In a survey of 600 managers, Lawler found virtually no relationship between their pay and their rated level of performance.

The third step is to design the contingencies in such a way that a reliable procedure for eliciting or inducing the desired response patterns is established; when desired responses rarely occur, there are few opportunities to influence behavior through contingency management. Training programs, goal-setting programs, and similar efforts should be undertaken to let workers know what is expected of them. If the criterion for reinforcement is unclear, unspecified, or set too high, most — if not all — of the worker's responses go unrewarded; eventually his or her efforts will be extinguished.

Escape conditioning

The second kind of contingency arrangement available to the manager is called escape or avoidance conditioning. Just as with positive reinforcement, this is a method of strengthening desired behavior. A contingency arrangement in which an individual's performance can terminate a noxious environment is called escape learning. When behavior can prevent the onset of a noxious stimulus, the procedure is called avoidance learning.

An employee is given an unpleasant task assignment, for example, with the promise that when he completes it, he can move on (escape) to a more pleasant job. Or a manager is such an unpleasant person to be around that the employees work when he is present in order to "avoid" him.

Let's note the distinction between strengthening behavior through positive reinforcement techniques and doing so through avoidance learning techniques. In one case, the individual works hard to gain the consequences from the environment (provided by the manager in most cases) that result from good work, and in the second case, the individual works hard to avoid the negative aspects of the environment itself (again, the manager is the source). In both cases the same behavior is strengthened over the short run. In escape learning, however, the manager is more process oriented; he or she must be present in order to elicit the desired level of performance. Under positive reinforcement, however, the manager is outcome oriented and does not have to be physically present at all times in order to maintain the desired level of performance.

Extinction

When positive reinforcement for a learned or previously conditioned response is withheld, individuals will still continue to exhibit that behavior for an extended period of time. With repeated nonreinforcement, however, the behavior decreases and eventually disappears. This decline in response rate as a result of nonrewarded repetition of a task is defined as *extinction*.

This method, when combined with a positive reinforcement method, is the procedure of behavior modification recommended by Skinner. It leads to the fewest negative side effects. Using the two methods together allows employees to get the rewards they desire and allows the organization to eliminate the undesired behavior.

Punishment

Punishment is the most controversial method of behavior modification. Punishment is defined as presenting an aversive or noxious consequence contingent upon a response, or removing a positive consequence contingent upon a response. The Law of Effect operates here, too: As rewards strengthen behavior, punishment weakens it. Notice carefully the difference between withholding rewards in the punishment process and withholding rewards in the extinction process. In the extinction process, we withhold rewards for behavior that has previously been rewarded because the behavior was previously desired. In punishment, we withhold a reward because the behavior is undesired, has never been associated with the reward before, and is plainly an undesirable consquence.

Rules for using operant conditioning techniques

Rule 1. Don't give the same level of reward to all

Differentiate rewards based on per-formance in relation to defined objectives or standards. We know that people compare their performance with the performance of their peers to determine how well they are doing and that they compare their rewards with peer rewards to determine how to evaluate theirs. Some managers may think that the fairest compensation system is one in which everyone in the same job classification gets the same pay, but employees want differentiation as evidence of how important their services are to the organization. Managers who reward all people at the same level are simply encouraging, at most, only average performance. Behavior leading to high performance is being extinguished (ignored), while average and poor performance are being strengthened by means of positive reinforcement.

Rule 2. Failure to respond to behavior has reinforcing consequences

Managers who find the job of differentiating between workers so unpleasant or so difficult that they fail to respond to their behavior must recognize that failure to respond is itself a form of response that, in turn, modifies behavior. Superiors are bound to shape the behavior of their subordinates by the way in which they utilize the rewards at their disposal. Therefore, managers must be careful that they examine the consequences on performance of their nonactions as well as their actions.

Rule 3. Tell a person what behavior gets reinforced

By making clear to a worker the contingencies of reinforcement, a manager may actually be increasing his individual freedom. The employee who has a standard against which to measure his job will have a built-in feedback system that allows him or her to make judgments about his or her own level of performance. The awarding of reinforcements in an organization where workers' goals are specified will be associated with worker performance, not supervisory bias. The assumption is, of course, that the supervisor rates the employee accurately and then reinforces the employee according to his ratings. If the supervisor fails to rate accurately or administer rewards based on peformance, then the worker will be forced to search for the "true" contingencies — that is, what behavior he or she should display in order to get rewarded (ingratiation? loyalty? positive attitude?).

Rule 4. Tell a person what he or she is doing wrong

As a general rule, very few people find failure rewarding. One assumption of behavior conditioning therefore is that a worker wants to be rewarded for positive accomplishments. A supervisor should never use extinction or punishment as the sole method for modifying behavior — but if one of these is used judiciously in conjunction with positive reinforcement techniques, such combined procedures can hasten the change process. If the supervisor fails to specify why a reward is being withheld, the employee may associate the withholding of the reward with past desired behavior instead of the behavior that the supervisor is trying to extinguish. Thus the supervisor extinguishes good performance while having no effect on the undesired behavior.

Rule 5. Don't punish in front of others

The reason for this rule is quite simple. The punishment (for example, a repri-

mand) should be enough to extinguish the undesired behavior. By administering the punishment in front of the work group, the worker is doubly punished; he also "loses face." This additional punishment may lead to negative side effects in three ways. First, the worker whose self-image is damaged may feel that he must retaliate in order to protect himself. Therefore, the supervisor has actually increased undesired responses. Second, the work group may associate the punishment with another behavior of the worker and, through "avoidance learning" techniques, may modify their own behavior in ways not intended by the supervisor. Third, the work group is also being punished — in the sense that observing a member of their team being reprimanded is unpleasant to most people. This may result in lowered performance of the total work group.

Rule 6. Make the consequences equal to the behavior

In other words, don't cheat the worker out of his just rewards. If he is a good worker, tell him. Many supervisors find it very difficult to praise an employee. Others find it very difficult to counsel an employee about what he is doing wrong. When a manager fails to use these reinforcement tools, he is actually reducing his effectiveness. Overrewarding a worker may make him feel guilty and certainly reinforces his current performance level. If the performance level is lower than that of others who get the same reward, he has no reason to increase his output. When a worker is underrewarded, he becomes angry with the system. His behavior is being extinguished and the company may be forcing the good employee (underrewarded) to seek employment elsewhere while encouraging the poor employee (over-rewarded) to stay on.

Setting up a positive reinforcement program in industry

Many organizations are setting up formal motivational programs in an attempt use the principles of positive reinforcement to increase employee productivity.

A positive reinforcement approach to management differs from traditional motivational theories in two basic ways. First, as noted above, a positive reinforcement program calls for the maximum use of reinforcement and the minimum use of punishment. Punishment tends to leave the individual feeling controlled and coerced. Second, a positive reinforcement program avoids psychological probing into the worker's attitudes as a possible cause of behavior. Instead, the work situation itself is analyzed, with the focus on the reward contingencies that cause a worker to act the way in which he does.

A positive reinforcement program, therefore, is results oriented rather than process oriented. Geary A. Rummler, president of Praxis Corporation, a management consultant firm, claims that the motivational theories of such behavioral scientists as Herzberg and Maslow, which stress workers' psychological needs, are impractical. "They can't be made operative. While they help classify a problem, a positive reinforcement program leads to solutions."

Stages in program development

Positive reinforcement programs currently used in industry generally involve at least four stages. The *first stage,* according to Edward J. Feeney, formerly vice-president, systems, of Emery Air Freight Corporation, is to define the behavioral aspects of performance and do a performance audit. This step is potentially one of the most difficult, since some companies do not have a formal performance evaluation program, especially for nonmanagerial employees, and those that do have a program often rate the employee's behavior or nonjob-related measures (such as friendliness, loyalty, cooperation, overall attitude, and so on). But once these behavioral aspects are defined the task of convincing managers that improvement is needed and of persuading them to cooperate with such a program is simplified. Feeney asserts, "Most managers genuinely think that operations in their bailiwick are doing well; a performance audit that proves they're not comes as a real and unpleasant surprise."

The *second stage* in developing a working positive reinforcement program is to develop and set specific goals for each worker. Failure to specify concrete behavioral goals is a major reason many programs do not work. Goals should be expressed in such terms as "decreased employee turnover" or "schedules met" rather than only in terms of "better identification with the company" or "increased job satisfaction." The goals set, therefore, should be in the same terms as those defined in the performance audit, goals that specifically relate to the task at hand. Goals should be reasonable — that is, set somewhere between "where you are" (as spelled out in the performance audit) and some ideal.

While it is important for the manager to set goals, it is also important for the employee to accept them. An approach that tends to build in goal acceptance is to allow employees to work with management in setting work goals. According to

John C. Emery, president of Emery Air Freight Corporation, the use of a participatory management technique to enlist the ideas of those performing the job not only results in their acceptance of goals, but also stimulates them to come up with goals.

The *third stage* in a positive reinforcement program is to allow the employee to keep a record of his or her own work. This process of self-feedback maintains a continuous schedule of reinforcement for the worker and helps him obtain intrinsic reinforcement from the task itself. Where employees can total their own results, they can see whether they are meeting their goals and whether they are improving over their previous performance audit stage). In other words, the worker has two chances of being successful — either by beating his previous record or by beating both his previous record and his established goal. E. D. Grady, general manager, operator services for Michigan Bell, maintains that the manager should set up the work environment in such a way that people have a chance to succeed. One way to do this, he says, is to "shorten the success interval." Grady says, "If you're looking for success, keep shortening the interval of measurement so you can get a greater chance of success which you can latch on to for positive reinforcements." Instead of setting monthly or quarterly goals, for example, set weekly or daily goals.

The *fourth stage* — the most important step in a positive reinforcement program — is one that separates it from all other motivation plans. The supervisor looks at the self-feedback report of the employee and/or other indications of performance (sales records, for example) and then praises the positive aspects of the employee's performance (as deter-mined by the performance audit and subsequent goal setting). This extrinsic reinforcement should strengthen the desired performance, while the withholding of praise for substandard performance should give the employee incentive to improve that performance level. Since the worker already knows the areas of his or her deficiencies, there is no reason for the supervisor to criticize the employee. In other words, negative feedback is self-induced, whereas positive feedback comes from both internal and external sources.

As noted previously, this approach to feedback follows the teachings of B. F. Skinner, who believes that use of positive reinforcement leads to a greater feeling of self-control, while the avoidance of negative reinforcement keeps the individual from feeling controlled or coerced. Skinner says, "You can get the same effect if the supervisor simply discovers things being done right and says something like 'Good, I see you're doing it the way that works best.'"

While the feedback initially used in step four of the positive reinforcement program is praise, it is important to note that other forms of reinforcement can have the same effect. M. W. Warren, the director of organization and management development at the Questor Corporation, says that the five "reinforcers" he finds most effective are (1) money (but only when it is a consequence of a specific performance and when the relation to the performance is known); (2) praise or recognition; (3) freedom to choose one's own activity; (4) opportunity to see oneself become better, more important, or more useful; and (5) power to influence both coworkers and management. Warren states, "By building these reinforcers into programs at various facilities, Questor is getting results." The need for using more than praise after the positive reinforcement program has proved effective is discussed by Skinner.

It does not cost the company anything to use praise rather than blame, but if the company then makes a great deal more money that way, the worker may seem to be getting gypped. However, the welfare of the worker depends on the welfare of the company, and if the company is smart enough to distribute some of the fruits of positive reinforcement in the form of higher wages and better fringe benefits, everybody gains from the supervisor's use of positive reinforcements. *(Organizational Dynamics,* Winter 1973, p. 35.)

Motivation — a diagnostic approach

David A. Nadler and Edward E. Lawler III

- What makes some people work hard while others do as little as possible?
- How can I, as a manager, influence the performance of people who work for me?
- Why do people turn over, show up late to work, and miss work entirely?

These important questions about employees' behavior can only be answered by managers who have a grasp of what motivates people. Specifically, a good understanding of motivation can serve as a valuable tool for *understanding* the causes of behavior in organizations, for *predicting* the effects of any managerial action, and for *directing* behavior so that organizational and individual goals can be achieved.

Existing approaches

During the past twenty years, managers have been bombarded with a number of different approaches to motivation. The terms associated with these approaches are well known — "human relations," "scientific management," "job enrichment," "need hierarchy," "self-actualization," etc. Each of these approaches has something to offer. On the other hand, each of these different approaches also has its problems in both theory and practice. Running through almost all of the approaches with which managers are familiar are a series of implicit but clearly erroneous assumptions.

Assumption 1: All employees are alike. Different theories present different ways of looking at people, but each of them assumes that all employees are basically similar in their makeup: Employees all want economic gains, or all want a pleasant climate, or all aspire to be self-actualizing, etc.

Assumption 2: All situations are alike. Most theories assume that all managerial situations are alike, and that the managerial course of action for motivation (for example, participation, job enlargement, etc.) is applicable in all situations.

Assumption 3: One best way. Out of the other two assumptions there emerges a basic principle that there is "one best way" to motivate employees.

When these "one best way" approaches are tried in the "correct" situation they will work. However, all of them are bound to fail in some situations. They are therefore not adequate managerial tools.

A new approach

During the past ten years, a great deal of research has been done on a new approach to looking at motivation. This approach, frequently called "expectancy theory," still needs further testing, refining, and extending. However, enough is known that many behavioral scientists have concluded that it represents the most comprehensive, valid, and useful approach to understanding motivation. Further, it is apparent that it is a very useful tool for understanding motivation in organizations.

The theory is based on a number of specific assumptions about the causes of behavior in organizations.

Assumption 1: Behavior is determined by a combination of forces in the individual and forces in the environment. Neither the individual nor the environment alone determines behavior. Individuals come into organizations with certain "psychological baggage." They have past experiences and a developmental history which has given them unique sets of needs, ways of looking at the world, and expectations about how organizations will treat them. These all influence how individuals respond to their work environment. The work environment provides structures (such as a pay system or a supervisor) which influence

the behavior of people. Different environments tend to produce different behavior in similar people just as dissimilar people tend to behave differently in similar environments.

Assumption 2: People make decisions about their own behavior in organizations. While there are many constraints on the behavior of individuals in organizations, most of the behavior that is observed is the result of individuals' conscious decisions. These decisions usually fall into two categories. First, individuals make decisions about *membership behavior* — coming to work, staying at work, and in other ways being a member of the organization. Second, individuals make decisions about the amount of *effort* they will direct *towards performing their jobs.* This includes decisions about how hard to work, how much to produce, at what quality, etc.

Assumption 3: Different people have different types of needs, desires, and goals. Individuals differ on what kinds of outcomes (or rewards) they desire. These differences are not random; they can be examined systematically by an understanding of the differences in the strength of individuals' needs.

Assumption 4: People make decisions among alternative plans of behavior based on their perceptions (expectancies) of the degree to which a given behavior will lead to desired outcomes. In simple terms, people tend to do those things which they see as leading to outcomes (which can also be called "rewards") they desire and avoid doing those things they see as leading to outcomes that are not desired.

In general, the approach used here views people as having their own needs and mental maps of what the world is like. They use these maps to make decisions about how they will behave, behaving in those ways which their mental maps indicate will lead to outcomes that will satisfy their needs. Therefore, they are inherently neither motivated nor unmotivated; motivation depends on the situation they are in, and how it fits their needs.

The theory

Based on these general assumptions, expectancy theory states a number of propositions about the process by which people make decisions about their own behavior in organizational settings. While the theory is complex at first view, it is in fact made of a series of fairly straightforward observations about behavior. Three concepts serve as the key building blocks of the theory:

Performance-outcome expectancy. Every behavior has associated with it, in an individual's mind, certain outcomes (rewards or punishments). In other words, the individual believes or expects that if he or she behaves in a certain way, he or she will get certain things.

Examples of expectancies can easily be described. An individual may have an expectancy that if he produces ten units he will receive his normal hourly rate while if he produces fifteen units he will receive his hourly pay rate plus a bonus. Similarly an individual may believe that certain levels of performance will lead to approval or disapproval from members of her work group or from her supervisor. Each performance can be seen as leading to a number of different kinds of outcomes and outcomes can differ in their types.

Valence. Each outcome has a "valence" (value, worth, attractiveness) to a specific individual. Outcomes have different valences for different individuals. This comes about because valences result from individual needs and perceptions, which differ because they in turn reflect other factors in the individual's life.

For example, some individuals may value an opportunity for promotion or advancement because of their needs for achievement or power, while others may not want to be promoted and leave their current work group because of needs for affiliation with others. Similarly, a fringe benefit such as a pension plan may have great valence for an older worker but little valence for a young employee on his first job.

Effort-performance expectancy. Each behavior also has associated with it in the individual's mind a certain expectancy or probability of success. This expectancy represents the individual's perception of how hard it will be to achieve such behavior and the probability of his or her successful achievement of that behavior.

For example, you may have a strong expectancy that if you put forth the effort, you can produce ten units an hour, but that you have only a 50-50 chance of producing fifteen units an hour if you try.

Putting these concepts together, it is possible to make a basic statement about motivation. In general, the motivation to attempt to behave in a certain way is greatest when:

a. The individual believes that the behavior will lead to outcomes (performance-outcome expectancy)
b. The individual believes that these outcomes have positive value for him or her (valence)
c. The individual believes that he or she is able to perform at the desired level (effort-performance expectancy)

Given a number of alternative levels of behavior (ten, fifteen, and twenty units of production per hour, for example) the

Figure 1. The basic motivation-behavior sequence.

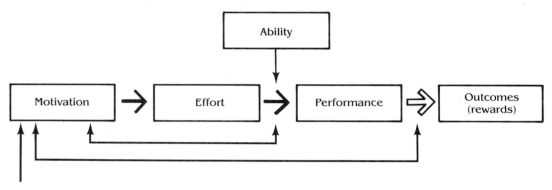

A person's motivation is a function of:
a. Effort-to-performance expectancies
b. Performance to outcome expectancies
c. Perceived valence of outcomes

individual will choose that level of performance which has the greatest motivational force associated with it, as indicated by the expectancies, outcomes, and valences.

In other words, when faced with choices about behavior, the individual goes through a process of considering questions such as, "Can I perform at that level if I try?" "If I perform at that level, what will happen?" "How do I feel about those things that will happen?" The individual then decides to behave in that way which seems to have the best chance of producing positive, desired outcomes.

A general model

On the basis of these concepts, it is possible to construct a general model of behavior in organizational settings (see Figure 1). Working from left to right in the model, motivation is seen as the force on the individual to expend effort. Motivation leads to an observed level of effort by the individual. Effort, alone, however, is not enough. Performance re-

sults from a combination of the effort that an individual puts forth *and* the level of ability which he or she has (reflecting skills, training, information, etc.). Effort thus combines with ability to produce a given level of performance. As a result of performance, the individual attains certain outcomes. The model indicates this relationship in a dotted line, reflecting the fact that sometimes people perform but do not get desired outcomes. As this process of performance-reward occurs, time after time, the actual events serve to provide information which influences the individual's perceptions (particularly expectancies) and thus influences motivation in the future.

Outcomes, or rewards, fall into two major categories. First, the individual obtains outcomes from the environment. When an individual performs at a given level he or she can receive positive or negative outcomes from supervisors, coworkers, the organization's rewards systems, or other sources. These environmental rewards are thus one source of outcomes for the individual. A second source of outcomes is the individual. These include outcomes which occur purely from the performance of the task itself (feelings of accomplishment, personal worth, achievement, etc.). In a sense, the individual gives these rewards to himself or herself. The environment cannot give them or take them away directly; it can only make them possible.

Supporting evidence

Over fifty studies have been done to test the validity of the expectancy-theory approach to predicting employee behavior. Almost without exception, the studies have confirmed the predictions of the theory. As the theory predicts, the best performers in organizations tend to see a strong relationship between performing their jobs well and receiving rewards they value. In addition they have clear performance goals and they feel they can perform well. Similarly, studies using the expectancy theory to predict how people choose jobs also show that individuals tend to interview for and actually take those jobs which they feel will provide the rewards they value. One study, for example, was able to correctly predict for 80 percent of the people studied which of several jobs they would take. Finally, the theory correctly predicts that beliefs about the outcomes associated with performance (expectancies) will be better predictors of performance than will feelings of job satisfaction since expectancies are the critical causes of performance and satisfaction is not.

Questions about the model

Although the results so far have been encouraging, they also indicate some problems with the model. These problems do not critically affect the managerial im-

plications of the model, but they should be noted. The model is based on the assumption that individuals make very rational decisions after a thorough exploration of all the available alternatives and on weighing the possible outcomes of all these alternatives. When we talk to or observe individuals, however, we find that their decision processes are frequently less thorough. People often stop considering alternative behavior plans when they find one that is at least moderately satisfying, even though more rewarding plans remain to be examined.

People are also limited in the amount of information they can handle at one time, and therefore the model may indicate a process that is much more complex than the one that actually takes place. On the other hand, the model does provide enough information and is consistent enough with reality to present some clear implications for managers who are concerned with the question of how to motivate the people who work for them.

Implications for managers

The first set of implications is directed toward the individual manager who has a group of people working for him or her and is concerned with how to motivate good performance. Since behavior is a result of forces both in the person and in the environment, you as manager need to look at and diagnose both the person and the environment. Specifically, you need to do the following:

Figure out what outcomes each employee values. As a first step, it is important to determine what kinds of outcomes or rewards have valence for your employees. For each employee you need to determine "what turns him or her on." There are various ways of finding this out, including (a) finding out employees' desires through some structured method of data collection, such as a questionaire, (b) observing the employees' reactions to different situations or rewards, or (c) the fairly simple act of asking them what kinds of rewards they want, what kind of career goals they have, or "what's in it for them." It is important to stress here that it is very difficult to change what people want, but fairly easy to find out what they want. Thus, the skillful manager emphasizes diagnosis of needs, not changing the individuals themselves.

Determine what kinds of behavior you desire. Managers frequently talk about "good performance" without really defining what good performance is. An important step in motivating is for you yourself to figure out what kinds of performances are required and what are adequate measures of indicators of performance (quantity, quality, etc.). There is also a need to be able to define those performances in fairly specific terms so that observable and measurable behavior can be defined and subordinates can understand what is desired of them (e.g., produce ten products of a certain quality standard — rather than only produce at a high rate).

Make sure desired levels of performance are reachable. The model states that motivation is determined not only by the performance-to-outcome expectancy, but also by the effort-to-performance expectancy. The implication of this is that the levels of performance which are set as the points at which individuals receive desired outcomes must be reachable or attainable by these individuals. If the employees feel that the level of performance required to get a reward is higher that they can reasonably achieve, then their mo-

tivation to perform well will be relatively low.

Link desired outcomes to desired performances. The next step is to directly, clearly, and explicitly link those outcomes desired by employees to the specific performances desired by you. If your employee values external rewards, then the emphasis should be on the rewards systems concerned with promotion, pay, and approval. While the linking of these rewards can be initiated through your making statements to your employees, it is extremely important that employees see a clear example of the reward process working in a fairly short period of time if the motivating "expectancies" are to be created in the employees's minds. The linking must be done by some concrete public acts, in addition to statements of intent.

If your employee values internal rewards (e.g., achievement), then you should concentrate on changing the nature of the person's job, for he or she is likely to respond well to such things as increased autonomy, feedback, and challenge, because these things will lead to a situation where good job performance is inherently rewarding. The best way to check on the adequacy of the internal and external reward system is to ask people what their perceptions of the situation are. Remember it is the perceptions of people that determine their motivation, not reality. It doesn't matter for example whether you feel a subordinate's pay is related to his or her motivation. Motivation will be present only if the subordinate sees the relationship. Many managers are misled about the behavior of their subordinates because they rely on their own perceptions of the situation and forget to find out what their subordinates feel. There is only one way to do this: ask. Questionnaires can be used here, as can personal interviews.

Analyze the total situation for conflicting expectancies. Having set up positive expectancies for employees, you then need to look at the entire situation to see if other factors (informal work groups, other managers, the organization's reward systems) have set up conflicting expectancies in the minds of the employees. Motivation will only be high when people see a number of rewards associated with good performance and few negative outcomes. Again, you can often gather this kind of information by asking your subordinates. If there are major conflicts, you need to make adjustments, either in your own performance and reward structure, or in the other sources of rewards or punishments in the environment.

Make sure changes in outcomes are large enough. In examining the motivational system, it is important to make sure that changes in outcomes or rewards are large enough to motivate significant behavior. Trivial rewards will result in trivial amounts of effort and thus trivial improvements in performance. Rewards must be large enough to motivate individuals to put forth the effort required to bring about significant changes in performance.

Check the system for its equity. The model is based on the idea that individuals are different and therefore different rewards will need to be used to motivate different individuals. On the other hand, for a motivational system to work it must be a fair one — one that has equity (not equality). Good performers should see that they get more desired rewards than do poor performers, and others in the system should see that also. Equity should not be confused with a system of equality where all are rewarded equally, with no regard to their

performance. A system of equality is guaranteed to produce low motivation.

Implications for organizations

Expectancy theory has some clear messages for those who run large organizations. It suggests how organizational structures can be designed so that they increase rather than decrease levels of motivation of organization members. While there are many different implications, a few of the major ones are as follows:

Implication 1: The design of pay and reward systems. Organizations usually get what they reward, not what they want. This can be seen in many situations, and pay systems are a good example. Frequently, organizations reward people for membership (through pay tied to seniority, for example) rather than for performance. Little wonder that what the organization gets is behavior oriented towards "safe," secure employment rather than effort directed at peforming well. In addition, even where organizations do pay for performance as a motivational device, they frequently negate the motivational value of the system by keeping pay secret, therefore preventing people from observing the pay-to-performance relationship that would serve to create positive, clear, and strong performance-to-reward expectancies. The implication is that organizations should put more effort into rewarding people (through pay, promotion, better job opportunities, etc.) for the performances which are desired, and that to keep these rewards secret is clearly self-defeating. In addition, it underscores the importance of the frequently ignored performance evaluation or appraisal process and the need to evaluate people based on how they perform clearly defined specific behaviors, rather than on how they score on ratings of general traits such as "honesty," "cleanliness," and other, similar terms which frequently appear as part of the performance appraisal form.

Implication 2: The design of tasks, jobs, and roles. One source of desired outcomes is the work itself. The expectancy-theory model supports much of the job enrichment literature, in saying that by designing jobs which enable people to get their needs fulfilled, organizations can bring about higher levels of motivation. The major difference between the traditional approaches to job enlargement or enrichment and the expectancy-theory approach is the recognition by expectancy theory that different people have different needs and, therefore, some people may not want enlarged or enriched jobs. Thus, while the design of tasks that have more autonomy, variety, feedback, meaningfulness, etc., will lead to higher motivation in some, the organization needs to build in the opportunity for individuals to make choices about the kind of work they will do so that not everyone is forced to experience job enrichment.

Implication 3: The importance of group structures. Groups, both formal and informal, are powerful and potent sources of desired outcomes for individuals. Groups can provide or withhold acceptance, approval, affection, skill training, needed information, assistance, etc. They are a powerful force in the total motivational environment of individuals. Several implications emerge from the importance of groups. First, organizations should consider the structuring of at least a portion of rewards around group members have to cooperate with each other to produce a group product or service, and where the individual's contribution is often hard to de-

termine. Second, the organization needs to train managers to be aware of how groups can influence individual behavior and to be sensitive to the kinds of expectancies which informal groups set up and their conflict or consistency with the expectancies that the organization attempts to create.

Implication 4: The supervisor's role. The immediate supervisor has an important role in creating, monitoring, and maintaining the expectancies and reward structures which will lead to good performance. The supervisor's role in the motivation process becomes one of defining clear goals, setting clear reward expectancies, and providing the right rewards for different people (which could include both organizational rewards and personal rewards such as recognition, approval, or support from the supervisor). Thus, organizations need to provide supervisors with an awareness of the nature of motivation as well as the tools (control over organizational rewards, skill in administering those rewards) to create positive motivation.

Implication 5: Measuring motivation. If things like expectancies, the nature of the job, supervisor-controlled outcomes, satisfaction, etc., are important in understanding how well people are being motivated, then organizations need to monitor employee perceptions along these lines. One relatively cheap and reliable method of doing this is through standardized employee questionnaires. A number of organizations already use such techniques, surveying employees' perceptions and attitudes at regular intervals (ranging from once a month to once every year-and-a-half) using either standardized surveys or surveys developed specifically for the organization. Such information is useful both to the individual manager and to top management in assessing the state of human resources and the effectiveness of the organization's motivational systems.

Implication 6: Individualizing organizations. Expectancy theory leads to a final general impliction about a possible future direction for the design of organizations. Because different people have different needs and therefore have different valences, effective motivation must come though the recognition that not all employees are alike and that organizations need to be flexible in order to accommodate individual differences. This implies the "building in" of choice for employees in many areas, such as reward systems, fringe benefits, job assignments, etc., where employees previously have had little say. A successful example of the building in of such choice can be seen in the experiments at TRW and the Educational Testing Service with "cafeteria fringe benefits plans" which allow employees to choose the fringe benefits they want, rather than taking the expensive and often unwanted benefits which the company frequently provides to everyone.

Summary

Expectancy theory provides a more com-plex model of man for managers to work with. At the same time, it is a model which holds promise for the more effective motivation of individuals and the more effective design of organizational systems. It implies, however, the need for more exacting and thorough diagnosis by the manager to determine (a) the relevant forces in the individual, and (b) the relevant forces in the environment, both of which combine to motivate different kinds of behavior. Following diagnosis, the model implies a need to act — to develop a system of pay, promotion, job assignments, group structures, supervision, etc. — to bring about effective motivation by providing different outcomes for different individuals.

Performance of individuals is a critical issue in making organizations work effectively. If a manager is to influence work behavior and performance, he or she must have an understanding of motivation and the factors which influence an individual's motivation to come to work, to work hard, and to work well. While simple models offer easy answers, it is the more complex models which seem to offer more promise. Managers can use models (like expectancy theory) to understand the nature of behavior and build more effective organizations.

A new strategy for job enrichment

J. Richard Hackman, Greg Oldham,
Robert Janson, and Kenneth Purdy

Practitioners of job enrichment have been living through a time of excitement, even euphoria. Their craft has moved from the psychology and management journals to the front page and the Sunday supplement. Job enrichment, which began with the pioneering work of Herzberg and his associates, originally was intended as a means to increase the motivation and satisfaction of people at work — and to improve productivity in the bargain. (Herzberg 1966, 1968; Herzberg, Mausner, and Snyderman 1959; Paul, Robertson, and Herzberg 1969; Ford 1969). Now it is being acclaimed in the popular press as a cure for problems ranging from inflation to drug abuse.

Much current writing about job enrichment is enthusiastic, sometimes even messianic, about what it can accomplish. But the hard questions of exactly what should be done to improve jobs, and how, tend to be glossed over. Lately, because the harder questions have not been dealt with adequately, critical winds have begun to blow. Job enrichment has been described as yet another "management fad," as "nothing new," even as a fraud. And reports of job enrichment failures are beginning to appear in management and psychology journals.

This article attempts to redress the excesses that have characterized some of the recent writings about job enrichment. As the technique increases in popularity as a management tool, top managers inevitably will find themselves making decisions about its use. The intent of this paper is to help both managers and behavioral scientists become better able to make those decisions on a solid basis of fact and data.

Succinctly stated, we present here a new strategy for going about the redesign of work. The strategy is based on three years of collaborative work and cross-fertilization among the authors — two of whom are active practitioners in job enrichment. Our approach is new, but it has been tested in many organizations. It draws on the contributions of both management practice and psychological theory, but it is firmly in the middle ground between them. It builds on and complements previous work by Herzberg and others, but provides for the first time a set of tools for *diagnosing* existing jobs — and a map for translating the diagnostic results into specific action steps for change.

What we have, then, is the following:

1. A theory that specifies when people will get personally "turned on" to their work. The theory shows what kinds of

jobs are most likely to generate excitement and commitment about work, and what kinds of employees it works best for.

2. A set of action steps for job enrichment based on the theory, which prescribe in concrete terms what to do to make jobs more motivating for the people who do them.

3. Evidence that the theory holds water and that it can be used to bring about measurable — and sometimes dramatic — improvements in employee work behavior, in job satisfaction, and in the financial performance of the organizational unit involved.

The theory behind the strategy

What makes people get turned on to their

J. Richard Hackman is Associate Professor of Administrative Sciences and of Psychology at Yale University. He is the author of numerous articles on organizational behavior and co-author of the recent book *Behavior in Organizations.*

Greg Oldham is Assistant Professor of Business Administration at the University of Illinois. His work has been published in several leading journals, and his current research interests include leadership, job design, and motivation.

Robert Janson is Vice-President of Roy W. Walters & Associates, a consulting firm specializing in applications of the behavioral sciences to the solution of organizational problems. He has contributed numerous articles to personnel and training journals, as well as to books on motivation and work design.

Kenneth Purdy is a senior associate with Roy W. Walters & Associates. He has written numerous articles on job design and the quality of work.

work? For workers who are really prospering in their jobs, work is likely to be a lot like play. Consider, for example, a golfer at a driving range, practicing to get rid of a hook. His activity is *meaningful* to him; he has chosen to do it because he gets a "kick" from testing his skills by playing the game. He knows that he alone is *responsible* what happens when he hits the ball. And he has *knowledge of the results* within a few seconds.

Behavioral scientists have found that the three "psychological states" experienced by the golfer in the above example also are critical in determining a person's motivation and satisfaction on the job.

• *Experienced meaningfulness:* The individual must perceive his work as worthwhile or important by some system of values he accepts.

• *Experienced responsibility:* He must believe that he personally is accountable for the outcomes of his efforts.

• *Knowledge of results:* He must be able to determine, on some fairly regular basis, whether or not the outcomes of his work are satisfactory.

When these three conditions are present, a person tends to feel very good about himself when he performs well. And those good feelings will prompt him to try to continue to do well — so he can continue to earn the positive feelings in the future. That is what is meant by "internal motivation" — being turned on to one's work because of the positive internal feelings that are generated by doing well, rather than being dependent on external factors (such as incentive pay or compliments from the boss) for the motivation to work effectively.

What if one of the three psychological states is missing? Motivation drops markedly. Suppose, for example, that our golfer has settled in at the driving range to practice for a couple of hours.

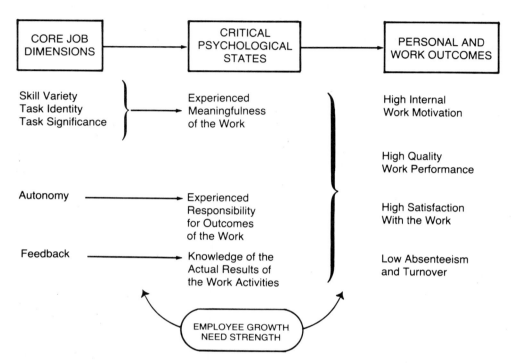

Figure 1. Relationships among core job dimensions, critical psychological states, and on-the-job outcomes.

Suddenly a fog drifts in over the range. He can no longer see if the ball starts to tail off to the left a hundred yards out. The satisfaction he got from hitting straight down the middle — and the motivation to try to correct something whenever he didn't — are both gone. If the fog stays, it's likely that he soon will be packing up his clubs.

The relationship between the three psychological states and on-the-job outcomes is illustrated in Figure 1. When all three are high, then internal work motivation, job satisfaction, and work quality are high, and absenteeism and turnover are low.

What job characteristics make it happen? Recent research has identified five "core" characteristics of jobs that elicit the psychological states described

above. (Turner and Lawrence 1965; Hackman and Lawler 1971; Hackman and Oldham 1974). These five core job dimensions provide the key to objectively measuring jobs and to changing them so that they have high potential for motivating people who do them.

• Toward meaningful work. Three of the five core dimensions contribute to a job's meaningfulness for the worker;

1. Skill variety — the degree to which a job requires the worker to perform activities that challenge his skills and abilities. When even a single skill is involved, there is at least a seed of potential meaningfulness. When several are involved, the job has the potential of appealing to more of the whole person, and also of avoiding

the monotony of performing the same task repeatedly, no matter how much skill it may require.

2. Task identity — the degree to which the job requires completion of a "whole" and identifiable piece of work — doing a job from beginning to end with a visible outcome. For example, it is clearly more meaningful to an employee to build complete toasters than to attach electrical cord after electrical cord, especially if he never sees a completed toaster. (Note that the whole job, in this example, probably would involve greater skill variety as well as task identity.)

3. Task significance — the degree to which the job has a substantial and perceivable impact on the lives of other people, whether in the immediate organization or the world at large. The worker who tightens nuts on aircraft brake assemblies is more likely to perceive his work as significant than the worker who fills small boxes with paper clips — even though the skill levels involved may be comparable.

Each of these three job dimensions represents an important route to experienced meaningfulness. If the job is high in all three, the worker is quite likely to experience his job as very meaningful. It is not necessary, however, for a job to be very high in three dimensions. If the job is low in any one of them, there will be a drop in overall experienced meaningfulness. But even when two dimensions are low the worker may find the job meaningful if the third is high enough.

• Toward personal responsibility. A fourth core dimension leads a worker to experience increased responsibility in his job. This is *autonomy*, the degree to which the job gives the worker freedom, independence, and discretion in scheduling work and determining how he will carry it out. people in highly autonomous jobs know that they are personally responsible for successes and failures. To the extent that their autonomy is high, then, how the work goes will be felt to depend more on the individual's own efforts and initiatives rather than on detailed instructions from the boss or from a manual of job procedures.

• Toward knowledge of results. The fifth and last core dimension is *feedback*. This is the degree to which a worker, in carrying out the work activities required by the job, gets information about the effectiveness of his efforts. Feedback is most powerful when it comes directly from the work itself — for example, when a worker has the responsibility for gauging and otherwise checking a component he has just finished and learns in the process that he has lowered his reject rate by meeting specifications more consistently.

• The overall "motivating potential" of a job. Figure 1 shows how the five core dimensions combine to affect the psychological states that are critical in determining whether or not an employee will be internally motivated to work effectively. Indeed, when using an instrument to be described later, it is possible to compute a 'motivating potential score" (MPS) for any job. The MPS provides a single summary index of the degree to which the objective characteristics of the job will prompt high internal work motivation. Following the theory outlined above, a job high in motivating potential must be high in at least one (and hopefully more) of the three dimensions that lead to experienced meaningfulness and high in both autonomy and feedback as well. The MPS provides a quantitative index of the degree to which this is in fact the case. As will be seen later, the MPS can be very useful in diagnosing jobs and in assessing the effectiveness of job enrichment activities.

Does the theory work for everybody? Unfortunately not. Not everyone is able to become internally motivated in his work, even when the motivating potential of a job is very high indeed.

Research has shown that the *psychological needs* of people are very important in determining who can (and who cannot) become internally motivated at work. Some people have strong needs for personal accomplishment, for learning and developing themselves beyond where they are now, for being stimulated and challenged, and so on. These people are high in "growth-need strength."

Figure 2 shows diagrammatically the proposition that individual growth needs have the power to moderate the relationship between the characteristics of jobs and work outcomes. Many workers with high growth needs will turn on eagerly when they have jobs that are high in the core dimensions. Workers whose growth needs are not so strong may respond less eagerly — or, at first, even balk at being "pushed" or "stretched" too far.

Psychologists who emphasize human potential argue that everyone has within

him at least a spark of the need to grow and develop personally. Steadily accumulating evidence shows, however, that unless that spark is pretty strong, chances are it will get snuffed out by one's experiences in typical organizations. So, a person who has worked for twenty years in stultifying jobs may find it difficult or impossible to become internally motivated overnight when given the opportunity.

We should be cautious, however, about creating rigid categories of people based on their measured growth-need strength at any particular time. It is true that we can predict from these measures who is likely to become internally motivated on a job and who will be less willing or able to do so. But what we do not know yet is whether or not the growth-need "spark" can be rekindled for those individuals who have had their growth needs dampened by years of growth-depressing experience in their organizations.

Since it is often the organization that is responsible for currently low levels of growth desires, we believe that the organization also should provide the individual with the chance to reverse that trend whenever possible, even if that means putting a person in a job where he may be "stretched" more than he wants

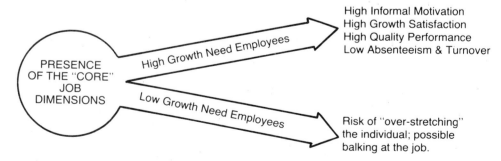

Figure 2. The moderating effect of employee growth-need strength.

to be. He can always move back to the old job — and in the meantime the embers of his growth needs just might burst back into flame, to his surprise and pleasure, and for the good of the organization.

From theory to practice: A technology for job enrichment

When job enrichment fails, it often fails because of inadequate *diagnosis* of the target job and employees' reactions to it. Often, for example, job enrichment is assumed by management to be a solution to "people problems" on the job and is implemented even though there has been no diagnostic activity to indicate that the root of the problem is in fact how the work is designed. At other times, some diagnosis is made — but it provides no concrete guidance about what specific aspects of the job require change. In either case, the success of job enrichment may wind up depending more on the quality of the intuition of the change agent — or his luck — than on a solid base of data about the people and the work.

In the paragraphs to follow, we outline a new technology for use in job enrichment which explicitly addresses the diagnostic as well as the action components of the change process. The technology has two parts: (1) a set of diagnostic tools that are useful in evaluating jobs and people's reactions to them prior to change — and in pinpointing exactly what aspects of specific jobs are most critical to a successful change attempt; and (2) a set of "implementing concepts" that provide concrete guidance for action steps in job enrichment. The implementing concepts are tied directly to the diagnostic tools;

the output of the diagnostic activity specifies which action steps are likely to have the most impact in a particular situation.

The diagnostic tools. Central to the diagnostic procedure we propose is a package of instruments to be used by employees, supervisors, and outside observers in assessing the target job and employees' reactions to it. (Hackman and Oldham 1975). These instruments gauge the following:

1. The objective characteristics of the jobs themselves, including both an overall indication of the "motivating potential" of the job as it exists (that is, the MPS score) and the score of the job on each of the five core dimensions described previously. Because knowing the strengths and weaknesses of the job is critical to any work redesign effort, assessments of the job are made by supervisors and outside observers as well as the employees themselves — and the final assessment of a job uses data from all three sources.
2. The current levels of motivation, satisfaction, and work performance of employees on the job. In addition to satisfacion with the work itself, measures are taken of how people feel about other aspects of the work setting, such as pay, supervision, and relationships with co-workers.
3. The level of growth-need strength of the employees. As indicated earlier, employees who have strong growth needs are more likely to be more responsive to job enrichment than employees with weak growth needs. Therefore, it is important to know at the outset just what kinds of satisfactions the people who do the job are (and are not) motivated to obtain

from their work. This will make it possible to identify which persons are best to start changes with, and which may need help in adapting to the newly enriched job.

What, then, might be the actual steps one would take in carrying out a job diagnosis using these tools? Although the approach to any particular diagnosis depends upon the specifics of the particular work situation involved, the sequence of questions listed below is fairly typical.

• *Step 1. Are motivation and satisfaction central to the problem?* Sometimes organizations undertake job enrichment to improve the work motivation and satisfaction of employees when in fact the real problem with work performance lies elsewhere — for example, in a poorly designed production system, in an error-prone computer, and so on. The first step is to examine the scores of employees on the motivation and satisfaction portions of the diagnostic instrument. (The questionnaire taken by employees is called the Job Diagnostic Survey and will be referred to hereafter as the JDS.) If motivation and satisfaction are problematic, the change agent would continue to Step 2; if not, he would look to other aspects of the work situation to identify the real problem.

• *Step 2. Is the job low in motivating potential?* To answer this question, one would examine the motivating potential score of the target job and compare it to the MPS's of other jobs to determine whether or not *the job itself* is a probable cause of the motivational problems documented in Step 1. If the job turns out to be low on the MPS, one would continue to Step 3: if it scores high, attention should be given to other possible reasons for the motivational difficulties

(such as the pay system, the nature of supervision, and so on).

• *Step 3. What specific aspects of the job are causing the difficulty?* This step involves examining the job on each of the five core dimensions to pinpoint the specific strengths and weaknesses of the job as it is currently structured. It is useful at this stage to construct a "profile" of the target job, to make visually apparent where improvements need to be made. An illustrative profile for two jobs (one "good" job and one job needing improvement) is shown in Figure 3.

Job A is an engineering maintenance job and is high on all of the core dimensions; the MPS of this job is a very high 260. (MPS scores can range from 1 to about 350; an "average" score would be about 125.) Job enrichment would not be recommended for this job; if employees working on the job were unproductive and unhappy, the reasons are likely to have little to do with the nature or design of the work itself.

Job B, on the other hand, has many problems.

This job involves the routine and repetitive processing of checks in the "back room" of a bank. The MPS is 30, which is quite low — and indeed, would be even lower if it were not for the moderately high task significance of the job. (Task significance is moderately high because the people are handling large amounts of other people's money, and therefore the quality of their efforts potentially has important consequences for their unseen clients.) The job provides the individuals with very little direct feedback about how effectively they are doing it; the employees have little autonomy in how they go about doing the job; and the job is moderately low in both skill variety and task identity.

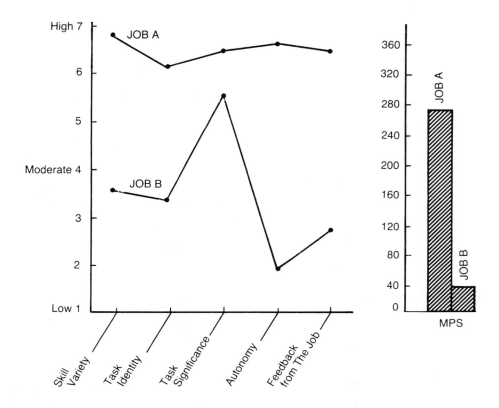

Figure 3. The JDS diagnostic profile for a "good" and a "bad" job.

For Job B, then, there is plenty of room for improvement — and many avenues to examine in planning job changes. For still other jobs, the avenues for change often turn out to be considerably more specific: for example, feedback and autonomy may be reasonably high, but one or more of the core dimensions that contribute to the experienced meaningfulness of the job (skill variety, task identity, and task significance) may be low. In such a case, attention would turn to ways to increase the standing of the job on these latter three dimensions.

• *Step 4. How "ready" are the employ-*

ees for change? Once it has been documented that there is need for improvement in the job — and the particularly troublesome aspects of the job have been identified — then it is time to begin to think about the specific action steps which will be taken to enrich the job. An important factor in such planning is the level of growth needs of the employees, since employees high on growth needs usually respond more readily to job enrichment than do employees with little need for growth. The JDS provides a direct measure of the growth-need strength of the employees. This measure can be very helpful in planning how to introduce the changes to the people (for instance, cautiously versus dramatically), and in deciding who should be among the first group of employees to have their jobs changed.

In actual use of the diagnostic package, additional information is generated which supplements and expands the basic diagnostic questions outlined above. The point of the above discussion is merely to indicate the kinds of questions which we believe to be most important in diagnosing a job prior to changing it. We now turn to how the diagnostic conclusions are translated into specific job changes.

The implementing concepts. Five "implementing concepts" for job enrichment are identified and discussed below. (Walters and Associates 1975). Each one is a specific action step aimed at improving both the quality of the working experience for the individual and his work pro-ductivity. They are: (1) forming natural work units, (2) combining tasks, (3) establishing client relationships, (4) vertical loading, (5) opening feedback channels.

The links between the implementing concepts and the core dimensions are shown in Figure 4 — which illustrates our theory of job enrichment, ranging from the concrete action steps through the core dimensions and the psychological states to the actual personal and work outcomes.

After completing the diagnosis of a job, a change agent would know which of the core dimensions were most in need of remedial attention. He could then turn to Figure 4 and select those implementing concepts that specifically deal with the most troublesome parts of the existing job. How this would take place in practice will be seen below.

• Forming natural work units. The notion

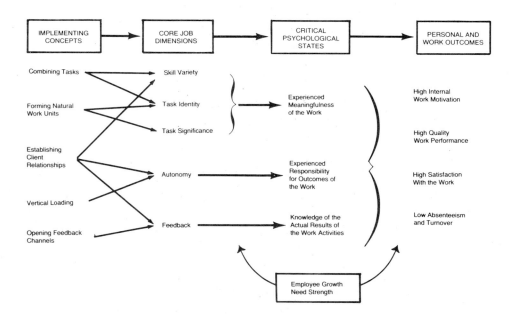

Figure 4. The full model: how use of the implementing concepts can lead to positive outcomes.

of distributing work in some logical way may seem to be an obvious part of the design of any job. In many cases, however, the logic is one imposed by just about any consideration except jobholder satisfaction and motivation. Such considerations include technological dictates, level of worker training or experience, "efficiency" as defined by industrial engineering, and current workload. In many cases the cluster of tasks a worker faces during a typical day or week is natural to anyone *but* the worker.

For example, suppose that a typing pool (consisting of one supervisor and ten typists) handles all work for one division of a company. Jobs are delivered in rough draft or dictated form to the supervisor, who distributes them as evenly as possible among the typists. In such circumstances the individual letters, reports, and other tasks performed by a given typist in one day or week are randomly assigned. There is no basis for identifying with the work or the person or department for whom it is performed, or for placing any personal value upon it.

The principle underlying natural units of work, by contrast, is "ownership" — a worker's sense of continuing responsibility for an identifiable body of work. Two steps are involved in creating natural work units. The first is to identify the basic work items. In the typing pool, for example, the items might be "pages to be typed." The second step is to group the items in natural categories. For example, each typist might be assigned continuing responsibility for all jobs requested by one or several specific departments. The assignments should be made, of course, in such a way that workloads are about equal in the long run. (For example, one typist might end up with all the work from one busy department, while another handles jobs from several smaller units.)

At this point we can begin to see specifically how the job-design principles relate to the core dimensions (cf. Figure 4). The ownership fostered by natural units of work can make the difference between a feeling that work is meaningful and rewarding and the feeling that it is irrelevant and boring. As the diagram shows, natural units of work are directly related to two of the core dimensions: task identity and task significance.

A typist whose work is assigned naturally rather than randomly — say, by departments — has a much greater chance of performing a whole job to completion. Instead of typing one section of a large report, the individual is likely to type the whole thing, with knowledge of exactly what the product of the work is (task identity). Furthermore, over time the typist will develop a growing sense of how the work affects coworkers in the department serviced (task significance).

• Combining tasks. The very existence of a pool made up entirely of persons whose sole function is typing reflects a fractionalization of jobs that has been a basic precept of "scientific management." Most obvious in assembly-line work, fractionalization has been applied to non-manufacturing jobs as well. It is typically justified by efficiency, which is usually defined in terms of either low costs or some time-and-motion type of criteria.

It is hard to find fault with measuring efficiency ultimately in terms of cost-effectiveness. In doing so, however, a manager should be sure to consider *all* the costs involved. It is possible, for example, for highly fractionalized jobs to meet all the time-and-motion criteria of efficiency, but if the resulting job is so unrewarding that performing it day after day leads to high turnover, absenteeism, drugs and alcohol, and strikes, then productivity is really lower (and costs higher) than data on efficiency might indicate.

The principle of combining tasks, then, suggests that whenever possible existing and fractionalized tasks should be put together to form new and larger modules of work. At the Medfield, Massachusetts plant of Corning Glass Works the assembly of a laboratory hot plate has been re-designed along the lines suggested here. Each hot plate now is assembled from start to finish by one operator, instead of going through several separate operations that are performed by different people.

Some tasks, if combined into a meaningfully large module of work, would be more than an individual could do by himself. In such cases, it is often usefull to consider assigning the new, larger task to a small *team* of workers — who are given great autonomy for its completion. At the Racine, Wisconsin plant of Emerson Electric, the assembly process for trash disposal appliances was restructured this way. Instead of a sequence of moving the appliance from station to station, the assembly now is done from start to finish by one team. Such teams include both men and women to permit switching off the heavier and more delicate aspects of the work. The team responsible is identified on the appliance. In case of customer complaints, the team often drafts the reply.

As a job-design principle, task combination, like natural units of work, expands the task identity of the job. For example, the hot plate assembler can see and identify with a finished product ready for shipment, rather than a nearly invisible junction of solder. Moreover, the more tasks that are combined into a single worker's job, the greater the variety of skills he must call on in performing the job. So task combination also leads to greater skill variety — the third core dimension that contributes to the overall experienced meaningfulness of the work.

• Establishing client relationships. One consequence of fractionalization is that the typical worker has little or no contact with (or even awareness of) the ultimate use of his product or service. By encouraging and enabling employees to establish direct relationships with the clients of their work, improvements often can be realized simultaneously on three of the core dimensions. Feedback increases, because of additional opportunities for the individual to receive praise or criticism of his work outputs directly. Skill variety often increases, because of the necessity to develop and exercise one's interpersonal skills in maintaining the client relationship. And autonomy can increase because the individual often is given personal responsibility for deciding how to manage his relationships with the clients of his work.

Creating client relationships is a three-step process. First, the client must be identified. Second, the most direct contact possible between the worker and the client must be established. Third, criteria must be set up by which the client can judge the quality of the product or service he receives. And whenever possible, the client should have a means of relaying his judgements directly back to the worker.

The contact between worker and client should be as great as possible and as frequent as necessary. Face-to-face contact is highly desirable, at least occasionally. Where that is impossible or impractical, telephone and mail can suffice. In any case, it is important that the performance criteria by which the worker will be rated by the client must be mutually understood and agreed upon.

• Vertical loading. Typically the split between the "doing" of a job and the "planning" and "controlling" of the work has evolved along with horizontal fractionalization. Its rationale, once again, has been "efficiency through specialization." And once again, the excess of specialization that has emerged has resulted in unexpected but significant costs in motivation, morale, and work quality. In vertical loading, the intent is to partially close the gap between the doing and the controlling parts of the job — and thereby reap some important motivational advantages.

Of all the job-design principles, vertical loading may be the single most crucial one. In some cases, where it has been impossible to implement any other changes, vertical loading alone has had significant motivational effects.

When a job is vertically loaded, responsibilities and controls that formerly were reserved for higher levels of management are added to the job. There are many ways to accomplish this:

• Return to the jobholder greater discretion in setting schedules, deciding on work methods, checking on quality, and advising or helping to train less experienced workers.

• Grant additional authority. The objective should be to advance workers from a position of no authority or highly restricted authority to positions of reviewed, and eventually, near-total authority for their own work.

• Time management. The jobholder should have the greatest possible freedom to decide when to start and stop work, when to break, and how to assign priorities.

• Troubleshooting and crisis decisions.

Workers should be encouraged to seek problem solutions on their own, rather than calling immediately for the supervisor.

• Financial controls. Some degree of knowledge and control over budgets and other financial aspects of a job can often be highly motivating. However, access to this information frequently tends to be restricted. Workers can benefit from knowing something about the costs of their jobs, the potential effect upon profit, and various financial and budgetary alternatives.

When a job is verticaly loaded it will inevitably increase in *autonomy*. And as shown in Figure 4, this increase in objective personal control over the work will also lead to an increased feeling of personal responsibility for the work, and ultimately to higher internal work motivation.

• Opening feedback channels. In virtually all jobs there are ways to open channels of feedback to individuals or teams to help them learn whether their performance is improving, deteriorating, or remaining at a constant level. While there are numerous channels through which information about performance can be provided, it generally is better for a worker to learn about his performances *directly as he does his job* — rather than from management on an occasional basis.

Job-provided feedback usually is more immediate and private than supervisor-supplied feedback, and it increases the worker's feelings of personal control over his work in the bargain. Moreover, it avoids many of the potentially disruptive interpersonal problems that can develop when the only way a worker has to find out how he is doing is through direct messages or subtle cues from his boss.

Exactly what should be done to open

channels for job-provided feedback will vary from job to job and organization to organization. Yet in many cases the changes involve simply removing existing blocks that isolate the worker from naturally occuring data about performance — rather than generating entirely new feedback mechanisms. For example:

• Establishing direct client relationships often removes blocks between the worker and natural external sources of data about his work.

• Quality control efforts in many organizations often eliminate a natural source of feedback. The quality check on a product or service is done by a person other than those reponsible for the work. Feedback to the workers — if there is any — is belated and diluted. It often fosters a tendency to think of quality as "someone else's concern." By placing control close to the worker (perhaps even in his own hands), the quantity and quality of data about performance available to him can dramatically increase.

• Tradition and established procedure in many organizations dictate that records about performance be kept by a supervisor and transmitted up (not down) in the organizational hierarchy. Sometimes supervisors even check the work and correct any errors themselves. The worker who made the error never knows it occured — and is denied the very information that could enhance both his internal work motivation and the technical adequacy of his performance. In many cases it is possible to provide standard summaries of performance records directly to the worker (as well as to his superior), thereby giving him personally and regularly the data he needs to improve his performance.

• Computers and other automated operations sometimes can be used to provide the individual with data now blocked from him. Many clerical operations, for example, are now performed on computer consoles. These consoles often can be programmed to provide the clerk with immediate feedback in the form of a CRT display or a printout indicating that an error has been made. Some systems even have been programmed to provide the operator with a positive feedback message when a period of error-free performance has been sustained.

Many organizations simply have not recognized the importance of feedback as a motivator. Data on quality and other aspects of performance are viewed as being of interest only to management. Worse still, the *standards* for acceptable performance often are kept from workers as well. As a result, workers who would be interested in following the daily or weekly ups and downs of their performance, and in trying accordingly to improve, are deprived of the very guidelines they need to do so. They are like the golfer we mentioned earlier, whose efforts to correct his hook are stopped dead by fog over the driving range.

Conclusions

In this article we have presented a new strategy for the redesign of work in general and for job enrichment in particular. The approach has four main characteristics:

1. It is grounded in a basic psychological theory of what motivates people in their work.
2. It emphasizes that planning for job changes should be done on the basis of *data* about the jobs and the people who do them — and a set of diagnostic instruments is provided to collect such data.

3. It provides a set of specific implementing concepts to guide actual job changes, as well as a set of theory-based rules for selecting *which* action steps are likely to be most beneficial in a given situation.

4. The strategy is buttressed by a set of findings showing that the theory holds water, that the diagnostic procedures are practical and informative, and that the implementing concepts can lead to changes that are beneficial both to organizations and to the people who work in them.

We believe that job enrichment is moving beyond the stage where it can be considered "yet another management fad." Instead, it represents a potentially powerful strategy for change that can help organizations achieve their goals for higher quality work — and at the same time further the equally legitimate needs of contemporary employees for a more meaingingful work experience. Yet there are pressing questions about job enrichment and its use that remain to be answered.

Prominent among these is the question of employee participation in planning and implementing work redesign. The diagnostic tools and implementing concepts we have presented are neither designed nor intended for use only by management. Rather, our belief is that the effectiveness of job enrichment is likely to be enhanced when the tasks of diagnosing and changing jobs are undertaken *collaboratively* by management and by the employees whose work will be affected.

Moreover, the effects of work redesign on the broader organization remain generally uncharted. Evidence now is accumulating that when jobs are changed, turbulence can appear in the surrounding organization — for example, in supervisory-surbordinate relationships, in pay and benefit plans, and so on. Such turbulence can be viewed by management either as a problem with job enrichment, or as an opportunity for further and broader organizational development by teams of managers and employees. To the degree that management takes the latter view, we believe, the oft-espoused goal of achieving basic organizational change through the redesign of work may come increasingly within reach.

The diagnostic tools and implementing concepts we have presented are useful in deciding on and designing basic changes in the jobs themselves. They do not address the broader issues of who plans the changes, how they are carried out, and how they are followed up. The way these broader questions are dealt with, we believe, may determine whether job enrichment will grow up — or whether it will die an early and unfortunate death, like so many other fledgling behavioral science approaches to organizational change.

Tear down the pyramids

Paul H. Thompson

It's not unusual to hear managers comment on the difficulties they have managing their professional employees. The most visible evidence of this problem has been union activity. An increasing number of doctors, teachers, and engineers are walking picket lines and pressing for improvements in pay, hours, and working conditions. Membership in professional unions or associations involved in collective bargaining has increased dramatically in the last decade.

Much of that increase has been in the public sector. For example, last year the American Federation of Teachers claimed 450,000 members, four and one-half times their 1963 membership. Nearly 20 percent of the college and university professors on 420 campuses have been organized.

However, the private sector cannot afford to ignore these developments because there has been a high level of interest in unionization among scientists, engineers, and other professional employees. And this is not the only evidence of unrest among what Peter Drucker calls "knowledge workers." Research interviews with over 400 accountants, scientists, engineers, bank loan officers, and professors have indicated frequent disenchantment with professional employment.

"Engineering doesn't have the prestige it once had. The glamour has worn off."

"I'd never let my son go into this field."

"My brother makes more money as a plumber than I do with a Ph.D."

Managing "knowledge workers"

We are not doing a very good job of managing our professional work force. Peter Drucker has written on our inadequate knowledge in managing this type of worker.

We also do not know how to satisfy the knowledge worker and to enable him to gain the achievement he needs. Nor do we as yet fully understand the social and psychological needs of the knowledge worker. . . . We also do not know how to manage the knowledge worker so that he wants to contribute and perform. But we do know that he must be managed quite differently from the way we manage the manual worker. (*The Age of Discontinuity*, Harper and Row, 1968, pp. 287–288).

Organizations are having difficulty with their professional employees because firms tend to think of career growth only in terms of climbing the corporate ladder. With that concept, career development consists of moving as high and as fast as possible. Whether the ladder is called the hierarchy, organization chart, or pyramid, upward movement has become the symbol of corporate success.

However, this concept of career growth can be completely inappropriate for professional organizations. We need a new way to think about careers if professionals are going to be motivated and productive members of organizations. Yet the pyramid problem must be studied before we can develop workable alternatives.

Winners and losers

In the last 15 to 20 years almost all medium-to-large organizations have employed increasing numbers of professionals — accountants, engineers, lawyers, scientists, and the like. As the numbers in each of these specialties increased, it seemed only natural to create a hierarchy and appoint supervisors, managers, vice-presidents, and so forth. Since many of these specialists were bright and well educated, some of the most competent were promoted into the top management to help the organization cope with increasingly complex situations. No one would argue that these professionals should not be promoted into top management. But management went beyond just promoting some capable people; they designed a whole reward system that inadvertently gave the signal that professional contributions were valued — but only secondarily. The reward system encouraged all the brightest people to move out of their specialties and into the management ranks as fast as possible. Those who had been promoted into management were labeled *winners,* and those still performing the prime tasks of the organization were pegged *losers.* In these organizations it became extremely

difficult for anyone to take pride in himself as a professional. Most power and status were given to the managers.

A recent article in *Business Week* advocates "career pathing" for those who want to "make something" of themselves. In describing "career pathing," the article gives some advice that illustrates the point very well:

Get out of your specialty fast, unless you decide that's all you ever want to do. This means rapid rejection of the notion that you are a professional engineer, lawyer, scientist, or anything but a manager.

This advice makes it very difficult for a person to feel successful if he chooses to make a contribution in his specialty. But organizations do more than just imply that promotion means success and not being promoted means failure. They tie most of the important rewards to the hierarchy.

"Mahogany Row"

Most pay systems are designed on the basis of a hierarchical system which emphasizes factors such as the number of people supervised. Before long, a chemist, who has the ability to develop a new product that may mean millions of dollars in profits, decides that he wants to become a manager because that's where the money is. The status symbols are also tied to the hierarchy. Most organizations make major distinctions between managers and nonmanagers — the accountants have desks in a large bull pen and their supervisor gets a large office on "Mahogany Row." Furthermore, for each promotion, the manager gets a larger office, more expensive furniture, and a parking space closer to the front door. These symbols don't go to those making significant contributions in nonmanagement areas. Such distinctions are often a real disincentive to individual contributors.

Managers are not deliberately trying to push all the best people out of professional work. They are aware that a chemical company needs top-notch chemists in the labs and an engineering company needs first-rate engineers at the drafting tables. If all the best professionals go into management, what will there be left to manage? The problem remains that managers and professionals alike have been locked into the concept of pyramid scaling. An alternative system is necessary.

Individual specialists, mentors . . .

Looking at careers of professionals, one becomes aware that many individuals remain high performers while others slip into mediocrity after age 35 or 40. Examination of these patterns makes it clear that the careers of professionals develop by stages. Each stage differs from the others in activities, relationships, and psychological adjustments. Moreover, successful performance at each stage is a prerequisite for moving on to the next. Individuals who continue to move through these stages retain their high performance ratings; those who do not move tend to be less valued by the organization. Four stages are identified, in the accompanying box, with Stage I noted as the apprenticeship period. Here an individual works under relatively close supervision and direction. In addition, most highly successful professionals have an informal "mentor" at this time. Surprisingly, some people stay in this stage most of their careers and are never able to assume independent responsibility for their own work. However, that

group represents a small minority. The majority of professionals make a successful transition into Stage II — the independent specialist.

A majority of professionals look forward to having their own project or area of responsibility. Earning this opportunity and taking advantage of it moves a person into Stage II. Most of the solid professional work in the organization is done by individuals in this category. About 40 percent of professionals are in Stage II. However, from an individual point of view, it is risky to remain in this stage because managers have rising expectations as a person's age and salary level increase. As a result those who remain in this stage after age 40 tend to receive lower performance ratings. Professionals who move into Stages III and IV are quite successful in avoiding that fate.

The last two stages are characterized by greater breadth of interest and activities and by involvement in the careers and development of others in the organization. The activities in Stages III and IV are highly valued in professional organizations, and people in these stages receive high performance rankings. The following table presents the average performance rating for the four stages in one research organization that was studied.

Stage	Average performance ranking
I	17th percentile
II	34th percentile
III	65th percentile
IV	89th percentile

Some have commented that these stages are just descriptions of different levels of management and that all that has been done is to give the pyramid another name. Yet research does not support this observation. In an effort to better understand this concept, third-level managers in five organizations were asked to list each person in their departments in one of the four stages. We then compared the descriptions with current performance rankings. On the average, people in the later stages were rated higher than those in early stages, as the table indicates. But an analysis of proportion of managers and nonmanagers in each stage reveals some interesting results:

Stage	Proportion of nonmanagers
I	100 percent
II	100 percent
III	65 percent
IV	26 percent

It is true there are many managers in Stages III and IV, but those stages are by no means reserved exclusively for managers. In fact, a majority of the people in

Stage I

Works under the supervision and direction of a more senior professional in the field

Is never entrusted with work entirely his own but is given assignments which are a portion of larger project or activity being overseen by senior professional

Lacks experience and status in organization

Is expected to accept supervision and direction willingly

Is expected to do most of the detailed and routine work on a project

Is expected to exercise "directed" creativity and initiative

Learns to perform well under pressure and accomplish a task within the time budgeted

Stage II

Goes into depth in one problem or technical area

Assumes responsibility for a definable portion of the project, process, or clients

Works independently and produces significant results

Develops credibility and a reputation

Relies less on supervisor or mentor for answers, develops more of his own resources to solve problems

Increases in confidence and ability

Stage III

Involved enough in his own work to make significant technical contributions but begins working in more than one area

Greater breadth of technical skills and application of those skills

Stimulates others through ideas and information

Involved in developing people in one or more of the following ways:
a. acts as an idea man for a small group
b. serves as a mentor to younger professionals
c. assumes a formal supervisory position

Deals with the outside to benefit others in organizations, i.e., works and relationships with client organizations, developing new business, etc.

Stage IV

Influences future direction of organization through:
a. original ideas, leading the organization into new areas of work
b. organizational leadership and policy formation
c. integrating the work of others to a significant end

Influence gained on the basis of:
a. past ability to assess environmental trends
b. ability to deal effectively with outside
c. ability to affect others inside the organization

Has the ability to engage in wide and varied interactions:
a. at all levels of the organization
b. with individuals and groups outside the organization

Involved in the development of future key people; a sponsor for promising people in other stages

Stage III were individual contributors. This indicates that a *person can remain an individual contributor doing work primarily in his specialty and still be highly valued by the organization.* Unfortunately, the pyramid and associated reward system in many organizations make it difficult, if not impossible, for managers to show the individual contributors in Stages III and IV that they are highly valued. It becomes evident that major changers must be made if organizations are going to succeed in keeping competent professionals working hard at their professional work.

Toppling the corporate ladder

In order to manage professionals effectively, executives need to tear down the pyramids. Instead of highlighting the corporate ladder and tying all rewards to promotion, that aspect of rewards needs to be substantially deemphasized. Some concrete recommendations may be helpful in meeting that objective.

Focus on stages, not ladders

Promotion as an indicator of career growth has serious consequences for a professional organization, but very few managers and professionals have had satisfactory ways to evaluate careers. The concept of career stages is one alternative. This idea has been received positively when presented to both professionals and their managers. They seem almost relieved that there is an alternative way to examine careers. The four-stage system is a useful tool in seminars focusing on careers as well as on a one-to-one basis in performance appraisal and long-range planning sessions between professionals and their supervisors.

Reward professional contributions

If an organization is going to keep talented employees doing professional work, it must provide meaningful rewards to high-performing individual contributors. An individual should be paid for his performance and not for his position or the number of people he supervises. If an individual contributor is doing Stage IV work, he should be paid more than the manager doing Stage III work.

A critical incentive for an experienced professional is the confidence that he is influential in making important decisions. The manager who makes all decisions on the basis of the authority of his position has a stifling effect on the whole organization. Managers who make use of the expertise of individual contributors have found the practice pays off.

One reason promotion into management is an important sign of success is that it provides increased visibility, often in the form of status symbols such as a private office, reserved parking, and the like. The distinction between managers and nonmanagers in these areas is often counterproductive. If distinctions must be made, it would be better to use stages as a basis rather than managerial status.

The pyramid, or corporate hierarchy, may be a major cause of unrest and disenchantment in the ranks of professional employees in organizations. Many competent professionals want to make their contribution to the corporation in their area of specialty. If they can believe that such a contribution is valued and rewarded, they will remain highly productive. It will not be an easy task for managers to communicate this view to their professionals, but tearing down the pyramid is a step in the right direction.

New light on adult life cycles

Freud, Spock and Piaget have charted almost every inch of childhood. Psychoanalyst Erik Erikson put the final touches on a convincing map of adolescence. Yet until very recently, most of the charting stopped near the age of 21 — as if adults escape any sequence of further development. Now a growing number of researchers are surveying the adult life cycle.

The research so far has been narrow, concentrating largely on white, middle-class American males. But in separate studies, three of the most important life-cycle scholars — psychiatrist Roger Gould of U.C.L.A., Yale psychologist Daniel Levinson and Harvard psychiatrist George Vaillant — have reached some remarkably similar conclusions that add new dimensions to the topography of postadolescent life. The main features:

16-22: Leaving the family

In this period, youthful fantasies about adulthood slowly give way. Young people begin to find their peers useful allies in an effort to break the hold of the family. Peer groups, in turn, tend to impose group beliefs. Emotions are kept under wraps, and friendships are brittle; any disagreement by a friend tends to be viewed as betrayal.

23-28: Reaching out

Following Erik Erikson, who found the dominant feature of the twenties to be a search for personal identity and an ability to develop intimacy, Gould, Levinson and Vaillant see this period as an age of reaching toward others. The growing adult is expansive, devoted to mastering the world; he avoids emotional extremes, rarely bothers to analyze commitments. To Levinson, this is a time for "togetherness" in marriage. It is also a time when a man is likely to acquire a mentor — a patron and supporter some eight to 15 years older.

29-34: Questions, questions

All the researchers agree that a crisis generally develops around age 30. Assurance wavers, life begins to look more difficult and painful, and self-reflection churns up new questions: "What is life all about? Why can't I be accepted for what I am, not what others (boss, society, spouse) expect me to be?" An active social life tends to decline during this period. So does marital satisfaction, and the spouse is often viewed as an obstacle instead of an asset. Marriage becomes particularly vulnerable to infidelity and divorce. Vaillant sees a crassness, callowness and materialism at this stage. Levinson detects a wrenching struggle among incompatible drives: for order and stability, for freedom from all restraints, for upward mobility at work. Says he: "If a man doesn't start to settle down by age 34, his chances of forming a reasonably satisfying life structure are quite small."

35-43: Mid-life explosion

Somewhere in this period comes the first emotional awareness that death will come and time is running out. The researchers see this stage as an unstable, explosive time resembling a second adolescence. All values are open to question, and the mid-lifer wonders, is there time to change? The mentor acquired in the mid-20s is cast aside, and the emphasis is on what Levinson calls BOOM — becoming one's own man. Parents are blamed for unresolved personality problems. There is "one last chance to make it big" in one's career. Does all this add up to disaster? Not necessarily. "Mid-life crisis does not appear to portend decay," says Vaillant. "It often heralds a new stage of man." The way out of this turbulent stage, say the researchers, is through what Erikson calls "generativity" — nurturing, teaching and serving others. The successful mid-lifer emerges ready to be a mentor to a younger man.

44-50: Settling down

A stable time: the die is cast, decisions must be lived with, and life settles down. There is increasing attention to a few old values and a few friends. Money is less important. Gould sees married people turning to their spouses for sympathy as they once did to their parents. Levinson notes that men tend to have fantasies of young, erotic girls as well as of older, nurturing women — all part of a final attempt to solve childhood problems and cut free from the mother.

After 50: The mellowing

These years are marked by a softening of feelings and relationships, a tendency to avoid emotion-laden issues, a preoccupation with everyday joys, triumphs, irritations. Parents are no longer blamed for personal problems. There is a little concern for either past or future.

Like Freud and Erikson, the life-cycle researchers argue that personality disorders arise when, for one reason or another, the orderly march of life stages is disrupted. Vaillant's studies suggest, for instance, that men who fail to achieve an identity in adolescence sometimes sail through life with a happy-go-lucky air, but never achieve intimacy, BOOM or generativity. "They live out their lives like latency boys," he says, not mentally ill, but developmentally retarded at the childhood level.

The researchers' findings are tentative. So far, few minority group members or working-class men have been studied, and the data on women are limited. Vaillant believes, however, that the female life pattern is much the same as the male, except that the drive for generativity that appears in men in their late 30s or early 40s may show up a decade earlier in women.

In any event, a thoroughly detailed portrait of adult life is still "many years away," as Gould concedes, and there is much skepticism in the academic world that one will ever appear. Yet the life-cycle researchers are confident that the threatening 30s and the mellowing 50s will some day become as universally accepted as, say, the terrible twos and the noisy nines of childhood.

On wasting time

James A. Michener

We all worry about wasting time, about the years sliding past, about what we intend to do with our lives. We shouldn't. For there is a divine irrelevance in the universe that defies calculation. Many men and women win through to a sense of greatness in their lives only by first stumbling and fumbling their way into patterns that gratify them and allow them to utilize their endowments to the maximum.

If Swarthmore College in 1925 had employed even a halfway decent guidance counselor, I would have spent my life as an assistant professor of education in some Midwestern university. Because when I reported to college it must have been apparent to everyone that I was destined for some kind of academic career. Nevertheless, I was allowed to take Spanish, which leads to nothing, instead of French or German, which everyone knows are important languages studied by serious students who wish to gain a Ph.D.

I cannot tell you how often I was penalized for having taken a frivolous language like Spanish instead of a decent, self-respecting tongue like French. In fact, it led to the sacrifice of my academic career.

Still, I continued to putter around with Spanish, eventually finding a deep affinity for it. In the end, I was able to write a book about Spain which will probably live longer than anything else I've done. In other words, I blindly backed into a minor masterpiece. There are thousands of people competent to write about France, and if I had taken that language in college I would have been prepared to add no new ideas to general knowledge. It was Spanish that opened up for me a whole new universe of concepts and ideas.

Actually, I wrote nothing at all until I was 40. This tardy beginning, one might say delinquency, stemmed from the fact that I had spent a good deal of my early time knocking around the country and Europe, trying to find out what I believe in, what values were large enough to enlist my sympathies during what I sensed would be a long and confused life. Had I committed myself at age 18, as I was encouraged to do, I would not even have known the parameters of the problem, and any choice I might have made then would have had to be wrong.

It took me 40 years to find out the facts.

As a consequence, I have never been able to feel anxiety about young people who are fumbling their way toward the enlightenment that will keep them going. I doubt that a young man — unless he wants to be a doctor or a research chemist in which case a substantial body of specific knowledge must be mastered within a prescribed time — is really capable of wasting time, *regardless* of what he does. I believe you have until 35 to decide finally on what you are going to do, and that any exploration you pursue in the process will in the end turn out to have been creative.

Indeed, it may well be that the years observers describe as "wasted" will prove to have been the most productive of those insights which will keep you going. The trip to Egypt. The two years spent working as a runner for a bank. The spell you spent on the newspaper in Idaho. Your apprenticeship at a trade. These are the ways in which a young man ought to spend his life . . . the ways of "waste" that lead to true knowledge.

Two more comments. First, I have recently decided that the constructive work of the world is done by an appallingly small percentage of the general population. The rest simply don't give a damn . . . or they grow tired . . . or they have failed to acquire when young the ideas that would vitalize them for the long decades.

I am not saying that such people don't matter. They are among the most precious items on earth. But they cannot be depended upon either to generate necessary new ideas or to put them into operation if someone else generates them. Therefore, those men and women who do have the energy to form new constructs and new ways to implement them just do the work of many. I believe it to be an honorable aspiration to want to be among those creators.

Second, I was about 40 when I retired from the rat race, having satisfied myself that I could handle it if I had to. I saw then that a man could count his life a success if he survived — merely survived — to age 70 without having ended up in jail (because he couldn't adjust to the minimum laws that society requires) or having landed in the booby hatch (because he could not bring his personality into harmony with the personalities of others).

I believe this now without question: income, position, the opinion of one's friends, the judgment of one's peers and all the other traditional criteria by which human beings are generally judged are for the birds. The only question is, "Can you hang on through the crap they throw at you and not lose your freedom or your good sense?"

I am now 67¾, and it looks as if I've made it. Whatever happens now is on the house . . . and of no concern to me.

Motivators: America's new glamour figures

Jeannye Thorton

There's big money to be made telling people how to gain success in their business and personal lives. For a look at who's earning it —

When sales growth slackened last year at TLC Associates, a Texas insurance company, President Burk Barr determined that what his staff needed was a pep talk of a different sort.

Rather than relying on a sales manager to outline new goals for employees, Barr turned to professional motivator Zig Ziglar, who laid on a hearty dose of his philosophy of success. Since then, the company has chalked up sales gains that are double those of 1981.

TLC's experience reflects a growing tendency among Americans to reach out for inspirational advice — a trend that has made the selling of motivation a highly lucrative business.

The market seemingly is limitless. Corporations seeking to get more work out of employees sponsor seminars by motivation gurus. Individuals searching for the secret of success jam hotel meeting rooms for training sessions, buy millions of audio cassettes and select from hundreds of book titles.

Motivational programs are even designed for children of kindergarten age and younger.

Big attractions

In major cities, rallies — which one motivator calls "a smorgasbord of renewal" — draw up to 10,000 people and are staged by promoters in the mold of rock concerts.

Success formulas aren't cheap. A seminar can cost a corporation $10,000, plus first-class travel expenses for the speaker. All told, industry experts estimate that the high priests of success pull in about 1 to 2 billion dollars annually.

Messages often borrow heavily from inspirational passages of the Bible. They are couched in catchy phrases: How to make your own luck, pull your own strings, win through negotiation or intimidation. The theme is the same: This book or this speaker will tell you how to get what you want out of life.

Whatever the message, its success in the marketplace hinges on the motivator, which makes the industry one built on personalities. They include entertainers, psychologists, educators, the clergy, successful business people and, occasionally, hucksters.

Some enter the success motivation circuit after having achieved celebrity status in other endeavors. Such was the case with news broadcaster Paul Harvey, whose $20,000 fee per engagement includes expenses, and television personality Art Linkletter, who collects about

$7,000 per speech, in addition to expenses.

But most professional motivators are little known outside of their industry. Typical is Ziglar, the man credited with revving up the TLC staff. His 12-year-old, Dallas-based company last year sold 3 million dollars' worth of seminars, video and audio training programs and booklets to schools, businesses and athletic groups. Charging corporations $5,000 per talk, Ziglar himself earns $350,000 annually on his speeches alone.

Ziglar claims his "I Can" course, taught in more than 2,000 schools in 48 states, has helped improve grades, cut vandalism and drug abuse and even reduce racial tension.

A born-again Christian, Ziglar delivers his message in the manner of an old-time evangelist holding forth in a tent meeting. He screams, cajoles, jokes with and teases his audience to hammer home his point: "You can change what you are and where you are by changing what goes into your mind."

Other motivators are more subdued: Wayne Dyer, author of *Your Erroneous Zones*, prefers writing and makes only three or four appearances a year, charging $10,000 and up for each.

Admirers of Denis Waitly of Rancho Sante Fe, California, author of *The Winner's Edge*, say he is "soft-spoken and low-key, but what he says is so mentally exciting."

Athletes and astronauts

A Naval Academy graduate and former pilot with the Navy's Blue Angels, Waitly has counseled Apollo astronauts and Super Bowl athletes as well as sales and management executives for Fortune 500 firms. He is working on a new project with the U.S. Olympic Committee to overcome what he sees as a big lead by the Soviet Union and East Germany in motivating athletes to "mentally enhance their performance."

Waitly, who charges his corporate customers $3,500 an hour, is amazed by the huge fees that motivators command. "I never in my life dreamed consultants could get as much money as I'm getting now," he says.

That money is well earned, motivators say. Tom Hopkins of Scottsdale, Arizona, who bills himself as "the No. 1 sales trainer in America" and charges his corporate customers up to $10,000 for seminars, has lived on the road 50 weeks a year for the past eight years doing a seminar every other day.

Like many of his colleagues, Hopkins uses his own life story as a storehouse of anecdotes. Now heading a business worth 18 million dollars annually, he reminds audiences that he was a college dropout and an unsuccessful real estate agent.

Likewise, Nido Qubein of High Point, North Carolina, tells how he arrived as a penniless immigrant from Lebanon at age 17 and now, at age 34, heads two firms promoting his success ideas to the tune of 1 million dollars in annual sales.

For some, the motivational-speaking circuit is a sideline. The Rev. Robert Schuller, the California pastor whose "Hour of Power" draws a large television audience each week, also makes about 100 motivational speeches a year, sometimes at no charge or for up to $10,000 each.

Joyce Brothers, psychologist, author and television personality, markets a cassette series called "Success Is a State of Mind." When not refereeing National Football League games, Jim Tunney conducts "personal-growth seminars" that bring in about $200,000 a year.

With so many people hawking success secrets, motivators often enhance their opportunities by targeting audiences.

Communications specialist Loretta Melandro of Denver grossed $300,000 after only three years of offering a program to help lawyers make "first and lasting impressions." Fat people can get inspiration not to shed pounds but to build a better self-image from Ruthanne Olds, author of *Big & Beautiful*. Her seminars cost $125.

The expanding electronics industry promises to open up still more avenues for spreading motivational advice. Xerox, IBM and Control Data have developed computerized motivational programs. Negotiations now under way also may bring to network television a program of interviews with 26 successful people conducted by Charles Garfield of Berkeley, California, a psychologist who says he has identified the characteristics of success.

While new to TV and computers, the motivational business has been around for a long time. Steel tycoon Andrew Carnegie set down success principles in the 19th century.

Dale Carnegie, author of the still popular *How to Win Friends and Influence People*, started offering motivational training in 1912. The firm he left behind supplied success, leadership and personal-development advice to more than 105,000 people in the U.S., Canada and 56 other countries last year.

In the 1950s, Norman Vincent Peale's *Power of Positive Thinking* outsold every book but the Bible. The 1956 motivational recording, "The Strangest Secret" by Earl Nightingale, is the only nonentertainment disc to earn the recording industry's "Gold Record" for sales of 1 million records.

Who is buying the motivation message? Surprisingly enough, many are people who already have achieved success. "We used to think it was the other people," says Lloyd Conant, chairman of Nightingale-Conant, for 27 years a producer of motivational records. "We tried to make winners. Now we find winners who want to become bigger winners."

Some people come to motivational programs through their jobs. General Motors, Tandy Corporation, General Electric, Nabisco and AT&T are just a few of the businesses that have in-house programs but also make use of outsiders.

One cereal maker this year purchased $120,000 worth of motivational tapes for employees. An accounting firm in Shreveport, Louisiana, closed down for one day and hired three temporaries to answer the phones so all of its employees could attend a time-management seminar by Dan Bellus of Richardson, Texas.

Behind the popularity of many such motivation programs, observers say, is the need of hard-pressed firms to get more production out of fewer employees. Adds Schuller: "So many people lack self-esteem. They are suffering from inertia, but we've got to get up and move."

Not everyone agrees that the methods and messages of professional motivators are the answer. Some motivators have run afoul of regulators or landed in court. The Federal Trade Commission ruled in the 1960s that the "Dare to Be Great" program of Glenn Turner was a pyramid scheme because it stressed recruitment of other sales people more than the selling of products.

Legal challenge

In October, a Boulder, Colorado, man filed a 3.5-million-dollar lawsuit against est Inc., claiming he suffers from "severe personality disruption" as a result of that widely publicized seminar program. Although est officials deny the charges, the man claims the practices used by est subjected him to sensory deprivation and ridicule.

Psychologist Harry Levinson of Cambridge, Massachusetts, notes that some image-building programs often follow a set formula: "They convince you you're a sinner and then come along and save you." As for the firms that hire motivational experts, he adds: "It astonishes me how often they are suckered by games and gimmicks."

Other psychologists stress that success comes from hard work, not from listening to tape recordings. Says Dr. Glenn Swogger, Jr., of the Menninger Foundation: "The implication of many of these programs is that if you smile right and intimidate your peers, everything will come your way. Such attitudes might set up great unattainable expectations."

David Elkind, head of the child-study center at Tufts University, is particularly concerned about the pressure put on children by motivational programs aimed at tots as young as 3 years old. "I doubt if children can be inspired by verbal harangues," he says.

Whatever the criticisms, signs point to still bigger profits for professional motivators. Says psychologist Richard Farson of the Western Behavioral Sciences Institute: "Everyone wants the short route to success — that magical hope."

Some individuals never see the relationship between their personal needs and organizational realities.

"Frankly, I believe your résumé would be much stronger if you were to condense it a bit . . . for instance . . . you might consider leaving out this entire section dealing with your pet hamster."

How to make an intelligent decision

Robert L. Heilbroner

There is nothing in the world so common and ordinary and yet so agonizingly difficult as a tough decision. Most of us have marched up to some crossroad in our lives — whether or not to get married, to change jobs, to choose this or that career — and experienced the awful feeling of not knowing which route to choose. Worse yet, many of us have known what it is like, after a paralyzing wait, to start down one road with the sinking sensation that we've picked the wrong one.

Ever since Adam and Eve made the wrong one, decisions have been bedeviling people. Damn-fool decisions and half-cocked decisions lie behind much of the unhappiness of life. More pathetic yet is the misery caused by no-decision. "Everything comes to him who waits," writes Bill Gibson, in *The Seesaw Log*, "— too late."

What makes us decide things badly, when we "know better?" What is it that sometimes stalls our decision-making machinery entirely? There is no single or simple reason why decisions are the pitfall of our lives. A high school senior who sits with his pencil wavering between the True and False answers on an examination may be baffled by the difficulty of the questions, or may simply be reduced to a blue funk by the pressure of taking an exam. A young woman in the throes of indecision over a marriage proposal may be trying to weigh the pros and cons of a tangled life situation, or may be panicked by the thought of marriage itself. Foolish decisions and indecision are the consequence not only of the complexity of the world about us, but of the complicated crosscurrents of the world within us.

Whatever their causes, the agonies of decision making are often magnified because we go about making up our minds so ineffectively. Faced with a hard choice, we allow our thoughts to fly around, our emotional generators to get overheated, rather than trying to bring our energies to bear as systematically as we can.

There is no ABC for decision making. But, there are a few guidelines that have helped others, and we can use them to help ourselves.

Marshal the facts

A lot of the mental anguish of decision making comes because we often worry in a factual vacuum. An endless amount of stewing can be avoided if we do what all good executives do with a problem that can't be settled: send it back for more data. Dale Carnegie once quoted a distinguished university dean as saying, "If I have a problem that has to be faced at three o'clock next Tuesday, I refuse to try to make a decision about it until Tuesday arrives. In the meantime I concentrate on getting all the facts that bear on the problem. And by Tuesday, if I've got all the facts, the problem usually solves itself."

But just gathering facts won't solve hard problems. "The problem in coming to a firm and clear-sighted decision," says Lt. General Thomas L. Harrold, veteran infantry commander and now Commandant of the National War College, "is not only to corral the facts, but to marshal them in good order. In the Army," General Harrold explains, "we train our leaders to draw up what we call an Estimate of the Situation. First, they must know their objective. Unless you know what you want, you can't possibly decide how to get it. Second, we teach them to consider *alternative* means of attaining that objective. It's very rarely that a goal, military or any other, can be realized in only one way. Next we line up the pros and cons of each alternative, as far as we can see them. Then we choose the course that appears most likely to achieve the results we want. That doesn't guarantee success. But at least it allows us to decide as intelligently as the situation permits. It prevents us from going off on a half-baked hunch that may turn out to be disastrous."

Some people, however, *misuse* the idea of fact collecting. They go on and on getting advice, gathering data, and never seem to be able to clinch the case. When we find ourselves assembling more and more facts without coming to any clear conclusions, without acting, it's time to be suspicious. Frequently we are merely waiting for the "right" fact which will rationalize a decision we have already made.

An executive of a New York placement agency tells of a young man who couldn't make up his mind whether or not to take a job that involved a move out of town. He kept coming back for more and more information until one day he learned that the company had had tough sledding during the 30's and nearly closed down. That clinched it. With obvious relief the young man "reluctantly" turned the job down.

"Actually," the placement official comments, "it was clear that he didn't want to move. But he had to find a 'fact' to make this decision respectable in his own eyes."

When we reach this point, it is time to stop fact collecting.

Consult your feelings

The psychiatrist Theodore Reik, when still a young man, once asked Sigmund Freud about an important decision he had to make. "I can only tell you of my personal experience," Freud replied. "When making a decision of minor importance I have always found it advantageous to consider all the pros and cons. In vital matters, however, such as the choice of a mate or a profession, the decision should come from the unconscious, from somewhere within ourselves. In the important decisions of our personal life, we should be governed, I think, by the deep inner needs of our nature."

We can usually tell when a decision accords with our nature by the enormous sense of relief that it brings. Good decisions are the best tranquilizers ever invented; bad ones often increase our mental tension. When we have decided something against the grain, there is a nagging sense of incompletion, a feeling that the last knot has been pulled out of the string.

Timing

We must learn to distinguish between our deep-running characteristics and our transient moods. There is an old rule that we should sleep on big decisions, and contemporary psychological research has established that the rule is sound.

Data from questionnaires answered by some 500 persons at Columbia University's Bureau of Applied Social Research show that our behavior is affected by our passing moods. When we are blue, low, our actions tend to be aggressive and destructive; when we are in good spirits, all fired up, our behavior swings toward tolerance and balance. Everyone knows that the boss is more apt to make lenient decisions when he's in a good mood, and that it's no time to ask him for a raise when he comes into the office glowering. We do well to take account of our emotional temperatures before we put important decisions on our *own* desks. On paydays, for example, we are all apt to be a little happy-go-lucky, especially about money decisions; on days when we've had a run-in with our wife or the day's work has gone all wrong, we are apt to decide things harshly, pessimistically, sourly.

A sense of timing also requires that we know when *not* to make a decision. "In surgery," says Dr. Abram Abeloff, Surgeon at New York's Lenox Hill Hospital, "a doctor often studies a situation for days or even weeks until he feels reasonably confident to go ahead. Time itself is an essential component of many decisions. It brings uncertain situations to a head. Premature decisions are the most dangerous a person can make."

In ordinary life, as well as in business and medicine, many of the most involved and difficult decisions are best not "made," but allowed to ripen. Facts accumulate, feelings gradually jell and, as Barnard says, other people take a hand in the situation. By holding ourselves back — refusing to plunge in the moment our adolescents ask us, "Should I go to college?" "Should I enlist in the Army now, or should I wait?" — we give complicated situations a chance to work themselves out, and sometimes save ourselves a great deal of exhausting and useless brain-cudgeling.

Consciously postponing a decision — deciding not to decide — is not the same as indecision. As Chester I. Barnard, first president of the New Jersey Bell Telephone Company, has put it in a famous book on business leadership, *The Functions of the Executive:* "The fine art of executive decision consists in not deciding questions that are not now pertinent, in not deciding prematurely, in not making decisions that others should make."

Follow-through

We all know that decisions do not mean much unless we back them with the will to carry them out. The alcoholic decides a thousand times to give up drink; the smoker vows again and again that this is his last cigarette. Many times an inability to make up our minds reflects just such an unwillingness to *go through* with a decision. "Thinking," wrote the great Swiss psychiatrist, Otto Fenichel, "is preparation for action. People who are afraid of actions increase the preparation."

Thus indecision can sometimes help us *clarify* our minds. It can be the signal flag that forces us to look beyond the immediate point at issue into the follow-through that a decision demands of us. Frequently, when we make fools of ourselves at a retail counter, trying to decide which gift to buy, we are really wrestling with a quite different problem — such as our unconscious feelings about the person for whom we're selecting the gift. At a more serious level, an unhappily married woman, endlessly debating with herself whether or not to ask for a divorce, may in fact be avoiding the more difficult question of what she would do with her life if she were divorced.

Flexibility

Part of the worrisomeness of decision making comes from a natural tendency to overstress the *finality*, the one-and-for-allness of our choices. There is much more "give" in most decisions than we are aware. Franklin D. Roosevelt, for example, was a great believer in making flexible decisions. "He rarely got himself sewed tight to a program from which there was no turning back," his Secretary of Labor, Frances Perkins, once observed.

"We have to do the best we know how at the moment," he told one of his aides. 'If it doesn't turn out all right, we can modify it as we go along."

Too many of us find decisions painful because we regard them as final and irrevocable. "Half the difficulties of man," Somerset Maugham has written, "lie in his desire to answer every question with yes or no. Yes or no may neither of them be the answer; each side may have in it some yes and some no."

Sometimes, naturally, we have to answer a question with a firm yes or no. But even then it is often possible to modify our answer later. That's why some advisers counsel: "When in doubt, say no. It's a lot easier to change a no to a yes, than vice versa."

The final ingredient

Finally, there is one last consideration to bear in mind. In making genuinely big decisions we have to be prepared to stand a sense of loss, as well as gain. A student who hesitates between a lifetime as a teacher or businessman, a talented young girl trying to make up her mind between marriage and a career, face choices in which sacrifice is involved, *no matter what they do.* That's one reason why big decisions in contrast to little ones, do not leave us exhilarated and charged with confidence, but humble and prayerful.

It helps to talk big decisions over with others — not only because another's opinion may illumine aspects of the dilemma that we may have missed, but because in the process of talking we sort out and clarify our own thoughts and feelings. Talk, as a clergyman and the psychiatrist both know, has a cathartic effect; it gives vent to feelings which may otherwise be expressed, not always wisely, in actions.

After this, meditation, reflections — letting the problem stew in its own juice — can also help. But in the end, after talk and thought, one ingredient is still essential. It is courage.

"One man with courage makes a majority," said Andrew Jackson; and this was never more true than in the election of our minds where the one vote we cast is the deciding one.

Working connections

by Reba Keele and Christine Russell

What women know about networking helps them live longer. What men know about networking helps them get jobs and promotions. Are we smart enough to learn from each other?

Reba Keele is an associate professor of organizational behavior at Brigham Young University, a member of the Utah State Board of Regents, and is currently coauthoring a book with Christine Russell on mentoring and support systems.

Christine Russell is completing a masters in organizational behavior at Brigham Young University in April and is currently networking for a corporate position.

Men have networks; women don't. Right? Men are successful in part because their "old boy network" maintains contacts which helps them find jobs, and to succeed once they're in them. Meanwhile, women struggle along alone, succeeding less often.

Some of that may be true, but before we contribute to building a myth which works against women, let's re-examine the realities of female networking. Good male networks do exist, and they do give men an edge in some ways. On the other hand, it's not as if women have no networking experience. Indeed, they excel in providing particular kinds of support, and, furthermore, they can learn other strategies which complement what they already know.

James House, author of *Work Stress and Social Support,* identifies four types of support which are needed by, and given to, persons in support systems or networks: *emotional support* (feelings, esteem, trust, and concern); *appraisal support* (feedback, social comparison information, and affirmation); *information support* (advice, suggestions, directives, and information); and *instrumental support* (aid-in-kind, money, labor, time, and modifying the environment). Each kind of support, for both men and women, assumes importance at different times in their lives, depending on the situation. Examining these different types of support helps us estimate the strengths and weaknesses of our own support systems.

We now know that support of all kinds is important to our health and longevity. Historically, women have suffered from fewer stress-related diseases than men. One of the reasons for this might be that women are better at giving and receiving emotional support. As women move into the paid work force in greater and greater numbers, they, too, are now afflicted by these diseases. This may be partly because they are, as women working outside the home, removed from some of their traditional support systems. The effects of support upon stress are well documented, and most of the studies refer to emotional support as a primary stress, mitigating influence. For instance, people who are widowed are less likely to become ill if they have a confidant. Women with high stress and low support show a significant increase in birth complications, while women with the same level of stress with high support show no significant differences from women with low stress. Women who have friends of their own, who don't share most relationships with their husbands, adjust better to divorce than women whose relationships are shared. Surgical patients who are given supportive care by the anesthetist require less medication for pain and return home an average of 2.7 days earlier than patients receiving no such support.

Research also shows that men emphasize gregariousness and similarity in their friendships, while women emphasize assistance, reciprocity, and intimacy. Men often have difficulty in offering emotional support to others and tend to interact with male friends in groups, women tend to interact in pairs.

Emotional support is important to both sexes in a variety of situations. For example, men who are unemployed for a long period of time do not suffer from depression if they have adequate support. On the job, supervisor support tends to reduce perceived work stress, In addition, high support from either supervisors or coworkers generally accompanies high skill use, full participation, increased commitment to organizational goals while it decreases employee confusion about job roles. As a result, these people experience less conflict with fellow employees.

In other words, emotional support

seems to be the most important of the four types of support in moderating the effects of stress. Women have learned to give that emotional support to those around them. They find it easier to express liking, esteem and concern than most men do, and most of them have learned to be good listeners. So, while some kinds of support may be more available to men, women have a distinct advantage from their social conditioning that allows them to absorb more stress with fewer health consequences.

Another kind of support, appraisal support (feedback, social comparison, and affirmation), is an important part of success on the job. This is true for women whether the job is paid or in the home. Here women have fewer skills because they often miss the feedback they need to improve. Rosabeth Moss Kanter, author of *Men and Women of the Corporation,* points out that women do not receive constructive criticism as often as men. Males who give feedback are not always sure how a women will respond to being given feedback. They tend to "protect" women, to worry that they'll cry. In addition, women do not *ask* for this vital information as often as men do. Too often they seek approval — not information.

The feedback process has other components which are alien to women as well. While women have been socialized to their "womanly" role, they have not been taught as effectively about career progression. Success in an organization comes, in part, from fitting in. Fitting in comes from knowledge about how to conform to regulations, rules, and norms that are implicit, not explicit, in the system. Men understand this informal, covert organization better than women. Here, individual behavior is judged by compliance with these implicity rules, and women (who are often not a part of the feedback process that teaches the informal success system) frequently find themselves feeling isolated without knowing why.

Another way of learning about the organization is through the process of comparing ourselves with others in the system. The continuing process of comparing oneself with others is difficult when the only role models in the organization are male. One female engineer I know of, in a Fortune 500 industrial plant in the South, who had been identified as a fast-track employee (one of high potential who is expected to advance rapidly) explains, "If you want to get ahead in this company you've got to fit the mold. That means the male image of overalls, short hair and aggression — which leads me to a lot of aggravation and identity conflict." Not all organizations have a macho orientation or culture, but a woman in management may find her responses so different from those of male co-managers that she is soon isolated and has no way to obtain adequate information about how she compares with others in essential ways. This problem is most intense when there are only one or two women and becomes less an issue as the number of women increases. Further, when there are only a few women to compare one's self to, women may take inappropriate comparisons. Most of us, for instance, feel inadequate in comparison to Utah Supreme Court Justice Christine Durham (*Network,* January 1982). Though it's vitally important to us to see such women of high achievement, we also need to find appropriate role models — women who are in jobs similar to ours or who are in positions just a step or two beyond us — in sufficient numbers that we can find ourselves among them.

The third type of support is infor-mational. Women often feel shut out of informational networks and this is especially true when the information is casually exchanged in group settings, because such groups, intentionally or unintentionally, exclude women. Men play golf, tennis or squash, and have drinks at the club for both social and business reasons. These activities appear to be strictly social but the information exchange which goes on in these settings is extensive. Men often are not aware themselves how much information is passed on casually. One feminist man I know was very surprised when he discovered that the men in the university department he headed were receiving all kinds of information from him the women were not. He had not intended to exclude the women; he simply wasn't associating with them as often and didn't realize how much he casually dropped information in conversations with the other men in the department. It was information that simply wasn't available to the women.

The availability for women of the fourth type of support — instrumental (aid-in-kind, time, money, modifying the environment) — is often reduced by women's discomfort with material, as opposed to emotional, support. Women are sometimes reluctant to solicit information, ask for opportunities, seek advice, or ask someone to intervene for them unless they can offer something they feel is of equal or greater value to the other person. They will ask only when there is a strong system of trust and concern, and even then, women tend to be uncomfortable with the concept of "using" connections. The concept of reciprocity is important in networking or support systems. To the extent that both people have something to gain, both are likely to continue to nurture a relationship. However, it is possible that women who see themselves as having too little to trade, or who have little sense of their own value or competency, avoid reciprocal relationships. In a graduate school of management in Utah it was found that graduate males call professors more for assistance than graduate females. Females may feel they are intruding and may be fearful of not being able to offer something the professor would find professionally valuable in return. A further complication is the fear of owing another in a way that might be interpreted as personal rather than professional — especially if the other is male.

As managers have recognized the value of all four types of support, some conscious attempts at networking are taking place. A recent *Fortune* article describes what is happening: "Perhaps for the betterment of us all, perhaps only as a measure of how brazen we've become, the subject of connections is coming out of the closet. The old-boy network as traditionally understood is still functioning . . . but it's rapidly giving ground. Taking its place is a new, deliberate, and relatively above board pattern of contact formation sanitized by feminists and others under the same 'networking'." More than a thousand women's networks have formed around the country in an attempt to provide not only emotional, but appraisal, informational, and instrumental support.

Build your own network

Different people need different kinds of networks, and different amounts of support. Information about many kinds of networks appears in the pages of this paper from month to month. The following are some principles that will be important in deciding whether a particular network might provide you the kind of support and networking you need.

1. Decide what kind of support you are looking for and what are the best means of obtaining that support. For instance, to ask a professional organization to provide emotional support may be more than it intended or is capable of doing. Emotional support may be better provided from the development of friendships with one or more persons than from a professional network. Constructive criticism may be more valid from your boss than from women professionals who don't know the requirements of your position. The kind of information you most need may determine the kind of network you need. It is better to make expectations explicit than to blame the network for not providing something it was never intended to provide.

2. Determine what you have to offer to the network. You may have skills, content, information, time, or money which would be of use. You will need to have a system of reciprocity established, both for your sake and the sake of the organization or relationship.

3. Look at the programs publicized by the network, and don't affiliate where programming does not meet your needs.

4. Make contact with individuals rather than with a formal network when appropriate. Be sure to leave the other person free to say no. The need for support is different for different people, and some people may already feel "overnetworked" and should not be punished for that feeling. Women in high positions may need a different

kind of support than is available to them from those who wish to network with them.

The surge of networks and support systems for women helps compensate for their number within individual organizations. Yet the support system itself shouldn't be a numbers game. Robert Kahn and Toni Antonucci, researchers into support systems, point out that one supportive relationship may be enough, and that the biggest distinction in capability to face stress is between those who must face stressful events with no close relationship and those who are supported by *at least* one. Yet, we shouldn't expect that one person to be able to provide all four kinds of support. In fact, relationships which are not close may be excellent for providing appraisal, informational, or instrumental support. We need a system in which someone can provide emotional support, someone (not necessarily the same person) can give information about how we compare with others, someone (still another) can help us learn what we need to know about the job or the organization, and someone can put us in contact with the resources or people who will help us achieve the particular task we are about at the moment. These people may be part of a shifting kaleidoscope of relationships, or they may be very stable across time. They might be few or many, either may be very effective.

Women's networks across the country take many forms, but most tend to be formally organized. They bind women within a particular organization or straddle several organizations. For instance, a group of women engineers in the Atlanta, Georgia and surrounding areas meet every Tuesday. In Salt Lake City, The Women Lawyers of Utah meet every third Thursday in a banquet/

speaker format. Women employees of Procter & Gamble in Georgia meet in individual plants to discuss plant issues, promotions, and departmental problems. The multistate Consortium for Utah Women in Higher Education and HERS/West meet several times a year for training sessions and the exchange of career information.

In contrast, men's groups are usually informal. Men are socialized on the playing field and in other activities to engage in friendly competition. They learn early to trade favors and see themselves as an active, independent, aggressive sex. Women, in contrast, stereotype themselves as dependent and less skilled than men. They are just learning how to compete professionally, not personally, with women, and are still learning the rules of organizational behavior. Further, the informal male system often develops outside work hours when women tend to be concerned with the demands of home, especially in dual career families. It is important to work for the time when women are integrated into the informal systems with men — in the meantime, the more formal organizations of women attempt to fill the gap.

Evidence suggests that people have less support than is optimal, and that most women have less support than most men. And though social support is not a panacea for all problems of occupational and personal stress, or a guarantee of career success, greater social support would provide most of us with more resiliency. We need to recognize that women are strong in one of the important qualities of effective support: emotional caring and concern. Our networks will continue to progress in learning to provide informational, instrumental, and appraisal support. We are learning more about the care and feeding of contacts and becoming less apologetic about seeking kinds of support we need. As we become more matter of fact about our requests we may learn to move from our present networks, which frequently focus on the individual woman and her training and professional associations, to broader networks which teach us about organizational change. Another future emphasis of support systems might be the integration of work and family.

We know the difference in our own lives when our personal and professional networks are functioning, and have seen it in the lives of colleagues. Paying conscious attention to the building of support systems offers the hope we may be able to build a more humane and egalitarian approach to our work lives as well as our private lives, thus allowing us more developmental opportunities. Whether the level of our support is buying from women-owned businesses, passing on a job or promotion tip, offering a training program, or being available when a friend needs to talk, we are participating in the weaving of a network of connections and contacts, and giving and receiving support. The question is not whether we need support, but rather how effective we are at building it. The potential reward makes the effort worthwhile.

Taking a look back at his 37 years in the automobile business, Iacocca reflected not long long ago: "I don't know what the hell I rushed for. It's a long race. I was trying to sprint all the time. Maybe if I had to do it again I would slow down a little." The thought is so outlandish that not even Lee Iacocca can sell it.
Time (March 21, 1983)

Many of our young managers are looking six steps ahead and pushing for every promotion while trying to break so and so's record to Vice-President. In the meantime, they seem to have forgotten what they were hired to do. They have lost interest in learning skills.
Fifty-year-old bank manager

The inquiring reporter asked the young woman why she wanted to be a mortician. "Because," she said, "I enjoy working with people."
The San Francisco Chronicle

CASES

State Bank

After graduating from college, I accepted a job with what I considered to be the best local bank, State Bank. My first year of employment consisted of a management development program that mixed a bit of formal book education with a generous amount of practical application. At the close of one year, I received a permanent assignment at the bank's computer processing and operations center as an operations officer. I received very little concrete explanation of my job from the officer I replaced. This was frustrating, considering that I now faced the task of overseeing seven departments that I knew very little about.

The first week on my own, Jack Freestone, the manager of the operations center, called me into his office to talk about a special assignment he had for me. Jack wanted me to give up one of my departments and take on the challenge of the Phone Inquiry Department. Trina Farr, the officer over the department, couldn't handle the job. Jack felt there was too much "goofing off," and discipline was terrible. My assignment was to "straighten things out" and "get some work out of those people." Jack told me to report to Fred Garcia, the assistant manager, about my progress in solving the problem (see Exhibit 1).

When I left Jack's office, I went right to Fred's desk to ask for some insight into the situation. Fred's response was, "You can ask Trina about the department, but she didn't get along well with the people there and probably won't have anything good to say. Jack does this once a year.

He assigns that department to another officer and hopes they'll do something . . . Let me know if you come up with an idea."

The Phone Inquiry Department

The Phone Inquiry Department was not essential to the work flow of the operations center. But it did play an important role in the check-cashing process for the branches. Tellers would call the phone operators to inquire as to whether the check they were about to cash would clear. The inquiry operator sat at a computer terminal, punched in the account number of the customer, checked for sufficient funds, and then reserved those funds on the computer until the check could be processed. If the operator gave permission to cash the check, the teller would go ahead with the transaction.

Phone Inquiry also handled customer questions, either directly or via branch personnel. Branch clerks would call to get information to solve the problems while customers waited. Customers could call to get their current balance and find out if a certain check had cleared the account. Sometimes operators would spend twenty minutes or more going through the processed checks of a particular account to help the customer balance his or her books. Both the computer terminals and cancelled checks waiting to be mailed in the next monthly statement were at the operators' disposal.

Exhibit 1

Operations Center organization chart

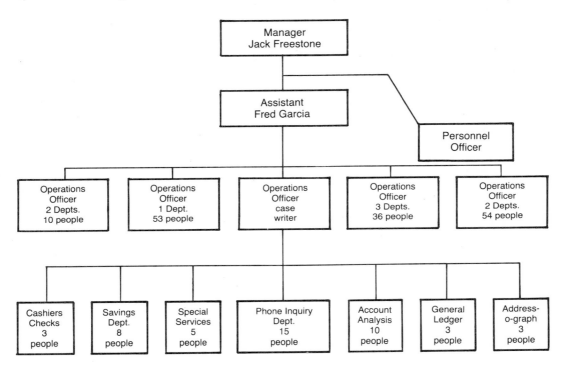

Fifteen young employees were employed in the department; twelve were full-time operators, two were alternates, and one was a supervisor. Each of the twelve full-time workers was assigned a small desk with a terminal on it. The desks were arranged in clusters of three, with partitions separating each work station (see Exhibit 2). Each desk had a phone board with twelve phone lines on it. No one was assigned to a particular line. When a phone rang, any free operator was expected to answer as quickly and courteously as possible. (The phones didn't actually ring, they beeped. The beep came over a central speaker in the middle of the department. If one phone needed answering the beep was slow.

The speed of the beep increased in proportion to the number of phones needing answering. Calls came constantly from 8:30 A.M. to 6:00 P.M. each work day.)

The two alternates in the department filled in for ill employees. Sometimes two were not enough and the department ran short. Very rarely was there a day when no one was ill. If the alternates were not needed on the phones, they did other miscellaneous duties: stuffing statement envelopes or filing copies of charge notices. When calls slowed down, the other operators were also supposed to help with these tasks.

Twenty-three-year-old Mary Anderson supervised the department. Mary had

Exhibit 2

Phone Inquiry Department physical layout

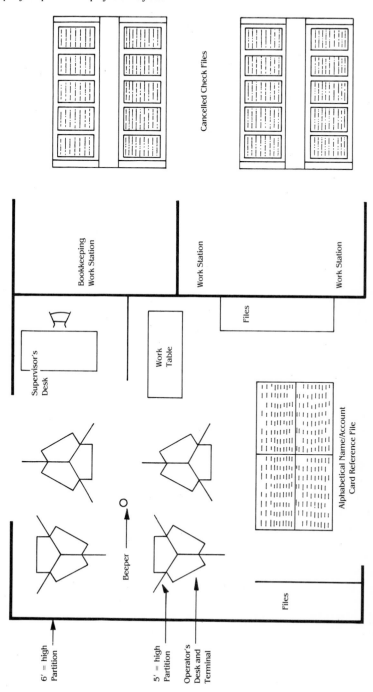

come from another department about a year earlier. She hadn't worked in Phone Inquiry before but was selected for her patience and her ability to relate to the young workers. When asked, all the operators said they liked Mary and thought she was easy to get along with. In her last annual appraisal Mary had been rated as "competent" in her position. Officer comments on the appraisal were "needs to be more strict." Her attendance had become a problem in the past few months due to problems with her pregnancy. Mary came at 8:00 A.M. each day, took a half-hour lunch, and left at 4:30 P.M. She gave daily work station assignments to the operators and determined where the alternates were needed. Operators "signed on" to their assigned terminal with a security code. This allowed the supervisor to monitor the number and length of time between transactions on each terminal daily and identify the operator who used the terminal. A hand tally of calls was also kept because (contrary to rules) operators sometimes used another operator's station. The total calls calculated by the computer and the total hand tallies for any given day usually did not match. Yet each operator insisted the tally they kept was accurate.

Operators were divided into three groups of four. Each group worked a shift for one week and then switched systematically to the next shift, which only varied by one-half hour. That is, Group 1 worked 8:30 to 5:00, Group 2 worked 9:00 to 5:30, and Group 3 worked 9:30 to 6:00. The next week Group 1 worked the middle shift, Group 2 the late shift, and Group 3 the early shift. The members of the group were changed only when someone was transferred to another department or quit — which occurred quite often.

Usually an operator was hired at a minimum wage because no previous experience or skill was required for the job. New employees trained with a more experienced worker for about two days and then were given their own station. After 90 days on the job an operator was evaluated on performance and given a ten to twelve percent raise. Shortly after the 90-day raise, most operators began to ask about opportunities in other departments. They wanted more challenge, were bored, or didn't like the other employees. Other departments had turnover problems too and were talking to the operators on the side. If a transfer was not granted, the operator would often quit. Only three workers had been in the department more than nine months. No other department wanted them.

Time for change

The challenge of overseeing seven departments kept me quite busy for the first few days. But I did manage to spend a few minutes observing the Phone Inquiry Department each afternoon. It was obvious that the operators liked to gossip among themselves and were not eager to answer the beeping phones. It was a game to wait long enough that another operator would break down and answer first. The winner was the worker who eventually answered the phone last.

The gossip and talking sometimes led to loud laughter and an occasional outburst of shouts and chasing around the department. The noise didn't seem too serious when I was there, but early one morning I received a call from one of the bank vice-presidents. He had received numerous complaints from customers about the background noise they heard when they called the Phone Inquiry Department. He had decided to check it out and had called the department about 5:30 the previous evening, after I had gone for the day. He said the giggling, shouting, and general commotion, were not professional and did not portray the proper bank image.

Now I knew something had to be done right away. The vice-president would probably anonymously check on the department again very soon.

The slab yard slowdown

E ven the tremendous roar of the nearby open-hearth furnace would not have drowned out Bob Flint's screams when he was handed the latest slab yard payroll report. Flint, a division superintendent at Midland Steel's Dayton, Ohio plant, was outraged to discover that a crew of "scarfers" had reported a 410 percent incentive pay performance level on last week's day shift. To earn the $41 hourly wage reported by the scarfers would have required a physically impossible work pace.

Background

The overall steel production process

Raw iron ore is melted down in large blast furnaces to form basic pig-iron soup. The soup is transported to open-hearth furnaces where certain alloys are added to produce a molten steel mixture of malleability and strength, tailored to unique specifications. This mixture is reheated, then poured into ingot molds and transported to a mill for further processing.

In the mill, the ingot molds are removed and the ingots rolled and chopped into steel slabs of predetermined dimensions. After the slabs cool to 1,000 degrees, jet streams of water are turned on them to further reduce their temperature. At this point, the scarfers mount the steel slabs and use their torches to burn off any cracks, scabs, or blemishes on the slab surface. When the scarfers have completed their work, the slabs are transferred to a rolling mill, reheated, and rolled into either plates or coils, depending on customer specifications.

The scarfing process

The scarfers were specifically responsible for burning all cuts, cracks, scabs, and blemishes off the surface of the steel slabs before they were reheated and rolled into plates or coils in the rolling mill. Their function was vital, since failure to remove defects in the steel slabs could have resulted in scrapping much of the metal during the rolling process. The defects could ruin the metal in two ways: (1) impurities could prevent the steel from reaching the required level of malleability during reheat, causing the metal to snap during the coiling process; or (2) even a small blemish could become greatly enlarged during the rolling process; e.g; a two-inch-wide blemish on the surface of a six-inch-thick slab of steel would be stretched out over the face of over 100 feet of finished product when the slab was rolled into a plate one-tenth of an inch thick.

The scarfers' task was achieved by standing on top of the steel slabs in thick, wooden-soled boots and cutting paths along the steel surface with a heavy blowtorch. Obviously, the working conditions were not comfortable. The workers endured the discomfort of extreme heat, bulky clothing and protective goggles, moisture from the water jets used to cool the slabs, and an immediate environment full of acid fumes from molten steel.

This harsh environment dictated that a scarfer be in top physical condition. Some of the workers were very large physically while others were not. Regardless of his size, each scarfer was exceptionally strong. The majority of the scarfers were either junior high or high school dropouts. Most scarfers would spend their entire working lives in the slab yard, working until well into their sixties; consequently, many had worked together for years. Over time, they had developed good friendships and did many things together after work.

Added to the physical discomforts of the environment and the monotony of the task were the inherent dangers of working in an enclosed area among eight-foot stacks of hot steel slabs. The slab yard was the division with the highest accident rate in the corporation. According to the shift foremen, a high percentage of Midland's scarfers had died on the job from accidents or from heart attacks caused by overexertion.

The current incentive plan

Because scarfing was one of the most difficult, dangerous, and dirty tasks at Midland Steel, the job was more financially attractive than others. Under the current incentive plan, scarfing had become the highest-paying blue-collar position in the steel plant. In fact, good scarfers would make over $50,000 a year; consequently, they were considered by themselves and others to be the "elite" of steelworkers. However, the large pay differential between scarfers and other blue-collar workers created tension between the two groups.

The scarfers' incentive system was based on measures of production output, i.e., actual number of slabs and amount of square inches scarfed. Measurement of square inches and slab counts were performed by inspectors who were also responsible for slab quality. Markers carried out another function, that of marking areas on the slabs that needed scarfing. Markers, as well as inspectors, received compensation based on the number of slabs scarfed.

In addition to the piece-rate incentive system, management provided scarfers with a base pay which was calculated by the dollar amount of rolled or coiled steel which would have been wasted in absence of the scarfing process. To increase their variable incentive pay, scarfers had often skipped their hourly heat breaks.

When the bargaining union negotiated the incentive plan in 1956, management had expected scarfers to average about 150 percent of their base pay, but scarfers saw the incentive plan as a much larger money-making opportunity. Throughout the twenty-five years of the plan's existence, scarfers had averaged 262 percent of base pay.

The problem

Under Midland Steel's quantity-oriented incentive system, division superintendent Flint knew that the scarfers had been cheating for years by altering their blowtorch tips so that they could scarf more steel slabs per shift, thereby earning a higher wage. The workers would simply drill larger holes in the tip of their blowtorch so that the flame broadened, enabling them to burn a larger path with one pass of the torch over the steel slab. The larger torch path enabled the scarfer to finish more slabs during a shift, thereby increasing his income. However, by broadening the torch flame, the worker also decreased the flame's intensity such that the burn into the steel would not penetrate deeply enough to lift out the defects and blemishes from the steel. Rather, the weaker flame would simply cover the defect with molten steel, hiding it from the inspector's visual check. These hidden defects resulted in costly scrap in the final steelmaking process.

In addition, markers would often mark slabs for scarfing that did not need treatment in order to increase slab count and total square inches scarfed. Since quantity incentives were also offered to inspectors, they typically qualified inferior steel as acceptable in order to increase their own and scarfers' pay.

The only real contact between the scarfers and management was via the shift foremen. The shift foremen were thought of as the bridge between white- and blue-collar workers (each shift had two foremen — one in each slab yard). Their function was to ensure that the scarfers worked safely, kept on schedule, and did quality work. This was not an easy task considering the strong-willed and independent-minded attitudes of the scarfers.

The shift foreman also had the task of inspecting the blowtorches. Because some of the scarfers had altered their tips, a large number of defects had caused the rejection of significant quan-

tities of finished steel products. In order to decrease their rejection rate, the shift foremen conducted periodic inspections to ensure that the tips met regulations. Management at any level higher than the shift foremen were prohibited by union contract from conducting these inspections themselves.

The raid

Management, including the shift foremen, believed that greed was the motivating force behind the scarfers' altering their blowtorch tips. Management also thought that the incentive plan was a problem in that it rewarded output but not quality. The newer scarfers particularly were seen as guilty because they had been under pressure to keep up with older employees. The tip alteration problem had been going on for a long time and the finished product rejection rate at the Dayton plant was twice the corporate rate. With the obvious abuse of the incentive plan (410 percent by one crew for one period), management felt that it was time to make an example of the violators and to correct the abuses.

Blowtorch tip checks had been conducted before on the initiative of the shift foremen to discover and replace altered torch tips and to mildly reprimand the men, but Flint felt the whole thing had gone too far this time. Now was the time for more drastic action. Flint felt that the recent 410 percent incentive pay performance level provided him with an opportunity to show the scarfers who was boss. It would also serve as an excuse for him to implement changes in the types of torch tips the scarfers used and in their incentive system.

Consequently, Bob Flint ordered his shift foremen to conduct an immediate torch tip check on all scarfing crews, telling them that any workers found using altered tips were, in his words, "to be dealt with." When Dee Colton, the shift foreman at the time, conducted a job-site tip check in the slab yard, he found 50 percent of the scarfers using altered tips. Following past procedure, he issued each guilty worker a reprimand requiring two days off without pay. When Colton reported his actions to Flint, however, Flint was incensed. He demanded that Colton fire the guilty men immediately and that he fire any other scarfers found cheating in the next two shifts. Despite the fact that the first shift had warned the next shift — swing shift — that a tip check was on, three men supposed that the action taken would not be any different from that of the usual inspections and therefore they did not bother to change their tips. They were subsequently fired. By the time the graveyard shift shuffled into the slab yard that night, the word had gotten around that top management had its hands in this crackdown. No altered tips were found during the graveyard shift.

Two days later the scarfers began a wildcat slowdown which created a bottleneck potentially costing the company millions of dollars.

The dilemma

Management's perspective

Management regarded the slowdown primarily as a show of strength and a protest against its attempts to invoke adherence to work regulations. However, management fully realized that it couldn't force the scarfers to work any faster either. A major source of embarrassment to upper management was that the scarfers were earning an average of 262 percent of base pay — by far the highest incentive in the corporation.

For several years, Flint had desired to change the incentive plan to eliminate upper management's embarrassment and to install new, more powerful blowtorch tips. The blowtorch incident emphasized the importance of making these changes.

Labor's perspective

Typically, when one scarfer was criticized by management, all of them took it personally. Never before in the Midland plant had any scarfer been fired for altering a torch tip. When they saw some scarfers suspended without pay for two days and others fired for similar tip alterations, they felt that management was out of line. When the shift foremen made the inspections and firings, they made sure the scarfers knew that the foremen were only following Flint's orders. The scarfers resented this heavy-handed intervention by top management. Therefore, they had staged the slowdown to protest the firings and top management's interference.

The problem had to be solved quickly because the Dayton plant had been only marginally productive even before the expensive slowdown began.

Denver Department Stores

(A)

In the early spring of 1974 Jim Barton was evaluating the decline in sales volume experienced by the four departments he supervised in the main store of Denver Department Stores, a Colorado retail chain. Barton was at a loss as to how to improve sales. He attributed the slowdown in sales to the current economic downturn affecting the entire nation. However, Barton's supervisor, Mr. Cornwall, pointed out that some of the other departments in the store had experienced a 15 percent gain over the previous year. Cornwall added that Barton was expected to have his departments up to par with the others in a short period of time.

Background

Jim Barton had been supervisor of the sporting goods, hardware, housewares, and toy departments in the main store of Denver Department Stores for three of the ten years he had worked for the chain. The four departments were situated adjacent to each other on the ground floor of the store. Each department had a head sales clerk who reported to Mr. Barton on merchandise storage and presentation, special orders, and general department upkeep. The head sales clerks were all full-time, long-term employees of Denver Department Stores, having an average of about eight years' experience with the chain. The head clerks were also expected to train the people in the department they supervised. The rest of the staff in each department was made up of part-time employees who lived in or near Denver. Most of the part-time people were students at nearby universities who worked to finance their education. In addition, there were two or three housewives who worked about ten hours a week in the evenings.

All sales personnel at Denver Department Stores were paid strictly on an hourly basis. Beginning pay was just slightly over the minimum wage and raises were given based on length of employment and work performance evaluations. The salespeople in the housewares and sporting goods departments were paid about forty cents an hour more than the clerks in the other departments because it was thought that more sales ability and experience were needed in dealing with the people who shopped for items found in those departments.

As a general rule the head sales clerk in each department did not actively sell, but kept the department well stocked and presentable, and trained and evaluated sales personnel. The part-time employees did most of the clerk and sales work. The role of the sales clerk was seen as one of answering customer questions and ringing up the sale rather than actively selling the merchandise except in the two departments previously mentioned where a little more active selling was done.

The sales clerks in Barton's departments seemed to get along well with each other. The four department heads usually ate lunch together. If business was brisk in one department and slow in another, the sales people in the slower area would assist in the busy department. Male clerks often helped female clerks unoad heavy merchandise carts. Store procedure was that whenever a cash register was low on change a clerk would go to a master till in the stationery department to get more. Barton's departments, however, usually supplied each other with change, thus avoiding the longer walk to the master till.

Barton's immediate supervisor, Mr.

Cornwall, had the reputation of being a skilled merchandiser and in the past had initiated many ideas to increase the sales volume of the store. Some of the longer-term employees said that Mr. Cornwall was very impatient and that he sometimes was rude to his subordinates while discussing merchandising problems with them.

The store manager, Mr. Blanding, had been with Denver Department Stores for twenty years and would be retiring in a few years. Earlier in his career Mr. Blanding had taken an active part in the merchandising aspect of the store, but recently he had delegated most of the mer-

(Exhibit 1 is an organization chart of the store.)

Exhibit 1

Denver Department Stores organization chart

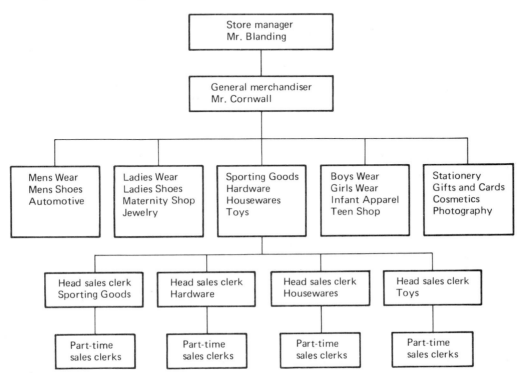

chandising and sales responsibilities to Mr. Cornwall.

Situation

Because of Mr. Cornwall's concern, Barton consulted with his department supervisors about the reason for the declining sales volume. The consensus reached was that the level of customer traffic had not been adequate to allow the departments to achieve a high sales volume. When Barton presented his problem to Mr. Cornwall, Cornwall concluded that since customer traffic could not be controlled and since the departments had been adequately stocked throughout the year, the improvement in sales would have to be a result of increased effort on the part of the clerks in each department. Cornwall added that if sales didn't improve soon the hours of both the full-and part-time sales clerks would have to be cut back. Later Barton found out that Cornwall had sent a letter around to each department informing employees of the possibility of fewer hours if sales didn't improve.

A few days after Barton received the assignment to increase sales in his department, Mr. Cornwall called him into his office again and suggested that each sales person carry a personal tally card to record daily sales. Each clerk would record his or her sales and at the end of the day the personal sales tally card would be totaled. Cornwall said that by reviewing the cards over a period of time he would be able to determine who were the "deadwood" and who were the real producers. The clerks were to be told about the purpose of the tally card and that those clerks who had low sales tallies would have their hours cut back.

Barton told Cornwall he wanted to consider this program and also discuss it with the head salespeople before implementing it. He told Mr. Cornwall that the next day was his day off but that when he returned to work the day after he would discuss this proposal with the head sales clerks.

(B)

Upon returning to the store after his day off, Mr. Barton was surprised to see each of his salespeople carrying a daily tally sheet. When he asked Mr. Cornwall why the program had been adopted so quickly, Cornwall replied that when it came to improvement of sales, no delay could be tolerated. Barton wondered what effect the new program would have on the personnel in each of his departments.

(C)

When Mr. Cornwall issued the tally cards to Barton's salespeople, the head sales clerks failed to fill them out. Two of the head clerks had lost their tally cards when Cornwall came by later in the day to see how the program was progressing. Cornwall issued the two head clerks new cards and told them that if they didn't "shape up" he would see some "new faces" in the departments.

The part-time salespeople filled out the cards completely, writing down every sale. The rumor that those clerks who had low sales tallies would have their hours cut spread rapidly. Soon the clerks became much more active and aggressive in their sales efforts. Customers were often approached more than once by different clerks in each department. One elderly lady complained that while making her way to the restroom in the back of the hardware deparment she was asked by four clerks if she needed assistance in making a selection.

When Barton returned the day after the institution of the program, the head sales clerks asked him about the new program. Barton replied that they had no alternative but to follow Cornwall's orders or quit. Later that afternoon the head clerks were seen discussing the situation on their regular break. After the break the head clerks began waiting on customers and filling out their sales tally cards.

Not long after the adoption of the program, the stock rooms began to look cluttered. Unloaded carts lined the aisles of the stock room. The shelves on the sales floor were slowly emptied and remained poorly stocked. Sales of items that had a large retail value were especially sought after and the head sales clerks were often seen dusting and rearranging these more expensive items. The head clerks' tally sheets always had the greatest amount of sales when the clerks compared sheets at the end of each day. (Barton collected them daily and delivered them to Cornwall.) The friendly conversations among salespeople and between clerks and customers were shortened and sales were rung up on the cash register and completed in a much shorter time. Breaks were no longer taken as groups and when they were taken they seemed to be much shorter than before.

When sales activity was slow in one department, clerks would migrate to other departments where there were more customers. Sometimes conflicts between clerks arose because of competition for sales. In one instance the head clerk of the hardware department interrupted a part-time clerk from the toy department who was demonstrating a large and expensive table saw to a customer. The head clerk of the hardware department introduced himself as the hardware specialist and sent the toy clerk back to his own department.

Often customers asked for items which were not on the shelves of the sales floor. When the clerk looked for the item it was found on the carts which jammed the stock room aisles. Some customers were told the item they desired wasn't in stock and later the clerk would find it on a cart in the stock room.

When Barton reported his observations of the foregoing situations to Mr. Cornwall, he was told that it was a result of the clerks' adjusting to the new program and to not worry about it. Cornwall pointed out, however, that sales volume had still not improved. He further noted that the sum of all sales reported on the tally sheets was often $500 to $600 more than total department sales according to the cash register.

A few weeks after the instigations of the tally card system Cornwall walked through the hardware department and stopped beside three carts of merchandise left in the aisle of the stock room from the morning of the day before. He talked to the head clerk in an impatient tone and asked him why the carts weren't unloaded. The clerk replied that if Mr. Cornwall had any questions about the department he should ask Mr. Barton. Cornwall picked up the telephone and angrily dialed Barton's office. Barton told him that the handling of merchandise had been preempted by the emphasis on the tally card system of recording sales. Cornwall slammed down the receiver and stormed out of the department.

That afternoon, at Barton's request, Blanding, Cornwall, and Barton visited the four departments. After talking with some of the salespeople, Mr. Blanding sent a memo announcing that the tally card program would be discontinued immediately.

After the program had been terminated, sales clerks still took their breaks separately and conversations seemed to be limited to only the essential topics needed to run the department. Barton and the head sales clerk didn't talk as freely as they had before and some of the head clerks said that Mr. Barton had failed to represent their best interests to Cornwall. Some of the clerks said they thought the tally card system was Barton's idea. The part-time people resumed the major portion of the sales and clerking jobs and the head clerks returned to merchandising. Sales volume in the departments didn't improve.

Margaret Jardine

(A)

Margaret Jardine was sure when she completed her bachelor's degree in business at Oregon State over thirteen years ago that she would go places at Pacific Security Bank. She had graduated with honors from OSU with an emphasis in finance and had joined PSB because she had felt it was a very progressive bank and sufficiently large to allow for movement into a variety of areas. She had done very well in the bank's credit training program and had gone, after one year with the bank, directly to the position of loan officer at the Albany branch of PSB. Albany was located in central Oregon about 100 miles south of Portland, where PSB had its headquarters.

She had been successful in her first assignment, she felt, because she had been able to work closely with Ben Compton, the branch manager, who had given her a good deal of direction and guidance on handling accounts during her first year or two. She had also put in a great deal of extra time in that assignment keeping up with pending loan requests and making sure of each analysis. The only disconcerting thing to Margaret was that she had spent a full seven years in the assignment. This, she felt, had been too long.

When Ben Compton left the bank, Margaret felt there were a lot of reasons why she should be his replacement. When she did get the position as Albany branch manager, this confirmed her faith that she was on her way up in the bank. She was only the second woman in PSB to attain the position of branch manager. Recently, though, she had begun again to wonder about her future with the bank.

She had now been branch manager for over five years, and from her current perspective she could see what kind of opportunities were open to her in the bank. The fact was that there was very little movement among officers in the bank. There was only one other branch manager in the division who had been in his position less time than she had, and there were several who had been branch manager for ten years or more. The division manager, Dan Martin, was new but had himself been a branch manager for twelve years at Corvallis before becoming division manager. Recently at a bank dinner, Dan had introduced her to someone from another division and had referred to her as "one of our new branch managers."

In her four years at Albany, the branch had done well, with substantial increases in loans outstanding and earnings. Recently, though, she felt that she had lost some of her motivation. Now if she put in extra time, it was only out of necessity of getting something done that had to be done. It certainly was not voluntary.

Margaret felt trapped, pigeonholed in some way. She felt like she had no idea where she was going in the bank. Others who had joined the bank and gone through the training program with her had stayed near PSB headquarters in Portland and had gotten a somewhat broader experience than she had. They were probably more promotable now than she was. She was at the stage with the bank where, although her market value was still high, her salary increases were getting smaller and smaller and her options were becoming more limited. Recently, Margaret had turned down a very attractive offer from Northwestern Security and Exchange, a small finance company in Salem near Albany, because there, too, she thought there would be little opportunity for advancement. Now she wondered if it would have been better to take the opportunity.

Still, there was an ambiguity in Margaret's feelings about the bank. She felt that a move to corporate headquarters would be advantageous for her at this point in her career. At least that seemed like the next logical move; and if she could do that, there was a great likelihood she would be made an AVP. Yet she had really come to enjoy living in Albany. She was not sure that she wanted to leave Albany for the big-city atmosphere of Portland even if a better opportunity presented itself there. Her dilemma was that as long as she stayed in Albany, there was no place for her to go in the bank, and realistically speaking, an offer to go to Portland was not exactly imminent.

After dialing Northwestern's number, only to hang up before it rang, Margaret decided she would put off any decision for at least a month so she could have plenty of time to think over her situation. Besides, Dan Martin had called from division headquarters and asked to see her on Monday morning. This would be a good time, she felt, to raise her concerns with Dan and to get his ideas.

(B)

Dan Martin had felt like he had it coming. After twelve years as manager of the Corvallis, Oregon, branch office of Pacific Security Bank, Dan had been made division manager of PSB's southern division. PSB was a large northwestern bank centered at Portland and the southern division covered most of the southern half of Oregon. Since division headquarters were in Corvallis, Dan had not had to move with the promotion.

Along with the benefits, the new position had brought its share of headaches. Dan's biggest challenge, he felt, was keeping the branch managers in his division motivated. Margaret Jardine, the branch manager at Albany, was of particular concern to Dan. Margaret was a very promising young employee who, at 36, still had a bright future with the bank. Margaret's problem was not exactly motivation, since she was one of the most outstanding performers in the division and her branch had significantly bettered its financial position during her term as branch manager. Nor was her problem one of complacency or stagnation. While several of the other branch managers had been in their positions for ten years or more, Margaret had only been a branch manager for five years or so.

From Dan's point of view, Margaret's problem was simply that she had become dissatisfied with the bank. She apparently felt, from comments she had made to Dan and Ed Finnerty, the former division manager, that she had not had sufficient opportunity to move around within the bank and to gain a broad exposure to PSB's operation. She also felt, according to Ed, that her advancement opportunities had not come quickly enough. Ed had said that he expected her to leave PSB sometime in the near future if she could not get the kind of opportunity she wanted within the bank.

Of late, Dan had noticed a subtle change in her attitude. Margaret seemed to be less enthusiastic than Dan had come to expect of her and had been, on occasion, very critical of PSB's operations. One or two of the other branch managers in the division had described her as being "cynical" and even "apathetic." Dan decided he had better bring her in to talk over her situation.

Dan turned to her file to learn more about her background and her history with PSB. Margaret had been at the Albany branch for twelve of her thirteen years with the bank. She had spent only seven years as a loan officer before becoming the branch manager. That she had been very highly rated in her appraisals throughout her career also corroborated Dan's impression of her. Her salary increases had been generally quite high. Considering the age at which she had become a branch manager and the kind of increases she had received, it

was difficult to understand her dissatisfaction.

Dan read through the appraisals Ed Finnerty had written on her in the last few years. The following comment from her most recent appraisal was typical:

"Margaret is a highly competent professional with sound quantitative skills and credit judgment as well as the skills necessary for bank leadership. She gets along well with the people who work with and for her and the Albany branch has shown consistent improvement under her directgion."

Dan found some of Ed's concluding remarks interesting:

"Margaret is anxious to continue her career at Pacific Security and looks forward in the future to taking on new and diverse assignments within the bank. She would like, however, to remain in the southern division and her preference would be to remain in or around Albany, where she has lived for some time."

It occurred to Dan that Margaret wanted to have her cake and eat it, too. She could never really advance in the bank without moving close to Portland. To remain in Albany was impossible if she really wanted to develop her career at the bank. Dan might be able to offer her a divisional assignment in Corvallis sometime down the line, but this would not really be a step up for her, and Dan was not sure she would want to move to Corvallis. Dan did not want to see her leave the bank, and he also felt that her present frame of mind needed to be changed if she ever wanted to advance beyond her present position at the bank. Not knowing exactly what he planned to say to Margaret or what he could do for her, Dan phoned her and arranged an appointment for the following Monday morning.

Biff Loman: To suffer fifty weeks of the year for the sake of two-week vacation, when all you really desire is to be outside with your shirt off. And always to have to get ahead of the next fella. And still that's how you build a future.
Arthur Miller, *Death of a Salesman*

Work expands so as to fill the time available for its completion . . . work (and especially paperwork) is thus elastic in its demands on time, it is manifest that there need be little or no relationship between the work to be done and the size of the staff to which it may be assigned.
C. Northcote Parkinson; *Parkinson's Law*

"The team that makes the most mistakes will probably win." There is much truth in that statement if you analyze it properly. The doer makes mistakes, and I want doers on my team — players who make things happen.
John Wooden, *They Call Me Coach*

EXERCISES

Motivational style exercise

We all have assumptions with respect to the motivating forces in behavior. Sometimes we find people have conflicting assumptions. Also, it often turns out that when we are required to state our assumptions we may not like some of them. An exercise such as this one allows you to approximate some of your own assumptions and then develop a profile where you can look at yourself compared to other students. Also, you can compare your adjusted score to that of the average middle manager.

Motivational style questionnaire

Instructions

Think about what you would do in a supervisory role in relation to handling your subordinates. There are 36 pairs of statements which may describe what you would do in that setting. Read each pair of statements and decide which one best applies to you. Then mark an "X" in the box next to that statement.

statement in item 1 best describes what you would do in your job, then place an "X" in the box which appears under column B.

You must answer all questions. Some questions you will find hard to distinguish because both seem to apply or neither seem to apply. Nevertheless a choice must be made as to which of the two is more characteristic of you.

Please be sure that you place your "X" in the box next to the statement you have chosen.

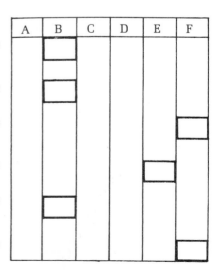

1. I believe that once the goals have been set, then each man should have enough motivation to achieve them.

or

I will give responsibility, but take it away if performance is not forthcoming.

2. I tell subordinates not to worry about others' performance but rather to concentrate on self-improvement.

or

I feel that reports are not very necessary in a situation where trust has been established.

3. I have high standards of performance and have less sympathy for those whose performance falls short.

or

When a subordinate's plan is inappropriate, I stimulate him to re-think and come up with another plan.

4. I believe that human rights and values are more important than the immediate job on hand.

or

I reward good work and feel that punishment for non-performance has limited use.

5. I suggest alternative ways of doing things rather than indicate the way I prefer it myself.

or

I think that subordinates should be able to overcome difficulties in the way to achievement by themselves.

6. When alternatives are described to me I am not long in indicating the course of action I prefer.

or

When a subordinate disagrees with me, I am careful to give my reasons why I want it done a certain way.

7. I think that disciplining employees does more harm than good.

or

I develop a close personal relationship with subordinates because I believe this marks out a good manager.

8. I reward good work and feel that punishment for non-performance has limited use.

or

When a subordinate fails to perform I let him know of the failure in a firm and reasoned manner.

9. I expect my subordinates to carry out plans I have prepared.

or

I think that subordinates should be able to overcome difficulties in the way to achievement by themselves.

10. When I make a decision, I take the additional step of persuading my subordinates to accept it.

or

I feel that accepted plans should generally represent the ideas of my subordinates.

11. I feel that people develop best in a trusting environment.

or

I believe that once goals have been set, then each man should have enough motivation to achieve them.

12. When I discipline a subordinate I am definite in letting him know what he has done wrong.

or

I feel that reports are not very necessary in a situation where trust has been established.

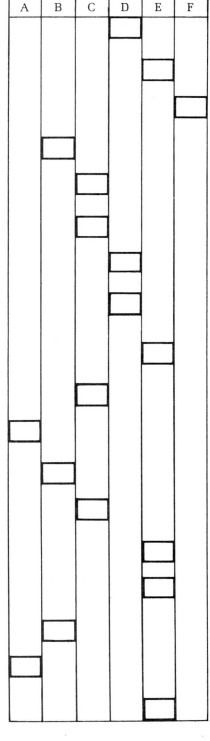

	A	B	C	D	E	F

13. I believe that firm discipline is important to keep the work moving. **[A]**

or

I insist subordinates submit detailed reports on their activities. **[A]**

14. I believe that a popular leader is better than an unpopular one. **[D]**

or

I believe that subordinates should not be too discouraged by setbacks in the job, but rather should be able to clear blockages themselves. **[B]**

15. I believe that it is a manager's job to arouse the will to achieve in subordinates. **[F]**

or

I am constantly concerned with high standards of performance and encourage subordinates to reach these standards. **[F]**

16. I am available to subordinates as a consultant and adviser when it is agreed they need help. **[E]**

or

I feel that people develop best in a trusting environment. **[E]**

17. When a subordinate's plan is inappropriate, I stimulate him to re-think and come up with another plan. **[F]**

or

I often give orders in the form of a suggestion, but make clear what I want. **[C]**

18. I believe that job security and benefits such as super-annuation plans are important for employee happiness. **[D]**

or

When a subordinate's plan is inappropriate I stimulate him to re-think and come up with another plan. **[F]**

19. In the long run, I will fire a man I consider to be unmanageable. **[A]**

or

I discourage arguments which upset the harmony amongst subordinates. **[D]**

20. I feel that reports are not very necessary in a situation where trust has been established. **[E]**

or

I expect my subordinates to carry out plans I have prepared. **[A]**

21. I am not so concerned with establishing close personal relationships as in getting subordinates to follow my example. **[B]**

or

Statement	A	B	C	D	E	F
I believe that human rights and values are more important than the immediate job on hand.				☐		
22. I watch for improvement in individual performance rather than insist on high level performance from subordinates.						☐
or I discourage arguments which upset the harmony amongst subordinates.				☐		
23. I believe that subordinates should not be too discouraged by setbacks in the job, but rather should be able to clear blockages themselves.		☐				
or When I make a decision, I take the additional step of persuading my subordinates to accept it.			☐			
24. When a subordinate disagrees with me, I am careful to give my reasons why I want it done a certain way.			☐			
or I think that disciplining employees does more harm than good				☐		
25. I am constantly concerned with high standards of performance and encourage subordinates to reach these standards.						☐
or I believe that firm discipline is important to keep the work moving.	☐					
26. I discourage arguments which upset the harmony amongst subordinates.				☐		
or I expect my subordinates to follow my instructions closely.	☐					
27. I develop a close personal relationship with subordinates because I believe this marks out a good manager.				☐		
or When alternatives are described to me I am not long in indicating the course of action I prefer.			☐			
28. When a subordinate fails to perform I let him know of the failure in a firm and reasoned manner.			☐			
or I am not so concerned with establishing close personal relationships as in getting subordinates to follow my example.		☐				
29. I expect my subordinates to follow my instructions closely.	☐					
or I often give orders in the form of a suggestion, but make it clear what I want.			☐			

	A	B	C	D	E	F

30. I will give responsibility, but take it away if performance is not forthcoming.

or

I am available to subordinates as a consultant and adviser when it is agreed that they need help.

31. I think that subordinates should be able to overcome difficulties in the way to achievement by themselves.

or

When I discipline a subordinate I am definite in letting him know what he has done wrong.

32. I tend to rely on self-direction and self-control rather than doing much controlling myself.

or

I suggest alternative ways of doing things rather than indicate the way I prefer it myself.

33. I seek to reduce resistance to my decision by indicating what subordinates have to gain from my decision.

or

I watch for improvement in individual performance rather than insist on high level performance from subordinates.

34. I often give orders in the form of a suggestion, but make clear what I want.

or

In the long run, I will fire a man I consider to be unmanageable.

35. I insist subordinates submit detailed reports on their activities.

or

I am constantly concerned with high standards of performance and encourage subordinates to reach these standards.

36. I feel that accepted plans should generally represent the ideas of my subordinates.

or

I believe that a popular leader is better than an unpopular one.

Scoring key and profile

To compute your motivational style, count the number of Xs you made in column A; then do the same for those you made in column B and so forth through column F.

Put the number of Xs for each column here:

A	B	C	D	E	F	
						=36
+1	0	+2	0	+1	-2	
A=	B=	C=	D=	D=	F=	

To shade in your Motivation Style Profile, simply shade the space using your adjusted score above. For instance, if your "A" for Coercer score is 6, then you shade your profile thus:

		1	2	3	4	5	6	7	8	9	10	11⁺

| A ☐ | Coercer | ░░░░░░░░░░░░ |

		1	2	3	4	5	6	7	8	9	10	11⁺

A ☐	Coercer	
B ☐	Pace-setter	
C ☐	Authoritarian	
D ☐	Affiliator	
E ☐	Democrat	
F ☐	Coach	

To further analyze your profile, you could compare yourself to the average middle manager adjusted score of 6 on each of the six scales. Also, you should turn back to the McClelland article, "That Urge to Achieve," (p. 00) and review his classification of needs. The categories in this profile fit McClelland's framework as follows:

You also might note that the "I" variable in each need category is the strongest or more extreme indicator of the need. The "II" variable is a less extreme emphasis. This means that you lean in that direction, but it is a more facilitating rather than obsessive force.

n Ach	Pace Setter	(I)
	Coach	(II)
n Power	Coercer	(I)
	Authoritarian	(II)
n Aff	Affiliator	(I)
	Democrat	(II)

Perception exercise

I magination and creative ability can be very useful to you in analyzing and interpreting organizational phenomena. The following exercise gives you the opportunity to use your imagination to describe and interpret common situations that occur in organizations. Four pictures are provided to give you a starting point from which you should describe, using your imagination, the people involved, their relationships, what has and what will happen, what they are saying or thinking, etc. Do not merely describe the picture, but make up a story based upon it. The pictures are intentionally very general and can be interpreted in many different ways. Look at the pictures briefly, then begin to write your stories.

Take no more than five minutes to write each story. They need not be long but should be as complete and yet as spontaneous as you can make them in the time allowed. When you have completed one, go directly to the next one. It is not necessary to go back and refine and revise your stories; just write what comes to mind as you interpret the pictures.

In order for this to be a meaningful learning experience, avoid looking ahead at the scoring key until you have completed your stories.

After you have completed your stories, form into groups of three. Each person in turn should read one story to the other two. Using the scoring summary, discuss the themes and motives that appear to be dominant in the story. Try to determine whether the story is primarily concerned with *n* Aff, *n* Ach, or *n* Pow. Try to understand why the story suggests the different needs that become evident as you relate the content of the story to the three basic needs that McClelland identified. How does the operation of these needs in yourself affect the manner in which you behave in organizations?

After you have each read and analyzed one of your stories, go on to another one and continue the process until you have completed all of your stories or until you run out of time.

The purpose of this exercise is not so much to analyze each individual's inner drives as to understand, through personal experience with these concepts, how these motives affect your behavior in relation to other people in organizations.

Just look at the picture briefly (10–15 seconds), and write the story it suggests.

Just look at the picture briefly (10–15 seconds), and write the story it suggests.

Just look at the picture briefly (10–15 seconds), and write the story it suggests.

Just look at the picture briefly (10–15 seconds), and write the story it suggests.

Scoring summary

Over the last twenty years, David McClelland has done a great deal of research into the inner motivations of people. In his research, he developed the Thematic Apperception Test, which consists of showing a series of pictures to his subjects asking them to respond to them in an imaginative story about what the people in the pictures were doing or thinking. He analyzed the content of these stories for a great number of people and determined that there were three basic motives or needs which occur in different mixtures in different people. He called these three motives: need for achievement (*n* Ach), need for affiliation *n* Aff), and need for power (*n* Pow). Other researchers used the same projective techniques as McClelland and included hunger, sex, fear, aggression, and a number of other drives in their research. For our purposes, we are primarily concerned with *n* Aff, *n* Ach, and *n* Pow as they relate to behavior of people in organizations.

The differing mixtures of these three factors in people may result in different behavior patterns in interpersonal relationships. The relationships between people, which are determined by the interplay of their behaviors, are strongly affected by the motives of the individuals involved. These factors influence many, if not all, of the interpersonal and organizational dynamics that are commonly observed where people must organize to accomplish some goal.

The following is a summary of the basic themes that McClelland and his associates used to identify their motives in scoring the T.A.T. Since we do not need the complexity and sophistication that McClelland developed, we have simplified and summarized the scoring key. Use the following key as a guideline to understand the motives evident in your stories.

Need for achievement.

Achievement motive, *n* Ach, is reflected in behavior which strives for performing excellence. Three main indications of *n* Ach are the following:

1. Competition with a standard of excellence
   a. Some competitive activity where winning or doing as well as or better than others is explicitly stated; winning a competition, the desire to show that one can indeed accomplish some stated task.
   b. The statement that someone feels "good" over success or "bitter" over a failure, anticipation of good feelings when a task is successfully completed, etc.
   c. Evidence of concern for a standard of excellence must be present; a statement that someone is "working hard" or accomplishing something, without mention of a goal or standard, should not be considered *n* Ach.
2. Unique accomplishment
   a. Someone is concerned with accomplishing something out of the ordinary, such as an invention, an artistic creation, or some other extraordinary accomplishment. An explicit statement of a goal or standard of excellence is not necessary when the task is unique and will be accepted as a personal accomplishment when completed.
3. Long-term involvement
   a. A character is concerned with or involved in the attainment of a long-term achievement goal. Career involvement or preparations for a profession make possible

the inference of a standard of excellence unless some other primary reason is clearly stated.

b. The relationship of a limited task to a long-term goal must be clearly stated if it is to be considered *n* Ach.

Need for affiliation

Affiliation Motive, *n* Aff, is concerned with the need to be with, liked by, and accepted by other people.

1. *n* Aff is scored when concern for establishing, maintaining, or restoring a positive affective relationship with another person is stated. Friendship is a key word. There must be a statement of liking or desire for acceptance or forgiveness concerning a relationship. Mere mention of a relationship, e.g., father-son, husband-wife, does not indicate affiliation motive — only social states.

2. Negative reaction toward a separation or disruption in social or interpersonal ties may be scored as *n* Aff.

3. Positive statement about generally accepted affiliation activities, such as parties, reunions, visits, bull sessions, can be considered evidence for *n* Aff.

4. Nurturant actions, such as consoling, helping, being concerned about the happiness or well-being of others, are evidence for *n* Aff.

Need for power

Power motive, *n* Pow, is evident where one person in the story is concerned with control of the means of influence of other people in the story. *n* Pow is characterized by the following:

1. Statements of feelings about attainment or maintenance of the control of the means of influencing a person. Feeling about winning an argument; feeling about the avoidance of weakness; desires to teach, inspire other people out of the context of teacher; etc.

2. A definite statement about someone actually doing something to gain control of the means of influence of another person, e.g., a character must be arguing a point, demanding or forcing something, giving a command, punishing someone, telling someone off, etc.

3. A statement of an interpersonal relationship which is culturally defined as a superior/subordinate one and in which there is some control of the means of influencing a person. There must be some mention of both the superior and the subordinate and some mention of the effect of the superior on the subordinate.

Career goals exercise

Most people spend time thinking about their future and what they would like to accomplish in their lifetime. Sometimes that thinking is really daydreaming, such as the thought of becoming a star quarterback for the Green Bay Packers or a movie star. Sometimes that thinking focuses on more immediate objectives, such as, How do I get a job when I graduate? Or, Do I want to go into marketing or accounting? While the future is very important to all of us, very few people think through and write out career goals that would help provide direction to their lives.

Written goals have a number of advantages over unwritten goals:

1. They are more concrete and specific.
2. They are easier to analyze, refine, update, etc.
3. They make it easier to identify and attempt to resolve areas of conflict between goals.

This exercise is designed to get a person started on the activity of analyzing, setting, and refining career goals. Plan to spend at least fifty minutes on this activity.

Part I: Identifying goals

A. Spend ten minutes writing your answers to each of the following questions.
   1. What are my lifetime goals?
      a. Some of the areas of life where goals might be specified include: job, finances, family, social life, community life, spiritual life, etc.
      b. Write down as many goals as possible in the first five minutes; then spend the remaining time refining or modifying those goals.
   2. What would I like to achieve in the next five years?
      (Once again, try to get the goals written down quickly and then spend some time refining them.)
   3. A year from now what would I like to look back on having accomplished during the past twelve months?
B. As a next step, compare the goals under each question and look for possible conflicts or inconsistencies. Then identify the three most important goals under each question and rank them in order of importance.

Part II: Career decisions

A. Make the assumption that in the next year you will have to make a decision that will have a significant impact on your career. This decision might be about choosing a major, whether to go on to graduate school, deciding to take a job with company A rather than company B, etc.
   Take a sheet of paper and write *Best possible decision* at the top of

the page on the left side. On the right side write *Worst possible decision.* Beginning with the best, write down the possible outcomes if you were to make the best possible decision in this situation. What is likely to come into your life as a result of your making such a good decision? What would happen to you in your career, your family, your social life, etc.?

Now move to the worst possible decision. Write down the possible outcomes if you were to make the worst possible decision in this situation.

What is likely to come into your life as result of your making such a bad decision? What would happen to you in your career, your family, your social life, etc.

B. As a next step, compare the outcomes under each heading and look for possible conflicts and inconsistencies. Be prepared to discuss your conclusions in class.

Married students may find it valuable to discuss this experience with their spouse.

The reluctant operator

Sometimes the perceptions of superior and subordinate are so different that neither understands the problem as seen by the other party. Motives often can be identified only through long and careful discussion. This role play is an opportunity to consider this problem through the experience of conflict from both superior and subordinate viewpoints.

Try to think and act as if you really were the character whose role you have been assigned. Think of the role in terms of contemporary implications and let your feelings develop as if you were actually involved. Should issues develop that are not covered by the role, adapt or innovate accordingly.

To conceptualize your role, it is usually best to read it carefully two or three times; then close the book and think about it for a few minutes. Do not read the other roles; try to develop an approach in terms of the information given and your own interpretation of how a person in that position would likely behave. After you have the role in mind, do not reread it during the process of the role play.

Role for Jim Johnson, supervisor

You are the supervisor for a crew of twelve individuals in a small production operation. You have the typical problems any supervisor must put up with — the crew horsing around at times, violation of safety rules, some absenteeism and tardiness — but basically a pretty good crew. The quality of the work is consistently high. It looks as if you are going to have an expanded work load in the future, and because of increased administrative demands — paperwork, meetings, and so on — you and the superintendent have decided that you need an assistant supervisor.

You have the feeling that the superintendent is going to be promoted and that you have the best chance among the five supervisors of making superintendent. This means that the assistant you choose has a good shot at becoming supervisor himself. In reviewing your crew, you have observed that the majority of the members are older and not very good prospects for the assistant supervisor job. Most of the younger crew members do not know the job well enough to assume any supervisory responsibility.

There is one individual, however, who might really be able to do the job — if he would just change his attitude. You have in mind Bill Black. Bill is a young fellow, about 25, who has mastered the various jobs in your area. He can do them all better and faster than anyone else. You think he would make an excellent supervisor with just a little more experience — especially in dealing with people. The problem is that, whenever you have asked him to do little extra things, he doesn't seem interested. He can perform any job, but that is all he wants to accomplish. When he has completed his job, he is through. Several times you have told him that he has a good future in the organization and you would like to help him develop his leadership ability. Again, he does not seem interested. You still think he is your best bet, however, and so you have decided to talk to him — to attempt once more to convince him that if he changed his attitude he could really get ahead. He is on his way to your office now.

Role for Bill Black, operator

You are one of twelve members of a production crew supervised by Jim Johnson. Most of the members of the crew are duds, but the jobs are simple and the work seems to get done. The pay is not very good, and you feel that any capable person would be crazy to stay with this organization. But then, you really do not care. You are just here temporarily while you save a little money so you can return to school. You want to finish your B.S. in engineering so that you can get a really good job. The only reason you are working is that your wife had a baby and the part-time job you had in school just didn't give you enough cash to meet all your financial obligations.

There are some difficulties with your present position, however. You can't let Jim know you see your job only as temporary or he would let you go. And lately he has been asking you to do all kinds of extra things. You don't understand what he is getting at. You just want to do your job and forget it. Why does he have to keep bugging you? Now he wants to see you again. He has asked you to come to his office. You wonder if it is about a job yesterday when one of the older guys messed up and you tried to help him. You weren't able to correct the problem, and it looked a little like your mistake, but that wasn't a very big deal. Oh, well, you can bluff your way through another session — it has always worked before. You will just complain about the poor pay — lowest in the area; the dumb workers — can't even figure out what is going on; the poor materials — purchasing must really mess up, and so on. You are just about to knock on Jim's door.

Things are not always as they first appear

3

Differing viewpoints on the impact of groups

Groups in organizations have become the subject of widely differing viewpoints in recent years. Many individuals underestimate the impact of groups; they believe that, to get along well in an organization, all they have to do is to meet their boss's expectations. For some it is surprising to discover that informal groups within an organization have real power to make their lives easy or difficult, depending on the acceptance of the individual into the group. Similarly, some managers tend to ignore informal groups and have little faith in committees. In their attempts to develop an effective organization, they focus exclusively on the relationship between manager and subordinates. These managers' attempts to introduce changes are often frustrated by resistance from informal groups.

On the other hand, some individuals overestimate the impact of groups. Such people focus only on the interests of the group and ignore the wishes of the boss. Usually that is a risky strategy. Likewise, some managers rely heavily on groups for making and implementing decisions. But involving every individual in every decision can lead to inefficiency and a very slow decision-making process.

These extreme positions are not helpful in dealing with work groups. However, the examples illustrate that groups do have a major impact on their members, on other groups, and on the parent organization. This section presents a variety of viewpoints on important issues concerning groups in organizations.

Levitt starts out this section with a proposal that organizations should be built around groups. He suggests that the small face-to-face group is the most powerful tool available to managers and that they should consider building organizations using this important material. He lists several reasons why groups should be used more extensively in organizations. Two cases in this section, Great Majestic and Claremont Instrument, provide an opportunity to analyze the impact of informal groups on individuals and the organization.

One area where groups can make a contribution is in decision making. Maier presents an analysis of group problem solving that may help people to be more effective in making decisions in groups. He suggests that a group can be an asset in some aspects of decision making but a liability in others. A better understanding of when and how to use a group in decision making should reduce much of the frustration that people experience in the decision-making process. One problem in decision making concerns the management of agreement. Harvey points out that most people want to be agreeable and get along with others. One negative result of this desire is that many times a group will agree to do something that none of the individuals want to do. He maintains that the inability to cope with agreement rather than the inability to cope with conflict is the most pressing issue of modern organizations. Three exercises in this section, NASA, Winter survival, and Giant Food Company, provide an opportunity to put some of the ideas in these articles into practice.

If we move up the organization ladder one more step, we see that organizations contain many groups that often compete for resources, prestige, power, and so forth. Being caught between conflicting groups can prove to be a very confusing and frustrating experience. Schein's article points out some consequences of intergroup competition and suggests ways of reducing negative outcomes. The Northwest Industries case and the Intergroup exercise provide an opportunity to apply those concepts in concrete situations.

Communication is important in all of the situations we have just described. In virtually any discussion of a problem involving people someone is bound to say, "It's a communication problem and if only that were straightened out everything would be okay." But what are the causes of communication problems and what can be done about them? Gibb's article identifies communication behaviors that are likely to be perceived as defensive or supportive. He maintains that when people are defensive they are less able to perceive accurately the motives, the values, and the emotions of the sender. Being aware of behaviors that cause defensiveness can help a person avoid some of them. The communications exercise and all of the cases in the section provide various opportunities to apply effective communication concepts.

In this section we have provided materials on several skill areas. Communications is a skill that most people need to improve. Decision making in groups is a skill that can be developed. In addition, we have focused on observing behavior in groups and in conducting meetings. The Group Observer Instructions present a set of questions that should help the student to be aware of a wide range of behaviors in a group setting. Students who frequently practice observing behavior in groups are most likely to significantly improve their skills in this area. The Blake article presents some useful ideas on how to hold effective meetings. This is also an area where practice should help improve one's effectiveness.

Finally, we look at some of the implications of power and obedience. Vandivier presents a case study of managers who order their sub-ordinates to carry out activities that are dishonest and unethical. The pressures in organizations that lead to these kinds of actions need to be carefully analyzed. This article raises a number of questions about power and obedience and usually stimulates a lively discussion.

Group behavior involves a complex set of relationships. This section provides concepts and ideas to help bring order to that chaotic world. In addition, applying those ideas to the cases and exercises should help develop relevant skills as well as increase awareness of the importance of this topic.

READINGS

Suppose we took groups seriously...

Harold J. Leavitt

Introduction

This chapter is mostly a fantasy, but not a utopian fantasy. As the title suggests, it tries to spin out some things that might happen if we really took small groups seriously; if, that is, we really used groups, rather than individuals, as the basic building blocks for an organization.

This seems an appropriate forum for such a fantasy. It was fifty years ago, at Hawthorne, that the informal face-to-face work group was discovered. Since then groups have been studied inside and out; they have been experimented with, observed, built, and taken apart. Small groups have become the major tool of the applied behavioral scientist. Organizational Development methods are groups methods. Almost all of what is called participative management is essentially based on group techniques.

So the idea of using groups as organizational mechanisms is by no means new or fantastic. The fantasy comes in proposing to start with groups, not add them in; to design organizations from scratch around small groups rather than around individuals.

But right from the start, talk like that appears to violate a deep and important value, individualism. But this fantasy will not really turn out to be anti-individualistic in the end.

The rest of this chapter will briefly address the following questions: (1) Is it fair to say that groups have not been taken very seriously in organizational design? (2) Why are groups even worth thinking about as organizational building materials? What are the characteristics of groups that might make them interesting enough to be worth serious attention? (3) What would it mean "to take groups seriously"? Just what kinds of things would have to be done differently? (4) What compensatory changes would probably be needed in other aspects of the organization, to have groups as the basic unit? And finally, (5) Is the idea of designing the organization around small face-to-face groups a very radical idea, or is it just an extension of a direction in which we are already going?

Haven't groups been taken seriously enough already?

The argument that groups have not been taken "seriously" doesn't seem a hard one to make. The contemporary ideas about groups didn't really come along until the thirties and fourties. By that time a logical, rationalistic tradition for the construction of organizations already existed. That tradition was very heavily based on the notion that the individual was the construction unit. The logic moved from the projected task backward. Determine the task, the goal, then find an appropriate structure and technology, and last of all fit individual human beings into predefined man-sized pieces of the action. That was, for instance, what industrial psychology was all about during its development between the two world wars. It was concerned almost entirely with individual differences and worked in the service of structuralists, fitting square human pegs to predesigned square holes. The role of the psychologist was thus ancillary to the role of the designers of the whole organization. It was a back-up, supportive role that followed more than it led design.

It was not just the logic of classical organizational theory that concentrated on the individual. The whole entrepreneurial tradition of American society supported it. Individuals, at least male individuals, were taught achievement motivation. They were taught to seek individual evaluation, to compete, to see the world, organizational or otherwise, as a place in which to strive for individual accomplishment and satisfaction.

In those respects the classical design of organizations was constant with the then existent cultural landscape. Individualized organizational structures blended with the environment of individualism. All the accessories fell into place: individual incentive schemes for hourly workers, individual merit rating and assessment schemes, tests for selection of individuals.

The unique characteristic of the organization was that it was not simply a race track within which individuals could compete, but a system in which somehow the competitive behavior of individuals could be coordinated, harnessed and controlled in the interest of the common tasks. Of course one residual of all that was a continuing tension between individual and organization, with the organization seeking to control and coordinate the individual's activities at the same time that it tried to motivate him; while the competitive individual insisted on reaching well beyond the constraints imposed upon him by the organization. One product of this tension became the informal organization discovered here at Western; typically an informal coalition designed to fight the system.

Then it was discovered that groups could be exploited for what management saw as positive purposes, *toward* productivity instead of away from it. There followed the era of experimentation with small face-to-face groups. We learned to patch them on to existing organizations as bandaids to relieve tensions between individual and organization. We promoted coordination through group methods. We learned that groups were useful to discipline and control recalcitrant individuals.

Groups were fitted onto organizations. The group skills of individual members improved so that they could coordinate their efforts more effectively, control deviants more effectively and gain more commitment from subordinate individuals. But groups were seen primarily as tools to be tacked on and utilized in the pre-existing individualized organizational system. With a few notable exceptions, like Rensis Likert (1961), most did not design organizations around groups. On the contrary, as some of the ideas about small groups began to be tacked onto existing organizational models, they generated new tensions and conflicts of their own. Managers complained not only that groups were slow, but that they diffused responsibility, vitiated the power of the hierarchy because they were too "democratic" and created small in-group empires which were very hard for others to penetrate. There was the period, for example, of the great gap between T-group training (which had to be conducted on "cultural islands") and the organization back home. The T-groupers therefore talked a lot about the "reentry problem," which meant in part the problem of movement from a new culture (the T-group culture) designed around groups back into the organizational culture designed around individuals.

But of course groups didn't die despite their difficulties. How could they die? They had always been there, though often unrecognized tools. For organizations were growing, and professionalizing, and the need for better coordination grew even as the humanistic expectations of individuals also grew. So "acknowledged" groups (as distinct from "natural," informal groups) became fairly firmly attached even to conservative organizations, but largely as compensating addenda very often reluctantly backed into by organizational managers.

Groups have never been given a chance. It is as though someone had insisted that automobiles be designed to fit the existing terrain rather than build roads to adapt to automobiles.

Are groups worth considering as fundamental building blocks?

Why would groups be more interesing than individuals as basic design units around which to build organizations? What are the prominent characteristics of small groups? Why are they interesting? Here are several answers:

First, small groups seem to be good for people. They can satisfy important membership needs. They can provide a moderately wide range of activities for individual members. They can provide support in times of stress and crisis. They are settings in which people can learn not only cognitively but empirically to be reasonably trusting and helpful to one another. Second, groups seem to be good problem finding tools. They seem to be useful in promoting innovation and creativity. Third, in a wide variety of decision situations, they make better decisions than individuals do. Fourth, they are great tools for implementation. They gain commitment from their members so that group decisions are likely to be willingly carried out. Fifth, they can control and discipline individual members in ways that are often extremely difficult through more impersonal quasi-legal disciplinary systems. Sixth, as organizations grow large, small groups appear to be useful mechanisms for fending off many of the negative effects of large size. They help to prevent communication lines from growing too long, the hierarchy from growing too steep, and the individual from getting lost in the crowd.

There is a seventh, but altogether different kind of argument for taking groups seriously. Thus far the designer of organizations seemed to have a choice. He could build an individualized *or* a groupy organization. A groupy organization will, de facto, have to deal with individuals; but what was learned here so long ago is that individualized organizations, must, de facto, deal with groups. Groups are natural phenomena, and facts of organizational life. They can be created but their spontaneous development cannot be prevented. The problem is not shall groups exist or not, but shall groups be planned or not? If not, the individualized organizational garden will sprout groupy weeds all over the place. By defining them as weeds instead of flowers, they shall continue, as in earlier days, to be treated as pests, forever fouling up the beauty of rationally designed individualized organizations, forever forming informally (and irrationally) to harass and outgame the planners.

It is likely that the reverse could also be true, that if groups are defined as the flowers and individuals as the weeds, new problems will crop up. Surely they will, but that discussion can be delayed for at least a little while.

Who uses groups best?

So groups look like interesting organizational building blocks. But before going on to consider the implications of designing organizations around groups, one useful heuristic might be to look around the existing world at those places in which groups seem to have been treated somewhat more seriously.

One place groups have become big is in Japanese organizations (Johnson and Ouchi 1974). The Japanese seem to be very groupy, and much less concerned than Americans about issues like individual accountability. Japanese organizations, of course, are thus consonant with Japanese culture, where notions of

individual aggressiveness and competitiveness are deemphasized in favor of self-effacement and group loyalty. But Japanese organizations seem to get a lot done, despite the relative suppression of the individual in favor of the group. It also appears that the advantages of the groupy Japanese style have really come to the fore in large technologically complex organizations.

Another place to look is at American conglomerates. They go to the opposite extreme, dealing with very large units. They buy large organizational units and sell units. They evaluate units. In effect they promote units by offering them extra resources as rewards for good performance. In that sense conglomerates, one might argue, are designed around groups, but the groups in question are often themselves large organizational chunks.

Groups in an individualistic culture

An architect can design a beautiful building which either blends smoothly with its environment or contrasts starkly with it. But organization designers may not have the same choice. If we design an organization which is structurally dissonant with its environment, it is conceivable that the environment will change to adjust to the organization. It seems much more likely, however, that the environment will reject the organization. If designing organizations around groups represents a sharp counterpoint to environmental trends maybe we should abort the idea.

Our environment, one can argue, is certainly highly individualized. But one can also make a less solid argument in the other direction; an argument that American society is going groupy rather than individual this year. Or at least it is going groupy as well as individual. The evidence is sloppy at best. One can reinterpret the student revolution and the growth of anti-establishment feelings at least in part as a reaction to the decline of those institutions that most satisfied social membership and belongingness motives. Certainly popular critics of American society have laid a great deal of emphasis on individualism. It seems possible to argue that, insofar as there has been any significant change in the work ethic in America, the change has been toward a desire for work which is socially as well as egoistically fulfilling, and which satisfies human needs for belongingness and affiliation as well as needs for achievement.

In effect, the usual interpretation of Abraham Maslow's need hierarchy may be wrong. Usually the esteem and self-actualization levels of motivation are emphasized. Perhaps the level that is becoming operant most rapidly is neither of those, but the social-membership level.

The rising role of women in American society also has implications for the groupiness of organizations. There is a moderate amount of evidence that American women have been socialized more strongly into affiliative and relational sorts of attitudes than men. They probably can, in general, more comfortably work in direct achievement roles in group settings, where there are strong relational bonds among members, than in competitive, individualistic settings. Moreover it is reasonable to assume that as women take a more important place in American society, some of their values and attitudes will spill over to the male side.

Although the notion of designing organizations around groups in America in 1974 may be a little premature, it is consonant with cultural trends that may take the idea much more appropriate ten years from now.

But groups are becoming more relevant for organizational as well as cultural reasons. Groups seem to be particularly useful as coordinating and integrating mechanisms for dealing with complex tasks that require the inputs of many kinds of specialized knowledge. In fact the development of matrix-type organizations in high technology industry is perhaps one effort to modify individually designed organizations toward a more groupy direction; not for humanistic reasons but as a consequence of tremendous increases in the informational complexity of the jobs that need to be done.

What might a seriously groupy organization look like?

Just what does it mean to design organizations around groups? Operationally how is that different from designing organizations around individuals? One approach to an answer is simply to take the things organizations do with individuals and try them out with groups. The idea is to raise the level from the atom to the molecule, and *select* groups rather than individuals, *train* groups rather than individuals, *pay* groups rather than individuals, *promote* groups rather than individuals, *design jobs* for groups rather than individuals, *fire* groups rather than individuals, and so on down the list of activities which organizations have traditionally carried on in order to use human beings in their organizations.

Some of the items on that list seem easy to handle at the group level. For example, it doesn't seem terribly hard to design jobs for groups. In effect that is what top management already does for itself to a great extent. It gives specific jobs to committees, and often runs itself as a group. The problem seems to be a manageable one: designing job sets which are both big enough to require a small number of persons and also small enough to require only a small number of persons. Big enough in this context means not only jobs that would occupy the hands of group members but that would provide opportunities for learning and expansion.

Ideas like evaluating, promoting, and paying groups raise many more difficult but interesting problems. Maybe the best that can be said for such ideas is that they provide opportunities for thinking creatively about pay and evaluation. Suppose, for example, that as a reward for good work the group gets a larger salary budget than it got last year. Suppose the allocation for increases within the group is left to the group members. Certainly one can think up all sorts of difficulties that might arise. But are the potential problems necessarily any more difficult than those now generated by individual merit raises? Is there any company in America that is satisfied with its existing individual performance appraisal and salary allocation schemes? At least the issues of distributive justice within small groups would presumably be open to internal discussion and debate. One might even permit the group to allocate payments to individuals differentially at different times, in accordance with some criteria of current contribution that they might establish.

As far as performance evaluation is concerned, it is probably easier for people up the hierachy to assess the performance of total groups than it is to assess the performance of individual members well down the hierarchy. Top

managers of decentralized organizations do it all the time, except that they usually reward the formal leader of the decentralized unit rather than the whole unit.

The notion of promoting groups raises another variety of difficulties. One thinks of physically transferring a whole group, for example, and of the costs associated with training a whole group to do a new job, especially if there are no bridging individuals. But there may be large advantages too. If a group moves, its members already know how to work with one another. Families may be less disrupted by movement if several move at the same time.

There is the problem of selection. Does it make sense to select groups? Initially, why not? Can't means be found for selecting not only for appropriate knowledge and skill but also for potential ability to work together? There is plenty of groundwork in the literature already.

After the initial phase, there will of course be problems of adding or subtracting individuals from existing groups. We already know a good deal about how to help new members get integrated into old groups. Incidentally, I was told recently by a plant manager in the midwest about an oddity he had encountered; the phenomenon of groups applying for work. Groups of three or four people have been coming to his plant seeking employment together. They wanted to work together and stay together.

Costs and danger points

To play this game of designing organizations around groups, what might be some important danger points? In general, a group-type organization is somewhat more like a free market than present organizations. More decisions would have to be worked out ad hoc, in a continually changing way. So one would need to schedule more negotiation time both within and between groups.

One would encounter more issues of justice, for the individual vis-s-vis the group and for groups vis-a-vis one another. More and better arbitration mechanisms would probably be needed along with highly flexible and rapidly adaptive recordkeeping. But modern record-keeping technology is, potentially, both highly flexible and rapidly adaptive.

Another specific issue is the provision of escape hatches for individuals. Groups have been known to be cruel and unjust to the deviant members. One existing escape route for the individual would of course continue to exist: departure from the organization. Another might be easy means of transfer to another group.

Another obvious problem: If groups are emphasized by rewarding them, paying them, promoting them, and so on, groups may begin to perceive themselves as power centers, in competitive conflict with other groups. Intergroup hostilities are likely to be exacerbated unless we can design some new coping mechanisms into the organization. Likert's proposal for solving that sort of problem (and others) is linking pin concept. The notion is that individuals serve as members of more than one group, both up and down the hierarchy and horizontally. But Likert's scheme seems to me to assume fundamentally individualized organizations in the sense that it is still individuals who get paid, promoted and so on. In a more groupy organization, the linking pin concept has to be modified so that an individual might be a part-time member of more than one group, but still a real member.

That is, for example, a portion of an individual's pay might come from each group in accordance with that group's perception of his contribution.

Certainly much more talk, both within and between groups, would be a necessary accompaniment of group emphasis; though we might argue about whether more talk should be classified as a cost or benefit. In any case careful design of escape hatches for individuals and connections among groups would be as important in this kind of organization as would stairways between floors in the design of a private home.

There is also the danger of over-designing groups. All groups in the orgainzation need not look alike. Quite to the contrary. Task and technology should have significant effects on the shapes and sizes of different subgroups within the large organization. Just as individuals end up adjusting the edges of their jobs to themselves and themselves to their jobs, we should expect flexibility within groups, allowing them to adapt and modify themselves to whatever the task and technology demand.

Another initially scary problem associated with groups is the potential loss of clear formal individual leadership. Without formal leaders how will we motivate people? Without leaders how will we control and discipline people? Without leaders how will we pinpoint responsiblilty? Even as I write those questions I cannot help but feel that they are archaic. They are questions which are themselves a product of the basic individual building block design of old organizations. The problem is not leaders so much as the performance of leadership functions. Surely groups will find leaders, but they will emerge from the bottom up. Given a fairly clear job description, some groups, in some settings, will set up more or less permanent leadership roles. Others may let leadership vary as the situation demands, or as a function of the power that individuals within any group may possess relative to the group's needs at that time. A reasonable amount of process time can be built in to enable groups to work on the leadership problem, but the problem will have to be resolved within each group. On the advantage side of the ledger, this may even get rid of a few hierarchical levels. There should be far less need for individuals who are chiefly supervisors of other individuals' work. Groups can serve as hierarchical leaders of other groups.

Two other potential costs: With an organization of groups, there may be a great deal of infighting, and power and conflict issues will come even more to the fore than they do now. Organizations of groups may become highly political, with coalitions lining up against one another on various issues. If so, the rest of the organizational system will have to take those political problems into account, both by setting up sensible systems of intercommunications among groups, and by allocating larger amounts of time and expertise to problems of conflict resolution.

But this is not a new problem unique to groupy organizations. Conflict among groups is prevalent in large organizations which are political systems now. But because these issues have not often been foreseen and planned for, the mechanisms for dealing with them are largely ad hoc. As a result, conflict is often dealt with in extremely irrational ways.

But there is another kind of intergroup power problem that may become extremely important and difficult in groupy organizations. There is a real danger that relatively autonomous and cohesive groups may be closed, not only to other groups but more importantly to staff advice or to new technological inputs.

These problems exist at present, of course, but they may be exacerbated by group structure. I cannot see any perfect way to handle those problems. One possibility may be to make individual members of staff groups part-time members of line groups. Another is to work harder to educate line groups to potential staff contributions. Of course the reward system, the old market system, will probably be the strongest force for keeping groups from staying old-fashioned in a world of new technologies and ideas.

But the nature and degree of many of the second order spinoff effects are not fully knowable at the design stage. We need to build more complete working models and pilot plants. In any case it does not seem obvious that slowdowns, either at the workplace or in decision-making processes, would necessarily accompany group-based organizational designs.

Some possible advantages to the organization

Finally, from an organizational perspective, what are the potential advantages to be gained from a group based organization? The first might be a share reduction in the number of units that need to be controlled. Control would not have to be carried all the way down to the individual level. If the average group size is five, the number of blocks that management has to worry about is cut to 20 percent of what it was. Such a design would also probably cut the number of operational levels in the organization. In effect, levels which are now primarily supervisory would be incorporated into the groups that they supervise.

By this means many of the advantages of the small individualized organization could be brought back. These advantages would occur within groups simply because there would be a small number of blocks, albeit larger blocks, with which to build and rebuild the organization.

But most of all, and this is still uncertain, despite the extent to which we behavioral scientists have been enamoured of groups, there would be increased human advantages of cohesiveness, motivation, and commitment, and via that route, both increased productivity, stronger social glue within the organization, and a wider interaction between organization and environment.

Summary

Far and away the most powerful and beloved tool of applied behavioral scientists is the small face-to-face group. Since the Western Electric researches, behavioral scientists have been learning to understand, exploit and love groups. Groups attracted interest initially as devices for improving the implementation of decisions and to increase human commitment and motivation. They are now loved because they are also creative and innovative, they often make better quality decisions than individuals, and because they make organizational life more livable for people. One can't hire an applied behavioral scientist into an organization who within ten minutes will not want to call a group meeting and talk things over. The group meeting is his primary technology, his primary tool.

But groups in organizations are not an invention of behavioral types. They are a natural phenomenon of organizations. Organizations develop informal groups, like it or not. It is both possible and sen-

sible to describe most large organizations as collections of groups in interaction with one another; bargaining with one another, forming coalitions with one another, cooperating and competing with one another. It is possible and sensible too to treat the decisions that emerge from large organizations as a resultant of the interplay of forces among groups within the organizations, and not just the resultant of rational analysis.

On the down side, small face-to-face groups are great tools for disciplining and controlling their members. Contemporary China, for example, has just a fraction of the number of lawyers in the United States. Partially this is a result of the lesser complexity of Chinese society and lower levels of education. But a large part of it, suprisingly enough, seems to derive from the fact that modern China is designed around small groups. Since small groups take responsibility for the discipline and control of their members many deviant acts which would be considered illegal in the United States never enter the formal legal system in China. The law controls individual deviation less, the group controls it more (Li 1971).

Control of individual behavior is also a major problem of large complex western organizations. This problem has driven many organizations into elaborate bureaucratic quali-legal sets of rules, ranging from job evaluation schemes to performance evaluations to incentive systems; all individually based, all terribly complex, all creating problems of distributive justice. Any organizational design that might eliminate much of that legalistic superstructure therefore begins to look highly desirable.

Management should consider building organizations using a material now understood very well and with properties that look very promising, the small group. Until recently, al least, the human group has primarily been used for patching and mending organizations that were originally built of other materials.

The major unanswered questions in my mind are not in the understanding of groups, nor in the potential utility of the group as a building block. The more difficult answered question is whether or not the approaching era is one in which Americans would willingly work in such apparently contra-individualistic units. I think we are.

Assets and liabilities in group problem solving: The need for an integrative function

Norman R.F. Maier

Research on group problem solving reveals that the group has both advantages and disadvantages over individual problem solving. If the potentials for group problem solving can be exploited and if its deficiencies can be avoided, it follows that group problem solving can attain a level of proficiency not ordinarily achieved. The requirement for achieving this level of group performance seems to hinge on developing a style of discussion leadership which maximizes the group's assets and minimizes its liabilities. Since members possess the essential ingredients for the solutions, the deficiencies that appear in group solutions reside in the processes by which group solutions develop. These processes can determine whether the group functions effectively or ineffectively. The critical factor in a group's potential is organization and integration. With training, a leader can supply these functions and serve as the group's central nervous system, thus permitting the group to emerge as a highly efficient entity.

The research reported in the following reading was supported by Grant No. MH-02704 from the United States Public Health Service. Grateful acknowledgment is made for the constructive criticism of Melba Colgrove, Junie Janzen, Mara Julius, and James Thurber.

A number of investigators have raised the question of whether group problem solving is superior, inferior, or equal to individual problem solving. Evidence can be cited in support of each position so that the answer to this question remains ambiguous. Rather than pursue this generalized approach to the question, it seems more fruitful to explore the forces that influence problem solving under the two conditions (see reviews by Hoffman 1965; Kelley and Thibaut 1954). It is hoped that a better recognition of these forces will permit clarification of the varied dimensions of the problem-solving process, especially in groups.

The forces operating in such groups include some that are assets, some that are liabilities, and some that can be either assets or liabilities, depending upon the skills of the members, especially those of the discussion leader. Let us examine these three sets of forces.

Group assets

Greater sum total of knowledge and information.

There is more information in a group than in any of its members. Thus problems that require the utilization of knowledge should give groups an advantage over individuals. Even if one member of the group (e.g., the leader) knows much more than anyone else, the limited unique knowledge of lesser-informed individuals could serve to fill in some gaps in knowledge. For example, a skilled machinist might contribute to an engineer's problem solving and an ordinary workman might supply information on how a new machine might be received by workers.

Greater number of approaches to a problem

It has been shown that individuals get into ruts in their thinking (Duneker 1945; Maier 1930; Wertheimer 1959). Many obstacles stand in the way of achieving a goal, and a solution must circumvent these. The individual is handicapped in that he tends to persist in his approach and thus fails to find another approach that might solve the problem in a simpler manner. Individuals in a group have the same failing, but the approaches in which they are persisting may be different. For example, one researcher may try to prevent the spread of a disease by making man immune to the germ, an-

other by finding and destroying the carrier of the germ, and still another by altering the environment so as to kill the germ before it reaches man. There is no way of determining which approach will best achieve the desired goal, but undue persistence in any one will stifle new discoveries. Since group members do not have identical approaches, each can contribute by knocking others out of ruts of thinking.

Participation in problem solving increases acceptance

Many problems require solutions that depend upon the support of others to be effective. Insofar as group problem solving permits participation and influence, it follows that more individuals accept solutions when a group solves the problem than when one person solves it. When one individual solves a problem he still has the task of persuading others. It follows, therefore, that when groups solve such problems, a greater number of persons accept and feel responsible for making the solution work. A low-quality solution that has good acceptance can be more effective than a higher-quality decision that lacks acceptance.

Better comprehension of the decision

Decisions made by an individual, which are to be carried out by others, must be communicated from the decision maker to the decision executors. Thus individual problem solving often requires an additional stage — that of relaying the decision reached. Failures in this communication process detract from the merits of the decision and can even cause its failure or create a problem of greater magnitude than the initial problem that was solved. Many organizational problems can be traced to inadequate communication of decisions made by superiors and transmitted to subordinates, who have the task of implementing the decision.

The chances for communication failures are greatly reduced when the individuals who must work together in executing the decision have participated in making it. They not only understand the solution because they saw it develop, but they are also aware of the several other alternatives that were considered and the reasons why they were discarded. The common assumption that decisions supplied by superiors are arbitrarily reached therefore disappears. A full knowledge of goals, obstacles, alternatives, and factual information is essential to communication, and this communication is maximized when the total problem-solving process is shared.

Group liabilities

Social pressure

Social pressure is a major force making for conformity. The desire to be a good group member and to be accepted tends to silence disagreement and favors consensus. Majority opinions tend to be accepted regardless of whether or not their objective quality is logically and scientifically sound. Problems requiring solutions based upon facts, regardless of feelings and wishes, can suffer in group problem-solving situations.

It has been shown (Maier and Solem 1952) that minority opinions in leaderless groups have little influence on the solution reached, even when these opinions are the correct ones. Reaching agreement in a group often is confused with finding the right answer, and it is for this reason that the dimensions of a decision's acceptance and its objective quality must be distinguished (Maier 1963).

Valence of solutions

When leaderless groups (made up of three of four persons) engage in problem solving, they propose a variety of solutions. Each solution may receive both critical and supportive comments, as well as descriptive and explorative comments from other participants. If the number of negative and positive comments for each solution are algebraically summed, each may be given a valence index (Hoffman and Maier 1964). The first solution that receives a positive valence value of .15 tends to be adopted to the satisfaction of all participants about 85 percent of the time, regardless of its quality. Higher-quality solutions introduced after the critical value for one of the solutions has been reached have little chance of achieving real consideration. Once some degree of consensus is reached, the jelling process seems to proceed rather rapidly.

The critical valence value of .15 appears not to be greatly altered by the nature of the problem or the exact size of the group. Rather, it seems to designate a turning point between the idea-getting process and the decision-making process (idea evaluation). A solution's valence index is not a measure of the number of persons supporting the solution, since a vocal minority can build up a solution's valence by actively pushing it. In this sense, valence becomes an influence in addition to social pressure in determining an outcome.

Since a solution's valence is independent of its objective quality, this group factor becomes an important liability in group problem solving, even when the value of a decision depends upon objective criteria (facts and logic).

It becomes a means whereby skilled manipulators can have more influence over the group process than their proportion of membership deserves.

Individual domination

In most leaderless groups a dominant individual emerges and captures more than his share of influence on the outcome. He can achieve this end through a greater degree of participation (valence), persuasive ability, or stubborn persistence (fatiguing the opposition). None of these factors is related to problem-solving ability, so that the best problem solver in the group may not have the influence to upgrade the quality of the group's solution (which he would have had if left to solve the problem by himself).

Hoffman and Maier (1967) found that the mere fact of appointing a leader causes this person to dominate a discussion. Thus, regardless of his problem-solving ability a leader tends to exert a major influence on the outcome of a discussion.

Conflicting secondary goal: Winning the argument

When groups are confronted with a problem, the initial goal is to obtain a solution. However, the appearance of several alternatives causes individuals to have preferences and once these emerge the desire to support a position is created. Converting those with neutral viewpoints and refuting those with opposed viewpoints now enter into the problem-solving process. More and more the goal becomes that of winning the decision rather than finding the best solution. This new goal is unrelated to the quality of the problem's solution and therefore can result in lowering the qual-

ity of the decision (Hoffman and Maier 1967).

Factors that serve as assets or liabilities, depending largely upon the skill of the discussion leader

Disagreement

The fact that discussion may lead to disagreement can serve either to create hard feelings among members or lead to a resolution of conflict and hence to an innovative solution (Hoffman 1961; Hoffman, Harburg, and Maier 1962; Hoffman and Maier 1961; Maier 1958, 1963; Maier and Hoffman 1965). The first of these outcomes of disagreement is a liability, especially with regard to the acceptance of solutions; while the second is an asset, particularly where innovation is desired. A leader can treat disagreement as undesirable and thereby reduce the probability of both hard feelings and innovation, or he can maximize disagreement and risk hard feelings in his attempts to achieve innovation. The skill of a leader requires this ability to create a climate for disagreement which will permit innovation without risking hard feelings. The leader's perception of disagreement is one of the critical factors in this skill area (Maier and Hoffman 1965). Others involve permissiveness (Maier 1953), delaying the reaching of a solution (Maier and Hoffman 1960b; Maier and Solem 1962), techniques for processing information and opinions (Maier 1963; Maier and Hoffman 1960a; Maier and Maier 1957), and techniques for separating idea-getting from idea-evaluation (Maier 1960, 1963; Osborn 1953).

Conflicting interests versus mutual interests

Disagreement in discussion may take many forms. Often participants agree with one another with regard to solutions, but when issues are explored one finds that these conflicting solutions are designed to solve different problems. Before one can rightly expect agreement on a solution, there should be agreement on the goal, as well as on the various obstacles that prevent the goal from being reached. Once distinctions are made between goals, obstacles, and solutions (which represent ways of overcoming obstacles), one finds increased opportunities for cooperative problem solving and less conflict (Hoffman and Maier 1959; Maier 1960, 1963; Maier and Solem 1962; Solem 1965).

Often there is also disagreement regarding whether the objective of a solution is to achieve quality or acceptance (Maier and Hoffman 1964b), and frequently a stated problem reveals a complex of separate problems, each having separate solutions so that a search for a single solution is impossible (Maier 1963). Communications often are inadequate because the discussion is not synchronized and each person is engaged in discussing a different aspect. Organizing discussion to synchronize the exploration of different aspects of the problem and to follow a systematic procedure increases solution quality (Maier and Hoffman 1960a; Maier and Maier 1957). The leadership function of influencing discussion procedure is quite distinct from the function of evaluating or contributing ideas (Maier 1950, 1953).

When the discussion leader aids in the separation of the several aspects of the problem-solving process and delays the solution-mindedness of the group (Maier 1958, 1963; Maier and Solem 1962), both solution quality and acceptance improve; when he hinders or fails to facilitate the isolation of these varied processes, he risks a deterioration in the group processes (Solem 1965). His skill thus determines whether a discussion drifts toward conflicting interests or whether mutual interests are located. Cooperative problem solving can only occur after the mutual interests have been established and it is surprising how often they can be found when the discussion leader makes this his task (Maier 1952, 1963; Maier and Hayes 1962).

Risk taking

Groups are more willing than individuals to reach decisions involving risks (Wallach and Kogan 1965; Wallach, Kogan, and Bem 1962). Taking risks is a factor in acceptance of change, but change may represent either a gain or a loss. The best guard against the latter outcome seems to be primarily a matter of a decision's quality. In a group situation this depends upon the leader's skill in utilizing the factors that represent group assets and avoiding those that make for liabilities.

Time requirements

In general, more time is required for a group to reach a decision than for a single individual to reach one. Insofar as some problems require quick decisions, individual decisions are favored. In other situations acceptance and quality are requirements, but excessive time without sufficient returns also represents a loss. On the other hand, discussion can resolve conflicts, whereas reaching consensus has limited value (Wallach and Kogan 1965). The practice of hastening a meeting can prevent full discussion, but failure to move a discussion forward can lead to boredom and fatigue-type solutions, in which members agree merely to get out of the meeting. The effective utilization of discussion time (a delicate balance between permissiveness and control on the part of the leader), therefore, is needed to make the time factor as asset rather than a liability. Unskilled leaders tend to be too concerned with reaching a solution and therefore terminate a discussion before the group potential is achieved (Maier and Hoffman 1960b).

Who changes

In reaching consensus or agreement, some members of a group must change. Persuasive forces do not operate in individual problem solving in the same way they operate in a group situation; hence, the changing of someone's mind is not an issue. In group situations, however, who changes can be an asset or a liability. If persons with the most constructive views are induced to change the end product suffers; whereas if persons with the least constructive point of view change, the end product is upgraded. The leader can upgrade the quality of a decision because his position permits him to protect the person with a minority view and increase his opportunity to influence the majority position. This protection is a constructive factor because a minority viewpoint influences only when facts favor it (Maier 1950, 1952; Maier and Solem 1952).

The leader also plays a constructive role insofar as he can facilitate communications and thereby reduce misunderstandings (Maier 1952; Solem 1965). The leader has an adverse effect on the end product when he suppresses minority views by holding a contrary position and when he uses his office to promote his own views (Maier and Hoffman 1960b, 1962; Maier and Solem

1952). In many problem-solving discussions the untrained leader plays a dominant role in influencing the outcome, and when he is more resistant to changing his views than are the other participants, the quality of the outcome tends to be lowered. This negative leader-influence was demonstrated by experiments in which untrained leaders were asked to obtain a second solution to a problem after they had obtained their first one (Maier and Hoffman 1960a). It was found that the second solution tended to be superior to the first. Since the dominant individual had influenced the first solution, he had won his point and therefore ceased to dominate the subsequent discussion which led to the second solution. Acceptance of a solution also increases as the leader sees disagreement as idea-producing rather than as a source of difficulty or trouble (Maier and Hoffman 1965). Leaders who see some of their participants as trouble-makers obtain fewer innovative solutions and gain less acceptance of decisions made than leaders who see disagreeing members as persons with ideas.

The leader's role for integrated groups

Two differing types of group process

In observing group problem solving under various conditions, it is rather easy to distinguish between cooperative problem-solving activity and persuasion or selling approaches. Problem-solving activity includes searching, trying out ideas on one another, listening to understand rather than to refute, making relatively short speeches, and reacting to differences in opinion as stimulating. The general pattern is one of rather complete participation, involvement. Persuasion activity includes the selling of opinions already formed, defending a position held, either not listening at all or listening in order to be able to refute, talking dominated by a few members, unfavorable reactions to disagreement, and a lack of involvement of some members. During problem solving the behavior observed seems to be that of members interacting as segments of a group. The interaction pattern is not between certain individual members, but with the group as a whole. Sometimes it is difficult to determine who should be credited with an idea. "It just developed," is a response often used to describe the solution reached. In contrast, discussions involving selling or persuasive behavior seem to consist of a series of interpersonal interactions with each individual retaining his identity. Such groups do not function as integrated units but as separate individuals, each with an agenda. In one situation the solution is unknown and is sought; in the other, several solutions exist and conflict occurs because commitments have been made.

The starfish analogy

The analysis of these two group processes suggests an analogy with the behavior of the rays of a starfish under two conditions; one with the nerve ring intact, the other with the nerve ring sectioned (Hamilton 1922; Moore 1924; Moore and Doudoroff 1939; Schneirla and Maier 1940). In the intact condition, locomotion and righting behavior reveal that the behavior of each ray is not merely a function of local stimulation. Locomotion and righting behavior reveal a degree of coordination and interdependence that is centrally controlled. However, when the nerve ring is sec-

tioned, the behavior of one ray still can influence others, but internal coordination is lacking. For example, if one ray is stimulated, it may step forward, thereby exerting pressure on the sides of the other four rays. In response to these eternal pressures (tactile stimulation), these rays show stepping responses on the stimulated side so that locomotion successfully can occur on the basis of external control. If, however, stimulation is applied to opposite rays, the specimen may be "locked" for a time, and in some species the conflicting locomotions may divide the animal, thus destroying it (Crozier 1920; Moore and Doudoroff 1939).

Each of the rays of the starfish can show stepping responses even when sectioned and removed from the animal. Thus each may be regarded as an individual. In a starfish with a sectioned nerve ring the five rays become members of a group. They can successfully work together for locomotion purposes by being controlled by the dominant ray. Thus if uniformity of action is desired, the group of five rays can sometimes be more effective than the individual ray in moving the group toward a source of stimulation. However, if "locking" or the division of the organism occurs, the group action becomes less effective than individual action. External control, through the influence of a dominant ray, therefore can lead to adaptive behavior for the starfish as a whole, but it can also result in a conflict that destroys the organism. Something more than external influence is needed.

In the animal with an intact nerve ring, the function of the rays is coordinated by the nerve ring. With this type of internal organization the group is always superior to that of the individual actions. When the rays function as a part of an organized unit, rather than as a group that is physically together, they become a higher type of organization — a single intact organism. This is accomplished by the nerve ring, which in itself does not do the behaving. Rather, it receives and processes the data which the rays relay to it. Through this central organization, the responses of rays become part of a larger pattern so that together they constitute a single coordinated total response rather than a group of individual responses.

The leader as the group's central nervous system

If we now examine what goes on in a discussion group we find that members can problem-solve as individuals, they can influence others by external pushes and pulls, or they can function as a group with varying degrees of unity. In order for the latter function to be maximized, however, something must be introduced to serve the function of a nerve ring. In our conceptualization of group problem solving and group decision (Maier 1963), we see this as the function of the leader. Thus the leader does not serve as the dominant ray and produce the solution. Rather, his function is to receive information, facilitate communications between individuals, relay messages, and integrate the incoming responses so that a single unified response occurs.

Solutions that are the product of good group discussions often come as surprises to discussion leaders. One of these is unexpected generosity. If there is a weak member, this member is given less to do, in much the same way as an organism adapts to an injured limb and alters the function of other limbs to keep the locomotion on course. Experimental evidence supports the point that group decisions award special consideration to needy members of groups (Hoffman and Maier 1959). Group decisions in industrial groups often give smaller assignments to the less gifted (Maier 1952). A leader could not effectually impose such differential treatment on group membrs without being charged with discriminatory practices.

Another unique aspect of group discussion is the way fairness is resolved. In a simulated problem situation involving the problem of how to introduce a new truck into a group of drivers, the typical group solution involves a trading of trucks so that several or all members stand to profit. If the leader makes the decision the number of persons who profit is often confined to one (Maier and Hoffman 1962; Maier and Zerfoss 1952). In industrial practice, supervisors assign a new truck to an individual member of a crew after careful evaluation of needs. This practice results in dissatisfaction, with the charge of *unfair* being leveled at him. Despite those repeated attempts to do justice, supervisors in the telephone industry never hit upon the notion of a general reallocation of trucks, a solution that crews invariably reach when the decision is theirs to make.

In experiments involving the introduction of change, the use of group discussion tends to lead to decisions that resolve differences (Maier 1952, 1953; Maier and Hoffman 1961, 1964a, 1964b). Such decisions tend to be different from decisions reached by individuals because of the very fact that disagreement is common in group problem solving and rare in individual problem solving. The process of resolving differences in a constructive setting causes the exploration of additional areas and leads to solutions that are integrative rather than compromises.

Finally, group solutions tend to be

tailored to fit the interests and personalities of the participants; thus group solutions to problems involving fairness, fears, facesaving, etc., tend to vary from one group to another. An outsider cannot process these variables because they are not subject to logical treatment.

If we think of the leader as serving a function in the group different from that of its membership, we might be able to create a group that can function as an intact organism. For a leader, such functions as rejecting or promoting ideas according to his personal needs are out of bounds. He must be receptive to information contributed, accept contributions without evaluating them (post contributions on a chalk board to keep them alive), summarize information to facilitate integration, stimulate exploratory behavior, create awareness of problems of one member by others, and detect when the group is ready to resolve differences and agree to a unified solution.

Since higher organisms have more than a nerve ring and can store information, a leader might appropriately supply information, but according to our model of a leader's role, he must clearly distinguish between supplying information and promoting a solution. If his knowledge indicates the desirability of a particular solution, sharing this knowledge might lead the group to find this solution, but the solution should be the group's discovery. A leader's contributions do not receive the same treatment as those of a member of the group. Whether he likes it or not, his position is different. According to our conception of the leader's contribution to discussion, his role not only differs in influence, but gives him an entirely different function. He is to serve much as the nerve ring in the starfish and to further refine this function so as to make it a higher type of

nerve ring.

This model of a leader's role in group processes has served as a guide for many of our studies in group problem solving. It is not our claim that this will lead to the best possible group function under all conditions. In sharing it we hope to indicate the nature of our guidelines in exploring group leadership as a function quite different and apart from group membership. Thus the model serves as a stimulant for research problems and as a guide for our analyses of leadership skills and principles.

Conclusions

On the basis of our analysis, it follows that the comparison of the merits of group versus individual problem solving depends on the nature of the problem, the goal to be achieved (high quality solution, highly accepted solution, effective communication and understanding of the solution, innovation, a quickly reached solution, or satisfaction), and the skill of the discussion leader. If liabilities inherent in groups are avoided, assets capitalized upon, and conditions that can serve either favorable or unfavorable outcomes are effectively used, it follows that groups have a potential which in many instances can exceed that of a superior individual functioning alone, even with respect to creativity.

This goal was nicely stated by Thibaut and Kelley (1961) when they

wonder whether it may not be possible for a rather small, intimate group to establish a problem-solving process that capitalizes upon the total pool of information and provides for great interstimulation of ideas without any loss of innovative creativity due to social restraints (p. 268).

In order to accomplish his high level of

achievement, however, a leader is needed who plays a role quite different from that of the members. His role is analogous to that of the nerve ring in the starfish which permits the rays to execute a unified response. If the leader can contribute the integrative requirement, group problem solving may emerge as a unique type of group function. This type of approach to group processes places the leader in a particular role in which he must cease to contribute, avoid evaluation, and refrain from thinking about solutions or group *products*. Instead he must concentrate on the group *process*, listen in order to understand rather than to appraise or refute, assume responsibility for accurate communication between members, be sensitive to unexpressed feelings, protect minority points of view, keep the discussion moving, and develop skills in summarizing.

The Abilene Paradox:
The management of agreement

Jerry B. Harvey

The July afternoon in Coleman, Texas (population 5,607) was particularly hot — 104 degrees as measured by the Walgreen's Rexall Ex-Lax temperature gauge. In addition, the wind was blowing fine-grained West Texas topsoil through the house. But the afternoon was still tolerable — even potentially enjoyable. There was a fan going on the back porch; there was cold lemonade; and finally, there was entertainment. Dominoes. Perfect for the conditions. The game required little more physical exertion than an occasional mumbled comment, "Shuffle 'em," and an unhurried movement of the arm to place the spots in the appropriate perspective on the table. All in all, it had the makings of an agreeable Sunday afternoon in Coleman — that is, it was until my father-in-law suddenly said, "Let's get in the car and go to Abilene and have dinner at the cafeteria."

I thought, "What, go to Abilene? Fifty-three miles? In this dust storm and heat? And in an unairconditioned 1958 Buick?"

But my wife chimed in with, "Sounds like a great idea. I'd like to go. How about you, Jerry?" Since my own preferences were obviously out of step with the rest I replied, "Sounds good to me," and added, "I just hope your mother wants to go."

"Of course I want to go," said my mother-in-law. "I haven't been to Abilene in a long time."

So into the car and off to Abilene we went. My predictions were fulfilled. The heat was brutal. We were coated with a fine layer of dust that was cemented with perspiration by the time we arrived. The food at the cafeteria provided first-rate testimonial material for antacid commercials.

Some four hours and 106 miles later we returned to Coleman, hot and exhausted. We sat in front of the fan for a long time in silence. Then, both to be sociable and to break the silence, I said, "It was a great trip, wasn't it?"

No one spoke.

Finally my mother-in-law said, with some irritation, "Well, to tell the truth, I really didn't enjoy it much and would rather have stayed here. I just went along because the three of you were so enthusiastic about going. I wouldn't have gone if you all hadn't pressured me into it."

I couldn't believe it. "What do you mean 'you all'?" I said. "Don't put me in the 'you all' group. I was delighted to be doing what we were doing. I didn't want to go. I only went to satisfy the rest of you. You're the culprits."

My wife looked shocked. "Don't call me a culprit. You and Daddy and Mama were the ones who wanted to go. I just went along to be sociable and to keep you happy. I would have had to be crazy to want to go out in heat like that."

Her father entered the conversation abruptly. "Hell!" he said.

He proceeded to expand on what was already absolutely clear. "Listen, I never wanted to go to Abilene. I just thought you might be bored. You visit so seldom I wanted to be sure you enjoyed it. I would have preferred to play another game of dominoes and eat the leftovers in the icebox."

After the outburst of recrimination we all sat back in silence. Here we were, four reasonably sensible people who, of our own volition, had just taken a 106-mile trip across a godforsaken desert in a furnace-like temperature through a cloud-like dust storm to eat unpalatable food at a hole-in-the-wall cafeteria in Abilene, when none of us had really wanted to go. In fact, to be more accurate, we'd done just the opposite of what we wanted to do. The whole situation simply didn't make sense.

At lest it didn't make sense at the time. But since that day in Coleman, I have observed, consulted with, and been a part of more than one organization that has been caught in the same situation. As a result, they have either taken a side trip, or, occasionally, a terminal journey to Abilene, when Dallas or Houston or Tokyo was where they really wanted to go. And for most of those organizations, the negative consequences of such trips, measured in terms of both human misery and economic loss, have been much greater than for our little Abilene group.

This article is concerned with that paradox — the Abilene Paradox. Stated simply, it is as follows: Organizations frequently take actions in contradiction to what they really want to do and therefore defeat the very purposes they are trying to achieve. It also deals with a major corollary of the paradox, which is that *the inability to manage agreement is a major source of organization dysfunction.* Last, the article is designed to help members of organizations cope more effectively with the paradox's pernicious influence.

As a means of accomplishing the above, I shall: (1) describe the symptoms exhibited by organizations caught in the paradox; (2) describe, in summarized case study examples, how they occur in a variety of organizations; (3) discuss the underlying causal dynamics; (4) indicate some of the implications of accepting this model for describing organizational behavior; (5) make recommendations for coping with the paradox; and, in conclusion (6) relate the paradox to a broader existential issue.

Symptoms of the Paradox

The inability to manage agreement, not the inability to manage conflict, is the essential symptom that defines organizations caught in the web of the Abilene Paradox. That inability effectively to manage agreement is expressed by six specific subsymptoms, all of which were present in our family Abilene group.

1. Organization members agree privately, as individuals, as to the nature of the situation or problem facing the organization. For example, members of the Abilene group agreed that they were enjoying themselves sitting in front of the fan, sipping lemonade, and playing dominoes.

2. Organization members agree privately, as individuals, as to the steps that would be required to cope with the situation or problem they face. For members of the Abilene group "more of the same" was a solution that would have adequately satisfied their individual and collective desires.

3. Organization members fail to accurately communicate their desires and/or beliefs to one another. In fact, they do just the opposite and thereby lead one another into misperceiving the collective reality. Each member of the Abilene group, for example, communicated inaccurate data to other members of the organization. The data, in effect, said, "Yeah, it's a great idea. Let's go to Abilene," when in reality members of the organization individually and collectively preferred to stay in Coleman.

4. With such invalid and inaccurate information, organization members make collective decisions that lead them to take actions contrary to what they want to do, and thereby arrive at results that are counterproductive to the organization's intent and purposes. Thus, the Abilene group went to Abilene when it preferred to do something else.

5. As a result of taking actions that are counterproductive, organization members experience frustration, anger, irritation, and dissatisfaction with their organization. Consequently, they form subgroups with trusted acquaintances and blame other subgroups for the organization's dilemma. Frequently, they also blame authority figures and one another. Such phenomena were illustrated in the Abilene group by the "culprit" argument that occurred when we had returned to the comfort of the fan.

6. Finally, if organization members do not deal with the generic issue — the inability to manage agreement — the cycle repeats itself with greater intensity. The Abilene group, for a variety of reasons, the most important of which was that it became conscious of the process, did not reach that point.

To repeat, the Abilene Paradox reflects a failure to manage agreement. In fact, it is my contention that the inability to cope with (manage) agreement, rather than the inability to cope with (manage) conflict is the single most pressing issue of modern organizations.

Other trips to Abilene

The Abilene Paradox is no respector of individuals, organizations, or institutions. Following are descriptions of two other trips to Abilene that illustrate both the pervasiveness of the paradox and its underlying dynamics.

Case No. 1: The Boardroom.

The Ozyx Corporation is a relatively small industrial company that has embarked on a trip to Abilene. The president of Ozyx has hired a consultant to help discover the reasons for the poor profit picture of the company in general and the low morale and productivity of the R&D division in particular. During the process of investigation, the consultant becomes interested in a research project in which the company has invested a sizable proportion of its R&D budget.

When asked about the project by the consultant in the privacy of their offices, the president, the vice-president for research, and the research manager each describes it as an idea that looked great on paper but will ultimately fail because of the unavailability of the technology required to make it work. Each of them also acknowledges that continued support of the project will create cash flow problems that will jeopardize the very existence of the total organization.

Furthermore, each individual indicates he has not told the others about his reservations. When asked why, the president says he can't reveal his "true" feelings because abandoning the project, which has been widely publicized, would make the company look bad in the press and, in addition, would probably cause his vice-president's ulcer to kick up or perhaps even cause him to quit, "because he has staked his professional reputation on the project's success."

Similarly, the vice-president for research says he can't let the president or the research manager know of his reservations because the president is so committed to it that "I would probably get fired for insubordination if I questioned the project."

Finally, the research manager says he can't let the president or vice-president know of his doubts about the project because of their extreme commitment to the project's success.

All indicate that, in meetings with one another, they try to maintain an optimistic facade so the others won't worry unduly about the project. The research director, in particular, admits to writing ambiguous progress reports so the president and the vice-president can "interpret them to suit themselves." In fact, he says he tends to slant them to the "positive" side, "given how committed the brass are."

The scent of the Abilene trail wafts from a paneled conference room where the project research budget is being considered for the following fiscal year. In the meeting itself, praises are heaped on the questionable project and a unanimous decision is made to continue it for yet another year. Symbolically, the organization has boarded a bus to Abilene.

In fact, although the real issue of agreement was confronted approximately eight months after the bus departed, it was nearly too late. The organization failed to meet a payroll and underwent a two-year period of personnel cutbacks, retrenchments, and austerity. Morale suffered, the most competent technical personnel resigned, and the organization's prestige in the industry declined.

Case No. 2: The Watergate

Apart from the grave question of who did what, Watergate presents America with the profound puzzle of why. What is it that led such a wide assortment of men, many of them high public officials, possibly including the President himself, either to instigate or to go along with and later try to hide a pattern of behavior that by now appears not only reprehensible, but stupid? (*The Washington Star and Daily News*, editorial, May 27, 1973.)

One possible answer to the editorial

writer's question can be found by probing into the dynamics of the Abilene paradox. I shall let the reader reach his own conclusions, though, on the basis of the following excerpts from testimony before the Senate investigating committee on "The Watergate Affair".

In one exchange, Senator Howard Baker asked Herbert Porter, then a member of the White House staff, why he (Porter) found himself "in charge of or deeply involved in a dirty tricks operation of the campaign." In response, Porter indicated that he had had qualms about what he was doing, but that he " . . . was not one to stand up in a meeting and say that this should be stopped. . . . I kind of drifted along."

And when asked by Baker why he had "drifted along," Porter replied, "In all honesty, because of the fear of the group pressure that would ensue, of not being a team player," and " . . . I felt a deep sense of loyalty to him [the President] or was appealed to on that basis." (*The Washington Post*, June 8, 1973, p. 20.)

Jeb Magruder gave a similar response to a question posed by committee counsel Dash. Specifically, when asked about his, Mr. Dean's, and Mr. Mitchell's reactions to Mr. Liddy's proposal, which included bugging the Watergate, Mr. Magruder replied, "I think all three of us were appalled. The scope and size of the project were something that at least in my mind were not envisioned. I do not think it was in Mr. Mitchell's mind or Mr. Dean's, although I can't comment on their states of mind at that time."

Mr. Mitchell, in an understated way, which was his way of dealing with difficult problems like this, indicated that this was not an "acceptable project." (*The Washington Post*, June 15, 1973, p. A14.)

Later in his testimony Mr. Magruder

said, " . . . I think I can honestly say that no one was particularly overwhelmed with the project. But I think we felt that this information could be useful, and Mr. Mitchell agreed to approve the project, and I then notified the parties of Mr. Mitchell's approval." (*The Washington Post*, June 15, 1973, p. A14.)

Although I obviously was not privy to the private conversations of the principal characters, the data seem to reflect the essential elements of the Abilene Paradox. First, they indicate agreement. Evidently, Mitchell, Porter, Dean, and Magruder agreed that the plan was inappropriate. ("I think I can honestly say that no one was particularly over-whelmed with the project.") Second, the data indicate that the principal figures then proceeded to implement the plan in contradiction to their shared agreement. Third, the data surrounding the case clearly indicate that the plan multiplied the organization's problems rather than solved them. And finally, the organization broke into subgroups with the various principals, such as the President, Mitchell, Porter, Dean, and Magruder, blaming one another for the dilemma in which they found themselves, and internecine warfare ensued.

In summary, it is possible that because of the inability of White House staff members to cope with the fact that they agreed, the organization took a trip to Abilene.

Analyzing the Paradox

The Abilene Paradox can be stated succinctly as follows: Organizations frequently take actions in contradiction to the data they have for dealing with problems and, as a result, compound their problems rather than solve them. Like all paradoxes, the Abilene Paradox deals with absurdity. On the surface, it makes little sense for organizations, whether they are couples or companies, bureaucracies or governments, to take actions that are diametrically opposed to the data they possess for solving crucial organizational problems. Such actions are particularly absurd since they tend to compound the very problems they are designed to solve and thereby defeat the purposes the organization is trying to achieve. However, as Robert Rapaport and others have so cogently expressed it, paradoxes are generally paradoxes only because they are based on a logic or rationale different from what we understand or expect.

Discovering that different logic not only destroys the paradoxical quality but also offers alternative ways for coping with similar situations. Therefore, part of the dilemma facing an Abilene-bound organization may be the lack of a map — a theory or model — that provides rationality to the paradox. The purpose of the following discussion is to provide such a map.

The map will be developed by examining the underlying psychological themes of the profit-making organization and the bureaucracy and it will include the following landmarks: (1) Action Anxiety; (2) Real Risk; (3) Separation Anxiety; and (4) the Psychological Reversal of Risk and Certainty. I hope that the discussion of such landmarks will provide harried organization travelers with a new map that will assist them in arriving at where they really want to go and, in addition, will help them in assessing the risks that are an inevitable part of the journey.

Action anxiety

Action anxiety provides the first land-mark for locating roadways that bypass Abilene. The concept of action anxiety says that the reason organization members take actions in contradiction to their understanding of the organization's problems lies in the intense anxiety that is created as they think about acting in accordance with what they believe needs to be done. As a result, they opt to endure the professional and economic degradation of pursuing an unworkable research project or the consequences of participating in an illegal activity rather than act in a manner congruent with their beliefs. It is not that organization members do not know what needs to be done — they do know. For example, the various principals in the research organization cited *knew* they were working on a research project that had no real possibility of succeeding. And the central figures of the Watergate episode apparently *knew* that, for a variety of reasons, the plan to bug the Watergate did not make sense.

Such action anxiety experienced by the various protagonists may not make sense, but the dilemma is not a new one. In fact, it is very similar to the anxiety experienced by Hamlet, who expressed it most eloquently in the opening lines of his famous soliloquy:

To be or not to be; that is the question:
Whether 'tis nobler in the mind to suffer
The slings and arrows of outrageous fortune
Or to take arms against a sea of troubles
And by opposing, end them? . . . (*Hamlet,* Act III, Scene II)

Real risk

Risk is a reality of life, a condition of existence. John Kennedy articulated it in another way when he said at a news conference, "Life is unfair." By that I believe he meant we do not know, nor can we predict or control with certainty, either the events that impinge upon us or the outcomes of actions we undertake in response to those events.

Consequently, in the business environment, the research manager might find that confronting the president and the vice-president with the fact that the project was a "turkey" might result in his being fired. And Mr. Porter's saying that an illegal plan of surveillance should not be carried out could have caused his ostracism as a non-team player. There are too many cases when confrontation of this sort has resulted in such consequences. The real question, though, is not, Are such fantasized consequences possible? but, Are such fantisized consequences likely?

Thus, real risk is an existential condition, and all actions do have consequences that, to paraphrase Hamlet, may be worse than the evils of the present. As a result of their unwillingness to accept existential risk as one of life's givens, however, people may opt to take their organizations to Abilene rather than run the risk, no matter how small, of ending up somewhere worse.

Again, though, one must ask, What is the real risk that underlies the decision to opt for Abilene? What is at the core of the paradox?

Fear of separation

One is tempted to say that the core of the paradox lies in the individual's fear of the unknown. Actually, we do not fear what is unknown, but we are afraid of things we do know about. What do we know about that frightens us into such apparently inexplicable organizational behavior?

Separation, alienation, and loneliness are things we do know about — and fear.

Both research and experience indicate that ostracism is one of the most powerful punishments that can be devised. Solitary confinement does not draw its coercive strength from physical deprivation. The evidence is overwhelming that we have a fundamental need to be connected, engaged, and related and a reciprocal need not to be separated or alone. Everyone of us, though, has experienced aloneness. From the time the umbilical cord was cut, we have experienced the real anguish of separation — broken friendships, divorces, deaths, and exclusions. C. P. Snow vividly described the tragic interplay between loneliness and connection:

"Each of us is alone; sometimes we escape from our solitariness, through love and affection or perhaps creative moments, but these triumphs of life are pools of light we make for ourselves while the edge of the road is black. Each of us dies alone."

That fear of taking risks that may result in our separation from others is at the core of the paradox. It finds expression in ways of which we may be unaware, and it is ultimately the cause of the self-defeating, collective deception that leads to self-destructive decisions within organizations.

Concretely, such fear of separation leads research committees to fund projects that none of its members want and, perhaps, White House staff members to engage in illegal activities that they don't really support.

The psychological reversal of risk and certainty

One piece of the map is still missing. It relates to the peculiar reversal that occurs in our thought processes as we try to cope with the Abilene Paradox. For example, we frequently fail to take action in an organizational setting because we fear that the actions we take may result in our separation from others, or, in the language of Mr. Porter, we are afraid of being tabbed as "disloyal" or are afraid of being ostracized as "non-team players." But therein lies a paradox within a paradox, because our very unwillingness to take such risks virtually ensures the separation and aloneness we so fear. In effect, we reverse "real existential risk" and "fantasied risk" and by doing so transform what is a probability statement into what, for all practical purposes, becomes a certainty.

Take the R&D organization described earlier. When the project fails, some people will get fired, demoted, or sentenced to the purgatory of a make-work job in an out-of-the-way office. For those who remain, the atmosphere of blame, distrust, suspicion, and backbiting that accompanies such failure will serve only to further alienate and separate those who remain.

The Watergate situation is similar. The principals evidently feared being ostracized as disloyal non-team players. When the illegality of the act surfaced, however, it was nearly inevitable that blaming, self-protective actions, and scapegoating would result in the very emotional separation from both the President and one another that the principals feared. Thus, by reversing real and fantasied risk, they had taken effective action to ensure the outcome they least desired.

One final question remains: Why do we make this peculiar reversal? I support the general thesis of Alvin Toffler and Philip Slater, who contend that our cultural emphasis on technology, competition, individualism, temporariness, and mobility has resulted in a population

that has frequently experienced the terror of loneliness and seldom the satisfaction of engagement. Consequently, though we have learned of the reality of separation, we have not had the opportunity to learn the reciprocal skills of connection, with the result that, like the ancient dinosaurs, we are breeding organizations with self-destructive decision-making proclivities.

A possible Abilene bypass

Existential risk is inherent in living, so it is impossible to provide a map that meets the no-risk criterion, but it may be possible to describe the route in terms that make the landmarks understandable and that will clarify the risks involved. In order to do that, however, some commonly used terms such as victim, victimizer, collusion, responsibility, conflict, conformity, courage, confrontation, reality, and knowledge have to·be redefined. In additioin, we need to explore the relevance of the redefined concepts for bypassing or getting out of Abilene.

• *Victim and victimizer.* Blaming and fault-finding behavior is one of the basic symptoms of organizations that have found their way to Abilene, and the target of blame generally doesn't include the one who criticizes. Stated in different terms, executives begin to assign one another to roles of victims and victimizers. Ironic as it may seem, however, this assignment of roles is both irrelevant and dysfunctional, because once a business or a government fails to manage its agreement and arrives in Abilene, all its members are victims. Thus, arguments and accusations that identify victims and victimizers at best become symptoms of the paradox, and, at worst, drain energy from the problem-solving efforts required to redirect the organization along the route it really wants to take.

• *Collusion.* A basic implication of the Abilene Paradox is that human problems of organization are reciprocal in nature. As Robert Tannenbaum has point out, you can't have an autocratic boss unless subordinates are willing to collude with his autocracy, and you can't have obsequious subordinates unless the boss is willing to collude with their obsequiousness.

Thus, in plain terms, each person in a self-defeating, Abilene-bound organization *colludes* with others, including peers, superiors, and subordinates, sometimes consciously and sometimes subconsciously, to create the dilemma in which the organization finds itself. To adopt a cliche of modern organization, "It takes a real team effort to go to Abilene." In that sense each person, in his own collusive manner, shares responsibility for the trip, so searching for a locus of blame outside oneself serves no useful purpose for either the organization or the individual. It neither helps the organization handle its dilemma of unrecognized agreement nor does it provide psychological relief for the individual, because focusing on conflict when agreement is the issue is devoid of reality. In fact, it does just the opposite, for it causes the organization to focus on managing conflict when it should be focusing on managing agreement.

• *Responsibility for problem-solving action.* A second question is, Who is responsible for getting us out of this place? To that question is frequently appended a third one, generally rhetorical in nature, with "should" overtones, such as,

Isn't it the boss (or the ranking government official) who is responsible for doing something about the situation?

The answer to that question is no.

The key to understanding the functionality of the no answer is the knowledge that, when the dynamics of the paradox are in operation, the authority figure — and others — are in unknowing agreement with one another concerning the organization's problems and the steps necessary to solve them. Consequently, the power to destroy the paradox's pernicious influence comes from confronting and speaking to the underlying reality of the situation, and not from one's hierarchical position within the organization. Therefore, any organization member who chooses to risk confronting that reality possesses the necessary leverage to release the organization from the paradox's grip.

In one situation, it may be a research director's saying, "I don't think this project can succeed." In another, it may be Jeb Magruder's response to this question of Senator Baker:

If you were concerned because the action was known to you to be illegal, because you thought it improper or unethical, you thought the prospects for success were very meager, and you doubted the reliability of Mr. Liddy, what on earth would it have taken to decide against the plan?

Magruder's reply was brief and to the point:

Not very much, sir. I am sure that if I had fought vigorously against it, I think any of us could have had the plan cancelled. (*Time*, June 25, 1973, p. 12.)

• *Reality, knowledge, confrontation.* Accepting the paradox as a model describing certain kinds of organizational dilemmas also requires rethinking the nature of reality and knowledge, as they are generally described in organizations. In brief, the underlying dynamics of the paradox clearly indicate that organization members generally know more about issues confronting the organization than they don't know. The various principals attending the research budget meeting, for example, knew the research project was doomed to failure. And Jeb Magruder spoke as a true Abilener when he said, "We knew it was illegal, probably, inappropriate." (*The Washington Post,* June 15, 1973, p. A16.)

Given this concept of reality and its relationship to knowledge, confrontation becomes the process of facing issues squarely, openly, and directly in an effort to discover whether the nature of the underlying collective reality is agreement or conflict. Accepting such a definition of confrontation has an important implication for change agents interested in making organizations more effective. That is, organization change and effectiveness may be facilitated as much by confronting the organization with what it knows and agrees upon as by confronting it with what it doesn't know or disagrees about.

The Abilene Paradox and the myth of Sisyphus

In essence, this paper proposes that there is an underlying organizational reality that includes both agreement and disagreement, cooperation and conflict. However, the decision to confront the possibility of organization agreement is all too difficult and rare, and its opposite, the decision to accept the evils of the present, is all too common. Yet those two decisions may reflect the essence of both our human potential and our human imperfectability. Consequently, the choice to confront reality in the family, the church, the business, or the bureaucracy, though made only occasionally, may reflect those "peak experiences" that provide meaning to the valleys.

In many ways, they may reflect the experience of Sisyphus. As you may remember, Sisyphus was condemned by Pluto to a perpetuity of pushing a large stone to the top of a mountain, only to see it return to its original position when he released it. As Camus suggested in his revision of the myth, Sisyphus' task was absurd and totally devoid of meaning. For most of us, though, the lives we lead pushing papers or hubcaps are no less absurd, and in many ways we probably spend about as much time pushing rocks in our organizations as Sisyphus did in his.

Camus also points out, though, that on occasion as Sisyphus released his rock and watched it return to its resting place at the bottom of the hill, he was able to recognize the absurdity of his lot, and for brief periods of time, transcend it.

So it may be with confronting the Abilene Paradox. Confronting the absurd paradox of agreement may provide, through activity, what Sisyphus gained from his passive but conscious acceptance of his fate. Thus, through the process of active confrontation with reality, we may take respite from pushing our rocks on their endless journeys and, for brief moments, experience what C. P. Snow termed "the triumphs of life we make for ourselves" within those absurdities we call organizations.

Intergroup problems in organizations

Edgar H. Schein

The first major problem of groups in organizations is how to make them effective in fulfilling both organizational goals and the needs of their members. The second major problem is how to establish conditions *between groups* which will enhance the productivity of each without destroying intergroup relations and coordination. This problem exists because as groups become more committed to their own goals and norms, they are likely to become competitive with one another and seek to undermine their rivals' activities, thereby becoming a liability to the organization as a whole. The overall problem, then, is how to establish high-productive, *collaborative* intergroup relations.

Some consequences of intergroup competition

The consequences of intergroup competition were first studied systematically by Sherif in an ingeniously designed setting. He organized a boys' camp in such a way that two groups would form and would become competitive. Sherif then studied the effects of the competition and tried various devices for reestablishing collaborative relationships between the groups (Sherif et al. 1961). Since his original experiments, there have been many replications with adult

groups; the phenomena are so constant that it has been possible to make a demonstration exercise out of the experiment. (Blake and Mouton 1961). The effects can be described in terms of the following categories:

A. What happens *within* each competing group?
    1. Each group becomes more closely knit and elicits greater loyalty from its members; members close ranks and bury some of their internal differences.
    2. Group climate changes from informal, casual, playful to work and task oriented; concern for members' psychological needs declines while concern for task accomplishment increases.
    3. Leadership patterns tend to change from more democratic toward more autocratic; the group becomes more willing to tolerate autocratic leadership.
    4. Each group becomes more highly structured and organized.
    5. Each group demands more loyalty and conformity from its members in order to be able to present a "solid front."
B. What happens *between* the competing groups?
    1. Each group begins to see the

other groups as the enemy, rather than merely a neutral object.

2. Each group begins to experience distortions of perception — it tends to perceive only the best parts of itself, denying its weaknesses, and tends to perceive only the worst parts of the other group, denying its strengths; each group is likely to develop a negative stereotype of the other (``they don't play fair like we do'').

3. Hostility toward the other group increases while interaction and communication with the other group decrease; thus it becomes easier to maintain negative stereotypes and more difficult to correct perceptual distortions.

4. If the groups are forced into interaction — for example, if they are forced to listen to representatives plead their own and the others' cause in reference to some task — each group is likely to listen more closely to their own representative and not to listen to the representative of the other group, except to find fault with his presentation; in other words, group members tend to listen only for that which supports their own position and stereotype.

Thus far, I have listed some consequences of the competition itself, without reference to the consequences if one group actually wins out over the other. Before listing those effects, I would like to draw attention to the generality of the above reactions. Whether one is talking about sports teams, or interfraternity competition, or labor-management disputes, or interdepartmental competition as between sales and production in an industrial organization, or about inter-

national relations and the competition between the Soviet Union and the United States, the same phenomena tend to occur. If you will give just a little thought to competing groups of which you have been a member, you will begin to recognize most of the psychological responses described. I want to stress that these responses can be very useful to the group in making it more effective and highly motivated in task accomplishment. However, the same factors which improve *intragroup* effectiveness may have negative consequences for *intergroup* effectiveness. For example, as we have seen in labor-management or international disputes, if the groups perceive themselves as competitors, they find it more difficult to resolve their differences.

Let us look at the consequences of winning and losing, as in a situation where several groups are bidding to have their proposal accepted for a contract or as a solution to some problem. Many intraorganizational situations become win-or-lose affairs, hence it is of particular importance to examine their consequences.

C. What happens to the *winner?*
1. Winner retains it cohesion and may become even more cohesive.
2. Winner tends to release tension, lose its fighting spirit, become complacent, casual, and playful (the ``fat and happy'' state).
3. Winner tends toward high intragroup cooperation and concern for members' needs, and low concern for work and task accomplishment.
4. Winner tends to be complacent and to feel that winning has confirmed the positive stereotype of itself and the negative stereotype

of the "enemy" group; there is little basis for reevaluating perceptions, or reexamining group operations in order to learn how to improve them.

D. What happens to the *loser*?
1. If the situation permits because of some ambiguity in the decision (say, if judges have rendered it or if the game was close), there is a strong tendency for the loser to deny or distort the reality of losing; instead, the loser will find psychological escapes like "the judges were biased," "the judges didn't really understand our solution," "the rules of the game were not clearly explained to us," "if luck had not been against us at the one key point, we would have won," and so on.
2. If loss is accepted, the losing group tends to splinter, unresolved conflicts come to the surface, fights break out, all in the effort to find the cause for the loss.
3. Loser is more tense, ready to work harder, and desperate to find someone or something to blame — the leader, itself, the judges who decided against them, the rules of the game (the "lean and hungry" state).
4. Loser tends toward low intragroup cooperation, low concern for members' needs, and high concern for recouping by working harder.
5. Loser tends to learn a lot about itself as a group because positive stereotype of itself and negative stereotype of the other group are upset by the loss, forcing a reevaluation of perceptions; as a consequence, loser is likely to re-

organize and become more cohesive and effective, once the loss has been accepted realistically.

The net effect of the win-lose situation is often that the loser is not convinced that he lost, and that intergroup tension is higher than before the competition began.

Reducing the negative consequences of intergroup competitions

The gains of intergroup competition may under some conditions outweigh the negative consequences. It may be desirable to have work groups pitted against one another or to have departments become cohesive loyal units, even if interdepartmental coordination suffers. Other times, however, the negative consequences outweigh the gains, and management seeks ways of reducing intergroup tension. Many of the ideas to be mentioned about how this might be accomplished also come from the basic researches of Sherif and Blake; they have been tested and found to be successful. As we will see, the problems derive not so much from being unable to think of ways for reducing intergroup conflicts as from being *unable to implement some of the most effective ways.*

The fundamental problem of intergroup competition is the conflict of goals and the breakdown of interaction and communication between the groups; this breakdown in turn permits and stimulates perceptual distortion and mutual negative stereotyping. The basic strategy of reducing conflict, therefore, is to find goals upon which groups can agree and to reestablish valid communication between the groups. The tactics to employ in implementing this strategy can be any combination of the following:

Locating a common enemy □ For example, the competing teams of each league can compose an all-star team to play the other league, or conflicts between sales and production can be reduced if both can harness their efforts to helping their company successfully compete against another company. The conflict here is merely shifted to a higher level.

Inventing a negotiation strategy which brings subgroups of the competing groups into interaction with each other □ The isolated group representative cannot abandon his group position but a subgroup which is given some power can not only permit itself to be influenced by its counterpart negotiation team, but will have the strength to influence the remainder of the group.

Locating a superordinate goal □ Such a goal can be a brand-new task which requires the cooperative effort of the previously competing groups or can be a task like analyzing and reducing the intergroup conflict itself. For example, the previously competing sales and production departments can be given the task of developing a new product line that will be both cheap to produce and in great customer demand; or, with the help of an outside consultant, the competing groups can be invited to examine their own behavior and reevaluate the gains and losses from competition.

Reducing intergroup competition through laboratory training methods

The last procedure mentioned above has been tried by a number of psychologists, notably Blake, with considerable success. (Blake and Mouton 1962). Assuming the organization recognizes that

it has a problem, and assuming it is ready to expose this problem to an outside consultant, the laboratory approach to reducing conflict might proceed as follows: (1) The competing groups are both brought into a training setting and the goals are stated to be an exploration of mutual perceptions and mutual relations. (2) Each group is then invited to discuss its perceptions of and attitudes toward itself and the other group. (3) In the presence of both groups, representatives publicly share the perceptions of self and other which the groups have generated, while the groups are obligated to remain silent (the objective is simply to report to the other group as accurately as possible the images that each group has developed in private). (4). Before any exchange has taken place, the groups return to private sessions to digest and analyze what they have heard; there is a great likelihood that the representative reports have revealed great discrepancies to each group between its self-image and the image that the other group holds of it; the private session is partly devoted to an analysis of the reasons for the discrepancies, which forces each group to review its actual behavior toward the other group and the possible consequences of that behavior, regardless of its intentions. (5) In public session, again working through representatives, each group shares with the other what discrepancies they have uncovered and their analysis of the possible reasons for them, with the focus on the actual behavior exhibited. (6) Following this mutual exposure, a more open exploration is then permitted between the two groups on the *now-shared goal* of identifying further reasons for perceptual distortions.

Interspersed with these steps are short

lectures and reading assignments on the psychology of intergroup conflict, the bases for perceptual distortion, psychological defense mechanisms, and so on. The goal is to bring the psychological dynamics of the situation into conscious awareness and to refocus the groups on the common goal of exploring jointly the problem they share. In order to do this, they must have valid data about each other, which is provided through the artifice of the representative reports.

The Blake model described above deals with the entire group. Various other approaches have been tried which start with numbers. For example, groups A and B can be divided into pairs composed of an A and B member. Each pair can be given the assignment of developing a joint product which uses the best ideas from the A product and the B product. Or, in each pair, members may be asked to argue for the product of the opposing group. It has been shown in a number of experiments that one way of changing attitudes is to ask a person to play the role of an advocate of the new attitude to be learned. (Janis and King 1954). The very act of arguing for another product, even if it is purely an exercise, exposes the person to some of its virtues which he had previously denied. A practical application of these points might be to have some members of the sales department spend time in the production department and be asked to represent the production point of view to some third party, or to have some production people join sales teams to learn the sales point of view.

Most of the approaches cited depend on a recognition of some problem by the organization and a willingness on the part of the competing groups to participate in some training effort to reduce negative consequences. The reality, however, is that most organizations neither recognize the problem nor are willing to invest time and energy in resolving it. Some of the unwillingness also arises from each competing group's recognition that in becoming more cooperative it may lose some of its own identity and integrity as a group. Rather than risk this, the group may prefer to continue the competition. This may well be the reason why, in international relations, nations refuse to engage in what seem like perfectly simple ways of resolving their differences. They resist partly in order to protect their integrity. Consequently, the *implementation* of strategies and tactics for reducing the negative consequences of intergroup competition is often a greater problem than the development of such strategies and tactics.

Preventing intergroup conflict

Because of the great difficulties of reducing intergroup conflict once it has developed, it may be desirable to prevent its occurrence in the first place. How can this be done? Paradoxically, a strategy of prevention must bring into question the fundamental premise upon which organization through division of labor rests. Once it has been decided by a superordinate authority to divide up functions among different departments or groups, a bias has already been introduced toward intergroup competition; for in doing its own job well, each group must to some degree compete for scarce resources and rewards from the superordinate authority. The very concept of division of labor implies a reduction of communication and interaction between groups, thus making it possible for perceptual distortions to occur.

The organization planner who wishes

to avoid intergroup competition need not abandon the concept of division of labor, but he should follow some of the steps listed in creating and handling his different functional groups.

1. Relatively greater emphasis given to *total organizational effectiveness* and the role of departments in contributing to it; departments measured and rewarded on the basis of their *contribution* to the total effort rather than their individual effectiveness.
2. *High interaction* and *frequent communication* stimulated between groups to work on problems of intergroup coordination and help; organizational *rewards given partly on the basis of help* which groups give to each other.
3. Frequent *rotation of members* among groups or departments to stimulate high degree of mutual understanding and empathy for one another's problems.
4. *Avoidance of any win-lose situation;* groups never put into the position of competing for some organizational reward; emphasis always placed on pooling resources to maximize organizational effectiveness; rewards shared equally with all the groups or departments.

Most managers find the last of the above points particularly difficult to accept because of the strong belief that performance can be improved by pitting people or groups against one another in a competitive situation. This may indeed be true in the short run, and in some cases may work in the long run, but the negative consequences we have described are undeniably a product of a competitive win-lose situation. Consequently, if a manager wishes to prevent

such consequences, he must face the possibility that he may have to abandon competitive relationships altogether and seek to substitute intergroup collaboration toward organizational goals. Implementing such a preventive strategy is often more difficult, partly because most people are inexperienced in stimulating and managing collabortive relationships. Yet it is clear from observing organizations such as those using the Scanlon Plan not only that it is possible to establish collaborative relationships, even between labor and management, but also that where this has been done, organizational and group effectiveness have been as high as or higher than under competitive conditions.

The problem of integration in perspective

I have discussed two basic issues in this chapter, both dealing with psychological groups: (1) the development of groups within organizations which can fulfill both the needs of the organization and the psychological needs of its members; and (2) the problems of intergroup competition and conflict. To achieve maximum integration, the organization should be able to create conditions that will facilitate a balance between organizational goals and member needs and minimize disintegrative competition between the subunits of the total organization.

Groups are highly complex sets of relationships. There are no easy generalizations about the conditions under which they will be effective, but with suitable training, many kinds of groups can become more effective than they have been. Consequently, group dynamics training by laboratory methods may be a more promising approach to effectiveness than attempting a *priority* to determine the right membership, type of leadership, and organization. All the factors must be taken into account, with training perhaps weighted more heavily than it has been, though the training itself must be carefully undertaken.

The creation of psychologically meaningful and effective groups does not solve all of the organization's problems if such groups compete and conflict with each other. We examined some of the consequences of competition under win-lose conditions and outlined two basic approaches for dealing with the problem: (1) reducing conflict by increasing communication and locating superordinate goals, and (2) preventing conflict by establishing from the outset organizational conditions which stimulate collaboration rather than competition.

The Prevention of intergroup conflict is especially crucial if the groups involved are highly interdependent. The greater the interdependence, the greater the potential loss to the total organization of negative stereotyping, withholding of information, efforts to make the other group look bad in the eyes of the superior, and so on.

It is important to recognize that the preventative strategy does not imply absence of disagreement and artificial "sweetness and light" within or between groups. Conflict and disagreement at the level of the group or organizational *task* is not only desirable but essential for the achievement of the best solutions to problems. What is harmful is *interpersonal* or *intergroup* conflict in which the task is not as important as gaining advantage over the other person or group. The negative consequences we described, such as mutual negative stereotyping, fall into this latter category and undermine rather than aid overall task performance. And it is these kinds of conflicts which can be reduced by establishing collaborative relationships. Interestingly enough, observations of cases would suggest that task-relevant conflict which improves overall effectiveness is greater under collaborative conditions because groups and members trust each other enough to be frank and open in sharing information and opinions. In the competitive situation, each group is committed to hiding its special resources from the other groups, thus preventing effective integration of all resources in the organization.

Defensive communication

Jack R. Gibb

One way to understand communication is to view it as a possible process rather than as a language process. If one is to make fundamental improvements in communication, he must make changes in interpersonal relationships.

One possible type of alteration — and the one with which this paper is concerned — is that of reducing the degree of defensiveness.

Defensive behavior is defined as that behavior which occurs when an individual perceives threat or anticipates threat in the group. The person who behaves defensively, even though he also gives some attention to the common task, devotes an appreciable portion of his energy to defending himself. Besides talking about the topic, he thinks about how he appears to others, how he may be seen more favorably, how he may win, dominate, impress, or escape punishment, and/or how he may avoid or mitigate a perceived or an anticipated attack.

Such inner feelings and outward acts tend to create similarly defensive postures in others; and, if unchecked, the ensuing circular response becomes increasingly destructive. Defensive behavior, in short, engenders defensive listening, and this in turn produces postural, facial, and verbal cues which raise the defense level of the original communicator.

Defense arousal prevents the listener from concentrating upon the message. Not only do defensive communicators send off multiple value, motive, and affect cues, but also defensive recipients distort what they receive. As a person becomes more and more defensive, he becomes less and less able to perceive accurately the motives, the values, and the emotions of the sender. My analyses of tape-recorded discussions revealed that increases in defensive behavior were correlated positively with losses in efficiency in communication (Gibb 1961). Specifically, distortions became greater when defensive states existed in the groups.

The converse, moreover, also is true. The more "supportive" or defense reductive the climate, the less the receiver reads into the communication distorted loadings which arise from projections of his own anxieties, motives, and concerns. As defenses are reduced, the receivers become better able to con-

centrate upon the structure, the content, and the cognitive meanings of the message.

In working over an eight-year peiod with recordings of discussions occuring in varied settings, I developed the six pairs of defensive and supportive categories presented in Table 1. Behavior which a listener perceives as possessing any of the characteristics listed in the left-hand column arouses defensiveness, whereas that which he interprets as having any of the qualities designated as supportive reduces defensive feelings. The degree to which these reactions occur depends upon the personal level of defensiveness and upon the general climate in the group at the time (Gibb 1960).

Speech or other behavior which appears evaluative increases defensiveness. If by expression, manner of speech, tone of voice, or verbal content the sender seems to be evaluating or judging the listener, then the receiver goes on guard. Of course, other factors may inhibit the reaction. If the listener thought that the speaker regarded him as an equal and was being open and spontaneous, for example, the evaluativeness in a message would be neutralized and perhaps not even perceived. This same principle applies equally to the other five categories of potentially defense-producing climates. The six sets are interactive.

Table 1
Categories of behavior characteristics of supportive and defensive climates in small groups

Defensive climates	Supportive climates
1. Evaluation	1. Description
2. Control	2. Problem orientation
3. Strategy	3. Spontaneity
4. Neutrality	4. Empathy
5. Superiority	5. Equality
6. Certainty	6. Provisionalism

Because our attitudes toward other persons are frequently, and often necessarily, evaluative, expressions which the defensive person will regard as non-judgmental are hard to frame. Even the simplest question usually conveys the answer that the sender wishes or implies the response that would fit into his value system. A mother, for example, immediately following an earth tremor that shook the house, sought for her small son with the question: "Bobby, where are you?" The timid and plaintive "Mommy, I didn't do it" indicated how Bobby's chronic mild defensiveness predisposed him to react with a project of his own guilt and in the context of his chronic assumption that questions are full of accusation.

Anyone who has attempted to train professionals to use information-seeking speech with neutral affect appreciates how difficult it is to teach a person to say even the simple "Who did that?" without being seen as accusing. Speech is so frequently judgmental that there is a reality base for the defensive interpretations which are so common.

When insecure, group members are particularly likely to place blame, to see others as fitting into categories of good or bad, to make moral judgments of their colleagues, and to question the value, motive, and affect loadings of the speech which they hear. Since value loadings imply a judgment of others, a belief that the standards of the speaker differ from his own, causes the listener to become defensive.

Descriptive speech, in contrast to that which is evaluative, tends to arouse a minimum of uneasiness. Speech acts which the listener perceives as genuine requests for information or as material with neutral loadings are descriptive. Specifically, presentations of feelings, events, perceptions, or processes which do not ask or imply that the receiver change behavior or attitude are minimally defense producing. The difficulty in avoiding overtone is illustrated by the problems of news reporters in writing stories about unions, communists, Negroes, and religious activities without tipping off the "party" line of the newspaper. One can often tell from the opening words in a news article which side the newspaper's editorial policy favors.

Speech which is used to control the listener evokes resistance. In most of our social intercourse someone is trying to do something to someone else — to change an attitude, to influence behavior, or to restrict the field of activity. The degree to which attempts to control produce defensiveness depends upon the openness of the effort, for a suspicion that hidden motives exist heightens resistance. For this reason, attempts of non-directive therapists and progressive educators to refrain from imposing a set of values, a point of view, or a problem solution upon the receivers meet with many barriers. Since the norm is control, noncontrollers must earn the perceptions that their efforts have no hidden motives. A bombardment of persuasiveness "messages" in the fields of politics, education, special causes, advertising, religion, medicine, industrial relations, and guidance has bred cynical and paranoidal responses in listeners.

Implicit in all attempts to alter another person is the assumption by the change agent that the person to be altered is inadequate. That the speaker secretly views the listener as ignorant, unable to make his own decisions, uninformed, immature, unwise, or possessed of wrong or inadequate attitudes is a subconscious perception which gives the latter a valid base for defensive reactions.

Methods of control are many and varied. Legalistic insistence on detail, restrictive regulations and policies, conformity norms, and all laws are among the methods. Gestures, facial expressions, other forms of nonverbal communication, and even such simple acts as holding a door open in a particular manner are means of imposing one's will upon another and hence are potential sources of resistance.

Problem orientation, on the other hand, is the antithesis of persuasion. When the sender communicates a desire to collaborate in defining a mutual problem and in seeking its solution, he tends to create the same problem orientation in the listener; and, of greater importance, he implies that he has no predetermined solution, attitude, or method to impose. Such behavior is permissive in that it allows the receiver to set his own goals, make his own decisions, and evaluate his own progress — or to share with the sender in doing so. The exact methods of attaining permissiveness are not known, but they must involve a constellation of cues and they certainly go beyond mere verbal assurances that the communicator has no hidden desires to exercise control.

When the sender is perceived as engaged in a stratagem involving ambiguous and multiple motivations, the receiver becomes defensive. No one wishes to be a guinea pig, a role player, or an impressed actor, and no one likes to be the victim of some hidden motivation. That which is concealed, also, may appear larger than it really is with the degree of defensiveness of the listener determining the perceived size of the suppressed element. The intense reaction of the reading audience to the material in *The Hidden Persuaders* indicates the prevalence of defensive reactions to multiple motivations behind strategy. Group members who are seen as "taking a role," as feigning emotion, as toying with their colleagues, as withholding information, or as having special sources of data are especially resented. One participant once complained that another was "using a listening technique" on him!

A large part of the adverse reaction to much of the so-called human relations training is a feeling against what are perceived as gimmicks and tricks to fool or to "involve" people, to make a person think he is making his own decision, or to make the listener feel that the sender is genuinely interested in him as a person. Particularly violent reactions occur when it appears that someone is trying to make a stratagem appear spontaneous. One person has reported a boss who incurred resentment by habitually using the gimmick of "spontaneously" looking at his watch and saying, "My gosh, look at the time — I must run to an appointment." The belief was that the boss would create less irritation by honestly asking to be excused.

Similarly, the deliberate assumption of guilelessness and natural simplicity is especially resented. Monitoring the tapes of feedback and evaluation sessions in training groups indicates the surprising extent to which members perceive the strategies of their colleagues. This perceptual clarity may be quite shocking to the strategist, who usually feels that he has cleverly hidden the motivational aura around the "gimmick."

This aversion to deceit may account for one's resistance to politicians who are suspected of behind-the-scenes planning to get his vote, to psychologists whose listening apparently is motivated by more than the manifest or content-level interest in his behavior, or to the sophisticated, smooth, or clever person whose "oneupmanship" is marked with guile. In training groups the role-flexible person frequently is resented because his changes in behavior are perceived as strategic maneuvers.

In contrast, behavior which appears to be spontaneous and free of deception is defense reductive. If the communicator is seen as having a clean id, as having uncomplicated motivations, as being straightforward and honest, and as behaving spontaneously in response to the situation, he is likely to arouse minimal defense.

When neutrality in speech appears to the listener to indicate a lack of concern for his welfare, he becomes defensive. Group members usually desire to be perceived as valued persons, as individuals of special worth, and as objects of concern and affection. The clinical, detached, person-is-an-object-of-study attitude on the part of many psychologist-trainers is resented by group members. Speech with low affect that communicates little warmth or caring is in such contrast with the affect-laden speech in social situations that it sometimes communicates rejection.

Communication that conveys empathy for the feelings and respect for the worth of the listener, however, is particularly supportive and defense reductive. Reassurance results when a message indicates that the speaker identifies himself with the listener's problems, shares his feelings, and accepts his emotional reactions at face value. Abortive efforts to deny the legitimacy of the receiver's emotions by assuring the receiver that he need not feel bad, that he should not feel rejected, or that he is overly anxious, though often intended as support giving, may impress the listener as lack of acceptance. The combination of under-standing and empathizing with the other person's emotions with no accompanying effort to change him apparently is supportive at a high level.

The importance of gestural behavioral cues in communicating empathy should be mentioned. Apparently spontaneous facial and bodily evidences of concern are often interpreted as especially valid evidence of deep-level acceptance.

When a person communicates to another that he feels superior in position, power, wealth, intellectual ability, physical characteristics, or other ways, he arouses defensiveness. Here, as with the other sources of disturbance, whatever arouses feelings of inadequacy causes the listener to center upon the affect loading of the statement rather than upon the cognitive elements. The receiver then reacts by not hearing the message, by forgetting it, by competing with the sender, or by becoming jealous of him.

The person who is perceived as feeling superior communicates that he is not willing to enter into a shared problem-solving relationship, that he probably does not desire feedback, that he does not require help, and/or that he will be likely to try to reduce the power, the status, or the worth of the receiver.

Many ways exist for creating the atmosphere that the sender feels himself equal to the listener. Defenses are reduced when one perceives the sender as being willing to enter into participate planning with mutual trust and respect. Differences in talent, ability, worth, appearance, status, and power often exist, but the low defense communicator seems to attach little importance to these distinctions.

The effects of dogmatism in producing defensiveness are well known. Those who seem to know the answers, to require no additional data, and to regard themselves as teachers rather than as co-workers tend to put others on guard. Moreover, in my experiment, listeners often perceived manifest expressions of certainty as connoting inward feelings of inferiority. They saw the dogmatic individual as needing to be right, as wanting to win an argument rather than solve a problem, and as seeing his ideas as truths to be defended. This kind of behavior often was associated with acts which others regarded as attempts to exercise control. People who were "right" seemed to have low tolerance for members who were "wrong" — that is, those who did not agree with the sender.

One reduces the defensiveness of the listener when he communicates that he is willing to experiment with his own behavior, attitudes, and ideas. The person who appears to be taking provisional attitudes, to be investigating issues rather than taking sides on them, to be problem solving rather than debating, and to be willing to experiment and explore tends to communicate that the listener may have some control over the shared quest or the investigation of the ideas. If a person is genuinely searching for information and data, he does not resent help or company along the way.

Conclusions

The implications of the above material for the parent, the teacher, the manager, the administrator, or the therapist are fairly obvious. Arousing defensiveness interferes with communication and thus makes it difficult — and sometimes impossible — for anyone to convey ideas clearly and to move effectively toward the solution of therapeutic, educational, or managerial problems.

"Why should my conscience bother me?"

Kermit Vandivier

The B. F. Goodrich Co. is what business magazines like to speak of as "a major American corporation." It has operations in a dozen states and as many foreign countries, and of these far-flung facilities, the Goodrich plant at Troy, Ohio, is not the most imposing. It is a small, one-story building, once used to manufacture airplanes. Set in the grassy flatlands of west-central Ohio, it employs only about six hundred people. Never-theless, it is one of the three largest manufacturers of aircraft wheels and brakes, a leader in a most profitable industry. Goodrich wheels and brakes support such well-known planes as the F111, the C5A, the Boeing 727, the XB70 and many others. Its customers include almost every aircraft manufacturer in the world.

Contracts for aircraft wheels and brakes often run into millions of dollars, and ordinarily a contract with a total value of less than $70,000, though welcome, would not create any special stir of joy in the hearts of Goodrich sales personnel. But purchase order P-23718, issued on June 18, 1967, by the LTV Aerospace Corporation, and ordering 202 brake assemblies for a new Air Force plane at a total price of $69,417, was received by Goodrich with considerable glee. And there was good reason. Some ten years previously, Goodrich had built a brake for LTV that was, to say the least, considerably less than a rousing success. The brake had not lived up to Goodrich's promises, and after experiencing considerable difficulty, LTV had written off Goodrich as a source of brakes. Since that time, Goodrich salesmen had been unable to sell so much as a shot of brake fluid to LTV. So in 1967, when LTV requested bids on wheels and brakes for the new A7D light attack aircraft it proposed to build for the Air Force, Goodrich submitted a bid that was absurdly low, so low that LTV could not, in all prudence, turn it down.

Goodrich had, in industry parlance, "bought into the business." Not only did the company not expect to make a profit on the deal; it was prepared, if necessary, to lose money. For aircraft brakes are not something that can be ordered off the shelf. They are designed for a particular aircraft, and once an aircraft manufacturer buys a brake, he is forced to purchase all replacement parts from the brake manufacturer. The $70,000 that Goodrich would get for making the brake would be a drop in the bucket when compared with the cost of the linings and other parts the Air Force would have to buy from Goodrich during the lifetime of the aircraft. Furthermore, the company which manufacturers brakes for one particular model of an aircraft quite nat-

urally has the inside track to supply other brakes when the planes are updated and improved.

Thus, that first contract, regardless of the money involved, is very important, and Goodrich, when it learned that it had been awarded the A7D contract, was determined that while it may have slammed the door on its own foot ten years before, this time, the second time around, things would be different. The word was soon circulated throughout the plant: "We can't bungle it this time. We've got to give them a good brake, regardless of the cost."

There was another factor which had undoubtedly influenced LTV. All aircraft brakes made today are of the disk type, and the bid submitted by Goodrich called for a relatively small brake, one containing four disks and weighing only 106 pounds. The weight of any aircraft part is extremely important. The lighter a part is, the heavier the plane's payload can be. The four-rotor, 106-pound brake promised by Goodrich was about as light as could be expected, and this undoubtedly had helped more LTV to award the contract to Goodrich.

The brake was designed by one of Goodrich's most capable engineers, John Warren. A tall, lanky blond and a graduate of Purdue, Warren had come from the Chrysler Corporation seven years before and had become adept at aircraft brake design. The happy-go-lucky manner he usually maintained belied a temper which exploded whenever anyone ventured to offer any criticism of his work, no matter how small. On these occasions, Warren would turn red in the face, often throwing or slamming something and then stalking from the scene. As his coworkers learned the consequences of criticizing him, they did so less and less readily, and when he submitted his preliminary design for the A7D brake, it was accepted without question.

Warren was named project engineer for the A7D, and he, in turn, assigned the task of producing the final production design to a newcomer to the Goodrich engineering stable, Searle Lawson. Just turned twenty-six, Lawson had been out of the Northrup Institute of Technology only one year when he came to Goodrich in January 1967. Like Warren, he had worked for a while in the automotive industry, but his engineering degree was in aeronautical and astronautical sciences, and when the opportunity came to enter his special field, via Goodrich, he took it. At the Troy plant, Lawson had been assigned to various "paper projects" to break him in, and after several months spent reviewing statistics and old brake designs, he was beginning to fret at the lack of challenge. When told he was being assigned to his first "real" project, he was elated and immediately plunged into his work.

The major portion of the design had already been completed by Warren, and major assemblies for the brake had already been ordered from Goodrich suppliers. Naturally, however, before Goodrich could start making the brakes on a production basis, much testing would have to be done. Lawson would have to determine the best materials to use for the linings and discover what minor adjustments in the design would have to be made.

Then, after the preliminary testing and after the brake was judged ready for production, one brake assembly would undergo a series of grueling, simulated braking stops and other severe trials called qualification tests. These tests are required by the military, which gives very detailed specifications on how they are to be conducted, the criteria for failure, and

so on. They are performed in the Goodrich plant's test laboratory, where huge machines called dynamometers can simulate the weight and speed of almost any aircraft. After the brakes pass the laboratory tests, they are approved for production, but before the brakes are accepted for use in military service, they must undergo further extensive flight tests.

Searle Lawson was well aware that much more had to be done before the A7D brake could go into production, and he knew that LTV had set the last two weeks in June 1968, as the starting dates for flight tests. So he decided to begin testing immediately. Goodrich's suppliers had not yet delivered the brake housing and other parts, but the brake disks had arrived, and using the housing from a brake similar in size and weight to the A7D brake, Lawson built a prototype. The prototype was installed in a test wheel and placed on one of the big dynamometers in the plant's test laboratory. The dynamometer was adjusted to simulate the weight of the A7D and Lawson began a series of tests, "landing" the wheel and brake at the A7D's landing speed, and braking it to a stop. The main purpose of these preliminary tests was to learn what temperatures would develop within the brake during the simulated stops and to evaluate the lining materials tentatively selected for use.

During a normal aircraft landing the temperatures inside the brake may reach 1000 degrees, and occasionally a bit higher. During Lawson's first simulated landings, the temperature of his prototype brake reached 1500 degrees. The brake glowed a bright cherry-red and threw off incandescent particles of metal and lining material as the temperature reached its peak. After a few such stops, the brake was dismantled and the linings were found to be almost completely dis-integrated. Lawson chalked this first fail-ure up to chance and, ordering new lin-ing materials, tried again.

The second attempt was a repeat of the first. The brake became extremely hot, causing the lining materials to crumble into dust.

After the third such failure, Lawson in-experienced though he was, knew that the fault lay not in defective parts or unsuitable lining material but in the basic design of the brake itself. Ignoring Warren's original computations, Lawson made his own, and it didn't take him long to discover where the trouble lay — the brake was too small. There simply was not enough surface area on the disks to stop the aircraft without generating the excessive heat that caused the linings to fail.

The answer to the problem was obvi-ous but far from simple — the four-disk brake would have to be scrapped, and a new design, using five disks, would have to be developed. The implications were not lost on Lawson. Such a step would require the junking of all the four-disk-brake subassemblies, many of which had now begun to arrive from the various suppliers. It would also mean several weeks of preliminary design and testing and many more weeks of waiting while the suppliers made and delivered the new subassemblies.

Yet, several weeks had already gone by since LTV's order had arrived, and the date for delivery of the first production brakes for flight testing was only a few months away.

Although project engineer John War-ren had more or less turned the A7D over to Lawson, he knew of the difficulties Lawson had been experiencing. He had assured the young engineer that the problem revolved around getting the right kind of lining material. Once that was found, he said, the difficulties would end.

Despite the evidence of the abortive tests and Lawson's careful com-putations, Warren rejected the sugges-tion that the four-disk brake was too light for the job. Warren knew that his superior had already told LTV, in rather glowing terms, that the preliminary tests on the A7D brake were very successful. Indeed, Warren's superiors weren't aware at this time of the troubles on the brake. It would have been difficult for Warren to admit not only that he had made a seri-ous error in his calculations and original design but that his mistakes had been caught by a green kid, barely out of college.

Warren's reaction to a five-disk brake was not unexpected by Lawson, and, see-ing that the four-disk brake was not to be abandoned so easily, he took his calcula-tions and dismal test results one step up the corporate ladder.

At Goodrich, the man who supervises the engineers working on projects slated for production is called, predictably, the projects manager. The job was held by a short, chubby and bald man named Rob-ert Sink. A man truly devoted to his work, Sink was as likely to be found at his desk at ten o'clock on Sunday night as ten o'clock on Monday morning. His outside interests consisted mainly of tinkering on a Model-A Ford and an occasional game of golf. Some fifteen years before, Sink had begun working at Goodrich as a lowly draftsman. Slowly, he worked his way up. Despite his geniality, Sink was neither respected nor liked by the ma-jority of the engineers, and his appoint-ment as their supervisor did not improve their feelings about him. They thought he had only gone to high school. It quite naturally rankled those who had gone through years of college and acquired impressive specialties such as thermodynamics and astronautics to be commanded by a man whom they considered their intellectual inferior. But, though Sink had no college training, he had something even more useful: a fine working knowledge of company politics.

Puffing upon a Meerschaum pipe, Sink listened gravely as young Lawson confided his fears about the four-disk brake. Then he examined Lawson's calculations and the results of the abortive tests. Despite the fact that he was not a qualified engineer, in the strictest sense of the word, it must certainly have been obvious to Sink that Lawson's calculations were correct and that a four-disk brake would never have worked on the A7D.

But other things of equal importance were also obvious. First, to concede that Lawson's calculations were correct would also mean conceding that Warren's calculations were incorrect. As projects manager, he not only was responsible for Warren's activities, but, in admitting that Warren had erred, he would have to admit that he had erred in trusting Warren's judgment. It also meant that, as projects manager, it would be he who would have to explain the whole messy situaton to the Goodrich hierarchy, not only at Troy but possibly on the corporate level at Goodrich's Akron offices. And, having taken Warren's judgment of the four-disk brake at face value (he was forced to do this since, not being an engineer, he was unable to exercise any engineering judgment of his own), he had assured LTV, not once but several times, that about all there was left to do on the brake was pack it in a crate and ship it out the back door.

There's really no problem at all, he told Lawson. After all, Warren was an experienced engineer, and if he said the brake would work, it would work. Just keep on testing and probably, maybe even on the very next try, it'll work out just fine.

Lawson was far from convinced, but without the support of his superiors there was little he could do except keep on testing. By now, housings for the four-disk brake had begun to arrive at the plant, and Lawson was able to build up a production model of the brake and begin the formal qualification tests demanded by the military.

The first qualification attempts went exactly as the tests on the prototype had. Terrific heat developed within the brakes and, after a few, short, simulated stops, the linings crumbled. A new type of lining material was ordered and once again an attempt to qualify the brake was made. Again, failure.

Experts were called in from lining manufacturers, and new lining "mixes" were tried, always with the same result. Failure.

It was now the last week in March 1968, and flight tests were scheduled to begin in seventy days. Twelve separate attempts had been made to formally qualify the brake, and all had failed. It was no longer possible for anyone to ignore the glaring truth that the brake was a dismal failure and that nothing short of a major design change could ever make it work.

In the engineering department, panic set in. A glum-faced Lawson prowled the test laboratory dejectedly. Occasionally, Warren would witness some simulated stop on the brake and, after it was completed, troop silently back to his desk. Sink, too, showed an unusual interest in the trials, and he and Warren would converse in low tones while poring over the results of the latest tests. Even the most inexperienced of the lab technicians and the men who operated the testing equipment knew they had a "bad" brake on their hands, and there was some grumbling about "wasting time on a brake that won't work."

New menaces appeared. An engineering team from LTV arrived at the plant to get a good look at the brake in action. Luckily, they stayed only a few days, and Goodrich engineers managed to cover the true situation without too much difficulty.

On April 4, the thirteenth attempt at qualification was begun. This time no attempt was made to conduct the tests by the methods and techniques spelled out in the military specifications. Regardless of how it had to be done, the brake was to be "nursed" through the required fifty simulated stops.

Fans were set up to provide special cooling. Instead of maintaining pressure on the brake until the test wheel had come to a complete stop, the pressure was reduced when the wheel had decelerated to around 15 mph, allowing it to "coast" to a stop. After each stop, the brake was disassembled and carefully cleaned, and after some of the stops, internal brake parts were machined in order to remove warp and other disfigurations caused by the high heat.

By these and other methods, all clearly contrary to the techniques established by the military specifications, the brake was coaxed through the fifty stops. But even using these methods, the brake could not meet all the requirements. On one stop the wheel rolled for a distance of 16,000 feet, nearly three miles, before the brake could bring it to a stop. The normal distance required for such a stop was around 3500 feet.

On April 11, the day the thirteenth test was completed, I became personally involved in the A7D situation.

I had worked in the Goodrich test laboratory for five years, starting first as an instrumentation engineer, then later becoming a data analyst and technical writer. As part of my duties, I analyzed the reams and reams of instrumentation data that came from the many testing machines in the laboratory, then transcribed it to a more usable form for the engineering department. And when a new-type brake had successfully completed the required qualification tests, I would issue a formal qualification report.

Qualification reports were an accumulation of all the data and test logs compiled by the tests, and were documentary proof that a brake had met all the requirements established by the military specifications and was therefore presumed safe for flight testing. Before actual flight tests were conducted on a brake, qualification reports had to be delivered to the customer and to various government officials.

On April 11, I was looking over the data from the latest A7D test, and I noticed that many irregularities in testing methods had been noted on the test logs.

Technically, of course, there was nothing wrong with conducting tests in any manner desired, so long as the test was for research purposes only. But qualification test methods are clearly delineated by the military, and I knew that this test had been a formal qualification attempt. One particular notation on the test logs caught my eye. For some of the stops, the instrument which recorded the brake pressure had been deliberately miscalibrated so that, while the brake pressure used during the stops was recorded as 1000 psi (the maximum pressure that would be available on the A7D aircraft), the pressure had actually been 1100 psi!

I showed the test logs to the test lab supervisor, Ralph Gretzinger, who said he had learned from the technician who had miscalibrated the instrument that he had been asked to do so by Lawson. Lawson, said Gretzinger, readily admitted asking for the miscalibration, saying he had been told to do so by Sink.

I asked Gretzinger why anyone would want to miscalibrate the data-recording instruments.

"Why? I'll tell you why," he snorted. "That brake is a failure. It's way too small for the job, and they're not ever going to get it to work. They're getting desperate, and instead of scrapping the damned thing and starting over, they figure they can horse around down here in the lab and qualify it that way."

An expert engineer, Gretzinger had been responsible for several innovations in brake design. It was he who had invented the unique brake system used on the famous XB70. A graduate of Georgia Tech, he was a stickler for detail and he had some very firm ideas about honesty and ethics. "If you want to find out what's going on," said Gretzinger, "ask Lawson, he'll tell you."

Curious, I did ask Lawson the next time he came into the lab. He seemed eager to discuss the A7D and give me the history of his months of frustrating efforts to get Warren and Sink to change the brake design. "I just can't believe this is really happening," said Lawson, shaking his head slowly. "This isn't engineering, at least not what I thought it would be. Back in school, I thought that when you were an engineer, you tried to do your best, no matter what it cost. But this is something else."

He sat across the desk from me, his chin proped in his hand. "Just wait," he warned. "You'll get a chance to see what I'm talking about. You're going to get in the act, too, because I've already had the word that we're going to make one more

attempt to qualify the brake, and that's it. Win or lose, we're going to issue a qualification report!"

I reminded him that a qualification report could only be issued after a brake had successfully met all military requirements, and therefore, unless the next qualification attempt was a success, no report would be issued.

"You'll find out," retorted Lawson. "I was already told that regardless of what the brake does on test, It's going to be qualified." He said he had been told in those exact words at a conference with Sink and Russell Van Horn.

This was the first indication that Sink had brought his boss, Van Horn, into the mess. Although Van Horn, as manager of the design engineering section, was responsible for the entire department, he was not necessarily familiar with all phases of every project, and it was not uncommon for those under him to exercise the what-he-doesn't-know-won't-hurt-him philosophy. If he was aware of the full extent of the A7D situation, it meant that matters had truly reached a desperate stage — that Sink had decided not only to call for help but was looking toward that moment when blame must be borne and, if possible, shared.

Also, if Van Horn had said, "regardless what the brake does on test, it's going to be qualified," then it could only mean that, if necessary, a false qualification report would be issued! I discussed this possibility with Gretzinger, and he assured me that under no circumstances would such a report ever be issued.

"If they want a qualification report, we'll write them one, but we'll tell it just like it is," he declared emphatically. "No false data or false reports are going to come out of this lab."

On May 2, 1968, the fourteenth and

final attempt to qualify the brake was begun. Although the same improper methods used to nurse the brake through the previous tests were employed, it soon became obvious that this too would end in failure.

When the tests were about half completed, Lawson asked if I would start preparing the various engineering curves and graphic displays which were normally incorporated in a qualification report. "It looks as though you'll be writing a qualification report shortly," he said.

I flatly refused to have anything to do with the matter and immediately told Gretzinger what I had been asked to do. He was furious and repeated his previous declaration that under no circumstances would any false data or other matter be issued from the lab.

"I'm going to get this settled right now, once and for all," he declared. "I'm going to see Line [Russell Line, manager of the Goodrich Technical Services Section, of which the test lab was a part] and find out just how far this thing is going to go!" He stormed out of the room.

In about an hour, he returned and called me to his desk. He sat silently for a few moments, then muttered, half to himself, "I wonder what the hell they'd do if I just quit?" I didn't answer and I didn't ask him what he meant. I knew. He had been beaten down. He had reached the point when the decision had to be made. Defy them now while there was still time — or knuckle under, sell out.

"You know," he went on uncertainly, looking down at his desk, "I've been an engineer for a long time, and I've always believed that ethics and integrity were every bit as important as theorems and formulas, and never once has anything happened to change my beliefs. Now this . . . Hell, I've got two sons I've got to put through school and I just . . ." His voice

trailed off.

He sat for a few more minutes, then, looking over the top of his glasses, said hoarsely, "Well, it looks like we're licked. The way it stands now, we're to go ahead and prepare the data and other things for the graphic presentation in the report, and when we're finished, someone upstairs will actually write the report.

"After all," he continued, "we're just drawing some curves, and what happens to them after they leave here, well, we're not responsible for that."

He was trying to persuade himself that as long as we were concerned with only one part of the puzzle and didn't see the completed picture, we really weren't doing anything wrong. He didn't believe what he was saying, and he knew I didn't believe it either. It was an embarrassing and shameful moment for both of us.

I wasn't at all satisfied with the situation and decided that I too would discuss the matter with Russell Line, the senior executive in our section.

Tall, powerfully built, his teeth flashing white, his face tanned to a coffee-brown by a daily stint with a sun lamp, Line looked and acted every inch the executive. He was a crossword puzzle enthusiast and an ardent golfer, and though he had lived in Troy only a short time, he had been accepted into the Troy Country Club and made an official of the golf committee. He had been transferred from the Akron offices some two years previously, and an air of mystery surrounded him. Some office gossips figured he had been sent to Troy as the result of some sort of demotion. Others speculated that since the present general manager of the Troy plant was due shortly for retirement, Line had been transferred to Troy to assume that job and was merely occupying his present position to "get the feel of things." Whatever the case, he commanded great respect and had come to be well liked by those of us who worked under him.

He listened sympathetically while I explained how I felt about the A7D situation, and when I had finished, he asked me what I wanted him to do about it. I said that as employees of the Goodrich Company we had a responsibility to protect the company and its reputation if at all possible. I said I was certain that officers on the corporate level would never knowingly allow such tactics as had been employed on the A7D.

"I agree with you," he remarked, "but I still want to know what you want me to do about it."

I suggested that in all probability the chief engineer at the Troy plant, H. C. "Bud" Sunderman, was unaware of the A7D problem and that he, Line, should tell him what was going on.

Line laughed, good-humoredly. "Sure, I could, but I'm not going to. Bud probably already knows about this thing anyway, and if he doesn't, I'm sure not going to be the one to tell him."

"But why?"

"Because it's none of my business, and it's none of yours. I learned a long time ago not to worry about things over which I had no control. I have no control over this."

I wasn't satisfied with this answer, and I asked him if his conscience wouldn't bother him if, say, during flight tests on the brake, something should happen resulting in death or injury to the test pilot.

"Look," he said, becoming somewhat exasperated, "I just told you I have no control over this thing. Why should my conscience bother me?"

His voice took on a quiet, soothing tone as he continued. "You're just getting all upset over this thing for nothing. I just do as I'm told, and I'd advise you to do

the same."

He had made his decision, and now I had to make mine.

I made no attempt to rationalize what I had been asked to do. It made no difference who would falsify which part of the report or whether the actual falsification would be by misleading numbers or misleading words. Whether by acts of commission or omission, all of us who contributed to the fraud would be guilty. The only question left for me to decide was whether or not I would become a party to the fraud.

Before coming to Goodrich in 1963, I had held a variety of jobs, each a little more pleasant, a little more rewarding than the last. At 42, with seven children, I had decided that the Goodrich Company would probably be my "home" for the rest of my working life. The job paid well, it was pleasant and challenging, and the future looked reasonably bright. My wife and I had bought a home and we were ready to settle down into a comfortable, middle-age, middle-class rut. If I refused to take part in the A7D fraud, I would have to either resign or be fired. The report would be written by someone anyway, but I would have the satisfaction of knowing I had had no part in the matter. But bills aren't paid with personal satisfaction, nor house payments with ethical principles. I made my decision. The next morning, I telephoned Lawson and told him I was ready to begin on the qualification report.

In a few minutes, he was at my desk, ready to begin. Before we started, I asked him, "Do you realize what we are going to do?"

"Yeah," he replied bitterly, "we're going to screw LTV. And speaking of screwing," he continued, "I know now how a whore feels, because that's exactly what I've become, an engineering whore.

I've sold myself. It's all I can do to look at myself in the mirror when I shave. I make me sick."

I was surprised at his vehemence. It was obvious that he too had done his share of soul-searching and didn't like what he had found. Somehow, though, the air seemed clearer after his outburst, and we began working on the report.

I had written dozens of qualification reports, and I knew what a "good" one looked like. Resorting to the actual test data only on occasion, Lawson and I proceeded to prepare page after page of elaborate, detailed engineering curves, charts, and test logs, which purported to show what had happened during the formal qualification tests. Where temperatures were too high, we deliberately chopped them down a few hundred degrees, and where they were too low, we raised them to a value that would appear reasonable to the LTV and military engineers. Brake pressure, torque values, distances, times — everything of consequence was tailored to fit the occasion.

Occasionally, we would find that some test either hadn't been performed at all or had been conducted improperly. On those occasions, we "conducted" the test — successfully, of course — on paper.

For nearly a month we worked on the graphic presentation that would be a part of the report. Meanwhile, the fourteenth and final qualification attempt had been completed, and the brake, not unexpectedly, had failed again.

During that month, Lawson and I talked of little else except the enormity of what we were doing. The more involved we became in our work, the more apparent became our own culpability. We discussed such things as the Nuremberg trials and how they related to our guilt and complicity in the A7D situation. Lawson often expressed his opinion that the brake was downright dangerous and that, once on flight test, "anything is liable to happen."

I saw his boss, John Warren, at least twice during that month and needled him about what we were doing. He didn't take the jibes too kindly but managed to laugh the situation off as "one of those things." One day I remarked that what we were doing amounted to fraud, and he pulled out an engineering handbook and turned to a section on laws as they related to the engineering profession.

He read the definition of fraud aloud, then said, "Well, technically I don't think what we're doing can be called fraud. I'll admit it's not right, but it's just one of those things. We're just kinda caught in the middle. About all I can tell you is, Do like I'm doing. Make copies of everything and put them in your SYA file."

"What's an 'SYA' file?" I asked.

"That's a 'save your ass' file." He laughed.

Although I hadn't known it was called that, I had been keeping an SYA file since the beginning of the A7D fiasco. I had made a copy of every scrap of paper connected even remotely with the A7D and had even had copies of 16mm movies that had been made during some of the simulated stops. Lawson, too, had an SYA file, and we both maintained them for one reason: Should the true state of events on the A7D ever be questioned, we wanted to have access to a complete set of factual data. We were afraid that should the question every come up, the test data might accidentally be "lost."

We finished our work on the graphic portion of the report around the first of June. Altogether, we had prepared nearly two hundred pages of data, containing dozens of deliberate falsifications and misrepresentations. I delivered the data to Gretzinger, who said he had been instructed to deliver it personally to the chief engineer, Bud Sunderman, who in turn would assign someone in the engineering department to complete the written portion of the report. He gathered the bundle of data and left the office. Within minutes, he was back with the data, his face white with anger.

"That damned Sink's beat me to it," he said furiously. "He's already talked to Bud about this, and now Sunderman says no one in the engineering department has time to write the report. He wants us to do it, and I told him we couldn't." The words had barely left his mouth when Russell Line burst in the door. "What the hell's all the fuss about this damned report?" he demanded loudly.

Patiently, Gretzinger explained. "There's no fuss. Sunderman just told me that we'd have to write the report down here, and I said we couldn't. Russ," he went on, "I've told you before that we weren't going to write the report. I made my position clear on that a long time ago."

Line shut him up with a wave of his hand and, turning to me, bellowed, "I'm getting sick and tired of hearing about this damned report. Now, write the goddam thing and shut up about it!" He slammed out of the office.

Gretzinger and I just sat for a few seconds looking at each other. Then he spoke.

"Well, I guess he's made it pretty clear, hasn't he? We can either write the thing or quit. You know, what we should have done was quit a long time ago. Now, it's too late."

Somehow, I wasn't at all surprised at this turn of events, and it didn't really make that much difference. As far as I was concerned, we were all up to our necks in the thing anyway, and writing the narrative portion of the report couldn't make me any more guilty than I already felt myself to be.

Still, Line's order came as something of a shock. All the time Lawson and I were working on the report, I felt, deep down, that somewhere, somehow, something would come along and the whole thing would blow over. But Russell Line had crushed that hope. The report was actually going to be issued. Intelligent, law-abiding officials of B.F. Goodrich, one of the oldest and most respected of American corporations, were actually going to deliver to a customer a product that was known to be defective and dangerous and which could very possibly cause death or serious injury.

Within two days, I had completed the narrative, or written portion of the report. As a final sop to my own self-respect, in the conclusion of the report I wrote, "The B.F. Goodrich P/N 2-1162-3 brake assembly does not meet the intent or the requirements of the applicable specification documents and therefore is not qualified."

This was a meaningless gesture, since I knew that this would certainly be changed when the report went through the final typing proces. Sure enough, when the report was published, the negative conclusion had been made positive.

One final and signficant incident occurred just before publication.

Qualification reports always bear the signature of the person who has prepared them. I refused to sign the report, as did Lawson. Warren was later asked to sign the report. He replied that he would "when I received a signed statement from Bob Sink ordering me to sign it."

The engineering secretary who was delegated the responsibility of "dogging" the report through publication, told me later that after I, Lawson, and Warren had all refused to sign the report, she had asked Sink if he would sign. He replied, "On something of this nature, I don't think a signature is really needed."

On June 5, 1968, the report was officially published and copies were delivered in person to the Air Force and LTV. Within a week, flight tests were begun at Edwards Air Force Base in California. Searle Lawson was sent to California as Goodrich's representative. Within approximately two weeks, he returned because some rather unusual incidents during the test had caused them to be canceled.

His face was grim as he related stories of several near crashes during landings — caused by brake troubles. He told me about one incident in which, upon landing, one brake was literally welded together by the intense heat developed during the test stop. The wheel locked, and the plane skidded for nearly 1500 feet before coming to a halt. The plane was jacked up and the wheel removed. The fused parts within the brake had to be pried apart.

Lawson had returned to Troy from California that same day, and that evening, he and others of the Goodrich engineering department left for Dallas for a high-level conference with LTV.

That evening I left work early and went to see my attorney. After I told him the story, he advised that, while I was probably not actually guilty of fraud, I was certainly part of a conspiracy to defraud. He adivsed me to go the Federal Bureau of Investigation and offered to arrange an appointment. The following week he took me to the Dayton office of the FBI, and after I had been warned that I would not immune from prosecution, I disclosed the A7D matter to one of the agents. The agent told me to say nothing about the episode to anyone and to re-

port any further incident to him. He said he would forward the story to his superiors in Washington.

A few days later, Lawson returned from the conference in Dallas and said that the Air Force, which had previously approved the qualification report, had suddenly rescinded that approval and was demanding to see some of the raw test data taken during the tests. I gathered that the FBI had passed the word.

Omitting any reference to the FBI, I told Lawson I had been to an attorney and that we were probably guilty of conspiracy.

"Can you get me an appointment with your attorney?" he asked. Within a week he had been to the FBI and told them of his part in the mess. He too was advised to say nothing but to keep on the job reporting any new development.

Naturally, with the rescinding of Air Force approval and the demand to see raw test data, Goodrich officials were in a panic. A conference was called for July 27, a Saturday morning affair at which Lawson, Sink, Warren and myself were present. We met in a tiny conference room in the deserted engineering department. Lawson and I, by now openly hostile to Warren and Sink, ranged ourselves on one side of the conference table while Warren sat on the ther side. Sink, chairing the meeting, paced slowly in front of a blackboard puffing furiously on a pipe.

The meeting was called, Sink began, "to see where we stand on the A7D." What we were going to do, he said, was to "level" with LTV and tell them the "whole truth" about the A7D. "After all," he said, "they're in this thing with us, and they have the right to know how matters stand."

"In other words," I asked, "we're going to tell them the truth?"

"That's right," he replied. "We're going to level with them and let them handle the ball from there."

"There's one thing I don't quite understand," I interjected. "Isn't it going to be pretty hard for us to admit to them that we've lied?"

"Now, wait a minute," he said angrily. "Let's don't go off half-cocked on this thing. It's not a matter of lying. We've just interpreted the information the way we felt it should be."

"I don't know what you call it," I replied, "but to me it's lying, and it's going to be damned hard to confess to them that we've been lying all along."

He became very agitated at this and repeated his "We're not lying," adding, "I don't like this sort of talk."

I dropped the matter at this point, and he began discussing the various discrepancies in the report.

We broke for lunch, and afterward, I came back to the plant to find Sink sitting alone at his desk, waiting to resume the meeting. He called me over and said he wanted to apologize for his outburst that morning. "This thing has kind of gotten me down," he confessed, "and I think you've got the wrong picture. I don't think you really understand everything about this."

Perhaps so, I conceded, but it seemed to me that if we had already told LTV one thing and then had to tell them another, changing our story completely, we would have to admit we were lying.

"No," he explained patiently, "we're not really lying. All we were doing was interpreting the figures the way we knew they should be. We were just exercising engineering license."

During this afternoon session, we marked some forty-three discrepant points in the report: forty-three points that LTV would surely spot on occasions where we had exercised "engineering license."

After Sink listed those points on the blackboard, we discussed each one individually. As each point came up, Sink would explain that it was probably "too minor to bother about," or that perhaps it "wouldn't be wise to open that can of worms," or that maybe this was a point that "LTV just wouldn't understand." When the meeting was over, it had been decided that only three points were "worth mentioning."

Similar conferences were held during August and September, and the summer was punctuated with frequent treks between Dallas and Troy, and demands by the Air Force to see the raw test data. Tempers were short and matters seemed to grow worse.

Finally, early in October 1968, Lawson submitted his resignation, to take effect on October 25. On October 18, I submitted my own resignation, to take effect on November 1. In my resignation, addressed to Russell Line, I cited the A7D report and stated: "As you are aware, this report contained numerous deliberate and willful misrepresentations which, according to legal counsel, constitute fraud and expose both myself and others to criminal charges of conspiracy to defraud . . . The events of the past seven months have created an atmosphere of deceit and distrust in which it is impossible to work . . ."

On October 25, I received a sharp summons to the office of Bud Sunderman. As chief engineer at the Troy plant, Sunderman was responsible for the entire engineering division. Tall and graying, impeccably dressed at all times, he was capable of producing a dazzling smile or a hearty chuckle or immobilizing his face into marble hardness, as the occasion required.

I faced the marble hardness when I reached his office. He motioned me to a chair. "I have your resignation here," he snapped, "and I must say you have made some rather shocking, I might even say irresponsible, charges. This is very serious."

Before I could reply, he was demanding an explanation. "I want to know exactly what fraud is in connection with the A7D and how you can dare accuse this company of such a thing!"

I started to tell some of the things that had happened during the testing, but he shut me off saying, "There's nothing wrong with anything we've done here. You aren't aware of all the things that have been going on behind the scenes. If you had known the true situation, you would never have made these charges." He said that in view of my apparent "disloyalty" he had decided to accept my resignation "right now," and said it would be better for all concerned if I left the plant immediately. As I got up to leave he asked me if I intended to "carry this thing further."

I answered simply, "Yes," to which he replied, "Suit yourself." Within twenty minutes, I had cleaned out my desk and left. Forty-eight hours later, the B. F. Goodrich Company recalled the qualification report and the four-disk brake, announcing that it would replace the brake with a new, improved, five-disk brake at no cost to LTV.

Ten months later, on August 13, 1969, I was the chief government witness at a hearing conducted before Senator William Proxmire's Economy in Government Subcommittee of the Congress's Joint Economic Committee. I related the A7D story to the committee, and my testimony was supported by Searle Lawson, who followed me to the witness stand. Air Force officers also testified, as well as a four-man team from the General Accounting Office, which had conducted an investigation of the A7D brake at the request of Senator Proxmire. Both Air Force and GAO investigators declared that the brake was dangerous and had not been tested properly.

Testifying for Goodrich was R. G. Jeter, vice-president and general counsel of the company, from the Akron headquarters. Representing the Troy plant was Robert Sink. These two denied any wrongdoing on the part of the Goodrich Company, despite expert testimony to the contrary by Air Force and GAO officials. Sink was quick to deny any connection with the writing of the report or of directing any falsifications, claiming to be on the West coast at the time. John Warren was the man who supervised its writing, said Sink.

As for me, I was dismissed as a high-school graduate with no technical training, while Sink testified that Lawson was a young, inexperienced engineer. "We tried to give him guidance," Sink testified, "but he preferred to have his own convictions."

About changing the data and figures in the report, Sink said: "When you take data from several different sources, you have to rationalize among those data what is the true story. This is a part of your engineering know-how," He admitted that changes had been made in the data, "but only to make them more consistent with the over-all picture of the data that is available."

Jeter pooh-poohed the suggestion that anything improper occurred, saying: "We have thirty-odd engineers at this plant . . . and I say to you that is incredible that these men would stand idly by and see reports changed or falsified . . . I mean you just do not have to do that working for anybody . . . Just nobody does that."

The four-hour hearing adjourned with no real conclusion reached by the committee. But, the following day the Department of Defense made sweeping changes in its inspection, testing and reporting procedures. A spokesman for the DOD said the changes were a result of the Goodrich episode.

The A7D is now in service, sporting a Goodrich-made five-disk brake, a brake that works very well, I'm told. Business at the Goodrich plant is good. Lawson is now an engineer for LTV and has been assigned to the A7D project. And I am now a newspaper reporter.

At this writing, those remaining at Goodrich are still secure in the same positions, all except Russell Line and Robert Sink. Line has been rewarded with a promotion to production superintendent, a large step upward on the corporate ladder. As for Sink, he moved up into Line's old job.

To what degree does concern with individual needs make the organization more effective or, conversely, render it incapable of taking essential action?

"All right, everything must stop. The merger decision can wait. Edgar has a problem. Tell us about your hang-up, Edgar."

Group Observer Instructions

Over the years considerable research has been conducted on the characteristics of groups, the dimensions of their growth, the functions that constitute their leadership, their decision-making processes, and other factors which provide insights into their effectiveness. A summary of this research follows which will enable an individual to understand the "how" and "why" of group behavior.

Basically, most groups are working toward some goal. Even informal bull sessions have informal goals. Our concern is to look at the dynamics that are present as a group moves along the "path" toward its goal. *Every* meeting and *every* group has its dynamics — its unique *pattern of forces. These forces describe the interaction in the group — the interpersonal relationships, the communications problems, the way the members make decisions. Although these forces may exist in varying degrees, an examination of any group shows that they are always present. Understanding these dynamics — these characteristic aspects of group life — will help us work more effectively in group settings.*

The following is a description of basic group dynamic concepts. In addition, a set of questions is presented to assist you in diagnosing your group's behavior.

1. *Background.* Every group has a history, consisting of both its previous experiences and the personal notions and attitudes which the members bring to the group. These bear directly upon the present activities of the group. Also, the previous responses and feelings of the group which have been developed affect its present interaction.

What is the history of the group?

How does this history affect the relationships of the members?

How does this history affect the work of the group?

2. *Participation.* Participation can be described in terms of who is speaking to whom, and how much speaking is being done and by whom. Participation patterns tell something about the status and the power in the group, and often indicate how effectively the group is using the resources of its members.

Who are the high and low participators? Why? Who talks to whom? Who keeps the ball rolling?

Do you see and shift in participation, e.g., highs become quiet; lows suddenly become talkative?

How are the silent people treated? How is their silence interpreted? Consent? Disagreement? Disinterest? Fear? Etc.

3. *Influence.* Influence and participation are not the same. Some people may speak very little, yet they capture the attention of the whole group. Others may talk a lot but are generally not listened to by other members.

Which members are high in influence? That is, when they talk others seem to listen.

Which members are low in influence? Others neither listen to nor follow them. Is there any shifting in influence? Who shifts?

Do you see any rivalry in the group?

4. *Communication.* This is primarily what people say, how they say it, and what effect it has. However, much significant communication is *nonverbal* — in posture, facial expression, gesture, etc. In verbal communication, the clarity of expression and coherence of the presentation have an important influence on group effectiveness.

Do some members move in and out of the group, e.g., lean forward or backward in their chairs or move their chairs in and out? Under what conditions do they come in or move out? Which members frequently look away from the group?

Which members present their ideas clearly?

5. *Atmosphere.* At any given time a group's atmosphee is somewhere between "defensive" and "accepting." In a *defensive* atmosphere members are unable to communicate freely, to disagree with other members, or to expose ideas and feelings which run counter to the direction in which the group is going. But if the atmosphere is one of *listening, understanding, trusting* — in short, *accepting* — then the group will develop greater creativity, with more effective member relations.

Who seems to prefer a friendly, congenial atmosphere? Is there any attempt to suppress conflict or unpleasant feelings?

Who seems to prefer an atmosphere of conflict and disagreement? Do any members provoke or annoy others?

What signs of feelings do you observe in group members? Anger? Irritation? Frustration? Warmth? Excitement? Boredom? etc.

6. *Subgroupings.* Subgroups (sometimes called "cliques") often develop in groups and can greatly influence the group's effectiveness. Sometimes such subgroups form on the basis of friendships, sometimes because of a common need or interest at a particular stage of the group life, or sometimes because of antipathy toward other members or opposition to the direction of the group.

Is there any subgrouping? Sometimes two or three members may consistently agree and support each other or consistently disagree and oppose one another.

Do some people seem to be "outside" the group? Do some members seem to be "in"? How are those "outside" treated?

What are the issues around which subgroups appear to form?

7. *Norms.* Standards or ground rules may develop in a group that control the behavior of its members. Norms usually express what behaviors *should* or *should not* take place in the group. These norms may be clear to all members (explicit), known or sensed by only a few (implicit), or operating completely below the level of awareness of any group members.

Are certain areas avoided in the group (e.g., sex, religion, talk about present feelings in group)?

Are group members overly nice or polite to each other? Are only positive feelings expressed? Do members agree with each other too readily? What happens when members disagree?

Do you see norms operating about participation or the kinds of questions that are allowed?

8. *Procedures.* All groups operate with a certain set of procedures — that is, defined ways of getting work done (e.g., how an agenda is prepared and used, how votes are taken [by ballot or by hand]). If a group is to be effective, it must vary its procedures so that they are appropriate to the task at hand.

Is there any attempt to get all members participating in a decision (consensus)?

Is there any evidence of a majority pushing a decision through over other members' objections? Do they call for a vote (majority support)?

Does anyone make any contributions which do not receive any kind of response or recognition (plop)? What effect does this have on the member?

9. *Goals.* Goals can be immediate and short-range, or long-range; they can emerge from the group or be imposed on it; they can be realistic in relation to the resources of the group, or completely unrealistic. Effective groups must continually check the appropriateness of their goals.

How does the group choose its goals?

Are the goals realistic and attainable, considering the resources of the group?

Does the group relate its immediate task to long-range group objectives?

10. *Dysfunctional behaviors.* These activities typically hinder the development of a group, its maintenance, and its ability to accomplish goals. In general, blocking functions are dysfunctional for group progression on any scale.

Aggressor — Deflating others' status; attacking the group or its values; joking in a barbed or semi-concealed way.

Blocker — Disagreeing and opposing beyond reason; resisting stubbornly the group's wish for personally oriented reasons; using hidden agenda to thwart the movement of a group.

Dominator — Asserting authority of superiority to manipulate group or certain of its members; interrupting contributions of others; controlling by means of flattery or other forms of patronizing behavior.

Showoff — Makng a scene over one's lack of involvement; abandoning the group while remaining physically with it; seeking recognition in ways not relevant to group task.

Avoidance Behavior — Pursuing special interests not related to task; staying off subject to avoid commitment; preventing group from facing up to controversy.

11. *Leadership.* Leader behavior in a group can range from almost complete control of the decision making by the leader to almost complete control by the group, with the leader contributing his/her resources just like any other group member. A number of leadership functions must be performed by both the leader and other members of the group.

A. *Task functions.* These leadership functions are to facilitate and coordinate group efforts in the selection and definition of a common problem and in the solution of that problem.

Initiator — Proposing tasks or actions; defining group problems; suggesting a procedure.

Informer — Offering facts; giving expression of feelings; giving an opinion.

Clarifier — Interrupting ideas or suggestions; defining terms; clarifying issues before group.

Summarizer — Pulling together related ideas; restating suggestions; offering a decision or conclusion for group to consider.

Reality tester — Making a critical analysis of an idea; testing an idea against some data trying to see if the idea would work.

B. *Maintenance functions.* Functions in this category describe leadership activity necessary to alter or maintain the way in which members of the group work together, developing loyalty to one another and to the group as a whole.

Harmonizer — Attempting to reconcile disagreements; reducing tension; getting people to explore differences.

Gate keeper — helping to keep communication channels open; facilitating the participation of others; suggesting procedures that permit sharing remarks.

Consensus tester — Asking to see if a group is nearing a decision; sending up a trial balloon to test a possible conclusion.

Encourager — Being friendly, warm, and responsive to others; indicating by facial expression or remark the acceptance of others' contributions.

Compromiser — When his/her own idea or status is involved in a conflict, offering a compromise which yields status; admitting error; modifying an interest of group cohesion or growth.

Guidelines for group observation

Although these various aspects of group dynamics that have been discussed can be easily memorized, and awareness of how and an understanding of why they occur within groups is more difficult to attain. Often when a group has a task to perform, the group becomes so involved in the *task* of organizing for the activity that it is not able to remember accurately the *process* by which the task was accomplished. It can be useful for a neutral person who is not involved in the activity to observe and give feedback about the behavior of individuals during an actual group meeting. This observation process can sensitize group members, as well as the observer, to be more aware of the subtleties of group behavior in their day-to-day involvement.

When you are serving as a group observer your task is to provide feedback to group members about their behavior in the experience you are observing. You are to take no active part, but you should position yourself at a point where you can hear what is being said, see nonverbal behavior of as many participants as possible, and observe people on the periphery of the group.

As the group meeting proceeds, take notes of specifically what happens, who is involved, and so forth, so that you can refer to the notes when you verbally elaborate on them to the group members after they have completed the exercise. Avoid evaluations such as *good* and *bad*; simply describe the behavior of the people involved. If necessary, refer back to the specific descriptions of group dynamics and member roles in order to give specific feedback to group members.

By familiarizing yourself with the dynamics of a work or social group, your ability to perform effectively in groups will increase.

8 tips on holding a staff meeting

Gary Blake

Many business meetings are expensive, unproductive and boring.

Here are a few tips on adding momentum to your meetings.

There's something about a group of executives gathered around a conference table that suggests *productivity*. But many staff meetings fall short of being productive because of poor planning or disorganization. Perhaps that's why Sue, at the end of the table, is stifling a yawn; Bill is covertly fiddling with Rubik's Cube, and Bob, looking so intent, is silently trying to decide whether he'd prefer the tortellini salad or the red snapper for lunch.

Shakespeare would have had a few words to describe many staff meetings — *A Comedy of Errors* or *Much Ado About Nothing*.

Well-run staff meetings don't just "happen." They have been planned by managers who, either through experience or training, have been able to absorb the skills necessary for holding successful meetings. And, since managers spend an average of 69% of their work life in meetings with two or more people — according to a McGill University survey — more and more companies are paying greater attention to the art of running a meeting.

As someone who has helped train managers in communications skills, here are my eight tips for improving the quality of your meetings:

Make sure the meeting is necessary

There are a variety of reasons why a staff meeting may be necessary. They are needed to gain feedback on important corporate policy, to receive and react to reports, and to solve problems of logistics. Hold a meeting whenever you feel a group will produce sounder solutions than those of a solitary decision maker. But remember: meetings are not a corporate cure-all. Sometimes a strong managerial decision will obviate a large get-together. And certainly meetings should not be held merely because "it's Monday again." Don't hold a meeting to vent your rage at something or someone (that just demoralizes a lot of innocent bystanders). However, meetings are usually perfect places to announce corporate decisions, especially sweeping changes which might otherwise generate rumors and time-consuming apprehension about the future. When a staff meeting is mandatory, try to include only those staffers whose presence is essential, and, if possible, limit the number of attendees to 12 or fewer.

Preparation is everything

According to Wallace Fisher, Eastern Marketing Manager of Hitchcock Publishing Company, "One should spend as much time preparing for a meeting as at the meeting itself." Fisher has seen a number of meetings go awry because the agenda was improvised, causing an annoying repetition of the refrain, "Well, what else do we have to talk about?"

Before you march into a meeting, think about the needs and interests of those people attending. If people of different managerial levels will attend, there may be some subtle politicking and jockeying for position. If you're ready for it, you can recognize it and steer the discussion in a different direction.

Do you want the business-like formality of a conference table, or the classroom-like formality of rows? Perhaps the informality of a semicircle is best when encouraging people to share their true feelings.

The meeting room itself is important. Check the ventilation, acoustics, and adaptability for visual aids. Is an extension cord, a fresh Magic Marker or spare overhead-projector bulb available in a pinch?

Prepare an agenda

The pivotal piece of planning is the agenda, and every staff meeting requires one. Set up objectives for your meeting, and outline a logical listing of specific topics you wish to cover. If you circulate your agenda prior to the meeting, you'll be giving your colleagues an opportunity to collect their thoughts as well as any tangible materials which may be needed during the meeting.

A good agenda is well ordered. It makes sense, for example, to first discuss whether you have the capability of handling an assignment before you determine whether or not to accept it. By the way, the best time for confronting dramatic decisions is early in the meeting, when people have had their first cup of coffee but not their first daily crisis.

A specific amount of time should be allotted for each agenda item (as a safeguard against letting a discussion dissolve into a digression), and every agenda should specify a finishing as well as a starting time for the meeting, so that everyone can plan the rest of his day. You'll prevent meetings from meandering by indicating on the agenda that a particular item is either for *information, discussion,* or *decision.*

One other thing: Don't make your agenda a shopping list of serendipitous subjects; if you load the agenda with too many topics, perhaps you should cover them in *two brief* meetings.

Use the decision-making process

Many discussions, including those held at staff meetings "get nowhere fast." People seem to insist on going over the same ground innumerable times. To help avoid aimlessness, use a decision-making process to help you arrive at well-thought-out decisions:

A. *Define objectives.* Determine specifically what you want to accomplish by this decision, preferably in terms of what can be measured.

B. *Gather and evaluate the data.* Get

as much input that relates to the decision as possible. Be realistic as to what you actually need and when you've had enough.

C. *Develop alternatives.* Don't stop short of considering all the possibilities. Then measure each realistically against objectives.

D. *Calculate the risks, giving due weight to the critical factors.* Assess the adverse consequences of the best alternatives.

E. *Make the decision and follow through.* Select the alternative that gives the most return for the least expenditure of energy and resources. Protect the decision rather than try to eliminate all risks. Do this by establishing controls, providing for feedback and making secondary support decisions.

The important thing is to not get ahead of yourself by jumping to an easy or quick solution (e.g. "I know how we'll solve the high turnover problem — we'll overstaff!") People try to settle issues hurriedly because it provides a comforting release from tension ("Well, I'm glad *that's* solved!"), but don't succumb to the temptation of believing that your first thought is necessarily your best thought.

Keep out interruptions

It's a nice idea, in theory. Ideally, a note is placed on the door, calls are held, messages are taken. However, according to Wallace Fisher, "In a marketing organization, we never want to be unavailable to a client. The same is true for many purveyors of merchandise. Perhaps the answer is to cut off calls, but only to a certain level."

Bridgford Hunt, President of The Hunt Company, a leading executive search firm, decreases the chance of interruptions by scheduling staff meetings about a half-hour before the work day begins. "That way," says Hunt, "people aren't always checking their watches, waiting to leave and resume their own work. Mornings are ideal, because most people are 'day people.' A late afternoon meeting may have as many open eyes but fewer functioning brains."

The ultimate in interruption-free settings is off-premises. I.B.M., among many other companies, often holds staff meetings at off-site locations. This has the double advantage of lowering the chances of interruption and providing a pleasant respite from moment to moment corporate chaos.

One more tip: Start promptly, but bend that rule if a key person asks you to wait a few minutes for him. It's sometimes better to start a few minutes late than to interrupt the meeting to recap everything for a tardy decision-maker.

Take into account your staff's collective attention span

Bob Bly, Advertising Manager for Koch Engineering Company, has a hint for keeping meetings brief: Stand-up meetings. "They're terrific," says Bly, "because they keep people from talking too long. They're especially good for getting projects started, not for making decisions. If you sit down, you start getting comfortable."

To keep the blood flowing, take a break when the meeting goes too long (few sit-down meetings should last more than an hour and a half). If papers are to be perused keep them short and simple since everyone will be reading them at his own pace (most people read slowly). And never attempt to draft a document around a table — if they tried to write the *Declaration of Independence* that way, we'd still be colonies. It's preferable to ask for suggestions for improvement before assigning someone to produce a new draft following the meeting.

Be a leader... but lightly!

There's a saying that goes: "When the best leader's work is done, the worker's say, 'We did it ourselves.'"

Your function as leader of a staff meeting is not to dominate the meeting but to elicit the best thinking from those attending.

By beginning your questions with a person's name, you'll help keep everyone tuned in to the discussion. As leader, you're surrounded by people who are helpful, some who are negative, and a few who are passive. It's up to you to control the garrulous, draw out the silent, and maintain a positive tone. At all cost, restrain yourself from the sarcastic putdown one is occasionally tempted to unleash.

To help the passive prove that their vital signs are still active, try asking them questions that make them think, questions that cannot be answered by a simple "yes" or "no." Another thing you can do to stimulate lively discussion is to call on senior staff last. That way, junior staff in meetings will not feel pressure to parrot their superiors.

For morale's sake, end the meeting on a note of accomplishment.

Accurate minutes can save hours.

Just as a well-organized agenda helps make a meeting run smoothly, accurate minutes avoid confusion after the meeting concludes. Minutes should include a brief summary of the items discussed, with each section concluding with a record of any decision reached or responsibility assigned.

Since minutes are a written record of the meeting, include the time of the meeting, the date, who chaired, and who attended. Often minutes detail the time and place of any suggested follow-up meeting.

Says Wallace Fisher: "The real reason for minutes is to keep everyone honest. All too often, when an idea doesn't fly, everyone tries to escape responsibility for having ever been part of it. Minutes assure everyone that the ideas brought up at a meeting don't die when the meeting ends."

Bob Bly suggests keeping a tickler file for any type of note or reminder while watching over a project.

Minutes and follow-up memos protect the integrity of what was said at the meeting.

If you'd like to remind yourself of some of these tips, take a look at an extraordinarily clever training film titled "Meetings Bloody Meetings." This 30-minute film, written and starring John Cleese of Monty Python fame, gently pokes fun at a businessman who obviously subscribes to the "play it by ear" school of running meetings. One night, following a particularly unproductive staff meeting, this poor guy dreams he is being put on trial for "cold-blooded time-wasting." In a courtroom dream sequence, he is charged with four "crimes": (1) chairing without due preparation, (2) failure to signal the intention of the meeting, (3) negligent ordering of the agenda, and (4) not being in full charge of the discussion.

How would you plead to each of these charges?

Think back to the last meeting you ran. Did it move swiftly and surely toward its goals or, like Ol' Man River, did it "just keep rolling along?" I'll conclude our meeting of the minds with this thought: meetings are to coordinate, not pontificate.

I fear uniformity. You cannot manufacture great men any more than you can manufacture gold.
John Ruskin

A camel is a horse designed by a committee.
Author unknown

The symptoms of groupthink arise when members of the decision-making groups become motivated to avoid being too harsh in their judgments of their leaders' or their colleagues' ideas. They adopt a softline of criticism, even in their own thinking. At their meetings, all the members are amiable and seek complete concurrence on every important issue, with no bickering or conflict to spoil the cozy 'we-feeling' atmosphere.
Irving L. Janis, *Victims of Groupthink*

In any exhaustive theory of organization, communication would occupy a central place.
Chester I. Barnard, *The Functions of the Executive*

Ranch Supplies Company

John Watson, executive vice-president and general manager of Ranch Supplies Company (RSC), sat at his desk mulling over the events of the past few months, which had just climaxed in a serious clash between two of his key employees — George Cox and Dale Johnson. When John hired Dale, he had expected that a marketing team combining George's long-time field sales experience with Dale's recent UCLA business school training would result in great benefits to RSC. However, almost since the day Dale came to work, his relationship with George had deteriorated. And now George had just stormed into John's office and stated that he didn't want Dale to work with him on any more projects. John wondered what, if anything, he could do to help resolve the conflict between Dale and George.

Background

Ranch Supplies was an international company that annually grossed close to 4 million dollars' worth of cattle tags, bull semen, and other herd management supplies. RSC was a subsidiary of Jones Enterprises, which was owned by Bill Jones. Bill had convinced John less than a year before to leave a prominent Chicago consulting firm to come to work for him at the head office of both companies, in Grand Junction, Colorado. John was promoted quickly from assistant to the president of Jones Enterprises to general manager of RSC (see Exhibit 1).

When John came into the RSC organization, he turned to George Cox to teach him the ropes of the cattle industry and RSC's part in it. George did not have a college education but had worked his way up through RSC's organization from one of the original salesmen to his present position as director of marketing. He was one of the old-timers in the organization, having been with RSC since before it was acquired by Jones Enterprises. He was responsible for setting up the original marketing distribution system for the Big Green Tag (considered the "Cadillac" of the cattle ear tag industry) and for organizing the company's A.I. (artificial insemination) program. George was considered by many at RSC to be one of the most valuable people in the organization because of his close involvement with the Big Green Tag and bull semen, the two major items distributed by the company.

In spite of George's long-time service with the company, Bill Jones had voiced the opinion that George was not vital to the organization. He recognized that George had great ability as a salesman and that he had successfully persuaded many of the owners of famous bulls to sign contracts granting RSC exclusive distributorship of their bulls' semen, but he did not think of George as a good administrator because he was hardheaded in many ways and didn't like to delegate authority.

John voiced similar impressions about George's lack of administrative ability.

He commented that George not only lacked administrative skill in keeping up on all the detail work that went along with the deals and commitments he made, but also liked to "feel as if he had total control over the company's marketing and distribution system." According to John, it seemed that George didn't like to have his operations subject to the approval of either John or Bill and that "he

MBA program at UCLA. Dale was much more theoretical in his approach to solving problems than was George.

Dale originally came to work with the understanding that he would devote half of his time to Jones Enterprises and half to RSC; but because John had hired him and there was a greater need for him to help solve some of RSC's problems, he spent most of his time at RSC and had his

Exhibit 1

Ranch Supplies Company organization chart

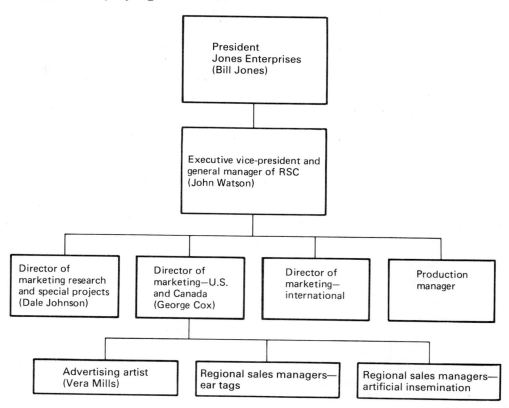

wants to be in my position as executive vice-president."

Unlike George, Dale Johnson had considerable formal business training. He and John had been classmates in the

office in the RSC building. John said that Dale was extremely creative in thinking of new ideas and ways to approach a problem but that he constantly hopped from one project to another, so that his work was disorganized. He often dreamed up projects on his own and started working on them. John also noted that Dale lacked the patience and skill needed to promote his ideas effectively within the organization. He added, however, that Dale was considered an important asset to the company because he had developed a point-of-purchase display that had proved successful in promoting RSC's new line of ear tag, the upright tag. RSC was planning to distribute another new tag in the near future, the stay-fast tag, which they hoped would be competitive in price with the "Fords and Chevrolets" of the industry and, at the same time, would not affect the sales of RSC's other ear tags. Dale was thought to be the person best qualified to develop a quality advertising and promotion campaign for the stay-fast tag.

The conflict

It was during the development of the promotion for the stay-fast tag that the clash between Dale and George first became evident. In deciding who would work on the project, John saw great potential in putting George and Dale together so that George's experience and Dale's training could be utilized. Dale and George were considered to be the best marketing men employed by RSC, and it was expected that they would cooperate with each other and coordinate their marketing efforts. However, even in the early stages of the project it was apparent that the relationship between the two was not cordial. It seemed that neither man was willing to compromise his own ideas. Soon the conflict became apparent to everybody in the office, for not only had George and Dale failed to present a unified proposal on the new

marketing strategy, but George visibly shunned Dale each time they passed each other in the hallway.

John felt that there was little organizational pressure to make Dale and George work together: both reported to John directly, and there was no superior-subordinate relationship between the two (see Exhibit 1). The fact that Dale was considered staff and George was a line manager seemed to add to their unwillingness to cooperate.

John made the following observations about the two men:

Dale likes to be a one-man show. He does not desire to be a leader in a large organization, but he likes to be in charge of his projects. He doesn't like too many people under him. Dale is extremely creative, but many of his ideas are impractical. He has not yet learned to screen himself. For example, he has sometimes come to me for advice; and then, after I have advised him to do something a certain way, he has ignored my advice and done it his way.

George, on the other hand, is resentful of Dale because I hired him, and he doesn't want someone who is working for me to be a success. He also has difficulty in accepting people's weaknesses as well as their strengths, and, because Dale's impulsive nature annoyed him, he refused to work with him.

The growing tension between Dale and George came to a head when Dale was assigned a new box for the Big Green Tag.

Dale developed a box that seemed to bring approval from a good number of people in the company. After a prototype was approved, several hundred thousand boxes were ordered from an outside firm. During the development of the new box, Verla Mills, the company artist with whom Dale had been working on the new design, complained several times to

George (her boss) that Dale was finicky and that he changed his mind too much.

After the newly designed box had been approved and ordered, Dale announced his decision that not only should the box graphics be changed, but all of RSC's products should be promoted under the acronym "RSC Tags," and new colors should be used in the graphics scheme. Dale took it upon himself to hire an outside advertising agency to come up with a new logo. When George found out about Dale's new project he nearly exploded. He stormed into John's office and told him that he flatly refused to work with Dale on any more projects. George refused to talk to Dale about the matter, but news of the problem soon got around to the rest of the office staff. John wondered what he could do to help resolve the conflict and get Dale and George to work together.

The Great Majestic Company

R obert Hoffman, the manager of the Great Majestic Lodge, was sitting at his desk and debating what he would say and what action he would take at a meeting with his bellmen, which was scheduled to begin in two hours. He had just weathered a stormy encounter with Mr. Tomblin, the general manager of the Great Majestic Lodge and several other recreational and lodging facilities in the area.

Mr. Tomblin was visibly upset by an action taken by the bellmen at Great Majestic Lodge three weeks ago. At the end of the explosive meeting, Mr. Tomblin roared, "Bob, I don't care if you fire the whole damn bunch! I want you to do something about this right now!"

Background

Great Majestic Lodge was located in a popular park in the western United States. It was rather remote, yet offered all the modern conveniences featured at any fine metropolitan hotel. Because of its size and accommodations, the lodge was a favorite spot for large, organized tours. Most of the tours stayed one night and none stayed over two days. They were good moneymakers for the lodge because they always kept their schedules, paid their bills promptly, and were usually gone very early on checkout day.

Most of the employees hired by the Great Majestic Company were college students. This was an ideal situation, because the opening and closing dates of the lodge corresponded to most universities' summer vacations. The employees lived and ate at the company facilities and were paid $105 a month.

The lodge bellmen

The bellmen at the Great Majestic Lodge were directly responsible to the lodge manager, Mr. Hoffman. They were college students who, before being chosen for the bellman position, had worked for the company at least three summers. A total of seven were chosen on the basis of their past work performance, loyalty, efficiency, and ability to work with the public. Mr. Tomblin, the general manager, chose the bellmen himself.

The position of bellman was considered by the employees to be prestigious and important. In the eyes of the public, the bellmen represented the Great Majestic Lodge in every aspect. They were the first ones to greet the guests upon arrival, the people the guests called when anything was needed or went wrong, and the last ones to see the guests off upon their departure. Clad in their special cowboy apparel complete with personalized name tags and company insignia, the bellmen functioned as an effective public relations force for the Great Majestic Lodge, as well as providing prompt and professional service for each guest.

The bellmen all lived together in the back area of the most secluded employees' dorm at the Great Majestic Lodge. This facility was shared with most of the other lodge employees who had been with the company for two years or more. The older student-employees were especially close-knit, and all were looking forward to the time they would have the opportunity to be chosen as bellmen. The first-year employees usually occupied a dorm to themselves, adjacent to the seniority dorm. For the most part, a warm comradeship was experienced among all the staff at the lodge.

Traditionally, the bellmen had a comfortable relationship with Mr. Tomblin. This latest incident was of great concern for Mr. Hoffman. He realized that Mr. Tomblin was dead serious about firing them. It was midsummer, and it would be difficult to find qualified replacements. The bellmen this year had been especially productive.

The bellmen were paid a dollar per hour plus tips, which they pooled and divided equally at the end of each week.

Daily tips averaged $20 per man. Hoffman was particularly concerned about the situation because it involved employees for whom he was directly responsible.

Organized tours

The bellmen had the responsibility of placing the tour luggage in the guests' rooms as soon as the bus arrived. The front desk provided them with a list of guests' names and the assigned cottage numbers. Speed was particularly important, because the guests wanted to freshen up and demanded that their bags be delivered promptly.

On the morning of departure, the guests left their packed bags in their rooms while they went to breakfast. The bellmen picked up the bags, counted them, and then loaded them on the bus.

As payment for the service rendered by the bellmen, the tour directors paid fifty cents per bag. This was the standard gratuity paid by all tours. It was considered a tip, but it was included in the tour expenses by each company. On large tours, the tip could range as high as $75, although the average was $40.

The Jones Transportation Agency

The Jones Transportation Agency had a reputation throughout the area of being fair and equitable with their gratuities. However, one of their tour directors, Mr. Sirkin, did not live up to the company's reputation. On a visit to the Great Majestic Lodge, Mr. Sirkin had not given a tip. The bellmen knew their service to Mr. Sirkin had been very good. They were upset about the situation but assumed Sirkin had forgotten the tip in the rush before his tour departed. The tour was large and the tip would have amounted to $65.

Mr. Sirkin's tour also stayed at several other nearby resorts. Several of the Majestic Lodge bellmen knew the bellmen at the other lodges and, in discussing the situation, discovered that Mr. Sirkin had neglected the tip at each of the other lodges. It was apparent that Mr. Sirkin had made a profit of more than $180 on his four-day tour through the region.

The letter

Upon hearing of Sirkin's actions, the Majestic Lodge bellmen decided that some action had to be taken. They immediately ruled out telling Mr. Hoffman. On previous occastions when there had been a problem, Mr. Hoffman had done very little to alleviate the situation.

Roger Sikes, a first-year bellman and a business undergraduate, suggested that a letter be written directly to the president of Jones Transportation Agency. He felt that the agency would appreciate knowing one of their tour directors had misused company funds. After some discussion, the other bellmen present agreed. Sikes prepared a detailed letter, which told the Jones president the details of the Sirkin incident. The bellmen didn't expect to recover the money from the tour, but they felt that this was the appropriate action to take.

Five of the bellmen signed the letter as soon as it was completed. Two more opposed but, after more discussion and considerable peer-group pressure, agreed to sign the letter. It was mailed with the expectation of a speedy reply and justice for the offending Mr. Sirkin.

Reaction to the letter

Three weeks after the bellmen's letter had been mailed to the Jones Transportation Agency, Mr. Tomblin was thumbing through his morning mail. He noticed a letter from his good friend Grant Cole, the president of the Jones Transportation Agency. Mr. Tomblin opened this letter first. Mr. Cole had written that there was a problem at the Great Majestic Lodge and he thought Mr. Tomblin should be made aware of it. He enclosed the letter from the bellmen and suggested that, if the bellmen had any problems with any Jones directors in the future, it might be wise for them to speak to Mr. Tomblin before any action was taken. Mr. Cole informed Mr. Tomblin that Jones was investigating the Sirkin incident.

Mr. Tomblin was enraged. The bellmen had totally ignored their supervisor and had written a letter without first consulting any of the managers of the entire Great Majestic Company. This was not only a breach of company policy, but a personal humiliation for Mr. Tomblin.

Mr. Tomblin, yelling with outrage, leaped to his feet and charged through the lobby to Hoffman's office. He spotted bellman George Fletcher and ordered him to get out of his sight. The bewildered Fletcher quickly obeyed.

Robert Hoffman's meeting with Mr. Tomblin was an unpleasant experience. He had never seen Mr. Tomblin so upset at actions of employees. Mr. Tomblin was a proud man, and, because his pride had been hurt, he wanted revenge. He showed Hoffman the bellmen's letter and the reply from Grant Cole. Mr. Tomblin made it clear that he expected some quick action. Hoffman knew that the action had to meet Mr. Tomblin's approval. Hoffman's position as manager was suddenly placed in a precarious position.

There had been several employees in the lobby when Mr. Tomblin roared through. Hoffman knew the gossip would spread quickly throughout the lodge. The bellmen were well liked by the other employees and he knew they would be concerned about the bellmen's fate.

Hoffman called the still shaken George Fletcher into his office and told him to summon the off-duty bellmen for a meeting. After Fletcher left, Robert Hoffman attempted to think of alternatives that would satisfy Mr. Tomblin and also provide the expected quality service to the guests.

Claremont Instrument Company

One of the problems facing the supervisory staff of the Claremont Instrument Company in the summer of 1948 was that of "horseplay" among employees in the glass department. For some time this question had troubled the management of the company. Efforts had been made to discourage employees from throwing water-soaked waste at each other and from engaging in water fights with buckets or fire hoses. Efforts to tighten up shop discipline had also resulted in orders to cut down on "visiting" with other employees. These efforts were made on the grounds that whatever took an employee away from his regular job would interfere with production or might cause injury to the employees or the plant machinery.

Production was a matter of some concern to the officials of the company, particularly since the war. In spite of a large backlog of unfilled orders, there were indications that domestic and foreign competition in the relatively near future might begin to cut into the company's business. Anything which could help to increase the salable output of the company was welcomed by the officers; at the same time, anything which might cut down overhead operating expenses, or improve the quality of the product, or cut down on manufacturing wastage was equally encouraged.

The Claremont Instrument Company had bee located for many years in a community in western Massachusetts with a population of approximately eighteen thousand. The company employed approximately five hundred people. None of these people was organized in a union for collective bargaining purposes. The company produced a varied line of laboratory equipment and supplies. Many of its products were fabricated principally from glass and over the years the company had built up a reputation for producing products of the highest quality. To a considerable extent this reputation for quality rested upon the company's ability to produce very delicate glass components to exacting quality standards. These glass components were produced from molten glass in the glass department. Exhibit 1 presents a partial organization chart of the company.

The entire glass department was located in one wing of the company's main factory. In this department the glass components such as tubes, bottles, decanters, and glass-measuring devices

Exhibit 1

Claremont Instrument Company partial organization chart

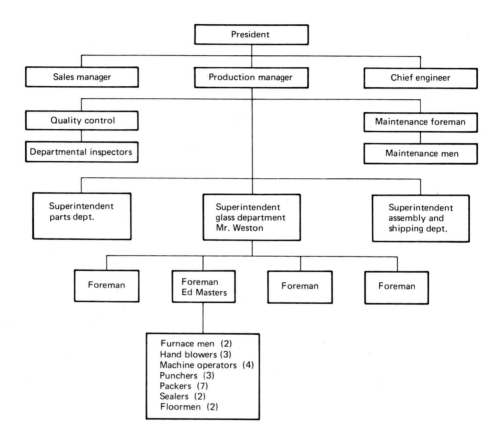

were made from molten glass. Some of these glass parts were produced by hand-blowing operations, but most of them were produced on bottle-making machinery which in effect blew the molten glass into a mold. This operation of blowing the glass by hand or by machine was the most critical operation in the department and required a high degree of skill. Immediately following the blowing operation some of the parts were "punched." The "puncher" was a mechanical apparatus into which the glass components were placed; as the machine revolved, a small gas flame melted the glass in a small area and blew a hole in the glass component. Next the parts were placed on a mechanical conveyor where they were annealed by an air-cooling process. Then the parts were picked off the conveyor by women known as packers whose duty was to inspect them for defects of many kinds and to give them temporary packaging in

Exhibit 2

Claremont Instrument Company — Floor plan of glass department

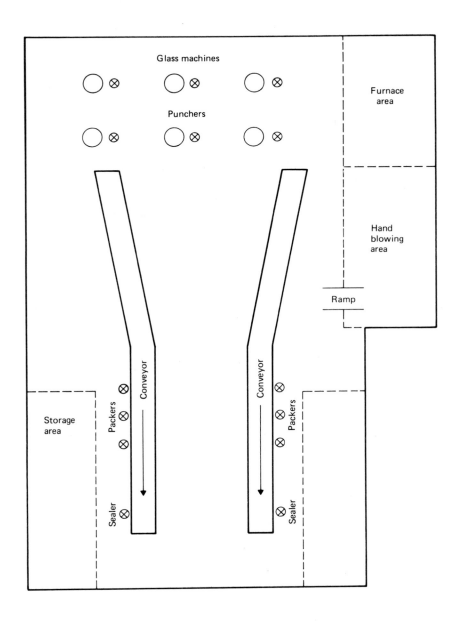

cardboard cartons for transit to other parts of the factory. The final operation in the department was performed by sealers whose job it was to seal these cardboard cartons and place them in a stack for temporary storage. Exhibit 2 is a floor plan of the glass department.

The glass department was operated on a continuous, 24-hour, 7-day-a-week basis, because of the necessity of keeping the tanks of molten glass hot and operating all the time. Four complete shifts worked in the department. The different shifts rotated as to the hours of the day they worked. Roughly each shift spent two weeks at a time on the day shift, on the evening shift, and on the night shift. Each shift worked on the average five days a week, but their days off came at varying times throughout the week. The glass department was located in a separate wing of the plant and the employees of the department used a special entrance and a special time clock.

Each of the four shifts employed about 23 people. Each shift had its own foreman and assistant foreman and hourly workers as indicated in Exhibit 1. All these workers were men with the exception of the packers. The foreman was a full-time supervisor but the assistant foreman usually operated a glass machine and only substituted for the foreman in his absence. The furnace men prepared the molten glass for the glass blowers while the floormen cleaned up broken glass and other waste and filled in on odd jobs.

An inspector from the quality-control department and a maintenance man from the maintenance department were assigned on a full-time basis to each of the four shifts. The inspector worked with the packers and was responsible for the quality of all glass components. The maintenance man was responsible for the maintenance and satisfactory operation of all machinery in the department.

Several physical conditions made work in the glass department unique in the plant. The fact that the glass furnaces were located in this department meant that the department was always unusually hot. The glass-blowing machines were run principally by compressed air and each movement of a machine part was accompanied by the hiss of escaping air. This noise combined with the occasional sound of breaking glass made it impossible for the members of the department to converse in a normal tone. An oil vapor was used to coat the inside of the molds on the glass machines, and when the hot glass poured into the mold, a smoke was given off that circulated throughout the department.

In the summer of 1948, Ralph Boynton, a student at the Harvard Business School, took a summer job as one of the floorman on one of the shifts working in the glass department. While on this job, he made the above observations about the Claremont Instrument Company in general and the glass department in particular. In the course of the summer Ralph became particularly interested in the practice of engaging in horseplay, and the description that follows was based on his observations.

The foreman of Boynton's shift, Ed Masters, had worked a number of years in the glass department and had been promoted to foreman from the position of operator of one of the glass machines. In Ralph's opinion the foreman was generally liked by the shift employees. One of them commented to Ralph, "If everything is going okay, you don't see Ed around. If anything goes wrong, he's right there to try and fix it up." Another one of them commented, "He pitches right in — gives us a hand — but he never says much." Frequently when a glass machine was producing glass components of unacceptable quality, Ralph noticed the foreman and the maintenance man working with a machine operator to get the machine in proper adjustment. On one occasion Ralph was assigned the job of substituting for one of the sealers. Shortly after Ralph had started his work Ed Masters came around and asked how he was doing. Ralph replied that he was doing fine and that it was quite a trick to toss the cartons into the proper positions on the stack. Ed replied, "You keep at it and it won't be long before you get the hang of it. You'll be tired for a while but you'll get used to it. I found I could do it and I'm a 97-pound weakling."

Ralph also picked up a variety of comments from the employees about one another. The shift maintenance man, Bert, referred to the men on the shift as "a good bunch of guys." One of the packers referred with pride to one of the machine operators, "That guy can get more good bottles than anybody else." On one occasion when the glass components were coming off the end of the conveyor at a very slow rate, one of the packers went around to the glass machines to find out what the trouble was. When she came back she reported to the rest of the packers, "Ollie is having trouble with his machine. It's out of adjustment but he will get it fixed in a few minutes." Ralph noticed that a record was kept of the total daily output of each shift of packers. These women seemed anxious to reach a certain minimum output on each shift. When the components were coming through slowly, he heard such comments as, "This is a bad night." If the work had been coming slowly, the packers regularly started "robbing the conveyor" toward the end of the shift. This was the practice of reaching up along the conveyor and picking off components for packaging before they reached the packer's usual work position.

A short time after Ralph started to work, the company employed another new floorman for the shift. This new man quickly picked up the nickname of Windy. The following were some of Windy's typical comments: "My objective is the paycheck and quitting time." "I love work so much I could lay down and go to sleep right beside it." "These guys were all dopes. If we had a union in here, we would get more money." "I hate his night work. I'm quitting as soon as I get anther job." Most of the other employees paid little attention to Windy. One of the sealers commented about him, "If bull were snow, Windy would be a blizzard." One night Windy commented to three of the men, "This is a lousy place. They wouldn't get away with this stuff if we had a union. Why don't the four of us start one right here?" None of the group replied to this comment.

Ralph had a number of opportunities to witness the horseplay that concerned the management. At least one horseplay episode seemed to occur on every eight-hour shift. For example, one night while Ralph stood watching Ollie, one of the machine operators, at his work, Ollie called Ralph's attention to the fact that Sam, the operator of the adjacent machine, was about to get soaked.

"Watch him now," Ollie said with a grin. "Last night he got Bert and now Bert is laying for him. You watch now." Ralph caught sight of Bert warily circling behind the machines with an oil can in his hand. Sam had been sitting and quietly watching the bottles come off his machine. Suddenly Bert sprang out and fired six or seven shots of water at Sam. When the water hit him, Sam immediately jumped up and fired a ball of wet waste which he had concealed for this occasion. He threw it at Bert and hit him in the chest with it. It left a large wet patch on his shirt. Bert stood his ground squirting his can until Sam started to chase him. Then he ran off. Sam wiped his face and sat down again. Then he got up and came over to Ollie and Ralph. Sam shouted, "By Jesus I am going to give him a good soaking." Ollie and Ralph nodded in agreement. Later Ollie commented to Ralph, it may take as long as three hours for Sam to work up a good plan to get even but Bert is going to get it good."

Sam was ready to get back at Bert as soon as he could be lured close enough to the machine. Sam pretended to watch his machine but kept his eye out for Bert. In a little while Bert walked jauntily by Sam's machine. They grinned at each other and shouted insults and challenges. Bert went over to a bench to fix something and Sam slipped around behind his machine, pulled down the fire hose and let Bert have a full blast, chasing him up along the conveyor as Bert retreated. Sam then turned off the hose, reeled it back up, and went back to his machine.

All the other employees on the scene had stopped to watch this episode and seemed to enjoy it. They commented that it was a good soaking. Bert came back to the machines after a while, grinning and hurling insults while he stood by Sam's machine to dry off from the heat of the machine. The other operators kidded him some and then everyone went back to work seriously.

A little later the foreman came through the department and noticed the large puddle of water on the floor. He instructed Bert to put some sawdust on the puddle to soak up the water. Ralph was told later that Ed Masters had told Bert, "I want more work and less of this horsing around." A few minutes later Ed Masters and Bert were discussing a small repair job that had to be done that evening.

On another occasion Ralph asked Ollie what he thought of the horseplay. Ollie commented, "It's something each guy has to make up his own mind about. Personally I don't go in for it. I have got all the raises and merit increases that have come along and I know Bert hasn't had a raise in over a year. Whenever something starts I always look back at my machine so that I can be sure nothing goes wrong while I am looking away. Personally, I just don't care — you have to have some fun, but personally, I don't go in for it."

Just at this point Al, one of the punchers, came down from the men's lavatory to take his turn on one of the punch machines. He was a moment or two early and stood talking to Sam. Ollie got up from where he had been talking to Ralph and started to holler, "Hey, Al, hey, Al." The other operators took up the chant and all of them picked up pieces of wood or pipe and started drumming on the waste barrels near their machines. Al took up a long piece of pipe and joined in. After a minute or two, one of the operators stopped and the drumming ended quickly. Al lit a cigarette and stepped up to take the machine for his turn.

Ralph later had an opportunity to ask Bert what he thought of the horseplay. Bert said, "You have to have some horseplay or you get rusty. You have to keep your hand in." Ralph noted that Bert's work kept him busy less than anyone else since his duties were primarily to act as an emergency repairman and maintenance man. Ralph asked, "Why doesn't Ollie get into the horseplay?" Bert replied, "Ollie can't take it. He likes to get other people, but he can't take it when he gets it. You have got to be fair about this. If you get some guy, you are surer than hell you will get it back yourself. Now you take Sam and me. We've been playing like that for a long time. He don't lose his temper and I don't lose mine. I knew I was going to get that hose the other night; that was why I was baiting him with a squirt gun." Ralph asked, "Does Ed Masters mind it very much?" Bert answered, "Hell, he's just like the rest of us. He knows you've got to have some of that stuff, only he gets bawled out by the superintendent if they see anything going on like that. That's why we don't play around much on the day shift. But on the night shift, that's when we have fun. The only reason we don't squirt the foreman is because he's the foreman. As far as we're concerned, he is no different from us. Besides he ain't my boss anyway. I'm maintenance. I don't care what he says."

About the middle of the summer the superintendent of the glass department returned from his vacation and immediately thereafter an effort was made by him through the foremen to 'tighten up" on shop discipline. The men on the machines and the punchers were forbidden to walk up to the other end of the conveyor to talk to the packers and sealers and vice versa. The foreman started making occasional comments like "keep moving" when he saw a small group together in conversation. On one occasion a small group stood watching some activity outside the plant. Ed came by and said curtly, "Break it up." Everyone seemed quite shocked at how abrupt he was.

About this same time, the word was passed around among the employees that a big push was on to step up the output of a certain product in order to make a tight delivery schedule. Everyone seemed to be putting a little extra effort into getting this job done. Ralph thought he noticed that the foreman was getting more and more "jumpy" at this time. On

one occasion Ed commented to some of the employees, "I am bitter today." One of the machine operators asked him what the trouble was and Ed made some comment about a foreman's meeting where the superintendent was telling them that the playing around and visiting would have to stop.

One night a short time later Ralph saw that preparations were being made for an unusually elaborate trap for soaking Jim, one of the sealers who had recently begun to take part in the water fights. A full bucket of water was tied to the ceiling with a trip rope at the bottom in such a way that the entire contents would be emptied on Jim when he least suspected it. Many of the employees made a point of being on hand when the trap was spring. It was worked perfectly, and Jim was given a complete soaking. Ralph thought Jim took it in good spirit since he turned quickly to counterattack the people who had soaked him. Shortly after all the crew had gone back to work, Ruth, one of the packers, was coming down the ramp from the area where the hand-blowing operations were performed. She was carrying some of the glass components. Ruth slipped on some of the water that had been spilled during the recent fight and fell down. She was slightly burned by some of the hot glass she was carrying. Those who saw this happen rushed to help her. The burn, while not serious, required first-aid attention and the assistant foreman went with Ruth to the company dispensary for treatment. Ralph thought that the employees all felt rather sheepish about the accident. Ruth was one of the more popular girls in the department. The word went around among the employees that a report on the nature and cause of the accident would have to be made out and sent to higher management. Everyone was wondering what would happen.

Northwest Industries

Northwest Industries was a growing company that manufactured recreational vehicles. One of the factories was located in Salem, Oregon. The recreational vehicle market was strong in the western United States and there was good demand for Northwest's products. The market reached its peak in mid-June and tapered off during the winter months. The factory tried to maintain a fairly constant production flow by building up inventories during the low winter months. During the summer months, a number of college students were hired to help boost production and bring inventory back to the desired level.

Organization

The Salem plant had a three-leveled management structure (see Exhibit 1). Craig Hansen, age 52, was the general plant foreman. He had started working on the lines and had worked up to his position after seventeen years. Mr. Hansen knew "everything about trailers and could perform any separate job involved in the construction of a trailer within forty-five minutes." He was in charge of schedules for each run of trailers that was sent through. He also decided which line the trailer would go on and how long it would take to construct them. Mr. Hansen was serious about the business and conferred with Northwest's home office several times each week.

Joe Mackay, age 35, was the assistant plant foreman. His job was to help the foremen solve any problems they couldn't handle and to see that all plant safety rules and regulations were complied with. He also was responsible for raw materials inventory and ordering. The men viewed Joe as a walking bomb and therefore tried to stay out of his way. When he was called to help correct an error that had been made, Joe demanded to know who had made it and an explanation of how the workman could be so dumb.

Eight foremen comprised the third management layer. During the winter four of them worked in other areas of the plant and weren't involved in construction. Each foreman was assisted by a lead man, who helped manage the sixteen-man production crew. Foremen were salaried at $1500 per month, while lead men received 20 cents extra per hour, or $6.70 per hour.

Ted Nelson, age 28, was one of the regular foremen. He didn't have much, good or bad, to say about the college kids. In fact, he didn't say much about anything. On Ted's line, when a mistake was made, he would correct it himself and not say anything to the one who had made the mistake. If it happened again, Ted would point out the mistake to the worker and then correct it himself while the worker went back to the job. Ted also managed the time cards and handed out the paychecks.

Quality control in the plant was maintained by three inspectors who reported directly to Mr. Hansen, The inspector's position was considered prestigious, perhaps even more prestigious than foreman, even though both received the same salary. Inspectors had to be especially knowledgeable and trustworthy and able to find production mistakes quickly.

Upon completion of each trailer, the foreman would call one of the inspectors, who would examine the trailer and test all components. Any defects were noted on a ''squawk sheet.'' These ''squawks'' then had to be fixed before the inspector would sign the release form. An average trailer generally had four or five minor squawks, which a good ''squawker'' could repair within twenty or twenty-five minutes. The idea was to have a good squawker, so that people would not be pulled off the line and lose time to fix production errors.

Workers with some experience were hired at $4.50 per hour, and unskilled help started at $3.75 per hour. Provided the unskilled workers produced well, a raise would be given after two months on the job to $4.50 per hour. After four or five years, the workers usually earned $6.50 per hour.

The inspectors, the year-round workers, and the foremen were a very close-knit group. They enjoyed many activities together, such as parties, bowling, raft races, and, occasionally, light refreshments. Lunch and break times were looked forward to. All participated in a regular contribution to support the highly enjoyed numbers game, which

Exhibit 1

Northwest Industries, Salem plant — Organization chart

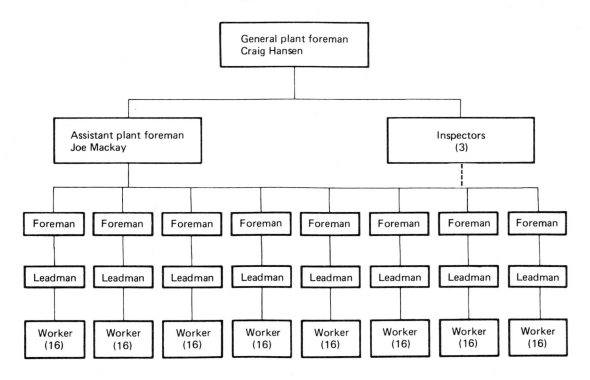

accompanied each pay period, as well as to fund such things as birthday and sympathy cards.

Most of the employees at Northwest had completed high school and then started work with the company. These fellows worked hard and took pride in what they were making. Most planned to stay with Northwest all their lives. About seventy-five employees worked year-round, with sixty-five seasonal workers helping out in the summer months.

Northwest's usual procedure was to run four of the eight production lines during the winter. During the summer, enough new people were hired to staff all eight lines. Most of the stations on a line required two people to complete each job, and ample space existed between stations to permit a trailer to sit between work areas. This spacing procedure facilitated line moves and allowed for the time differences in performing each job.

The new plan

This year, Mr. Hansen had decided to eliminate some of the problems experienced in the past. Six of the foremen had been complaining about the inefficiency of those college kids, who were reported to be slow, stubborn know-it-alls. They admitted that the kids were hard to train and got bored easily but for the most part did a good job.

Mr. Hansen decided to run four lines as normal, leaving most of the older, regular employees on those lines. The younger people who were already working for the company were distributed to two of the other lines, and, as the college kids were hired, they were paired up with the younger but experienced workers for training. Mr. Hansen's strategy was that, as the college kids learned, they would be able to expand to the other two lines,

and eventually all eight lines would be in full production.

The plan was readily adopted by the foremen. Four were assigned to the four lines with the regulars, and the other four were assigned in pairs to the two new lines, with one designated as the foreman and the other as assistant foreman.

The new plan seemed to be working well. Halfway through July, the plant was running at full production. The lines with the newer workers enjoyed working together, and a substantial rivalry had been created between them and the older workers. Mr. Hansen had seen to it that the younger lines were given routine, long production runs to work on. These runs generally consisted of thirty or forty units that were exactly the same and thus the training period was minimized and errors were reduced. The other, more experienced lines were given the shorter runs to work on.

At first the rivalry was in fun, but after a few weeks the older workers became resentful of the remarks that were being made and felt that those kids should have to work on some of the more difficult runs. The younger lines easily met production schedules, and thus some spare time was left for goofing around. It wasn't uncommon for someone from the younger lines to go to another line, in guise of looking for some material, and then give the older workers a hard time. Some of the older workers resented this treatment and soon began to retaliate with sabotage. They would sneak over during breaks and hide tools, dent metal, install something crooked, or in other small ways do something that would slow production in the lines with the younger workers.

To Mr. Hansen everything seemed to be going quite well, and he was proud of himself and his plan. Toward the end of

July, however, he began hearing reports of the rivalry and sabotage. As most of the longer production runs had been completed, Mr. Hansen decided that "those kids needed to quit playing around and get to work." He gave them some of the new runs, which were basically the same as before, except for a few changes in the interior walls and the wood roof.

Ted Nelson, the foreman of line C, one of the younger ones, heard about the new run coming on his line and decided to go ahead of the first trailer to help each station with the forthcoming changes. He carefully explained each change to the workers as the lead trailer came into their station and then went on to the next. The kids seemed to be picking up the changes okay, so that Ted didn't worry too much about the new run.

As the first trailer was pushed out, ready for inspection, Ted called the inspector. A half hour later, the inspector emerged with two pages of squawks — forty-nine of them. Not seeing Ted anywhere, the inspector called in Mr. Hansen and Joe to point out the uncommonly high number of squawks. It took about five minutes for things to completely explode. Ted walked on the scene just in time to hear Mr. Hansen yell to Joe, "Get that line into gear in one week and get those squawks fixed or fire the whole bunch!"

. . . I would work extra hard at whatever I was doing to become so good at it and that I would never have to kiss anyone's fanny to keep my job and I never have and I never will.

John A. DeLorean

. . . The law of triviality. Briefly stated, it means that the time spent on any item of the agenda will be in inverse proportion to the sum involved.

C. Northcote Parkinson, Parkinson's Law

Too often it is assumed that the organization of a company corresponds to . . . an organization chart. Actually, it never does.

Fritz J. Roethlisberger and William J. Dickson

At the very highest level there is very little knowledge. They do not understand the opinion of the masses . . . Their bureaucratic manner is immense. They beat their gongs to blaze the way. They cause people to become afraid just by looking at them.

Mao Tse-Tung

EXERCISES

Communications exercise

There are several ways to give instructions to people. Some of them are quicker or more accurate than others. Some generate more satisfaction in or greater compliance by the recipient. It is important that you be able to recognize different communication models with their resulting costs and benefits. Our purpose in this exercise is to illustrate forms of communication and investigate the differing outcomes as well as the processes resulting from these means of communication.

Part 1

1. One student should be selected to act as sender. (It may be useful for control purposes to have the same sender for both parts of the exercise.)
2. Participants should leave their books closed during the exercise.
3. The sender will give the receiver directions to draw a design of a series of figures. The receiver should draw the figures exactly as told. He may ask no questions and give no audible responses, such as moans, groans, and laughter, or facial expressions. The sender is asked to face away from the class, so that they will not pick up nonverbal cues.
4. The sender should then describe, quickly, accurately, and completely, the series of figures designated as Figure 1. Have someone time the exercise from the beginning of the description to the end.
5. At the conclusion of the sender's description, receivers are asked to guess how many figures they drew correctly. Record their guesses and average them for the group. Enter this average on the scorecard.
6. Ask the sender to show the group the figure that he or she described. Instruct them to count the number of figures they were able to draw correctly. Average this for the group and enter it on the scorecard. Enter the elapsed time on the scorecard.

Part 2

1. For the second, or two-way step, ask the sender to describe a second figure (Figure 2). This time, the receivers will be encouraged to ask questions and clarify the descriptions until they are satisfied they have understood. Time the description as before.
2. Ask the participants to estimate their

For further discussion of the ideas in this exercise, see Leavitt, Harold J. *Managerial Psychology*, University of Chicago Press, 1972, Chapter 11.

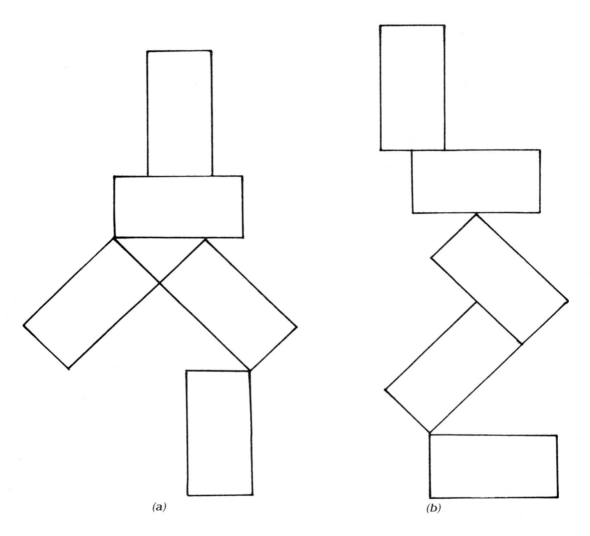

(a)   (b)

Figure 1

accuracy. Then show them the figure and have them score themselves for accuracy. Average their estimated and actual scores as before and enter them on the scorecard.

Compare the two trials. As a class, try to determine the causes for the differences. Ask the sender to relate his or her feel-

ings and the difference between the two experiences. The group should also discuss the different feelings they experienced with the two different types of communication. What conclusions can you draw from the experience? Relate this experience to your experience in organizations.

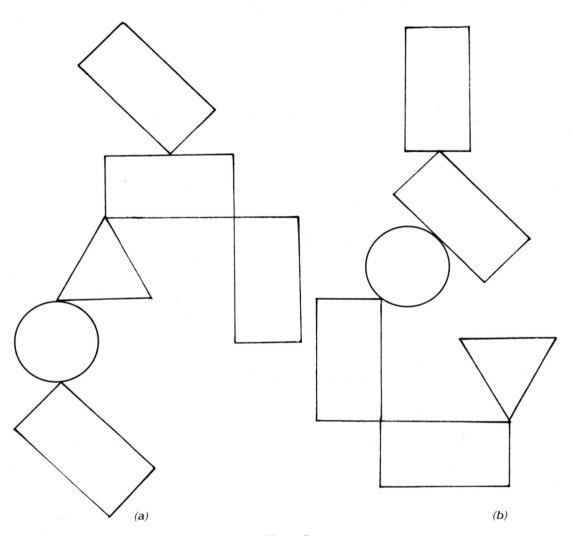

(a)   *(b)*

Figure 2

Scorecard

	One-way	Two-way
Time elapsed		
Average guess accuracy		
Average actual accuracy		

NASA exercise

The challenge in decision making is to obtain the best information within limits of time and other resources. This is often very difficult because information does not exist in pure form. It is always filtered through people who may or may not get along with each other and who might not even care about a good decision. This exercise is a means to help you look at the process of gathering information, working out group procedures, analyzing different contributions, and handling conflict and motivation. The exercise is intended to help you examine the strengths and weaknesses of individual decision making.

The NASA exercise is used quite frequently; alternative situations based on the same behavioral principles include Winter Survival and Desert Survival. The Winter Survival scenario follows the NASA exercise and can be used in the same way.

Instructions

You are a member of a space crew originally scheduled to rendezvous with a mother ship on the lighted surface of the moon. Due to mechanical difficulties, however, your ship was forced to land at a spot some 200 miles from the rendezvous point. During landing, much of the equipment aboard was damaged, and because survival depends on reaching the mother ship, the most critical items available must be chosen for the 200-mile trip. On the next page are listed the fifteen items left intact and un-damaged after the landing. Your task is to rank them in terms of their importance to your crew in reaching the rendezvous point. In the first column (step 1) place the number *1* by the most important item, the number *2* by the second most important, and so on, through number *15,* the least important. You have fifteen minutes to complete this phase of the

exercise.

After the individual rankings are completed, participants should be formed into groups having from four to seven members. Each group should then rank the fifteen items as a team. This group ranking should be a general consensus after a discussion of the issues, not just the average of each individual ranking. While it is unlikely that everyone will agree exactly on the group ranking, an effort should be made to reach at least a decision that everyone can live with. It is important to treat differences of opinion as a means of gathering more information and clarifying issues and as an incentive to force the group to seek better alternatives. The group ranking should be listed in the second column (step 2). The third phase of the exercise consists of the instructor's providing the expert's rankings, which should be entered in the third column (step 3). Each participant should compute the differ-

NASA tally sheet

Items	Step 1 Your individual ranking	Step 2 The team's ranking	Step 3 Survival expert's ranking	Step 4 Difference between Steps 1 & 3	Step 5 Difference between Steps 2 & 3
Box of matches					
Food concentrate					
50 feet of nylon rope					
Parachute silk					
Portable heating unit					
Two .45 calibre pistols					
One case dehydrated Pet milk					
Two 100-lb. tanks of oxygen					
Stellar map (of the moon's constellation)					
Life raft					
Magnetic compass					
5 gallons of water					
Signal flares					
First aid kit containing injection needles					
Solar-powered FM receiver-transmitter					
TOTAL					
(The lower the score the better)				Your score	Team score

ence between the individual ranking and the expert's ranking (step 4), and between the group ranking and the expert's ranking (step 5). Then add the two "difference" columns — the smaller the score, the closer the ranking is to the view of the experts.

Winter survival exercise

The situation

You have just crash-landed somewhere in the woods of northern Minnesota or southern Manitoba. It is 11:32 A.M. in mid-January. The small plane in which you were traveling was destroyed except for the frame. The pilot and copilot have been killed, but no one else is seriously injured.

The crash came suddenly before the pilot had time to radio for help or inform anyone of your position. Since your pilot was trying to avoid a storm, you know the plane was considerably off course. The pilot announced shortly before the crash that you were eighty miles northwest of a small town that is the nearest known habitation.

You are in a wilderness area made up of thick woods broken by many lakes and rivers. The last weather report indicated that the temperature would reach minus twenty-five degrees in the daytime and minus forty at night. The men and women in your party are wearing business attire (including pants and jacket), street shoes, and overcoats.

While escaping from the plane your group salvaged the fifteen items listed below. Your task is to rank these items according to their importance to your survival.

You may assume that the number of persons in the group is the same as the number in your group and that you have agreed to stick together.

Winter survival
decision form

Rank the following items to their importance to your survival, starting with "1" for the most important and proceeding to "15" for the least important:

Items	Step 1 Your individual ranking	Step 2 The team's ranking	Step 3 Survival expert's ranking	Step 4 Difference between Steps 1 & 3	Step 5 Difference between Steps 2 & 3
Compress kit with 28 ft., 2 in.-gauze					
Ball of steel wool					
Cigarette lighter without fluid					
Loaded .45 calibre pistol					
Newspaper (1 per person)					
Compass					
Two ski poles					
Knife					
Secitonal air map made of plastic					
30 feet of rope					
Family-size chocolate bar (1 per person)					
Flashlight with batteries					
Quart of 85-proof whiskey					
Extra shirt and pants for each person					
Can of shortening					
			TOTAL		
		(The lower the score the better)		Your score	Team score

Intergroup exercise

One of the interesting dimensions of organizational behavior is the relationship among individual goals, formally stated goals, and actual organizational activities. The way we assess our own and others' motives, the assumptions regarding criteria and strategy, and the dynamics of intragroup and intergroup relationships all have an important impact on what really happens.

This exercise will provide an opportunity to examine these and other aspects of group behavior and, perhaps more importantly, your own attitudes and values with respect to significant organizational issues.

Exercise objective: □ To win as many points as possible.

Exercise rules:
1. Each team will select a captain who transmits the team's decisions. The captain gives the referee the team's decision after each move. Also, each team will select two negotiators.
2. Each team has ten tanks and starts the game fully armed (i.e., all ten tanks are armed). When you disarm a tank you have a "dove." Normally each team has ten 3 × 5 cards with a tank on one side and a dove on the other. (A suitable substitute for tanks and doves would be a 3 × 5 card with an X on one side [armed] and the other side blank [unarmed].)
3. A game consists of at least two "sets." A set ends whenever a team "attacks," or after five moves, whichever comes first.
4. A "move" consists of a two-minute period when each team decides on its

strategy. During each move a team may change two, one, or zero cards from an armed to an unarmed position. Or it may change two, one, or zero cards from an unarmed to an armed position. At the end of the two-minute period the captain must announce the team's decision to the referee. The referee will *not* give either team information about the other team's move.
5. Either team can request negotiations [through the referee] with the other team after any move. The request to negotiate may be accepted or rejected by the other team. However, the team *must* negotiate after the first and third moves. Negotiations, on neutral ground, will last two minutes in the presence of the referee.
6. At the end of moves one through four, either team may announce an "attack" to the referee. At this time the set ends. The attacking team is charged five points for attacking. (If both teams announce an attack, they are both charged five points). Then the team with the greater number of

Adapted from game originally designated by N. Berkowitz and H. Hornstein.

tanks (determined by the referee, who has the score sheet) wins ten points for each tank it has over and above the tanks held by the other team.

7. If there is no attack prior to the fifth move, at the end of the fifth move each team receives five points for each dove.

Giant Food Company

To understand the subtleties of group decision making, it is necessary to have a keen awareness of the process by which individual objectives are translated into behavior in a dynamic group setting. This role play is an opportunity to try to achieve a decision satisfactory to you by acting as if you really were the character whose role you have been assigned. Try to accept the role in terms of contemporary implications. Let your feelings develop as if you actually were that individual. Should issues develop that are not covered by the role, adapt or innovate accordingly.

To conceptualize your role, it is usually best to read it carefully two or three times; then close the book and think about it for a few minutes. Do not read the other roles; try to develop an approach in terms of the information given and your own interpretation of how a person in that position would likely behave. After you have the role in mind, do not reread it during the process of the role play.

General situation

You are a sales representative for Giant Food Company, a wholesale supplier of packaged food products. Most of your customers are large grocery chains, but you deal with the stores on an individual basis, depending upon their inventory needs. You also supply smaller independent grocery stores and some restaurants. You have a territory assigned to you in the Los Angeles area, and it is your responsibility to generate as much business as possible. You are compensated on a commission basis, and you must pay your own expenses.

You are responsible to check the stock in your customers' stores and to take orders to replace sold items. You also make recommendations to the store manager about marketing and display of your products, and you must compete with other distributors and products for shelf and display space. Your relationship with the store manager affects how your products will be displayed and stocked, and display and stocking greatly affect the sales volume.

Your sales manager has an office in the main warehouse. He is responsible for the allocation of company property that you may use in your work. A new car has been ordered and will soon be available to one of the sales representatives in your division.

The sales representatives pride themselves on the appearance and running condition of their cars and on their economy, as they must pay all of their own automobile expenses. The sales representatives often entertain their customers as part of their sales program; they feel that the car plays a vital part in the impression they make and therefore affects subsequent sales.

Some facts about the sales manager and the sales representatives and their cars are the following:

Phil	14 years with the company, male, white, sales manager
Tom	19 years with the company, male white, 2-year-old Toyota sedan
José	9 years with the company, male, Chicano, 5-year-old Chevrolet full-size sedan
Henry	5 years with the company, male, white, 4-year-old Ford mid-size sedan
Susan	3 years with the company, female, white, 4-year-old Datsun station wagon
Paul	6 months with the company, male, white, 6-year-old Plymouth mid-size sedan

Individual roles

Phil ☐ You are the sales manager of the five sales representatives. Every year or two you get a new car for one of them and are faced with the problem of whom to give it to and how the other vechicles should be reallocated. Often there are hard feelings about your decision, because each person has reasons for feeling that he or she is entitled to the new car. In the past, no matter what you have decided, most of them have considered it wrong. You are now faced with the problem of who is to receive the new car, a Ford subcompact station wagon, next week. This year you have decided to allow the group to solve the problem, and

you will make them live with their decision. They can decide what is the fairest way to redistribute the cars that are now available. You don't want to take a position because you want to do what they think is equitable.

Tom ☐ You have a two-year-old Toyota, which runs well and has been an economical little car. You have been with the company in this position for nineteen years, however, and the Toyota is just not large enough to handle the promotion and display material you must take to your many customers. Sometimes you are forced to use your family station wagon. You have the greatest dollar volume of sales of all the sales representatives, and often you can't sevice your customers adequately or economically because you must make several trips to an area when you begin a new promotional campaign. You think the extra room in the Ford station wagon will be adequate, and you like the economy of the subcompact. You also feel that your seniority (longer service than the sales manager) and the volume of business entitles you to the new car.

José ☐ You have a five-year-old Chevrolet sedan, which in its day was a very nice car. You enjoy the roomy interior, because you have developed a good volume of business over the last nine years. The car is something of a gas hog and is getting very expensive to run the distances you must go to reach your area, which is mostly in the suburbs. You also feel that you need a newer car to take your customers to lunch. The Chevrolet is getting somewhat shabby. You feel that one of the reasons why you still have this old car, when newer representatives have better cars, may be that you are a Chicano.

Henry ☐ You have been with the company for five years and have a four-year-old Ford sedan. It is in fairly good shape, except for the right door, which is sprung and doesn't close tightly. That door has been an irritation since Susan backed into it two years ago in the parking lot. You feel that you deserve either the new car or her car, because she damaged yours. You don't think she should be trusted with the new car; she would probably just wreck it anyway. And she doesn't have enough business to justify it. You feel that you should receive the new car because it will help you build up your business.

Susan ☐ You are the only women in this position in a virtually all-male company. You feel that you are seen as an intruder and a radical, although you make every attempt to avoid that image. You expect to be treated as an equal. You have shown that your salesmanship is equal to or better than the men's. You have a four-year-old Datsun wagon. The body is OK, but the engine and the transmission, which were treated badly by the last person to use the car, are constantly giving you trouble. The Datsun has often been in the shop when you needed it, and the engine needs to be rebuilt or replaced.

You need the new car so that you can be more reliable in the eyes of your customers. You think the men in the department would like to see you fail and have given you the old Datsun as a handicap. You have a good driving record, except for the time when Henry opened the door of his car just as you were backing up to the building to load display materials. He still blames you for his door, although it was really his fault.

Paul ☐ You have been with the company only six months. You have taken over the area and the car of a sales representative who retired and who for the past few years had been coasting and doing little to build up the business. In the past six months you have shown the company what can be done to turn around such a stagnant area. You have doubled your business and have begun to generate a group of prospective customers, whom you must win away from the competitors. You have the oldest car and feel that is is a definite hindrance to your work. It is also uneconomical, and it needs repair. You feel that you have shown what you can do and should be rewarded with the new car, as a shot in the arm to help you build up momentum.

The whole concept of organization depends on some degree of collective action

"I did it! I just fired all 324 of them! I'm going to run the plant by myself."

4

Some comments on the challenge of leadership

I n ancient as well as modern times, few questions have so pre-occupied people's minds as that of the nature of effective leadership. Individuals in every kind of organized activity have tried to grasp the secret; that is, how does one mobilize human resources in the accomplishment of a task? Although simple or universal explanations have so far proven to be inadequate, some considerations can be useful in approaching the concept of leadership.

First, most people ascribe real power to leaders. As organization members, professional consultants, or causal observers try to explain what is wrong in an organization, a likely diagnosis is "bad leadership." Conversely, when a company performs well, when an athletic team wins, or when a national economy is strong, the common explanation is "good leadership." Even with our limited understanding, leadership is still regarded as the panacea or the scapegoat in a high percentage of explanations of organizational performance.

Second, most people have strong value assumptions about how leaders *ought* to think, behave, and treat their subordinates. These assumptions can be drawn from philosophical, political, economic, military, or religious principles. And, although the evidence supporting the effectiveness of a leadership concept may be limited, that concept is still believed and preached as a matter of fundamental truth. Consequently, rational analysis is difficult.

A third problem is the description or classification of leadership styles. In past research we attempted to label leaders *authoritarian* or *democratic*, on the assumption that authoritarian leaders were interested in the *task* and that democratic leaders were interested in *people*. This over-simplification suggested that you could either be tough and get the job done or be soft and make the people happy. Subsequent evidence indicated that a leader could show both traits strongly, or both weakly, or some other combination. But the evidence also revealed that task-emphasis and people-emphasis were not necessarily opposite ends of the continuum.

Putting the leadership issue in historical perspective also helps clarify it. Early discussions of leadership focused almost exclusively on personality traits of individual leaders. It was felt that, by observing great military or religious leaders, identifying their character traits, and imitating them, the imitators in turn could become great leaders. But experience has shown us that people cannot easily adopt the characteristics of great leaders. Furthermore, we found that we could not define a precise set of leadership characteristics anyway. Great leaders seemed to have many different traits.

Successive studies concentrated on styles. It was argued that, even if we could not all be like great leaders of the past, we might be able to learn general principles of leadership. The vast number of "human relations" training programs reflected this emphasis. But this approach has enjoyed limited success.

Recent studies have shown that some authoritarian leaders were successful and some were not and that some democratic or participative leaders experienced great success and some seemed to flounder. The implication is that there is no optimal style that everyone could use. Clearly, circumstances have a significant impact on leadership. This realization led us to a contingency approach, which argues that leadership effectiveness is a function of many different factors — some of which are beyond the leader's control: (a) the characteristics of the leader, (b) the characteristics of subordinates, (c) the nature of the task, (d) the organization structure and climate, and (e) the external environment of the organization.

A continuing indicator of the felt need for more effective leadership is the large number of leadership training programs. From the time of the "human relations" movement in the 1940s we have observed an almost unlimited number of training techniques and courses. The earlier supervisory training programs evolved into management development, which had a broader focus, and finally into organization development, which looks at the whole organization as a system. Organization development (OD) (for further discussion of OD see the article by Sherwood in Section 5) recognizes the inappropriateness of looking only at the leader in the analysis of organizational performance. The leader is very important but is not the only variable in the equation.

The articles in this section explore factors that affect the quality of leadership. While no article offers a list of simple steps on how to become a good leader, all suggest factors that need to be considered in the development of a leadership strategy.

Hoffer's article provides a view from the other side of the leadership equation — the worker's perspective. Hoffer is a longshoreman — philosopher who presents a case for a clear division between management and labor. It is a perspective that students of organizations need to understand.

Mintzberg suggests a very different perspective. He considers some common assumptions about the manager's role. He offers a descriptive model of the complex set of roles that managers perform and suggests that an effective manager is skilled at both introspection and the analysis of tasks and available resources. Kotter addresses the issue of power in organizations. He maintains that as organizations have grown more complex, managers have become more dependent on other people and organizations. Therefore, if they are going to be effective they need to be skilled at acquiring and using power to do their jobs. It is interesting to analyze Kotter's approach to power particularly as it applies to the issues raised by Vandivier in Section 3.

Two articles in this section focus more specifically on leadership style. Miles and Ritchie examine the appropriateness and impact of participative management. The topic of different leadership styles and when to use them is discussed by Tannenbaum and Schmidt. They develop a useful framework for analyzing the leadership situation.

The materials for skill development include an article on "Managing Your Manager." Hill and Thompson discuss leadership from the subordinate's perspective and suggest ways that subordinates can be proactive in their management of a superior-subordinate relationship. This is a skill that is very important for almost everyone in an organization to master. Managerial decision making is an exercise that helps students improve their skill in selecting the most effective decision strategy for each situation. Finally, Thompson presents some suggestions on the appraisal interview that should help students to handle this challenging managerial responsibility.

Workingman and management

Eric Hoffer

There are many of us who have been workingmen all our lives and, whether we know it or not, will remain workingmen till we die. Whether there be a God in heaven or not; whether we be free or regimented; whether our standard of living be high or low — I and my like will go on doing more or less what we are doing now.

This sober realization need not be unduly depressing to people who have acquired the habit of work and who, like the American workingman, have the ingredients of a fairly enjoyable life within their reach. Still, the awareness of being an eternal workingman colors one's attitudes; and it might be of some interest to indicate briefly what the relations between management and labor look like when seen from his point of view.

To the eternal workingman, management is substantially the same whether it is made up of profit seekers, idealists, technicians, or bureaucrats. The allegiance of the manager is to the task and the results. However noble his motives, he cannot help viewing the workers as a means to an end. He will always try to get the utmost out of them; and it matters not whether he does it for the sake of profit, for a holy cause, or for the sheer principle of efficiency.

One need not view management as an enemy or feel self-righteous about doing an honest day's work to realize that things are likely to get tough when management can take the worker for granted; when it can plan and operate without having to worry about what the worker will say or do.

The important point is that this taking of the worker for granted occurs not only when management has unlimited power to coerce, but also when the division between management and labor ceases to be self-evident. Any doctrine which preaches the oneness of management and labor — whether it stresses their unit in a party, class, race, nation, or even religion — can be used to turn the worker into a compliant instrument in the hands of management. Both Communism and Fascism postulate the oneness of management and labor, and both are devices for the extraction of maximum performance from an underpaid labor force. The preachment of racial unity facilitated the exploitation of labor in our South, in French Canada, and in South Africa. Pressure for nationalist and religious unity served, and still serves, a similar purpose elsewhere.

Seen from this point of view, the nationalization of the means of production is more a threat than a promise. For we shall be bossed and managed by someone, no matter who owns the means of production — and we can have no defenses against those who can tell us in all truth that we, the workers, own everything in sight and they, our taskmasters, are driving us for our own good. The battle between Socialism and Capitalism is to a large extent a battle between bosses, and it is legitimate to size up the dedicated Socialist as a potential boss.

One need not call to mind the example of Communist Russia to realize that the idealist has the making of a most formidable taskmaster. The ruthlessness born of self-seeking is ineffectual compared with the ruthlessness sustained by dedication to a holy cause. "God wishes," said Calvin, "that one should put aside all humanity when it is a question of striving for his glory." So it is better to be bossed by men of little faith, who set their hearts on toys, than by men animated by lofty ideals who are ready to sacrifice themselves and others for a cause. The most formidable employer is he who, like Stalin, casts himself in the role of a representative and champion of the workers.

Our sole protection lies in keeping the division between management and labor obvious and matter of fact. We want management to manage the best it can, and the workers to protect their interests the best they can. No social order will seem to us free if it makes it difficult for the worker to maintain a considerable degree of independence from management.

The things which bolster this independence are not utopian. Effective labor unions, free movement over a relatively large area, a savings account, a tradition of individual self-respect — these are some of them. They are within the worker's reach in this country and most of the free world, but are either absent or greatly weakened in totalitarian states.

In the present Communist regimes, unions are tools of management, worker mobility is discouraged by every means, savings are periodically wiped out by changes in the currency, and individual self-respect is extirpated by the fearful technique of Terror. Thus it seems that the worker's independence is as good an index as any for measuring the freedom of a society.

The next question is whether an independent labor force is compatible with efficient production. For if the attitude of the workers tends to interfere with the full unfolding of the productive process, then the workingman's independence becomes meaningless.

It has been my observation for years on the docks of San Francisco that, while a wholly independent labor force does not contribute to management's peace of mind, it can yet goad management to perfect its organization and to keep ever on the lookout for more efficient ways of doing things. Management on the San Francisco waterfront is busy twenty-four hours a day figuring out ways of loading and discharging ships with as few men as possible.

Mechanization became very marked on the waterfront after the organization of the present militant labor union in 1934. The fork lift and the pallet board are almost in universal use. There are special machines for handling sugar, newsprint, and cotton bales. There are new methods for handling coffee, rice, and wool. New arrangements and refinements appear almost every day. Here nobody has to be told that management is continually on the job. Certainly there are other factors behind this incessant alertness, and some of them play perhaps a more crucial role in the process of mechanization. But it is quite obvious that a fiercely independent labor force is not incompatible with efficient production.

Contrary to the doctrine propounded by some in the heyday of the Industrial Revolution, mechanization has not taught docility to "the refractory hand of labor." At least here on the docks, we know that we shall manage to get our full share no matter what happens. And it is a dull workingman who does not see in the machine the only key to the true millenium. For only mechanization can mitigate — if not cure — "the disease of work," as de Tocqueville calls it, which has tortured humanity since the first day of its existence.

To me the advent of automation is the culmination of the vying with God which began at the rise of the modern Occident. The skirmish with God has now moved all the way back to the gates of Eden. Jehovah and his angels, with their flaming and revolving swords, are now holed up inside their Eden fortress, while the blasphemous multitude with their host of machines are clamoring at the gate. And right there, in the sight of Jehovah and his angels, we are annulling the ukase that with the sweat of his brow man shall eat bread.

It is true, of course, that the cleavage between management and labor is a source of strain and strife. But it is questionable whether tranquility is the boon it is made out to be. The late William Randolph Hearst shrewdly observed that "whatever begins to be tranquil is gobbled up by something that is not tranquil." The constant effort to improve and advance is neither automatic nor the result of a leisurely choice between alternatives. In human affairs, the best stimulus for running ahead is to have something we must run from. The chances are that the millennial society, where the wolf and the lamb shall dwell together, will be a stagnant society.

The manager's job: Folklore and fact

Henry Mintzberg

If you ask a manager what he does, he will most likely tell you that he plans, organizes, coordinates, and controls. Then watch what he does. Don't be surprised if you can't relate what you see to these four words.

When he is called and told that one of his factories has just burned down, and he advises the caller to see whether temporary arrangements can be made to supply customers through a foreign subsidiary, is he planning, organizing, coordinating, or controlling? How about when he presents a gold watch to a retiring employee? Or when he attends a conference to meet people in the trade? Or on returning from that conference, when he tells one of his employees about an interesting product idea he picked up there?

The fact is that these four words, which have dominated management vocabulary since the French industrialist Henri Fayol first introduced them in 1916, tell us little about what managers actually do. At best, they indicate some vague objectives managers have when they work.

The field of management, so devoted to progress and change, has for more than half a century not seriously addressed the basic question: What do managers do? Without a proper answer, how can we teach management? How can we design planning or information systems for managers? How can we improve the practice of management at all?

Our ignorance of the nature of managerial work shows up in various ways in the modern organization — in the boast by the successful manager that he never spent a single day in a management training program; in the turnover of corporate planners who never quite understood what it was the manager wanted; in the computer consoles gathering dust in the back room because the managers never used the fancy on-line MIS some analyst thought they needed. Perhaps most important, of our ignornance shows up in the inability of our large public organizations to come to grips with some of their most serious policy problems.

Somehow, in the rush to automate production, to use management science in the functional areas of marketing and finance, and to apply the skills of the behavioral scientists to the problem of worker motivation, the manager — that person in charge of the organization or one of its submits — has been forgotten.

My intention in this article is simple: to break the reader away from Fayol's words and introduce him to a more supportable, and what I believe to be a more useful, description of managerial work. This description derives from my review and synthesis of the available research on how various managers have spent their time.

In some studies, managers were observed intensively (''shadowed'' is the term some of them used); in a number of others, they kept detailed diaries of their activities; in a few studies, their records were analyzed. All kinds of managers were studied — foremen, factory supervisors, staff managers, field sales managers, hospital administrators, presidents of companies and nations, and even street gang leaders. These ''managers'' worked in the United States, Canada, Sweden, and Great Britain. In the ruled insert is a brief review of the major studies that I found most useful in developing this description, including my own study of five American chief executive officers.

A synthesis of these findings paints an interesting picture, one as different from Fayol's classical view as a cubist abstract is from a Renaissance painting. In a sense, this picture will be obvious to anyone who has ever spent a day in a manager's office, either in front of the desk or behind it. Yet, at the same time, this picture may turn out to be revolutionary, in that it throws into doubt so much of the folklore that we have accepted about the manager's work.

I first discuss some of this folklore and contrast it with some of the discoveries of systematic research — the hard facts about how managers spend their time. Then I synthesize these research findings in a description of ten roles that seem to describe the essential content of all managers' jobs. In a concluding section, I discuss a number of implications of this synthesis for those trying to achieve more effective management,

Research on managerial work

Considering its central importance to every aspect of management, there has been surprisingly little research on the manager's work, and virtually no systematic building of knowledge from one group of studies to another. In seeking to describe managerial work, I conducted my own research and also scanned the literature widely to integrate the findings of studies from many diverse sources with my own. These studies focused on two very different aspects of managerial work. Some were concerned with the characteristics of the work — how long managers work, where, at what pace and with what interruptions, with whom they work, and through what media they communicate. Other studies were more concerned with the essential content of the work — what activities the managers actually carry out, and why. Thus, after a meeting, one researcher might note that the manager spent 45 minutes with three government officials in their Washington office, while another might record that he presented his company's stand on some proposed legislation in order to change a regulation.

A few of the studies of managerial work are widely known, but most have remained buried as single journal articles or isolated books. Among the more important ones I cite (with full references in the bibliography) are the following:

■

Sune Carlson developed the diary method to study the work characteristics of nine Swedish managing directors. Each kept a detailed log of his activities. Carlson' results are reported in his book *Executive Behavior*. A number of British researchers, notably Rosemary Stewart, have subsequently used Carlson's method. In *Managers and Their Jobs*, she describes the study of 160 top and middle managers of British companies during four weeks, with particular attention to the differences in their work.

■

Leonard Sayles's book *Managerial Behavior* is another important reference. Using a method he refers to as "anthropological," Sayles studies the work content of middle- and lower-level managers in a large U.S. corporation. Sayles moved freely in the company, collecting whatever information struck him as important.

■

Perhaps the best-known source is *Presidential Power*, in which Richard Neustadt analyzes the power and managerial behavior of Presidents Roosevelt, Truman, and Eisenhower. Neustadt used secondary sources — documents and interviews with other parties — to generate his data.

■

Robert H. Guest, in *Personnel*, reports on a study of the foreman's working day. Fifty-six U.S. foremen were observed and each of their activities recorded during one eight-hour shift.

■

Richard C. Hodgson, Daniel J. Levinson, and Abraham Zaleznik studied a team of three top executives of a U.S. hospital. From that study they wrote *The Executive Role Constellation*. These researchers addressed in particular the way in which work and socioemotional roles were divided among the three managers.

■

William F. Whyte, from his study of a street gang during the Depression, wrote *Street Corner Society*. His findings about the gang's leadership, which George C. Homans analyzed in *The Human Group*, suggest some interesting similarities of job content between street gang leaders and corporate managers.

My own study involved five American CEO's of middle- to large-size organizations — a consulting firm, a technology company, a hospital, a consumer goods company, and a school system. Using a method called "structural observation," during one intensive week of observation for each executive I recorded various aspects of every piece of mail and every verbal contact. My method was designed to capture data on both work characteristics and job content. In all, I analyzed 890 pieces of incoming and outgoing mail and 368 verbal contacts.

both in classrooms and in the business world.

Some folklore and facts about managerial work

There are four myths about the manager's job that do not bear up under careful scrutiny of the facts.

I. *Folklore: The manager is a reflective, systematic planner.* ☐ The evidence on this issue is overwhelming, but not a shred of it supports this statement.

Fact: Study after study has shown that managers work at an unrelenting pace, that their activities are characterized by brevity, variety, and discontinuity, and that they are strongly oriented to action and dislike reflective activities. ☐ Consider this evidence:

Half the activities engaged in by the five chief executives of my study lasted less than nine minutes, and only 10% exceeded one hour (Mintzberg 1973). A study of 56 U.S. foremen found that they averaged 583 activities per eight-hour shift, an average of 1 every 48 seconds (Guest 1956). The work pace for both chief executives and foremen was unrelenting. The chief executives met a steady stream of callers and mail from the moment they arrived in the morning until they left in the evening. Coffee breaks and lunches were inevitably work related, and ever-present subordinates seemed to usurp any free moment.

A diary study of 160 British middle and top managers found that they worked for a half hour or more without interruption only about once every two days. (Stewart 1967, Carlson 1951).

Of the verbal contacts of the chief executives in my study, 93% were arranged on an ad hoc basis. Only 1% of the executives' time was spent in open-ended observational tours. Only 1 out of 368 verbal contacts was unrelated to a specific issue and could be called general planning. Another researcher finds that "in *not one single case* did a manager report the obtaining of important external information from a general conversation or other undirected personal communication" (Aguiler 1967).

No study has found important patterns in the way managers schedule their time. They seem to jump from issue to issue, continually responding to the needs of the moment.

Is this the planner that the classical view describes? Hardly. How, then, can we explain this behavior? The manager is simply responding to the pressures of his job. I found that my chief executives terminated many of their own activities, often leaving meetings before the end, and interrupted their desk work to call in subordinates. One president not only placed his desk so that he could look down a long hallway but also left his door open when he was alone — an invitation for subordinates to come in and interrupt him.

Clearly, these managers wanted to encourage the flow of current information. But more significantly, they seemed to be conditioned by their own work loads. They appreciated the opportunity cost of their own time, and they were continually aware of their ever-present obligations — mail to be answered, callers to attend to, and so on. It seems that no matter what he is doing, the manager is plagued by the possibilities of what he might do and what he must do.

When the manager must plan, he

seems to do so implicitly in the context of daily actions, not in some abstract process reserved for two weeks in the organization's mountain retreat. The plans of the chief executives I studied seemed to exist only in their heads — as flexible, but often specific, intentions. The traditional literature nothwithstanding, the job of managing does not breed reflective planners; the manager is a real-time responder to stimuli, an individual who is conditioned by his job to prefer live to delayed action.

II. *Folklore: The effective manager has no regular duties to perform.* □ Managers are constantly being told to spend more time planning and delgating, and less time seeing customers and engaging in negotiations. These are not, after all, the true tasks of the manager. To use the popular analogy, the good manager, like the good conductor, carefully orchestrates everything in advance, then sits back to enjoy the fruits of his labor, responding occasionally to an unforseeable exception.

But here again the pleasant abstraction just does not seem to hold up. We had better take a closer look at those activities managers feel compelled to engage in before we arbitrarily define them away.

Fact: in addition to handling exceptions, managerial work involves performing a number of regular duties, including ritual and ceremony, negotiations, and processing of soft information that links the organization with its environment. • Consider some evidence from the research studies:

A study of the work of the presidents of small companies found that they engaged in routine activities because their companies could not afford staff specialists and were so thin on operating personnel that a single absence often required the president to substitute (see Choran).

One study of field sales managers and another of chief executives suggest that it is a natural part of both jobs to see important customers, assuming the managers wish to keep those customers (Davis 1957; Copeman 1963).

Someone, only half in jest, once decribed the manager as that person who sees visitors so that everyone else can get his work done. In my study, I found that certan ceremonial duties — meeting visiting dignitaries, giving out gold watches, presiding at Christmas dinners — were an intrinsic part of the chief executive's job.

Studies of managers' information flow suggest that managers play a key role in securing "soft" external information (much of it available only to them because of their status) and in passing it along to their subordinates.

III: *Folklore: The senior manager needs aggregated information, which a formal management information system best provides.* □ Not too long ago, the words *total information system* were everywhere in the management literature. In keeping with the classical view of the manager as that individual perched on the apex of a regulated, hierarchical system, the literature's manager was to receive all his important information from a giant, comprehensive MIS.

But lately, as it has become increasingly evident that these giant MIS systems are not working — that managers are simply not using them — the enthusiasm has waned. A look at how managers actually process information makes the reason quite clear. Managers have five media at their command — documents, telephone calls, scheduled and unscheduled meetings, and observational tours.

Fact: Managers strongly favor the verbal media — namely, telephone calls and meetings. ☐ The evidence comes from every single study of managerial work. Consider the following:

In two British studies, managers spent an average of 66 percent and 80 percent of their time in verbal (oral) communication (Stewart 1967; Burns 1954). In my study of five American chief executives, the figure was 78 percent.

These five chief executives treated mail processing as a burden to be dispensed with. One came in Saturday morning to process 142 pieces of mail in just over three hours, to "get rid of all the stuff." This same manager looked at the first piece of "hard" mail he had received all week, a standard cost report, and put it aside with the comment, "I never look at this."

These same five chief executives responded immediately to 2 of the 40 routine reports they received during the five weeks of my study and to four items in the 104 periodicals. They skimmed most of these periodicals in seconds, almost ritualistically. In all, these chief executives of good-sized organizations initiated on their own — that is, not in reponse to something else — a grand total of 25 pieces of mail during the 25 days I observed them.

An analysis of the mail the executives received reveals an interesting picture — only 13 percent was of specific and immediate use. So now we have another piece in the puzzle: not much of the mail

provides live, current information — the action of a competitor, the mood of a government legislator, or the rating of last night's television show. Yet this is the information that drove the managers, interrupting their meetings and rescheduling their workdays.

Consider another interesting finding. Managers seem to cherish "soft" information, especially gossip, hearsay, and speculation. Why? The reason is its timeliness; today's gossip may be tomorrow's fact. The manager who is not accessible for the telephone call informing him that his biggest customer was seen golfing with the main competitor may read about a dramatic drop in sales in the next quarterly report. But then it's too late.

To assess the value of historical, aggregated, "hard" MIS information, consider two of the manager's prime uses for his information — to identify problems and opportunites (Wrapp 1967) and to build his own mental models of the things around him (e.g., how his organization's budget system works, how his customers buy his product, how changes in the economy affect his organization, and so on). Every bit of evidence suggests that the manager identifies decision situations and builds models not with the aggregated abstractions an MIS provides, but with specific tidbits of data.

Consider the words of Richard Neustadt, who studied the information-collecting habits of Presidents Roosevelt, Truman, and Eisenhower:

It is not information of a general sort that helps a President see personal stakes; not summaries, not surveys, not the *bland amalgams.* Rather … it is the odds and ends of *tangible detail* that pieced together in his mind illuminate the underside of issues put before him. To help himself he must reach out as widely as he can for every scrap of fact, opinion, gossip, bearing on his interests and relationships as President. He must become his own director of his own central intelligence (Neustadt 1960, 153-154).

The manager's emphasis on the verbal media raises two important points:

First, verbal information is stored in the brains of people. Only when people write this information down can it be stored in the files of the organization — whether in metal cabinets or on magnetic tape — and managers apparently do not write down much of what they hear. Thus the strategic data bank of the organization is not in the memory of its computers but in the minds of its managers.

Second, the manager's extensive use of verbal media helps to explain why he is reluctant to delegate tasks. When we note that most of the manager's important information comes in verbal form and is stored in his head, we can well appreciate his reluctance. It is not as if he can hand a dossier over to someone; he must take the time to "dump memory" — to tell that someone all he knows about the subject. But this could take so long that the manager may find it easier to do the task himself. Thus the manager is damned by his own information system to a "dilemma of delegation" — to do too much himself or to delegate to his subordinates with inadequate briefing.

IV. *Folklore: Management is, or at least is quickly becoming, a science and a profession.* ☐ By almost any definitions of *science* and *profession,* this statement is false. Brief observation of any manager will quickly lay to rest the notion that managers practice a science. A science involves the enaction of systematic, analytically determined procedures or programs. If we do not even know what pro-

cedures managers use, how can we prescribe them by scientific analysis? And how can we call management a profession if we cannot specify what managers are to learn? For after all, a profession involves "knowledge of some department of learning or science" *(Random House Dictionary).* (Andrews 1969).

Fact: The managers' programs — to schedule time, process information, make decisions, and so on — remain locked deep inside their brains. ☐Thus, to describe these programs, we rely on words like *judgment* and *intuition,* seldom stopping to realize that they are merely labels for our ignorance.

I was struck during my study by the fact that the executives I was observing — all very competent by any standard — are fundamentally indistinguishable from their counterparts of a hundred years ago (or a thousand years ago, for that matter). The information they need differs, but they seek it in the same way — by word of mouth. Their decisions concern modern technology, but the procedures they use to make them are the same as the procedures of the nineteenth-century manager. Even the computer, so important for the specialized work of the organization, has apparently had no influence on the work procedures of general managers. In fact, the manager is in a kind of loop, with increasingly heavy work pressures but no aid forthcoming from management science.

Considering the facts about managerial work, we can see that the manager's job is enormously complicated and difficult. The manager is overburdened with obligations; yet he cannot easily delegate his tasks. As a result, he is driven to overwork and is forced to do many tasks superficially. Brevity, fragmentation, and verbal communications characterize his work. Yet these are the very characteristics of managerial work that have impeded scientific attempts to improve it. As a result, the management scientist has concentrated his efforts on the specialized functions of the organization, where he could more easily analyze the procedures and quantify the relevant information (Gragson 1973).

But the pressures of the manager's job are becoming worse. Where before he needed only to respond to owners and directors, now he finds that subordinates with democratic norms continually reduce his freedom to issue unexplained orders, and a growing number of outside influences (consumer groups, government agencies, and so on) expect his attention. And the manager has had nowhere to turn for help. The first step in providing the manager with some help is to find out what his job really is.

Back to a basic description of managerial work

Now let us try to put some of the pieces of this puzzle together. Earlier, I defined the manager as that person in charge of an organization or one of its subunits. Besides chief executive officers, this definition would include vice presidents, bishops, foremen, hockey coaches, and prime ministers. Can all of these people have anything in common? Indeed they can. For an important starting point, all are vested with formal authority over an organizational unit. From formal authority comes status, which leads to various interpersonal relations, and from these comes access to information. Information, in turn, enables the manager to make decisions and strategies for his unit.

The manager's job can be described in terms of various "roles," or organized sets of behaviors identified with a position. My description, shown in Exhibit 1, comprises ten roles. As we shall see, formal authority gives rise to the three interpersonal roles, which in turn give rise to the three interpersonal roles; these two sets of roles enable the manager to play the four decisional roles.

Interpersonal roles

Three of the manager's roles arise directly from his formal authority and involve basic interpersonal relationships.

1. First is the *figurehead* role. By virtue of his position as head of an organizational unit, every manager must perform some duties of a ceremonial nature. The president greets the touring dignitaries, the foreman attends the wedding of a lathe operator, and the sales manager takes an important customer to lunch.

The chief executives of my study spent 12% of their contact time on ceremonial duties; 17% of their incoming mail dealt

Exhibit 1
The manager's roles

Formal authority and status		
Interpersonal roles	Informational roles	Decisional roles
Figurehead	Monitor	Entrepreneur
Leader	Disseminator	Disturbance handler
Liaison	Spokesman	Resource allocator
		Negotiator

with acknowledgments and requests related to their status. For example, a letter to a company president requested free merchandise for a crippled schoolchild; diplomas were put on the desk of the school superintendent for his signature.

Duties that involve interpersonal roles may sometimes be routine, involving little serious communication and no important decision making. Nevertheless, they are important to the smooth functioning of an organization and cannot be ignored by the manager.

2. Becuase he is in charge of an organizational unit, the manager is responsible for the work of the people of that unit. His actions in this regard constitute the *leader* role. Some of these actions involve leadership directly — for example, in most organizations the manager is normally responsible for hiring and training his own staff.

In addition, there is the indirect exercise of the leader role. Every manager must motivate and encourage his employees, somehow reconciling their individual needs with the goals of the organization. In virtually every contact the manager has with his employees, subordinates seeking leadership clues probe his actions: "does he approve?" "How would he like the report to turn out?" "Is he more interested in market share than high profits?"

The influence of the manager is most clearly seen in the leader role. Formal authority vests him with great potential power; leadership determines in large part how much of it he will realize.

3. The literature of management has always recognized the leader role, particularly those aspects of it related to motivation. In comparison, until recently it has hardly mentioned the *liaison* role,

in which the manager makes contacts outside his vertical chain of command. This is remarkable in light of the finding of virtually every study of managerial work that managers spend as much time with peers and other people outside their units as they do with their own subordinates — and, surprisingly, very little time with their own superiors.

In Rosemary Stewart's diary study, the 160 British middle and top managers spent 47% of their time with peers, 41% of their time with people outside their unit, and only 12% of their time with their superiors. For Robert H. Guest's study of U.S. foremen, the figures were 44%, 46%, and 10%. The chief executives of my study averaged 44% of their contact time with people outside their organizations, 48% with subordinates, and 7% with directors and trustees.

The contacts the five CEOs made were with an incredibly wide range of people: subordinates; clients, business associates, and suppliers; and peers — managers of similar organizations, government and trade organization officials, fellow directors on outside boards, and independents with no relevant organizational affiliations. The chief executives' time with and mail from these groups is shown in Exhibit 2. Guest's study of foremen shows, likewise, that their contacts were numerous and wide ranging, seldom involving fewer than 25 individuals, and often more than 50.

As we shall see shortly, the manager cultivates such contacts largely to find information. In effect, the liaison role is devoted to building up the manager's own external information system — informal, private, verbal, but nevertheless, effective.

Informational roles

By virtue of his interpersonal contacts,

both with his subordinates and with his network of contacts, the manager emerges as the nerve center of his organizational unit. He may not know everything, but he typically knows more than any member of his staff.

Studies have shown this relationship to hold for all managers, from street gang leaders to U.S. presidents. In *The Human Group,* George C. Homans explains how, because they were at the center of the information flow in their own gangs and were also in close touch with the other gang leaders, street gang leaders were better informed than any of their followers (Homans 1950). And Richard Neustadt describes the following account from his study of Franklin D. Roosevelt:

Exhibit 2
The chief executives' contacts

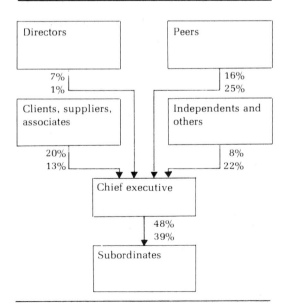

Note: The top figure indicates the proportion of total contact time spend with each group and the bottom figure, the proportion of mail from each group.

The essence of Roosevelt's technique for information gathering was competition. "He would call you," one of his aides once told me, "and he'd ask you to get the story on some complicated business, and you'd come back after a couple of days of hard labor and present the juicy morsel you'd uncovered under a stone somewhere, and *then* you'd find out he knew all about it, along with something else you *didn't* know. Where he got this information from he wouldn't mention, usually, but after he had done this to you once or twice you got damn careful about *your* information (Neustadt 1960, 1957).

We can see where Roosevelt "got this information" when we consider the relationship between the interpersonal and informational roles. As leader, the manager has formal and easy access to every member of his staff. Hence, as noted earlier, he tends to know more about his own unit than anyone else does. In addition, his liaison contacts expose the manager to external information to which his subordinates often lack access. Many of these contacts are with other managers of equal status, who are themselves nerve centers in their own organization. In this way, the manager develops a powerful data base of information.

The processing of information is a key part of the manager's job. In my study, the chief executives spent 40% of their contact time on activities devoted exclusively to the transmission of information; 70% of their incoming mail was purely informational (as opposed to requests for action). The manager does not leave meetings or hang up the telephone in order to get back to work. In large part, communication *is* his work. Three roles describe these informational aspects of managerial work.

1. As *monitor,* the manager perpetually

scans his environment for information, interrogates his liaison contacts and his subordinates, and receives unsolicited information, much of it as a result of the network of personal contacts he has developed. Remember that a good part of the information the manager collects in his monitor role arrives in verbal form, often as gossip, hearsay, and speculation. By virtue of his contacts, the manager has a natural advantage in collecting this soft information for his organization.

2. He must share and distribute much of this information. Information he gleans from outside personal contacts may be needed within his organization. In his *disseminator* role, the manager passes some of his privileged informaiton directly to his subordinates, who would otherwise have no access to it. When his subordinates lack easy contact with one another, the manager will sometimes pass information from one to another.

3. In his *spokesman* role, the manager sends some of his information to people outside his unit — a president makes a speech to lobby for an organization cause, or a foreman suggests a product modification to a supplier. In addition, as part of his role as spokesman, every manager must inform and satisfy the influential people who control his organizational unit. For the foreman, this may simply involve keeping the plant manager informed about the flow of work through the shop.

The president of a large corporation, however, may spend a great amount of his time dealing with a host of influences. Directors and shareholders must be advised about financial performance; consumer groups must be assured that the organizaton is fulfilling its social responsiblilities; and government officials must be satisfied that the organization is abiding by the law.

Decisional roles

Information is not, of course, an end in itself; it is the basic input to decision making. One thing is clear in the study of managerial work: the manager plays the major role in his unit's decision-making system. As its formal authority, only he can commit the unit to important new courses of action; and as its nerve center, only he has full and current information to make the set of decisions that determines the unit's strategy. Four roles describe the manager as decision-maker.

1. As *entrepreneur,* the manager seeks to improve his unit, to adapt it to changing conditions in the environment. In his monitor role, the president is constantly on the lookout for new ideas. When a good one appears, he initiates a development project that he may supervise himself or delegate to an employee (perhaps with the stipulation that he must approve the final proposal.).

There are two interesting features about these development projects at the chief executive level.

First, these projects do not involve single decisions or even unified clusters of decisions. Rather, they emerge as a series of small decisions and actions sequenced over time. Apparently, the chief executive prolongs each project so that he can fit it bit by bit into his busy, disjointed schedule and so that he can gradually come to comprehend the issue, if it is a complex one.

Second, the chief executives I studied supervised as many as 50 of these projects at the same time. Some projects entailed new products or processes; others involved public relations campaigns, improvement of the cash position, reorganization of a weak department, resolution of a morale problem in a foreign division, integration of computer operations, various acquisitions at different stages of development, and so on.

The chief executive appears to maintain a kind of inventory of the development projects that he himself supervises — projects that are at various stages of development, some active and some in limbo. Like a juggler, he keeps a number of projects in the air; periodically, one comes down, is given a new burst of energy, and is sent back into orbit. At various intervals, he put new projects onstream and discards old ones.

2. While the entrepreneur role describes the manager as the voluntary initiator of change, the *disturbance handler* role depicts the manager involuntarily reponding to pressures. Here change is beyond the manager's control. He must act because the pressures of the situation are too severe to be ignored: strike looms, a major customer has gone bankrupt, or a supplier reneges on his contract.

It has been fashionable, I noted earlier, to compare the manager to an orchestra conductor, just as Peter F. Drucker wrote in *The Practice of Management:*

The manager has the task of creating a true whole that is larger than the sum of its parts, a productive entity that turns out more than the sum of the resources put into it. One analogy is the conductor of a symphony orchestra, through whose effort, vision and leadership individual instrumental parts that are so much noise by themselves become the living whole of music. But the conductor has the composer's score; he is only interpreter. The manager is both composer

and conductor (Drucker 1954).

Now consider the words of Leonard R. Sayles, who has carried out systematic research on the manager's job:

[The manager] is like a symphony orchestra conductor, endeavouring to maintain a melodious performance in which the contributions of the various instruments are coordinated and sequenced, patterned and paced, while the orchestra members are having various personal difficulties, stage hands are moving music stands, alternating excessive heat and cold are creating audience and instrument problems, and the sponsor of the concert is insisting on irrational changes in the program (Sayles 1964).

If effect, every manager must spend a good part of his time responding to high-pressure disturbances. No organization can be so well run, so standardized, that it has considered every contingency in the uncertain environment in advance. Disturbances arise not only because poor managers ignore situations until they reach crisis proportions, but also because good managers cannot possibly anticipate all the consequences of the actions they take.

3. The third decisional role is that of *resource allocator.* To the manager falls the responsibility of deciding who will get what in his organizational unit. Perhaps the most important resource the manager allocates is his own time. Access to the manager constitutes exposure to the unit's nerve center and decision-maker. The manager is also charged with designing his unit's structure, that pattern of formal relationships that determines how work is to be divided and coordinated.

Also, in his role as resource allocator, the manager authorizes the important decisions of his unit before they are implemented. By retaining this power, the manager can ensure that decisions are interrelated; all must pass through a single brain. To fragment this power is to encourage discontinuous decision making and a disjointed strategy.

There are a number of interesting features about the manager's authorizing others' decisions. First, despite the widespread use of capital budgeting procedures — a means of authorizing various capital expenditures at one time — executives in my study made a great many authorization decisions on an ad hoc basis. Apparently, many projects cannot wait or simply do not have the quantifiable costs and benefits that capital budgeting requires.

Second, I found that the chief executives faced incredibly complex choices. They had to consider the impact of each decision on other decisions and on the organization's strategy. They had to ensure that the decision would be acceptable to those who influence the organization, as well as ensure that resources would not be overextended. They had to understand the various costs and benefits as well as the feasibility of the proposal. They also had to consider questions of timing. All this was necessary for the simple approval of someone else's proposal. At the same time, however, delay could lose time, while quick approval could be ill considered and quick rejection might discourage the subordinate who had spent months developing a pet project.

One common solution to approving projects is to pick the man instead of the proposal. That is, the manager authorizes those projects presented to him by people whose judgment he trusts. But he cannot always use this simple dodge.

4. The final decisional role is that of *negotiator.* Studies of managerial work at all levels indicate that managers spend considerable time in negotiations: the president of the football team is called in to work out a contract with the holdout superstar; the corporation president leads his company's contingent to negotiate a new strike issue; the foreman argues a grievance problem to its conclusion with the shop steward. As Leonard Sayles puts it, negotiations are a ''way of life'' for the sophisticated manager.

These negotiations are duties of the manager's job; perhaps routine, they are not to be shirked. They are an integral part of his job, for only he has the authority to commit organizational resources in "real time," and only he has the nerve center information that important negotiations require.

The integrated job

It should be clear by now that the ten roles I have been describing are not easily separable. In the terminology of the psychologist, they form a gestalt, an integrated whole. No role can be pulled out of the framework and the job be left intact. For example, a manager without liaison contacts lacks external information. As a result, he can neither disseminate the information his employees need nor make decisions that adequately reflect external conditions. (In fact, this is a problem for the new person in a managerial position, since he cannot make effective decisions until he has built up his network of contacts.)

Here lies a clue to the problem of team management. (Hodgson, Levinson, and Zaleznik 1965). Two or three people cannot share a single managerial position unless they can act as one entity. This means that they cannot divide up the ten roles unless they can very carefully reintegrate them. The real difficulty lies with the informational roles. Unless there can be full sharing of managerial information — and, as I pointed out earlier, it is primarily verbal — team management breaks down. A single manageral job cannot be arbitrarily split, for example, into internal and external roles, for information from both sources must be brought to bear on the same decisions.

To say that the ten roles form a gestalt is not to say that all managers give equal attention to each role. In fact, I found in my review of the various research studies that . . .

sales managers seem to spend relatively more of their time in the interpersonal roles, presumably a reflection of the extrovert nature of the marketing activity; . . .

production managers give relatively more attention to the decisional roles, presumably a reflection of their concern with efficient work flow; . . .

staff managers spend the most time in the informational roles, since they are experts who manage departments that advise other parts of the organization.

Nevertheless, in all cases the interpersonal, informational, and decisional roles remain inseparable.

Toward more effective management

What are the messages for management in this description? I believe, first and foremost, that this description of managerial work should prove more important to managers than any prescription they might derive from it. That is to say, *the manager's effectiveness is significantly influenced by his insight into his own work.* His performance depends on how well he understands and responds to the pressures and dilemmas of the job. Thus managers who can be introspective about their work are likely to be effective at their jobs. The ruled insert on page 290 offers 14 groups of self-study questions for managers. Some may sound rhetorical; none is meant to be. Even though the questions cannot be answered simply, the manager should address them.

Let us take a look at three specific areas of concern. For the most part, the managerial logjams — the dilemma of delegation, the data base centralized in one brain, the problems of working with the management scientist — revolve around the verbal nature of the manager's information. There are great dangers in centralizing the organization's data bank in the minds of its managers. When they leave, they take their memory with them. And when subordinates are out of convenient verbal reach of the manager, they are at an informational disadvantage.

I. *The manager is challenged to find systematic ways to share his privileged information.* ☐ A regular debriefing session with key subordinates, a weekly memory dump on the dictating machine, the maintaining of a diary of important information for limited circulation, or other similar methods may ease the logjam of work considerably. Time spent disseminating this information will be more than regained when decisions must be made. Of course, some will raise the question of confidentiality. But managers would do well to weigh the risks of exposing privileged information against having subordinates who can make effective decisions.

If there is a single theme that runs through this article, it is that the pressures of his job drive the manager to be superficial in his actions — to overload

Self-study questions for managers

1. Where do I get my information, and how? Can I make greater use of my contacts to get information? Can other people do some of my scanning for me? In what areas is my knowledge weakest, and how can I get others to provide me with the information I need? Do I have powerful enough mental models of those things I must understand within the organization and in its environment?

2. What information do I disseminate in my organization? How important is it that my subordinates get my information? Do I keep too much information to myself because dissemination of it is time-consuming or inconvenient? How can I get more information to others so they can make better decisions?

3. Do I balance information collecting with action taking? Do I tend to act before information is in? Or do I wait so long for all the information that opportunities pass me by and I become a bottleneck in my organization?

4. What pace of change am I asking my organization to tolerate? Is this change balanced so that our operations are neither excessively static nor overly disrupted? Have we sufficiently analyzed the impact of this change on the future of our organization?

5. Am I sufficiently well informed to pass judgment on the proposals that my subordinates make? Is it possible to leave final authorization for more of the proposals with subordinates? Do we have problems of coordination because subordinates in fact now make too many of these decisions independently?

6. What is my vision of direction for this organizaion? Are these plans primarily in my own mind in loose form? Should I make them explicit in order to guide the decisions of others in the organization better? Or do I need flexibility to change them at will?

7. How do my subordinates react to my managerial style? Am I sufficiently sensitive to the powerful influence my actions have on them? Do I fully understand their reactions to my actions? Do I find an appropriate balance between encouragement and pressure? Do I stifle their initiative?

8. What kind of external relationships do I maintain, and how? Do I spend too much of my time maintaining these relatinships? Are there certain types of people whom I should get to know better?

9. Is there any system to my time scheduling, or am I just reacting to the pressures of the moment? Do I find the appropriate mix of activities, or do I tend to concentrate on one particular functin or one type of problem just because I find it interesting? Am I more efficient with particular kinds of work at special times of the day or week? Does my schedule reflect this? Can someone else (in addition to my secretary) take responsibility for much of my scheduling and do it more systematically?

10. Do I overwork? What effect does my work load have on my efficiency? Should I force myself to take breaks or to reduce the pace of my activity?

11. Am I too superficial in what I do? Can I really shift moods as quickly and frequently as my work patterns require? Should I attempt to decrease the amount of fragmentation and interruption in my work?

12. Do I orient myself too much toward current, tangible activities? Am I a slave to the action and excitement of my work, so that I am no longer able to concentrate on issues? Do key problems receive the attention they deserve? Should I spend more time reading and probing deeply into certain issues? Could I be more reflective? Should I be?

13. Do I use the different media appropriately? Do I know how to make the most of the written communication? Do I rely excessively on face-to-face communication, thereby putting all but a few of my subordinates at an informational disadvantage? Do I schedule enough of my meetings on a regular basis? Do I spend enough time touring my organization to observe activity at first hand? Am I too detached from the heart of my organization's activities, seeing things only in an abstract way?

14. How do I blend my personal rights and duties? Do my obligations consume all my time? How can I free myself sufficiently from obligations to ensure that I am taking this organization where I want it to go? How can I turn my obligations to my advantage?

himself with work, encourage interruption, seek the tangible and avoid the abstract, make decisions in small increments, and do everything abruptly.

II. *Here again, the manager is challenged to deal consciously with the pressures of superficiality by giving serious attention to the issues that require it, by stepping back from his tangible bits of information in order to see a broad picture, and by making use of analytical inputs.* ☐ Although effective managers have to be adept at responding quickly to numerous and varying problems, the danger in managerial work is that they will respond to every issue equally (and that means abruptly) and that they will never work the tangible bits and pieces of informational input into a comprehensive picture of their world.

As I noted earlier, the manager uses these bits of information to build models of his world. But the manager can also avail himself of the models of the specialists. Economists describe the functioning of markets, operations researchers simulate financial flow processes, and behavioral scientists explain the needs and goals of people. The best of these models can be searched out and learned.

In dealing with complex issues, the senior manager has much to gain from a close relationship with the management scientists of his own organization. They have something important that he lacks — time to probe complex issues. An effective working relationship hinges on the resolution of what a colleague and I have called "the planning dilemma." (Hekimian and Mintzberg 1968). Managers have the information and the authority; analysts have the time and the technology. A successful working relationship between the two will be ef-

fected when the manager learns to share his information and the analyst learns to adapt to the manager's needs. For the analyst, adaptation means worrying less about the elegance of the method and more about its speed and flexibility.

It seems to me that analysts can help the top manager especially to schedule his time, feed in analytical information, monitor projects under his supervision, develop models to aid in making choices, design contingency plans for disturbances that can be anticipated, and conduct "quick-and-dirty" analysis for those that cannot. But there can be no cooperation if the analysts are out of the mainstream of the manager's information flow.

III. *The manager is challenged to gain control of his own time by turning obligations to his advantage and by turning those things he wishes to do into obligations.* ☐ The chief executives of my study initiated only 32% of their own contacts (and another 5% by mutual agreement). And yet to a considerable extent they seemed to control their time. There were two key factors that enabled them to to so.

First, the manager has to spend so much time discharging obligations that if he were to view them as just that, he would leave no mark on his organization. The unsuccessful manager blames failure on the obligations; the effective manager turns his obligations to his own advantage. A speech is a chance to lobby for a cause; a meeting is a chance to reorganize a weak department; a visit to an important customer is a chance to extract trade information.

Second, the manager frees some of his time to do those things that he — perhaps no one else — thinks important by turning them into obligations. Free time is made, not found, in the manager's job; it is forced into the schedule. Hoping to leave some time open for contemplation or general planning is tantamount to hoping that the pressures of the job will go away. The manager who wants to innovate initiates a project and obligates others to report back to him; the manager who needs certain environmental information establishes channels that will automatically keep him informed; the manager who has to tour facilities commits himself publicly.

The educator's job

Finally, a word about the training of managers. Our management schools have done an admirable job of training the organization's specialists — management scientists, marketing researchers, accountants, and organizational development specialist. But for the most part they have not trained managers (Livingston 1971).

Management schools will begin the serious training of managers when skill training takes a serious place next to cognitive learning. Cognitive learning is detached and informational, like reading a book or listening to a lecture. No doubt much important cognitive material must be assimilated by the manager-to-be. But cognitive learning no more makes a manager than it does a swimmer. The latter will drown the first time he jumps into the water if his coach never takes him out of the lecture hall, gets him wet, and gives him feedback on his performance.

In other words, we are taught a skill through practice plus feedback, whether in a real or a simulated situation. Our management schools need to identify the skills managers use, select students who show potential in these skills, put the students into situations where these skills can be practiced, and then give them systematic feedback on their performance.

My description of managerial work suggests a number of important managerial skills — developing peer relationships, carrying out negotiations, motivating subordinates, resolving conflicts, establishing information networks and subsequently disseminating information, making decisions in conditions of extreme ambiguity, and allocating resources. Above all, the manager needs to be introspective about his work so that he may continue to learn on the job.

Many of the manager's skills can, in fact, be practiced, using techniques that range from role playing to videotaping real meetings. And our management schools can enhance the entrepreneurial skills by designing programs that encourage sensible risk taking and innovation.

No job is more vital to our society than that of the manager. It is the manager who determines whether our social institutions serve us well or whether they squander our talents and resources. It is time to strip away the folklore about managerial work, and time to study it realistically so that we can begin the difficult task of making significant improvements in its performance.

Power, dependence, and effective management

John P. Kotter

A mericans have probably always been suspicious of power — the United States was born out of a rebellion against it, and our political processes seem to confirm that distrust. We have equated power with exploitation and corruption. But, the author of this article asserts, the negative aspects of power have blinded people to its positive points, to its uses, and to the fact that without it, people cannot accomplish very much anywhere. And that is especially true in management. The author maintains that, as organizations have grown more complex, it has become more difficult, if not impossible, for managers to achieve their ends either independently or through persuasion and formal authority alone. They increasingly need power to influence other people on whom they are dependent. Furthermore, he says, effective managers tend to be very successful at developing four different types of power, which they use along with persuasion to influence others. And they do so, the author concludes, with maturity, great skill, and a sensitivity to the obligations and risks involved.

John P. Kotter is associate professor of business admninistration at the Harvard Business School. He is currently conducting research and writing books on three topics — organizational design and change, managerial careers, and general management jobs.

Americans, as a rule, are not very comfortable with power or with its dynamics. We often distrust and question the motives of people who we think actively seek power. We have a certain fear of being manipulated. Even those people who think the dynamics of power are inevitable and needed often feel somewhat guilty when they themselves mobilize and use power. Simply put, the overall attitude and feeling toward power, which can easily be traced to the nation's very birth, is negative. In his enormously popular *Greening of America*, Charles Reich reflects the views of many when he writes, "It is not the misuse of power that is evil; the very existence of power is evil" (Reich 1970).

One of the many consequences of this attitude is that power as a topic for rational study and dialogue has not received much attention, even in managerial circles. If the reader doubts this, all he or she need do is flip through some textbooks, journals, or advanced management course descriptions. The word *power* rarely appears.

This lack of attention to the subject of power merely adds to the already enormous confusion and misunderstanding surrounding the topic of power and management. And this misunderstanding is becoming increasingly burdensome because in today's large and complex organizations the effective performance of most managerial jobs requires one to be skilled at the acquisition and use of power.

From my own observations, I suspect that a large number of managers — especially the young, well-educated ones — perform significantly below their potential because they do not understand the dynamics of power and because they have not nurtured and developed the instincts needed to effectively acquire and use power.

In this article I hope to clear up some of the confusion regarding power and managerial work by providing tentative answers to three questions:

1. Why are the dynamics of power necessarily an important part of managerial process?
2. How do effective managers acquire power?
3. How and for what purposes do effective managers use power?

I will not address questions related to the misuse of power, but not because I think they are unimportant. The fact that some managers, some of the time, acquire and use power mostly for their own aggrandizement is obviously a very important issue that deserves attention and careful study. But that is a complex topic unto itself and one that has already received more attention than the subject of this article.

Recognizing dependence in the manager's job

One of the distinguishing characteristics of a typical manager is how dependent he is on the activities of a variety of other people to perform his job effectively (Sayles 1964; Stewart 1967, 1976). Unlike doctors and mathematicians, whose performance is more directly dependent on their own talents and efforts, a manager can be dependent in varying degrees on superiors, subordinates, peers in other parts of the organization, the subordinates of peers, outside suppliers, customers, competitors, unions, regulating agencies, and many others.

These dependency relationships are an inherent part of managerial jobs because of two organizational facts of life: division of labor and limited resources. Because the work in organizations is divided in specialized divisions, departments, and jobs, managers are made directly or indirectly dependent on many others for information, staff services, and cooperation in general. Because of their organization's limited resources, managers are also dependent on their external environments for support. Without some minimal cooperation from suppliers, competitors, unions, regulatory agencies, and customers, managers cannot help their organizations survive and achieve their objectives.

Dealing with these dependencies and the manager's subsequent vulnerability is an important and difficult part of a manager's job because, while it is theoretically possible that all of these people and organizations would automatically act in just the manner that a manager wants and needs, such is almost never the case in reality. All the people on whom a manager is dependent have limited time, energy, and talent, for which there are competing demands.

Some people may be uncooperative because they are too busy elsewhere, and some because they are not really capable of helping. Others may well have goals, values, and beliefs that are quite different and in conflict with the manager's and may therefore have no desire whatsoever to help or cooperate. This is obviously true of a competing company and sometimes of a union, but it can also apply to a boss who is feeling threatened by a manager's career progress or to a peer whose objectives clash with the manager's.

Indeed, managers often find themselves dependent on many people (and things) whom they do not directly control and who are not "cooperating." This is the key to one of the biggest frustrations managers feel in their jobs, even in the top ones, which the following example illustrates:

After nearly a year of rumors, it was finally announced in May 1974 that the president of ABC Corporation had been elected chairman of the board and that Jim Franklin, the vice president of finance, would replace him as president. While everyone at ABC was aware that a shift would take place soon, it was not at all clear before the announcement who would be the next president. Most people had guessed it would be Phil Cook, the marketing vice president.

Nine months into his job as chief executive officer, Franklin found that Phil Cook (still the marketing vice president) seemed to be fighting him in small and subtle ways. There was never anything blatant, but Cook just did not cooperate with Franklin as the other vice presidents did. Shortly after being elected, Franklin had tried to bypass what he saw as a potential conflict with Cook by telling him that he would understand if Cook would prefer to move somewhere else where he could be a CEO also. Franklin said that it would be willing to help Cook in a number of ways if he wanted to look for a presidential opportunity elsewhere. Cook had thanked him but had said that family and community commitments would prevent him from relocating and all CEO opportunities were bound to be in a different city.

Since the situation did not improve after the tenth and eleventh months, Franklin seriously considered forcing Cook out. When he thought about the consequences of such a move, Franklin became more and more aware of just how dependent he was on Cook. Marketing and sales were generally the keys to success in their industry, and the company's sales force was one of the best, if not the best, in the industry. Cook had been with the company for 25 years. He had built a strong personal relationship with many of the people in the sales force and was universally popular. A mass exodus just might occur if Cook were fired. The loss of a large number of salesmen, or even a lot of turmoil in the department, could have a serious effect on the company's performance.

After one year as chief executive officer, Franklin found that the situation between Cook and himself had not improved and had become a constant source of frustration.

As a person gains more formal authority in an organization, the areas in which he or she is vulnerable increase and become more complex rather than the reverse. As the previous example suggests, it is not at all unusual for the president of an organization to be in a highly dependent position, a fact often not apparent to either the outsider or to the lower level manager who covets the president's job.

A considerable amount of the behavior of highly successful managers that seems inexplicable in light of what management texts usually tell us managers do becomes understandable when one considers a manager's need for, and efforts at, managing his or her relationships with others (Mintzberg 1975). To be able to plan, organize, budget, staff, control, and evaluate, managers need some control over the many people on whom they are dependent. Trying to control others solely by directing them and on the basis of the power associated with one's position simply will not work — first, because managers are always dependent on some people over whom they have no formal authority, and second, because virtually no one in modern organizations will passively accept and completely obey a constant stream of orders from someone just because he or she is the "boss."

Trying to influence others by means of persuasion alone will not work either. Although it is very powerful and possibly the single most important method of influence, persuasion has some serious drawbacks too. To make it work requires time (often lots of it), skill, and information on the part of the persuader. And persuasion can fail simply because the other person chooses not to listen or does not listen carefully.

This is not to say that directing people on the basis of the formal power of one's position and persuasion are not important means by which successful managers cope. They obviously are. But, even taken together, they are not usually enough.

Successful managers cope with their dependence on others by being sensitive to it, by eliminating or avoiding unnecessary dependence, and by establishing power over those others. Good managers then use that power to help them plan, organize, staff, budget, evaluate, and so on. *In other words, it is primarily because of the dependence inherent in managerial jobs that the dynamics of power necessarily form an important part of a manger's processes.*

An argument that took place during a middle management training seminar I participated in a few years ago helps illustrate further this important relationship between a manager's need for power and the degree of his or her dependence on others:

Two participants, both managers in their thirties, got into a heated disagreement regarding the acquisition and use of power by managers. One took the position that power was absolutely central to managerial work, while the other argued that it was virtually irrelevant. In support of their positions, each described a very "successful" manager with whom he worked. In one of these examples, the manager seemed to be constantly developing and using power, while in the other, such behavior was rare. Subsequently, both seminar participants were asked to describe their successful managers' jobs in terms of the dependence *inherent* in those jobs.

The young manager who felt power was unimportant described a staff vice president in a small company who was dependent only on his immediate subordinates, his peers, and his boss. This person, Joe Phillips, had to depend on his subordinates to do their jobs appropriately, but, if necessary, he could fill in for any of them or secure replacement for them rather easily. He also had considerable formal authority over them; that is, he could give them raises and new assignments, recommend promotions, and fire them. He was moderately dependent on the other vice presidents in the company for information and cooperation. They were likewise dependent on him. The president had considerable formal authority over Phillips but was also moderately dependent on him for help, expert advice, the service his staff performed, other information, and general cooperation.

The second young manager — the one who felt power was very important — described a service department manager, Sam Weller, in a large, complex, and growing company who was in quite a different position. Weller was dependent not only on his boss for rewards and information, but also on 30 other individuals who made up the divisional and corporate top management. And while his boss, like Phillips's was moderately dependent on him too, most of the top managers were not. Because Weller's subordinates, unlike Phillips's, had people reporting to them, Weller was dependent not only on his subordinates but also on his subordinates' subordinates. Because he could not himself easily replace them or do most of their technical jobs, unlike Phillips, he was very dependent on all these people.

In addition, for critical supplies, Weller was dependent on two other department managers in the division. Without their timely help, it was impossible for his department to do its job. These departments, however, did not have similar needs for Weller's help and cooperation. Weller was also dependent on local labor union officials and on a federal agency that regulated the division's industry. Both could shut his division down if they wanted.

Finally, Weller was dependent on two outside suppliers of key materials. Because of the volume of his department's purchase relative to the size of these two companies, he had little power over them.

Under these circumstances, it is hardly surprising that Sam Weller had to spend considerable time and effort acquiring and using power to manage his many dependencies, while Joe Phillips did not.

As this example also illustrates, not all management jobs require an incumbent to be able to provide the same amount of successful power-oriented behavior. But most management jobs today are more like Weller's than Phillip's. And, perhaps more important, the trend over the past two or three decades is away from jobs like Phillip's and toward jobs like Weller's. So long as our technologies continue to become more complex, the average organization continues to grow larger, and the average industry con-

tinues to become more competitive and regulated, that trend will continue; as it does so, the effective acquisition and use of power by managers will become even more important.

Establishing power in relationships

To help cope with the depencency relationships inherent in their jobs, effective managers create, increase, or maintain four different types of power over others (French and Raven 1968; Weber 1947). Having power based in these areas puts the manager in a position both to influence those people on whom he or she is dependent when necessary and to avoid being hurt by any of them.

Sense of obligation

One of the ways that successful managers generate power in their relationships with others is to create a sense of obligation in those others. When the manager is successful, the others feel that they should — rightly — allow the manager to influence them within certain limits.

Successful managers often go out of their way to do favors for people who they expect will feel an obligation to return those favors. As can be seen in the following description of a manager by one of his subordinates, some people are very skilled at identifying opportunities for doing favors that cost them very little but that others appreciate very much:

"Most of the people here would walk over hot coals in their bare feet if my boss asked them to. He has an incredible capacity to do little things that mean a lot to peole. Today, for example, in his junk mail he came across an advertisement for something that one of my subordinates had in passing once mentioned that he was shopping for. So my boss routed it to him. That probably took 15 seconds of his time, and yet my subordinate really appreciated it. To give you another example, two weeks ago he somehow learned that the purchasing manager's mother had died. On his way home that night, he stopped off at the funeral parlor. Our purchasing manager was, of course, there at the time. I bet he'll remember that brief visit for quite a while."

Recognizing that most people believe that friendship carries with it certain obligations ("A friend in need . . ."), successful managers often try to develop true friendships with those on whom they are dependent. They will also make formal and informal deals in which they give something up in exchange for certain future obligations.

Belief in a manager's expertise

A second way successful managers gain power is by building reputations as "experts" in certain matters. Believing in the manager's expertise, others will often defer to the manager on those matters. Managers usually establish this type of power through visible achievement. The larger the achievement and the more visible it is, the more power the manager tends to develop.

One of the reasons that managers display concern about their "professional reputations" and their "track records" is that they have an impact on others' beliefs about their expertise. These factors become particularly important in large settings, where most people have only secondhand information about most other people's professional competence, and the following shows:

Herb Randley and Bert Kline were both 35-year-old vice-presidents in a large research and development organization. According to their closest associates, they were equally bright and competent in their technical fields and as managers. Yet Randley had a much stronger professional reputation in most parts of the company, and his ideas generally carried much more weight. Close friends and associated claim the reason that Randley is so much more powerful is related to a number of tactics that he has used more than Kline has.

Randley has published more scientific papers and managerial articles than Kline. Randley has been more selective in the assignments he has worked on, choosing those that are visible and that require his strong suits. He has given more speeches and presentations on projects that are his own achievements. And in meetings in general, he is allegedly foreceful in areas where he has expertise and silent in those where he does not.

Identification with a manager

A third method by which managers gain power is by fostering others' unconscious identification with them or with ideas they "stand for." Sigmund Freud was the first to describe this phenomenon, which is most clearly seen in the way people look up to "charismatic" leaders. Generally, the more a person finds a manager both consciously and (more important) unconsciously an ideal person, the more he or she will defer to that manager.

Managers develop power based on others' idealized views of them in a number of ways. They try to look and behave in ways that others respect. They go out of their way to be visible to their employees and to give speeches about their organizational goals, values, and ideals. They even consider, while making hiring and promotion decisions, whether they will be able to develop this type of power over the candidates:

One vice-president of sales in a moderate-size manufacturing company was reputed to be so much in control of his sales force that he could get them to respond to new and different marketing programs in a third of the time taken by the company's best competitors. His power over his employees was based primarily on their strong identification with him and what he stood for. Immigrating to the United States at age 17, this person worked his way up "from nothing." When made a sales manager in 1965, he began recruiting other young immigrants and sons of immigrants from his former country. When made vice-president of sales in 1970, he continued to do so. In 1975, 85% of his sales force was made up of people whom he hired directly or who were hired by others he brought in.

Perceived dependence on a manager

The final way that an effective manager often gains power is by feeding others' beliefs that they are dependent on the manager either for help or for not being hurt. The more they perceive they are dependent, the more most people will be inclined to cooperate with such a manager.

There are two methods that successful managers often use to create perceived dependence.

Finding and acquiring resources

In the first, the manager identifies and secures (if necessary) resources that another person requires to perform his job, that he does not possess, and that are not readily available elsewhere. These resources include such things as authority to make certain decisions; control of

money, equipment, and office space; access to important people; information and control of information channels; and subordinates. Then the manager takes action so that the other person correctly perceives that the manager has such resources and is willing and ready to use them to help (or hinder) the other person. Consider the following extreme — but true — example.

When young Tim Babcock was put in charge of a division of a large manufacturing company and told to "turn it around," he spent the first few weeks studying it from afar. He decided that the division was in disastrous shape and that he would need to take many large steps quickly to save it. To be able to do that, he realized he needed to develop considerable power fast over most of the division's management and staff. He did the following:

He gave the division's management two hours' notice of his arrival.

He arrived in a limousine with six assistants.

He immediately called a meeting of the 40 top managers.

He outlined briefly his assessment of the situation, his commitment to turn things around, and the basic direction he wanted things to move in.

He then fired the four top managers in the room and told them that they had to be out of the building in two hours.

He then said he would personally dedicate himself to sabotaging the career of anyone who tried to block his efforts to save the division.

He ended the 60-minute meeting by announcing that his assistants would set up appointments for him with each of them starting at 7:00 A.M. the next morning.

Throughout the critical six-months period that followed, those who remained at the division generally cooperated energetically with Mr. Babcock.

Affecting perceptions of resources

A second way effective managers gain these types of power is by influencing other persons' perceptions of the manager's resources (Newstedt 1960). In settings where many people are involved and where the manager does not interact continuously with those he or she is dependent on, those people will seldom possess "hard facts" regarding what relevant resources the manager commands directly or indirectly (through others), what resources he will command in the future, or how prepared he is to use those resources to help or hinder them. They will be forced to make their own judgments.

Insofar as a manager can influence people's judgments, he can generate much more power than one would generally ascribe to him in light of the reality of his resources.

In trying to influence people's judgments, managers pay considerable attention to the "trappings" of power and to their own reputations and images. Among other actions, they sometimes carefully select, decorate, and arrange their offices in ways that give signs of power. They associate with people or organizations that are known to be powerful or that others perceive as powerful. Managers selectly foster rumors concerning their own power. Indeed, those who are particularly skilled at creating power in this way tend to be very sensitive to the impressions that all their actions might have on others.

Formal authority

Before discussing how managers use their power to influence others, it is useful to see how formal authority relates to power. By *formal authority,* I mean those elements that automatically come with a managerial job — perhaps a title, an office, a budget, the right to make certain decisions, a set of subordinates, a reporting relationship, and so on.

Effective managers use the elements of formal authority as resources to help them develop any or all of the four types of power previously discussed, just as they use other resources (such as their education). Two managers with the same formal authority can have very different amounts of power entirely because of the way they have used that authority. For example:

By sitting down with employees who are new or with people who are starting new projects and clearly specifying who has the formal authority to do what, one manager creates a strong sense of obligation in others to defer to his authority later.

By selectively withholding or giving the high-quality service his department can provide other departments, one manager makes other managers clearly perceive that they are dependent on him.

On its own, then, formal authority does not guarantee a certain amount of power; it is only a resource that managers can use to generate power in their relationships.

Exercising power to influence others

Successful managers use the power they develop in their relationships, along with persuasion, to influence people on whom they are dependent to behave in ways that make it possible for the managers to get their jobs done effectively. They use their power to influence others directly, face to face, and in more indirect ways.

Exhibit
Methods of influence

Face-to-face methods	What they can influence	Advantages	Drawbacks
Exercise obligation-based power.	Behavior within zone that the other perceives as legitimate in light of the obligation.	Quick. Requires no outlay of tangible resources.	If the request is outside the acceptable zone, it will fail; if it is too far outside, others might see it as illegitimate.
Exercise power based on perceived expertise.	Attitudes and behavior within the zone of perceived expertise.	Quick. Requires no expenditure of tangible resources.	If the request is outside the acceptable zone, it will fail; if it is too far outside, others might see it as illegitimate
Exercise power based on identification with a manager.	Attitudes and behavior that are not in conflict with the ideals that underlie the identification.	Quick. Requires no expenditure of limited resources.	Restricted to influence attempts that are not in conflict with the ideals that underlie the identification.
Exercise power based on perceived dependence.	Wide range of behavior that can be monitored.	Quick. Can often succeed when other methods fail.	Repeated influence attempts encourage the other to gain power over the influencer.
Coercively exercise power based on perceived dependence.	Wide range of behavior that can be easily monitored.	Quick. Can often succeed when other methods fail.	Invites retaliation. Very risky.
Use persuasion.	Very wide range of attitudes and behavior.	Can produce internalized motivation that does not require monitoring. Requires no power or outlay of scarce material resources.	Can be very time-consuming. Requires other person to listen.
Combine these methods.	Depends on the exact combination.	Can be more potent and less risky than using a single method.	More costly than using a single method.

Indirect methods	What they can influence	Advantages	Drawbacks
Manipulate the other's environment by using any or all of the face-to-face methods.	Wide range of behavior and attitudes.	Can succeed when face-to-face methods fail.	Can be time-consuming. Is complex to implement. Is very risky, especially if used frequently.
Change the forces that continuously act on the individual: Formal organizational arrangements. Informal social arrangements. Technology. Resources available Statement of organizational goals.	Wide range of behavior and attitudes on a continuous basis.	Has continuous influence, not just a one-shot effect. Can have a very powerful impact.	Often requires a considerable power outlay to achieve.

Face-to-face influence

The chief advantage of influencing others directly by exercising any of the types of power is speed. If the power exists and the manager correctly understands the nature and strength of it, he can influence the other person with nothing more than a brief request or command:

— Jones thinks Smith feels obliged to him for past favors. Furthermore, Jones thinks that his request to speed up a project by two days probably falls within a zone that Smith would consider legitimate in light of his own definition of his obligation to Jones. So Jones simply calls Smith and makes his request. Smith pauses for only a second and says yes, he'll do it.

— Manager Johnson has some power based on perceived dependence over manager Baker. When Johnson tells Baker that he wants a report done in 24 hours, Baker grudgingly considers the costs of compliance, of noncompliance, and of complaining to higher authorities. He decides that doing the report is the least costly action and tells Johnson he will do it.

— Young Porter identifies strongly with Marquette, an older manager who is not his boss. Porter thinks Marquette is the epitome of a great manager and tries to model himself after him. When Marquette asks Porter to work on a special project "that could be very valuable in improving the company's ability to meet new competitive products," Porter agrees without hesitation and works 15 hours per week above and beyond his normal hours to get the project done and done well.

When used to influence others, each of the four types of power has different advantages and drawbacks. For example, power based on perceived expertise or on identification with a manager can often be used to influence attitudes as well as someone's immediate behavior and thus can have a lasting impact. It is very difficult to influence attitudes by using power based on perceived dependence, but if it can be done, it usually has the advantage of being able to influence a much broader range of behavior than the other methods do. When exercising power based on perceived expertise, for example, one can only influence attitudes and behavior within that narrow zone defined by the "expertise."

The drawbacks with the use of power based on perceived dependence are particularly important to recognize. A person who feels dependent on a manager for rewards (or lack of punishments) might quickly agree to a request from the manager but then not follow through — especially if the manager cannot easily find out if the person has obeyed or not. Repeated influence attempts based on perceived dependence also seem to encourage the other person to try to gain some power to balance the manager's. And perhaps most important, using power based on perceived dependence in a coercive way is very risky. Coercion invites retaliation.

For instance, in the example in which Tim Babcock took such extreme steps to save the division he was assigned to "turn around," his development and use of power based on perceived dependence could have led to mass resignation and the collapse of the division. Babcock fully recognized this risk, however, and behaved as he did because he felt there was simply *no other way* that

he could gain the very large amount of quick cooperation needed to save the division.

Effective managers will often draw on more than one form of power to influence someone, or they will combine power with persuasion. In general, they do so because a combination can be more potent and less risky than any single method, as the following description shows:

"One of the best managers we have in the company has lots of power based on one thing or another over most people. But he seldom if ever just tells or asks someone to do something. He almost always takes a few minutes to try to persuade them. The power he has over people generally induces them to listen carefully and certainly disposes them to be influenced. That, of course, makes the persuasion process go quickly and easily. And he never risks getting the other person mad or upset by making what that person thinks is an unfair request or command."

It is also common for managers not to coercively exercise power based on perceived dependence by itself, but to combine it with other methods to reduce the risk of retaliation. In this way, managers are able to have a large impact without leaving the bitter aftertaste of punishment alone.

Indirect influence methods

Effective managers also rely on two types of less direct methods to influence those on whom they are dependent. In the first way, they use any or all of the face-to-face methods to influence other people, who in turn have some specific impact on a desired person.

Product manager Stein needed plant manager Billings to "sign off" on a new product idea (Product X) which Billings thought was terrible. Stein decided that there was no way he could logically persuade Billings because Billings just would not listen to him. With time, Stein felt, he could have broken through that barrier. But he did not have that time. Stein also realized that Billings would never, just because of some deal or favor, sign off on a product he did not believe in. Stein also felt it not worth the risk of trying to force Billings to sign off, so here is what he did:

On Monday, Stein got Reynolds, a person Billings respected, to send Billings two market research studies that were very favorable to Product X, with a note attached saying, "Have you seen this? I found them rather surprising. I am not sure if I entirely believe them, but still . . ."

On Tuesday, Stein got a representative of one of the company's biggest customers to mention casually to Billings on the phone that he had heard a rumor about Product X being introduced soon and was "glad to see you guys are on your toes as usual."

On Wednesday, Stein had two industrial engineers stand about three feet away from Billings as they were waiting for a meeting to begin and talk about the favorable test results on Product X.

On Thursday, Stein set up a meeting to talk about Product X with Billings and invited only people whom Billings liked or respected and who also felt favorably about Product X.

On Friday, Stein went to see Billings and asked him if he was willing to sign off on Product X. He was.

This type of manipulation of the environments of others can influence both behavior and attitudes and can often succeed when other influence methods fail. But it has a number of serious drawbacks. It takes considerable time and energy, and it is quite risky. Many people think it is wrong to try to influence others in this way, even people who, without consciously recognizing it, use this technique themselves. If they think someone is trying, or has tried, to manipulate them, they may retaliate. Furthermore, people who gain the reputation of being manipulators seriously undermine their own capacities for developing power and for influencing others. Almost no one, for example, will want to identify with a manipulator. And virtually no one accepts, at face value, a manipulator's sincere attempts at persuasion. In extreme cases, a reputation as a manipulator can completely ruin a manager's career.

A second way in which managers indirectly influence others is by making permanent changes in an individual's or group's environment. They change job descriptions, the formal systems that measure performance, the extrinsic incentives available, the tools, people, and other resources that the people or groups work with, the architecture, the norms or values of work groups, and so on. If the manager is successful in making the changes, and the changes have the desired effect on the individual or group, that effect will be sustained over time.

Effective managers recognize that changes in the forces that surround a person can have great impact on that person's behavior. Unlike many of the other influence methods, this one doesn't require a large expenditure of limited resources or effort on the part of the manager on an ongoing basis. Once such a change has been successfully made, it works independently of the manager.

This method of influence is used by all managers to some degree. Many, however, use it sparingly simply because they do not have the power to change the forces acting on the person they wish to influence. In many organizations, only the top managers have the power to change the formal measurement systems, the extrinsic incentives available, the architecture, and so on.

Generating and using power successfully

Managers who are successful at acquiring considerable power and using it to manage their dependence on others tend to share a number of common characteristics:

1. They are sensitive to what others consider to be legitimate behavior in acquiring and using power. They recognize that the four types of power carry with them certain "obligations" regarding their acquisition and use. A person who gains a considerable amount of power based on his perceived expertise is generally expected to be an expert in certain areas. If it ever becomes publicly known that the person is clearly not an expert in those areas, such a person will probably be labeled a "fraud" and will not only lose his power but will suffer other reprimands too.

   A person with whom a number of people identify is expected to act like an ideal leader. If he clearly lets people down, he will not only lose that power, he will also suffer the righteous anger of his ex-followers. Many managers who have created or used power based on perceived dependence in ways that their employees have felt unfair, such as in requesting overtime work, have ended up with unions.

2. They have good intuitive understanding of the various types of power and methods of influence. They are sensitive to what types of power are easiest to develop with different types of people. They recognize, for example, that professionals tend to be more influenced by perceived expertise than by other forms of power. They also have a grasp of all the various methods of

influence and what each can accomplish, at what costs, and with what risks (see the *Exhibit*) They are good at recognizing the specific conditions in any situation and then at selecting an influence method that is compatible with those conditions.

3. They tend to develop all the types of power, to some degree and they use all the influence methods mentioned in the exhibit. Unlike managers who are not very good at influencing people, effective managers usually do not think that only some of the methods are useful or that only some of the methods are moral. They recognize that any of the methods, used under the right circumstances, can help contribute to organizational effectiveness with few dysfunctional consequences. At the same time, they generally try to avoid those methods that are more risky than others and those that may have dysfunctional consequences. For example, they manipulate the environment of others only when absolutely necessary.

4. They establish career goals and seek out managerial positions that allow them to successfully develop and use power. They look for jobs, for example, that use their backgrounds and skills to control or manage some critically important problem or environmental contingency that an organization faces. They recognize that success in that type of job makes others dependent on them and increases their own perceived expertise. They also seek jobs that do not demand a type or a volume of power that is inconsistent with their own skills.

5. They use all of their resources, formal authority, and power to develop still more power. To borrow Edward Banfield's metaphor, they actually look for ways to "invest" their power where they might secure a high positive return (Banfield 1965). For example, by asking a person to do him two important favors, a manager might be able to finish his construction

program one day ahead of schedule. That request may cost him most of the obligation-based power he has over that person, but in return he may significantly increase his perceived expertise as a manager of construction projects in the eyes of everyone in his organization.

Just as in investing money, there is always some risk involved in using power this way; it is possible to get a zero return for a sizable investment, even for the most powerful manager. Effective managers do not try to avoid risks. Instead, they look for prudent risks, just as they do when investing capital.

6. Effective managers engage in power-oriented behavior in ways that are tempered by maturity and self-control (McClelland and Burnham 1976). They seldom, if ever, develop and use power in impulsive ways or for their own aggrandizement.

7. Finally, they also recognize and accept as legitimate that, in using these methods, they clearly influence other people's behavior and lives. Unlike many less effective managers, they are reasonably comfortable in using power to influence people. They recognize, often only intuitively, what this article is all about — that their attempts to establish power and use it are an absolutely necessary part of the successful fulfillment of their difficult managerial role.

You can't learn to acquire power by rules: it has to come from inside. But by following certain rules, you can develop an awareness of it. We all have a power potential, but few of us use it, or even know it's there.

In more "primitive" cultures, youths are initiated into the rites of power, sometimes in very complicated ways. The rules are absolute and clear-cut, and must be followed exactly, but they are intended to increase the initiate's awareness of himself — simply carrying out the rituals isn't enough. If in certain American Indian tribes young men bury themselves in pits up to the neck on lonely hills in the desert, it is to learn patience, concentration and the ability to stay motionless when necessary, however uncomfortable it may be. There's nothing mysterious about the process — a hunter who is fidgety or has to scratch himself when bitten by flies is unlikely to trap much in the way of game. Survival lies in the ability to control one's body and one's mind.

Our world is not so very different, noisy and complex as it seems, but we are less fortunate than the Indians. We are educated, at considerable expense and effort, but no wise teacher prepares us for the world we will face as adults. If we are lucky, we learn how to do a job, but for most people the price of survival is surrender. There is a place for almost everyone in our world, but usually on other peole's terms rather than our own. Some of us learn how to *succeed* and may even become rich and famous; few learn how to use the world, instead of being used by it.

From *Power: How to Get It, How to Use It,* by Michael Korda. Copyright © 1975 by Michael Korda and Paul Gitlin, Trustee for the Benefit of Christopher Korda. Reprinted by permission of Random House, Inc.

Participative management: Quality vs. quantity

Raymond E. Miles and J. B. Ritchie

Just as other vintage theoretical vehicles have demonstrated amazing durability on the academic stage, the theory of participative management has shown a remarkable facility for holding the spotlight of debate in the management literature. For this and other theories, however, it should be noted that it is often clever direction and staging, rather than substance, which sustains audience interest.

Having signaled this caveat, we must admit to some feeling of trepidation as we suggest another inquiry into this now middle-aged set of concepts. We do so, however, because we believe some of the recent findings from our continuing research on the process and effects of participation justify further examination of this theory. We should add that our research and its implications are unlikely to do much to resolve the polemics between those who view participation as the solution to all organizational ailments and those who consider it a humanistic palliative which threatens the moral fiber of managerial prerogatives. Nevertheless, we feel our findings may prove valuable to the much larger group for whom the concept of participation is neither panacea nor plague, but simply confusing.

In our view, a prime source of confusion surrounding the concept of participation is its purpose. We noted this confusion a few years ago (Miles 1965), drawing from our research the conclusion that most managers appeared to hold at least two different "theories" of participation. One of these, which we labeled the **Human Relations** model, viewed participation primarily as a means of obtaining cooperation — a technique which the manager could use to improve morale and reduce subordinate resistance to his policies and decisions. The second, which we labeled the **Human Resources** model, recognized the untapped potential of most organizational members and advocated participation as a means of achieving direct improvement in individual and organizational performance. Predictably, managers viewed the **Human Relations** model as appropriate for their subordinates while wanting their superior to follow the **Human Resources** logic.

Our recent research draws attention to a closely related, and probably equally important, source of confusion involving the *process* of participation. Our earlier descriptions of the purpose of participation under the Human Relations and Human Resources models implied that it is not only the degree of participation which is important, but also the nature of the superior-subordinate interaction. Upon reflection, the notion that both the quality and quantity of participation must be considered seems patently obvious. Rather surprisingly, however, the quality variable in the participative process has been infrequently specified in management theory, and even more rarely researched.

The lack of specific focus in theory or research on the quality aspect of the participative process has led, in our view, to the promulgation of a simple "quantity theory of participation," a theory which implies only that some participation is better than none and that more is better than a little. Clearly, a concept which, whether intended or not, appears to lump all participative acts together in a common category ignores individual and situational differences and is therefore open to a variety of justified criticism. It is just such a simplified view that allows its more vitriolic critics to draw caricatures extending the participative process to include a chairman of the board consulting with a janitor concerning issues of capital budgeting — the sort of criticism which brings humor to journal pages but contributes little to our understanding of participation.

Recognizing these key sources of confusion, our current studies have been aimed at increasing our understanding of the process of participation under the Human Relations and Human Resources models. Specifically, we have attempted, within a large sample of management teams, to identify and measure the amount of superior-subordinate consultation and a dimension of the quality of this interaction — the superior's attitude which reflects the degree to which he has confidence in his subordinates' capabilities. (Our research approach and findings are described in a later section.) As indicated, in our theoretical framework both the quantity and quality of participation are important determinants of subordinate satisfaction and performance. For these analyses, we have focused on the impact of these variables, both separately and jointly, on the subordinate's satisfaction with his immediate superior. Our findings, we believe, clarify the role which quality plays in the participative process and add substance to the Human Relations — Human Resources differentiation.

In the following sections we explore further the concepts of quantity and quality of participation, integrate these into existing theories of participative management, and examine the implications of our research for these theories and for management practice.

The quality concept and management theory

A simple, and we believe familiar, example should assist us in firmly integrating the quantity-quality variables into the major theories of participative management and perhaps demonstrate, in part at least, why we are concerned with this dimension. Most of us have had the following experience:

An invitation is received to attend an important meeting (we know it is important because it is carefully specified as such in the call). A crucial policy decision is to be made and our views and those of our colleagues are, according to the invitation, vital to the decision.

Having done our homework, we arrive at the meeting and begin serious and perhaps heated discussion. Before too long, however, a light begins to dawn, and illuminated in that dawning light is the fact that the crucial decision we had been called together to decide . . .

With a cynical, knowing smile, the typical organization member completes the sentence by saying "had already been made." It is helpful, however, to push aside the well-remembered frustration of such situations and examine the logic of the executive who called the meeting and the nature of the participative process flowing from his logic.

We can easily imagine (perhaps because we have frequently employed the same logic) the executive in our example saying to himself, "I've got this matter pretty well firmed, but it may require a bit of selling — I'd better call the troops in and at least let them express their views." He may even be willing to allow some minor revisions in the policy to overcome resistance and generate among his subordinates a feeling of being a part of the decision.

Purposes of participation

Clearly defined in our example and discussion is the tight bond between the purpose of participation and the quality of ensuing involvement. And, underlying the purpose of participation is the executive's set of assumptions about people — particularly his attitudes concerning the capabilities of his subordinates.

Three theoretical frameworks describe this linkage between the manager's basic attitudes toward people and the amount and kind of consultation in which he is likely to engage with his subordinates. It is worth a few lines to compare these theory systems and to apply them to our example. Listed chronologically, these frameworks are:

The Theory X–Theory Y dichotomy described by the late Douglas McGregor (1960, 1967).
The System I, II, III, IV continuum defined by Rensis Likert (1961, 1967).
Our own Traditional Human Relations,

Human Resources classification (Miles 1966; Miles, Porter, and Craft 1966).

Terminology

We have been criticized for referring to an essentially autocratic (nonparticipatory) style of management as traditional. Such a style is no longer traditional in the sense that it is prescribed, taught, or openly advocated by a majority of modern managers. Our research suggests that most managers consider such a style to be socially undesirable and few will admit adherence to it in concept or practice.

Nevertheless, we would argue that many if not most of our institutions and organizations are still so structured and operated that this style is alive and well today in our society. Many schools, hospitals, labor unions, political parties, and a substantial number of business enterprises frequently behave, particularly at the lower levels, in a manner which can only be described as autocratic. Thus even though their policy statements have been revised and some participative trappings have been hung about, the main thrust of their activity is not greatly changed from what it was twenty, thirty, perhaps even fifty years ago — they behave in a traditional manner toward the structure and direction of work. Further, the assumptions of the Traditional model are, in our view, still widely held and espoused in our society — the rhetoric has improved, but the intent is the same. These assumptions seem to us still to be a part of our "traditional" approach to life. If our views are accurate, Traditional model is therefore still an appropriate tag.

McGregor's Theory X, Likert's System I, and our Traditional model describe autocratic leadership behavior coupled with tight, unilateral control, and little or no subordinate participation in the decision process. Theory X and the Traditional model explicitly delineate the superior's assumptions that most people, including subordinates, are basically indolent, self-centered, gullible, and resistant to change and thus have little to contribute to the decision-making or control process. Focusing more on descriptive characteristics and less on an explicit set of assumptions, Likert's System I manager is pictured only as having no confidence or trust in his subordinates. At the other extreme, Theory Y, System IV, and our Human Resources model define a style of behavior which involves subordinates deeply in the decision process and emphasizes high levels of self-direction and self-control. Again, both Theory Y and the Human Resources model make the logic underlying such behavior explicit — that most organization members are capable of contributing more than demanded by their present jobs and thus represent untapped potential for the organization, potential which the capable manager develops and invests in improved performance. A System IV superior is described simply as one having complete confidence and trust in subordinates in all matters. In between these extremes fall Likert's Systems II and III and our Human Relations model. Systems II and III describe increasing amounts of subordinate participation and self-control, as their superior's attitudes toward them move from "condescending" to "substantial, but not complete" confidence and trust. Our Human Relations model views the superior as recognizing his subordinates' desire for involvement but doubting their ability to make meaningful contributions.

Theory and management practice

Comparing these frameworks with our example, it is clear that the executive calling the meeting was not operating at the Theory X, System I, Traditional end of the participative continuum. Had he followed the assumptions of these models, he would simply have announced his decision, and if a meeting were called, use it openly to explain his views. Similarly, it seems doubtful that our executive was following the Theory Y, System IV, or Human Resource models. Had he been, he would have called the meeting in the belief that his subordinates might make important contributions to the decision process and that their participation would possibly result in constructing a better overall policy. He would have had confidence and trust in their ability and willingness to generate and examine alternatives and take action in the best interest of the organization.

Instead, the meeting in the example and those from our own experience seem to be defined almost to the letter by our Human Relations logic and the behavior described in Likert's Systems II and III. The casual observer, and perhaps even the more naive participant, unaware of the reasoning of the executive calling the meeting, might well record a high level of involvement during the session — participation high both in quantity and quality. Most of the participants, however, would be much less charitable, particularly about the meaningfulness of the exercise. They would sense, although the guidance was subtle, that at least the depth of their participation was carefully controlled, just as they would be equally alert to the logic underlying the meeting strategy.

Alternative theories

Having described varying degrees of quantity and quality of participation flowing from alternative theories of management, and having attempted to link to common experience through our meeting example, it is not difficult to conjecture about the relationships between these variables and subordinate satisfaction. We would expect subordinate satisfaction to move up and down with both the quantity and the quality of participation, and there is already some evidence, with regard to the amount of participation, at least, that it does. Thus, we would expect, particularly within the managerial hierarchy, that their satisfaction would be lowest when both quantity and quality of participation were lowest — as the Traditional model is approached — the highest when both quantity and quality are high — when participation moves toward the type described in the Human Resources model.

Predicting satisfaction under the Human Relations model is less easy. If the superior's behavior is blatantly manipulative, we might expect satisfaction to be quite low despite high participation. But, if the superior's logic were less obvious, even to himself, we might expect his subordinates to be somewhat pleased to be involved in the decision process, even if their involvement is frequently peripheral.

We cannot precisely test the impact of these models on subordinate satisfaction, but our recent research does provide some evidence with regard to these conjectures, and it is therfore appropriate that we briefly describe the method of our investigation and look at some of our findings.

Research approach

The findings reported here were drawn from a broader research project conducted among management teams (a superior and his immediate subordinates) from five levels in six geographically separated operating divisions of a west coast firm (Blankenship and Miles 1968; Roberts, Blankenship, and Miles 1968). The 381 managers involved in the study ranged from the chief executive of each of the six divisions down through department supervisors.

From extensive questionnaire responses we were able to develop measures of the three variables important to these analyses: *quantity of participation, quality of participation,* and *satisfaction with immediate superiors.* Our measure of quantity of participation was drawn from managers' responses to questions concerning how frequently they felt they were consulted by their superior on a number of typical department issues and decisions (Ritchie and Miles 1970). This information allowed us to classify managers as high or low in terms of the amount of participation they felt they were allowed. For a measure of quality of this participation, we turned to the responses given by each manager's superior. The superior's attitudes toward his subordinates — his evaluation of their capabilities with regard to such traits as judgement, creativity, responsibility, perspective, and the like — were analyzed and categorized as high or low compared to the attitudes of other managers at the same level. Finally, our satisfaction measure was taken from a question on which managers indicated, on a scale from very satisfied to very dissatisfied, their reactions to their own immediate superiors.

Findings

The first thing apparent in our findings, as shown in each of the accompanying figures, is that virtually all the subjects in our study appear reasonably well satisfied with their immediate superiors. This is not surprising, particularly since all subjects, both superiors and subordinates, are in managerial positions. Managers generally respond positively (compared to other organization members) on satisfaction scales. Moreover, supporting the organization's reputation for being forward looking and well managed, most participants reported generally high levels of consultation, and superiors' scores on confidence in their subordinates were typically higher than the average scores in our broader research.

Nevertheless, differences do exist, differences which, given the restricted range of scores, are in most instances highly significant in statistical terms. Moreover, they demonstrate that both the quantity and the quality of participation are related to managers' feelings of satisfaction with their immediate superiors.

As shown in Figure 1, the quantity of participation achieved is apparently related to managers' feelings of satisfaction with their superiors. (The taller the figure — and the smaller the numerical score — the more satisfied is that group of managers.) Managers classified as low (relative to the scores of their peers) in terms of the extent to which they are consulted by their superiors are less well satisfied than those classified as high on this dimension. The difference in the average satisfaction score for the low consultation group (2.13) falls between the satisfied and the so-so (somewhat satisfied — somewhat dissatisfied) categories. For the high consultation group, the score (1.79) falls between the satisfied and the highly satisfied categories.

A slightly stronger pattern of results is apparent when managers are grouped in terms of the amount of confidence which their superiors have in them (Figure 2). Managers whose superiors have relatively high trust and confidence scores are significantly more satisfied (1.72) than their colleagues (2.16) whose superiors have relatively lower scores on this dimension.

Finally, our results take on their most interesting form when managers are cross-classified on both the quantity and the quality dimensions of participation. As shown in Figure 3, the progression in satisfaction is consistent with our theoretical formulation. Especially obvious is the comparison between managers classified as low both in amount of consultation received and the extent to which their superior has confidence in them (2.26) and managers who are rated high on both variables (1.55). Of interest, and relevant to our later discussion, managers whose superiors have high confidence in them but who are low in amount of participation appear slightly more satisfied (1.95) than their counterparts who are high in amount of participation but whose superiors are low in terms of confidence in their subordinates (2.05).

Linking findings to theory

The bulk of our findings, particularly as illustrated in Figure 3, thus appear to support our conjectures. Managers who least value their subordinates' capabilities and who least often seek their contributions on department issues have the least well satisfied subordinates in

Figure 1

Amount of superior consultation and subordinate satisfaction

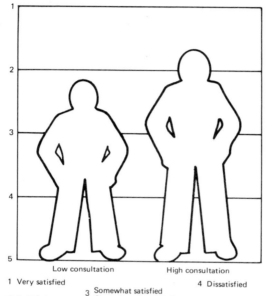

Low consultation   High consultation

1 Very satisfied   4 Dissatisfied
                    3 Somewhat satisfied
2 Satisfied   Somewhat dissatisfied   5 Very dissatisfied

Figure 2

Superior's confidence in subordinates and subordinate satisfaction

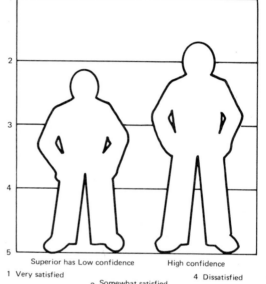

Superior has Low confidence   High confidence

1 Very satisfied   4 Dissatisfied
                    3 Somewhat satisfied
2 Satisfied   Somewhat dissatisfied   5 Very dissatisfied

Figure 3

Effects of amount of consultation and superior's confidence in subordinates on subordinate satisfaction.

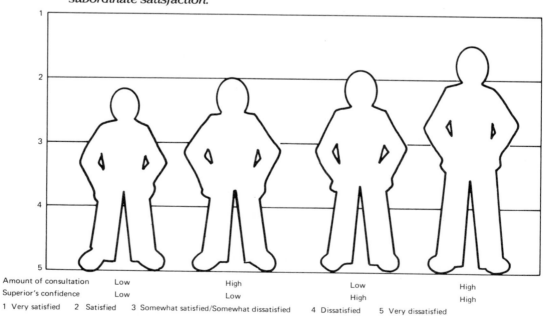

Amount of consultation   Low   High   Low   High
Superior's confidence   Low   Low   High   High

1 Very satisfied   2 Satisfied   3 Somewhat satisfied/Somewhat dissatisfied   4 Dissatisfied   5 Very dissatisfied

our study. It would probably be incorrect to place the Traditional (Theory X, System I) label on any of the managers in our sample, yet those who, relative to their peers, lean closest to these views do so with predictable results in terms of subordinate satisfaction.

Similarly, managers who, relative to their peers, are both high in their respect for their subordinates' capabilities and who consult them regularly on departmental issues also achieve the expected results. Precise labeling is again probably inappropriate, yet managers whose attitudes and behavior are closest to the Human Resources (Theory Y, System IV) model do in fact have the most satisfied subordinates.

Further, those managers who consult their subordinates frequently but who have little confidence in their ability to make a positive contribution to department decision making, and thus who fall nearest to our Human Relations model, have subordinates who are more satisfied than those under the more Traditional managers but are significantly less satisfied than the subordinates of Human Resources managers.

The majority of our findings support the major formulations of participative management theory, but they also suggest the need for elaboration and clarification. This need is brought to attention by the total pattern of our findings, and particularly by the results for one of our categories of managers — those high in superiors' confidence but relatively low in participation. Recall that, while the differences were not large, this group had the second highest average satisfaction score in our sample — the score falling between that of the Human Relations (high participation, low superior confidence) group and that of the Human Resources (high on each) group.

Moreover, for the two groups characterized by high participation, there is substantially higher satisfaction for those whose superior reflects high confidence in his subordinates. Clearly, any theory which focused on the amount of participation would not predict these results. Rather, for these managers at least, the quality of their relationship with their superiors as indicated by their superiors' attitude of trust and confidence in them appears to modify the effects of the amount of participation.

Implications for the theory

The quality demension of the theory of participative management has not been fully developed, but its outlines are suggested in our own Human Resources model and in McGregor's Theory Y framework. McGregor stressed heavily the importance of managers' basic attitudes and assumptions about their subordinates. In expanding on this point (McGregor 1967, 79), he suggested that a manager's assumptions about his subordinates' traits and abilities do not bind him to a single course of action. Rather, he argued that a range of possible behaviors are appropriate under Theory Y or Human Resources assumptions — a manager with high trust and confidence in his subordinates could and should take into account a variety of situational and personality factors in deciding, among other things, when and how to consult with them. Extending this reasoning, one can even imagine a Theory Y or Human Resources manager actually consulting with his subordinates less often than some of his colleagues. Nevertheless, the nature and quality of participation employed by such a manager, when it occurs, would presumably be deeper and more meaningful, which would be reflected in high levels of subordinate satisfaction and performance.

This view of the super-subordinate interaction process, emphasizing as it does the quality of the interaction rather than only the amount, can be employed to answer three of the more pervasive criticisms of participative management. These criticisms — each of which is probably most accurately aimed at the simple quantity theory of participation — focus on the inappropriateness of extensive consultation when the superior is constrained by time, technology, and his own or his subordinate's temperament.

The time constraint

"In a crisis, you simply do not have time to run around consulting people." This familiar explication is difficult to debate, and in fact, would receive no challenge from a sophisticated theory of participation. In a real building-burning crisis, consultation is inappropriate, and unnecessary. A crisis of this nature is recognized as such by any well-informed subordinate and his self-controlled cooperation is willingly supplied. The behavior of both superior and subordinate in such a situation is guided by the situation and each may turn freely and without question to the other or to any available source of expertise for direction or assistance in solving the problem at hand.

Many crises, however, do not fit the building-burning category, and may be much more real to one person, or to one level of management, than to those below him. Our experience suggests that managers may not be nearly as bound by their constraints as they frequently claim to be, or if they are constrained, these limits are either known in advance or are open to modification if circumstances

demand. Rather, in many instances it appears that managers employ the "time won't permit" argument primarily to justify autocratic, and at least partially risk-free behavior. If he succeeds, the credit is his; if he fails, he can defend his actions by pointing out that he had no time to explore alternatives.

Such self-defined, or at least self-sustaining, crises are most frequently employed by the manager with a Human Relations concept of participation — one who views participation primarily as a means of obtaining subordinate cooperation and who focuses mainly on the amount of formal involvement required. The crisis itself can be employed in place of participation as the lever to obtain cooperation and there is clearly no time for the sort of routine, frequently peripheral consultation in which he most often indulges.

Conversely, the manager with high trust and confidence in his subordinates' capabilities, the Human Resources manager, is less likely to employ the time constraints as a managerial tactic. In real crises he moves as rapidly as the situation demands. He is, however, more likely, because of his normal practices of sharing information with his subordinates, to have a group which is prepared to join him in a rapid review of alternatives. He is unconcerned with involvement for the sake of involvement and thus his consultation activities are penetrating and to the point. His subordinates share his trust and feel free to challenge his views, just as he feels free to question their advice and suggestions openly.

The technology barrier

"Look, I've got fifteen subordinates scattered all over the building. What do you expect me to do — shut down the plant and call a meeting every time something happens?" This argument is obviously closely linked to the time constraint argument — technology is a major factor in determining the flow and timing of decisions. Similarly, it too flows from a Human Relations — quantity oriented view of participation.

A good manager obviously does not regularly "stop the presses" and call a conference. He has confidence in his subordinates' abilities to handle problems as they appear and to call him in when the problem demands his attention. This confidence is, however, reinforced by joint planning, both one-to-one and across his group of subordinates, before the operation gets under way. Having agreed in advance on objectives, schedules, priorities, and procedures, involvement on a day-to-day basis may be minimal. The manager in this instance does not seek participation to obtain cooperation with his views. Both the manager and his subordinates view the regularly scheduled work planning and review sessions as important because they result in well-considered solutions to real problems.

The temperament barrier

"I'm simply not the sort who can run around to his subordinates asking them how things are going — it's just not my style." The manager who made this statement did so somewhat apologetically, but there was little for him to be apologetic about. He had a high-performing group of subordinates, in whom he placed high trust and confidence, who were in turn highly satisfied with their boss. Further, while he did not seek their views on a variety of routine departmental matters, and his sub-

ordinates did not drop in to his office to chat, he freely shared all departmental information with them and on a regular basis worked with his subordinates in coordinating department plans and schedules. In addition, he practiced a somewhat formal but effective form of management by objectives with each of his subordinates.

This manager and, unfortunately, many of the more outspoken critics of participative management, tend to feel that consultation must be carried out in a gregarious, back-slapping manner. Joint planning is a decision-making technique, and not a personality attribute. Extreme shyness or reserve may be an inhibiting factor, but is not an absolute barrier. Trust and confidence in subordinates can be demonstrated as effectively, if not more effectively, by action, as by words.

Similarly, as suggested earlier, the manager who holds a Human Resources view of participation acknowledges personality and capability differences among his subordinates. He feels a responsibility to the organization and to his subordinates to assist *each* to develop continuously his potential for making important contributions to department performance. He recognizes that individuals move toward the free interchange of ideas, suggestions, and criticisms at different paces. However, by demonstrating his own confidence in his subordinates' capabilities and in their potential, he tends to encourage more rapid growth than other managers.

Concluding comments

Our continuing research on the purpose and process of participative management has, in our view, contributed additional support for the Human Resources theory of participation. It has emphasized that when the impact on subordinates is considered, the superior's attitude toward the traits and abilities of his subordinates is equally as important as the amount of consultation in which he engages.

This not-so-startling finding allows expansions and interpretations of modern theories of participation to counter criticisms which may be properly leveled at a simple quantity theory of participation. However, although our findings have obvious implications for both theory and management behavior, they too are open to possible misinterpretation. It is possible to read into our findings, as some surely will, that subordinate consultation may be neglected, that all that matters is that the superior respect his subordinates.

Such a philosophy — tried, found wanting, and not supported by our findings — is embodied in the frequent statement that "all you need to do to be a good manager is hire a good subordinate and turn him loose to do the job as he sees fit." Such a philosophy, in our view, abdicates the superior's responsibility to guide, develop, and support his subordinates. The most satisfied managers in our sample were those who received high levels of consultation from superiors who valued their capabilities. It is our view that effective participation involves neither "selling" the superior's ideas nor blanket approval of all subordinate suggestions. Rather, it is most clearly embodied in the notion of joint planning where the skills of both superior and subordinate are used to their fullest.

Our findings emphasize the importance of attitudes of trust and confidence in subordinates, but they do not indicate their source. It is possible, but unlikely, that those superiors in our sample who reported the highest levels of trust and confidence in their subordinates did so because their subordinates were in fact of higher caliber than those of their colleagues. Within our large sample of managers, several indicators — education, age, experience, for example — suggest that managers' capabilities are roughly evenly distributed across levels and divisions within the organization.

Another possible reason for differences in superiors' attitudes on this dimenion is that they are caused by interaction with subordinates, rather than being a determinant of the nature of this interaction. That is, the manager, who attempts consultation which is highly successful increases his confidence in his subordinates and thus develops broader involvement. This seems to be a highly plausible explanation which has implications for management development. In fact, there is growing evidence that managers who experiment with participative techniques over lengthy periods do develop both a commitment to such practices and additional trust in their subordinates.

How to choose a leadership pattern

Robert Tannenbaum and Warren H. Schmidt

Since its publication in *HBR's* March–April 1958 issue, this article has had such impact and popularity as to warrant its choice as an "*HBR Classic.*" Robert Tannenbaum and Fred Schmidt succeeded in capturing in a few succinct pages the main ideas involved in the question of how a manager should lead his organization. For this publication, the authors have written a commentary in which they look at their article from a 15-year perspective (see page 000). Mr. Tannenbaum is Professor of the Development of Human Systems at the Graduate School of Management, University of California, Los Angeles. He is also a consulting editor of the *Journal of Applied Behavioral Science* and coauthor (with Irving Weschler and Fred Massarik) of *Leadership and Organization: A Behavioral Science Approach* (New York, McGraw-Hill, 1961). Mr. Schmidt is also affiliated with the UCLA Graduate School of Management, where he is senior lecturer in behavioral science. Besides writing extensively in the fields of human relations and leadership and conference planning, Mr. Schmidt wrote the screenplay for a film, "Is It Always Right to Be Right?" which won an Academy Award in 1970.

Should a manager be democratic or autocratic in dealing with his subordinates — or something in between?

"I put most problems into my group's hands and leave it to them to carry the ball from there. I serve merely as a catalyst, mirroring back the people's thoughts and feelings so that they can better understand them."

"It's foolish to make decisions oneself on matters that affect people. I always talk things over with my subordinates, but I make it clear to them that I'm the one who has to have the final say."

"Once I have decided on a course of action, I do my best to sell my ideas to my employees."

"I'm being paid to lead. If I let a lot of other people make the decisions I should be making, then I'm not worth my salt."

"I believe in getting things done. I can't waste time calling meetings. Someone has to call the shots around here, and I think it should be me."

Each of these statements represents a point of view about "good leadership." Considerable experience, factual data, and theoretical principles could be cited to support each statement, even though they seem to be inconsistent when placed together. Such contradictions point up the dilemma in which the modern manager frequently finds himself.

New problem

The problem of how the modern manager can be "democratic" in his relations with subordinates and at the same time maintain the necessary authority and control in the organization for which he is responsible has come into focus increasingly in recent years.

Earlier in the century this problem was not so acutely felt. The successful executive was generally pictured as possessing intelligence, imagination, initiative, the capacity to make rapid (and generally wise) decisions, and the ability to inspire subordinates. People tended to think of the world as being divided into "leaders" and "followers."

New focus

Gradually, however, from the social sciences emerged the concept of "group dynamics" with its focus on *members* of the group rather than solely on the leader. Research efforts of social scientists underscored the importance of employee involvement and participation in decision making. Evidence began to challenge the efficiency of highly directive leadership, and increasing attention was paid to problems of motivation and human relations.

Through training laboratories in group development that sprang up across the country, many of the newer notions of leadership began to exert an impact. These training laboratories were carefully designed to give people a firsthand experience in full participation and decision making. The designated "leaders" deliberately attempted to reduce their own power and to make group members as responsible as possible for setting their own goals and methods within the laboratory experience.

It was perhaps inevitable that some of the people who attended the training laboratories regarded this kind of leadership as being truly "democratic" and went home with the determination to build fully participative decision making into their own organizations. Whenever their bosses made a decision without convening a staff meeting, they tended to perceive that as authoritarian behavior. The true symbol of democratic leadership to some was the meeting — and the less directed from the top, the more democratic it was.

Some of the more enthusiastic alumni of these training laboratories began to get the habit of categorizing leader behavior as "democratic" or "authoritarian." The boss who made too many decisions himself was thought of as an authoritarian, and his directive behavior was often attributed solely to his personality.

New need

The net result of the research findings and of the human relations training based upon them has been to call into question the stereotype of an effective leader. Consequently, the modern manager often finds himself in an uncomfortable state of mind.

Often he is not quite sure how to behave; there are times when he is torn between exerting "strong" leadership and "permissive" leadership. Sometimes new knowledge pushes him in one direction ("I should really get the group to help make this decision"), but at the same time his experience pushes him in another direction ("I really understand the problem better than the group and therefore I should make the decision"). He is not sure when a group decision is really appropriate or when holding a staff meeting serves merely as a device for avoiding his own decision-making responsibility.

The purpose of our article is to suggest a framework which managers may find useful in grappling with this dilemma. First we shall look at the different patterns of leadership behavior that the manager can choose from in relating himself to his subordinates. Then we shall turn to some of the questions suggested by this range of patterns. For instance, how important is it for a manager's subordinates to know what type of leadership he is using in a situation? What factors should he consider in deciding on a leadership pattern? What difference do his long-run objectives make as compared to his immediate objectives?

Range of behavior

Exhibit 1 presents the continuum or range of possible leadership behavior available to a manager. Each type of ac-

tion is related to the degree of authority used by the boss and to the amount of freedom available to his subordinates in reaching decisions. The actions seen on the extreme left characterize the manager who maintains a high degree of control while those seen on the extreme right characterize the manager who releases a high degree of control. Neither extreme is absolute; authority and freedom are never without their limitation.

Now let us look more closely at each of the behavior points occurring along this continuum:

The manager makes the decision and announces it ☐ In this case the boss identifies a problem, considers alternative solutions, chooses one of them, and then reports this decision to his subordinates for implementation. He may or may not give consideration to what he believes his subordinates will think or feel about his decision; in any case, he provides no opportunity for them to par-

Exhibit 1

Continium of leadership behavior

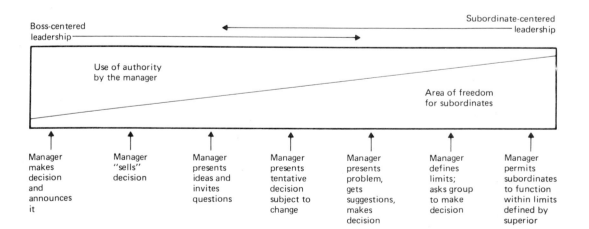

Boss-centered leadership ← → Subordinate-centered leadership

Use of authority by the manager

Area of freedom for subordinates

| Manager makes decision and announces it | Manager "sells" decision | Manager presents ideas and invites questions | Manager presents tentative decision subject to change | Manager presents problem, gets suggestions, makes decision | Manager defines limits; asks group to make decision | Manager permits subordinates to function within limits defined by superior |

ticipate directly in the decision-making process. Coercion may or may not be used or implied.

The manager "sells" his decision □ Here the manager, as before, takes responsibility for identifying the problem and arriving at a decision. However, rather than simply announcing it, he takes the additional step of persuading his subordinates to accept it. In doing so, he recognizes the possibility of some resistance among those who will be faced with the decision, and seeks to reduce this resistance by indicating, for example, what the employees have to gain from his decision.

The manager presents his ideas, invites questions □ Here the boss who has arrived at a decision and who seeks acceptance of his ideas provides an opportunity for his subordinates to get a fuller explanation of his thinking and his intentions. After presenting the ideas, he invites questions so that his associates can better understand what he is trying to accomplish. This "give and take" also enables the manager and the subordinates to explore more fully the implications of the decision.

The manager presents a tentative decision subject to change □ This kind of behavior permits the subordinates to exert some influence on the decision. The initiative for identifying and diagnosing the problem remains with the boss. Before meeting with his staff, he has thought the problem through and arrived at a decision — but only a tentative one. Before finalizing it, he presents his proposed solution for the reaction of those who will be affected by it. He says in effect, "I'd like to hear what you have to say about this plan that I have de-

veloped. I'll appreciate your frank reactions, but will reserve for myself the final decision."

The manager presents the problem, gets suggestions, and then makes his decision □ Up to this point the boss has come before the group with a solution of his own. Not so in this case. The subordinates now get the first chance to suggest solutions. The manager's initial role involves identifying the problem. He might, for example, say something of this sort: "We are faced with a number of complaints from newspapers and the general public on our service policy. What is wrong here? What ideas do you have for coming to grips with this problem?"

The function of the group becomes one of increasing the manager's repertory of possible solutions to the problem. The purpose is to capitalize on the knowledge and experience of those who are on the "firing line." From the expanded list of alternatives developed by the manager and his subordinates, the manager then selects the solution that he regards as most promising (Moore 1956).

The manager defines the limits and requests the group to make a decision □ At this point the manager passes to the group (possibly including himself as a member) the right to make decisions. Before doing so, however, he defines the problem to be solved and the boundaries within which the decision must be made.

An example might be the handling of a parking problem at a plant. The boss decided that this is something that should be worked on by the people involved, so he calls them together and points up the existence of the problem. Then he tells them:

There is the open field just north of the main plant which has been designated for additional employee parking. We can build underground or surface multilevel facilities as long as the cost does not exceed $100,000. Within these limits we are free to work out whatever solution makes sense to us. After we decide on a specific plan, the company will spend the available money in whatever way we indicate.

The manager permits the group to make decisions within prescribed limits ☐ This represents an extreme degree of group freedom only occasionally encountered in formal organizations, as, for instance, in many research groups. Here the team of managers or engineers undertakes the identification and diagnosis of the problem, develops alternative procedures for solving it, and decides on one or more of these alternative solutions. The only limits directly imposed on the group by the organization are those specified by the superior of the team's boss. If the boss participates in the decision-making process, he attempts to do so with no more authority than any other member of the group. He commits himself in advance to assist in implementing whatever decision the group makes.

Key questions

As the continuum in Exhibit 1 demonstrates, there are a number of alternative ways in which a manager can relate himself to the group or individuals he is supervising. At the extreme left of the range, the emphasis is on the manager — on what *he* is interested in, how *he* sees things, how *he* feels about them. As we move toward the subordinate-centered end of the continuum, however, the focus is increasingly on the subordinates — on what *they* are interested in, how *they* look at things, how *they* feel about them.

When a business leadership is regarded in this way, a number of questions arise. Let us take four of especial importance:

Can a boss ever relinquish his responsibility by delegating it to someone else? ☐ Our view is that the manager must expect to be held responsible by his superior for the quality of the decisions made, even though operationally these decisions may have been made on a group basis. He should, therefore, be ready to accept whatever risk is involved whenever he delegates decision-making power to his subordinates. Delegation is not a way of "passing the buck." Also, it should be emphasized that the amount of freedom the boss gives to his subordinates cannot be greater than the freedom which he himself has been given by his own superior.

Should the manager participate with his subordinates once he has delegated responsibility to them? ☐ The manager should carefully think over this question and decide on his role prior to involving the subordinate group. He should ask if his presence will inhibit or facilitate the problem-solving process. There may be some instances when he should leave the group to let it solve the problem itself. Typically, however, the boss has useful ideas to contribute, and should function as an additional member of the group. In the latter instance, it is important that he indicate clearly to the group that he sees himself in a member role rather than in an authority role.

How important is it for the group to recognize what kind of leadership behavior the boss is using? ☐ It makes a great deal of difference. Many relationship problems between the boss and subordinate occur because the boss fails to make clear how he plans to use his authority. If, for example, he actually intends to make a certain decision himself, but the subordinate group gets the impression that he has delegated this authority, considerable confusion and resentment are likely to follow. Problems may also occur when the boss uses a "democratic" facade to conceal the fact that he has already made a decision which he hopes the group will accept as its own. The attempt to "make them think it was their idea in the first place" is a risky one. We believe that it is highly important for the manager to be honest and clear in describing what authority he is keeping and what role he is asking his subordinates to assume in solving a particular problem.

Can you tell how "democratic" a manager is by the number of decisions his subordinates make? □ The sheer number of decisions is not an accurate index of the amount of freedom that a subordinate group enjoys. More important is the significance of the decisions which the boss entrusts to his subordinates. Obviously a decision on how to arrange desks is of an entirely different order from a decision involving the introduction of new electronic data processing equipment. Even though the widest possible limits are given in dealing with the first issue, the group will sense no particular degree of responsibility. For a boss to permit the group to decide equipment policy, even with rather narrow limits, would reflect a greater degree of confidence in them on his part.

Deciding how to lead

Now let us turn from the types of leadership that are practical and desirable. What factors or forces should a manager consider in deciding how to manage? Three are of particular importance:

Forces in the manager.
Forces in the subordinates.
Forces in the situation.

We should like briefly to describe these elements and indicate how they might influence a manger's actions in a decision-making situation (Tannenbaum and Massarik 1950). The strength of each of them will, of course, vary from instance to instance, but the manager who is sensitive to them can better assess the problems which face him and determine which mode of leadership behavior is most appropriate for him.

Forces in the manager

The manager's behavior in any given instance will be influenced greatly by the many forces operating within his own personality. He will, of course, perceive his leadership problems in a unique way on the basis of his background, knowledge, and experience. Among the important internal forces affecting him will be the following:

1. *His value system.* How strongly does he feel that individuals should have a share in making decisions which affect them? Or, how convinced is he that the official who is paid to assume responsibility should personally carry the burden of decision making? The strength of his convictions on questions like these will tend to move the manager to one end or the other of the continuum shown in Exhibit 1. His behavior will also be influenced by the relative importance that he attaches to organizational efficiency, personal growth of subordinates, and

company profits (Argyris 1955).

2. *His confidence in his subordinates.* Managers differ greatly in the amount of trust they have in other people generally, and this carries over to the particular employees they supervise at a given time. In viewing his particular group of subordinates, the manager is likely to consider their knowledge and competence with respect to the problem. A central question he might ask himself is: "Who is best qualified to deal with this problem?" Often he may, justifiably or not, have more confidence in his own capabilities than in those of his subordinates.

3. *His own leadership inclinations.* There are some managers who seem to function more comfortably and naturally as highly directive leaders. Resolving problems and issuing orders come easily to them. Other managers seem to operate more comfortably in a team role, where they are continually sharing many of their functions with their subordinates.

4. *His feelings of security in an uncertain situation.* The manager who releases control over the decision-making process thereby reduces the predictability of the outcome. Some managers have a greater need than others for predictability and stability in their environment. This "tolerance for ambiguity" is being viewed increasingly by psychologists as a key variable in a person's manner of dealing with problems.

The manager brings these and other highly personal variables to each situation he faces. If he can see them as forces which, consciously or unconsciously, influence his behavior, he can better understand what makes him prefer to act in a given way. And understanding this, he can often make himself more effective.

Forces in the subordinate

Before deciding how to lead a certain group, the manager will also want to consider a number of forces affecting his subordinates' behavior. He will want to remember that each employee, like himself, is influenced by many personality variables. In addition, each subordinate has a set of expectations about how the boss should act in relation to him (the phrase "expected behavior" is one we hear more and more often these days at discussions of leadership and teaching). The better the manager understands these factors, the more accurately he can determine what kind of behavior on his part will enable his subordinates to act more effectively.

Generally speaking, the manager can permit his subordinates greater freedom if the following essential conditions exist:

If the subordinates have relatively high needs for independence. (As we all know, people differ greatly in the amount of direction that they desire.)

If the subordinates have a readiness to assume responsibility for decision making. (Some see additional responsibility as a tribute to their ability; others see it as "passing the buck.")

If they have a relatively high tolerance for ambiguity. (Some employees prefer to have clear-cut directives given to them; others prefer a wider area of freedom.)

If they are interested in the problem and feel that it is important. If they understand and identify with the goals of the organization.

If they have the necessary knowledge and experience to deal with the problem.

If they have learned to expect to share in decision making. (Persons who have come to expect strong leadership and are then suddenly confronted with the request to share more fully in decision making are often upset by this new experience. On the other hand, persons who have enjoyed a considerable amount of freedom resent the boss who begins to make all the decisions himself.)

The manager will probably tend to make fuller use of his own authority if the above conditions do not exist; at times there may be no realistic alternative to running a "one-man show."

The restrictive effect of many of the forces will, of course, be greatly modified by the general feeling of confidence which subordinates have in the boss. Where they have learned to respect and trust him, he is free to vary his behavior. He will feel certain that he will not be perceived as an authoritarian boss on those occasions when he makes decisions by himself. Similarly, he will not be seen as using staff meetings to avoid his decision-making responsibility. In a climate of mutual confidence and respect, people tend to feel less threatened by deviations from normal practice, which in turn makes possible a higher degree of flexibility in the whole relationship.

Forces in the situation

In addition to the forces which exist in the manager himself and his subordinates, certain characteristics of the general situation will also affect the manager's behavior. Among the more critical environmental pressures that surround him are those which stem from the organization, the work group, the nature of the problem, and the pressures of time. Let us look briefly at each of these:

Type of organization. ☐ Like individuals, organizations have values and traditions which inevitably influence the behavior of the people who work in them. The manager who is a newcomer to a company quickly discovers that certain kinds of behavior are approved while others are not. He also discovers that to deviate radically from what is generally accepted is likely to create problems for him.

These values and traditions are communicated in many ways — through job descriptions, policy pronouncements, and public statements by top executives. Some organizations, for example, hold to the notion that the desirable executive is one who is dynamic, imaginative, decisive, and persuasive. Other organizatons put more emphasis upon the importance of the executive's ability to work effectively with people — his human relations skills. The fact that his superiors have a defined concept of what the good executive should be will very likely push the manager toward one end or the other of the behavioral range.

In addition to the above, the amount of employee participation is influenced by such variables as the size of the working units, their geographical distribution, and the degree of inter- and intra-organizational security required to attain company goals. For example, the wide geographical dispersion of an organization may preclude a practical system of participative decision making, even though this would otherwise be desirable. Similarly, the size of the working units or the need for keeping plans confidential may make it necessary for the boss to exercise more control then would otherwise be the case. Factors like these may limit considerably the manager's ability to function flexibly on the continuum.

Group effectiveness ☐ Before turning decision-making responsibility over to a subordinate group, the boss should consider how effectively its members work together as a unit.

One of the relevant factors here is the experience the group has had in working together. It can generally be expected that a group which has functioned for some time will have developed habits of cooperation and thus be able to tackle a problem more effectively than a new group. It can also be expected that a group of people with similar backgrounds and interests will work more quickly and easily than people with dissimilar backgrounds, because the communication problems are likely to be less complex.

The degree of confidence that the members have in their ability to solve problems as a group is also a key consideration. Finally, such group variables as cohesiveness, permissiveness, mutual acceptance, and commonality of purpose will exert subtle but powerful influence on the group's functioning.

The problem itself ☐ The nature of the problem may determine what degree of authority should be delegated by the manager to his subordinates. Obviously he will ask himself whether they have the kind of knowledge which is needed. It is possible to do them a real disservice by assigning a problem that their experience does not equip them to handle.

Since the problems faced in large or growing industries increasingly require knowledge of specialists from many different fields, it might be inferred that the more complex a problem, the more anxious a manager will be to get some assistance in solving it. However, this is not

always the case. There will be times when the very complexity of the problem calls for one person to work it out. For example, if the manager has most of the background and factual data relevant to a given issue, it may be easier for him to think it through himself than to take the time to fill in his staff on all the pertinent background information.

The key question to ask, of course, is: "Have I heard the ideas of everyone who has the necessary knowledge to make a significant contribution to the solution of this problem?"

The pressure of time ☐ This is perhaps the most clearly felt pressure on the manager (in spite of the fact that it may sometimes be imagined). The more that he feels the need for an immediate decision, the more difficult it is to involve other people. In organizations which are in a constant state of "crisis" and "crash programming" one is likely to find managers personally using a high degree of authority with relatively little delegation to subordinates. When the time pressure is less intense, however, it becomes much more possible to bring subordinates in on the decision-making process.

These, then, are the principal forces that impinge on the manager in any given instance and that tend to determine his tactical behavior in relation to his subordinates. In each case his behavior ideally will be that which makes possible the most effective attainment of his immediate goal within the limits facing him.

Long-run strategy

As a manager works with his organization on the problems that come up day by day, his choice of a leadership pattern is usually limited. He must take account of the forces just described and, within the restrictions they impose on him, do the best that he can. But as he looks ahead months or even years, he can shift his thinking from tactics to large-scale strategy. No longer need he be fettered by all of the forces mentioned, for he can view many of them as variables over which he has some control. He can, for example, gain new insights or skills for himself, supply training for individual subordinates, and provide participative experiences for his employee group.

In trying to bring about a change in these variables, however, he is faced with a challenging question: At which point along the continuum *should* he act?

Attaining objectives

The answer depends largely on what he wants to accomplish. Let us suppose that he is interested in the same objectives that most modern managers seek to attain when they can shift their attention from the pressure of immediate assignments:

1. To raise the level of employee motivation.
2. To increase the readiness of subordinates to accept change.
3. To improve the quality of all managerial decisions.
4. To develop teamwork and morale.
5. To further the individual development of employees.

In recent years the manager has been deluged with a flow of advice on how best to achieve these longer-run objectives. It is little wonder that he is often both bewildered and annoyed. However, there are some guidelines which he can usefully follow in making a decision.

Most research and much of the experience of recent years give a strong factual basis to the theory that a fairly high degree of subordinate-centered behavior is associated with accomplishment of the five purposes mentioned (Schmidt and Buchanan 1954; Viteles 1953). This does not mean that a manager should always leave all decisions to his assistants. To provide the individual or the group with greater freedom than they are ready for at any given time may very well tend to generate anxieties and therefore inhibit rather than facilitate the attainment of desired objectives. But this should not keep the manager from making a continuing effort to confront his subordinates with the challenge of freedom.

Conclusion

In summary, there are two implications in the basic thesis that we have been developing. The first is that the successful leader is one who is keenly aware of those forces which are relevant to his behavior at any given time. He accurately understands himself, the individuals and group he is dealing with, and the company and broader social environment in which he operates. And certainly he is able to assess the present readiness for growth of his subordinates.

But this sensitivity or understanding is not enough, which brings us to the second implication. The successful leader is one who is able to behave appropriately in the light of these perceptions. If direction is in order, he is able to direct; if considerable participative freedom is called for, he is able to provide such freedom.

Thus, the successful manager of men can be primarily characterized neither as a strong leader nor as a permissive one. Rather, he is one who maintains a high batting average in accurately assessing the forces that determine what his most appropriate behavior at any given time should be and in actually being able to behave accordingly. Being both insightful and flexible, he is less likely to see the problems of leadership as a dilemma.

Retrospective commentary

Since this *HBR* Classic was first published in 1958, there have been many changes in organizations and in the world that have affected leadership patterns. While the article's continued popularity attests to its essential validity, we believe it can be reconsidered and updated to reflect subsequent societal changes and new management concepts.

The reasons for the article's continued relevance can be summarized briefly:

The article contains insights and perspectives which mesh well with, and help clarify, the experiences of managers, other leaders, and students of leadership. Thus it is useful to individuals in a wide variety of organizations — industrial, governmental, educational, religious, and community.

The concept of leadership the article defines is reflected in a continuum of leadership behavior (see Exhibit 1 in original article). Rather than offering a choice between two styles of leadership, democratic or authoritarian, it sanctions a range of behavior.

The concept does not dictate to managers but helps them to analyze their own behavior. The continuum permits them to review their behavior within a context of other alternatives, without any style being labeled right or wrong.

(We have sometimes wondered if we have, perhaps, made it too easy for any-

one to justify his or her style of leadership. It may be a small step between being nonjudgmental and giving the impression that all behavior is equally valid and useful. The latter was not our intention. Indeed, the thrust of our endorsement was for the manager who is insightful in assessing relevant forces within himself, others, and the situation, and who can be flexible in responding to these forces.)

In recognizing that our article can be updated, we are acknowledging that organizations do not exist in a vacuum but are affected by changes that occur in society. Consider, for example, the implications for organizations of these recent social developments:

The youth revolution that expresses distrust and even contempt for organizations identified with the establishment.

The civil rights movement that demands all minority groups be given a greater opportunity for participation and influence in the organizational processes.

The ecology and consumer movements that challenge the right of managers to make decisions without considering the interest of people outside the organization.

The increasing national concern with the quality of working life and its relationship to worker productivity, participation, and satisfaction.

These and other societal changes make effective leadership in this decade a more challenging task, requiring even greater sensitivity and flexibility than was needed in the 1950s. Today's manager is more likely to deal with employees who resent being treated as subordinates, who may be highly critical of any organizational system, who expect to be consulted and to exert influence, and who often stand on the edge of alienation from the institution that needs their loyalty and commitment. In addition, he is frequently confronted by a highly turbulent, unpredictable environment.

In response to these social pressures, new concepts of management have emerged in organizations. Open-system theory, with its emphasis on subsystems' interdepency *and* on the interaction of an organization with its environment, has made a powerful impact on managers' approach to problems. Organization development has emerged as a new behavioral science approach to the improvement of individual, group, organizational, and interorganizational performance. New research has added to our understanding of motivation in the work situation. More and more executives have become concerned with social responsibility and have explored the feasibility of social responsibility and have explored the feasibility of social audits. And a growing number of organizations, in Europe and in the United States, have conducted experiments in industrial democracy.

In light of these develoments, we submit the following thoughts on how we would rewrite certain points in our original article.

The article described forces in the manager, subordinates, and the situation as givens, with the leadership pattern a resultant of these forces. We would now give more attention to the *interdependency* of these forces. For example, such interdependency occurs in: (a) the interplay between the manager's confidence in his subordinates, their readiness to assume responsibility, and the level of group effectiveness; and (b) the impact of the behavior of the manager

on that of his subordinates, and vice versa.

In discussing the forces in the situation, we primarily identified organizational phenomena. We would now include forces lying outside the organization, and would explore the relevant interdependencies between the organization and its environment.

In the original article, we presented the size of the rectangle in Exhibit 1 as a given, with its boundaries already determined by external forces — in effect, a closed system. We would now recognize the possibility of the manager and/or his subordinates taking the initiative to change those boundaries through interaction with relevant external forces — both within their own organization and in the larger society.

The article portrayed the manager as the principal and almost unilateral actor. He initiated and determined group functions, assumed responsibility, and exercised control. Subordinates made inputs and assumed power only at the will of the manager. Although the manager might have taken into account forces outside himself, it was *he* who decided where to operate on the continuum — that is, whether to announce a decision instead of trying to sell his idea to his subordinates, whether to invite questions, to let subordinates decide an issue, and so on. While the manager has retained this clear prerogative in many organizations, it has been challenged in others. Even in situations where he has retained it, however, the balance in the relationship between manager and subordinates at any given time is arrived at by interaction — direct or indirect — between the two parties.

Although power and its use by the manager played a role in our article, we now realize that our concern with cooperation and collaboration, common goals, commitment, trust, and mutual caring limited our vision with respect to the realities of power. We did not attempt to deal with unions, other forms of joint worker action, or with individual workers' expressions of resistance. Today, we would recognize much more clearly the power available to *all* parties, and the factors that underlie the interrelated decisions on whether to use it.

In the original article, we used the terms "manager" and "subordinate." We are now uncomfortable with "subordinate" because of its demeaning, dependency-laden connotations and prefer "nonmanager." The titles "manager" and "nonmanager" make the terminological difference functional rather than hierarchical.

We assumed fairly traditional organizational structures in our original article. Now we would alter our formulation to reflect newer organizational modes which are slowly emerging, such as industrial democracy, intentional communities, and "phenomenarchy" (McWhinneg 1973). These new modes are based on observations such as the following:

Both manager and nonmanagers may be governing forces in their group's environment, contributing to the definition of the total area of freedom.

A group can function without a manager, with managerial functions being shared by group members.

A group, as a unit, can be delegated authority and can assume responsibility within a large organizational context.

Our thoughts on the question of leadership have prompted us to design a new behavior continuum (see Exhibit 2) in which the total area of freedom shared by manager and nonmanagers is constantly redefined by interactions between them and the forces in the environment.

The arrows in the exhibit indicate the continual flow of interdependent influence among systems and people. The points on the continuum designate the types of manager and nonmanager behavior that become possible with any given amount of freedom available to each. The new continuum is both more complex and more dynamic than the 1958 version, reflecting the organization and societal realities of 1973.

Exhibit 2

Continuum of manager-nonmanager behavior

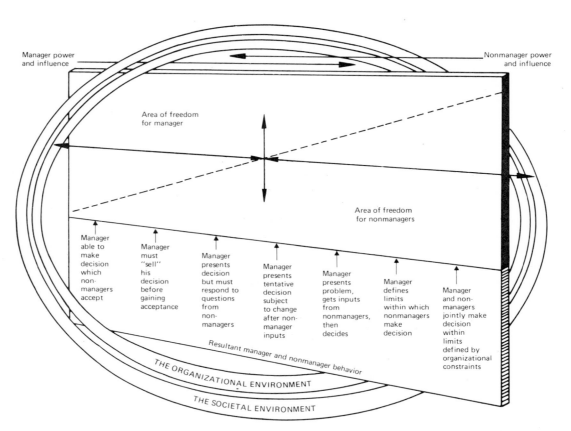

How do you identify a potential leader?

"Leadership experience? . . . Well, I organized a strike once!"

Managing your manager: The effective subordinate

Norman C. Hill and Paul H. Thompson

> After weeks of futile maneuvering to save his job, Lee Iacocca, 53, the hard-driving, cigar-chomping president of the world's fourth largest manufacturing company, found himself quite bluntly sacked by his equally toughminded boss, Chairman Henry Ford II. It was the culmination of months of behind-the-scenes quarreling between two of the auto industry's most respected — and often feared — executives.
>
> Reprinted by permission from *Time,* The Weekly Newsmagazine; Copyright Time Inc. 1978.

As president of the Ford Motor Company, Lee Iacocca was widely respected as one of the most skillful managers in the auto industry's history; but his problems with his boss apparently cost him his job.

People at all levels in organizations have difficulties with their bosses. And the name doesn't have to be Lee Iacocca, Andrew Young, Billy Martin, or Midge Constanza for the word to get around. A career may be terminated, jeopardized, or, at the very least, slowed by failing to establish a workable superior-subordinate relationship.

Nearly everyone is a subordinate to someone, no matter how high he or she rises in the organizational hierarchy. The value of a widespread concern for a better understanding of the relationship between superiors and subordinates would appear obvious — especially when so many managers are frustrated by their subordinates' lack of motivation and general low level of performance. Likewise, individuals often complain about their bosses' apparent lack of interest, supervision, or concern. Yet from university classrooms to slick paperbacks, the focus has been largely limited to "management style" — i.e., building your career by successfully directing those *beneath* you. Little attention has been paid to the other side of the issue — establishing your career based on your ability to manage those who formally manage you.

In the traditional role definition, the boss gives the orders and the subordinate carries them out. Many individuals expect a manager to define the job, make assignments, and then check to see that the work is completed. When the boss doesn't behave in this manner, frustration for many is evident. However, for professionals and other highly trained employees, the relationship is seldom that simple. Very often the two parties have different expectations about roles. These differing expectations can lead to tension, conflicts, missed deadlines, and even transfers or terminations.

A way to avoid these problems for some individuals is to have the two parties clarify expectations right at the beginning. One highly regarded manager described doing this:

Whenever I get a new boss, I sit down with him and ask him to make his expectations explicit. We try to list not my job activities but the main purposes of my job. To do that, we continue each statement of activity with "In order to ...," and try to complete the sentence. By recording my job purposes, we get a clear picture of what I should be accomplishing; and that's what counts — results.

This approach works very well for this individual, but most bosses are not able (or willing) to be nearly that clear about their expectations. In most cases, communication between superiors and subordinates is an ongoing, shifting dynamic. Most issues are not resolved in a one-shot conversation. In writing about superior-subordinate communications, Rensis Likert concluded:

A number of recent studies are providing disturbing evidence that communications between managers and supervisors is seriously deficient on such important matters as what a subordinate understands his job to be. The data shows that superiors fail to make clear to subordinates precisely what the job is and what is expected of them. Moreover, the subordiantes do not tell the superior about the obstacles and problems they encounter in doing the job. (*New Pattens of Management,* McGraw-Hill, New York, 1961, pp. 52-53.)

What is so difficult about communications in this relationship? Why do so many people have trouble spelling out their expectations? First, frequent changes in work assignments and relationships lead to frequent changes in expectations. Many professionals work on projects for periods of two weeks to six months. In addition, they may be working on two or three projects at the same time. This might even involve two or more bosses simultaneously. In such environments there is seldom adequate time to develop mutually agreed upon expectations.

Second, an effective working relationship is complex and involves a number of different facets. Specific issues need to be resolved in building an effective relationship. It obviously takes time and skill for two people to reach a mutual understanding in so many areas. It is probably not possible to resolve these issues in one two-hour session, but sooner or later they need to be addressed either explicitly or implicitly.

Job content

Reaching agreement on the subordinate's responsibilities is an important issue in defining the relationship. However, this is often difficult for professional jobs. It is seldom easy to define measurable standards of performance. For example, how do you define individual performance measures for a team of engineers designing a computer component? It is possible to set objectives in terms of time (meeting deadlines), cost, and quality. But engineers often do not have control over all of these factors. Furthermore, if the objectives are not achieved, how do you decide which engineer(s) is to blame? In addition, as mentioned earlier, job assignments change frequently, so there is often inadequate time to spell out responsibilities in detail. Many professionals are given "state of the art" assignments, so the work has never been done before. If professionals are exploring a new field, it is difficult to write a detailed job description of just how to proceed on the project. For these reasons, detailed job descriptions may be of little value for most professional workers. However, job descriptions may be more useful where assignments are more stable and the work more routine. (For example, it may be quite realistic to define responsibilities for a team conducting a routine audit of a division that the firm has audited many times before.)

Taking iniative

A good subordinate is one who thinks of the things I would do before I do them. What this means is that he tries to adopt my perspective and look at things from my position in the organization, not just his own.

Another executive said:

I have people coming back to me all of the time saying they couldn't do what I ask because of such and such or so and so. They may call a guy and he's sick or on vacation or something else. But they don't ask themselves, "Is there some other way to get this information?" They just report back to me, thinking that I'll accept their efforts and good intentions as a substitute for what I need.

The message becomes evident: individuals are expected to take initiative on the job. However, the degree of initiative varies with each manager. One boss means that a person should be willing to complete an assignment even when there are obstacles to overcome. Another wants a subordinate to anticipate what the boss wants done. These different perspectives suggest an important point: a person needs to find out how much initiative is expected. Some bosses may be threatened by subordiantes who anticipate their desires, others would welcome it.

A means of resolving this dilemma is to look at the different levels of initiative that might be exercised. One article suggests that there are five degrees of initiative that an individual can exercise in relation to the boss. (W. Oncken, Jr., and D.L. Wass, *Harvard Business Review,* Nov.-Dec. 1974, p. 79.) These are:

1. Wait until told (i.e., "But I haven't been told yet to put out the fire.")
2. Ask what to do.
3. Recommend, then take resulting action.
4. Act, but advise at once.
5. Act on own, then routinely report (i.e., "September 5 — Fire in factory. Damage: approximately $25,000. Cause: Under Investigation.")

A famous case is brought to mind. A technician at a large company invented a transparent adhesive. But he found no one that was particularly interested in his discovery. Everyone ignored what he felt would be a useful product. During a break in the company's board of directors meeting, the technician taped all the directors' papers to the table. It was the beginning of Scotch tape and a windfall for the 3M Company. Of course, the technician jumped ten levels in the organization to find a responsive audience, and this degree of initiative, itself, is not without risk.

Rather than asking the boss, "What are your expectations?", it might be more useful to talk about levels of initiative. A discussion of those alternatives is likely to lead to a better understanding of the expectations. However, using such an approach could result in oversimplifying the relationship. On some matters the boss may want the subordinate to operate on level five, but on other matters he or she may prefer that the subordinate operate on level two. This suggests that they may also need to talk about activities inside the department versus outside the department — decisions that are within existing policies versus those that might require a change of policy, etc. Individuals should not merely ask how they are expected to operate, but also *observe* carefully over a period of months the boss's reaction when they take different levels of initiative on various kinds of problems. This can do much to clarify expectations.

Keeping the boss informed

The information-to-the-boss issue is closely tied to initiative, but there are some aspects that deserve separate consideration. Subordinates need to learn how to keep the boss advised on *appropriate* matters.

One rule of thumb to follow is letting the boss know about the progress that is being made on particular projects and avoid reporting all of the *activities* engaged in to achieve those results.

Some subordinates think they must report everything they do. Those who do may find their boss becoming increasingly inaccesssible to them. Managers have neither the time nor the desire to know all that the subordinate knows about a particular situation. If the boss has to spend that much time on a project, of what use is the subordinate?

One of the most difficult issues in this area concerns negative information. Often individuals fail to call attention to problems, mistakes, or misjudgments because they believe that "someone up there must know what's going on around here." Individuals may feel that they do not have all of the facts in a situation and thus say nothing. By assuming that superiors have complete information or answers, subordinates ease themselves out of taking responsibility for what goes on in the division or organization. Taking the "it's-not-my-job" position shifts more burden from a subordinate back to the boss — a burden that few bosses need or want to carry.

John and Mark Arnold have documented a number of cases where subordinates in an organization knew that something was wrong, but failed to do anything about it. Two examples:

The president of a manufacturing company ordered work to begin on a new type of photocopying machine. Although those with direct responsibility believed the machine would take two years to build, they cooperated in forecasting that it could be developed in a matter of months. Working furiously, they managed to complete a prototype to meet their deadline. The president inspected and left the test room with assurances that it was ready for production. Shortly after, however, the machine burst into flames and was destroyed.

In one electronics firm, shipments were being predated and papers falsified to meet sales targets. Sales representatives had accepted the targets rather than complain for fear that they would be labeled as uncommitted. It took months before upper-level managers realized what was happening. (The *Wall Street Journal,* June 5, 1978, p. 9.)

Even though these may be extreme cases, they are real examples, and they are repeated on a smaller scale hundreds of times every day.

Reasons given for withholding negative information from the boss are varied. While the subordinate's well-meant *intent* might be to protect others (the manager or the organization), the *outcome,* generally, will negatively impact any or all of them. Frequent comments in this area include:

"Don't worry the boss about this, she's got enough trouble as it is."

"Don't tell Frank, he has a terrible temper and he'll really chew you out."

"We need to insulate Mr. Layton from all of these details or he'll get overloaded and won't be able to get anything done."

These are nice rationalizations, but managers need negative as well as positive information.

Asking for help

A sensitive matter for both the manager and the subordinate is the issue of requesting help. Some bosses want to be deeply involved in a project, and they use requests for help as an opportunity to teach their subordinates. Others only want to see the final product and do not want to be bothered with frequent questions. A bank manager presented his views on this issue:

Some subordinates will take an assignment, work as hard on it as possible, then come back to you when they get stuck or when it's completed. Other people start coming back to you to do their work for them. People in the second group don't do very well in our bank.

Asking for help too often undermines the manager's confidence in the subordinate. However, there are times when the individual is new or has a difficult assignment and a great deal of help is needed. One way to solve this dilemma is to seek help from peers in the department. The more experienced people are usually able to help, and such requests are less likely to affect the boss's opinion of the employee's ability.

Another factor to consider is the amount of risk involved in a situation. A promising young accountant described

his strategy on seeking advice from the boss:

My boss had high expectations for me when he hired me, and I believe I have lived up to them. To ensure that I would perform successfully, I adopted a strategy of taking risks — not gambles — but calculated risks. If a decision involved a high level of risk, I would consult with my boss and didn't assume full responsibility on my own. However, if a job was not overly risky or of crucial importance, I would do as much of it on my own as I could and not waste my boss's time with the details. I assumed it was important to look out for my boss's welfare, not just my own. If I could make him look good or make his job easier and less time consuming, then it would benefit me as well. However, when I made a decision that turned out to be a mistake, I told my boss about it and didn't try to cover my errors.

This suggests some important guidelines in deciding when to go to the boss for help and when an individual should handle the situation alone:

Take risks, not gambles (and recognize the differences between the two).

Handle the details, but keep the manager informed.

Check with the boss on decisions that will impact work units outside the department.

Take the boss a recommendation each time he asks for an analysis of a project.

Initiate an appointment only when prepared to suggest some action that should be taken.

The last recommendation may meet with mixed reactions. For some managers it works very well, but others want to be kept informed and have the opportunity to talk through the issues as work progresses. This is another area where the boss's style must be considered.

Frequency and length of contact

Many individuals are upset because they don't get more time with their managers. They feel that the boss doesn't appreciate them because he doesn't spend more time with them. Often subordinates feel they are delayed on projects waiting for a decision. On the other hand, many managers are frustrated because they lack information from their subordinates. They don't want to be continually checking up on their people, but neither do they want to be surprised because projects aren't done on time.

The amount of time spent working together involves the previous issues of keeping informed and asking for help, but is also concerns the nature of the relationship. Differing expectations about frequency of contact and the amount of time spent together can be a major sore spot. In practice, people take quite different approaches in deciding how often to get together, including:

Getting together whenever something comes up. (These contacts might be initiated by the superior or the subordinate).

Setting up another appointment at the end of each session together.

Establishing regular meetings (e.g., Wednesday at 9:00 *a.m.*) with one individual or an entire staff.

Any of these approaches can be effective depending on the nature of the relationship. However, it is important that both individuals work out an agreement regarding their approach to this issue.

A reciprocal relationship

The young accountant in the last example made an important point that should not be overlooked. He said:

"I assumed it was important to look out for my boss's welfare, not just my own. If I could make him look good or make his job easier and less time consuming, then it would benefit me as well."

The most effective superior-subordinate relationships are reciprocal. Both individuals gain substantial benefits from the relationship. The boss gains because the accountant saves him time and produces high-quality work. The boss rewards the subordinate by spending extra time with him, giving him challenging work assignments, and increasing his responsibilities. In addition, the young accountant is given opportunities to make presentations to higher levels of management, thus providing him visibility in the firm. This kind of reciprocity contributes to a productive relationship and increases the motivation level of both individuals. When a manager and employee see that the efforts of each individual contribute to the reputation of both, they begin to see the reciprocal process. A boss who thoroughly outlines pitfalls in a specific project or a client's past association with the organization may invest several hours, but he will be rewarded with extra time to devote to other assignments. Undoubtedly he must recognize that his reputation will, to a great extent, rest with his subordinates and the quality of work they produce. Likewise, subordinates' reputations will, to a large degree, stem from the extent to which they are able to handle increasingly complex, significant, or otherwise valued assignments. Investing time in doing a highly competent job for a manager will put both the boss and subordinate in a good light. Future assignments and other rewards will generally reflect the manager's opinion of extra-mile work. The wise subordinate should take the stance of what-I-do-for-my-boss-I-do-for-myself.

Such an alliance contributes to a mentor-protégé relationship, a reciprocal coalition in which the boss, serving as a mentor, agrees to let the subordinate gain the experience and acquire the skills valued in the organization. In exchange, the subordinate must be prepared to perform the necessary detail work that goes with every project and assure its accuracy. He must do the routine but essential groundwork — and do it well — if he expects to gain a reputation that both will value.

The advantages of having a mentor are many. As the primary link in the development of coalitions, a mentor can do such things as guide a subordinate through the unwritten rules and policies that govern routine affairs or show the protégé how to design and carry a project to successful completion. Moreover, as his or her advocate, a mentor can show how to have upward influence with other managers and even be a force in getting the subordinate's ideas accepted.

At this point it must be acknowledged that all organizations are, by definition, political entities, and individuals must manage their careers with this in mind. To say that organizations are by their very nature political is to neither commend nor condemn them. This political aspect is simply an expression of the network of power relationships that may or may not be represented on formal organizational charts. Unfortunately, many professionals view the power relationships from one of two extremes: either they cynically ignore them and claim to be above politics, or they pursue their goals with Machiavellian tactics and coercive techniques. Neither approach optimizes either personal objectives or

organizational goals. Nevertheless, mentors can be extremely valuable to those trying to learn the political ropes of the organization.

Developing a condition of trust with the boss

E.E. Jennings suggests that an effective subordinate achieves a condition of trust with his superior (See *The Mobile Manager*, New York, McGraw-Hill, 1967, pp. 47-50). He views four conditions as being necessary for trust to develop.

Accessibility ☐ This is defined as a person who takes in ideas easily and gives them out freely. Both individuals need to demonstrate that they value each other's ideas. If two people are going to develop a productive relationship they must respect each other's ideas and give them careful thought and consideration. A subordinate who does not respect the boss's ideas will never be trusted and will not obtain the help needed in developing his own ideas. This does not mean that two people always have to agree with one another. "The minimum requirement of trust in this sense is that the subordinate respects new and different ideas enough to think them through carefully and energetically" (Jennings, p. 48).

Availability ☐ This subordinate should be attentive and available physically, mentally, and emotionally when the manager is under pressure and needs support. Recently, one of the authors was under pressure to complete several projects with very tight deadlines. One of his subordinates became upset because he was not receiving the help he needed on a project that the author felt was of less importance. Another subordinate took a different approach. In one of their meetings, he said:

I know you're under a lot of pressure right now trying to complete high-priority projects. This article we're working on is less important, so I'm quite willing to let it wait for a while. In addition, if I can be of help on any of your projects, just let me know. I've got a little extra time, and I'm willing to pitch in and help any way I can.

The second subordinate was invited to work on two of the projects and not only helped his boss but helped himself as well. It is not difficult to guess which individual received the most favorable letters of recommendation.

Predictability □ By predictability, Jennings means that the subordinate will handle delicate administrative circumstances with good judgment and thoroughness. This bears on the kinds of assignments a manager will feel free to give a subordinate. If an individual demonstrates early that he can be trusted to handle relationships with customers on a sensitive project, this will free the manager to work on other projects. However, if the subordinate lacks sensitivity or interpersonal skills and jeopardizes relationships with the customer, it means that in the future the subordinate will not be as trusted, and thus, will be of much less value to the boss.

Predictability has another important facet that relates to dependability. An accounting manager described the importance of this factor:

Recently, I was supervising some tax work with one of our major clients. I assigned one member of the team to a specific part of the project. He kept saying, "I can do it." Each time I checked he'd say, "I will get it done," but it was not ready when I went out to the job on Friday night. We had to make a major adjustment that night in order to meet a filing deadline. The client had gone to Las Vegas and was very upset when we called him. You can be sure that I don't take that young accountant's word anymore on important matters.

Needless to say, managers don't like surprises that embarrass them or make them look bad.

Loyalty □ In this context Jennings is not referring to organizational loyalty but personal loyalty. A manager is not likely to trust a subordinate with important information if he or she fears that the information might be used to further the subordinate's own interests at the manager's expense.

But loyalty must also be considered in a broader context. There are times when loyalty to an immediate superior will come in conflict with loyalty to the organization or to society. What is good for the boss is not always good for the organization; and what is good for the organization is not always good for society. But recognizing and acting upon such situations is not without costs to the individual. A case in a Big 8 accounting firm relates such a conflict: A housing project was being audited, and a supervisor in the firm wanted to give a qualified opinion. A partner in charge of the audit said that the project should be given a clear opinion. The supervisor refused to have his name associated with the working paper unless he could include a memo stating his objections. While some others involved in the case also sided with the supervisor and admired him for stating his view, he remained the only one who held out. Today he has yet to make promotion to manager.

Other professionals work to maintain a certain distance, a degree of objectivity, about projects — even those that appear to be critical to the organization's future success. One highly regarded middle manager described his strategy:

I'm not a yes man. I know the importance of speaking up and saying what's on my mind. I also know that other people in the organization may have a better perspective than I do. So I follow this rule of thumb: I argue forcefully one time for my position. If my boss then does not accept my recommendation, I try to make his decision an effective one through my support and commitment. That is, of course, unless I feel a conflict with my personal values.

Watergate brings to mind a wide range of activities associated with the problems of conflicting loyalties. Focusing on the role of subordinates does not imply that a person should always be a loyal subordinate at the expense of individual conscience, the organization, or society. Rather, individuals need to understand their own values and adhere to them even if it means running into conflict with the boss or losing a job. In fact, an individual should take the initiative and seek out another boss when there is a major conflict of values. Some things are far more important than being an "effective subordinate" to a manager of doubtful or even differing values.

The relationship between two individuals in a superior-subordinate relationship is critical, and mutual expectations must be achieved if the individual is to become a valued subordinate.

Those subordinates interested in accomplishing this objective are advised to remember the following points:

Very few bosses will do all that is necessary to clarify expectations in a superior-subordinate relationship.

Most managers will respond favorably to a discussion of the manager-subordinate relationship. However, managers have varying styles, so an individual is well advised to find out how the boss is *likely* to respond before initiating such a discussion.

Subordinates will usually learn more in such a discussion if they present their perceptions of the expectations and ask for a response. Just asking "What are my responsibilites?" will not generate as much dialogue as, "My understanding of my assignment is that I am to . . . and . . . Is this in agreement with your viewpoint?"

Managerial decision-making exercise

Considering all the arguments as to which leadership decision-making style is best, a manager is hard pressed to know just which approach to adopt. Most managers agree that participative decision making with subordinates makes sense, yet these same managers often behave in very nonparticipative ways. Are these managers wrong when they behave nonparticipatively? Is there one best way to make decisions?

Victor H. Vroom and Philip Yetton maintain that the manager's first task is one of determining how problems should be solved, not one of selecting a solution. They asked the question, "What decision-making process should managers use to deal effectively with the problems they encounter in their jobs?" Their search led them to the conclusion that there is no one best way to make decisions; rather, different styles of decision making and leadership should be used, depending on the demands of the situation.

Out of their research, Vroom and Yetton developed a framework to help managers analyze the various situations they encounter in a way that allows the manager to pick the appropriate decision-making style for a given situation. A major portion of this model is a breakdown of six types of management decision styles. Each style of decision making is represented by a symbol (AI, AII, CI, etc.). The first letter of the symbol represents the "basic properties" of the process (A stands for autocratic, C for consultative, G for group, D for delegation). The roman numerals represent variations on these basic properties.

Types of management decision styles

AI   You solve the problem or make the decision yourself, using information available to you at that time.

AII   You obtain the necessary information from your subordinate(s), then decide on the solution to the problem yourself. You may or may not tell your subordinates what the problem is in getting the information from them. The role played by your subordinates in making the decision is clearly one of providing the necessary information to you, rather than generating or evaluating alternative solutions.

CI   You share the problem with relevant subordinates individually, getting their ideas and suggestions without bringing them together as a group. Then you make the decision which may or may not reflect your subordinates' influence.

CII   You share the problem with your subordinates as a group, collectively obtaining their ideas and suggestions. Then you make the decision which may or may not reflect your subordinates' influence.

G   You share a problem with your subordinates as a group. Together you generate and evaluate alternatives and attempt to reach agreement (consensus) on a solution. Your role is much like that of coordinator. You do not try to influence the group to adopt "your" solution and you are willing to accept and implement any solution which has the support of the entire group.

D   You delegate the authority to solve the problem to subordinates, providing them with any relevant information that you possess, but giving them responsibility for solving the problem. You may or may not request that you be informed regarding the outcome of the decision.

In order to better understand the context where one approach (or perhaps a combination of approaches) would be most appropriate, the following questions are suggested as a means of focusing on the relevant dimensions.

1.   What is the cost of a bad decision? The higher the cost, the more care needs to be taken to ensure that the appropriate individual(s) are involved.

2.   What types of information are needed? The availability of information may

suggest including or eliminating certain individuals. Access to relevant information is a key determinant in structuring the decision-making process.

3. Which individuals are important in implementing the decision?
   It is not always obvious who will be significant in the implementation phase. The more important and complex the decision, the more important that those responsible for implementation be included in the decision making.

4. How fast must the decision be made?
   As time pressure on the decision increases, you would normally involve less people and have the decision made closer to the source of information and/or implementation.

5. Who is affected by the decision?
   The more far-reaching the effects of the decision, the more important it is to include relevant areas of the organization so they can contribute information and coordinate the impact of the decision in their areas of responsibility.

By considering the above diagnostic questions, the manager can then determine which decision-making style would be useful. In the following cases you have an opportunity to apply the concepts outlined in selecting a decision-making strategy. Read each case carefully, review probable answers to the questions, then develop an argument for the best strategy.

Case 1

You are the manufacturing manager in a large electronics plant. The company's management has always been searching for ways of increasing efficiency. They have recently installed new machines and put in a new, simplified work system, but to the surprise of everyone, including yourself, the expected increase in productivity was not realized. In fact, production has begun to drop, quality has fallen off, and the number of employee separations has risen.

You do not believe that there is anything wrong with the machines. You have had reports from other companies who are using them and they confirm your opinion. You have also had representatives from the firm that built the machines go over them, and they report that they are operating at peak efficiency.

You suspect that some parts of the new work system may be responsible for the change, but this view is not widely shared among your immediate subordinates — four first-line supervisors, each in charge of a section, and your supply manager. The drop in production has been variously attributed to poor training of the operators, lack of an adequate system of financial incentives, and poor morale. Clearly, this is an issue about which there is considerable depth of feeling within individuals and potential disagreement between your subordinates.

This morning you received a phone call from your division manager. He had just received your production figures for the last six months and was calling to express his concern. He indicated that the problem was yours to solve in any way that you think best, but that he would like to know within a week what steps you plan to take.

You share your division manager's concern with the falling productivity and know that your subordinates are also concerned. The problem is to decide what steps to take to rectify the situation.

Case 2

You are supervising the work of twelve engineers. Their formal training and work experience are very similar, permitting you to use them interchangeably on projects. Yesterday your manager informed you that a request had been received from an overseas affiliate for four engineers to go abroad on extended loan for a period of six to eight months. For a number of reasons, he argued and you agreed that this request should be met from your group.

All your engineers are capable of handling this assignment, and from the standpoint of present and future projects there is no particular reason why any one should be retained over any other. The problem is somewhat complicated by the fact that the overseas assignment is in what is generally regarded in the company as an undesirable location.

Case 3

You are the head of a staff unit reporting to the vice-president of finance. He has asked you to provide a report on the firm's current portfolio to include recommendations for changes in the selection criteria currently employed. Doubts have been raised about the efficiency of the existing system in view of current conditions, and there is considerable dissatisfaction with prevailing rates of return.

You plan to write the report, but at the moment you are quite perplexed about the approach to take. Your own specialty is the bond market and it is clear to you that a detailed knowledge of the equity market, which you lack, would greatly enhance the value of the report. Fortunately, four members of your staff are specialists in different segments of the equity market. Together, they possess a vast amount of knowledge about the intricacies of investment. However, they seldom agree on the best way to achieve anything when it comes to the stock market. While they are obviously conscientious as well as knowledgeable, they have major differences when it comes to investment philosophy and strategy.

You have six weeks before the report is due. You have already begun to familiarize yourself with the firm's current portfolio and have been provided by management with a specific set of constraints that any portfolio must satisfy. Your immediate problem is to come up with some alternatives to the firm's present practices and select the most promising alternative for detailed analysis in your report.

Some thoughts on the appraisal interview

Paul H. Thompson

I. Preparation for the interview. The appraisal interview is too important to be left to chance. The appraiser needs to be well prepared for the interview:

A. Know the person's record thoroughly. It will seriously undermine the results of the interview for the appraiser to get into the interview and find that he or she lacks important information about the appraisee's performance. Be prepared with specific information, not just a general overall evaluation.

B. Make an appointment for the interview well in advance and tell the person the purpose of the interview.

C. Arrange to hold the interview in a physical setting that will enhance the interviewing process. The basic requirement is a private room where the conversation cannot be overheard. There should be no distractions such as telephone calls or other outside interruptions.

D. Allow adequate time so the interview will not have to be terminated in the middle of an important discussion.

II. Conducting the interview:

A. Restate the purpose of the interview and indicate what is to be accomplished during the session. Do what you can to put the subordinate at ease.

B. Ask for the subordinate's opinion of his or her performance since the last appraisal.

C. Recognize the subordinate's accomplishments and contributions to the organization.

D. Identify one or two areas where performance might be improved, then ask for reactions, suggestions, etc.

E. Facilitate an open discussion of the issues that have been raised. Some suggestions on how to open up the discussion include:

1. Listen actively — Show that you are interested in what the person has to say, but most importantly, be quiet and give him or her a chance to talk.

2. Use the reflective summary — Every once in a while you can summarize what you believe to be the other person's perception of a particular situation (e.g., you're afraid you're falling behind technically?).

3. Use silence — There may be times when the subordinate appears reluctant to discuss a particular topic. If it is desirable that he or she talk more about it, silence may bring pressure on the subordinate to talk.

4. Be honest in your answers — If you are open, natural, and honest, then this helps develop similar behavior in the appraisee.

5. Minimize criticism — Criticism may evoke defensive behavior from the subordinate which may lead to argument and disagreement. However, we're not suggesting that criticism should be eliminated completely. The subordinate must know when the superior is not satisfied with progress. But too much criticism can be a threat to self-esteem and lead to lower performance.*

F. List disagreements — If possible, disagreements should be resolved before the end of the interview. But if a disagreement cannot be resolved, then perhaps an assignment involving the collection of more information on the issue may eventually lead to a resolution.

G. Summarize overall performance to put things in perspective — This will make it more likely that both individuals come away from the interview with a common understanding and set of expectations.

H. Develop a plan — Unless a plan is developed, the time and energy expended on identifying problems are likely to be wasted.

I. Document the conclusions — A good set of notes on the interview will be very helpful in preparing for the next review.

*Additional information on these ideas can be found in *Management By Objectives*, edited by S.J. Carroll, and H.C. Tosi (New York: Macmillan, 1973, pp. 94–97).

"Leadership is figuring out which way your people are going and running fast enough to get in front of them."
Gandhi

"The effective executive focuses on contribution. He looks up from his work and outward toward goals. He asks: What can I contribute that will significantly affect the performance and the results of the institution I serve?"
Peter Drucker, The Effective Executive

Managers are hired to be fired.
Sports Illustrated **(April 13, 1981)**

BILLY MARTIN, Manager

	HIRED	FIRED
Minnesota Twins	1969	1969
Detroit Tigers	1971	1973
Texas Rangers	1973	1975
New York Yankees	1975	1978
New York Yankees (Rehired)	1979	1979
Oakland A's	1980	1982
New York Yankees (Rehired)	1982	1983

CASES

Hural Corporation

Bill Rogers, a summer intern with the Hural Corporation, was contemplating his final interview with Mr. Christensen. Bill had been hired by Hural Corporation for three months as an accounting intern. He had worked during the summer with an internal auditing team supervised by Jay Randall. Bill knew that his interview would coincide with the yearly evaluation interviews that the other men on his audit team had with Mr. Christensen. Most of the men had voiced dissatisfaction with Jay Randall's conduct on audit trips, but they seemed unsure about the situation. Bill wondered whether he should mention Jay's escapades in his interview. Bill would be leaving to go back to school in a couple of weeks, but he didn't want to jeopardize his chances for full-time employment with Hural after graduation, and neither did he want to cause problems for the other men on the team.

Background

The Hural Corporation manufactured rubber products. It was a large corporation with several plants throughout the United States. The operations of every division of Hural were audited once each year. The corporation maintained twelve audit staffs — one for each division plus various specialty staffs.

Jay Randall, an accounting graduate, joined Hural Corporation at the age of 25. He worked many hours each week learning the audit procedures of the company. Jay mastered the many diversified operations of Hural quickly and within three months began auditing some of the operations himself.

The supervisor of the research and development audit staff was favorably impressed with Jay's performance and picked him as a man with a good future at Hural. Consequently, Jay was given broad exposure to different activities of the company. His first transfer came after he had been with the company a little over one year.

During the next eight years, Jay was transferred five more times within Hural Corporation. Each transfer brought new exposure and experience. However, the process of continual transfers, coupled with the travel required of the audit staff, seemed to keep Jay from passing the CPA exam. Jay, however, did pass the CIA (Certified Internal Auditor) exam and thus was able to distinguish himself as a certified internal auditor. Shortly thereafter, he was promoted to the position of auditing supervisor in the marketing division auditing staff.

After a year and a half in the position of supervisor, Jay was transferred to the San Francisco office to become the auditing supervisor in the marketing division of the Pacific region (see Exhibit 1 for an organization chart). The audit staff was responsible for auditing retail and wholesale operations of Hural Corporation in California, Arizona, Nevada,

Exhibit 1

Hural Corporation organization chart — Market division audit staff

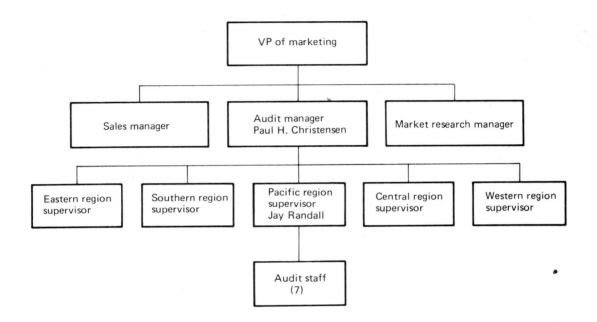

Oregon, and Washington. As auditing supervisor Jay was responsible for directing and evaluating the work of the seven people on the audit staff (see Exhibit 2). Each audit team included a head auditor, who planned and coordinated the work of the staff and reported to Jay.

After the staff compiled and wrote up the audit, Jay studied the report and reviewed it with the supervisor in charge of the operation being audited. Jay then discussed the audit in an evaluation session with Paul Christensen, the audit manager.

In addition to his auditing duties, Jay attended many corporate meetings at the middle management level. There he received various assignments and projects, most of which were not related to audit work. He also was in a position to make many decisions relating to the audit staff and review each audit assignment personally. However, Jay made no decisions with respect to salary, transfers, or promotions.

Each wholesale outlet, as well as all retail outlets, was audited once each year. The auditors did a great deal of travel while an audit was being conducted in the field. The actual audit report, however, was always written in the home office. Besides the hard data that were collected, the members of the audit staff were supposed to include any impressions they might have concerning fraud, theft, violation of company policy, and so on, in the audit report.

Jay held an informal review with each member of the audit staff every two to

Exhibit 2

Hural Corporation marketing division audit staff — Pacific Region

Name	Tenure	Family status	Professional status	Age	Education
Jay Randall	9 years 7 — other 2 — S.F.	Married 2 children	CIA, no CPA	34	B.S. — Acct.
Pat Willis	2½ years All in S.F.	Married 2 children	CPA certified	28	M.B.A. — Bus. Admin.
Dick Smith	2 years 1¾ — L.A. ¼ — S.F.	Unmarried	No CPA	25	B.S. — Acct.
Bob Hansen	1½ years 1¼ — Portland ¼ — S.F.	Unmarried	No CPA	27	B.S. — Acct.
Dave Hillam	1 year ¾ — L.A. ¼ — S.F.	Married 1 child	No CPA	24	B.S. — Acct.
Don Meyers	1 year All in S.F.	Married 2 children	CPA Needs 1 more year's experience to certify	26	B.S. — Acct.
Randy Bergess	3 months All in S.F.	Unmarried	No CPA	26	M.A. — Finance
Bill Rogers	Undergraduate intern	Married No children	No CPA	23	B.S. — Acct. (candidate)

three months. Jay also met with Mr. Christensen, the audit manager, every two weeks. Each member of the audit staff met with Mr. Christensen once a year in a formal review. Mr. Christensen made the decisions concerning promotions, raises, and transfers.

Problem

About two years after Jay had become a supervisor in San Francisco, Bill Rogers was assigned to his office as an accounting intern. Bill became a member of the team almost immediately and was soon on the road conducting an audit. Jay made the trip with the team, and Bill was somewhat surprised at his behavior. Ap-

parently Jay was quite a ladies' man. He was good looking and liked to wine and dine his girl friends. Bill was told that Jay had girl friends in most of the large cities in the region. No one knew whether Jay's wife was aware of this, but most felt that she wasn't. Dick and Bob liked to go out at night with Jay and some girls and have a good time. However, most of the time Jay went alone. One of the auditors told Bill that Jay always requested a room in the back of the motel, so that he could sneak his girl friends in at night. Bill later noticed that Jay did in fact always have a room in the rear of the motel.

Bill was also told that Jay was very little help when it came to auditing the different operations. When he went on a job with some of the auditors, he only stayed for about two hours and then he left. An auditor reported that once he returned to the motel room at lunch time and found Jay still in bed. Apparently, Jay gave instructions but did very little supervising. Opinions were expressed that, after Jay's promotion to audit supervisor, he lost his desire to work. Some said that he obtained more satisfaction from being in charge than from being involved in the mundane mechanics of audit work. Jay's current attitude seemed to be that he could now relax a little and enjoy the benefits of his previous efforts. The staff members felt that they could get more done by not having Jay with them. One auditor commented that he didn't like babysitting the boss.

Near the end of July, Dave was assigned to be the head auditor to audit the Nevada district. Dave prepared all of the audit materials and a tentative schedule showing which outlets would be audited by each auditor on each day. After submitting this schedule to Jay, Dave was told that the visit to the district office in Las Vegas would have to be postponed a week because Jay wanted to go with them to see the district manager and get the audit started. Dave and some of the other auditors were quite upset about this delay. They felt that they were being unnecessarily detained by Jay. He did not need to go. He would not accomplish anything that couldn't be done without him. Most of them felt that real reason for Jay's accompanying them was that then he could go see his favorite girl friend. Nonetheless, Dave changed the schedule to accommodate Jay's wishes.

The day after the delay of the Nevada district audit was announced, Jay informed the audit staff members that they would soon be having their yearly interview with Mr. Christensen. The interviews would be held immediately after the field work for the Nevada district audit was completed. Each person was told to discuss progress and experiences with Hural Corporation during the interview, as well as any frustrations experienced. Jay pointed out that, if any inefficiencies or problems were noted by the staff members, such items were to be discussed with Mr. Christensen. Bill wondered if any of the auditors would discuss Jay's behavior in their interviews. He also wondered if any of the district managers had mentioned anything about Jay to Mr. Christensen. These questions ran through his mind as he tried to decide what he should say in his interview.

How Iacocca won the big one

In the summer of 1961, a varying group of six to 12 men began to meet one night a week in the Fairlane Inn, a motel on Michigan Avenue in Dearborn, Mich. Their leader was Lee A. Iacocca, vice-president of Ford Motor Co. and general manager of its Ford Div. since November, 1960. Out of those meetings, free from the pressures of the office a mile or so away, came the Mustang. And out of the success of the Mustang came first a group vice-presidency, an executive vice-presidency, and finally, last week, the presidency of Ford Motor Co. for Lee Iacocca, just past his 46th birthday.

The Mustang was the great divide in Iacocca's career, a career that has brought him to the top so rapidly that the stops along the way have been blurred. Before the Mustang, he was brash, opinionated, aggressive — and unknown. When he was made vice-president, recalls Donald N. Frey, now president of General Cable Corp. and, for several incandescent years a principal Iacocca lieutenant, "half the people in the company didn't know who he was, and the other half couldn't pronounce his name." After the Mustang sold 419,000 in a 12-month period, Iacocca was brash, opinionated, aggressive — and successful. "The worst that was said of him," says Frey, "was that he would be president or be fired. The best was that he would be president."

Winning style

The motel meetings and the subsequent Mustang history were typical of Iacocca's management mode and illustrate how he rose so fast, developed his loyal team, and was able to supplant in Henry Ford II's esteem such an experienced auto man as Semon E. Knudsen, whom Chairman Ford fired as president in September, 1969, only 19 months after recruiting him from General Motors. The presidency has been vacant since then. They also hint at how he now will handle the challenges of imports and markets of the future.

The Fairlane meetings were held to study population trends, Ford's product line, the auto market, and assorted other factors. Iacocca believes in ideas, in rubbing people together to create ideas — about their own jobs or someone else's. He grabs for facts and seems to absorb them by osmosis. The "Fairlane Group" eventually decided Ford needed a new car for the young people coming into the market.

Selling a new car to the company's top men "took tremendous courage," a participant recalls. "It was so soon after the Edsel that you can imagine the cold stares." Iacocca marshaled his material, and put on a brilliant performance that convinced his hostile audience.

Iacocca had earlier demonstrated his ability to present his ideas, when, as car marketing manager of the Ford Division, he was charged with introducing the Falcon in 1959. Chase Morsey, Jr., now executive vice-president of RCA Corporation and formerly a Ford marketing executive, remembers the Falcon presentation well. "His instincts are good and he has great taste in the way things are done," he says. The Falcon performance caught the eye of Henry Ford, but Iacocca already had his sponsors in the company: Robert S. McNamara, briefly Ford president in 1960, and Charles Beecham, the man Iacocca calls his mentor.

Fast learner

Beecham, who retired a few years ago as vice-president of marketing, has a blunt and simple explanation of how and why Lee Iacocca rose so fast: "Lee learned how the wheels meshed together to make money for Ford Motor Co." Iacocca began learning under Beecham's tutelage in 1946 in the Chester (Pa.) district sales office. "The basic fundamentals in this business are how to make more money," says Beecham, "and he learned that by working with dealers." One time, Beecham sent Iacocca out to a dealer who was having sales and business problems and told him not to come back until he straightened the dealer out. It took three months.

Iacocca was still in the Chester office when he pushed a program called "56 for 56" (a 1956 Ford on a $56-a-month installment plan); most people now say Iacocca conceived the program; Beecham agrees, but with some hesitation. The program attracted the attention of McNamara, then Ford Div. general manager. When Beecham, by that time sales manager of the division, needed more staff, McNamara approved Iacocca's appointment as truck manager. "Suddenly," recalls Thomas Tierney, now head of his own Dallas-based public relations firm, but then in truck promotion, "everybody in the division began to think and talk trucks. He believes in what he is doing, and has the ability to put together a team that believes in him."

Iacocca is the first man with actual dealer selling experience at the helm of Ford Motor Co. He knows what will sell cars, though his way of selling sometimes abrades associates. After he became car marketing manager in 1957, he went hell-for-leather for racing — when the company was trying to demonstrate a concern for safety. "He knew Ford was right on the safety thing, but he knew racing would sell cars." Indeed, one Iacoccaism well known around Ford is: "You race 'em on Sunday and sell 'em on Monday."

Bookkeeping

By all accounts, Iacocca has a tremendous capacity to learn, as well as a tremendous drive to work. He is widely regarded as a marketing man, but in-

siders respect his knowledge of finance and management. One man remembers that Iacocca began keeping books on people early in his career at the Ford Div. "He would take the books over to Mr. Ford and discuss people with him."

The key book was one in which Iacocca kept a record of a manager's own objectives for each quarter, along with the manager's own grading of how he had done. Says one close associate in awe: "I looked at mine one time and it was all marked up. He actually keeps track of you."

In that way, Iacocca has built up his own team, with a nucleus of men who were with him in the Chester office: Matthew S. McLaughlin, now president of Ford Marketing Corp.; John Naughton, vice-president and general manager, Ford Div.; Bennett Bidwell, vice-president and general manager of Lincoln-Mercury Div.; Frank Zimmerman, marketing manager of Ford Div.; and J. William Benton, sales manager of Lincoln-Mercury.

He drives his men hard, and in return, he pays them well — "one year my bonus exceeded my salary," recalls an aide — and exacts fierce loyalty. He is going to need all of that. The auto industry has entered the most difficult period in its history. Detroit has not yet found the answer to competition from abroad — unless it is in Ford's Pinto and GM's Vega. The pressures for greater safety and a cleaner environment will substantially change the design and performance of cars and emphasize the cost squeeze, and yet-undetermined living patterns may demand new types of cars. The auto market abroad is growing faster than in this country.

To these problems, Iacocca brings weaknesses as well as strengths. He knows little about the foreign segments of the business, which now will come under his direction, along with the company's other operations. His bluntness is building up opponents in Washington. Along with GM President Edward N. Cole, Iacocca has been getting firmer and firmer in his public statements that the industry cannot meet the stringent 1975 antipollution requirements. He and Henry Ford have derided the air bag as a safety device, defying government opinion.

But when it comes to product and profit, Iacocca's record is sparkling — with the Mustang, Maverick, and Pinto. Few outsiders ever recognized that the Mustang's drive train — the most expensive part of the car — was largely paid for by its prior use in the Falcon, and that this helped Ford's first car named for a horse to make money like crazy.

So Iacocca watchers are confident he will come up with products to meet all problems. Says one: "He's damned smart. He knows the company and knows products. I really think the company may do some dramatic things under him."

Upheaval in the House of Ford

Power struggles are nothing new at Ford Motor Co., but the one that climaxed last week was a stunner. After weeks of futile maneuvering to save his job, Lee Iacocca, 53, the hard-driving, cigar-chomping president of the world's fourth largest manufacturing company, found himself quite bluntly sacked by his equally tough-minded boss, Chairman Henry Ford II. It was the culmination of months of behind-the-scenes quarreling between two of the auto industry's most respected — and often feared — executives. The end came for Iacocca following a day of stormy meetings of the ten-member organization committee of the company's outside directors at Ford's headquarters in Dearborn, Mich. Afterward, Iacocca denied widely published reports that he had asked his boss, "I have been with the company 32 years. What have I done wrong?" And that Ford had replied, "I just don't like you." In fact, Ford was recently heard to say, "I haven't liked you for two years."

The icily frank appraisal, like a line out of *Wheels*, sums up a relationship between two strong-willed men that was never warm and has been deteriorating for several years. "The body chemistry wasn't right," said Henry W. Gadsden, one of the several outside directors who hoped that the president could stay on. Both Ford and Iacocca can be at times charming, abrasive, cordial and arch. A clash of their personalities was all but inevitable from the moment that Ford, the celebrated heir who liked to remind subordinates that "my name is on the building," elevated Iacocca, the ambitious hired manager, to president in 1970. Early rumored to have the inside track on the job of chief executive upon Ford's retirement at the age of 65 in

1982, Iacocca made the mistake of encouraging subordinates to regard him as the dauphin. That did not sit well with Chairman Ford, who thought that Iacocca had too many rough edges, and whose company has always been headed by a member of the first family of American industry.

Ford has grown increasingly preoccupied with providing for an orderly transition before the eventual takeover of his job by another Ford — most likely his only son, Edsel, 29, an executive of Ford of Australia Ltd. The first open signs of Henry Ford's determination to nudge Iacocca aside came 15 months ago. In a maneuver that infuriated Iacocca, who throughout his presidency had alone reported directly to the chairman, Ford set up a three-man "office of the chief executive" composed of himself, Iacocca and Vice Chairman Philip Caldwell, 57.

The change diluted Iacocca's control over day-to-day operations, and sent him on a supersecret scouting mission for a possible job as assistant and heir apparent to J. Stanford Smith, chief executive of International Paper Co. The talks came to nothing. Iacocca's role at Ford was reduced still further only a month ago when Ford expanded the office of the chief executive to include his brother William Clay Ford, 53, owner of the Detroit Lions football team. At the time the internal structure of the office was modified so that Iacocca could no longer report to the chairman at all but instead had to deal through Caldwell.

In the past several weeks, Iacocca launched a fevered campaign to gather support from among the company's outside directors. Though some backed him, it was a pointless effort, since the chairman has the power to pick whomever he wishes as president.

Iacocca has been one of the most skillful managers in the auto industry's modern history. His quick decisions and his flair for styling not only brought him a spectacular rise at Ford in the early 1960s but was a key reason that the company overcame its stodgy image of earlier years. He made the Falcon a hot seller by adding bucket seats and a bigger engine as an option, captured a large piece of the youth market by making Ford cars conspicuous on the racing circuit. He is proudest of his revitalization of the company's dealer network, but industry historians may remember him most for the Mustang. He helped design the sporty car for Everyman with his own hands, and put it into production in 1964. By personally orchestrating a snappy marketing campaign, Iacocca logged 419,000 Mustang sales in the first year, still a record for new models.

The company that he leaves is in fine shape (last year sales jumped from $29 billion to $38 billion, and earnings rose from $983 million to $1.7 billion), but it will miss Iacocca's talents. Warned Ed Mulane, president of the Ford Dealer Alliance, which represents 1,200 car and truck outlets; "Iacocca is the only guy with charisma. He was able to slot in the right product at the right time."

In the past year the company has also been distracted by a series of lawsuits and reported scandals. Executives are worried by persistent rumors within the company that one top official may have misused hundreds of thousands of dollars in business-related travel expenses. In a totally unrelated matter, Henry Ford himself last month became the subject of a bizarre stockholder lawsuit by New York Attorney Roy Cohn, which accused Ford and other company officers of taking $750,000 in illegal kickbacks from a catering concern, Canteen Corp., a charge that Ford denies vigorously. The

Justice Department is also investigating allegations that Ford executives paid $900,000 to an Indonesian government official in return for an aerospace communications contract.

On top of that, Iacocca's firing could lead to further departures by managers. Almost always when a top executive is removed, his close supporters and recruits become vulnerable. Chairman Ford is said to be looking closely at a number of General Motors executives to replace some Iacocca loyalists. The automakers may be in for a period of industry wide executive raiding.

Iacocca is not the first mighty executive to be cast off by Henry Ford II. When Ford was only 27, he led other family members in a celebrated coup that forced his aged and autocratic grandfather, the original Henry Ford, to relinquish power. Then, in a series of historic confrontations in 1945, he forced the resignation of Director Harry Bennett, who to keep his own *de facto* control over the company had surrounded himself with a gang of hired thugs. In 1969 Ford unceremoniously canned President Semon ("Bunky") Knudsen, in large part at the urging of Iacocca, who was Knudsen's rival for power. When asked why he was letting Knudsen go, Ford simply answered: "It just didn't work out."

Nine years later, Lee Iacocca sat on the gold-colored couch in his office and remarked that the boss had used ironically similar words to justify his own ouster. "Mr. Ford said it's just one of those things, we're going to do it and that's it."

Mr. Upward Automobility

Lee Iacocca thought he had a better idea. An eager young sales manager in the 1950s, he figured he would pep up a dull convention of 1,100 Ford salesmen by proving in a live demonstration that if he dropped an egg from a 10-ft.-high ladder onto Ford's new crash-padded dashboard, the egg would not break. He was wrong. Until last week, that was one of the very few times that Iacocca came close to having egg on his face. After 32 years with Ford, the plain-spoken son of an Italian immigrant was a Horatio Alger — hero on wheels, a paradigm of upward automobility. Yet unlike others who have risen through the sober, polyester-clad ranks of America's most important industry, Iacocca is perpetually outspoken, fashionably dressed in European worsteds and as obviously at ease in a barroom throbbing with used-Ford salesmen as in a hearing room full of Senators. If humans can be said to have automotive analogues, Iacocca suggests nothing so much as a Ford Mustang, that stylish-yet-democratic car whose creation is perhaps Iacocca's greatest triumph.

Lido Anthony Iacocca was born in Allentown, Pa., into what can be described as a Ford family. His father drove a Model T, launched one of the nation's earliest rent-a-car agencies, made and lost several pre-

Depression fortunes by renting Fords and trading in local real estate. Young Lido decided he wanted to enter the auto business, preferably with Ford. He got an engineering degree at nearby Lehigh University, signed on with Ford as a trainee, earned a master's in engineering at Princeton and then surprised Ford recruiters by rejecting a quiet career in automatic transmissions for the tough world of sales.

In ten years as a salesman, Iacocca sold so many cars that Ford Vice-President Robert McNamara brought him to Detroit as marketing director for Ford trucks. In 1960, at the precocious age of 36, Iacocca attained what was at one time his life's goal, a Ford vice presidency (in charge of the Ford Division). It was not a complete triumph; his plan had been to be there by age 35. "He had a schedule for himself as to what amount of money he would like to be making," his wife Mary once said, "Like maybe in five years he might like to be making $5,000 and in ten years $10,000. It was on a little scrap of paper."

Though a millionaire several times over by now, he lives with his wife and younger daughter (their other daughter is at college in the East) in a comparatively modest 13-room Colonial home in suburban Bloomfield Hills, and is active in Detroit area civic and charitable groups. He likes jazz and Big Band music, but has no hobbies. His close friends tend to come from outside the auto industry, and he has made a point of avoiding the social circles of "Mister Ford," as Iacocca ad other Ford executives respectfully call their ruler. Iacocca once explained, "I don't want to be fired for something I said to Mister Ford at the 21 Club."

By that standard, Iacocca will be officially free to buy the boss a drink after Oct. 15, the day he goes off the payroll and, not coincidentally, his 54th birthday. By allowing Iacocca to stay on until then, Ford will be swelling Iacocca's annual pension to more than $100,000, though the de-hired executive is hardly the retiring type. He has given "no thought to what I'm going to do at all, literally none," he says. "Education, business, government, fishing — I don't know." He would not mind being an independent Ford dealer. "Maybe there is such a thing as a new life. I've got to do a lot of thinking about it."

Editor's note:

In November 1978, just a few months after he was fired as President at Ford, Iacocca became President of Chrysler Corporation. In the next three years Chrysler lost $3.5 billion — the largest loss of any American company in history. In 1979, it took an act of Congress to grant federal guarantees on $1.5 billion of Chrysler loans. This congressional "bailout" was, and still is, a very controversial issue. In 1982 Iacocca announced a profit for the troubled company, and in 1983 repaid the federal loan. *Time* magazine said (March 12, 1983), "Chrysler's recovery is largely Iacocca's doing, a triumph of brains, bluster and bravado." Some at Chrysler "worship the guy" and others refer to him as the "Ayatollah" Iacocca.

L. J. Summers Company

Jon Reese couldn't think of a time in the history of L. J. Summers Company when there had been as much anti-company sentiment among the workers as had emerged in the past few weeks. He knew that Mr. Summers would place the blame on him for the problems with the production workers because Jon was supposed to be helping Mr. Summer's son, Blaine, to become oriented to his new position. Blaine had only recently taken over as production manager of the company (see Exhibit 1). Blaine was unpopular with most of the workers, but the events of the past weeks had caused him to be resented even more. This resentment had increased to the point that several of the male workers had quit and all the women in the assembly department had refused to work.

The programs that had caused the resentment among the workers were instituted by Blaine to reduce waste and lower production costs, but they had produced completely opposite results. Jon knew that on Monday morning he would have to explain to Mr. Summers why the workers had reacted as they did and that he would have to present a plan to resolve the employee problems, reduce waste, and decrease production costs.

Company history

L. J. Summers Company manufactured large sliding doors made of many narrow aluminum panels held together by thick rubber strips, which allowed the door to collapse as it was opened. Some of the doors were as high as eighteen feet and were used in buildings to section off large areas. The company had grown rapidly in its early years due mainly to the expansion of the building program of the firm's major customer, which accounted for nearly 90 percent of Summers' business.

When L. J. Summers began the business, his was the only firm that manufactured the large sliding doors. Recently, however, several other firms had begun to market similar doors. One firm in particular had been bidding to obtain business from Summers' major customer. Fearing that the competitor might be able to underbid his company, Mr. Summers began urging his assistant, Jon, to increase efficiency and cut production costs.

Conditions before the cost reduction programs

A family-type atmosphere had existed at Summers before the cost reduction programs were instituted. There was little direct supervision of the workers from the front office, and no pressure was put on them to meet production standards. Several of the employees worked overtime regularly without supervision. The foremen and workers often played cards together during lunchtime, and company

Exhibit 1

L. J. Summers Company organization chart

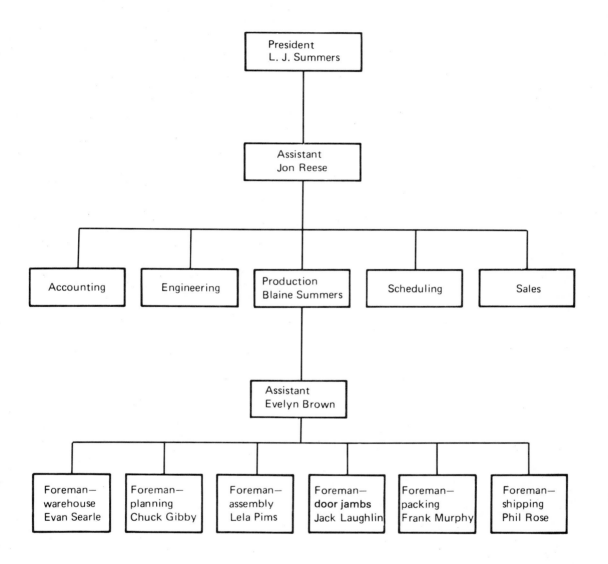

parties after work were common and popular. Mr. Summers was generally on friendly terms with all the employees, although he was known to get angry if something displeased him. He also participated freely in the daily operations of the company.

As Mr. Summers' assistant, Jon was responsible for seeing to it that the company achieved the goals established by

Mr. Summers. Jon was considered hard-working and persuasive by most of the employees and had a reputation of not giving in easily to employee complaints.

Blaine Summers had only recently become the production manager of Summers. He was in his early twenties, married, and had a good build. Several of the workers commented that Blaine liked to show off his strength in front of others. He was known to be very meticulous about keeping the shop orderly and neat, even to the point of making sure that packing crates were stacked "his way." It was often commented among the other employees how Blaine seemed to be trying to impress his father. Many workers voiced the opinion that the only reason Blaine was production manager was that his father owned the company. They also resented his using company employees and materials to build a swing set for his children and to repair his camper.

Blaine, commenting to Jon one day that the major problem with production was the workers, added that people of such caliber as the Summers' employees did not understand how important cost reduction was and that they would rather sit around and talk all day than work. Blaine rarely spoke to the workers but left most of the reprimanding and firing up to his assistant, Evelyn Brown.

Summers employed about seventy people to perform the warehousing, assembly, and door-jamb building, as well as the packing ahd shipping operations done on the doors. Each operation was supervised by a foreman, and crews ranged from three men in warehousing to twenty-five women in the assembly department. The foremen were usually employees with the most seniority and were responsible for quality and on-time production output. Most of the foremen had good relationships with the workers.

The majority of the work done at Summers consisted of repetitive assembly tasks requiring very little skill or training; for example, in the pinning department the workers operated a punch press, which made holes in the panels. The job consisted of punching the hole and then inserting a metal pin into it. Workers commented that it was very tiring and boring to stand at the press during the whole shift without frequent breaks.

Wages at Summers were considered to be low for the area. The workers griped about the low pay but said that they tried to compensate by taking frequent breaks, working overtime, and "taking small items home at night." Most of the workers who worked overtime were in the door-jamb department, the operation requiring the most skill. Several of these workers either worked very little or slept during overtime hours they reportedly worked.

The majority of the male employees were in their mid-twenties; about half of them were unmarried. There was a great turnover among the unmarried male workers. The female employees were either young and single or older married women. The twenty-five women who worked in production were all in the assembly department under Lela Pims.

The cost reduction programs

Shortly after Mr. Summers began stressing the need to reduce waste and increase production, Blaine called the foremen together and told them that they would be responsible for stricter discipline among the employees. Unless each foreman could reduce waste and improve production in his department, he would either be replaced or receive no pay increases.

The efforts of the foremen to make the workers eliminate wasteful activities and increase output brought immediate resistance and resentment. The employees' reactions were typified by the following comment: "What has gotten into Chuck lately? He's been chewing us out for the same old things we've always done. All he thinks about now is increasing production." Several of the foremen commented that they didn't like the front office making them the "bad guys" in the eyes of the workers. The workers didn't change their work habits as a result of the pressure put on them by the foremen, but a growing spirit of antagonism between the workers and the foremen was apparent.

After several weeks of no apparent improvement in production, Jon called a meeting with the workers to announce that the plant would go on a four-day, ten-hour-a-day work week in order to reduce operating costs. He stressed that the workers would enjoy having a three-day weekend. This was greeted with enthusiasm by some of the younger employees, but several of the older women complained that the schedule would be too tiring for them and that they would rather work five days a week. The proposal was voted on and passed by a two-to-one margin. Next Jon stated that there would be no more unsupervised overtime and that all overtime had to be approved in advance by Blaine. Overtime would be allowed only if some specific job had to be finished. Those who had been working overtime protested vigorously, saying that this would only result in lagging behind schedule, but Jon remained firm on this new rule.

Shortly after the meeting, several workers in the door-jamb department made plans to stage a work slowdown so that the department would fall behind schedule and they would have to work overtime to catch up. One of the workers, who had previously been the hardest working in the department, said, "We will tell them that we are working as fast as possible and that we just can't do as much as we used to in a five-day week. The only thing they could do would be to fire us, and they would never do that." Similar tactics were devised by workers in other departments. Some workers said that if they couldn't have overtime they would find a better paying job elsewhere.

Blaine, observing what was going on, told Jon, "They think I can't tell that they are staging a slowdown. Well, I simply won't approve any overtime, and after Jack's department gets way behind I'll let him have it for fouling up scheduling."

After a few weeks of continued slowdown, Blaine drew up a set of specific rules, which were posted on the company bulletin board early one Monday morning (see Exhibit 2). This brought immediate criticism from the workers. During the next week they continued to deliberately violate the posted rules. On Friday two of the male employees quit

Exhibit 2

Production shop regulations

---

1. Anyone reporting late to work will lose one half hour's pay for each five minutes of lateness. The same applies to punching in after lunch.

2. No one is to leave the machine or post without the permission of the supervisor.

3. Anyone observed not working will be noted and if sufficient occurrences are counted the employee will be dismissed.

---

because they were penalized for arriving late to work and for "lounging around" during working hours. As they left they said they would be waiting for their foreman after work to get even with him for turning them in.

That same day the entire assembly department (all women) staged a work stoppage to protest an action taken against Myrtle King, an employee of the company since the beginning. The action resulted from a run-in she had with Lela Pims, foreman of the assembly department. Myrtle was about 60 years old and had been turned in by Lela for resting too much. She became furious, saying she couldn't work ten hours a day. Several of her friends had organized the work stoppage after Myrtle had been sent home without pay credit for the day. The stoppage was also inspired by some talk among the workers of forming a union. The women seemed to favor this idea more than the men.

When Blaine found out about the incident he tried joking with the women and in jest threatened to fire them if they did not begin working again. When he saw he was getting nowhere he returned to the front office. One of the workers commented, "He thinks he can send us home and push us around and then all he has to do is tell us to go back to work and we will. Well, this place can't operate without us."

Jon soon appeared and called Lela into his office and began talking with her. Later he persuaded the women to go back to work and told them that there would be a meeting with all the female employees on Monday morning.

Jon wondered what steps he should take to solve the problems at L.J. Summers Company. The efforts of management to increase efficiency and reduce production costs had definitely caused resentment among the workers. Even more disappointing was the fact that the company accountant had just announced that waste and costs had increased since the new programs had been instituted, and the company scheduler reported that Summers was farther behind on shipments than ever before.

Fables for management: The ill-informed walrus

"**H**ow's it going down there?" barked the big walrus from his perch on the highest rock near the shore. He waited for the good word.

Down below, the smaller walruses conferred hastily among themselves. Things weren't going well at all, but none of them wanted to break the news to the Old Man. He was the biggest and wisest walrus in the herd, and he knew his business — but he had such a terrible temper that every walrus in the herd was terrified of his ferocious bark.

"What will we tell him?" whispered Basil, the second-ranking walrus. He well remembered how the Old Man had raved and ranted at him the last time the herd caught less than its quota of herring, and he had no desire to go through that experience again. Nevertheless, the walruses noticed for several weeks that the water level in the nearby Arctic bay had been falling constantly, and it had become necessary to travel much farther to catch the dwindling supply of herring. Someone should tell the Old Man; he would probably know what to do. But who? and how?

Adapted, by permission of the publisher, from "A New Look at Managerial Decision Making," Victor H. Vroom, *Organizational Dynamics, Vol. 1, #4,* Spring 1973, © 1973 by AMACOM, a division of American Management Associations. All rights reserved.

Finally Basil spoke up: "Things are going pretty well, Chief," he said. The thought of the receding water line made his heart grow heavy, but he went on: "As a matter of fact, the beach seems to be getting larger."

The Old Man grunted. "Fine, fine," he said. "That will give us a bit more elbow room." He closed his eyes and continued basking in the sun.

The next day brought more trouble. A new herd of walruses moved in down the beach, and with the supply of herring dwindling, this invasion could be dangerous. No one wanted to tell the Old Man, though only he could take the steps necessary to meet this new competition.

Reluctantly, Basil approached the big walrus who was still sunning himself on the large rock. After some small talk, he said, "Oh, by the way, Chief, a new herd of walruses seems to have moved into our territory." The Old Man's eyes snapped open, and he filled his great lungs in preparation for a mighty bellow. But Basil added quickly, "Of course, we don't anticipate any trouble. They don't look like herring-eaters to me. More likely interested in minnows. And as you know, we don't bother with minnows ourselves."

The Old Man let out the air with a long sigh. "Good, good," he said. "No point in our getting excited over nothing then, is there?"

Things didn't get any better in the weeks that followed. One day, peering down from the large rock, the Old Man noticed that part of the herd seemed to be missing. Summoning Basil, he grunted peevishly, "What's going on, Basil? Where is everyone?" Poor Basil didn't have the courage to tell the Old Man that many of the younger walruses were leaving every day to join the new herd. Clearing his throat nervously he said, "Well, Chief, we've been tightening up things a bit. You know, getting rid of some of the deadwood. After all, a herd is only as good as the walruses in it."

"Run a tight ship, I always say," the Old Man grunted. "Glad to hear that all is going so well."

Before long, everyone but Basil had left to join the new herd, and Basil realized that the time had come to tell the Old Man the facts. Terrified but determined, he flopped up to the large rock. "Chief," he said, "I have bad news. The rest of the herd has left you." The Old Walrus was so astonished that he couldn't even work up a good bellow. "Left me?" he cried. "All of them? But why? How could this happen?"

Basil didn't have the heart to tell him, so he merely shrugged helplessly.

"I can't understand it," the Old Walrus said. "And just when everything was going so well."

MORAL: What you like to hear isn't always what you need to know.

"There re no bad regiments only bad colonels."

Napoleon

"These people only work for the organization. The ones I am talking about belong to it as well. There are the ones of the middle class who have left home, spiritually as well as physically, to take the vows of organization life, and it is they who are the mind and soul of our great self-perpetuating institutions. Only a few are top managers or ever will be ... But they are the dominant members of our society nonetheless. They have not joined together into a recognizable elite — our country does not stand still long enough for that — but it is from their ranks that are coming most of the first and second echelons of our leadership, and it is their values which will set the American tempo."
William H. Whyte, Jr., The Organization Man

"All decisions should be made as low as possible in the organization. The charge of the Light Brigade was ordered by an officer who wasn't looking at the territory."
Robert Townsend, Up the Organization

It's said that a good manager may get his team between five and ten more wins a year than a middling skipper would, and a bad manager may cost his team even more games than that.
The game is basically very simple. If you get good players, you win. I've never seen a manager win a pennant. Players win pennants.
Sports Illustrated (April 13, 1981)

EXERCISES

Supervisory style exercise

While many factors can determine the effectiveness of supervisory behavior, this exercise highlights the relationship between a supervisor's assumptions about people and his or her leadership strategy.

Part of the class should develop a supervisory approach based on the first set of assumptions (Supervisor X) and another part on the second set (Supervisor Y). Then compare the strategies based on different assumptions.

Supervisor X

You are a supervisor in a manufacturing plant and are responsible for the production of a small group of workers. According to personnel manning requirements, your group is fully staffed. As far as you know, there is no problem with machine operation, and the quality of raw materials seems to be consistently high.

While your group has had a good history of satisfactory performance, in recent weeks the quality and quantity of production have both declined substantially.

On the basis of the following assumptions, which you believe to be true regarding people generally, what would you do to correct the current situation and to prevent it from recurring in the future?

1. People are basically lazy, have an inherent dislike of work, and will go to great lengths to avoid work assignments.
2. People generally must be closely controlled, directed, and threatened with punishment in order to obtain satisfactory performance.
3. People generally want to avoid responsibility and prefer the security of a less demanding job.
4. People need a clear-cut organization hierarchy with each job spelled out in great detail.

Supervisor Y

You are a supervisor in a manufacturing plant and are responsible for the production of a small group of workers. According to personnel manning requirements, your group is fully staffed. As far as you know, there is no problem with machine operation, and the quality of raw materials seems to be consistently high.

While your group has had a good history of satisfactory performance, in recent weeks the quality and quantity of production have both declined substantially.

On the basis of the following assumptions, which you believe to be true regarding people generally, what would you do to correct the current situation and to prevent it from recurring in the future?

1. People basically enjoy productive work and receive a great deal of satisfaction from making a worthwhile contribution to the organization.
2. People will exercise a great deal of self-direction and self-control in solving organizational problems and performing their job.
3. People generally will accept and seek responsibility in order to satisfy achievement and ego needs.
4. People have a great deal of untapped potential and can make a substantial contribution in defining their job.

Leadership exercise

In your attempt to achieve results through different leadership approaches, you might focus on one technique or goal. For example, you may see some leaders dealing with general directions, leaving details to subordinates. Other leaders focus on specific details with the expectation that subordinates will carry out orders. Depending on the situation, both approaches can be effective. The important issue is the ability to identify relevant dimensions of the situation and behave accordingly.

In this exercise you can identify your relative emphasis on two dimensions of leadership — "task orientation" and "people orientation." These are not opposite approaches, and an individual can be high or low on either or both.

T–P Leadership Questionnaire: An assessment of style

Goal

To evaluate oneself in terms of task orientation and people orientation.

Group size
Unlimited.

The T-P Leadership Questionnaire was adapted from Sergiovanni, Metzcus, and Bruden's revision of the Leadership Behavior Description Questionnaire, *American Educational Research Journal* 6 (1969): 62–79.

Time required

Approximately forty-five minutes.

Materials

1. T–P Leadership Questionnaire.
2. T–P Leadership-Style Profile Sheet.

Process

1. Fill out the T–P Leadership Questionnaire.
2. Before the questionnaires are scored, it may be appropriate to discuss the

concept of shared leadership as a function of the combined concern for task and people.

3. In order to locate oneself on the Leadership-Style Profile Sheet, each group participant will score his own questionnaire on the dimensions of task orientation (T) and people orientation (P).

4. The T–P Leadership Questionnaire is scored as follows:
   a. Circle the item number for items 8, 12, 17, 18, 19, 30, 34, and 35.
   b. Write the number 1 in front of a *circled item number* if you responded S (seldom) or N (never) to that item.
   c. Also write a number 1 in front of *item numbers not circled* if you responded A (always) or F (frequently).
   d. Circle the number 1's which you have written in front of the following items: 3, 5, 8, 10, 15, 18, 19, 22, 24, 26, 28, 30, 32, 34, and 35.
   e. *Count the circled number 1's.* This is your score for concern for people. Record the score in the blank following the letter P at the end of the questionnaire.
   f. *Count uncircled number 1's.* This

is your score for concern for task. Record this number in the blank following the letter T.

5. Follow directions on the Leadership-Style Profile Sheet. A discussion of implications members attach to their location on the profile would be appropriate.

Variations

1. Participants can predict how they will appear on the profile prior to scoring the questionnaire.

2. Paired participants already acquainted can predict each other's scores. If they are not acquainted, they can discuss their reactions to the questionnaire items to form some basis for this prediction.

3. The leadership styles represented on the profile sheet can be illustrated through role-playing. A relevant situation can be set up, and the "leaders" can be coached to demonstrate the styles being studied.

4. Subgroups can be formed of participants similarly situated on the shared leadership scale. These groups can be assigned identical tasks to perform. The data generated can be processed in terms of morale and productivity.

T–P Leadership Questionnaire

Directions: The following items describe aspects of leadership behavior. Respond to each item according to the way you would most likely act if you were the leader of a work group. Circle whether you would most likely behave in the described way: always (A), frequently (F), occasionally (O), seldom (S), or never (N).

A F O S N   1. I would most likely act as the spokesman of the group.

A F O S N   2. I would encourage overtime work.

A F O S N   3. I would allow members complete freedom in their work.

A F O S N   4. I would encourage the use of uniform procedures.

A F O S N   5. I would permit members to use their own judgment in solving problems.

A F O S N   6. I would stress being ahead of competing groups.

A F O S N   7. I would speak as a representative of the group.

A F O S N   8. I would needle members for greater effort.

A F O S N   9. I would try out my ideas in the group.

A F O S N   10. I would let members do their work the way they think best.

A F O S N   11. I would be working hard for a promotion.

A F O S N   12. I would tolerate postponement and uncertainty.

A F O S N   13. I would speak for the group if there were visitors present.

A F O S N   14. I would keep the work moving at a rapid pace.

A F O S N   15. I would turn the members loose on a job and let them go to it.

A F O S N   16. I would settle conflicts when they occur in the group.

A F O S N   17. I would get swamped by details.

A F O S N   18. I would represent the group at outside meetings.

A F O S N   19. I would be reluctant to allow the members any freedom of action.

A F O S N   29. I would decide what should be done and how it should be done.

A F O S N   21. I would push for increased production.

A F O S N   22. I would let some members have authority which I could keep.

A F O S N   23. Things would usually turn out as I had predicted.

A F O S N   24. I would allow the group a high degree of initiative.

A F O S N   25. I would assign group members to particular tasks.

A F O S N   26. I would be willing to make changes.

A F O S N   27. I would ask the members to work harder.

A F O S N   28. I would trust the group members to exercise good judgment.

A F O S N   29. I would schedule the work to be done.

A F O S N   30. I would refuse to explain my actions.

A F O S N   31. I would persuade others that my ideas are to their advantage.

A F O S N   32. I would permit the group to set its own pace.

A F O S N   33. I would urge the group to beat its previous record.

A F O S N   34. I would act without consulting the group.

A F O S N   35. I would ask that group members follow standard rules and regulations.

T_____ P_____

T–P Leadership-Style Profile Sheet

Name_____ Group_____

Directions: To determine your style of leadership, mark your score on the *concern for task* dimension (T) on the left-hand arrow below. Next, move to the right-hand arrow and mark your score on the *concern for people* dimension (P). Draw a straight line that intersects the P and T scores. The point at which the line crosses the *shared leadership* arrow indicates your score on that dimension.

SHARED LEADERSHIP RESULTS FROM BALANCING CONCERN FOR TASK AND CONCERN FOR PEOPLE.

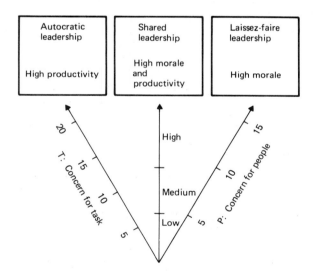

Who's in charge around here?

Those in leadership roles never have perfect information regarding people or performance. Making good decisions with limited information is a real challenge. This role play is an opportunity for you to explore the process of deciding on an acceptable strategy in an awkward situation.

Try to think and act as if you really were the character whose role you have been assigned. Think of the role in terms of contemporary implications, and let your feelings develop as if you actually were involved. Should issues develop that are not covered by the role, adapt or innovate accordingly.

To conceptualize your role, it is usually best to read it carefully two or three times; then close the book and think about it for a few minutes. Do not read the other roles; try to develop an approach in terms of the information given and your own interpretation of how a person in that position would likely behave. After you have the role in mind, do not reread it during the process of the role play.

General information

This incident takes place in a government agency in a large metropolitan area. Mr. Hall is the division manager, Cynthia is currently working as his staff assistant for special projects, and Jason is the supervisor in the department where Cynthia was previously a case worker.

Jason has been in his position for three months. He replaced Louise, who moved to another agency. One month ago Jason fired Cynthia. She immediately filed a complaint and, after a hearing by Mr. Hall, was reinstated. However, her case worker position had been filled in the meantime, and she was appointed as staff assistant to Mr. Hall, Jason's immediate superior.

Role for Jason

You are the department supervisor responsible for ten case workers and several supporting staff members. When you replaced Louise three months ago, you realized that things were very sloppy in the department. Many people were putting in six-hour days, and complaints were coming from clients and other agency units that depended on your department. After you talked to each case worker and held several department meetings, most of the staff members really went to work — all except Cynthia and one other, a man who voluntarily resigned. Cynthia acted as if she owned the place. She did a poor job with her clients, and no one in the department could stand her. Finally, after working with her for two months, you couldn't see any hope for changing her and feared that, if you didn't let her go, the morale of the unit would go down. So, you called her in and, following what you thought were the proper steps, terminated her.

Then, a few days later, she filed a complaint with Mr. Hall, your boss. Without even calling you in to discuss the issue, he considered the situation and rehired her. This made you a little suspicious. You remembered hearing that Cynthia "Had something" on Mr. Hall. Anyway, you were grateful that you had filled her slot prior to her rehiring, so that she couldn't be reassigned to your department. But instead, of all things, she was assigned to work as Mr. Hall's staff assistant.

With her appointment, morale really did go down. Everyone was saying that the way to get promoted was to do a bad job. Things were beginning to settle down until last week, when Cynthia came to your office to give you instructions on a project she was responsible for. This was too much; you blew up and told her where to go. Then Mr. Hall called to tell you that you would have to work with Cynthia. You requested to talk to him about the whole situation. You must somehow warn Hall about Cynthia — you think she will ruin his operation just as she almost ruined yours. He agreed to talk, and you are now on your way to his office.

Role for Mr. Hall

One thing after another! Why can't your department supervisors do their job and quit griping over every little thing! Jason, one of your new supervisors, who is sort of on trial, has just requested a conference to complain about your staff assistant, Cynthia. So, you guess you will have to talk to him.

Before he comes in, you try to reconstruct in your mind the events preceding the incident. Jason took over a pretty good department from Louise, who left to take a better job. At first you thought he would be OK. He did eliminate some recurring problems, but then you started getting a few complaints. One guy quit and wrote a nasty letter to you, claiming that Jason would ruin the department. You assumed this was sour grapes. Then Cynthia, whom you have known for some time, said that things were really bad and that anyone who showed any initiative was suppressed. In fact, Jason seemed irritated by anyone who moved out on his or her own. Anyway, he did a dumb thing when he fired Cynthia. He didn't even follow the civil service procedure. In addition, all of Cynthia's performance reports said she was exceptional. You couldn't fire someone who didn't have even one bad mark in her personnel file.

Cynthia filed a complaint and came in to talk to you. You had always thought she had a lot of potential, and because a formal hearing would reinstate her anyway, you decided to hire her as your staff assistant.

That turned out to be a great move. She has taken responsibility for many projects, followed up on them, and relieved you of several troublesome details. Everything is going well except for Jason. His department has shown steady improvement in several areas, but in situations where he must occasionally work with Cynthia, he seems totally unwilling to cooperate. This can't go on, and so you have agreed to talk to him about the problem and resolve it once and for all. Because Cynthia is involved in the whole thing, you have invited her to join the meeting. Both of them are on their way to your office.

Role for Cynthia

For the last three weeks you have been working as a staff assistant for special projects. Your boss, Mr. Hall, is a great guy to work for, and he supports you whenever you have a problem with any of the department supervisors. This job is a great improvement over your previous assignment as a case worker under Jason.

You are not exactly sure what happened when you were working under Jason, but somehow you think he was out to get you. Things were great when Louise was department supervisor. Everyone got along well. Then Jason came in and really turned things upside down. He kept the staff so long in meetings that no one ever had time to do his or her job. Jason seemed to give you ten things to do at once, and then he blew up when you didn't get them all done. He

harassed another case worker so much that the poor guy had to quit, or have a nervous breakdown. Morale and efficiency dropped, and finally you had a little discussion with Mr. Hall, whom you knew socially, to tell him what was going on. Mr. Hall said he would look into it. You think Jason found out, because the next day he told you you were through.

You waited a couple of days and then filed a complaint with Mr. Hall. He called you in, listened carefully to your account, and then told you he would be glad to have you come to work for him. Besides, Jason had not followed proper procedures for termination.

Things went well until you had to contact Jason in connection with a project. When you went to talk to him, he acted as though he had gone crazy. He told you to get out of his office and never come back. You reported this to Mr. Hall, who called Jason to straighten things out. This didn't seem to solve the problem, and Jason requested a conference with Mr. Hall. Because you are a central figure in the whole thing, Mr. Hall invited you to join in. You are on your way to Mr. Hall's office.

In the future people may demand more than a formal role; they want genuine meaning in relationships

"Of course I love you. I'm your husband. That's my job!"

5

Survival and growth in organizations of the future

I n a time of declining productivity, increasing foreign competition, frequent plant closings, and record numbers of bankruptcies, organizations can no longer just assume that they will continue to grow or even that they will survive. Developments in our society are forcing organizations to change at an ever-increasing rate. Pressures for change come from many different directions.

Consumer groups have demanded safer, pollution-free, and more reliable products at lower prices. Their activities include class action suits against automobile manufacturers, product boycotts, and requests for drug recalls, increased airline safety, and more specific labeling information.

Another source of change is employees. Almost daily we find a new group pressing its demands: public school teachers strike, farm workers demonstrate for a more livable wage, air traffic controllers participate in a work slowdown. Employees, individually and in groups, have long been active in encouraging organizations to change.

The number of state and federal government agencies pressing for change has increased dramatically in recent years: the Equal Employment Opportunity Commission enforces affirmative action in the hiring and promoting of minorities and women; the Environmental Protection Agency is trying to reduce water and air pollution; the Occupational Safety and Health Act was passed to require employers to make workplaces safer for employees; the National Labor Relations Board can require a company to bargain collectively with a certified bargaining agent.

Special-interest groups, such as the Sierra Club, the Veterans of Foreign Wars, the American Medical Association, the NAACP, and Common Cause, have adopted a variety of strategies to change organizations (The list of interested groups also includes foreign governments, suppliers, stockholders, political parties, and the like.) They have used the courts to force organizations to respond to their wishes. They have used demonstrations, published reports on abuses, boycotted other organizations, lobbied state and federal legislatures, and engaged in mass media campaigns.

Organizations that respond well to environmental pressures survive and grow. Other organizations, less responsive to changes in their environment, become less competitive. For example, major changes in federal regulation of the airline industry during the late 1970s brought new challenges and problems to companies in the United States. Why were some firms able to respond quickly to these changes and continue as viable operations while other firms were slow to respond? There is no simple answer. But, as we have suggested, there are many pressures for change, and an organization needs a strategy for responding to those pressures.

A simple cone can help us think about the process of coping with environment.

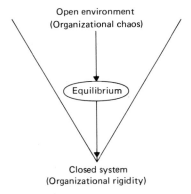

The top of the cone represents the openness of the environment and the almost unlimited resources (e.g., products, technologies, ideas, organization structures, assumptions) that the organization can use to cope with its environment. As an organization adopts a strategy with its accompanying limitations, it is forced to move down the cone into a more structured situation affording fewer alternatives. Ideally, an organization reaches a point of equilibrium if it acquires sufficient structure to operate effectively but retains adequate flexibility to cope with environmental pressures for change. As the organization loses its ability to cope, it encounters serious difficulty and may eventually die. In fact, because of external variables, self-imposed restrictions, and rigidity, the natural tendency of an organization is to die. Only through great skill on the part of its members can an organization achieve equilibrium with its environment and avoid death.

But how can managers and employees help their organizations find equilibrium and be appropriately responsive to the environment? The materials in this section were selected to present concepts and ideas for thinking about these issues.

The first article in this section, "A New Era for Management," describes the impact that the technological revolution is having on people in organizations. Initially middle managers are feeling the greatest pain, but eventually people at all levels will be affected. Adaptation to radical changes will be a major challenge in the 1980s. Dyer presents several concepts to help people think about change including the processes that are likely to be present in successful organizational change. A major problem in organizations is a tendency for people to resist change. Kotter and Schlesinger describe four basic reasons why people resist change. They also describe various methods for dealing with the resistance and provide a guide to what kinds of approaches will work when the different types of resistance occur. In the next article Sherwood presents a brief description of some of the objectives, assumptions, and technologies of organization development (OD), a widely used practice for managing planned change in organizations.

One of the major developments of the 1970s and 1980s is a significant change in the relationship between individuals and organizations. Woodworth explores one aspect of that change in an article titled "Hard Hats in the Boardroom." He summarizes processes for formally increasing worker participation in the management and control of the business enterprise. Cray provides an account of the efforts of one major corporation to be socially responsible. The increasing emphasis on social responsibility of business reflects the growing awareness that organizations not only adapt to, but also affect, people in their environments. The next three articles look at current and future issues for blacks and women in organizations. Schwartz and Rago describe some of the problems male executives have had in accepting women as peers. They suggest policies and actions that will help organizations to move toward a greater sense of equality between men and women. The article, "Breaking Through: Women on the Move," describes the progress that women have made in the last decade in their efforts to achieve equality in the workplace. The article includes stories of six women who have demonstrated that it is possible for women to reach high levels in almost any career. The article from *Black Enterprise* lists the best companies to work for from the point of view of their overall commitment to equal opportunity. In this article Gayle and Gray identify the factors that determine the success of affirmative action programs. Hines approaches this issue from a different perspective. He takes the viewpoint of black workers and presents some typical situations that they are confronted with in organizations. Improving one's skill in race relations should be a high priority for all students of behavior in organizations. Finally, Ritchie and Gregersen suggest an attitude toward change that will help people to develop a more constructive approach to the future. They present some concepts which might provide insight regarding the fast-moving and complex environment in which we live. The organizational profile exercise enables a student to analyze some organization with which he or she is familiar and identify areas where change might be needed. Four of the cases illustrate the point that there may be problems in bringing about change in organizations — whether a change in technology (Hovey and Beard), in police officers' uniforms (Metropolitan Police Department), in a computer system (Builders Plumbing and Heating Supply), or in integrating more women into the professional work force (DMG Corporation). One case explores the problems that people encounter when they move to another culture and then return to their home country (Universal Bank).

Change is often painful, and therefore many people try to avoid it. But there is no way to avoid change. People in organizations need to find ways to deal with the challenge of change; otherwise, they and their organizations will become less effective — or worse! Reading and discussing materials and concepts in this section is at least a first step in equipping individuals for that challenge.

A new era for management

As companies grew rapidly after World War II, middle management — whose function was to turn the policy decisions of top managment into the dollars and cents of revenues — grew even faster. And their function changed. More and more, they became collectors of information, which they then analyzed, interpreted, and passed on to top executives. The staff middle manager did not run anything: He was merely supposed to advise others on strategic planning, marketing, engineering, and manufacturing. But from that position he gradually came to dominate the line operations that produced and sold the goods and services that brought in the company's dollars.

Suddenly, that is being turned upside down. The onrushing electronics revolution is changing the role of the middle manager and forcing a radical restructuring of the corporation's middle ranks, shrinking them drastically in the best-managed companies. Just as the industrial revolution changed hierarchies, radicalized labor, realigned political forces, and created widespread social and psychological disruption, the technological revolution is producing pain and strain. The initial impact is being felt by the middle manager, who typically earns $25,000 to $80,000. And, as in the earlier upheaval, the woes overshadow even the most glowing promises of the future.

Redundant

Ironically, many of those in the first skirmishes have not yet perceived the magnitude of the revolution. It started with modest modernization of bookkeeping chores — the purchase of computers for data processing — and quickly gathered steam. Now it is being fueled by hard times. As more top managers see that much of the information once gathered by middle managers can be obtained faster, less expensively, and more thoroughly by computers, they have begun to view many middle managers as "redundant." They look on the very fiefdoms they have created as vast cost centers, contributing little to profits and much to overhead. Where once they eagerly added to staff as symbols of their power, today they enviously eye Japanese competitors who all along realized that less meant more.

That attitude is showing up in employment patterns. Eugene E. Jennings, a professor at Michigan State University, estimates that one-third of the 100 largest U.S. industrial companies are paring management, and there are clear signs that others will follow. The Bureau of Labor Statistics places unemployment among managers and administrators in nonfarm industries at its highest levels since World War II. And that does not include the thousands of managers who accepted early retirement or opened their own businesses.

To be sure, the severe recession has contributed to cutbacks. But relatively slow economic growth is likely to be a fact of life throughout the 1980's. The average annual rate for the decade will be only 2.3 percent, according to Data Resources Inc. Competition from abroad is increasing, too. And executives are realizing that only the leanest, fittest companies will survive through the rest of the century.

Economic necessity and technological forces are thus combining to keep a permanent crunch on middle managers. And some of the broad implications of that are beginning to emerge:

• Corporate structure is changing to accomodate broader information gathering and to let data flow from shop floor to executive suite without the editing, monitoring, and second-guessing that have been the middle manager's function.

• Middle managers who survive find their roles expanded and their functions changed. Generalists, not specialists, are needed, as companies demand solutions to interdisciplinary problems.

• Fewer business-school graduates are hired; those who are find the ladder harder to climb. As corporate pyramids are flattened, with fewer levels, there are more lateral moves and lowered expectations.

• Marketplace and manufacturing decisions are made by first-line managers, whose power had been eroded by staff. Foremen now serve in pivotal roles, managing better-educated, more demanding workers and knitting maintenance, engineering, and personnel managers into integrated operating teams.

• Business education will focus less on analysis, financial maneuvers, and gamesmanship and more on teaching manufacturing, marketing, and computer skills. For the next generation, retraining will become as important as initial training.

• Displaced managers will need safety nets as their health and pension benefits are lost. Many will find it impossible to maintain their standards of living. Higher drug and alcohol abuse and family problems are reflecting the psychological devastation of this group.

• Middle managers, who have traditionally been politically conservative, may become radicalized under pressure, demanding welfare benefits they once only grudgingly conceded to the poor.

It is becoming clear that the restructuring is essential if companies are to survive in the tougher environment. Yet the hard choices for top managers are equally clear. No matter the cost, they must be able to react quickly to change, push their companies to be more productive, and upgrade their products as rapidly as technology dictates.

Recognizing this, experts are beginning to see that organizations and cultures must be overhauled and even rebuilt. Indeed, helping companies accomplish this appears to be replacing strategic planning as the new growth business of such big consultants as McKinsey & Co. and Booz, Allen & Hamilton Inc. "Implementation — making a strategy happen — is increasingly what consulting is all about," says John M. Harris, a Booz-Allen senior vice-president. "Companies have had to rethink a lot of things they've done over the last 20 to 30 years in adding staff, middle management, and analytical jobs," says Daniel M. Glasner of Hay Management Consultants. "What they're saying is, 'We used to do without these things. The recession is forcing us to do without them. And we'll continue to do without them in the future.' "

The new heroes

That view is pervading executive suites. Declares Rene C. McPherson, retired chairman of Dana Corp.; "The fat is not going to come back." Even with an economic upturn, increased competition means every penny counts. So cuts in middle-management staffs of old-line companies, ranging, for example, from 20 percent at Firestone and Crown Zellerbach to 40 percent at Chrysler, are not likely to be reversed. Indeed, they might deepen.

Even industries anticipating steady, albeit slower, growth have slashed staff. Texaco, Exxon, and Mobil have cut planning and marketing staffs, while Alcoa, with demand growth averaging 3 percent per year — down from 8 percent in the 1960s and early 1970s — trimmed total management by about 15%. Mergers have resulted in still more reductions. Allied's alliance with Bendix and Occidental Petroleum's with Cities Service, for example, have made or probably will make scores of middle managers superfluous.

Those who remain find little security. Instead of serving as monitors of operations, staff managers are now servants of the divisions they ruled, and they must justify their existence. The new corporate heroes actually make, sell, or service products, and are rewarded on how well those jobs are done.

"The 1980s will be a decade in which manufacturing and line operations will be stressed much more than in the last 20 years," notes Robert S. Kaplan, dean of Carnegie-Mellon University's Graduates School of Industrial Administration.

Adds Jack F. Reichert, president of Brunswick Corp.: "We've been rewarding bookkeepers as if they created wealth. U.S. business has to make more beans rather than count them several times.

At some companies these sentiments have been put into action. General Electric Co.'s new chairman is John F. Welch Jr., an engineer who built the company's plastic business. Picked by his predecessor, Reginald Jones, a financial expert who had made a careful study of the technological needs of the future. Welch was chosen because he demonstrated entrepreneurial and technical abilities. General Motors Corp.'s president, F. James McDonald, is using his engineering and managerial skills in an effort to improve car quality.

These leaders share a common background and value system: They all have operating experience, and they have succeeded in the new environment, assimilating new technology into products and forging blue-and white-collar workers into teams. They respect accomplishment and promote accordingly. Typical is James A. Meehan's rise at GE (box).

If Meehan is the new corporate hero, less accomplished managers are viewed as enemies. Within weeks of assuming control of Honeywell's computer operation, Vice-Chairman James J. Renier lopped off 1,371 staff and other middle managers. Says Renier: "There are two ways of managing: One requires a lot of useless staff, and the other lets people do their jobs and tell you what expertise they need. If you've got a staff that is either trying to do the line job or has turned into a large group of scorekeepers, you had better get rid of that staff."

"People who make decisions, not recommendations," are the only middle

'You get a sense that you
own the business'

*James A. Meehan, 41, who is leading
General Electric Co.'s push into robot-
ics, exemplifies the kind of middle
manager that Chairman John F. Welch
Jr. wants others to emulate. The engineer helped build GE's European
semi-conductor business and led a
small group that developed a low-
cost appliance motor. To an ever-
increasing extent, says Meehan,
"you get a sense that you own the
business. What that means is that
you're going to spend a lot less
time worrying about whose toes
you're going to tread on and much
more time worrying about how
you're going to move that business
forward."*

managers currently in demand, reports J. Gerald Simmons, president of Handy Associates Inc., a New York-based executive recruiter. Even McKinsey, one of the management consultants famous for hiring MBAS, is shifting its recruiting focus from business schools to industry.

Freedom to err

But cultures are hard to change. In its battle to become more competitive, Xerox Corp. has had to fight its entrenched system. Managers are still reluctant to use their newfound authority for fear of being second-guessed. Executive Vice-President William F. Glavin recalls a line vice-president vacillating over a pricing move because it differed from the view of the staff man who once made such decisions. "The corporate culture change is huge," Glavin acknowledges.

So even when GE's Welch warns his managers that there is room only for the "better than the best," that does not guarantee instant compliance. Freedom to make decisions brings with it freedom to make mistakes, and middle managers want to see what the penalties are before they embrace the new autonomy. Asked to take new risks, they fear reprisals if their performance falls off. Even managers whose specialties are in strong demand have to worry. Stan B. Osenar, director of data processing at Medical Mutual of Cleveland Inc., somberly notes that "even the computer jock is no longer immune. I am safer than a sales district manager, but both of us live and die by our performance."

To make good decisions today, managers must deal with several issues, including the internationalization of their markets, complex financial transactions, and the impact of technology on their products. Technology is also changing the very nature of and need for middle management jobs. Sales staff in industries ranging from brokerages to pharmaceuticals are, or soon will be, consulting their computers — rather than their managers — for pricing, inventory, and market information. With less paperwork, sales managers can cover larger territories and get faster feedback on performance and problems. Similarly, computer-aided design and manufacturing allowed Chrysler Corp. to halve its engineering group to 4,000 without sacrificing its product-development programs.

Only one element could reverse such cuts: an information-management staff that would rival in size the middle-management group it replaces. Many companies are determined to avoid that pitfall. GE's Drive Systems Div. uses a single data base for all departments to prevent a rise in "infocrat" empires. "The biggest single thing that will make information technology a monster is if information bureaucracies grow up in each function," says Donald E. Dane, GE's manager for corporate organizational planning.

Nowhere to climb

Other problems are not as tractable. Fewer managment layers mean fewer chances for promotions. "It used to be if you weren't promoted in two years, you weren't on the fast track. But the rapid promotions are ending. We're looking at two to five years, and we won't (promote) sooner unless it's vitally important," says

---

*'All of a sudden you
don't have to be anywhere'*

You might say I feel rootless, like I'm drifting or floating," says Jack L. Shanafelt, 49, who was, until last September, a $50,000-a-year district sales manager at B.F. Goodrich Co. in Akron. Notes Shanafelt: Eight years ago Goodrich had 18 district managers. Two years ago there were 10. Last June there were six. "It's the first time in my life I haven't been attached to something. For 25 years, you get up at 6. All of a sudden you ... don't have to be anywhere," he says. He has searched and searched and found nothing remotely comparable to his old job. "If I were to start analyzing all of this, I would wind up in a deep depression."

Gerald G. Carlton, vice president for human resources at Diamond Shamrock Corp.

But this creates new problems. "We can't afford to have a person between the ages of 28 and 35 spend five years on one job, (but) it's hard in our culture today to get people to move laterally," concedes GE's Kane. Adds Howard V. Knicely, vice-president for human relations at TRW Inc.: "American business must escape the syndrome that everything must go up, including people."

All these trends mean that middle managment jobs are becoming tougher, more competitive, and less secure. "It used to be that there was always another rung in the ladder. For many, there is no longer anywhere to climb," mourns a manager in Ohio who was fired and had to settle for a much lower salary.

The fallout will hurt companies as well. Only a few have established retraining programs. Warns Walter K. Joelson, chief economist at GE: "How to get rid of unwanted workers is the name of the game right now. But 7 to 10 years from now it will be tough to find the people we want to hire." Unless companies and universities face up to this, declares Columbia Business School Dean John C. Burton, "we will be writing off a whole generation." One thing is certain: Revolutions never retreat. They may collapse, but considering the impetus behind the electronics revolution, these early changes may represent only the first tremors of an earthquake.

Planned change

William Dyer

Almost everyone would like to be an expert in planned change at one time or another. We are often in a position where we would consciously like to produce change in certain conditions or people. Parents sometimes want their children to change their behavior, and teachers, bosses, ministers, and administrators desire at times to see change or improvement in the performance of students, members, or workers. Managers in organizations sometimes long for an upturn in profits, quality of product, amount of service, or amount of production. And usually, if the need for change is strong enough, we try to do something to stimulate, encourage, direct, or influence the desired changes to occur. What kinds of change strategies actually work, and which lead us into unproductive pathways?

Force field analysis

During World War II, the government of the United States became interested in an area of change. At the time meat was rationed, and scarce ration stamps were required to secure the choice cuts of meats — roasts, steaks, and chops. Other cuts of meat were not rationed (liver, brain, tongue, heart), but for a variety of reasons people would not use them. Kurt Lewin, a professor at the University of Iowa, was asked to do some research on planned change. The issue:

Was it possible to get housewives to change their meat buying and eating habits and to start using these nonrationed products? With his research assistants, Lewin set up some experimental conditions. Some housewives were put in groups that listened to "attractive lectures ... which linked the problem of nutrition with the war effort, emphasized the vitamin and mineral value of the (nonrationed) meats ... Both the health and economic aspects were stressed. The preparation of these meats was discussed in detail ... Mimeographed recipes were distributed" (Lewin 1958). Yet despite all these extensive efforts, only 3 percent of the women who heard the lectures served any of the nonrationed cuts of meats.

Other housewives were asked to participate in discussion groups and were requested to discuss food, nutrition, and the war effort — to see what housewives could do to assist in this area. Following the discussion sessions it was found that 32 percent of the women served at least one of the previously avoided products. Apparently something happened in the group sessions that was not present in the lectures to produce change. Lewin's own analysis indicates he felt the differences were due to (1) the degree of involvement of people in the discussion and decision, (2) the motivation in actually being a party to the decision, and (3) group influence and support of others in reinforcing the decision.

From this and other similar research, Lewin developed a model for analyzing the planned-change process. He visualized any existing condition as in a state of balance or equilibrium (with some fluctuation) locked between two sets of forces — driving and restraining. He called his model of counterbalancing forces "force field analysis."

In Lewin's meat-eating problem, the restraining forces that kept housewives from buying and using the nonrationed meats seemed to be taste, smell, appearance, family reactions, low status attached to eating these meats, lack of approval by others, and lack of information about preparation. Driving forces that pushed toward change were patriotism, hunger, nutrition, no stamps needed, new experience. Apparently drive was not enough to overcome the strength of resistance.

Change strategies

Given the field-of-forces model, there are really three basic change strategies:
1. *Increase* the driving forces.
2. *Decrease* the restraining forces.
3. Do both.

There is good evidence to suggest that just increasing the driving forces results in a certain degree of increased resistance, and it may not maintain the change unless pressure is constantly applied. According to Lewin, change occurs when the existing situation could be "unfrozen," moved to a new level, and then "refrozen" at the new position. Just applying more pressure does not seem adequate to get the change fixed or refrozen at the new level.

More appropriate is the strategy of either reducing or eliminating restraints, or even better, moving previously restraining forces around to the driving side. In the meat-eating case, the lecture made an effort to put more pressures on — appealing to patriotism, helping the war effort, and trying to reduce the one restraint of lack of preparation knowledge by passing out recipes.

The group discussion–decision method changed peer-group pressure from a restraining force to a driving force. Women who formerly had been uneasy about the reactions of their peers were now getting support from those very peers. Even the group-process method was not strong enough to overcome the resistance forces, for more than 65 percent of the women still would not use the undersirable cuts of meat.

Force Field Analysis — Model of an Existing Condition

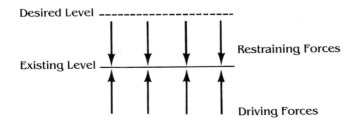

Force field analysis and action research

In more recent years a systematic method for planning change has emerged. It is called *action research* and can be related to Lewin's earlier model. Action research involves the following steps and follows what would need to be done if one were to utilize Lewin's model:

1. *Define the problem and determine the change goals*

In planned change one moves from the existing situation, which is seen as a "problem" or a condition to be altered. The change target or goal is also identified. Lewin's model suggests the same beginning.

2. *Gather the data*

In order to determine what the *real* forces in the situation are, it is important to gather accurate information about both resistance forces and positive factors. If possible, it is helpful to learn which forces are most critical and which are amenable to change. Some factors may be open to change but are really not important, and some very important forces may be outside the ability of people to influence to any greater degree. Data gathering may be accomplished by interviews, questionnaires, instruments, or direct observations in which the data about the forces in the situation are collected. However it is done, the results are fed back into the system as the basis for achieving change.

3. *Summarize and analyze the data*

After being accumulated, the data are put into some type of summary form. For larger amounts of data, sophisticated computer and statistical analyses may be necessary. For interviews or direct observations, dominant "themes" or issues mentioned by several respondents should be identified. Analysis of the data should help determine which factors are most important, which are amenable to change, which cannot be influenced or modified, and which have the greatest probability for lending themselves to a successful change endeavor.

4. *Plan the action*

Following analysis of the data, the plan of action to be utilized is prepared. In a good action plan the following matters are considered:

   a. Who are the significant people who need to support a change program?

   b. Where should action taking begin?

   c. Who should be assigned to take what specific action?

   d. When should first reports of action be prepared for review?

   e. What resources (time, money, equipment, personnel) are needed for the change program?

   f. What is the estimated completion time?

5. *Take action*

After the plan of action has been carefully worked out, the next logical step is to put the plan into effect. Lewin's model would encourage the following in the action-taking stage:

   a. Work on reducing restraining forces.

   b. Involve people in planning their own change.

   c. Develop social supports for change.

   d. Get people to make their own decisions to change.

6. *Evaluate*

Any good action research program has built into it the criteria for its own success. How do you know if you have reached your goals? Goals should be stated in such a way that evaluation criteria are evident and easily applied. For example, if an organization stated its change goal as "improve communications," its success would be very difficult to measure. Any increase in talking could be said to "improve communications." A more measurable goal would be one like this: "Have every manager conduct a sharing and evaluation session with each of his subordinates every three months." Measurement is possible to see if this change goal has been achieved. If not, recycling the action-research model must be initiated: gathering new data, analyzing it, and repeating the whole process.

Conditions of successful change

In planning a change program, it would be well to check the change plan against the findings of Gene Dalton (1970). He reviewed most of the literature on personal and organizational change and identified the following six conditions associated with successful change efforts:

1. There was a strongly felt need, tension, or "hurt" that moved people to want to change.
2. The person assisting in change was highly esteemed by the persons involved in changing.
3. The change effort moved from general proposals to specific plans and workable subgoals.
4. The change plan increased the self-esteem of the people who were changing.

5. The change plan resulted in new social ties or reformulation of old ties around new behaviors and attitudes.
6. The people changing shifted from an external motive for changing to an internal understanding and commitment.

The change plan should include as many of the above elements as are feasible, given the conditions surrounding the change effort.

Change and anxiety

An important consideration in implementing a change plan is coping with the anxiety that results, particularly when the initiation of the change at first results in an even less productive effort. Early research by Coch and French (1948) found that even under the best of change conditions, when workers are asked to change assignments and begin new, unfamiliar work, their production falls off. This dropoff in performance is usually accompanied by an increase in anxiety on the part of those who began the change program: an anxiety gap (see diagram) develops.

At the point of heightened anxiety and decreasing performance, there is a terrible tendency to want to cancel out the whole change effort and return to the earlier state; for, as bad as it was, it seems better than the new condition. There are times when a change program

Anxiety Gap

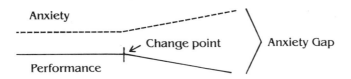

is not well conceived and should be cancelled, but if it has been based on data, the people changing have been involved in choosing the change, plans have been thought through, and people are committed to them, the major issue is to manage the anxiety — not the change. The Coch-French study found that in motor skill performance it takes about two weeks for a turnaround in peformance to occur. In some other areas it may take many months before improvement is noticeable. One manages his anxiety best by talking honestly about his concerns, reviewing the progress and the plans, and making additional modifications as needed. No one can guarantee the success of every change program. There will always be elements of risk and surprise and sometimes failure. One plans for change because action seems a better course than inaction. If the plan is well conceived, initiated, and carried out, the chances for success seem better than the slow erosion of a deteriorating situation where nothing is done.

Choosing strategies for change

John P. Kotter and Leonard A. Schlesinger

"From the frying pan into the fire," let sleeping dogs lie," and "you can't teach an old dog new tricks" are very well-known sayings born of the fear of change. When people are threatened with change in organizations, similar maxims about certain people and departments are trotted out to prevent an altercation in the status quo. Fear of change is understandable, but because the environment changes rapidly, and it has been doing so increasingly, organizations cannot afford not to change. One major task of a manager, then is to implement change, and that entails overcoming resistance to it. In this article, the authors describe four basic reasons people resist change. They also describe various methods for dealing with the resistance and provide a guide to what kinds of approaches will work when the different types of resistance occur.

Mr. Kotter is associate professor of business administration at the Harvard Business School. His most recent books include *Self Assessment and Career Development* (with Victor Faux and Charles McArthur, Prentice-Hall, 1978), as well as *Power in Management* (AMACOM, 1979). Mr. Schlesinger is assistant professor in organizational behavior at the Harvard Business School. He and Mr. Kotter are coauthors, with Vijay Sathe, of *Organization* (Richard D. Irwin, 1979) and *Managing the Human Organization* (Dow Jones-Irwin, 1979).

"**I**t must be considered that there is nothing more difficult to carry out, nor more doubtful of success, nor more dangerous to handle, than to initiate a new order of things" (Mauhiavelli).

In 1973, The Conference Board asked 13 eminent authorities to speculate what significant management issues and problems would develop over the next 20 years. One of the strongest themes that runs through their subsequent reports is a concern for the ability of organizations to respond to environmental change. As one person wrote: "It follows that an acceleration in the rate of change will result in an increasing need for reorganization. Reorganization is usually feared, because it means disturbance of the status quo, a threat to people's vested interests in their jobs, and an upset to established ways of doing things. For these reasons, needed reorganization is often deferred, with a resulting loss in effectiveness and an increase in costs." (Bower and Walton 1973).

Subsequent events have confirmed the importance of this concern about organizational change. Today, more and more managers must deal with new government regulations, new products, growth, increased competition, technological developments, and a changing work force. In response, most companies or divisions or major corporations find that they must undertake moderate organizational changes at least once a year and major changes every four or five (Allen 1978).

Few organizational change efforts tend to be complete failures, but few tend to be entirely successful either. Most efforts encounter problems; they often take longer than expected and desired, they sometimes kill morale, and they often cost a great deal in terms of managerial time or emotional upheaval. More than a few organizations have not even tried to initiate needed changes because the managers involved were afraid that they were simply incapable of successfully implementing them.

In this article, we first describe various causes for resistance to change and then outline a systematic way to select a strategy and set specific approaches for implementing an organizational change effort. The methods described are based on our analyses of dozens of successful and unsuccessful organizational changes.

Diagnosing resistance

Organizational change efforts often run into some form of human resistance. Although experienced managers are generally all too aware of this fact, surprisingly few take time before an organizational change to assess systematically who might resist the change initiative and for what reasons. Instead, using past experiences as guidelines, managers all too often apply a simple set of beliefs — such as "engineers will probably resist the change because they are independent and suspicious of top management." This limited approach can create serious problems. Because of the many different ways in which individuals and groups can react to change, correct assessments are often not intuitively obvious and require careful thought.

Of course, all people who are affected by change experience some emotional turmoil. Even changes that appear to be "positive" or "rational" involve loss and uncertainty (1973). Nevertheless, for a number of different reasons, individuals or groups can react very differently to change — from passively resisting it, to aggressively trying to undermine it, to sincerely embracing it.

To predict what form resistance might take, managers need to be aware of the four most common reasons people resist change. These include: a desire not to lose something of value, a misunderstanding of the change and its implications, a belief that the change does not make sense for the organization, and a low tolerance for change.

Parochial self-interest

One major reason people resist organizational change is that they think they will lose something of value as a result. In these cases, because people focus on their own best interests and not on those of the total organization, resistance often results in "policies" or "political behavior." (Zaleznik and Kets de Vries 1975; Miles 1978). Consider these two examples:

• After a number of years of rapid growth, the president of an organization decided that its size demanded the creation of a new staff function — New Product Planning and Development — to be headed by a vice-president. Operationally, this change eliminated most of the decision-making power that the vice-presidents of marketing, engineering, and production had over new products. Inasmuch as new products were very important in this organization, the change also reduced the vice-presidents' status which, together with power, was very important to them.

During the two months after the president announced his idea for a new product vice-president, the existing vice-presidents each came up with six or seven reasons the new arrangement might not work. Their objections grew louder and louder until the president shelved the idea.

• A manufacturing company had traditionally employed a large group of personnel people as counselors and "father confessors" to its production employees. This group of counselors tended to exhibit high morale because of the professional satisfaction they received from the "helping relationships" they had with employees. When a new performance appraisal system was installed, every six months the counselors were required to provide each employee's supervisor with a written evaluation of the employee's "emotional maturity," "promotional potential," and so forth.

As some of the personnel people immediately recognized, the change would alter their relationships from a peer and helper to more of a boss and evaluator with most of the employees. Predictably, the personnel counselors resisted the change. While publicly arguing that the new system was not as good for the company as the old one, they privately put as much pressure as possible on the personnel vice president until he significantly altered the new system.

Political behavior emerges before and during organizational change efforts when what is in the best interests of one individual or group is not in the best interests of the total organization or of other individuals and groups.

While political behavior sometimes takes the form of two or more armed camps publicly fighting things out, it usually is much more subtle. In many cases, it occurs completely under the surface of public dialogue. Although scheming and ruthless individuals sometimes initiate power struggles, more often than not those who do are people who view their potential loss from change as an unfair violation of their implicit, or psychological, contract with the organization (Schein 1965).

Misunderstandng and lack of trust

People also resist change when they do not understand its simplications and perceive that it might cost them much more than they will gain. Such situations often occur when trust is lacking between the person initiating the change and the employees. (Argyris 1970). Here is an example:

• When the president of a small midwestern company announced to his managers that the company would implement a flexible working schedule for all employees, it never occurred to him that he might run into resistance. He had been introduced to the concept at a management seminar and decided to use it to make working conditions at his company more attractive, particularly to clerical and plant personnel.

Shortly after the announcement, numerous rumors begin to circulate among plant employees — none of whom really knew what flexible working hours meant and many of whom were distrustful of the manufacturing vice-president. One rumor, for instance, suggested that flexible hours meant that most people would have to work whenever their supervisors asked them to — including evenings and weekends. The employee association, a local union, held a quick meeting and then presented the management with a nonnegotiable demand that the flexible hours concept be dropped. The president, caught completely by surprise, complied.

Few organizations can be characterized as having a high level of trust between employees and managers; consequently, it is easy for misunderstandings to develop when change is introduced. Unless managers surface misunderstandings and clarify them rapidly, they can lead to resistance. And that resistance can easily catch change initiators by surprise, especially if they assume that people only resist change when it is not in their best interest.

Different assessments

Another common reason people resist organizational change is that they assess the situation differently from their managers or those initiating the change and see more costs than benefits resulting from the change, not only for themselves but for their company as well. For example:

• The president of one moderate-size bank was shocked by his staff's analysis of the bank's real estate investment trust (REIT) loans. This complicated analysis suggested that the bank could easily lose up to $10 million, and that the possible losses were increasing each month by 20%. Within a week, the president drew up a plan to reorganize the part of the bank that managed REITs. Because of his concern for the bank's stock price, however, he chose not to release the staff report to anyone except the new REIT section manager.

The reorganization immediately ran into massive resistance from the people involved. The group sentiment, as articulated by one person, was: "Has he gone mad? Why in God's name is he tearing apart this section of the bank? His actions have already cost us three very good people (who quit), and have crippled a new program we were implementing (which the president was unaware of) to reduce our loan losses."

Managers who initiate change often assume both that they have all the relevant information required to conduct an adequate organization analysis and that those who will be affected by the change have the same facts, when neither assumption is correct. In either case, the difference in information that groups work with often leads to difference in analyses, which in turn can lead to resistance. Moreover, if the analysis made by those not initiating the change is more accurate than that derived by the initiators, resistance is obviously "good" for the organization. But this likelihood is not obvious to some managers who assume that resistance is always bad and therefore always fight it. (Lawrence 1954).

Low tolerance for change

People also resist change because they fear they will not be able to develop the new skills and behavior that will be required of them. All human beings are limited in their ability to change, with some people much more limited than others. (Watson 1969). Organizational change can inadvertently require people to change too much, too quickly.

Peter F. Drucker has argued that the major obstacle to organizational growth is managers' inability to change their attitudes and behavior as rapidly as their organizations require. (Drucker 1954). Even when managers intellectually understand the need for changes in the way they operate, they sometimes are emotionally unable to make the transition.

It is because of people's limited tolerance for change that individuals will sometimes resist a change even when they realize it is a good one. For example, a person who receives a significantly more important job as a result of an organizational change will probably be very happy. But it is just as possible for such a person to also feel uneasy and to resist giving up certain aspects of the current situation. A new and very different job will require new and different behavior, new and different relationships, as well as the loss of some satisfactory current activities and relationships. If the changes are significant and the individual's tolerance for change is low, he might begin actively to resist the change for reasons even he does not consciously understand.

People also sometimes resist organizational change to save face; to go along

with the change would be, they think, an admission that some of their previous decisions or beliefs were wrong. Or they might resist because of peer group pressure or because of a supervisor's attitude. Indeed, there are probably an endless number of reasons why people resist change. (Zaltman and Duncan 1977).

Assessing which of the many possiblilities might apply to those who will be affected by a change is important because it can help a manager select an appropriate way to overcome resistance. Without an accurate diagnosis of possibilities of resistance, a manager can easily get bogged down during the change process with very costly problems.

Dealing with resistance

Many managers underestimate not only the variety of ways people can react to organizational change, but also the ways they can positively influence specific individuals and groups during a change. And, again because of past experiences, managers sometimes do not have an accurate understanding of the advantages and disadvantages of the methods with which they *are* familiar.

Education and communication

One of the most common ways to overcome resistance to change is to educate people about it before-hand. Communication of ideas helps people see the need for and the logic of a change. The education process can involve one-on-one discussions, presentations to groups, or memos and reports. For example:

• As a part of an effort to make changes in a division's structure and in measurement and reward systems, a division manager put together a one-hour audiovisual presentation that explained the changes and the reasons for them. Over a four-month period, he made this presentation no less than a dozen times to groups of 20 or 30 corporate and division managers.

An education and communication program can be ideal when resistance is based on inadequate or inaccurate information and analysis, especially if the initiators need the resistors' help in implementing the change. But some managers overlook the fact that a program of this sort requires a good relationship between initiators and resistors or that the latter may not believe what they hear. It also requires time and effort, particularly if a lot of people are involved.

Participation and involvement

If the initiators involve the potential resistors in some aspect of the design and implementation of the change, they can often forestall resistance. With a participative change effort, the initiators listen to the people the change involves and use their advice. To illustrate:
• The head of a small financial services company once created a task force to help design and implement changes in his company's reward system. The task force was composed of eight second- and third-level managers from different parts of the company. The president's specific charter to them was that they recommend changes in the company's benefit package. They were given six months and asked to file a brief progress report with the president once a month. After they had made their recommendations, which the president largely accepted, they were asked to help the company's personnel director implement them.

We have found that many managers have quite strong feelings about participation — sometimes positive and sometimes negative. That is, some managers feel that there should always be participation during change efforts, while others feel this is virtually always a mistake. Both attitudes can create problems for a manager, because neither is very realistic.

When change initiators believe they do not have all the information they need to design and implement a change, or when they need the whole-hearted commitment of others to do so, involving others makes very good sense. Considerable research has demonstrated that, in general, participation leads to commitment, not merely compliance (Marrow, Bowers, and Seashore 1967). In some instances, commitment is needed for the change to be a success. Nevertheless, the participation process does have its drawbacks. Not only can it lead to a poor solution if the process is not carefully managed, but also it can be enormously time consuming. When the change must be made immediately, it can take simply too long to involve others.

Facilitation and support

Another way that managers can deal with potential resistance to change is by being supportive. This process might include providing training in new skills, or giving employees time off after a demanding period, or simply listening and providing emotional support. For example:
• Management in one rapidly growing electronics company devised a way to help people adjust to frequent organizational changes. First, management staffed its human resource department with four counselors who spent most of

their time talking to people who were feeling "burnt out" or who were having difficulty adjusting to new jobs. Second, on a selective basis, management offered people four-week minisabbaticals that involved some reflective or educational activity away from work. And, finally, it spent a great deal of money on in-house education and training programs.

Facilitation and support are most helpful when fear and anxiety lie at the heart of resistance. Seasoned, tough managers often overlook or ignore this kind of resistance, as well as the efficacy of facilitative ways of dealing with it. The basic drawback of this approach is that it can be time consuming and expensive and still fail (Zaltman and Duncan 1977). If time, money, and patience just are not available, then using supportive methods is not very practical.

Negotiation and agreement

Another way to deal with resistance is to offer incentives to active or potential resistors. For instance, management could give a union a higher wage rate in return for a work rule change; it could increase an individual's pension benefits in return for an early retirement. Here is an example of negotiated agreements:
• In a large manufacturing company, the divisions were very interdependent. One division manager wanted to make some major changes in his organization. Yet, because of the interdependence, he recognized that he would be forcing some inconvenience and change on other divisions as well. To prevent top managers in other divisions from undermining his efforts, the division manager negotiated a written agreement with each. The agreement specified the outcomes the other division managers would receive and when, as well as the kinds of cooper-

ation that he would receive from them in return during the change process. Later, whenever the division managers complained about his changes or the change process itself, he could point to the negotiated agreements.

Negotiation is particularly appropriate when it is clear that someone is going to lose out as a result of a change and yet his or her power to resist is significant. Negotiated agreements can be a relatively easy way to avoid major resistance, though, like some other processes, they may become expensive. And once a manager makes it clear that he will negotiate to avoid major resistance, he opens himself up to the possibility of blackmail (Nierenberg 1968).

Manipulation and co-optation

In some situations, managers also resort to covert attempts to influence others. Manipulation, in this context, normally involves the very selective use of information and the conscious structuring of events.

One common form of manipulation is co-optation. Co-opting an individual usually involves giving him or her a desirable role in the design or implementation of the change. Co-opting a group involves giving one of its leaders, or someone it respects, a key role in the design or implementation of a change. This is not a form of participation, however, because the initiators do not want the advice of the co-opted, merely his or her endorsement. For example:
• One division manager in a large multibusiness corporation invited the corporate human relations vice president, a close friend of the president, to help him and his key staff diagnose some problems the division was having. Because of his busy schedule, the corporate vice-

president was not able to do much of the actual information gathering or analysis himself, thus limiting his own influence on the diagnoses. But his presence at key meetings helped commit him to the diagnoses as well as the solutions the group designed. The commitment was subsequently very important because the president, at least initially, did not like some of the proposed changes. Nevertheless, after discussion with his human relations vice-president, he did not try to block them.

Under certain circumstances co-optation can be a relatively inexpensive and easy way to gain an individual's or a group's support (cheaper, for example, that negotiation and quicker than participation). Nevertheless, it has its drawbacks. If people feel they are being tricked into not resisting, are not being treated equally, or are being lied to, they may respond very negatively. More than one manager has found that, by his effort to give some subordinate a sense of participation through co-optation, he created more resistance than if he had done nothing. In addition, co-optation can create a different kind of problem if those co-opted use their ability to influence the design and implementation of changes in ways that are not in the best interests of the organization.

Other forms of manipulation have drawbacks also, sometimes to an even greater degree. Most people are likely to greet what they perceive as covert treatment and/or lies with a negative response. Furthermore, if a manager develops a reputation as a manipulator, it can undermine his ability to use needed approaches such as education/communication and participation/involvement. At the extreme, it can even ruin his career.

Nevertheless, people do manipulate others successfully — particularly when all other tactics are not feasible or have failed. (Kotter 1977, 125). Having no other alternative, and not enough time to educate, involve, or support people, and without the power or other resources to negotiate, coerce, or co-opt them, managers have resorted to manipulating information channels in order to scare people into thinking there is a crisis coming which they can avoid only by changing.

Explicit and implicit coercion

Finally, managers often deal with resistance coercively. Here they essentially force people to accept a change by explicitly or implicitly threatening them (with the loss of jobs, promotion possibilities, and so forth) or by actually firing or transferring them. As with manipulation, using coercion is a risky process because inevitably people strongly resent forced change. But in situations where speed is essential and where the changes will not be popular, regardless of how they are introduced, coercion may be the manager's only option.

Successful organizational change efforts are always characterized by the skillful application of a number of these approaches, often in very different combinations. However, successful efforts share two characteristics: managers employ the approaches with a sensitivity to their strengths and limitations (see *Exhibit 1*) and appraise the situation realistically.

The most common mistake managers make is to use only one approach or a limited set of them *regardless of the situation.* A surprisingly large number of managers have this problem. This would include the hard-boiled boss who often

Exhibit I
Methods for dealing with resistance to change

Approach	Commonly used in situations	Advantages	Drawbacks
Education + communication	Where there is a lack of information or inaccurate information and analysis.	Once persuaded, people will often help with the implementation of the change.	Can be very time-consuming if lots of people are involved
Participation + involvement	Where the initiators do not have all the information they need to design the change, and where others they have considerable power to resist.	People who participate will be committed to implementing change, and any relevant information they have will be integrated into the change plan.	Can be very time-consuming if participators design an inappropriate change.
Facilitation + support	Where people are resisting because of adjustment problems.	No other approach works as well with adjustment problems.	Can be time-consuming, expensive, and still fail.
Negotiation + agreement	Where soneoone or some group will clearly lose out in a change, and where that group has considerable power to resist.	Sometimes it is a relatively easy way to avoid major resistance.	Can be too expensive in many cases if it alerts others to negotiate for compliance.
Manipulation + co-optation	Where other tactics will not work, or are too expensive.	It can be a relatively quick and inexpensive solution to resistance problems.	Can lead to future problems if people feel manipulated.
Explicit + implicit coercion	Where speed is essential, and the change initiators possess considerable power.	It is speedy, and can overcome any kind of resistance.	Can be risky if it leaves people mad at the initiators.

coerces people, the people-oriented manager who constantly tries to involve and support his people, the cynical boss who always manipulates and co-opts others, the intellectual manager who relies heavily on education and communication, and the lawyerlike manager who usually tries to negotiate (Kotter 1977, 135).

A second common mistake that managers make is to approach change in a disjointed and incremental way that is not a part of a clearly considered strategy.

Choice of strategy

In approaching an organizational change situation, managers explicitly or implicitly make strategic choices regarding the speed of the effort, the amount of preplanning, the involvement of others, and the relative emphasis they will give to different approaches. Successful change efforts seem to be those where these choices both are internally consistent and fit some key situational variables.

The strategic options available to managers can be usefully thought of as existing on a continuum (see *Exhibit 2*). (Greiner 1967; Greiner and Barnes 1970). At one end of the continuum, the change strategy calls for a very rapid implementation, a clear plan of action, and little involvement of others. This type of strategy mows over any resistance and, at the extreme, would result in a fait accompli. At the other end of the continuum, the strategy would call for a much slower change process, a less clear plan, and involvement on the part of many people other than the change initiators. This type of strategy is designed to reduce resistance to a minimum (Tagiuri 1979).

The further to the left one operates on the continuum in *Exhibit 2,* the more one tends to be coercive and the less one tends to use the other approaches — especially participation; the converse also holds.

Organizational change efforts that are based on inconsistent strategies tend to run into predictable problems. For example, efforts that are not clearly planned in advance and yet are implemented quickly tend to become

Exhibit 2
Strategic continuum

Fast	Slower
Clearly planned.	Not clearly planned at the beginning.
Little involvement of others.	Lots of involvement of others.
Attempt to overcome any resistance.	Attempt to minimize any resistance.

Key situational variables

The amount and type of resistance that is anticipated.	
The position of the initiators vis-a-vis the resistors (in terms of power, trust, and so forth).	
The locus of relevant data for designing the change, and of needed energy for implementing it.	
The stakes involved (e.g., the presence or lack of presence of a crisis, the consequences of resistance and lack of change).	

bogged down owing to unanticipated problems. Efforts that involve a large number of people, but are implemented quickly, usually become either stalled or less participative.

Situational factors

Exactly where a change effort should be strategically positioned on the continuum in *Exhibit 2* depends on four factors:

1. The amount and kind of resistance that is anticipated. All other factors being equal, the greater the anticipated resistance, the more difficult it will be simply to overwhelm it, and the more a manager will need to move toward the right on the continuum to find ways to reduce some of it. (Lorsch 1976).

2. The position of the initiator vis-a-vis the resistors, especially with regard to power. The less power the initiator has with respect to others, the more the initiating manager *must* move to the left on the continuum. (Lorsch 1976). Conversely, the stronger the initiator's position, the more he or she can move to the right.

3. The person who has the relevant data for designing the change and the en-

ergy for implementing it. The more the initiators anticipate that they will need information and commitment from others to help design and implement the change, the more they must move to the right (Lorsch 1976). Gaining useful information and commitment requires time and the involvement of others.

4. The stakes involved. The greater the short-run potential for risks to organizational performance and survival if the present situation is not changed, the more one must move to the left.

Organizational change efforts that ignore these factors inevitably run into problems. A common mistake some managers make, for example, is to move too quickly and involve too few people despite the fact that they do not have all the information they really need to design the change correctly.

Insofar as these factors still leave a manager with some choice of where to operate on the continuum, it is probably best to select a point as far to the right as possible for both economic and social reasons. Forcing change on people can have just too many negative side effects over both the short and the long term. Change efforts using the strategies on the right of the continuum can often help develop an organization and its people in useful ways. (Been 1979).

In some cases, however, knowing the four factors may not give a manager a comfortable and obvious choice. Consider a situation where a manager has a weak position vis-a-vis the people whom he thinks need a change and yet is faced with serious consequences if the change is not implemented immediately. Such a manager is clearly in a bind. If he somehow is not able to increase his power in the situation, he will be forced to choose some compromise strategy and to live through difficult times.

Implications for managers

A manager can improve his chance of success in an organizational change effort by:

1. Conducting an organizational analysis that identifies the current situation, problems, and the forces that are possible causes of those problems. The analysis should specify the actual importance of the problems, the speed with which the problems must be addressed if additional problems are to be avoided, and the kinds of changes that are generally needed.
2. Conducting an analysis of factors relevant to producing the needed changes. This analysis should focus on questions of who might resist the change, why, and how much; who has information that is needed to design the change, and whose cooperation is essential in implementing it; and what is the position of the initiator vis-a-vis other relevant parties in terms of power, trust, normal modes of interaction, and so forth.
3. Selecting a change strategy, based on the previous analysis, that specifies the speed of change, the amount of preplanning, and the degree of involvement of others; that selects specific tactics for use with various individuals and groups; and that is internally consistent.
4. Monitoring the implementation process. No matter how good a job one does of initially selecting a change strategy and tactics, something unexpected will eventually occur during implementation. Only by carefully monitoring the process can one identify the unexpected in a timely fashion and react to it intelligently.

Interpersonal skills, of course, are the key to using this analysis. But even the most outstanding interpersonal skills will not make up for a poor choice of strategy and tactics. And in a business world that continues to become more and more dynamic, the consequences of poor implementation choices will become increasingly severe.

An introduction to organization development

John J. Sherwood

Organization development is an educational process by which human resources are continuously identified, allocated, and expanded in ways that make these resources more available to the organizations, and therefore, improve the organization's problem-solving capabilities.

The most general objective of organizational development — OD — is to develop self-renewing, self-correcting systems of people who learn to organize themselves in a variety of ways according to the nature of their tasks, and who continue to expand the choices available to the organization as it copes with the changing demands of a changing environment. OD stands for a new way of looking at the human side of organizational life.

What is OD?

a. A long-range effort to introduce planned change based on a diagnosis which is shared by the members of an organization.
b. An OD program involves an entire organization, or a coherent "system" or part thereof.
c. Its goal is to increase organizational effectiveness and enhance organizational choice and self-renewal.
d. The major strategy of OD is to intervene in the ongoing activities of the organization to facilitate learning and to make choices about alternative ways to proceed.

Objectives of typical OD programs

Although the specific objectives of an OD effort vary according to the diagnosis of organizational problems, a number of objectives typically emerge. These objectives reflect problems which are common in organizations and which prevent the creative release of human potential within organizations:

1. To build trust among individuals and groups throughout the organization, and up and down the hierarchy.
2. To create an open, problem-solving climate throughout the organization — where problems are confronted and differences are clarified, both within groups and between groups, in contrast to "sweeping problems under the rug" or "smoothing things over."
3. To locate decision-making and problem-solving responsibilities as close to the information sources and the relevant resources as possible, rather than in a particular role or level of the hierarchy.
4. To increase the sense of "ownership" of organizational goals and objectives throughout the membership of the organization.
5. To move toward more collaboration between interdependent persons and interdependent groups within the organization. Where relationships are clearly competitive, e.g., limited resources, then it is important that competition be open and be managed so the organization might benefit from the advantages of open competition and avoid suffering from the destructive consequences of subversive rivalry.
6. To increase awareness of group "process" and its consequences for performance — that is, to help persons become aware of what is happening between and to group members while the group is working on the task, e.g., communications, influence, feelings, leadership styles and struggles, relationships between groups, how conflict is managed, etc.

The objectives of organizational development efforts are achieved through planned interventions based on research findings and theoretical hypotheses of the behavioral sciences. The organization is helped to examine its present ways of work, its norms and values, and to generate and evaluate alternative ways of working, or relating, or rewarding members of the system.

Some assumptions underlying the concept of OD

Using knowledge and techniques from the behavioral sciences, organization development attempts to integrate organizational goals with the needs for growth of individual members in order to design a more effective and fully functioning organization, in which the potential of members is more fully realized. Some of the basic assumptions underlying the concept of OD are as follows:

1. The attitudes most members of organizations hold toward work and their resultant work habits are usually more *reactions* to their work environment and how they are treated by the organization, than they are intrinsic characteristics of an individual's personality. Therefore, efforts to change attitudes toward work and toward the organization should be directed more toward changing how the person is treated than toward attempting to change the person.

2. Work which is organized to meet people's needs as well as to achieve organizational requirements tends to produce the highest productivity and quality of production.

3. Most members of organizations are not motivated primarily by an avoidance of work for which tight controls and threats of punishment are necessary — but rather, most individuals seek challenging work and desire responsibility for accomplishing organizational objectives to which they are committed.

4. The basic building blocks of organizations are groups of people; therefore, the basic units of change are also groups, not simply individuals.

5. The culture of most organizations tends to suppress the open expression of feelings which people have about each other and about where they and their organization are heading. The difficulty is that the suppression of feelings adversely affects problem solving, personal growth, and satisfaction with one's work. The expression of feelings is an important part of becoming committed to a decision or a task.

6. Groups which learn to work in a constructively open way by providing feedback for members become more able to profit from their own experience and become more able to fully utilize their resources on the task. Furthermore, the growth of individual members is facilitated by relationships which are open, supportive, and trusting.

7. There is an important difference between *agreement* and *commitment*. People are committed to and care about that which they help create. Where change is introduced, it will be most effectively implemented if the groups and individuals involved have a sense of ownership in the process. Commitment is most assuredly attained where there is active participation in the planning and conduct of the change. Agreement is simpler to achieve and results in a simpler outcome — people do what they are told, or something sufficient or similar.

8. The basic value underlying all OD theory and practice is that of *choice*. Through the collection and feedback of relevant data — made available by trust, openness, and risk — more choice becomes available to the organization, and to the individual, and hence better decisions can be made.

Organization Development technology

Basic to all OD efforts is an attempt to make the human resources of the organization optimally available. Outside consultants often share the responsibility for this process, but they also work toward increasing the organization's own capacity to understand and manage its own growth.

In contrast to management development which is oriented toward the individual manager, OD focuses on groups and changing relations between people. The system — be it a unit of the organization, or the entire organization — is the object of an OD effort.

A frequent strategy in OD programs is the use of an *action-research* model of intervention. There are three processes in an action-research approach, all of which involve extensive collaboration between a consultant and the organization: data gathering from individuals and groups; feedback to key client or client group in the organization; and joint action planning based on the feedback. Action-research is designed to make data available from the entire system and then to use that information to make plans about the future of that system.

Some OD interventions or building blocks of an OD program are the following:

1. *Team building:* focus is on early identification and solution of the work group's problems, particularly interpersonal and organizational roadblocks which stand in the way of the team's collaborative, cooperative, creative, competent functioning.

   A group's work procedures can be made more effective by using different decision-making procedures for different tasks and learning to treat leadership as a function to be performed by members of the group, not just as a role or a characteristic of an individual's personality.

   The interpersonal relationships within a team can be improved by working on communication skills and patterns; skills in openness and expression of what one thinks and feels; the degree of understanding and acceptance among team members; authority and hierarchical problems; trust and respect; and skills in conflict management.

2. *Intergroup problem solving:* groups are brought together for the purpose of reducing unhealthy competitiveness between the groups or to resolve intergroup conflicts over such things as overlapping responsibilities or confused lines of authority, and to enhance interdependence when it appropriately exists.

   Intergroup problems sometimes exist between different functional groups which must work together, e.g., sales and engineering; or between line and staff; or labor and management; or between separate organizations involved in a merger.

3. *Confrontation meeting:* is a problem-solving mechanism when problems are known to exist. An action-research format is used. The entire management group of an organization is brought together, problems and attitudes are collected and shared, priorities are established, commitments to actions are made through setting targets and assigning task forces.

4. *Goal setting and planning:* supervisor-subordinate pairs and teams throughout the organization engage in systematic performance

improvement and target setting with mutual commitment and review. Goal setting becomes a way of life for the organization.

5. *Third party facilitation:* involves the use of a skilled third person to help in the diagnosis, understanding, and resolution of difficult human problems — e.g., difficult one-to-one relationships between two persons or two groups.

6. *Consulting pairs:* often a manager can benefit from a close and continuing relationship with someone outside his own organization (a consultant, either internal or external to the organization), with whom he can share problems early.

In the effective OD effort each member of the organization begins to see himself as a resource to others and becomes willing to provide help to others when asked to do so. Such attitudes become norms or shared expectations. Once such a norm is established, members of the organization become potential consultants for one another, and the dependence of the organization on outside resources becomes less and less.

A major characteristic or organization development is that it relies heavily on an educational strategy emphasizing *experience-based learning* and on the skills such a procedure develops. Thus, the data feedback of the action-research model and the confrontation meeting are examples of how the experiences people have with each other and with the organization are shared and become the basis upon which learning occurs and upon which planning and action proceed. To be sure, OD is not simply human relations training (nor is it sensitivity training); however, openness about one's own experiences — including feelings, reactions, and perceptions — represents a cornerstone of many organizational development efforts. Furthermore, laboratory training experiences are often used to help members of the organization develop more interpersonal competence, including communication skills, ability to better manage conflict, and insights into oneself and into groups and how they form and function. Laboratory training programs are, therefore, a good preliminary step to an organization development effort.

Hard hats in the boardroom: New trends in workers' participation

Warner P. Woodworth

> I asked the young, long-haired worker on the truck assembly line what it was like to have a job in this company. "They're running this plant like F. W. Taylor back in 1910!" Later, I returned to the front office for a meeting with the company's top management. Upon hearing of the assembly-worker's comment, the response of the executives was unanimous: "Who is F. W. Taylor?"
>
> — Organizational consultant

This incident in the late 1970s was a jarring revelation to these truck company officials that a chasm was growing between the executive suite and the workers on the factory floor. To them, it suggested a different world of work, conflicting values within the organization's culture, and a poignant lesson about the growing sophistication of today's new generation of workers.

Fueled by declining productivity rates and a national economic crisis, American managers and trade unions are seeking to invent new organizational approaches to industrial effectiveness. Numerous firms have launched quality circle programs as executives became enamored with the ideas and techniques of Japanese practices. Instead of looking eastward to the Orient for answers, we may see that the trends most significant to American industry are to be found in Europe. It is from there that we derive our roots — the Judeo-Christian ethic, our major theories of political democracy, economic development, and indeed, most of the underpinnings of our contemporary culture.

I propose to review the thrust of recent events in the European workplace and perhaps extrapolate from them shifts America might expect in the coming decade. As we reflect on changes in European political and economic spheres, are there any signs that similar seeds have been planted in American soil? What parallels are emerging in the United States? Finally, we will explore several frameworks for a restructuring of organizational power that are beginning to emerge in the 1980s and discuss their implications.

Industrial democracy: The new revolution

For us, the question is whether the workers are to control their own destinies, or be subjected to ever more intensive and minute control themselves, as the power of the oligarchs becomes ever more arbitrary and ever more irresponsible.

— Coates & Topham (p.240)
Great Britain

We demand steps be taken to fight against the extreme divisions of labor, loss of skills, and the subservience of man to machines.

— Policy Paper on Industrial Democracy, French Trade Union, CGT

After 150 years, Europe is again giving birth to a new industrial age. The first was a technological revolution, an era of mechanization and mass production, of assembly-line organizational logic and the triumph of the machine. The second industrial revolution going on now is a transformation of power, a shifting of economic and political control in society from the few to the masses, from the owners to the producers of labor, from the haves to the have-nots. The results are yielding significant outcomes as the social structure is altered, as political expectations change, as a new psychology of entitlement emerges, and the nature of work itself is redefined.

Today in many advanced countries of Europe, a job no longer means simply arriving on time, operating a machine, and producing one's quota of quality products. Work has been infused with the notion of individual rights, the quality of working life, and the democratizing of corporate bureaucracy from the shop floor to the boardroom. Whether the national rhetoric is capitalistic or socialistic, the underlying thrust is a push for participation and power. For millions of workers across Europe, new institutional forms have been created in order to guarantee the redistribution of power. The range of these mechanisms makes up a phenomenon known as Industrial Democracy.

Instead of merely reporting to work and receiving orders for the day, the new worker's role is one of decision maker and policy setter. The experiments of the 1950s and 1960s have become institutionalized in the 1970s. Indeed, the past decade in Europe can be characterized as the most sweeping economic reform of the century. While the arguments from the political left and right vary on *how* to distribute the fruits of labor throughout society, the debate about whether to share the benefits of production more widely is all but over.

Immediately after World War II, France began the drive toward industrial democracy by establishing mandatory works councils in 1945. Germany went further in 1947, allocating to workers one-third of the board of directors' seats in the coal and steel industries. However, an explosion giving rise to full-fledged industrial democracy has culminated in over thirty changes in corporate-union relations among some ten countries in the past decade alone. Below is a sampling of these developments which empower workers and labor with new organizational and economic clout in different nations:

— The Netherlands establishes works councils (1971)
— Sweden passes one-third codetermination law (1972)
— Austria legislates labor constitution (1973)

— Britain creates Bullock Commission (1974)
— Denmark establishes codetermination system (1974)
— Sweden considers Meidner profit-sharing plan (1975)
— Norway creates work environment act (1976)
— Germany passes 50-50 codetermination law (1978)

A Smorgasbord of Workplace Democratization

What we are insisting from Lucas is a move away from weapons production for the arms trade — toward socially useful production: goods accessible to all, products which conserve resources and improve the environment.
— Member of Lucas Aerospace Combine Shop Stewards Committee (British labor strategy to combat mass layoffs through creation of alternative technology).

The sum total of these legislative and social innovations means profound industrial change. A more focused description of major types of change will suggest the flavor of these alternatives in the reform of industrial relations.

Collective bargaining

The fundamental basis for union-management relations in Europe is still the labor contract, although it is built on a foundation of cooperation, in contrast to the adversary system of the United States. Trade union membership is high, often exceeding 90 percent of the work force, and includes not only blue-collar employees, but white-collar and mana-gerial personnel in many countries. In contrast to the dominant bread-and-butter concerns of bargaining in America, the agenda of European labor unions in recent years has been broadened to include safety and health, joint decisionmaking, and social rights of workers. Sweden, for example, established a Democracy at Work law in 1977 which essentially tore the lid off issues once considered managerial prerogatives. On the other hand, Italian unions have achieved industrial democracy gains through collective bargaining rather than political means. in many cases the unions have used arbitration along with legislation to widen the focus from wages and working conditions to employment policies, capital investments, production schedule, and new plant construction.

Workplace democracy

The participation of workers at the shop-floor level of the firm has become a major focal point for industrial democracy. Early experiments in British coal mines and Swedish automobile assembly plants have led to widespread attempts to alter the relationship between the individual and the machine. Specific tactics and terms may vary: Norwegian work restructuring, job enrichment, British sociotechnical systems, Swedish autonomous work teams, and labor-management cooperation. The important goal is to restore meaning and growth to the work experience. Most European nations have as a high priority the improving of the quality of working life, illustrated in Germany's expenditure of over $100 million in the past five years to carry out research under the Humanization of the Work Act. The underlying prinicple seems to be that if workers participate in the design and execution of shopfloor activities, there will ensue a more productive process and higher-quality results, as well as a closer correspondence between bureaucratic organizational life and genuine societal democracy.

Works councils

National legislation exists which mandates the formation of a works council at the enterprise in numerous European countries — France, the Netherlands, Sweden, Belgium, and so on. Usually the councils are established as union-management consultative bodies to monitor factory working conditions and strengthen operations. These councils may range from groups of "all talk/no action" to very powerful committees which basically run the business. Usually between 10 and 20 in number, membership is either decided by one's formal position in the company or union hierarchy or by the election of representatives. In Belgium, the works councils are mainly an advisory body to top management, while in Italy and the Netherlands they are union-dominated and heavily control company decisions. In the latter case the councils have access to corporate information about future plans and financial data. Executives must involve the council in such decisions as plant relocations, mergers, product development, and layoffs. The councils have veto power over safety issues, changes in pensions and profit-sharing, and disciplinary policies. Operating a works council consumes a good deal of the time and energy of management and labor, but many argue the effort pays off as the council becomes a vehicle through which decisions get reached and plans are implemented.

Co-determination

In attempting to mitigate against a rebirth of nazism after World War II, the West German government attempted to democratize the economy by giving workers board of directors representation in key industries. Since then, the percentage of workers' board seats has grown from 33 percent to parity (50 percent) in Germany, and similar legislation is now on the books in the Scandinavian countries, France, the Netherlands, and Austria. The Bullock Commission Report of Great Britain advocated a similar structure for U.K. industries, but the political support for such a move has not yet been achieved. Recently, the European Economic Community organization has recommended a two-tier board system for all European companies in which the top level would have equal representation for workers and owners, with a second-level board consisting wholly of upper management, accountable as a group to the top board. Some nations mandate codetermination only in certain industries, and only in large companies. On the other hand, Sweden requires labor representation on the board of all firms employing (25) or more people. In most cases of codetermination, the trade union power seems to be mostly information; i.e., access to profit-and-loss statements and employee relations data rather than workers' using their power to redirect or block corporate activities.

Income redistribution

Perhaps the potentially most profound and far-reaching European changes have to do with worker participation in the corporate financial picture. The essence of sharing in the profits of a firm, however, is not simply a question of depositing an extra bonus in one's bank, but broad-ranging societal control. The ultimate goal is for the masses to obtain decision-making power through widespread stock ownership — a fundamental form of democratizing the economy. Such ideas are largely in the proposal stage at present, as labor leaders and economists advocate trade union control of the means of production throughout Europe. The first of this legislation to succeed will probably occur in Sweden, where the Meidner Plan is likely to be implemented since the Social Democrats' return to power in late 1982. This plan would turn 20 percent of the country's corporate profits over to a central fund administered by the union. Such a move would give labor virtual control of Sweden's economy within several years by creating a political economy of a Third Way, and alternative to the traditional dichotomy of having to choose between capitalism or socialism. Another illustration of a macro approach to economic democracy can be seen developing out of Yugoslavia's system in Eastern Europe. There, workers' self-management has emerged as a radical and unique means by which all factories are socially owned, workers are elected to manage the firm, and major corporate decisions are decided democratically by voting.

While the shifts toward worker participation have perhaps been more dramatic in Europe, the American case suggests the seeds of change. From human relations training and organizational development techniques which emphasized trust and working together but left the central issue of organizational power untouched, the push today in countless firms is on the Quality of Working Life (QWL). The underlying thrust seems to be that *it is not enough*

Parallels in America

There are no bad people, only bad management.
— Group Executive Vice-President, General Electric Corporation

I think most of us are looking for a calling, not a job. Most of us, like the assembly-line worker, have jobs that are too small for our spirit. Jobs are not big enough for people.
— Working, by Studs Terkel (p. xxiv)

---

to do things differently; what is needed is to do different things.

Hundreds of firms, like Procter & Gamble and Westinghouse, have designed and built new plants based on a logic of "small is beautiful." These new wave factories tend to be single-storied facilities with plenty of sunlight, access to the out-of-doors, and brightly colored work spaces. Rather than ten thousand workers packed into crowded pigeonholes, the new firms usually have 500 employees at the maximum, a size that is more consistent with human-scale organizations. Such enterprises do not suffer from hierarchical overkill, but are simpler to understand and generate feelings of belonging to the company family. Smallness enhances the possibility that when difficulties emerge, the organization is not so large and complex that problems are unchangeable. A number of other aspects of today's new plants reveal the cumulative effect of change: no time clocks; no uniforms; teams of workers doing their own scheduling, hiring, and firing; quality control; light maintenance; often without even immediate supervisors.

Meanwhile, dramatic alterations are also appearing in the old manufacturing industries of the Northeast. To combat community deterioration caused by strikes, low productivity, and runaway plants, dozens of cities have created area labor-management committees. Among the most widely heralded successes are those of Muskegon, Michigan and Jamestown, New York, where union officials, industrial owners and managers, and elected representatives of the public have created regional councils engaged in cooperative problem-solving. In many cases such efforts have led to reduced work stoppages, improved health and safety records, the retention of once-threatened jobs, and revitalization of the regional economy. These new forums for anticipatory joint planning, rather than post facto reactions to a crisis, have resulted in job guarantees, improved percentages of corporate bids on new work, redesign of plant layouts, and community-wide commitment to a different quality of life.

The present "era of labor concessions' has not been so much a period of union givebacks, but a tradeoff. In numerous cases workers have agreed to not demand wage increases and even to reductions in benefits or other settlements which minimize costs to the firm. However, labor has sought and gained power in exchange for such agreements, illustrated by the following recent sampling of new contracts: Ford and General Motors agreed with the United Auto Workers not to close down assembly plants and to reduce outside competitive buying of parts; American Telephone and Telegraph agreed to consult electrical workers' "technological change committees" before any innovations were implemented; the United Rubber Workers won the right to inspect Uniroyal's books in exchange for concessions; workers at Pan American, Chrysler, and a

number of smaller firms gained seats on the board of directors so they could monitor corporate performance and have access to critical financial data.

Perhaps a fundamental sign of the new industrial revolution in America is the shift toward workers' self-management and employee ownership. Sharing in the fruits of one's labors has been an evolutionary idea for some years, illustrated by the proliferation of profit-sharing schemes, Scanlon plans, and the more recent program of Improshare. However, more recently, employee stock ownership has mushroomed. In some cases, the workers simply obtain stock through special company arrangements, illustrated by Hallmark Cards or Sears, Roebuck, and Company (which is 20 percent employee-owned). In other instances, employees gained major blocks of stock through some sort of financing package, such as the Chrysler autoworkers obtaining 15 percent of the company's stock, 12 million shares, as part of the bailout plan, a figure which will rise to 25 percent by 1984. In hundreds of cases during the last five years, small business entrepreneurs have turned their firms over to their employees upon retirement, workers and communities have fought imminent plant closings through the tactic of a worker buyout, and thousands of jobs have been salvaged.

All told, today there are over 5,000 worker-owned firms across the country. In Poland when the heroic trade union, Solidarity, demanded as one of its core economic reforms a program of workers' self-management and ownership, the regime criticized the union proposal as bourgeois capitalism. In contrast, in the United States when one speaks of worker ownership, the idea is often rejected as socialism. Curiously, recent legislation reveals the notion of employee ownership to have widespread bipartisan support in Congress and even in the White House. So today worker ownership is growing, from 17 plywood corporations in the Northwest to an insurance company in Washington where workers elect their own managers. From a New Jersey automotive parts plant GM agreed to sell to its UAW workers to the $500 million-a-year Rath Packing Company in Iowa where workers control 11 of 17 seats on the board of directors. From the Chicago and Northwestern Railroad to the *Milwaukee Journal*. From large-scale agricultural co-ops to new wave collectives in light industry, crafts, and other economic alternatives. The idea was embraced by the newest and largest employee-owned firm in the country, a steel mill in Weirton, West Virginia which is being bought by 10,000 steelworkers and has become the eighth largest steel company in America. It has also caught hold in Philadelphia, where over 20 A&P food stores were closed late last year. Now an ingenious plan has been launched to reopen the stores under a new name with a heavy dose of worker participation and the funneling of profits into a fund to buy up the stores by the employees.

While the transporting of the new industrial revolution across the Atlantic is far from complete, the winds seem to be blowing in this direction. Although we should not overstate the similarities between Europe and America, the "Europeanization" of U.S. industry tends to look like the future. A key difference is that much of the shift in power to American workers is coming about through voluntary agreements between unions and companies, not because of political alliances and state-mandated legislation typified by much of Europe. In other words, while the thrust of the change is

similar, the means differ and seem to be based on a distinctly American approach in which the federal government stays out. Another factor which distinguishes change between the two continents is that in the United States there is generally not a coherent policy among employers' associations or international labor organizations regarding workers' participation. Rather, the process is occuring in piecemeal fashion. There have been several exceptions, such as the creation of plant-level labor-management committees throughout the steel industry and the General Motors-UAW formal commitment to participative structurers which ensure a higher quality of working life. But the norm seems to be that the union local and/or plant management propose changes which lead to bottom-up empowerment.

Quality of Working Life Frameworks

For 30 years Earl Murray has been tagging meat in the shipping department of the Rath Packing Company. Currently, he spends one day a month in a new role as a worker on the firm's board of directors. Out in the plant, he's a typical member of the 2,000-member union. In the boardroom he's a champion of the view from below in the analysis of company operations.

In attmepting to analyze QWL as an approach to organizaional change, it may be useful to look at the whole picture from different angles. One view that might be taken arises from consideration of the *level* of worker participation (shown in Table 1).

Table 1
Levels of organizational participation

Ownership — Stock control
Governance — co-determination of policy
Management — administration
Terms and working conditions — Labor Agreements

To explain this chart, let us begin with the lowest level of participation, *Terms and working conditions.* In America, the labor contract has been the historical vehicle for worker participation, as collective bargaining set the pay, benefits, duties, and otherwise defined the relationship between management and labor. Essentially, it boiled down to an assumption that "management's job is to manage and workers do the work."

A step-up in participation has developed over the past few years in cases where the union has been invited to become a partner with management in the administration of the firm. Under the rubric of *participative management,* Ford Motor Company has created employee involvement committees in over a hundred plants across the country in which workers and supervisors jointly assess problems and brainstorm possible solutions. Quality of working life specialists at General Motors have labored for a number of years to bring UAW and management representatives together for team-building programs in which trust and a new level of open dialogue are established for joint management of the factory.

During the decade of the 1970s, Dana Corporation increased productivity 126 percent by involving most of its 24,000 workers in participative management programs. Cummins Engine, General Foods, and others began to restructure decision making so that work teams became self-managing. Prominent European parallels consist of the Swedish new plant designs, sociotechnical redesign of work experiments in Britain, and so on.

Other efforts have raised the degree of organizational participation even higher, to a third level — the inclusion of workers in a firm's *governance.* Examples from Europe consist of work councils at the plant level in France, the Netherlands, and Belgium, and codetermination of the corporation in the cases of West Germany, Austria, and Scandinavia. The most widely heralded example of codetermination in the U.S. was the election of United Auto Workers President Douglas Fraser to the board of Chrysler Corporation in 1980. More recently, a union representative was elected to the board of Pan American World Airways to improve organizational effectiveness in the face of mounting losses. In other firms, such as Donnelly Mirrors, all employees are represented in an elected committee which sets all policy for personnel issues in the corporation.

Perhaps the most powerful level of participation is that of *legally owning a business.* European instances include Yugoslavian self-management, worker buyouts in Sweden, Britain's Scott Baker Commonwealth, and the 80 industrial cooperatives in Mondragon, Spain, which employ 20,000 workers in an intricate network which includes a worker bank, R&D center, engineering school, and housing complex. Worker ownership in America may arise from a profit-sharing program which gives employees a stake in the business, as illustrated by firms like Eastman Kodak which are partially owned by employees. Or the ownership may include over 50 percent of the stock held by the workers as is the case with South Bend Lathe, Bates Fabric, Rath Packing Company, and Hyatt-Clark Industries. In the latter case, for instance, workers are empowered to elect three directors of the company. They have set up an extensive system of worker participation and will directly own 100 percent of the stock ten years after taking over what was once a General Motors roller bearing facility.

To look at QWL from another angle, three basic *forms* of participation may exist (see Table 2).

Table 2
Forms of participation

Individual — Direct
Group — Direct
Organizational — Representative

One form is the involvement of the *individual* — an employee approaches management with ideas and criticisms. These may be verbal or written, solicited or unsolicited, and are often obtained through such programs as an open-door policy or suggestion box. A second form is that of *group* activity — quality circles, Scanlon committees, semi-autonomous or autonomous work teams, and so on. The third form is *organizational,* which, in contrast to the two direct approaches, is representational. Illustrations of this include the Management Councils cre-

ated in Westinghouse Corporation in which representatives from supervisory ranks in various departments are elected to open up channels of communication, make recommendations regarding management needs, and so on.

Another angle from which a different perspective of organizational change appears is to look at a scale of participative power. Table 3 attempts to suggest a hierarchy of decision making and is illustrated with examples from cases discussed above. While the range of worker input varies considerably, one might argue that the higher on the ladder worker participation in decisions goes, the more potential exists for genuine workers' control and organizational democracy.

The Future

We encourage and support the shared responsibility of all people at Oldsmobile toward a common goal: producing a quality product at a competitive price, in an atmosphere of cooperation and shared recognition, in which everyone has the opportunity to participate in the decision-making process.

— Mission statement, Management-Union Steering Committee, Oldsmobile Division and United Auto Workers Local 652

Table 3
Range of participation in decisions

Work Station Decisions	Day-to-day Team Management	Technology and Planning	Business Products	Profits: Distribution and Investment
(Collective bargaining decisions regarding job bidding, pace of work, etc.)	(Labor-management committees, quality circles: GM, Ford)	(Socio-technical design, layout, new plant start-ups: Volvo, Saab, Procter & Gamble, General Foods)	(Worker involvement in the creation of new product lines, socially beneficial products: Scott Baker, Rath Packing)	(Control of financial budget and corporate investments: Mondragon, U.S. Plywood co-ops)

A central thesis of this report is that the impetus for organizational change in the United States has its roots in European culture, not Japan. Shifting worker expectations, "new breed" values about one's job, and the current economic crisis enlarge the context for an increasingly democratic organizational life. The range of recent behavioral science theories, managerial practices, and labor proposals are designed to give workers more of a voice, heightened autonomy, and an enlarged share of responsibility in company operations.

There seem to be two basic premises for changes toward worker participation, whether at the factory floor or in the boardroom. One is pragmatic rationale which argues that such participation will ensure corporate profits, improve productivity, and better utilize the firm's human resources. The other view stems from an ideological premise that until the rights of the individual penetrate the company gates, the fundamental ideals of a participatory democracy in society will not be achieved.

While the thrust of industrial democracy seems to portend a future of dramatic alterations in the social and economic infrastructure of modern society, this movement in America is not without its problems and failures. One of the best-known cases of a worker takeover, the Vermont Asbestos Group, was a large financial success, but the worker-owners eventually lost a controlling interest in the stock and the firm has recently reverted to a more traditional system. Similarly, the worker participation experiments that the Harvard Project on Technology, Work, and Character launched in 1972 with Harmon Internationl Industries and the UAW in Bolivar, Tennessee have either been dismantled or extensively altered from an earlier, progressive form to more of a status quo organization.

Doubts and resistance to genuine democratization of industry are articulated in many management and trade union circles. Executive attitudes often reflect the view a CEO recently expressed to me that the current crisis over productivity and hard economic times is forcing business to seek employee input and listen to shopfloor-level ideas. His expectation, though, is couched in the hope that when the economy bounces back, channels from below will be blocked and the fortress-type practices of the past will again become the *modus operandi.*

Organized labor also has its concerns about joint union-management problem-solving. Said an official of the International Association of Machinists and Aereospace Workers, "We have a feeling that if we get into bed with management, there's going to be two people screwing the workers instead of one." And certain aspects of industrial democracy are referred to as "rainbow chasing" by Thomas Donahue, executive assistant to the president of the AFL-CIO, who argues: "We do not seek to be a partner in management — to be most likely the junior partner in success and the senior partner in failure."

Regardless of the controversies surrounding these new mechanisms for change and worker participation, the likelihood is that the radical alterations of the recent past will become norm within a decade or two. Cosmetic changes of the organization's facade will die quickly. But the substantive shifts of power beginning to occur suggest a future groundswell that will lead us into the twenty-first century. These changes are exploding from the guts and the heart of middle America. Top management and union officials who do not begin to articulate a coherent vision of a truly democratized society may be overthrown by the hard hats now clamoring at the gates.

A billion Levi's later

Ed Cray

How the Levi Strauss Company has combined business success with its own brand of social responsibility.

They are ubiquitous, virtually universal, 60 threads to the inch, the seams sewn in orange. Their fading indigo stretches from San Francisco to the Far East and beyond. They are even bootlegged to the walls of the Kremlin. Their brand name has become the generic term for all blue denim pants, and, despite competition, Levi Strauss & Co.'s 100-year-old western work pants still lead an industry caught up in the great leisure-time boom.

Guaranteed to shrink and fade, workaday Levi's are an unlikely foundation on which to build the world's largest clothing manufacturer, a $1.5-billion-a-year corporation marketing 1,500 different garments in 70 countries. But then Levi Strauss is an unlikely company. Publicly traded just since 1971, the 125-year-old multinational is still controlled by heirs of the founder Levi Strauss, a Bavarian Jew who migrated to the United States in 1848. The family tradition runs deep, infusing the corporation with a sense of social responsibility much praised in the business press and rarely imitated in the business world.

"It's in the genes," punned the shirt-sleeved chairman of the board, Walter Haas, Jr. It *is* the jeans, and their off-spring, that have made it possible for Haas and his brother Peter, president and chief executive officer, to pursue their youthful ambition to make Levi Strauss the best corporation in America.

What Wall Street once regarded as a funny little San Francisco pants manufacturer may not be the best corporation in America; it depends on one's measure. But it has been an unparalleled financial success.

Just 30 years ago, the company had modest sales of $11 million. Some $3 million of that total came from wholesaling other firms' products. But a succession of shrewd business moves and some serendipitous sociological trends transformed the mundane pants first into a youthful symbol of protest, and then into the vestment of leisure in America. As the post-World War II baby boom children grew, faded blue denim became a national uniform associated with the relaxed lifestyle of the West. California, as in other things, set the pace. Levi's dominated the market there before they took over the rest of the nation.

The denim phenomenon carried with it the three major jeans manufacturers: Levi Strauss; Blue Bell with its lower-priced Wrangler brand; and VF with its high-quality H.D. Lee label. With its strong western image and a youth-oriented advertising campaign, Levi Strauss consistently outsells its combined rivals by wide margins (by $214 million this year alone).

The Haas brothers themselves rose through the ranks, gradually assuming control from their father, Walter Haas, Sr., and from their uncle, Daniel Koshland. And as they did they methodically expanded the company's product line. First slacks, then boys' pants; a women's wear line and sportswear followed. Meanwhile, the jeans business prospered beyond the most optimistic of corporate forecasts.

In 1964 Levi Strauss introduced Sta-Prest, the first successful permanent press, and that caught on with even the most haughty department stores. By 1968, the company (then privately held) had annual sales of more than $200 million. Ten years later, that figure has grown more than 700 percent. Profits have more than stayed apace, rising from $12.1 million in 1968 to $129.8 million this year. (If one looks at profits as a percentage of capital investment, the company's performance is particularly impressive: according to *Fortune*, in 1977 Levi Strauss was among the ten most profitable firms in the country.)

The great leisure-time boom — and the ''California'' lifestyle contagion — spread overseas, carried by Levi's jeans. Levi Strauss International has become a $500 million-a-year enterprise with 27 factories dotted about the globe. (Last year the firm signed an agreeemnt with the Hungarian government that will introduce red-tabbed Levi's to Iron Curtain countries on a formal basis. That might reduce the black market price in Russia: $100-a-pair, used.)

In conventional terms, Levi Strauss is a rousing success. It is the largest of 22,000 American clothing manufacturers; beyond the men's jeans market, it is the second largest manufacturer of branded boy's wear (just behind Sear's house brand), the largest of sport-coat manufacturers, and, in just five years, one of the four largest shirtmakers in the country. But the Haas borthers, and the executives they have brought up through the ranks with them, do not measure success solely by the bottom line. The firm's first stock prospectus, issued when Levi Strauss went public, devoted one of three paragraphs in the legal description of the company to this:

The Company's social responsibilities have for many years been a matter of strong conviction on the part of its management. Well before legal requirements were imposed, the Company was an ''equal opportunity employer.'' In 1969, the Company received one of *Business Week* magazine's first two ''Business Citizenship'' awards in the field of human resources.

The corporation's underwriters think this paragraph was the first such announcement in a stock prospectus. The Haases have worked to institutionalize within the company their personal sense of social concern. The brothers have also tried to inspire similar feelings in other companies, where ''social responsibility'' is most often confined to self-serving institutional advertising, tax-deductible charity, and legally mandated equal employment opportunity.

The Haases see social responsibility as more. ''It's really integrity in dealing with the public, with customers, with employees, with the communities in which we live. And this is where business has such a bad image,'' said Walter Haas. ''There hasn't been integrity there.''

For Levi Strauss, intregrity begins with high quality, backed by a liberal merchandise-return policy. That was the case in 1873, when the company introduced the Two House brand denim pants, and it still applies, a billion pairs of pants later. The quality of the garments produced at Levi Strauss factories is closely monitored. Eighty-four people, with a budget of $1.3 million annually, police the company's purchases and the end product. Levi Strauss customarily rejects as substandard about 5 percent of the more than 250 million yards of fabric it buys annually. (The total yardage used would wrap a bandage around the equator almost five times; the rejected fabric would stretch from San Francisco to Melbourne.)

The standards are rigidly applied. The 13.5-ounce denim used in the famed jeans is produced largely by one American mill, and has been for more than 35 years. What is found to be flawed is rejected by Levi Strauss. Denim has been in short supply, and what Strauss rejects gets snapped up by less persnickety competitors in the United States and abroad.

Standards are not relaxed for expediency's sake. The company postponed for a year production of double-knit leisure suits, and thus missed the great boom of 1972, because Product Integrity repeatedly rejected the sampled piece goods as substandard. While Levi's merchandisers fretted and other companies scored, Product Integrity stood firm. Similarly, designers and merchandisers in women's wear, acutely aware of timing in that fashion-oriented market, repeatedly seek relief, and repeatedly find their fabrics rejected and returned to the mills.

Such striving for quality is not unique to Levi Strauss, to be sure; other corporations undertake similar efforts, but how many of them are willing to exchange a million garments (with a wholesale value of $7 million) to back up the pledge each year? Despite the costs, the return policy has been in effect for as long as anyone can remember. Walter Haas, Sr., who is now 88 years old, recalls that it hasn't changed since he joined the company in 1919. "If you don't give quality," he says, "you're responsible. It's as simple as that. Maybe that is one of the reasons we have been successful — because we have curious ideas."

The idea that Levi's should be durable, whether it's curious or not, has generated customer loyalty beyond dollar measure. The company regularly gets unsolicited letters from customers bragging that *their* pants lasted five or ten years, or seven unwashed months in a Cuban prison, or through high school, marriage and pregnancy. Doctors and grateful parents write in claiming that little Johnny's Levi's saved him from severe injury when he fell off: (a) his bike, (b) the cliff, or (c) the roof.

Consumer affection for Levi's is unrivaled by any product since Henry Ford's Model T. Presumably, the affection could be meaured in dollars if one but knew how.

But profit is not the only motive here. In an era of inch-thick contracts and phalanxes of attorneys, Levi Strauss still feels free to do business with suppliers in its own quirky fashion. For 30 years the company has contracted for the manufacture of pants with a relatively small firm in Sedalia, Missouri. The J.A. Lamy Co. gave up its own branded lines long ago and now makes only Levi's. It is totally vulnerable to takeover, yet for 30 years the contract between Lamy and Levi Strauss has been no firmer than a handshake.

Levi Strauss & Co. has unique values,

and a new employee has some learning to do. The president of Levi's Womenswear Division, Jim McDermott, explains that "If you make a mistake in buying a fabric, you don't go back to the mill and say, 'I'm Levi's, and if you don't bury it I'll cut you off.' You eat your mistake. We made a commitment and we live with it."

Commitment means a lot to McDermott, who came to Levi Strauss because of a broken promise. He had been a salesman for General Foods' Jello Division when the company "screwed around with the bonus arrangement they had and I got pissed off." McDermott quit, went to an employment agency, and was dispatched to Levi Strauss as a clerk. Thirteen years later, McDermott is president of a $62-million-a-year division and a corporate vice-president.

The commitment also turns inward. Managers of many corporations refer to their workers as "family." The decision lasts as long as labor relations are amicable.

Levi Strauss managers, especially the older ones with the most seniority, also look upon their coworkers warmly. And they reminisce about when the company was small, when the production manager knew every woman on the line and knew her husband's name and how her children were doing in school, when the Haases loaned money to hard-put workers, or paid extraordinary medical bills.

In 30 years of explosive growth, from 2,000 to 32,000 employees around the world, much of the paternalism has dissipated. "The Haases are trying to hold onto it," says Ed Pera, manager of the company's Canadian operations. "We're losing that feeling for people. The Haases are extremely upset about it."

Because the Haases themselves can no longer personally give employees that sense of family, they have tried to insti-tutionalize it. When Levi Strauss first topped the billion-dollar sales mark in 1975, the board of directors voted to give the 2,700 home-office employees company stock. And a $50 check went to each of the firm's 23,000 far-flung workers. The company paid the income taxes on the bonuses. Altogether, the gesture cost Levi Strauss $2.1 million.

On its own motion — no union contract or retirement plan mandated it — the company increased pensions of its 800 retirees in 1975 and 1976 by as much as 80 percent in order to cover increases in the cost of living. The additional outlay of $250,000 each year is modest, though over the next 15 years it will likely total some $1.75 million.

Past retirees automatically get boosts to keep them abreast of present retirees, again at the instance of the company. The only rationale is that "it's the right thing to do," as vice-president and director Paul Glasgow put it.

The examples go on and on. After purchasing a clothing maker called Oberman in an effort to expand Levi's production quickly, Strauss gave the 3,000 Oberman employees who came with the factory full credit for the years they had worked in Oberman plants.

To a corporation selling 40 percent of men's denim pants in the United States and making $129 million in profits, these sums are not great burdens. Still, how many of the other 241 U.S. companies with more than a billion dollars in annual sales are so keen to share their wealth?

The generosity, according to Ernest Griffes, the manager of employee benefits, stems from a "basic tradition of sincere concern for the welfare and security of employees." Because of their scope, such efforts are necessarily impersonal, the corporate equivalent of a family tradition. So it isn't particularly surprising that Walter Haas should be proudest of a more modest program of his, one that could be funded from petty cash. It was his idea to hire older people to pay monthly visits to retirees in San Francisco and Knoxville, Tennessee. The visitors bring gifts, sometimes food, and make certain that the retirees are cared for. "I really don't understand why more companies don't do it. It doesn't cost much, and we want people to know that we care about them, even after they've stopped working for us."

It is hard to see how unpublicized visits to old people have any bearing on Wall Street's yardstick of corporate excellence — return on investment. Certainly, there are no more hours at the salvage table to be wrung from Mary Rossi, who, at 101 years of age, remembers Levi Strauss himself.

In 1978 Levi Strauss began awarding shares of stock to all employees with five years of service, one share for each year. The initial distribution to 8,800 workers dealt off 60,000 shares with a market value of $1.7 million.

Employee stock ownership is not a new concept at Levi Strauss. The firm seems to have been one of the first to permit employees to be shareholders. Between 1912 and 1971, the year the company went public, about a thousand workers bought shares, frequently at bargain prices. When "LeviStr" went on the Big Board, 29 current and former employees became instant millionaires, and scores of others, including a stock clerk whose shares were worth more than $340,000, found themselves comfortably fixed for life.

As a matter of practice, union-negotiated benefit increases are automatically extended to the 25 percent of the workers not enrolled in unions. And that turns out to be good for business. Levi Strauss has lost just five week's work to strikes since it was first unionized in 1935. Negotiations with the three unions in Strauss plants — Teamsters in one distribution center, the United Garment Workers, and the Amalgamated Clothing and Textile Union elsewhere — are low-key. "As long as you're fair," said Max Cowan, national production manager of the $700-million-a-year Jeans Division, "it doesn't make much diffeence whether you have a labor union or you don't."

Levi Strauss has been a corporate overachiever in equal employment opportunity. Already integrated in its California facilities, the firm began hiring blacks in segrated Blackstone, Virginia, in 1957. Community opposition was strong, and at one point the company feared it was going to lose the plant's output. But Levi Strauss insisted on integrating and since it was the town's biggest employer, it prevailed. Levi Strauss has been totally integrated since.

With many companies, entry-level jobs for unskilled blacks and browns are one thing, promotions another. Levi Strauss is doing relatively well, but management is acutely aware that its proportions of minorities don't reflect the population. Minorities now constitute 14 percent of all company managers, 20 percent of the professionals, and one-third of the technicians. Percentages are inching up year by year largely because of promotions from within. Sewing machine operators rise to jobs as line managers; clerks become merchandisers. It is, in fact, an extension of the company policy of old: "Hire an office boy when the president retires." Two of the five current division presidents began as shipping clerks in the stock room.

Though women make up 80 percent of Levi Strauss's employees, until the women's movement became strong, the company was no more sensitive to sexual discrimination than other corporations were. Only a few women survived competition and prejudice to rise to middle management positions. Once discrimination was understood for what it was, Levi Strauss moved to put things right. According to its 1977 annual report, women now make up 22 percent of the officials and managers, 40 percent of the professionals, and 8 percent of its (at one time all-male) domestic sales force of 600 persons.

The Haases and others at Levi Strauss are very much aware that social responsibility is good business and that it contributes to profits. Walter Haas explains, "We can compete with IBM or Procter and Gamble and all the others for the top graduate school students because they want to identify with a company that has this philosophy. And that assures our success 20 years from now."

If Levi Strauss does right by its customers, suppliers and employees, with whom it has a direct mercantile relationship, the corporation also perceives a responsibility to the larger community. Its company-sponsored community relations teams in the towns and cities in which the corporation has facilities are the broadest based, most innovative, and probably the most altruistic of the Levi Strauss programs.

Volunteers at each of the domestic facilities seek out worthy local projects, then support them. The Levi Strauss foundation sometimes helps with cash contributions, but it has other interests.

The Clovis, New Mexico boyswear manufacturing plant was selected as having the outstanding community relations team in 1976. Its members had, among other things, visited nursing homes, given a Christmas party at a

mental retardation center, collected toys and clothes for a children's home, and so on. In an era of six-figure corporate donations to causes, such efforts appear modest, and they are. But in Clovis, which has a population of 28,495, they are noticed, and they have counterparts in teams at 50 other company plans and distribution centers.

Indeed such employee teams are mandated company policy. Not all plant managers are enthusiastic, but the efforts of their CRT are taken into account when bonuses are awarded.

Approximately one-third of the firm's sales, and something less than one-third of its profits, come from overseas operations. Corporate policy stresses strongly identifying Levi Strauss with the host country. Only 10 percent of its international managers are American citizens. Each of the overseas groups has been transformed into a self-sustaining manufacturing and sales entity; European goods are made and distributed in Europe. Far Eastern goods are marketed in the Orient. Prices are necessarily higher, and sales are thus limited, but Levi Strauss thereby becomes a local manufacturer, without the aura of a rich American corporation exploiting the local economy.

Except for some sweaters made in the Far East, Levi Strauss does not take advantage of cheaper foreign labor to manufacture goods overseas for sale in the United States. That, of course, places Levi Strauss at a substantial disadvantage domestically. Smaller, more fashion-oriented manufacturers such as Faded Glory, Brittania, Jag and Chemin-de-fer rely on cheap foreign labor, workers paid as little as 40 cents an hour (compared to the American minimum wage of $3.60), to produce their one-season, high-markup garments. Geared for the long haul, and for repeat business, Levi Strauss forgoes the quick profits.

Overseas operations are governed by a thick book of corporate policy statements, the most important of which are two from its "Code of International Business Principles":

The Company is committed to operating well above the minimum legal standard such that its conduct and intentions are above question ... The Company subscribes to the belief that its operations should provide benefits to ... the host country as well as its stockholders and investors. The Company affirms that all its investments will be in harmony with the social, economic and environmental priorities of the host countries and that it intends to conduct its business in such a way as to earn acceptance and respect.

Every multinational company doing business today makes policy statements of platitudes. At Levi Strauss, they are taken seriously. The company does no business in South Africa and Rhodesia. And it has closed its operations in Indonesia, in part because of the common local practice of paying bribes for the most routine of services.

For all the good intentions, overseas managers do transgress. In 1976 and 1977, Levi Strauss anounced that four of its people had passed $145,000 in bribes, in the form of so-called license fees expected to be paid by foreigners. Levi Strauss reported the payments to the Securities and Exchange Commission and dismissed the officers involved for violating corporate policy.

In June the company agreed to pay $3.5 million to Californians who had bought Levi's jeans between 1972 and 1975. The agreement settled a suit filed by the state's attorney general charging that Levi Strauss salesmen had threatened to close accounts with retailers who discounted Levi's jeans. The company, in this matter, did not admit guilt but settled nevertheless.

Good corporate citizenship of the sort practiced by Levi Strauss does not just happen. Nor can it be legislated, not exactly. Governments may permit tax credits for charitable contributions and corporations will make charitable contributions. But no tax credit could account for Levi Strauss's charitable impulses. Congress may mandate reforms in pension plans, and cunning tax lawyers will find loopholes. Making certain that retired workers are well cared for stems from a sense of duty foreign to bottom-line economics and legal obligation.

Walter Haas, Jr., much honored for his efforts to promote social responsibility among his peers, now has stopped giving speeches about it. "They don't do any good," he says.

Of course what business and industry are not inclined to do government will require. Business people can complain that there is too much government regulation already — of air and water pollution, of occupational safety and equal employment opportunity, of product safety and efficacy, of warranties, pension plans and energy conservation. But the government intruded only after the private sector flagrantly failed to live up to minimal standards of social responsibility.

For the most part corporations now care mainly about a single measure of business performance: profit and loss. Which is why Levi Strauss is such a fascinating anomaly.

Ed Cray is The Director of Metro Training at the Los Angeles Times whose book, *Levi's*, was published by Houghton Mifflin. Cray, who also teaches journalism at the University of Southern California, is at work on a history of General Motors and a biography of George C. Marshall.

Beyond tokenism: Women as true corporate peers

Eleanor Brantley Schwartz and James J. Rago, Jr.

Can organizations cope with male executives who resist working with women as peers? The authors explore this phenomenon and suggest individual and corporate strategies to deal with it.

Traditional organizational roles have evolved with men as peers and women as their subordinates. Most men respond with a resounding "Never!" to the prospect of being a subordinate, or even a peer, to a woman. Endless rationalizations have supported their position, including such charges as "Women are too emotional to be good decision makers" and "They use femininity to get their way." These rationalizations are manifestations of childhood learning about ourselves and the other sex. These attitudes are carried over into organizational roles and act against the effective integration of women and men as corporate peers.

Where women have been introduced into management, pressures have been exerted far too often to "keep them in their place." An obvious tactic, which is similar to one used for handling the obsolete male executive, calls for the following treatment: Give her a title, an office with all the trappings, including a secretary and a good salary, "but keep her away from operations!" Put her someplace where people can see her, "but make sure she doesn't say anything." This procedure has prevented the formation of relationships in which the participants are coequals, or colleagues, and thus has avoided threatening executive masculinity.

As a result of increasing pressure for equal opportunity and affirmative action programs, however, corporate management finds that integration of females into executive positions must be faced. This challenge is difficult in that women and men as management peers must experience each other in nontraditional, and therefore threatening, ways. This threat results partly from the individual's severely limited peer contacts with the opposite sex. A more disturbing and deeply rooted cause of threat and resistance lies in what they personally have come to need and expect from the other sex.

In our work with male and female executives, we continually encounter such threatening situations. Our principal concern is with the phenomenon involving restricted dimensions in which a male is dependent upon a female (and vice versa) for personal fulfillment. Particularly troublesome are chronic deficiencies involving ego needs: the need to validate manhood or womanhood, the need to satisfy nurturing not provided by a parent, and the need to punish a sister or brother. A person who is continually dependent upon one of the opposite sex to fulfill such deprivations tends to behave as if he were in an unchanging, closed system. Our experience is that far too many executives are chronically deprived-dependent people. Although many of these executives intellectually believe women should use their talents and education, emotionally they have mixed feelings about offering them the same professional opportunities as men. On the one hand, equal opportunity is desirable. On the other hand, it tilts organizational norms. The executive fears the psychic trauma that he and his organization will feel with women as equals.

Are organizations prepared to cope with the behavioral effects of men and women working together as professional peers? We suspect not. For instance, consider the destructive potential for the organization and the individual in the common situation of the executive indoctrinated to be a "man's man." He prides himself as a department manager, and he believes that "only a real man can do my job." Now, a woman, as a manager of an adjacent department — or worse, his immediate superior — jeopardizes his self-image of strength. Some of the destructive reactions we have found occurring in such situations included the following:

He attempts to ruin the effectiveness of the woman through conscious or un-conscious sabotage. He may use her as a scapegoat for errors he has made.

He seeks to avoid the situation by isolating his department as much as possible from the influence of the woman.

He withholds help and information she needs to learn her job.

He withdraws into himself, letting his capabilities wither. The reality of his being on a par with a woman has shattered his concept of being a man's man that kept his self-worth intact. He either remains at this zero level or re-develops to live with himself as he really is — with weaknesses and strengths — as well as with women as they really are.

Resolving a male-female threat tends to involve substantial changes for many executives in terms of the way they view themselves and the opposite sex. Although not in business to produce substantial behavioral changes in its employees, corporate management can provide circumstances that minimize female-male role conflicts and resolve them when they occur. To some extent, the problem can be cured by time, but only if appropriate reorientation begins now. The process requires a committed corporate management, one that tackles the problem at its source, and develops and implements a strategy leading to complementary relationships between male and female peers. Management is required to understand the resistance to women as organizational peers and superiors, and to provide individuals with methods — as well as supportive action — for coping with the resistance.

Social propaganda

Except for biological differences in physical strength and sex, studies show no actual trait differences between females and males. Any differences that can be generalized result more from cultural training and indoctrination than from biological fact. People become the expectations of their social propaganda (Mead 1971).

Societal and family role demands for males stress culturally approved masculine achievement. Achievements in dress design or nursing are not culturally approved. High social self-esteem for males results from extrinsic accomplishments (good college grades and executive salary, for example), while for females it results from intrinsic qualities (sociability and sensitivity, for example) (Hollander 1972; Connell and Johnson 1970; Doavan and Adelson 1966). Moreover, the male is pressured to keep producing: "If the next step is not taken, then the approval becomes only a remembered happiness, now withdrawn, which must be worked for again" (Mead 1971).

Overall, the male role incorporates an emphasis upon self and self-expression leading to achievement-oriented, autonomous, aggressive, and masterful types of behavior and attitudes. In contrast, the female role focuses upon others rather than self, leading to supportive, dependent, and passive types of behavior and attitudes (Gray-Shelberg et al. 1972).

Currently, women tend to be caught in a dilemma of conflicting role demands. Their socialization runs counter to executive occupational demands defined by the culture as ''masculine'' (independence, aggressiveness, self-expression, for example).

Socialization tends to mitigate against career interests in women, but among those women who do elect to enter the occupational arena, advancement in status is more likely to be achieved by women who diverge from the traditional feminine sex-role (Block 1972).

Such ambivalence can create psychological barriers, which may be expressed by avoiding success in competitive achievement situations because of negative social consequences (male disapproval, loss of affection, or decreased marital prospects). Furthermore, women so motivated tend to underachieve in competitive intellectual situations when a male is present (Horner 1963). "Can I remain a woman and still be successful?" they wonder. "Or must I become like a man to play and win in their game?" (Schwarts 1970).

All of us are indoctrinated to varying degrees about what women and men are like, what each can and cannot do, and what each should and should not be. Men are taught that females are not as cool under stress as they, certainly not as trustworthy, nor as open and confronting. They are told they must be strong, manly, and protective. Women are taught that men are aggressive, less emotional, less sensitive than they. Thus, prescribed sex roles restrict what a person can be. Living a role limits what one feels, senses, and believes, as well as how he acts to fit its image. The man's man rejects nonmasculine feelings (tenderness or compassion) within himself and in other men; the woman's woman disowns nonfeminine emotions within herself and other women (aggressiveness or hardness).

Become deprived-dependent

Heavily indoctrinated into a culturally approved masculine or femine role, one tends to become closed to experiences and behavior unacceptable to the learned role. Thus, for the most part, males and females grow up encountering each other in only limited ways: as mother-son, father-daughter, sister-brother, date-date, or neighbor-"pain in the neck next door." There is little contact as peers — males and females working together toward common goals. Consequently, men and women are strangers as peers, unknown quantities to each other. Furthermore, family influences often intensify one's restrictiveness toward the opposite sex by creating a chronic deprived-dependent situation. These following factors affect the nature and development of an individual.

Family environment □ One is most influenced by family environment, in which he learns to relate with other people within the family. These early interactions, particularly with the mother, provide models through which a person develops knowledge of who he is and others are. Behavioral results range from healthy growth to crippling psychosis.

Expectations of family members □ Critical to development is the degree to which one is forced to fulfill expectations of others in the family, especially the mother and father. These expectations represent models of what one should be. For instance, to meet the mother's expectations, a boy may "sissify" himself to be her "good little boy" or he may harden himself to avoid unmanly thoughts, emotions, and activities to fulfill a Gary Cooper image.

Parental deprivation □ Expectations often are manifestations of parental deprivation. Unable to develop and express their own talents and desires, parents may live through their children to fulfill

their deprivations (Janov 1970). The "stage mother" pushing her child to stardom and the "athlete father" living each game more than his dutiful son are examples. Other behaviors stemming from deprivations are less obvious, but still quite harmful: unexpressed husband-wife resentment acted out verbally or physically upon a child, parents' unfulfilled nurtural needs causing forced development of a little "adult" to care for his childlike parent, and on and on.

Satisfaction of others' deprivations □ A person indoctrinated to meet others' expectations (particularly if he is used to satisfying their deprivtions) tends to develop his own deprivations. Since he had to distort himself to become what others want, he is deprived of full development of the person he really is.

Satisfaction of personal deprivations □ Unable to meet certain needs himself, a person may seek others who fill roles needed to satisfy these deprivations. A man may seek from a woman warmth that he did not have from his mother. Men often marry to find a mother; women frequently marry to have a father.

Life as a closed system □ Locked in the past with his unfulfilled needs and the need to keep them buried by self-control and compensating behaviors, the chronically deprived person encounters others on a restricted basis. He also pressures others into constricted roles: "You must be what I want you to be." His deprivations limit his Gestalt — the wholeness he perceives of others and their circumstances. The derelict looks for a prospect good for a handout; similarly, the deprived person depends upon others in a static, fixed way.

Critical to a closed system is a particular set of beliefs about oneself and others. One develops these "truths" from what he encounters early and from what he learns in subsequent experiences: men and women are like that and act like this (Rokeach 1960). New informatiion which does not fit is either censored or distorted to fit within the system. An abundance of myths about the nature of women and men furnish supportive learning for any and all kinds of deprived-dependent people. Furthermore, if a particular truth is not there, the mind will create one on demand. Table 1 illustrates some common deprivations and corresponding limited perceptions of the opposite sex.

The relationship

A woman's relationship with a male whose behavior is restricted in a closed system requires her to play a role that feeds his deprivation (mother, strength giver, or doormat). This person sees women as stereotypes, mostly as objects for satisfaction of this insatiable ego deprivation. Women must meet these expectations or they become a threat because they may expose his weaknesses or other "bad" traits that he has learned to hide from himself and, hopefully, others. Dependent, he must keep women in circumstances which assure nourishment for his deprivations and which render the woman harmless.

Control is attempted through punishment and reward (support and recognition versus nonsupport and rejection) so that she is corralled into living his "do's and don'ts." If the woman allows herself to be drawn into such a relationship, she

Table 1
Some common deprivations and perceptions (myths) about the opposite sex

Dependent men	
Nature of deprivation	View of woman
Lack of self-worth	Possession, support to status
Lack of mother's nurturing	Warm, caring mother
Lack of potency and strength	Weak, soft, in need of protection
Lack of competency	Professionally less capable
Lack of recognition	Admiring audience
Lack of aggressiveness and competitiveness	Champion to provide strength and support
Lack of acceptance of "bad" parts of self	Villainess in need of punishment
Lack of closure on early hurts and setbacks	Healer, nurse
Dependent women	
Nature of deprivation	View of man
Lack of self-worth	Possession, adds to status
Lack of father's love	Kindly father
Lack of potency and strength	Strong protector without weaknesses
Lack of competency	All-knowing sage
Lack of aggressiveness and competitiveness	Forgiving, patient leader
Lack of closure on early hurts and setbacks	Healer, doctor
Lack of acceptance of "bad" parts of self	Villain in need of punishment
Lack of attractiveness	Admiring seeker

becomes part of the deprived person's closed system. The greater a man's chronic dependency toward women, the stronger will be his need to control them, to be "closed" in his relationships with them, and the more resistant to change.

Women as subordinates

Where women are subordinate to men, traditional organizational roles have evolved that support both male and female dependency needs. In the boss-secretary relationship, the secretary provides status for her boss by behaving in certain ways, ranging from how she dresses and answers the telephone to the little extras she performs to make his life more pleasant. She can be his office wife, office mother, or office shrew. In turn, her boss can be her office father, office admirer, or office villain. If her behavior is outside his expectations, the deprived executive punishes his secretary. He, most likely, does not feel free to "blast" her openly (though some do), but if she also is dependent he withholds what she needs from him to soothe her deprivations (for example, compliments and recognition.).

Although he is her boss, she can punish him in return if he does not meet her expectations. She knows what "buttons to push" to aggravate him where he is deprived. This may be his need to feel potent or his need to be cared for. In a way, just as deprived-dependent married couples, they become prisoners of each other.

Women as peers and superiors

It is natural for the deprived executive to develop a dependent relationship with his new woman colleague. Partly, the process involves manipulations to make her fit his myths about females. If she is also a deprived-dependent person, she may develop a rapport with him in which they give each other what each wants, and all is well. In this case, she fits his role-expectations for a woman, and he fits hers for a man. Thus, if the male executive can successfully manipulate and subsequently control his female counterpart, his myths are undisturbed. She is defined by job and money as a peer, but in actions she fits his mold for women.

What happens if she is not a deprived-dependent person and resists pressure to fit his expectations? Since he needs her to be less competent than he, he may withhold help and information she needs to learn her job. If necessary, he could escalate his pressure by using her as a scapegoat for errors and, thereby, sabotaging her efforts. If he is extensively closed, he has erected formidable barriers to protect himself against change.

Where such events have occurred, higher management has been less than adequate in dealing with them successfully. Usually, the role-bound male executive prevails, his world intact, while the woman loses. His superiors, as well as the new woman on the job, tend not to recognize and understand the fixed-role phenomenon and its symptoms. Consequently, management is not organizationally geared to handle them. The woman-man peer situation is still too new in most organizations. thus, the woman's professional survival and subsequent success depend largely upon her own efforts.

Counteractions against the deprived-dependent male executive depend upon the woman's freedom within herself. She may take any of the following courses:

Disengage ☐ Hide, minimize contacts, keep a low profile
Feed his deprivations ☐ Buy him off, be-

come indispensable use his weakness to manipulate him

Resist passively ☐ Humor him without giving in, ignore him, resist without open confrontation, take what he gives without striking back

War openly ☐ Overwhelm him, put him on the defensive, go for his weakness to unhinge him, work toward removing him from the office.

Tactfully but aggressively resist ☐ Refuse to feed his deprivations, minimize dependency by developing marketability to move on if necessary, push back without destructiveness, support behaviors opposite from dependency behaviors, gain his trust, support him professionally without playing his games.

What the organization can do

Some say if women are just "thrown in," co-workers will get used to them. The solution, as indicated, is not that simple. It is not enough to filter women into management training programs, place them on important committees, and promote them to higher positions. Full acceptance of women as professional peers or superiors requires relearning by both sexes to dispel previously learned male-female role expectations. In most corporations such relearning has been painfully slow, with only minimal progress. Women and men who attempt to break out of these fixed roles need substantial inner strength as they risk rejection and failure in their attempt to discover and develop themselves along unchartered courses.

Top management action must, through policies and attitudes that genuinely express the responsiveness of corporate managements, set the exam-

ple the entire organization follows. Crucial to success is a clear communication of the commitment to integration from the top of the organization. Support must start with the chief executive who follows up his decree all down the line. Trouble comes when management pays lip service to integration, but in reality is committed to tokenism. Overtly, management goes all out to get good talent, while covertly blocking these competent females from traditionally sacred male executive areas. Not only does management waste effort and resources hiring these women, but, in neutralizing them against doing anything, management plants an eventual time bomb for itself. Table 2 summarizes several goals with concomitant policies and actions found to be important to the successful integration of males and females in exempt salary positions.

Until women and men are freed from absolute sex roles that imprison both, hostility between the sexes will continue. Both sexes must revolt. Men are not the enemy; women are not the enemy. To be anti-woman or anti-man is to be anti-life.

We are brought up with each sex directed into "his and her" roles and slots. Children do not have any prejudices — they must be carefully taught. Men have been taught from childhood to be rational, unemotional, brave, and strong. A process of erosion goes on within a man because of the demands of the role. Manhood prescribes certain behavior around men and women. In fact, that is where real pressure is: "I do not want to become like a woman." Men are dominant because they are cast in that role by society. Women then become subversively dominant. They exploit the exploiter.

Women learn to feed the male ego deprivations and use his fears and weak-

Table 2
Organizational goals and some corresponding policies and actions

Goal	Policy	Action
Replace myths with new learning about the realities of people.	Provide a wide breadth of experience with many people.	Allow people to assume a variety of roles in training experiences. Expose stereotyping and camouflaging. Use male-female task groups in actual operations where success depends upon cooperation.
Maximize performance and development of people.	Give firm support to individual initiative and success promoted by supervisors. Increase total human resources available to the organization.	Set up systems of objectives, action plans, and measurements to produce and account for performance and development. Use teams of mature judges to evaluate performance.
Minimize organizational trauma.	Avoid attempting to change views rapidly. Companies are not in the psychotherapy business.	Survey attitudes to place people with most receptive associates. Screen males' views toward working with women. Avoid teaming a female with a deprived-dependent male and vice versa.
Minimize a person's isolation and other defenses.	Prevent a person from losing visibility and getting sandbagged.	Assure that an individual's career growth is followed by a third party who has the power to provide opportunities and make fair evaluations. Provide mobility and exposure to a variety of work situations and contacts with various higher management people.
Achieve openness to issues.	Give firm support to people who openly bring out issues and risk trying to resolve them.	Have periodic development sessions with an internal consultant to work out issues, and/or have sessions with a group comprising a diagonal slice of the organizational hierarchy.
Minimize tokenism to achieve true integration.	Be committed to the person most qualified for a task.	Express strong top-level support for integration. Set specific developmental objectives to which people can assume commitment.

nesses to manipulate him. One of the reasons deprived-dependent women do not want to work for women is because they cannot use manipulative behavior to get what they want. Each behavior generates hostility in the other, and a vicious cycle continues.

Most men and women are unaware of the process. One of the objectives of the article is to shed light on the process we use in influencing each other — and the price we pay for doing so. A relationship between equals is more rewarding, more honest, and most lasting. Management's concentration on men and women as contributors, each with unique talents and potentials which are unrelated to their sex, will move us further toward a greater sense of equality and cooperation.

Breaking Through

Women on the Move

In one of the most significant trends of the 1980s, women are steadily toppling barriers and assuming leadership in fields that traditionally have been closed to them.

The process is slow, arduous, often unnoticed. While the numbers are still small, the attitude changes they signal are enormous.

A decade ago, the nation's space program allowed no women as astronauts. Now it has eight.

Ten years ago, even the largest U.S. banks could count on one finger their number of female vice-presidents. Now some giant banks have more than 100 women as vice-presidents and one or two as senior vice-presidents.

In 1972, women in companies with 100 or more employees held only 1 of 8 management jobs. Now they occupy 1 of 5. Ten years ago, 13 women served in the House of Representatives. Next January, 21 will serve, a record. Just over 300 women sat in state legislatures in 1972. The current figure exceeds 900.

And until last year, the Supreme Court was a monastic sanctum. Now it has Associate Justice Sandra O'Connor.

Statistics can deceive. A different set of figures, equally valid, shows that women — who are 51.3 percent of the U.S. population — still comprise only 5 percent of executives in the 50 top corporations, 10 percent of the astronauts, 12 percent of state legislators, 2 percent of U.S. senators.

Clearly, though the walls are crumbling around preserves that are still male dominated. Once the trailblazers breach the barriers, others follow close behind.

The momentum can be seen in the legal field. In 1960, only 3.3 percent of lawyers and judges were women. Since then, the figure has jumped four times. And, as Justice O'Connor has noted, women make up a third to a half of today's law-school classes.

Some women leaders in nontraditional fields are well known: Rosalyn Yalow, the second woman in history — after France's Marie Curie — to win the Nobel

Prize in medicine; Sherry Lansing, the ex-model and script reader who became president of 20th Century-Fox movie studios; Sarah Caldwell, the conductor who founded the Opera Company of Boston and was the first woman to wield a baton at the Metropolitan Opera in New York.

Yet most of today's female pioneers are not household names. Thelma Estrin? A professor of engineering at the University of California at Los Angeles who helped pioneer the application of computer technology to brain research. Eugenie Clark? Biologist, University of Maryland professor of zoology, world renowned as an expert on sharks. Barbara Newell? Former president of Wellesley, now chancellor of Florida's university system. Nelle Nugent and Liz McCann? Toast-of-New-York producers whose hits include "Dracula," "The Elephant Man" and "The Life and Adventures of Nicholas Nickleby."

They and the six women whose stories follow demonstrate that it is now possible for women to reach high levels in almost any career. Numerically, women are still getting off the ground in positions of leadership. But, as the space program shows, they are finding that literally even the sky is no limit.

"Just another astronaut"

HOUSTON

When Sally Ride slips into her fireproof blue coveralls and blasts into orbit next April aboard the Challenger shuttle, she will become an instant heroine as the first U.S. woman in space.

A 31-year-old astrophysicist with a doctorate from Stanford, Ride takes pains to downplay her gender: "I am just another astronaut. There's nothing I'm going to be doing in space that I will be doing because I am a woman."

Still, women in space are a rare breed. Only two, both from the Soviet Union, have orbited the earth so far. Women in the physical sciences are not all that common, either. Of 3,124 people who earned U.S. doctorates in that field last year, only 380 were females.

Ride, who will help operate the spacecraft's intricate robot arm during a six-day mission, says she entered her field at a good time "in that the women's movement, coming when it did, helped me a lot. Women now are coming at an even better time."

Her own timing was perfect. She began job hunting in 1977 — the year the National Aeronautics and Space Administration announced it was accepting astronaut applications for the first time since the late 1960s and that women would be considered. Until then, Ride says, "it hadn't occurred to me that it was even an option."

Mailing a postcard, she applied — as did 1,000 other women and 7,000 men. Nine months later, in January of 1978, Ride was one of six women chosen among the space agency's 35 new astronaut recruits. Two more women were selected in 1980, and females now number eight of the total corps of 78.

When Ride joined the space program, she found many male engineers "in white shirts, ties and short haircuts who had been working on the space program 20 years and didn't know what to expect" of their new female colleagues.

The way to overcome their suspicions, she found, was to prove right off the bat that she knew what she was doing. Now she spends 12 to 16 hours a week in shuttle-flight simulations and 15 hours a month in a T-38 jet trainer. Recently she married astronaut Steven Hawley.

Ride says she has not thought much beyond the April mission, noting: "Going up in the shuttle is enough of a major milestone." But one thing is certain: She wants to stay with NASA and hopes to fly in space again.

SARAH PETERSON

"Women have to be twice as good"

ORLANDO, Fla. Pauline Hartington grew up in Rhode Island and prepared herself for a traditionally feminine job — schoolteacher. But when she looked for work 29 years ago, beginning teachers were earning $2,400 a year. So she joined the Naval Reserve, which offered $4,200.

That started a military career that eventually saw her vault to the rank of rear admiral — the second woman to achieve such status — and to her present job as commander of the Naval Training Center here. At 51, she oversees a staff of 2,500 military personnel, 3,000 civilians and a student population of 10,000.

Even though her family has been supportive, she says: "I guess my mother could not understand a daughter who never married. I told her I married the Navy."

Along the way, Hartington became the first woman naval officer to attend the National War College for advanced military studies. She also was the first woman appointed secretary of the Joint Chiefs of Staff. On loan from the Navy, she helped set up the civilian personnel office for President Johnson's war on poverty program. As a young officer, she handled policy decisions involving the Navy's undergraduate education and foreign language programs.

Looking back, Hartington recalls that 29 years ago the highest Navy rank women could achieve was commander,

"and you had only a 1 percent chance of that." Since last year, women have been allowed to compete for any rank, and their duties have become more varied. "I envy the young women who have the opportunity to go to sea," she says. "I wish I'd been born later. God, I would have loved to have gone to sea."

Hartington wears her uniform almost everywhere, but she remains a species many men cannot identify. In an airport once, an elderly man noticed her gold braid, shook his head and marveled: "You must fly the really big ones." Waitresses still often call her "Hon," and she grits her teeth when male civilians great her at social gatherings by kissing her on the cheek and cooing: "That's the first time I've ever kissed an admiral!"

The admiral worries about some of the Navy's new women recruits. "They're content to be mediocre," she laments. In her own trek to the top, she says, "everywhere you went, you had to keep reinventing the wheel, re-proving that you were indeed capable. If somebody else went home at 4, you had to stay until 6." On her desk is a plaque that reads: "Women have to be twice as good."

Hartington, who says she has had "a grand time" in the Navy, recalls the sacrifices — "the theater tickets I've torn up, the dinners I've called off or arrived at 2 hours late." But she insists: "It's paid off. I'm 'Good Old Dependable' — and that's not a bad reputation to have."

LINDA K. LANIER

Believe in yourself

WASHINGTON, D.C. Anne Wexler is a consummate "pol." She's a lobbyist on occasion for big business and, at other times, a strategist for the Democratic party.

She heads a political consulting firm,

Wexler and Associates, which she started last year. Before that, she was the top female adviser to Jimmy Carter with the title of assistant to the President for public liaison.

Now, as a lobbyist, she represents such firms as Bendix Corporation and Aetna Life & Casualty Company. As a politician, she is an adviser to former Vice President Walter Mondale, the Democratic Congressional Campaign Committee and the House Democratic Caucus. In the recent campaign, the Democratic leadership accepted one bit of advice from a select group of six consultants that includes Wexler: Raise the issue of whether GOP-inspired federal budget cuts are fair to minorities, the poor and the elderly.

Wexler, 52, is equally at home dealing with Republicans. "She works both sides of the aisle," notes one admiring Washington insider.

Wexler says she got into politics "because I love it." She started as a volunteer in Connecticut in Eugene McCarthy's 1968 presidential campaign. In 1970, she was one of two women in the country managing campaigns for U.S. Senate candidates. "We both lost," she recalls. Later she married her candidate, Joseph Duffey. He recently became Chancellor of the University of Massachusetts.

Professionally, Wexler's forte is rallying apparently disparate local-interest groups into a coalition behind a cause. Her guiding principle: "All politics is local, which means a national policy cannot succeed unless it has local support. You can't ignore the people. You have to reach out." A key congressional staffer calls her "the best grass-roots lobbyist in town."

Wexler insists that being a woman has never hindered her in politics. "I was not aware of any problem," she says. "Or if there was one, I just ignored it. My advice to other women wanting to enter politics is: Believe in yourself. Trust your own judgement. If you're a pro, you'll be taken seriously."

SUSANNA McBEE

I didn't think it was possible

SUN PRAIRIE, Wis. In 1980, Marjorie S. Matthews of the United Methodist Church became the first woman to be elected bishop of a major U.S. denomination. Yet she does not consider herself a pioneer in the women's movement.

"I never felt I was doing anything unusual," says the 66-year-old bishop, who is serving a four-year term as leader of Wisconsin's 131,000 United Methodists.

But the question of her sex was critical when she decided, while working as a secretary in 1959, that she would become a missionary. "I never dreamed of being a preacher or pastor because I didn't think it was possible for a woman," she recalls.

At the time, Matthews did not have the educational background for missionary work, and her minister in Alma, Mich., suggested that she take Methodist correspondence courses to become a "local pastor," one who serves congregations too small to have a full-time preacher.

She did, and spent many Sundays in the 1960s driving rural roads between two tiny Michigan churches. Later she attended seminary, becoming a full pastor in the United Methodist Church in 1970. Ultimately she earned master's and doctor's degrees from Florida State University. Divorced, she has a son and three grandchildren.

As pastor and preacher, Bishop Matthews recalls, she found that objections to female clergy did not originate in her congregations as might have been expected but instead came from pastors of other denominations: "I remember calling on an elderly couple in Michigan who said another clergyman told them they were doomed because they had a woman pastor. That's pretty upsetting to elderly people, but I convinced them it wasn't so. I said what the church was doing was proper, or it would fade away."

Even male colleagues in her own church did not accept her instantly. Recalling her early days as a district superintendent, she says: "The first time I met with my peers, the other superintendents — all male — carried on business just as if I were not there and as though I didn't have anything to say. It took some tuning on their part to recognize that I was speaking with some ability about the district I was in."

Even now the bishop occasionally gets letters quoting the Bible for support in questioning the propriety of a woman's holding high religious office. "If you read the Bible literally," she notes in reply to such criticism, "then you're going to say no one could be a disciple unless you were 30 years old and of the Jewish faith."

Such letters indicate that changes in attitudes come slowly. "Women in seminaries today who think all the problems have been solved aren't seeing the situation correctly," Bishop Matthews says. "They would face culture shock if they were appointed to a highly conservative area."

STEVE HUNTLEY

Dealing at the top

NEW YORK
Dalila Rodriguez is 36, married, mother of two children ages 6 and 11 — and a vice-president of Manufacturers Hanover Trust Company, one of the nation's largest banks.

Rodriguez says she always thought of herself as a career woman: "I never set any limitations."

Working for "Manny-Hanny" is like working for a small city: The bank has 20,900 employees, 800 of them vice presidents and 110 senior vice-presidents. Rodriguez is one of about 80 women to reach the vice-presidential level, including two senior VPs.

She grew up in Puerto Rico, daughter of a San Juan businessman. After four years of studying to become a pharmacist at the University of Puerto Rico, she left school without getting a degree.

Rodriguez and her husband came to New York, and in 1971 she was hired as a credit investigator at Manufacturers Hanover. She quickly moved into a year-long management-training program "because I had shown some initiative and a certain amount of aggressiveness."

Promotions have come steadily — from branch lending officer to branch assistant secretary to an assistant vice-president in international lending and finally, last February, to vice-president. Rodriguez manages a 650-million-dollar Latin American lending portfolio. On occasion she travels there and deals with banks, governments and private businesses in a region unaccustomed to treating females as equals. To her, the male environment she works in is a challenge.

"One should always try to excel," she says. "I make it a point to be organized. I had to prove that I could handle anything a single person or a man with a family could. I've never said I can't travel because of my children. I make arrangements to have my family well taken care of while I'm gone."

Whatever reservations her male colleagues may have had about women in banking, Rodriguez says attitudes are changing — especially in younger men. "They treat women on an equal basis, and they are more receptive to having a woman as a boss," she reports.

How does a woman make it in banking? Says Rodriguez: "Success is a matter of ability and performance — and personality. For a job like mine, you need to be self-confident and aggressive. You are dealing with people at the top. It's a matter of how you protect assets. Are you going to give the bank away, or improve its profits?"

PAT LYNCH

There's a real difference

CHICAGO

Hanna Holborn Gray, president of the University of Chicago, was not sure she could pursue an academic career when she got married in graduate school 28 years ago.

At that time, she recalls, "it was kind of assumed that if you got married, you dropped out of the academic job market. I thought I would have to be flexible."

She was. After her marriage to Charles M. Gray, she did not drop out. Instead, she taught at Harvard for five years. When her husband was appointed to the history faculty of the University of Chicago in 1960, she moved, too, becoming a fellow at a private research institution.

The next year, Gray joined the UC faculty herself, also teaching history. Gradually she shifted from teaching to administration. "For a long time, I didn't think it was the kind of work I was ready for."

But soon she became dean of the College of Arts and Sciences at Northwestern University, then provost of Yale University, later acting president there and finally, in 1978, president of UC. The fact that her husband, still a Chicago history professor, now works for her "is no problem at all," she says. "We think of ourselves as independent professionals and colleagues. It's kind of built into us."

On difficulties women face in higher education, Gray says: "It isn't terribly easy for women to be encouraged in academic institutions." But she adds: "I haven't experienced any sense that the men of the university regarded me as somewhat different or strange — someone requiring them to change their locker-room language."

Gray, 52, recalls her early days as a dean at Northwestern: "The naval commander in charge of the ROTC unit came to meet me in his dress whites and addressed me as 'Sir.' It was almost a caricature. He didn't salute, but I thought he might."

However, she contends that the academic realm is different from other professions once women overcome initial hurdles: "After you've been accepted as a colleague, the move as a woman to becoming president doesn't reawaken the early opposition — unlike the situation that often occurs when a woman becomes a chief executive in a corporation."

Gray contends that the job she holds "is a symptom of a larger change that's coming about." She adds: "It would be great to have it come along faster. Yet, you can see there's a real difference from the way things were before."

MARY GALLIGAN

Ten best places to work

Stephen Gayle and Lovett Gray

BE examines effective corporate affirmative action and turns up some familiar names — as well as a few surprises

Are there really "ten best places to work?" When we asked ourselves that question at *Black Enterprise,* we quickly discovered there were no simple answers. For blacks, life inside the corporation can be a subtle and sometimes mysterious mélange of ingredients that can add up to heaven for one person and hell for another. We found that no corporation is perfect; all had weaknesses as well as strengths. Some companies are good for blacks at the highest levels, while others have their strong suit in middle management. Some are heavy on minority employment at the bottom, while others stress hiring females over black males. But a number of companies did emerge as generally good places to work because of their overall commitment to equal opportunity. It is also clear that no company would be a good place to work without a strong policy of affirmative action and equal employment opportunity coming from the federal government.

But the federal programs that benefit minorities and prescribe remedies for discrimination now hover in a nebulous Washington twilight between survival and extinction, and top Reagan Administration officials are pushing minority concerns off the national agenda.

"None of this is as yet irreversible," warns Eleanor Holmes Norton, chair of the Equal Employment Opportunity Commission during the Carter Administration, "but black inattention to preserving the remedies for systematic discrimination could be fatal." Says J. Clay Smith, acting head of EEOC, "I kid you not when I say we are in a desperate fight for survival."

But other observers contend that many companies are already in a holding pattern because of the confused signals being called in the White House huddle. "The companies that are reacting to this sort of thing in Washington are those companies that never had a good record to begin with," says executive recruiter Richard Clarke. "They were always sitting on the fence waiting to see what side to fall on." Clarke says he has already had one firm tell him about their policy of hiring blacks: "Look, we don't have to do that anymore." People, says Clarke, "tend to follow secret messages, coded words, innuendo."

In order to determine which companies have the most effective affirmative action programs and why, *Black Enterprise* conducted a nationwide survey of a cross section of business people and government officials. The major factor that determines the success of any affirmative action program is the tone set by the chief executive officer and executive committee and the interplay between affirmative action officers and department heads. (The tying of affirmative action efforts to evaluations and bonuses has added a concrete, often effective and sometimes disputed, tool to the hiring and promotion arsenal.) In our survey and in conversations with company officials, the executive whose name was most frequently mentioned in connection with shaping his company's commitment to minorities was Coy Eklund, CEO of the Equitable Life Assurance Society in New York. Eklund has emerged as a sort of corporate pacesetter and when minority recruiters and personnel officials talk of effective programs they speak less about corporations as a whole and more about the individuals who lead them. Just below the CEO is his cadre of executives who, usually, will be charged with implementing the CEO's ideas. For this reason, it is "important to get black folks into meaningful positions where decisions are made — into boardrooms and senior-level positions with clout and not just title," says Charles Fields, an executive recruiter.

Once the tone is set, translating concept to reality rests on the personnel (or more recently "human management resources") department or on an affirmative action officer and his staff. They must coax lower and middle management to hire minorities, and often their liability to do so depends on personal relationships.

"There's a lot of resistance and resentment directed against EEO and affirmative action officers," says Goeffrey A. Atkins, president of New York Con-

sultant Groups, Ltd., an executive search company. "It's really the department head who makes the decision. If he or she is prejudiced, there's nothing you can do. And many times, personnel doesn't have the necessary rapport with the department head."

Eleanor Holmes Norton also identifies personnel as the key department to monitor for effective change within a company. "The numbers of minorities and women hired essentially measures whether personnel reforms are working."

Norton says that the strongest remedy offered by affirmative action is aggressive recruitment. Next is job-related tests and credentials. "When I first began working in this field as commissioner of New York City's Human Rights office, IQ tests were routinely given in pre-employment testing. It was a handy tool, but totally unrelated to employment. The work place was plagued through and through with such non-job-related credentials. Military rank, for example, might show leadership qualities, but it doesn't usually apply to women."

To emphasize their commitment to hire more minorities and women, some companies base evaluations and compensation packages partly on a manager's efforts to reach that goal. This tactic is viewed by some as counterproductive. "There has not been a need to push people into affirmative action, to beat people over the head," says June Clarke-Doar, director of employee relations and personnel development for Westinghouse Broadcasting. "People know if you're sincere; when you're not brow-beating someone, things get done faster."

But James Jones, director of affirmative action, recruitment, and community relations for Gannett Company, Inc., says that including affirmative action in performance evaluations insures that the concept plays a part in hiring and promotion, and that the executive does not "lose sight of corporate policy."

In some corporations, affirmative action may not be in "good faith." Atkins tells of one company that claimed it wanted to add a minority person to its economic advisory committee. After soliciting applicants through minority recruitment firms, one of whom was "superqualified," the comany ended up not filling the position but still satisfying its affirmative action "efforts."

Saddled to the concept of affirmative action is the age-old complaint that there aren't enough qualified blacks, particularly in the fields of engineering, science, and mathematics. "The question of availability, and not population statistics, is paramount," concedes Norton. "A generation ago, blacks stayed in 'safe fields' like education and social sciences, which prepared them for a very narrow range of professions. But young black people today are the first generation to ever have anything remotely like equal access to the job market. Blacks must continue to pursue education and penetrate new industries."

Even in the comparatively new field of affirmative action and equal employment opportunity, minorities are often placed in highly visible "window" jobs, while the real power to implement company programs still rests with whites.

Determining how well a company does can be elusive. Such an evaluation must be based not only on the plan on paper but also on the intangible inner workings of companies and on statistics that can be misleading, and often are not considered public information. Many companies that are good do not appear on our list, and that is not meant as a slight.

The companies presented have their shortcomings, but the elements of their programs seem to be working and have produced results.

AT&T
New York, New York

Since 1973, AT&T has seen a steady increase in the number of minority and women employees, largely the result of a consent decree. For the first five years of the agreement, women received an average 36 percent and minorities a quarter of the total hires and promotions into all job classifications.

The percentage of minorities in management increased from 4.5 in 1972 to 12 in 1981, and the total minority employees rose from 14 to 20 percent. Second-level managers rose from one to 7.5 percent from 1972 to 1980 and third-level executives — the highest level — increased from less than one percent to 3.5 percent.

To achieve its affirmative action goals, AT&T used a management assessment program to identify women with management potential and enroll them in career development programs. The Upgrade and Transfer Plan encouraged women and minorities to identify their own interests, which the company then tried to match with jobs. A technical preparation program helped train women and minorities for technical and management positions, and the Recruitment and Career Education Program attempted to inform students about opportunities at AT&T.

Since the decree expired in 1979, these programs have been expanded to include all employees. Says manager Ann Diomede: "The Bell System's position on why they don't have anything just for minorities is that it would be discriminatory. The programs are geared for minorities and women, but they don't exclude anybody."

Ed Anderson, an AT&T district manager, adds that now that the women and minorities are in place, they will grow professionally and move into the higher ranks.

Equitable
New York, New York

The Equitable Life Assurance Society was the company most frequently referred to as having the best affirmative action and EEO programs in the country. Says Ed Swan, national chairman of Minority Interchange, an insurance organization: "They have a commitment to develop those minorities already on board; they bring minorities into the company at a senior level and they have institutionalized a dialogue between senior management and minorities."

Equitable shows up best at the top, where there is a 17-member Black Officers Council, formed to assist and advise top management on companywide matters involving black development.

Officers and managers of the company are held accountable for meeting affirmative action goals in a twice yearly review, and part of the company's bonus and evaluation process for top managers is pegged to meeting these goals. There is also a voluntary Black Mentor Program, in which a participating black officer teams with a senior officer to offer job counseling. "We view affirmative action as a management-by-objectives approach," says vice-president Dorothy Orr.

In the category of officials and managers, 186 are black, or 6.2 percent. In the professionals category, there are 145 (10.2 percent), and for technicians, 738

(16.3 percent). Of the office and clerical workers, 20.9 percent, or 1866 are black. Throughout the company, the work force is 16.1 percent black.

But some outside observers say "pockets of resistance" to change exist at Equitable. On lower-management levels, "palace politics" is sometimes a stumbling block. Counters Orr: "When the right blacks come into the company and produce, then those who were resistant will change."

Exxon
New York, New York

Exxon is trying to shake off a perceived posture it feels may have scared off minorities. "We're very conservative at Exxon but not conservative to blacks," says Walter J. O'Neill, manager of EEO, communications and training.

Exxon's percentage of minorities jumped from 13.3 to 16.8 between 1977 and 1980. Among professionals, the percentage rose from 8.9 to 14.9 percent and among officials and managers, from 3.4 to 6.8 percent. Exxon declined to release the number of minorities among its top executives but acknowledges there are few.

O'Neill says the paucity of minorities in top management results from their relative lack of progressive management and technical experience and Exxon's practice of hiring from within the company. About 40 percent of the new employees come from outside Exxon's ranks.

Most of Exxon's minorities are hired from college campuses, where company officials say there is still a small but growing number of black engineering students. Recently Exxon gave a grant to an organization seeking alternative resources of minority members with technical experience.

In nontechnical areas — accounting, finance, employee relations — L. Mark Voight Jr., equal employment opportunity administrator, says there has been progress but offers no statistics.

Key to Exxon's program are the line managers who formulate and help meet affirmative action goals. Officials say they can avoid the resentment that can come from mandates issued by higher executives if they allow managers at the local level to handle affirmative action.

Gannett
Rochester, New York

Gannett Company, Inc., a chain of newspapers and radio and television stations, has been in the news in recent months for its appointment of two blacks to the position of newspaper publisher. Bob Maynard at the Oakland *Tribune* became the only black publisher of a major metropolitan newspaper, and Pam Johnson at the Ithaca (N.Y.) *Journal* became the first black woman to head a general circulation daily.

In addition, Gannett has named two blacks — Dolores Wharton and Andrew Brimmer — to its board of directors and has increased its total minority employment from 11 to 14.6 percent in the last three years. Statistics on individual job categories were incomplete, but data placed the percentage of minority officers and managers at 7 and the percentage of minority professionals at 8.5. Gannett spend $1 million with minority vendors in 1980, an increase of 63 percent over 1979.

The pace, says James "Jimmy" Jones, has been set by Gannett president Allen H. Neuharth and his executives. "They have set the tone so everyone knows that this is corporate policy," says Jones, director of affirmative action, recruitment,

and community relations. Jones adds that Gannett actively recruits minorities on college campuses, works with school department chairmen on curriculum, and ties salaries and bonuses to affirmative action efforts.

"In many cases, we find there are other priorities before affirmative action concerns," says Jones. With a performance evaluation, he adds, the executive "doesn't lose sight of corporate policy."

General Electric
Fairfield, Connecticut

General Electric's program for attracting, hiring and promoting minorities is woven into the fabric of the company's personnel practices. Fred H. Black, manager of special-interest group programs, calls it a systematic approach, a fair and modern employment policy that applies to all.

Overall, minorities constitute 12 percent of G.E.'s 285,000 domestic employees, and in 1980, the number of minority managers increased 8 pecent to 1,432 and professionals jumped 9 percent to 3,663. Black says G.E. was a leader among corporations in the hiring of black engineers. A minority executive recruiter described as excellent G.E.'s management training program.

"Good, sound personnel practices, equally applied, is good business," says Black. The positive effects can be seen in the company's growth and share of the market, Black adds, and in the absense of adverse litigation and strikes.

Black declines to be specific about the company's practices, saying it would be "trite." He also shies from using the term affirmative action, which he says suggests a company has been unfair in the past and is trying to catch up.

In general, Black says G.E. has, since

1969, attempted to apply to minorities and women policies used for whites. "We planned it, organized it, integrated it among our staff, and now we measure it," Black says. "The results have been good."

General Motors
Detroit, Michigan

Economics has given General Motors' affirmative action program a tough wringing over the last few years. Still, despite a slump in business and mounting layoffs, the auto manufacturer has been able to offset some of the effects of the last-hired, first-fired syndrome.

The number of minority blue-collar employees declined from 1978 to 1980 by a little more than one percent (from 22.4 to 21.1 percent) but the percent of minority white-collar workers increased by one-tenth of one percent to 11.7 — not much of a jump but in a troubled industry "we held our own," says John B. Holmes, director of employment relations.

G.M. uses a "human resources management" system designed to make sure all types of candidates have a shot at any position. At each of its plants, an equal employment opportunity coordinator works with department heads who are told, says Holmes, that affirmative action "is a way of doing business, just like designing cars and buying materials."

Geoffrey A. Atkins, an executive recruiter, says G.M. has a strong affirmative action program that varies in effectiveness according to an area of employment and state.

On the sales side, there were 156 minority-owned G.M. car and truck dealerships in the United States at the end of 1980, a net increase of 14 over 1979. In 1980, G.M. spent $224 million with minority suppliers and approved 12 loan and investment applications totalling $558,000 from minority-owned companies.

Hewlett-Packard
Palo Alto, California

Hewlett-Packard is the General Motors of the high technology, semiconductor industry in northern California's Silicon Valley. "There are a lot of opportunities for minorities in this field. The growth potential is enormous," says Harry Portwood, H-P's corporate affirmative action manager. "Our major strength at H-P is our willingness to improve that pool of minorities who want to join us."

Portwood says that of the company's 47,000 domestic employees, 18.2 percent are minority, as are 9.7 percent of the 6,717 managers and supervisors. Minorities comprise 11.2 percent of the 12,799 professionals, 15.8 percent of the 5,059 technicians. On the skills and crafts level, 18.2 percent of 2,577 employees are minorities.

H-P's purchases from minority-owned businesses reached an all-time high of $13.2 million last year, and a minority bank was selected to manage a portion of the H-P Foundation Fund. The company also has an extensive program involving participation in engineering curricula at black colleges and universities. "If we have a weakness," says Portwood, "it is our inability to recruit as many minority professionals in technical fields as we'd like."

But statistics show that pool is growing. In 1966, there were only 12,000 black engineering graduates in the United States. In 1978, the figure jumped to 41,000. Now, says Portwood, there is a new challenge. "Many AA and EEO programs were designed in the

1960s," he points out. "Today, we need to look at designing new and improved models to take us through the next 20 years and really make an impact."

Effective Affirmative Action

• Strong commitment from top officers of the corporation
• A rating system for top managers that pegs their compensation to the progress of minorities in their departments and divisions
• Strong affirmative action guidelines and aggressive minority recruitment policies
• Minorities in senior management positions involved in genuine corporate decision-making
• A company image that stresses community involvement.

IBM
Armonk, New York

IBM was one of the very first corporations to get involved in affirmative action. "They identified their social responsibility even before 1964," says executive recruiter W. Kirk Truitt, who worked with the company from 1963 to 1976.

Even so, IBM was reluctant to release hard information on how their AA and EEO plans work, an attitude they share with many other corporations.

Nearly 27,000 of IBM's 197,000 employees are from minority groups, and 15,600 are black. The company has provided grants to a number of engineering schools with predominantly black enrollments and has loaned hundreds of workers to black colleges, universities, and other institutions. In 1978, IBM moved into a newly constructed manu-

facturing plant in Brooklyn's Bedford-Stuyvesant. Of the plant's more than 400 employees, 80 percent are black and most of the managers are minorities, including the plant's general manager, Henry Bing Jr., who has been with the company since 1963. An IBM spokesman says that between 1975 and 1980, the company's minority population increased by 56 percent and during the same period, the company's minority managers increased by 97 percent. More than 11,200 new employees were hired by IBM in 1980, and 21.4 percent of them were minorities.

Of the 5,100 graduates of major training programs supported by IBM, 4,000 have been placed in jobs. The number of minority suppliers doing business with IBM has grown from seven in 1968 to more than 600, doing over $55 million in business in 1980. Minority-owned insurance companies underwrite approximately $136 million of IBM's group life insurance.

Sea-Land
Edison, New Jersey

Sea-Land Industries, Inc., is a water transportation and trucking company with 18 facilities around the country and the nation's largest and oldest merchant marine fleet. It also has some impressive figures for minority employees. Of its 3,500 US workers (the 25-year-old company also has international operations), minorities represent 13 percent of the officers and managers, 17 percent of the professionals, and 21.4 percent of the salespeople.

"The company is dealing with a moral obligation in relation to civil rights legislation," says Paul M. McGuire, director of equal opportunity affairs. Eight to 10 percent of the company's business is with the government.

Sea-Land uses minority recruiting agencies to broaden its net of minority candidates once it has searched for prospects within the company. A management training program takes entry-level employees and prepares them for the upper ranks. "This is a basic management program which is a vehicle for bringing in inexperienced people," says McGuire.

McGuire says the company offers good salaries and benefits, which help attract minorities who might normally go to larger corporations. However, the company has no black vice-presidents. The problem, says McGuire, is the lack of expertise in water transportation among minority members. The company gives money to colleges to train minorities in this area and is cultivating its middle management for the top positions. Says McGuire: "That's a developmental thing" that will take time.

Xerox
Stamford, Connecticut

"Affirmative action doesn't just happen. It only happens by design and that takes a lot of creativity. It takes desire and more than anything else, a commitment to do it."

That's how George Jabbour, manager of equal employment opportunity compliance, sums up Xerox's approach to affirmative action. This approach is reflected in the number of minorities in the company's ranks. In the last decade, the number of minority officers and managers has jumped from 3.5 percent to 14.6 percent, the number of professionals from 6.4 to 16.3 percent. The president of one of its smaller companies, Xerox Electro-Optical in Pasadena, California, is black, as is the vice-

president of a major division. "We still have a way to go in top executives," says Jabbour, "but we're probably doing better than most of the corporations."

Xerox has a variety of programs to aid affirmative action. Among them is a training program, averaging 16 weeks, that over the last few years has trained more than 150 technicians. Jabbour says no one has failed the qualifying test, which guarantees the trainee a job at Xerox. The company offers scholarships and a summer internship program. It helps math and science teachers by giving technical assistance. Xerox's Earn and Learn Program allows inner-city youths to work at the company while studying for a technical career. The company also ties affirmative action efforts to evaluations of department managers.

The Bottom Line At The Top Ten

Company	Gross Sales (000)	No. of Employees
AT&T	57,300,000	1,000,000
Equitable	20,000,000	27,250
Exxon	103,142,834	176,615
Gannett	1,214,983	23,000
GE	24,959,000	402,000
GM	57,728,500	746,000
Hewlett-Packard	3,099,000	57,000
IBM	26,213,000	341,279
Sea-Land	1,400,000	9,000
Xerox	8,196,500	120,480

Today's success — tomorrow's challenge: An attitude toward the future

J.B. Ritchie and Hal B. Gregersen

Mark Twain is said to have remarked that he was concerned with the future because that was where he was going to spend the rest of his life. We suspect that it is the inevitability of that logic that both frightens and encourages managers or other individuals as they contemplate the transition from present to future states. They find themselves trying to decide along the lines of maintaining and protecting the present world (and protecting themselves in the process) versus pursuing a new world and preparing to take advantage of stimulating and exciting opportunities. An individual's reaction to the challenge can be placed somewhere between two extremes. At one end of the continuum is an almost catatonic state induced by the fear and frustration of a changing and uncertain future. At the other end is a sort of euphoric attitude generated by the feeling that any change will be an interesting experience and very likely an improvement. As people place themselves along that continuum, a variety of issues must be considered.

What are some of the important points to consider as we attempt to understand our attitude toward changes in the future? One of the first points that should be mentioned is that in the process of formulating our attitude toward change, we are also determining a part of that future. Within certain constraints one can only think what one is prepared to think and do what one is prepared to do. Short of a catastrophe, our response to impending events — the cognitive and behavior patterns we are prepared to employ — will be substantially determined by the attitudes and skills we are now forming (or have already formed). Except for a forced confrontation, people will not be receptive to a better way of doing something if their minds are only prepared to mentally repeat yesterday's procedure. One cannot respond to a threatening situation in an analytical probelm-solving fashion without preparation to receive, process, and evaluate information under stress. The attitude that facilitates this behavior must exist prior to the decision situation; otherwise, the individual will simply be a victim of events. A classic illustration of this point is a major corporation's response to the prospects of a copying machine during the mid-1950s. After considering the potential future uses of such a device, the following conclusion was stated: "Nothing will ever replace carbon paper." Someone was not very well prepared to think about the future!

Failures versus successes

A second dimension of our attitude toward the future is whether we can distinguish between "problems of failure" and "problems of success." The problem of failure comes when an action does not produce the desired result. In contrast, if the action does produce a positive outcome, the problem of success comes when we cannot cope with the results of psychological, organization, or technical reality created by the new situation. The question has some interesting implications because we are not accustomed to thinking about problems resulting from success.

As you think about it, so often when we hear about the challenge of our times we are presented with an inventory of the many failures of our social, economic, and political institutions. We hear criticisms of virtually every program and organization. These accusations are stated by a variety of individuals: politicians who do not like an incumbent administration, students who do not like the university curriculum, business executives who are chafing under the restrictive regulations of a government bureaucracy, the young who reject the rules and values of the old, environmentalists who want clean air and water, minorities who desire their share of economic returns. Clearly, it is not difficult to generate a lengthy list of serious problems which await solution; however, is it reasonable to portray present problems as always being a result of past failures?

We would argue that a negative array of failures is only one way to view the problems created by a series of events. Rather than focusing on the failures of the system as the cause of a problem — or source of a challenge — we contend that it is most often the successes or achievements of our complex organizational society which pose the more significant challenge. In many areas where criticism is directed, we find that we have attained exactly what we set out to achieve — whether we now agree or disagree with the set of criteria for that achievement, by some measure we have been successful. However, success in one area does not necessarily replicate itself in other areas. A singular success must be understood, controlled, and integrated into a larger or newly established organizational framework. For example, recent implementation of the quality circles concept into hundreds of American organizations was mainly a replication of singular success in the Japanese business world. With little regard for the different aspects of American industry, many innovative U.S. organizations are now recognizing the futility of blindly expanding a singular success into broader organizational contacts. On the other hand, the failure of a program is more straightforward — you drop it, or try to make it work next time. But with success you must create new ways to incorporate the results of the success into the overall system. The new, offtimes unanticipated demands which have been generated as a result of affluence or education, growth or technology, are usually much more challenging than correcting the past mistakes of a static system.

Some examples

It seems to us unfortunate, for example, to talk about the failure of our education systems (although there are some dramatic failures) when a more interesting challenge is to cope with the success of it. We set out to educate and train more of our population, and now we are upset when that educated, trained population demands exactly what we taught them to look for in life: opportunities to achieve their goals in the workplace, equality under the law, credibility in business and government, answers supported by good evidence rather than authoritarian fiat, etc. The dilemma comes when the rest of our societal institutions are not equipped to respond to the needs and demands of educated and affluent individuals.

Another example comes from the field of data processing, computers, and management information systems. Some years ago we observed great enthusiasm to make dramatic movement into this area. Many organizations made enormous expenditures installing new systems. Over a period of time, many of these investments were not recovered; consequently, people were asking why. We heard many managers say that the system was a failure. But, was it really the system? The system often did exactly what it was supposed to do — generate a great deal of information to be used in management decision-making. The problems was that many people did not know what information they needed or wanted. The information overload was not a failure of the system; it was the success of the system. The failure was that managers did not know how to use it — they became victims rather than masters of technology.

Future Shock

A third consideration in thinking about the future can be drawn from Alvin Toffler's books, *Future Shock* and *The Third Wave*. Nearly two decades ago, Bennis and Slater expressed many predictions about the composition of future organizations in *The Temporary Society*. Briefly, Bennis and Slater predicted that the most constant thing within our future organizations would be continual change. Drawing upon Bennis and Slater's perspective, Toffler stretches their predictions beyond the organizations of the late '70s into the society of tomorrow. In *Future Shock*, Toffler argued that we are now a part of an "environment so ephemeral, unfamiliar, and complex as to threaten millions with adaptive breakdown." This breakdown is "future shock." Future shock is what happens to individuals when the substance and pace of change overpower the individual, "when he is required to operate above his adaptive range." The problem comes not from a particular change which we cannot handle; rather, it is the fact that so many things are changing that we need a new set of assumptions to deal with the "temporary society." Toffler says we are living in a world of transience, novelty, and diversity. Our norms have become a temporary house, car, neighborhood, friendship, job, etc. Things move so fast that all of our possessions, relationships, and values become part of a "throwaway" society. Demands change so fast that there is no time for long-term stability in our activities. "Good" products, procedures, and criteria are often outdated or obsolete before they are even generally known. The solution Toffler suggests to help us come to terms with the future is his "theory of adaptation" — an understanding of trends, how people respond to change, and most importantly, how *you* respond. With that understanding, he claims, the individual can attain serenity within an environment of confusion.

In addition to individuals confronting a state of "future shock," organizations which are merely collectives of individuals will also need to contend with the various pressures toward substantive organizational change. For example, in *The Third Wave*, Toffler raises an intriguing question about what goals organizations of the future will pursue. Instead of a corporation maximizing its profit as its sole goal, Toffler suggests that the effective corporation of the future will have multiple bottom lines. Such a corporation will probably pursue a variety of goals in areas such as "social, environmental, informational, political, and ethical" issues "in addition to the traditional financial bottom line."

From yet another perspective, the novelist Chaim Potok approaches the concept of "future shock" in terms of a core identity. For him, individuals need to have firm roots in a culture that provides a clear identity. After they comprehend their own values and those of their immediate environment (e.g., family, friends, religious or occupational community), then they can more confidently venture out into the broader environment of other cultures and ideas without being overcome by "future shock." Instead, by knowing one's own culture, people encounter a newly found world of ideas, peoples, or technology with a core-to-core confrontation which will not only be destructive but can be the basis of great creativity and innovation. In short, one must first know what ideas and values influence actions; and only then can one consistently enter the broader "marketplace of ideas." The challenge, then, is to develop ways to learn about your environment and yourself.

Needs and motivation

Our last issue deals specifically with the elusive problem of understanding behavior. It has already been suggested that the future may be influenced by what an individual thinks, values, and anticipates. When we ask why one thinks and behaves in certain ways, we are talking about motivation. In order to understand or change how we feel about the future, it may be helpful to explore a concept of motivation. For purposes of illustration, we shall build on the theory of Abraham Maslow. In *Toward a Psychology of Being*, Maslow's thesis is that we operate on a hierarchy of needs and that a satisfied need is not a motivator. These needs are rank ordered as follows (see figure 1):

1. Basic needs — physiological demands, rest, food
2. Security needs — order, control, predictability
3. Social needs — affection, belongingness, love
4. Ego needs — presitge, self-respect, identity
5. Self-actualization needs — ultimate self-fulfillment

The argument is that a lower need must be reasonably satisfied before the next higher level need can command a major part of the individual's attention. All of the needs are likely operating at all times to some extent — it is a question of relative emphasis or dominance of a certain need depending on the degree of overall need satisfaction. The logic that "man lives by bread alone" has some basis when man has no bread. But, what happens when there is plenty of bread? Does the intensity of effort in acquiring food remain the same? At this point the concern over having a secure home, community, nation, and future may lead to substantial effort. As a certain degree of security is attained, the individual is more concerned with having a status home, car, country club membership, or whatever else provides social recognition. At this point he becomes more concerned with pleasing other individuals because the lower-order needs are basically taken care of.

As you move up the hierarchy (to the right on Figure 1), it becomes more and more difficult to satisfy the complex interaction of needs. This nexus of needs also seems to require more sophisticated manipulation in order to fulfill them. Such is the case in moving from social to ego types of needs. The ego needs play to the "identity crisis" of our current generation.

Many of our current human resource training and development programs are formulated around the pop psychology emphasis of past years which encouraged people to "look out for number one," to "win through intimidation," and to "pull your own strings." Such programs are a reflection of the quest to answer such questions as: "Who am I?" "Where do I fit in?" and "What do I think of myself?", and "How can I get more out of the organization that I put into it?"

A major problem in this pursuit of self-interests is the disregard for others' dignity and well-being. A prime example of these egotistic pursuits is when managers return from certain training programs anxious to try out new skills in confrontation and assertiveness when others have not attended the program. Many of these "politically sensitized" managers are convinced that they will never become the victim of organizational politics. But, does that individual care about someone else becoming the victim? In our experience, rarely. As this quest for "self" turns into a competitive game at the cost of other individuals or organizations, one slowly becomes trapped in the culture of narcissism — unless one moves to a more noble definition of self-actualization.

Significance of self-actualization

The last need on the hierarchy — self-actualization — is most difficult to de-

Figure 1

Need hierarchy in individual motivation

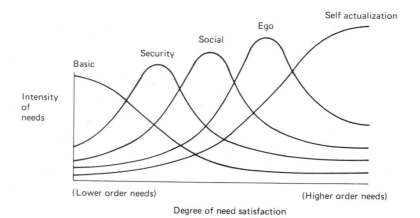

scribe. The youth talk about "doing their own thing" as a way to express a desire for self-fulfillment. We search for examples of individuals who act only for the intrinsic satisfaction which comes from the process rather than just the external rewards. The ultimate "religious ethic" of serving one's fellow men may be this type of phenomenon. While we may debate the purity of an individual's motives when altruism or selflessness is imputed to someone's behavior, the idea of intrinsic satisfaction is very strong. And, there doen seem to be some evidence of a higher order quest where values are most important. These have found success on another level, when higher values lead to more successful organizations. (See Peters and Waterman's *In Search of Excellence.*)

From this very abbreviated framework we can observe some possible explanations for current and future problems. For example, it is estimated that forty years ago about 40 percent of the population were confronted with low-income poverty conditions. That means that most of the people in the United States were close to the bottom of the need hierarchy. Their goals were quite direct — higher income and greater security. Since the beginning of World War II, however, that percentage has declined remarkably. By 1950 it was down to about 30 percent, 1960 about 20 percent, 1970 about 10 percent. Following that trend line, poverty should now be eradicated. Instead, it is up to about 15 percent. What we saw was a large block of society moving up the need hierarchy until the early eighties. In the seventies, education and economic growth had placed the majority of the population in that area of need satisfaction where social and ego needs dominate. This does not mean that we forgot lower-order needs — we just added to them. There were at least three important consequences which resulted from this "progress."

Striving for higher order needs

One consequence was that these people were demanding satisfaction of more complex needs. They still required that lower-order needs continued to be satisfied, but greater energy was going into social- and ego-type goals. Money was for prestige and pleasure rather than only food and security. This made many more conflicting demands on our institutions than had been made before the seventies. Part of the problem was that most of our insititutions were created during a time when lower-order needs had been dominant, and therefore many jobs reflected those inappropriate assumptions. Many managers assumed that employees were like they were in the forties and fifties. They should be thankful for a job and be loyal to the boss. These older assumptions may hold for those at the lower end of the hierarchy; however, they appear inadequate as you move toward the middle and upper end. In fact, with a skilled, mobile, affluent work force you heard a well-known management consultant saying that "organization loyalty is a weakness, not a virtue."

A second consequence of the general movement to higher-order needs came from a special sector of the educated, affluent population — women. How could one expect an educated or trained woman with a house full of labor-saving devices, a car, no small children, and a world full of things to be done, to sit home and be content? It seemed that women's liberation pressures inevitably came from women in whom higher-order needs were waiting to be realized.

A third consequence resulting from a majority of people striving after higher-order needs was seen in the minority who were still at the lower end of the needs hierarchy. When the poor had a lot of company during the great Depression, things were not so bad. But by the seventies the distance was more obvious, and they clearly saw "coercive comparisons" between the rich and the poor. The conclusions of the statistical comparisons were brutal, frustrating, and insulting. About 8 percent of the total population was at the bottom, while over 30 percent of the black population was in the same cellar position. Since advertising and other norms of society were geared to people with higher-order needs, the realization of the poor's position was more poignant. Also, people at the bottom of the hierarchy seemed to feel as a matter of right that they should have been at the point where the majority of people had established the "standard of living." This meant that the greater the education and affluence of a society, the greater the tension and strain from those still at the bottom.

What we observe, then, is that we had been very successful in providing higher income with a relative degree of security for many people. But, by default, we expected the same organizations and policies which provided for satisfaction of those lower-order needs to also take care of the higher-order ones. And, we have good evidence that it did not automatically work — our corporations, schools, and governments were continually challenged because they were trying to serve needs which were no longer predominant. We continually yearned for the "good old days"; in fact, the goals of those people who had lived

in the "good old days" were very clearly to obtain education and affluence — the very conditions which created incompatability with the organizations of the "good old days." The situation is analogous to giving someone a great deal of money and then being upset when he or she buys expensive things. Over a period of time, we realized that by developing people who had acquired higher-order needs through schooling or other forms of socialization, we created a very incongruous world by expecting them to continue behaving on the assumptions of lower-order needs.

The shift in needs

Resulting from the past organizational emphasis on fulfilling lower needs, we wanted in the early eighties to modify our organizations in order to satisfy higher needs. With a major push toward a society which would fulfill our social, ego and self-actualization needs, many organizations began to shift their direction. As reported and advocated in books such as Ouchi's *Theory Z* or Peters and Waterman's *In Search of Excellence*, many managers are set on the infusion of deeply held values into the organization's members on an explicit and/or implicit basis. Peters and Waterman argue that the most successful organizations of today are those which inculate their organizations with an overarching value system which would satisfy the higher-order needs. In hopes of attaining a fulfillment of social, ego, and self-actualization needs, the apparent organizational success of these changes is that employees will probably act upon deeply held organizational values rather than just to satisfy external constraints.

Clearly, the success of the "best companies" presented by Peters and Waterman is the permeation of commonly shared values — an answer to the question of "Who am I?" or "Who are we?" However, with the development of loyal and obedient employees, what might be a failure of this "success"?

If an organization demands loyalty to an overarching set of organizational values, what might happen to the individual who refuses to wholly accept the organization's values? Individuals now seek a feeling of who they are from other organizations in addition to their work organization. In fact, the actual success of a value-laden organization may well cause the subsequent failure of forcing a single set of values upon a wide variety of individuals. Indeed, Toffler suggests that the corporation of the future will not be homogenous. Rather, the future organization will be a breeding ground for heterogeneity. Following the logic of organizational variety, Toffler asserts that organizations will not be single-purpose organizations. On the contrary, such future organizations will be multi-purpose.

Another part of this shift in needs can be placed in historical perspective. Most of the people in current leadership positions in formal institutions experienced two dramatic events which influenced their assumptions about needs, goals, and behavior. These events were the Depression and World War II. Here we saw the two lower-order needs under attack. The success of our victory over these threats carried with it a strong commitment to carefully protect oneself against any future threat in those areas. Thus, we observed a great emphasis on financial security and military protection. These concerns are not felt in the same way by the current generation. For the most part they have not experienced real threats to the basic and security needs — although many more are beginning to experience these threats. For the most part, however, they start out at a social need level and take the lower ones for granted. The lesson seems clear: We must learn how to live with the consequences of our achievement or lack thereof.

We have discussed some considerations relating to an attitude toward the future. We have tried to raise some questions, which if carefully answered might help in developing a constructive approach to the future. We have tried to suggest some concepts, which if incorporated into those answers might provide insight regarding the fast-moving and complex environment we must live in. And lastly, we have tried to suggest that the conditions we find ourselves in are not cause to give up in despair — the new demands and conflicts we observe are not because of failure; rather, they reflect progress. The challenge of the future is to understand our world and develop the competence to deal with it — it is not an easy task. We must study. We must think. We must be open-minded. And many of us must change! But this is not a new demand — it has been done before, and it can be done again!

*Most people (and organizations) would sooner die than change —
and most do*

"And here, Mr. J.P. Babbit, Vice-President in charge of resistance to change."

When the boss calls you a ...

Coping with the intricacies of corporate racism

William Watson Hines III

Employment professionals say that the indispensable ingredient for job advancement is improved technical skills. But for minority employees, it is equally important to develop communications abilities in order to deal effectively with the boss and their coworkers. Herewith, we present some typical office situations, along with suggested techniques for black workers to use when they find themselves confronted with corporate-style racism.

On being ignored

One day you encounter your boss and several of his peers talking in the corridor. Although he usually says hello when he is alone, he does not speak when he is with his white friends. Since all agree that the minority is a nonperson, acknowledging you would violate their beliefs about you. Instead, you should say a general "good morning" and keep on walking. Don't underestimate the impact of being polite and in control.

On other occasions when you experience rudeness from the boss when he is part of a group, don't respond in kind; to do so is to be manipulated. Wait until the boss is alone in his office. Ask him *quietly* if he is feeling okay. Tell him you're inquiring because you have never seen him behave that way.

The snarling boss

When Sam's boss snarled at him in a meeting, Sam afterward went to the boss's office with a bottle of aspirin and a cup of water. Sam said he knew the boss was under a lot of stress, and wondered if this would help. As a result of their discussion, the boss apologized for his rudeness.

A gentle reminder of inappropriate behavior can put the boss on guard and make him think before again acting in such a manner. He becomes aware that you will not suffer abuse. Remaining cool throws the boss off guard. Don't let slights pass without doing something about them. Otherwise you will give a misleading impression of acquiescence. You can certainly mention a transgression at a later date, but do it on your own terms.

Another way to deal with a snarling boss is to thank him (or her) after the yelling is finished, and leave the room. Quietly confronting rude behavior is an effective way of making the offender aware of his rudeness. It is a means of permitting them to look at themselves realistically, and from a different perspective. This is disconcerting, because it is not the anticipated response. Developing proper office conduct requires dealing with people without provoking them into more negative behavior. Keep in mind that you are actually aiding your boss by making him or her more effective when working with people, particularly those of different ethnic groups.

Another consideration to bear in mind is that the snarling boss's behavior can be what psychologists term "displacement." He is angry because *his* boss yelled at him. Though angry with his boss, he can't very well rage at him. So you become the focus of his anger. Be aware that the "displacement" principle supports the notion that victims are likely to return anger. Instead, level with the boss by stating that something he said or did is offensive to you. Show your concern. For example, you might say, "I'm sharing this with you because I am sure you are not aware of the implication of your remarks. I know you will tell me if I've made a mistake." Make it clear to the boss that you are objecting to a specific behavior, and not disapproving of him personally. Be firm but gentle.

The veiled insult and the direct slur

John, a black manager, is assigned a new office. A white manager says, "Oh, the office area is changing here." The reference is similar to one that is often made when blacks move into a new neighborhood. Remembering that some comments, though subtle, have derogatory meanings, John might respond in a nice tone, "Yes, it has changed with you and me here. We are both distinct personalities." Or, John might ask him to tell what he meant by the comment. He may or may not make a feeble effort to

explain. At all events, he will think twice before he makes such a quick, possibly racist remark in the future.

"You people are doing okay"

The old comments: "You people are doing okay" or "What else do they want?" aren't heard much these days in the corporate environment. Now the comments run along the line of "We want qualified employees" or "Affirmative action is weakening the quality of our work force." As used in this situation, the comment is an intentional putdown of minorities. An effective reply might be: "I think you are oversimplifying a complex economic problem. We need to get to the root of what you are really saying.

"We all know the problem we are having with productivity and the pressures resulting from technological change. Let us look further. It's not affirmative action; it's the younger generation's emphasis on getting more out of a job than a paycheck. Let us consider the death of the Protestant Ethic — work hard and you will be rewarded. It's not really a minorities problem, but a general problem of motivating all workers. You are misapprehending by seeing the problem in affirmative action terms only."

Joking relationships

Teasing and joking relationships reek of hostility. This behavior is another way of making fun of and putting one down. (We're not talking about banter among friends or humor which often arises spontaneously when a work team has to get through a tough assignment.) If you find yourself part of a group which resorts to joking relationships, don't laugh or retaliate. Keep in mind that if you laugh, you are showing approval and appreciation, and encouraging what is basically a vicious game in which people get hurt.

Many of us have had the following experience: The boss starts a meeting by telling an ethnic joke about Poles or Italians, or a sexist joke about women. Never laugh at these jokes, no matter how funny they are. If it gets too bad, you can take a chance and say that you really don't like these jokes because you find them offensive. He may even try to start the day-to-day transaction in a one-on-one situation by joking. This is where you may tell him that you don't like such joking because it leads to underplaying the seriousness of a situation, and a lot of helpful information can be lost in this sort of climate. A risk is involved, but there are benefits to be gained by your willingness to risk growth for both yourself and your supervisor. Your supervisor might recognize your effectiveness with people as useful to the company. This may result in increased respect or other rewards. Always appeal to the boss's vested interest in the work environment.

Another way to deal with this situation is to pretend you don't understand what is being said, and ask for clarification. Make sure instructions are repeated straight. You may want to say, "Let's move on. We are wasting time and we have work to finish." Or you may simply break it off by changing the subject. Refusing to play along will lead offenders to drop their destructive behavior and may move them toward respecting you more. You should choose tactics that best reflect your ability to recognize and redirect hostile behavior.

Joking and teasing may reflect the inability of a supervisor to take seriously the credentials and abilities of a minority employee. This may be because the boss has never come in contact with a minority of equal or higher socioeconomic status. He may feel that joking is the only way to communicate with blacks. However, this style of communication puts you in a Step-in Fetchit position because of the boss/subordinate relationship.

One way to handle this type of situation is to approach your boss about his joking. Ask him if he takes you seriously. If the boss says, "Yes, and why are you asking the question?" you can simply reply that his constant joking and teasing seem to indicate the opposite. Tell him that psychologists say teasing is "displaced hostility." Tell your boss that you think his intentions are honorable, but these overly familiar expressions of easy acceptance and friendship may be misinterpreted by others.

Situation reversed

In the reverse situation, with a black supervisor and a white subordinate, here is another example of employing interpersonal skills to combat racism on the job.

Georgiana, a young, white professional was trained, counseled and assisted by a black manager for six months. A few weeks afterward, he went to her new office to get some information on a project, and to say hello. She immediately scowled and looked at him with great contempt. After she left the area in order to get some material, he spoke to the woman who shared the office, wondering what had happened to Georgiana, her disposition had become so hostile and unfriendly. "After all," he said, "I trained her and showed her the ropes." At that moment, Georgiana returned. He told her how unfriendly and even hostile she had appeared. Georgiana immediately said she was exhausted and he was misreading her behavior. He said, "Well, I hope you are right." Then he ended the conversation, wished her a good day, and left.

Although the episode occurred on her turf, the supervisor maintained control because he spoke quietly and firmly and kept his language timely and specific to the situation. Most importantly, he mentioned her previous behavior and showed an interest in understanding her point of view.

Acknowledging previous relationships is another technique for letting offenders know that you see what they are up to, and not allowing them to slip unnoticed

into negative behavior. Perhaps Georgiana felt unsure of how her white office mate would react to a black manager, so she went into more comfortable racist behavior. When confronted, she blamed her actions on hard work and exhaustion.

The responsibility for how you are treated in office relationships mostly lies with you. Part of your lifelong job is to develop skills that effectively improve work relationships. Taking the time to meet this need is critical. Just as you develop and refine job skills, you must also refine those interpersonal skills needed for success.

A powerful tide is surging across much of the world today, creating a new, often bizarre, environment in which to work, play, marry, raise children, or retire. In this bewildering context, businessmen swim against highly erratic economic currents; politicians see their ratings bob wildly up and down; universities, hospitals, and other institutions battle desperately against inflation. Value systems splinter and crash, while the lifeboats of family, church, and state are hurled madly about.

Alvin Toffler, *The Third Wave*

In contemporary America the needs of organization overwhelm all other considerations, whether those of family, religion, art, science, law or the individual. This has had a shattering impact on us, for it has caused us to become a different people than we thought we would be.

D.K. Hart and W.G. Scott, *The Organizational Imperative*

I was to learn later in life that we tend to meet any new situation by reorganizing; and a wonderful method it can be for creating the illusion of progress while producing confusion, inefficiency, and demoralization.

Petronius Arbiter (Circa A.D. 60)

CASES

Universal Bank

Introduction

Brian Baker had just come from a meeting with one of Universal Bank's executive vice-presidents, Bob Jasper, and his head was spinning. Jasper has asked Brian to go to Mexico City and put out some fires in the bank's local branch. During the oil boom years, Universal Bank's Mexico operation had been one of the most profitable units in the organization. No one anticipated the severity of the economic collapse which sent banks reeling. Universal was no different — they had over a hundred million dollars in outstanding loans in Mexico. Although they had been able to renegotiate most loans, top management was on edge because several big loans were due in the next six to twelve months. Bob Jasper decided that Brian Baker was the bank's best shot at guiding Universal through a rough year ahead. His technical competence in loan operations, his language ability, and his international experience and savvy made him the obvious choice.

Background

Brian had an MBA from the University of Michigan. He came to work for Universal Bank in New York after graduating, and quickly demonstrated both his technical and leadership skills. The first few years were exciting and challenging. In addition, his fast-track status had given him both prestige and financial comforts more quickly

than he had hoped for. Brian, his wife Kathryn, and their two children lived in an old, but very attractive, house in a nice suburb. Kathryn finished her law degree at Michigan at the same time that Brian graduated, and they moved to New York. For two years, Kathryn worked on the legal staff of a large, multinational chemical company. When her first child was born, she decided to take time off to be with her child and redecorate the house — something she had wanted to do for some time. But the second child was born soon after the first, and the strain of two small children eventually caused a mild depression for Kathryn. Brian encouraged her to go back to work. She was able to go back to work part-time for her previous employer, and with the variety and outside stimulation she was soon feeling much better.

However, shortly after Kathryn started back to work, Brian began to feel restless. He had thrived on the challenge and adventure that he received from his work for the first few years. Now he had settled into a more comfortable routine at work. Also, with two children, he felt the burden of family responsibilities. Life wasn't as exciting as it once was.

It wasn't long, though, before that all changed. Universal was opening a branch in Buenos Aires, and Brian was selected to go down and get it off the ground. His technical skill, leadership, energy, and language ability made him an excellent candidate. "This is just the break you need, Brian," his boss, Sam Stewart, told him when he offered him the position. "A stint abroad is all you need to make you top management material. Management is really high on the branch down there and you'll be in the limelight. Do a good job and you'll probably come back as my boss!"

Brian had no doubts about accepting the position, but Kathryn was much less enthusiastic. Her company wanted her to come to work full-time now, and for the first time she was feeling confident about her abilities as a lawyer. In addition, the kids were just starting school and she was concerned how they would react to such a major change. Where would they live? What about school for the kids? How long would they be down there? She was unable to get a satisfactory answer to any of these questions and the uncertainty was overwhelming.

But eventually Brian was able to convince her to go, with the promise that they would be gone no longer than a couple of years and that when they got back she could return to her career. When Brian accepted the job, they had less than a month to sell the house and make all of the necessary arrangements before they had to leave.

Argentina

For the first year in Buenos Aires, Brian hardly saw his family. He worked 16-hour days and traveled frequently. It was exactly what Brian wanted: challenge, autonomy, responsibility, and excitement. Professionally, he felt good about his own development, and the new branch was progressing well. His only major complaint was that headquarters didn't seem to take much notice of what he was doing. In contrast to what Sam Stewart

told Brian when he offered him the job, there was no limelight. If a report was late or inaccurate, he would get a phone call from someone in accounting; otherwise, Brian felt as if no one back home was really paying much attention — especially to him. Brian's major source of information and help was the South American regional supervisor — but he only came by every two or three months.

Brian's fluency in Spanish helped him to adjust quickly to the Argentine culture. He developed a taste for the local food and enjoyed participating in holiday festivities. This helped his Argentine subordinates to accept him and to work well with him.

Unfortunately, it took longer for Kathryn to adjust to Argentina. With Brian rarely home and the kids attending a British school, she was lonely, and her depression began to creep back. She fought it by immersing herself in studying the language and by visiting museums and other cultural and historical sites.

After about a year in Buenos Aires, Brian became aware of a legal position at the U.S. Embassy there. The job included working with immigration cases, visas, and some sticky international licensing problems. Kathryn applied for the position and was hired. Although apprehensive of her ability to speak the language, she was happy to be using her legal skills again, and quickly made some good friends.

At that point, things were going pretty well for the Bakers. Even though Brian still wasn't around much, Kathryn and the kids took advantage of school breaks and holidays to travel to scenic spots along Argentina's vast coastline. Five years passed, and the Bakers were still not anxious to return to the states. But a series of events combined to quickly force their return.

First, Kathryn had become involved with a local human rights movement that was ruffling some feathers in the Argentine government. Some local government officials who were acquainted with Brian began to put some pressure on him to rein her in, but to no avail. Then suddenly, Brian's father died of a heart attack, and Brian returned to New York for the funeral. While he was there he talked with top management about the progress he was making in Buenos Aires.

"You've done an outstanding job down there, Brian," said one executive vice-president, "and we're appreciative of what you've done. You've single-handedly put Universal Bank on the map in South America. None of our other branches have been able to do so well in so short a time. But it's time for you to move on, Brian. You're too talented to be stuck in right field for your whole career. Train one of your local subordinates down there to replace you, and come back as soon as you can."

Brian couldn't help but feel like the rug had just been pulled out from under him. The ostensible reason that management wanted him back was to further his career. But he wondered if the real reason had more to do with Kathryn's human rights activities and the bank's wanting to prevent any conflict with the Argentine government.

A spirit of gloom hung over the Bakers as they prepared to leave Buenos Aires. Eventually, they resigned themselves to returning, and even decided it was for the best. Brian's mother was calling almost weekly wondering when they would be home. She would need to depend on Brian more now that her husband had died. Moreover, the kids were almost teenagers, and both Brian and Kathryn believed that it was important for the kids

to have more stability through these years. If they waited any longer to return to the U.S., it would just make it more difficult for the kids to make the transition. With a feeling of sadness, yet also a feeling of pride for what they had accomplished during the last five and a half years, Brian and Kathryn shipped the last boxes, packed their bags, and returned home to New York.

The repatriation

Coming home wasn't easy. There were no "Welcome Back" banners for Brian when he came back to work. In fact, the first day back he wondered if he was even in the right place. He had never seen half the employees before, and some major restructuring of the organization left him confused about the direction of the domestic operation. But there were bigger problems. All of his peers that he used to work with in New York were well up the hierarchy. There was no clear position open for Brian when he returned, and no one seemed all that interested in taking him on board.

"They're out of touch with domestic operations," was an opinion frequently expressed about repatriated managers at Universal Bank. "They walk around dazed for six months, and when they finally come out of shock, they think they should run the show. Overseas they had it all to themselves, but back here they forget we're a team."

Brian was assigned to work on a few projects while waiting for some position to open up for him. He felt that the projects hardly used the skills and abilities he had developed over the past five years in Buenos Aires. His lack of commitment to the projects only aggravated the situation, confirming to other people in the company that he was no longer a team player.

Meanwhile, the Baker children were having a difficult time making the readjustment to American life. In terms of their educational level, they were well ahead of their peers. Socially, though, they were seen as odd, even stuffy, and had difficulty making friends. They had missed a crucial socializaton period, and they were now being "socialized" the hard way. The $125 a week the Bakers were paying a child psychologist didn't seem to help much. Brian felt responsible for the problems his kids were having, and had a hard time dealing with the resultant guilt. We should never have gone to Buenos Aires in the first place, he thought to himself.

Kathryn was the only member of the family who seemed to be adjusting well. She went to work full-time on the legal staff of the same company that she had worked for before they left. The company had recently opened up a new manufacturing facility in Argentina, and her language ability, her familiarity with the local legal system and cultural norms, and her contacts made her extremely valuable to the company. She had several opportunities to travel back to Argentina on business. Brian tried not to be jealous of her success, but with his career seemingly stalled and her career just beginning to skyrocket, there was tension between them. Brian was hoping that returning to the U.S. would give him more time to spend with the family. He did spend more time with the kids, but Kathryn's work didn't allow her as much time at home as Brian would have liked. It was evident to Brian that five and a half years in Buenos Aires working 70-hour weeks had left their marriage relationship strained. But he was uncertain how to change things.

After six months of Brian's working on insignificant projects, no position had opened up for him. He was angry, frustrated, and wanted to quit but didn't feel they could affort it. Despite Kathryn's income, they were still struggling financially. When they returned to the U.S., real estate prices had soared and their new mortgage required both incomes. They had become accustomed to the perks and the good life they were able to enjoy while in Buenos Aires due to Brian's large salary and bonuses. Financially, they felt worse off than before they left for Argentina six years earlier. Because of their current money situation, Brian hung on, hoping that he would soon be able to find a more challenging position.

That's when Bob Jasper called Brian into his office and asked him to put out the fires in Universal's Mexico City branch. "I know you've been a little dissatisfied since you got back from Buenos Aires, Brian. I admit that we've really screwed up with a lot of our repatriated managers. But things are going to change. I want you to go down to Mexico and get them through this rough period ahead. I give you my word that I'll bring you back in one year as a senior vice-president. You're the best manager we've got, Brian. We're counting on you. I'll need your decision on Monday. Take a few days off to think about it."

Brian was excited by the offer, but uncertain what to do. How would the family react? When Brian mentioned the offer to Kathryn, she was visibly shaken and upset. They tried to talk about it, but the discussion didn't get anywhere.

"We'll talk about it Saturday when I get back," Kathryn said. The next morning she left on a business trip. Brian asked his mother to come and stay with the kids for a couple of days. Then he jumped in the car and headed for the Catskills to do some hard thinking.

DMG Corporation

Dennis Brown and Sharon Wayment had been hired as consultants at DMG Corporation to conduct a survey of the attitudes of the professional employees. Over the past months they had been gathering data through employee interviews on various issues of concern. From the data, they determined that top management needed to consider employee concerns in four areas: (1) career development for professionals, (2) the role of professional women, (3) computer training, and (4) communications.

In each of these areas Sharon and Dennis were conducting more specific interviews and also checking with a number of other organizations to see what they had been doing to successfully address these concerns. For each of these four areas, Sharon and Dennis were preparing a summary of employee concerns and recommendations for Richard Chrisman, the Vice-President of Employee Relations, to review and submit to top management. Currently, they were working on the issues which were of concern to the professional women at DMG.

In 1977, there had been only two professional women employed by DMG — one in accounting and one in personnel — in addition to the secretaries and clerks. Over the next five years, the number of women in professional positions had increased to 27 women working in engineering, marketing, accounting, and administration (see Table 1). Considering the small number of women compared with the number of men in the organization, management felt that significant progress had been made toward increasing the number of women in professional positions. Interviews with managers indicated they felt very good about the women they had hired because they had qualifications equal to or better than those of the men who had been hired in the same time period, and they were doing very good work.

However, as Sharon and Dennis reviewed the information they had gathered, they observed that there were differing views of what women were experiencing in the organization. For example, the response to a survey taken in the engineering department about

Table 1
Professional employees of DMG Corporation

	Engineering	Marketing	Accounting	Administration	Total
Men	337	36	57	48	478
Women	13	4	3	7	27
Total	350	40	60	55	505

whether women were treated the same as men underscored this difference in perception. Of the 45 engineers interviewed, 39 reported that there was no problem — women and men were treated the same. However, of the six respondents who indicated that women were not being treated equally, five were women.

In preparation for the meeting with Mr. Chrisman, Sharon and Dennis compiled a set of interviews which represented the most frequently expressed attitudes concerning professional women (Appendix A). They also prepared a summary of programs which had been implemented in other companies to address the needs of women (Appendix B).

Appendix A
Individual Interviews

1. Product specialist in marketing

Marilyn: I found no discrimination against women here. Oh, a few people make uncalled-for comments, but that's not the company's fault. Most people here try to accept women.

Consultant: Are there any who don't?

Marilyn: It's usually secretaries who are a problem. It makes me mad when women won't accept women. They say, "Are you a *secretary?*" Women have as much problem accepting women professionals as men do. For example, men flirt with our secretary, but I can't flirt with her. So we have to develop a whole new role relationship just for us. I'm the only woman she types for, so it's hard for us to learn to work together. With customers, it's different. I've had some customer contact in the eight months I've been here, but I've had no problems because I'm a woman. But people from other countries sometimes comment on my being the only woman in the meeting.

Consultant: What about the men you work with? Are they ever a problem?

Marilyn: I work with a lot of men my age. That's no problem. You just have to establish the rules. For example, if we travel, we just set the rules. I don't see problems with stereotyping either. My boss is a bit unusual in hiring a woman. He thinks women can do the job. He is nice and courteous.

Consultant: How has your boss been helpful to you?

Marilyn: He has asked me if I've had any problems being accepted, and that has helped. I don't make a big issue of sexist comments. He also is responsible for helping me get a mentor. My mentor isn't up-and-coming in the company, but he's helped me to understand the market, the job, etc. He's older and is not going much higher. I initiated the contact after my boss told me to go talk to him. Now we talk almost every day. He's been very helpful to make me more effective. He's the best resource I could have.

Consultant: Why do you think he helps you?

Marilyn: He wants to help the company be more effective. He also has three daughters and is aware of women's need for mentors. He says, "I want you to help me learn how to work with women." So I tell him if he makes a sexist comment.

Consultant: Do you think a women's support group would be helpful here?

Marilyn: I suppose a support group would be helpful if it were positive. They could suggest things to do. Women don't have the hard times they used to; they can take more initiative now. I go out to eat with women and with guys in our department. For a while I was the one who organized the group to eat lunch.

2. Financial analyst

Cindy: Some of us (all women) have discussed the issue among ourselves and feel a support group or women's association could make a very positive contribution to the company. So three weeks ago a couple of us approached some our managers to get some feedback on the idea. Those we talked to directly were quite positive about the matter, but now we're hearing rumors that some people think we're planning to picket the plant. Somehow it got blown all out of proportion. We've never even thought of picketing the plant.

Consultant: What did you hope to accomplish with a support group?

Cindy: Mostly an opportunity to get together and develop constructive ideas about how to cope with problems. There is a danger that it could just become a complaining session. We need to focus on something positive and have company sponsorship to support and direct us to work constructively.

We want to make other women and men aware of the problem. We'd like to see them do something for male managers on this issue. They have the responsibility to prevent discrimination against women.

Consultant: What kind of discrimination do you see?

Cindy: All kinds. Sexism is rampant in my department. My boss is very sexist. He lets it be known by frequently joking about women. He makes comments on women drivers, women should stay at home, etc. His favorite line is "Some dumb broad did it." I confront him by joking back, but it's not very effective. His boss is aware of this, but he doesn't confront him on it. There are not enough women in the organization to stand up and create an awareness. Top management doesn't have to deal with it. There aren't many women in management.

Consultant: Is the problem just with your boss, or do other men in your department act the same way?

Cindy: It's all of them. The men play racquetball together. I play racquetball, but I'm never invited to play with them. The boss and the men go to lunch together; I'm never invited. The men go out together after work; I'm not invited. The boss has had all of the men reporting to him over to his house, but I've never been invited to his house. My peers make negative comments about other women. Maybe they are threatened by women. They'll come in and a woman will be using the computer terminal. They'll say, "She's always at the terminal. I'm tired of waiting for her." She's not at the terminal any more then they are.

You know, it's funny. The men seem to feel at ease with the female secretaries. They go to lunch with them all the time. But they ignore the female professionals. They seem to be trying to isolate the women professionals. All of the men in our department are married and their wives stay home with the kids. So these men don't have any way to understand women professionals.

Consultant: If the general manager wanted to improve the situation for women, what could he do?

Cindy: He could do more for the development of women's careers. There is no company commitment to this. For example, I feel like I've been stuck in a corner of the accounting department. I'm not even trained to be an accountant. I'm a financial analyst. And I know a woman MBA who was hired at the same time as two male MBAs. She was hired at a lower salary and one job grade lower. She was just as well qualified. It really upsets me that this company doesn't recognize and reward qualified women.

Consultant: Anything else besides job assignment and career development?

Cindy: Well, yes. It would be nice to have a combined task force of men and women to discover and deal with problems, to make sure that women are supported by their superiors and peers. Recently, I was left in charge for two days when the boss was gone. One of the men went to our boss's boss and said, "I don't have to report to a 28-year-old woman, do I? I don't have to do what she tells me, do I?" The boss said no. That really made me mad. What am I supposed to do? Where do I go for support when my own superiors won't back me up?

3. Engineering Department: Group interview with Male Supervisors

Consultant: Let's talk about the situation for women. What kind of experience are they having here?

Joe: It's better than it used to be.

Mack: They have hired a lot of women in recent years. The company has really made an effort to get women into the organization.

Fred: We just hired a chemical engineer. She's our best little girl.

Steve: The women are getting recognized. They're pulling their own weight.

Joe: Women are accepted just like the men. They are treated just like any other engineer. The real problem is out in the plant.

Consultant: What do you mean?

Joe: They have a different attitude down there. They think women are sick all the time.

Fred: The real problem is that the women aren't able to lift things, so men back off and don't work as hard. They only respond to the tough approach.

Mack: That's true. I sometimes hesitate to send one of the girls out to the plant because she may not be forceful enough to deal with them.

Fred: Yeah, I've seen the guys out there give some of our girls a real hard time.

Consultant: "You mean" sexual harassment?

Fred: Well, it's mostly teasing. They'll whistle or say something about how nice they look. Sometimes they are real slow about doing what the girls ask them to do.

Consultant: What about here? Are the women treated equally in the Engineering department?

Mack: No problem, the company has

given us lectures on discrimination and awareness. We have very specific instructions on sexual harassment.

Joe: The company has done a lot for women. One girl is in upper management already. I don't think they have done as much for minorities. The women are moving very fast. The company is not promoting minorities as fast.

Consultant: Do you mean women are being given special treatment?

Fred: Women take more sick leave than men. The company has been lenient on that.

Mack: Yes, and some of the men are resentful of women who have more time off on sick leave.

Joe: But there are also plenty of guys who take lots of sick leave; they just aren't as noticeable as the women. Before, when I said women were being promoted faster than the minorities, I didn't mean they were getting special treatment. I meant that the minorities were being neglected more. I haven't seen anything special in treatment or recruitment of women.

Fred: I've noticed it's easier for women to switch departments than it is for men.

Consultant: Why would that be?

Fred: I don't know. I guess they're trying to fill quotas.

Consultant: Have you noticed any times when women are specifically discriminated against on a particular job?

Steve: We had a case like that just last month.

Consultant: What happened?

Steve: I got a report from the plant that produces one of the electrical components we design. They'd hit some real snags. I wanted to take all four members of my design team down there so we could work on the problem on site. It was a two- or three-day trip. I took the request to my boss, who okayed the trip, but then he said, "Of course, Susan won't be going." I couldn't change his mind. He just didn't think it was proper for a woman to make that trip with us.

Consultant: What about informal gatherings? Do you involve the women in activities such as going to lunch or playing tennis or golf after work?

Mack: Sometimes we do, but they don't like to do the same kinds of things we do. They'd be bored.

Joe: Anyway, they always get together and do "girl things" like have parties when someone has a baby.

4. Female engineers: Group interview

Consultant: What has hindered you in your effort to become effective engineers?

Pam: Mainly the fact that I have a math degree rather than an engineering degree. But there has also been some kidding about my being a woman.

Consultant: How do you respond?

Pam: I say, "Women have as many brains as you do." Some men don't take it very well when I say that.

Karen: Kidding isn't the only difficult part about being a woman here. There is a lot of stereotyping. At school there was a more liberal atmosphere. But coming to work here was like stepping back ten years. Here men compare you to their wives, not to other engineers. They treat you more like a woman than another engineer. It's a subtle influence, but it's there.

Pam: Some men ask me, "What are you doing here? Why aren't you home having a family?" Other men are jealous; they say, "You ought to be rich because you have two salaries in your family." You can hear jealousy in their comments.

Karen: Some of the managers get upset when women take sick leave. One woman told her supervisor that she was pregnant, and he said, "I don't like that; you'll miss too much work." I think his reaction was discriminatory.

Consultant: Does she still work here?

Karen: No; when the baby came, she requested a one-year leave of absence, but the company wouldn't do it, so she had to just quit. I've seen her recently. She does a little consulting on the side to keep a toe in the door. She'd like to continue full-time when her son gets older.

Pam: Another problem is that managers treat exempt and non-exempt people quite differently. If exempt women take extra sick leave, they don't get in trouble, but if non-exempt women take extra sick leave, they get into trouble.

Consultant: What do you do when someone makes a sexist comment?

Karen: Sometimes I get mad, then I confront him. I try to make him look stupid. The people who are five years older than me are more conservative than those who are 50 years old. The 30-year-olds are more of a problem. Maybe it's because I'm more tolerant of the older engineers.

Consultant: I note that the men call women "girls" here.

Pam: I don't mind being called a girl, but some women don't like it. Our secretary keeps correcting them when they call her a girl. But to me, the way they treat me is more important than what they call me. My supervisor does something I don't like. He walks by the copy machine and comes to my desk and asks me to make two copies for him. It would be faster for him to do it for himself.

Consultant: Do you tell him you don't like that?

Pam: No, I don't like it, but I don't tell him.

Consultant: Does he do the same to others in the department?

Pam: Yes, he gives copying work to the other two women and the one man who is new. The old-timers say that it used to get to them, to do copying for him. Maybe he just does it with new employees. But since three of us are women, it doesn't look right to me.

Consultant: Who do you talk with about your work?

Pam: I talk with my husband and the other women in the department. I don't go to my supervisor very often.

Karen: My husband has also helped me a lot. He tells me when I'm being too sensitive. He helps me keep a good perspective on what's happening. I often get told by men in the department that I'm too sensitive. I don't know if I'm too sensitive. Sometimes it bothers me to hear negative comments about women.

Consultant: What do you think about having a women's support group?

Pam: A lot of managers would get upset if there was such a group. They'd be afraid that it would become a union; so women don't want a support group. A lot of managers discriminate against women in promotions. We have only one woman supervisor out in the plant, and the men call her names behind her back. Many men don't want to work for a woman. We don't have a women's support group in the company, but we know what's happening with other women because we talk to each other.

Consultant: What improvements would you like to see?

Pam: Equal promotion for men and women. Equal job assignments. I have problems — for example, I go to the plant to check a motor and men will say, "What is a pretty girl like you doing down here getting dirty?" I get less harassment here because my husband works in the department.

Karen: Don't treat women differently. Treat men and women the same. Back up the women, be supportive, don't laugh at sexist comments. Women don't need special assistance, but they need confidence building. Many women lack self-confidence. Women are treated as second-class citizens in their upbringing.

Appendix B
Programs Implemented by Other Companies
To Deal With Professional Women's Issues

1. Awareness Seminars (one- or two-day sessions):
   -Men and women working together
   -Professional development for women
   -Career opportunities within the corporation
   -Managing a diverse workforce
2. Support Groups for Women:
   -A peer group who could meet to discuss common challenges and problems
3. Monthly Noontime Programs for Women
   -Educational programs
   -Networking
   -Scientific and engineering development
   -Guest speakers
   -Career discussions
4. Company Newsletter-
   -Include articles about women and issues of concern to professional women
5. Task Force:
   -Enlist both men and women to study management practices, policies, behaviors, etc. which discriminate against women, and recommend action to be taken.

Hovey and Beard Company

Part 1

The Hovey and Beard Company manufactured wooden toys of various kinds: wooden animals, pull toys, and the like. One part of the manufacturing process involved spraying paint on the partially assembled toys. The operation was staffed entirely by women.

The toys were cut, sanded, and partially assembled in the wood room. Then they were dipped into shellac, following which they were painted. The toys were predominantly two-colored; a few were made in more than two colors. Each color required an additional trip through the paint room.

For a number of years, production of these toys had been entirely handwork. However, to meet tremendously increased demand, the painting operation had recently been re-engineered so that the eight women who did the painting sat in a line by an endless chain of hooks. These hooks were in continuous motion, past the line of women and into a long horizontal oven. Each woman sat at her own painting booth, so designed as to carry away fumes and to backstop excess paint. The women would take a toy from the tray beside her, position it in a jig inside the painting cubicle, spray on the color according to a pattern, then release the toy and hang it on the hook passing by. The rate at which the hooks moved had been calculated by the engineers so that each woman, when fully trained, would be able to hang a painted toy on each hook before it passed beyond her reach.

The women working in the paint room were on a group bonus plan. Since the operation was new to them, they were receiving a learning bonus which decreased by regular amounts each month. The learning bonus was scheduled to vanish in six months, by which time it was expected that they would be on their own — that is, able to meet the standard and to earn a group bonus when they exceeded it.

Part 2

By the second month of the training period, trouble had developed. The women learned more slowly than had been anticipated, and it began to look as though their production would stabilize far below what was planned for. Many of the hooks were going by empty. The women complained that the hooks were going by too fast, and that the time-study man had set the rates wrong. A few women quit and had to be replaced with new women, which further aggravated the learning problem. The team spirit that the management had expected to develop automatically through the group bonus was not in evidence except as an expression of what the engineers called "resistance." One woman whom the group regarded as its leader (and the management regarded as the ringleader) was outspoken in making the various complaints of the group to the foreman: The job was a messy one, the hooks moved too fast, the incentive pay was not being correctly calculated, and it was too hot working so close to the drying oven."

Part 3

A consultant who was brought into this picture worked entirely with and through the foreman. After many conversations with him, the foreman felt that the first step should be to get the women together for a general discussion of the working conditions. He took this step with some hesitation, but he took it on his own volition.

The first meeting, held immediately after the shift was over at 4:00 in the afternoon, was attended by all eight women. They voiced the same complaints again: The hooks went by too fast, the job was too dirty, the room was hot and poorly ventilated. For some reason, it was this last item that they complained of most. The foreman promised to discuss the problem of ventilation and temperature with the engineers, and he scheduled a second meeting to report back to the women. In the next few days the foreman had several talks with the engineers. They and the superintendent felt that this was really a trumped-up complaint, and that the expense of any effective corrective measure would be prohibitively high.

The foreman came to the second meeting with some apprehension. The women, however, did not seem to be much put out, perhaps because they had a proposal of their own to make. They

felt that if several large fans were set up so as to circulate the air around their feet, they would be much more comfortable. After some discussion, the foreman agreed that the idea might be tried out. The foreman and the consultant discussed the question of the fans with the superintendent, and three large propeller-type fans were purchased.

Part 4

The fans were brought in. The women were jubilant. For several days the fans were moved about in various positions until they were placed to the satisfaction of the group. The women seemed completely satisfied with the results, and relations between them and the foreman improved visibly.

The foreman, after this encouraging episode, decided that further meetings might also be profitable. He asked the women if they would like to meet and discuss other aspects of the work situation. The women were eager to do this. The meeting was held, and the discussion quickly centered on the speed of the hooks. The women maintained that the time-study man had set the hooks at an unreasonably fast speed and that they would never be able to reach the goal of filling enough of them to make a bonus.

The turning point of the discussion came when the group's leader frankly explained that the point wasn't that they couldn't work fast enough to keep up with the hooks, but they couldn't work at that pace all day long. The foreman explored the point. The women were unanimous in their opinion that they could keep up with the belt for short periods if they wanted to. But they didn't want to because if they showed they could do this for short periods, they would be expected to do it all day long. The meeting ended with an unprecedented request: "Let us adjust the speed of the belt faster or slower, depending on how we feel." The foreman agreed to discuss this with the superintendent and the engineers.

The reaction of the engineers to the suggestion was negative. However, after several meetings, it was granted that there was some latitude within which variations in the speed of the hooks would not affect the finished product. After considerable argument with the engineers, it was agreed to try out the women's ideas.

With misgivings, the foreman had a control with a dial marked "low, medium, fast" installed at the booth of the group leader; she could now adjust the speed of the belt anywhere between the lower and upper limits that the engineers had set.

Part 5

The women were delighted, and spent many lunch hours deciding how the speed of the belt should be varied from hour to hour throughout the day. Within a week the pattern had settled down to one in which the first half hour of the shift was run on what the women called medium speed (a dial setting slightly above the point marked "medium"). The next two and one-half hours were run at high speed; the half hour before lunch and the half hour after lunch were run at low speed. The rest of the afternoon was run at high speed with the exception of the last 45 minutes of the shift, which was run at medium.

In view of the women's reports of satisfaction and ease in their work, it is interesting to note that the constant speed at which the engineers had originally set the belt was slightly below medium on the dial of the control that had been given the women. The average speed at which the women were running the belt was on the high side of the dial. Few, if any, empty hooks entered the oven, and inspection showed no increase of rejects from the paint room.

Production increased, and within three weeks (some two months before the scheduled ending of the learning bonus) the women were operating at 30 to 50 percent above the level that had been expected under the original arrangement. They were collecting their base pay, a considerable piece-rate bonus, and the learning bonus which, it will be remembered, had been set to decrease with time and not as a function of current productivity. The women were earning more now than many skilled workers in other parts of the plant.

Part 6

Management was besieged by demands that this inequity be taken care of. With growing irritation between superintendent and foreman, engineers and foreman, superintendent and engineers, the situation came to a head when the superintendent revoked the learning bonus and returned the painting operation to its original status. The hooks moved again at their constant, time-studied designated speed; production dropped again; and within a month, all but two of the eight girls had quit. The foreman himself stayed on for several months but, feeling aggrieved, then left for another job.

Metropolitan Police Department

O n June 17, 1968, Verl Iverson, commander of the ninth division of the Metropolitan Police Department, was trying to figure out some way of motivating the people in his division to wear the new equipment provided by the city as accessories to the basic uniform. For two years, the city and department officials had been trying to institute a change in the accessories to the uniform worn by the city police and had met with much unanticipated resistance from both the old-timers and the rookies on the force. Verl had just had an encounter with Phil Snead, a deputy chief of the department, over the long-drawn-out process of changing over to the new equipment. Chief Snead left Verl with an ultimatum: that officers who had not changed over to the new equipment in two weeks should be given an official reprimand including days off without pay.

The new uniform

In the mid-sixties, the chief of police of the Metropolitan Police Department as well as a number of city officials received numerous letters from the public suggesting that the police uniforms worn by the force were outdated and that they gave the policemen a "gestapo" look. Being concerned about public image, the chief of police formed a committee and assigned it the task of recommending changes in the uniform to remove the gestapo look while maintaining the efficiency of the uniform as a piece of equipment. After months of research and evaluation, the committee selected several items of new equipment to be field tested. The results of the field tests, in general, were seen as favorable, and a go-ahead was given to start to issue the new equipment to academy graduates.

The parts of the uniform that were changed included the hat, the pants belt, and the Sam Browne belt (the belt used to carry handcuffs, holster, and other accessories). The hat was changed to a rounded-top style instead of the old eight-pointed style. The new pants belt had a Velcro fastener instead of the conventional buckle and was lined with Velcro strips on the inside. The new Sam Browne was very different from the traditional style. Like the pants belt, it was lined with Velcro on the inside; to fasten it to the pants belt, the pants belt was reversed and its exposed Velcro lining was pressed against the Velcro on the reverse side of the Sam Browne. (The old Sam Browne belt was attached to the old pants belt with leather straps.)

The city had gone to considerable expense to make the uniform convey what was thought to be the image of an efficient police officer. It was felt that the removal of the silver buckles from the pants and accessories belts, the rounding of the crown of the hat, and other minor modifications achieved the goal of obtaining a uniform without the gestapo look.

Response to the change

Verl knew that the city officials and high-echelon law enforcement officers who were pushing the change in uniform were very committed to the change, and there appeared to be no way to convince them to return to the old-style accessories. All of this had been decided two years ago after heated discussions between the committee and representatives of the law enforcement officers. Verl also knew that many of the officers on the force were opposed to wearing some of the new pieces of equipment.

The opposition to the new gear had been so strong that twice the city had had to postpone the date set for it to be worn by all personnel. Until this point, the city had supplied all new academy graduates with the new equipment and had allowed those who were on the force prior to the introduction of the new pieces to wear what was initially issued them or, in the case of the older officers, what they had purchased themselves.

The opposition to the new equipment was mainly directed at the new pants belt and the new Sam Browne belt. The officers complained that the Velcro cut through the belt loops of their pants, that the Sam Browne belt was uncomfortable, and that it didn't hold up well. Verl knew that many of the old-timers were a little on the heavy side and that the old wide leather belt slipped down comfortably underneath the "overhang" but the new Velcro-lined belt was not as adjustable.

The older officers had voiced the opinion that the new Sam Browne was unsafe. The Sam Browne was a very important accessory to a police officer. Almost every piece of equipment was attached to the belt, including keys, handcuffs, whistle, and revolver. Each officer had a slightly different way of wearing the Sam Browne. Each could find any piece of equipment in a split second. In emergencies and dangerous situations, it was vital that the officer have easy and quick access to his equipment. The old-timers complained that once they had become accustomed to their particular way of carrying equipment on the belt, a change to a new system could cause confusion and delay in an emergency and might cost an officer's life.

The newer officers had also voiced a strong bias against the new belts. After graduating from the academy and beginning service on the force, almost without exception each officer bought the old-style Sam Browne and pants belt and discarded the new ones issued by the city. The younger officers said that the new belt was not worn by anyone but rookies on the force and that wearing the belts identified a "green" officer both to other officers on the force and to people on the street, who might treat a new cop with less respect than they would an experienced policeman.

During the course of the last two years, the department had tried everything to get the officers to wear the belts, from threats of days off to an animated cartoon showing the benefits of the new equipment. Verl agreed with the points brought up by the officers. He also thought that the equipment change was a waste of time and money. He knew that within a year or two he would retire and that he had reached the highest level he would attain on the force. Nevertheless, he felt a great deal of pressure to get the officers to change. Verl felt that he was in a difficult spot, and the wondered how he could develop a strategy that would satisfy the city council, the chief of police, and the policemen in his department.

Builders Plumbing and Heating Supply

In October 1973 Steve Baker, warehouse foreman at Builders Plumbing and Heating Supply, was experiencing some problems with the introduction of a computer system into the organization. He felt that in getting the system off the ground they had experienced a number of problems, but they were to be expected in any organization making a transition to computer. However, he was especially concerned about the attitudes of a number of the employees toward the new system. Many people were very critical of the changes being made and would make jokes or snide comments about the computer. It was becoming a daily activity to find some new problems caused by the system. Steve wondered why people seemed so hostile to the changes being made and was searching for some way to get these people to develop a more favorable attitude toward the computer system.

Background

Builders Plumbing and Heating Supply was located in Lincoln, Nebraska and had been in operation for nearly fifty years. The company had the reputation in the community of handling a complete line of plumbing, heating, and air conditioning equipment, parts, and supplies. The employees prided themselves on giving customers good service. This required the stocking of over 12,000 items in inventory. The company had a wide variety of customers, including contractors, plumbers, and electricians as well as individual homeowners. Most of the customers had been buying from Builders for many years.

About half of the twenty-eight employees had been with the company for more than ten years; the other half were relatively new and had been employed for less than five years. Most of the old-timers and the younger employees were able to work together with no friction, and there was a cooperative climate in the organization (an organizational chart is presented in Exhibit 1).

In 1970 Steve Baker was promoted from counter salesman to warehouse foreman. In his new position Steve instituted a change in the inventory system: He tried to decrease the amount of each item kept on hand by placing smaller and more frequent orders. His goal was to make the company more liquid by a reduction in the amount of money tied up in idle or obsolete inventory. The results were increased inventory turnover and higher profits. During the implementation of Steve's inventory system there were times when stockouts occurred in important and high-demand items, and sales were lost. Many of the old-timers who used to handle part of the ordering process began to criticize Steve and his system. Often the criticisms were quite severe, causing bad feelings and heated arguments. The salespeople began to call the system "the Ouija board." Eventually Steve was able to work out almost all of the problems, but the criticism seemed to continue even after he stopped making mistakes.

In 1971 Builders Plumbing and Heating began to use the computer of a sister company in Omaha to handle the pricing of all of its items. However, in April 1973 the sister company informed the general manager at Builders that they would have to find access to another computer, because the extra capacity being used by Builders for pricing was needed by the Omaha operation. After some discussion between the president, the general manager, and Steve Baker, it was decided to buy a small computer that could be used not only for pricing but also for all of the inventory and accounting work. Steve was given responsibility for implementation of the new system. One other employee, Tom Burbank, had taken some computer courses in college, and so he was assigned to help on the project. To implement the new system, it was necessary to make a number of changes. Mate-

Exhibit 1

Builders Plumbing and Heating Supply organization chart

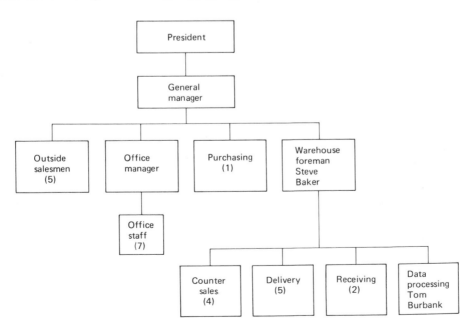

rials and parts had to be physically re-located. Each item had to be assigned a number, which had to be entered on the sales slip when a sale was written up. These changes brought a renewal of the criticism that Steven had received when he introduced his own system in 1970.

The salespeople complained about the requirement that they use a number for each item on the sales slip. They had to look up the numbers in a book, and this meant it took longer to wait on a customer. As a result, customers were kept waiting and salespeople became frustrated and upset. Sometimes one would write down the wrong number, and then an angry customer would call, complaining that the bill showed the wrong amount for the parts purchased. Some customers had historically received dis-counts on the purchases they made at Builders, but the computer system made it very difficult to give different discounts to customers. Even some of the secretaries commented that they were afraid the computer might eliminate the need for their jobs.

Steve and Tom worked long hours to solve the problems in the system. They met with the employees to assure them that no one would lose his or her job because of the computer and to deal with any questions or complaints about the system. Steve felt that most of the bugs in the system had been solved, but still the criticisms and jokes about the computer continued. He wanted to take some action to improve the situation, but he didn't know what to do.

It is remarkable how willing American business people are to make the current quarter look better at the expense of the future, to sacrifice the future to make this year's bottom line a little more attractive or less embarrassing. The American approach stands in sharp contrast to Japan's sophisticated business leadership, which often does just the opposite, sacrificing now in order to have a healthy future.

John Naisbitt, *Megatrends*

"It may be too bad that our society isn't further along and that this (a woman astronaut) is such a big deal."

Sally Ride, *Astronaut, June 1983*

"We have no problems with sex discriminating in our company. Women are treated the same as men. Recently we hired a female chemical engineer. She is a great little girl and is working out very well."

Male middle manager

EXERCISES

Organizational profile exercise

Many comments have been made with respect to accurate identification of the strengths and weaknesses of organizations. It is important that you develop more than just an intuitive feel for what is going on. There are a variety of different ways to obtain such a profile. (Discussion with different management or organizational consultants would clearly illustrate this point.) However, many of the methods involve some sort of questionnaire. The following exercise is an abbreviated version of one of the best known instruments in the field. It was developed by Rensis Likert and is more fully explained in his books, *New Patterns of Management* and *The Human Organization*.

In this exercise you should think of an organization you are familiar with (perhaps one in which you are currently involved or one you have been part of in the past). Describe that organization by indicating the most accurate statement with respect to each organizational variable. You have a range of twenty points along the scale to describe the relative degree of each item.

After describing this organization, you should now think of an *ideal* organization — not a mythological one, but one you think would be most effective. What characteristics do you think you would see in this type of organization? Describe this organization with another color or marking. Then connect the set of points for your actual organization in a vertical profile. Do the same for your ideal organization.

If you are like most people, the ideal organization will be a profile to the right of your actual organization. This raises the question of changing organizations to make them more effective and, in turn, more rewarding. You might discuss this topic in groups or in class.

You will notice the systems referred to in the headings on the profile sheet. These classifications identify the differences in overall description of the general organization climate. In Likert's model overall responses which fall in the range of each of the four systems are defined as follows: System 1 — Exploitive authoritative; System 2 — Benevolent authoritative; System 3 — Consultative; System 4 — Participative Group.

Exhibit 1

Profile of organization characteristics

	Organizational variables	System 1	System 2	System 3	System 4
Leadership	1. How much confidence is shown in subordinates?	None	Condescending	Substantial	Complete
	2. How free do they feel to talk to superiors about job?	Not at all	Not very	Rather free	Fully free
	3. Are subordinates' ideas sought and used, if worthy?	Seldom	Sometimes	Usually	Always
Motivation	4. Is predominant use made of (1) fear, (2) threats, (3) punishment, (4) rewards, (5) involvement?	1, 2, 3 occasionally 4	4, some 3	4, some 3 and 5	5, 4 based on group
	5. Where is responsibility felt for achieving organization's goals?	Mostly at top	Top and middle	Fairly general	At all levels
	6. How much cooperative teamwork exists?	None	Little	Some	Great deal
Communication	7. What is the direction of information flow?	Downward	Mostly downward	Down and up	Down, up and sideways
	8. How is downward communication accepted?	With suspicion	Possibly with suspicion	With caution	With a receptive mind
	9. How accurate is upward communication?	Often wrong	Censored for the boss	Limited accuracy	Accurate
	10. How well do superiors know problems faced by subordinates?	Know little	Some knowledge	Quite well	Very well

(continued)

Exhibit 1 (continued)

	Organizational	System 1	System 2	System 3	System 4
Decisions	11. At what level are decisions made?	Mostly at top	Policy at top, some delegation	Broad policy at top, more delegation	Throughout but well integrated
	12. Are subordinates involved in decisions related to their work?	Not at all	Occasionally consulted	Generally consulted	Fully involved
	13. What does decision-making process contribute to motivation?	Nothing, often weakens it	Relatively little	Some contribution	Substantial contribution
Goals	14. How are organizational goals established?	Orders issued	Orders, some comments invited	After discussion, by orders	By group action (except in crisis)
	15. How much covert resistance to goals is present?	Strong resistance	Moderate resistance	Some resistance at times	Little or none
Control	16. How concentrated are review and control functions?	Highly at top	Relatively highly at top	Moderate delegation to lower levels	Quite widely shared
	17. Is there an informal organization resisting the formal one?	Yes	Usually	Sometimes	No—same goals as formal
	18. What are cost, productivity, and other control data used for?	Policing, punishment	Reward and punishment	Reward, some self-guidance	Self-guidance problem-solving

What — me change?

Organizations often encounter obstacles in their attempts to change or to adapt to a changing environment. Sometimes this obstacle is a person or persons in key positions within the organization. This role play is an opportunity to understand the frustrations and the dynamics of confronting roadblocks and dealing with them. Let your feelings develop as they would if you actually were the individuals described in your role. Should issues develop that are not covered by the role, adapt or innovate accordingly.

To conceptualize your role, it is usually best to read it carefully two or three times. Do not read the other roles. Then close the book and think about it for a few minutes. Try to develop an approach in terms of the limited information given and your own interpretation of how a person in that position would probably behave. After you have the role in mind, do not reread it during the process of the role play.

Role for Mike

You have been with a small manufacturing firm for eighteen years. For the past seven years you have been plant manager. You have developed your management and control systems over the years, and you feel that you have been doing a pretty good job. The plant had been doing pretty well until the last two years. Recently a competitor has taken away some of your old accounts. These past customers have told you that they are getting a better price, better service, and better quality from the competitor. You think that the supervisors who work for you probably are to blame for the slow orders and lowered quality as well as the salespeople who deal directly with the accounts. In the past few weeks you have become aware of some problems among the supervisors. Not only have they seemed very dissatisfied and surly to you, but they have not been following established procedures that you have developed. The company president has called you in and told you that several of the supervisors have reported that they have met with resistance from you every time they have tried to improve and change things. You resent the implication that you are against improvement. It is just that tried-and-true methods have been developed and have worked until now. Some of their new schemes are too radical even to consider. The supervisors have apparently been doing things behind your back for some time now and finally they have made this attempt to undermine your position with the president. You resent this deeply, because if you hadn't brought them along and trained them, they would still be working on the production line. The president has told you to work out the problem with them. He is tired of hearing about it, and, if you can't solve it internally, he will have to take some action. You think it is about time that these young upstarts be put in their place and understand who is boss. You think George is the ringleader and have called him in to lay down the law. You want to talk to George and George alone, and when you have straightened him out you will bring all the supervisors together.

Role for George

You have been with a small manufacturing firm for six years. You worked into your present position, supervisor of the assembly department, from the production line. You have been supervisor for two years. In those two years you have tried to implement changes that you had recognized as necessary even when you worked on the line. Mike, the plant manager and your immediate supervisor, has been a roadblock to every change you have tried to make. You are becoming very frustrated, and the feeling is shared by the other supervisors as well as the salespeople who have to face customers when the orders are not on time or are of poor quality. You have gotten them together and have talked about the problem but have come to no solutions. You and Jim, a salesman, have gone to the president to explain what is happening and what you have tried to do about it. He was sympathetic but told you that he expected you to handle it at your level and go directly to Mike about it. If you can't come to any reasonable solutions, then he may have to take more drastic action, but not until Mike has had a chance to deal with the problem himself.

You are now prepared to confront Mike directly with your feelings about the way things are going. You expect him to react negatively and defensively, because he always has before when you make suggestions. He reacts as if any suggestion for improvement is a personal attack on his competence. Things have finally gone on long enough, and if changes aren't made you will quit. You have just received a call from Mike to come to his office immediately. You can tell he is mad. Jim is here with you right now, and you invite him to go along even though Mike implied that you come alone.

Role for Jim

You are a sales representative for a small manufacturing firm. Over the years you have built up a sizable clientele who use your company's products. You have recently lost some major accounts, and it is hurting your income, because you work on a commission. You are no longer sure how much quality or reliability you can promise your customers, because your promises have repeatedly been broken by the plant in the past year or two;. You have expanded your sales, while the plant is still running as it did several years ago. They have made no effort to gear up for increased business. The plant manager's response to having lost the business is, "We have all we can do anyway, we don't need their work." This hurts you, and furthermore you have no incentives to acquire new customers, because you don't expect to be able to keep them. You have tried to talk to Mike about the problem, but he doesn't even recognize it as a problem. He thinks things are going along fine, and if he does see problems, he always blames them on someone else. You have talked to the supervisors of the different departments, and they have tried but haven't been allowed to innovate. Finally you and George went to see the company president about it. You are talking to George when he gets a call from Mike to come and see him immediately. The tone of his voice tells you he is mad.

Probably he got wind of the visit with the president. He tells George to come to his office alone, but the two of you decide that you will go together. You intend to stay at the meeting with Mike and tell him what's on your mind.

Annotated Bibliography

Section 2
Selection no.

13 "On the Folly of rewarding A, While Hoping for B" (Kerr, S.)

Barnard, C.I. *The Functions of the Executive.* Cambridge, Mass.: Harvard University Press, 1964.

Blau, P.F. and Scott, W.R. *Formal Organizations.* San Francisco: Chandler, 1962.

Fiedler, F.E. "Predicting the Effects of Leadership Training and Experience from the Contingency Model." *Journal of Applied Psychology* 56 (1972): 114-119.

Garland, L.H. "Studies of the Accuracy of Diagnostic Procedures." *American Journal Roentgenological, Radium Therapy Nuclear Medicine* 82 (1959): 25-38. In one study of 14,867 films for signs of tuberculosis, 1,216 positive readings turned out to be clinically negative; only 24 negative readings proved clinical active, a ratio of 50 to 1.

Kerr, S. "Some Modifications in MBO as an OD Strategy." *Academy of Management Proceedings* (1973): 39-42. (a)

Kerr, S. "What Price Objectivity?" *American Sociologist* 8 (1973): 92-93. (b)

Litwin, G.H. and Stringer, R.A., Jr. *Motivation and Organizational Climate.* Boston: Harvard University Press, 1968.

Perrow, C. "The Analysis of Goals in Complex Organizations." In A. Etzioni (Ed.), *Readings on Modern Organizations.* Englewood Cliffs, N.J.: Prentice-Hall, 1969.

Scheff, T.J. "Decision Rules, Types of Error, and Their Consequences in Medical Diagnosis." In F. Massarik and P. Ratoosh (Eds.), *Mathematical Explorations in Behavioral Science.* Homewood, Ill.: Irwin, 1965.

Simon, H.A. *Administrative Behavior.* New York: Free Press, 1957. In Simon's terms, a decision is "subjectively rational" if it maximizes an individual's valued outcomes so far as his knowledge permits. A decision is "personally rational" if it is oriented toward the individual's goals.

Swanson, G.E. "Review Symposium: Beyond Freedom and Dignity." *American Journal of Sociology* 78 (1972):702-705.

Webster, E. *Decision Making in the Employment Interview.* Montreal: Industrial Relations Center, McGill University, 1964.

Selection No.

15 "Behavior Modification on the Bottom Line" (Hamner, W.C. and Hamner, E.P.)

Hamner, W.C. "Reinforcement Theory and Contingency Management." In Tosi and Hamner (Eds.), *Organizational Behavior and Management: A Contingency Approach.* St. Clair Press, 1974. Pp. 188-204. Previous comments on behavior modification by the author.

Hamner, W.C. "Worker Motivation Programs: Importance of Climate, Structure and Performance Consequences." In Hamner and Schmidt (Eds.), *Contemporary Problems in Personnel.* St. Clair Press, 1974. Pp. 280-308. Previous comments on behavior modification by the author.

"An Interview with B. F. Skinner." *Organizational Dynamics* (Winter 1973): 31-40. Skinner's views on the applications of his ideas in industry. Also see pp. 41-50 for an account of Skinner's ideas in action.

Lawler, E.E., III. *Pay and Organizational Effectiveness.* McGraw-Hill, 1971. The best discussion of the general subject of pay and performance.

Nord, W.R. "Beyond the Teaching Machine: The Negative Area of Operant Conditioning." In *The Theory and Prac-*

tice of Management, Organizational Behavior and Human Performance 4 (1969): 375-401.

Skinner, B.F.*Contingencies of Reinforcement.* Appleton-Century-Crofts, 1969. An understandable view of Skinner's basic ideas in his own words.

Skinner, B.F. and Rogers, C.R. "Some Issues Concerning the Control of Human Behavior." *Science* 24 (1965): 1057-66.

"Where Skinner's Theories Work." *Business Week* (December 2, 1972): 64-69.

Whyte, W.F. "Pigeons, Persons, and Piece Rates." *Psychology Today* (April 1972): 67-68. Highly critical of the application of Skinner's ideas in industry.

Selection No.

17   "A New Strategy for Job Enrichment" (Hackman, J.R. et al.)

Ford, N.R. *Motivation Through the Work Itself.* New York: American Management Association, 1969.

Hackman, J.R. and Lawler, E.E."Employee Reactions to Job Characteristics." *Journal of Applied Psychology Monograph* (1971): 259-286.

Hackman, J.R. and Oldham, G.R. *Motivation Through the Design of Work: Test of a Theory.* Technical Report No. 6. Department of Administrative Sciences, Yale University, 1974.

Hackman, J.R. and Oldham, G.R. "Development of the Job Diagnostic Survey." *Journal of Applied Psychology* (1975): 159-170.

Herzberg, F. *Work and the Nature of Man.* Cleveland: World, 1966.

Herzberg, F. "One More Time: How Do You Motivate Employees?" *Harvard Business Review* (1968): 53-62.

Herzberg, F., Mausner, B., and Snyderman, B. *The Motivation to Work.* New York: John Wiley & Sons, 1959.

Paul, W.J., Jr., Robertson, K.B. and Herzberg, F. "Job Enrichment Pays Off." *Harvard Business Review* (1969): 61-78.

Turner, A.N. and Lawrence, P.R. *Industrial Jobs and the Worker.* Cambridge, Mass.: Harvard Graduate School of Business Administration, 1965.

Walters, R.W. and Associates. *Job Enrichment for Results.* Cambridge, Mass.: Addison-Wesley, 1975.

30   Career goals exercise

Bolles, R. *What Color is Your Parachute?* Berkeley, Ten Speed Press, 1972.

Haldane, B. *Career Satisfaction and Success: A Guide to Job Freedom.* New York: AMACOM, 1974.

Kotter, J., Faux, V., and McArthur, C. *Self-Assessment and Career Development.* Englewood Cliffs, N.J.: Prentice-Hall, 1978.

Lakein, A. *How to Get Control of Your Time and Your Life.* New York: Signet, 1973.

Section 3
Selection No.

32   "Suppose We Took Groups Seriously . . ." (Leavitt, H.)

Johnson, R.T. and Ouchi, W.G. "Made in America (Under Japanese Management)." *Harvard Business Review* (September-October 1974).

Li, V. "The Development of the Chinese Legal System." In John Lindbeck (Ed.), *China: The Management of a Revolutionary Society.* Seattle: University of Washington Press, 1971.

Likert, R. *New Patterns of Management.* New York: McGraw-Hill, 1961.

33   "Assets and Liabilities in Group Problem Solving: The Need For an Integrative Function" (Maier, N.R.F.)

Crozier, W.J. "Notes on Some Problems of Adaptation." *Biological Bulletin* 39 (1920): 116-129.

Duneker, K. "On Problem Solving." *Psychological Monographs* 58 (1945): 5, Whole No. 270.

Hamilton, W.F. "Coordination in the Starfish. III. The Righting Reaction as a Phase of Locomotion (Righting and

Locomotion)." *Journal of Comparative Psychology* 2 (1922): 81-94.

Hoffman, L.R. "Conditions for Creative Problem Solving." *Journal of Psychology* 52 (1961): 429-444.

Hoffman, L.R. "Group Problem Solving." In L. Berkowitz (Ed.), *Advances in Experimental Social Psychology.* Vol. 2 New York: Academic Press, 1965. Pp. 99-132.

Selection No.

33 Hoffman, L.R., Harburg, E., and Maier, N.R.F. "Differences and Disagreement as Factors in Creative Group Problem Solving." *Journal of Abnormal and Social Psychology* 64 (1962): 206-214.

Hoffman, L.R., and Maier, N.R.F., "The Use of Group Decision to Resolve a Problem of Fairness." *Personnel Psychology* 12 (1959): 545-559.

Hoffman, L.R., and Maier, N.R.F., "Quality and Acceptance of Problem Solutions by Members of Homogenous and Heterogeneous Groups." *Journal of Abnormal and Social Psychology* 69 (1964): 264-271.

Hoffman, L.R., and Maier, N.R.F., "Valence in the Adoption of Solutions by Problem-Solving Groups. II. Quality and Acceptance as Goals of Leaders and Members." Unpublished manuscript, 1967 (mimeo).

Kelley, H.H., and Thibaut, J.W. "Experimental Studies of Group Problem Solving and Process." In G. Lindzey (Ed.), *Handbook of Social Psychology.* Cambridge, Mass.: Addison-Wesley, 1954. Pp. 735-785.

Maier, N.R.F., "Reasoning in Humans. I. On Direction." *Journal of Comparitive Psychology* 10 (1930): 115-143.

Maier, N.R.F. "The Quality of Group Decisions As Influenced By the Discussion Leader." *Human Relations* 3 (1950): 155-174.

Maier, N.R.F. *Principles of Human Relations.* New York: Wiley, 1952.

Maier, N.R.F. "An Experimental Test of the Effect of Training on Discussion Leadership." *Human Relations* 6 (1953): 161-173.

Maier, N.R.F. *The Appraisal Interview.* New York: Wiley, 1958.

Maier, N.R.F. "Screening Solutions to Upgrade Quality: A New Approach to Problem Solving Under Conditions of Uncertainty." *Journal of Psychology* 49 (1960): 217-231.

Maier, N.R.F. *Problem-Solving Discussions and Conferences: Leadership Methods and Skills.* New York: McGraw-Hill, 1963.

Maier, N.R.F., and Hayes, J.J. *Creative Management.* New York: Wiley, 1962.

Maier, N.R.F., and Hoffman, L.R. "Using Trained 'Developmental' Discussion Leaders to Improve Further the Quality of Group Decisions." *Journal of Applied Psychology* 44 (1960): 247-251. (a)

Maier, N.R.F., and Hoffman, L.R. "Quality of First and Second Solutions in Group Problem Solving." *Journal of Applied Psychology* 44 (1960): 278-283. (b)

Maier, N.R.F. and Hoffman, L.R. "Organization and Creative Problem Solving." *Journal of Applied Psychology* 45 (1961): 277-280.

Maier, N.R.F. and Hoffman, L.R. "Group Decision in England and the United States." *Personnel Psychology* 15 (1962): 75-87.

Maier, N.R.F. and Hoffman, L.R. "Financial Incentives and Group Decision in Motivating Change." *Journal of Social Psychology* 64 (1964): 369-378. (a)

Maier, N.R.F. and Hoffman, L.R. "Types of Problems Confronting Managers." *Personnel Psychology* 17 (1964): 261-269. (b)

Maier, N.R.F. and Hoffman, L.R. "Acceptance and Quality of Solutions as Related to Leaders' Attitudes Toward Disagreement in Group Problem Solving." *Journal of Applied Behavioral Science* 1 (1965): 373-386.

Maier, N.R.F. and Maier, R.A. "An Experimental Test of the Effects of 'Developmental' vs. 'free' Discussions on the Quality of Group Decisions." *Journal of Applied Psychology* 41 (1957): 320-323.

Maier, N.R.F. and Solem, A.R. "The Contribution of a Discussion Leader to the Quality of Group Thinking: The Effective Use of Minority Opinions." *Human Relations* 5 (1952): 277-288.

Maier, N.R.F. and Solem, A.R. "Improving Solutions by Turning Choice Situations Into Problems." *Personnel Psychology* 15 (1962): 151-157.

Maier, N.R.F. and Zerfoss, I.F. "MRP: A Technique for Training Large Groups of Supervisors and Its Potential Use in Social Research." *Human Relations* 5 (1952): 177-186.

Moore, A.R. "The Nervous Mechanism of Coordination in the Crinoid Antedon rosaceus." *Journal of Genetic Psychology* 6 (1924): 281-288.

Moore, A.R. and Doudoroff, M. "Injury, Recovery and Function In an Aganglionic Central Nervous System." *Journal of Comparitive Psychology* 28 (1939): 313-328.

Osborn, A.F. *Applied Imagination.* New York: Scribner's, 1953.

Schneirla, T.C. and Maier, N.R.F. "Concerning the Status of the Starfish." *Journal of Comparitive Psychology* 30 (1940): 103-110.

Solem, A.R. "Almost Anything I Can Do, We Can Do Better." *Personnel Administration* 28 (1965): 6-16.

Thibaut, J.W. and Kelley, H.H. "*The Social Psychology of Groups.*" New York: Wiley, 1961.

Wallach, M.A. and Kogan, N. "The Roles of Information, Discussion and Consensus in Group Risk Taking." *Journal of Experimental and Social Psychology* 1 (1965): 1-19.

Wallach, M.A., Kogan, N. and Bem, D.J. "Group Influence on Individual Risk

Taking." *Journal of Abnormal and Social Psychology* 65 (1962): 75-86.

Wertheimer, M. *Productive Thinking.* New York: Harper, 1959.

24 "The Abilene Paradox: The Management of Agreement" (Harvey, J.B.).

Argyris, C. *Intervention Theory and Method: A Behavioral Science View.* Addison-Wesley, 1970. Gives an excellent description of the process of "owning up" and being "open," both of which are major skills required if one is to assist his organization in avoiding or leaving Abilene.

Camus, A. *The Myth of Sisyphus and Other Essays.* Vintage Books, Random House, 1955. Provides an existential viewpoint for coping with absurdity, of which the Abilene Paradox is a clear example.

Harvey, J.B. and Albertson, R. "Neurotic Organizations: Symptoms, Causes and Treatment." Parts I and II. *Personnel Journal* (September and October 1971). A detailed example of a third-party intervention into an organization caught in a variety of agreement-management dilemmas.

Janis, I.L. *Victims of Groupthink.* Houghton-Mifflin Co., 1972. Offers an alternative viewpoint for understanding and dealing with many of the dilemmas described in the "Abilene Paradox." Specifically, many of the events that Janis describes as examples of conformity pressures (that is, group tyranny) I would conceptualize as mismanaged agreement.

Slater, P. *The Pursuit of Loneliness.* Beacon Press, 1970. Contributes an in-depth description of the impact of the role of alienation, separation, and loneliness (a major contribution to the Abilene Paradox) in our culture.

Walton, R. *Interpersonal Peacemaking: Confrontation and Third Party Consultation.* Addison-Wesley, 1969. Describes a variety of approaches for dealing with conflict when it is real, rather than phony.

Selection No.

35 "Intergroup Problems in Organizations" (Schein, E.H.)

Blake, R.R. and Mouton, J.S. "Reactions to Intergroup Competition under Win-Lose Conditions." *Management Science* 7 (1961): 420-435.

Blake, R.R. and Mouton, J.S. "Headquarters — Field Team Training for Organizational Improvements." *Journal of the American Society of Training Directors* 16 (1962).

Janis, I.L. and King, B.T. "The Influence of Role Playing on Opinion Change." *Journal of Abnormal and Social Psychology* 69 (1954): 211-218.

Sherif, M., et al. *Intergroup Conflict and Cooperation: The Robbers Cave Experiment.* Norman, Oklahoma: University Book Exchange, 1961.

36 "Defensive Communication" (J.R. Gibb)

Gibb, J.R. "Sociopsychological Processes of Group Instruction." In N.B. Henry (Ed.), *The Dynamics of Instructional Groups.* Fifty-ninth Yearbook of the National Society for the Study of Education, Part II, 1960. Pp. 115-135.

Section 4
Selection No.

49 "The Manager's Job: Folklore and Fact" (Mintzberg, H.)

Aguilar, F.J. *Scanning the Business Environment.* New York: Macmillan, 1967. P. 102.

Andrews, K.R. "Toward Professionalism in Business Management." (March-April 1969): 49. A more thorough, though rather different, discussion of this issue.

Burns, T. "The Directions of Activity and Communication in a Departmental Executive Group." *Human Relations* 7, no. I (1954): 73.

Carlson, S. *Executive Behaviour.* Stockholm: Strömbergs, 1951. The first of the diary studies.

Choran, I. Unpublished study. Reported in Mintzberg, *The Nature of Managerial Work.*

Copeman, G.H. *The Role of the Managing Director.* London: Business Publications, 1963.

Davis, R.T. *Performance and Development of Field Sales Managers.* Boston: Division of Research, Harvard Business School, 1957.

Drucker, P.F. *The Practice of Management.* New York: Harper & Row, 1954. Pp. 341-342.

Grayson, C.J., Jr. in "Management Science and Business Practice." (July-August 1973): 41. Grayson explains why, as chairman of the Price Commission, he did not use those very techniques that he himself promoted in his earlier career as a management scientist.

Guest, R.H. "Of Time and the Foreman." *Personnel* (May 1956): 478.

Hekimian, J.S. and Mintzberg, H. "The Planning Dilemma." *The Management Review* (May 1968): 4.

Hodgson, R.C., Levinson, D.J. and Zaleznik, A. *The Executive Role Constellation.* Boston: Division of Research, Harvard Business School, 1965. Discussion of the sharing of roles.

Homans, G.C. *The Human Group.* New York: Harcourt, Brace & World, 1950. Based on the study by William F. Whyte entitled *Street Corner Society,* rev. ed. (Chicago: University of Chicago Press, 1955).

Livingston, J.S. "Myth of the Well-Educated Manager." (January-February 1971): 79.

Mintzberg, H. *The Nature of Managerial Work.* New York: Harper & Row, 1973. Contains all the data from my study.

Neustadt, R.E. *Presidential Power.* New York: John Wiley, 1960. Pp. 153-154 (italics added) and p. 157.

Sayles, L.R. *Managerial Behavior.* New York: McGraw-Hill, 1964. P. 162.

Stewart, R. *Managers and Their Jobs.*

London: Macmillan, 1967.

Wrapp, W.E. "Good Managers Don't Make Policy Decisions." (September-October 1967): 91. Wrapp refers to this as spotting opportunities and relationships in the stream of operating problems and decisions: in his article Wrapp raises a number of excellent points related to this analysis.

Selection No.

50 "Power, Dependence, and Effective Management" (Kotter, J.P.)

Banfield, E.C. *Political Influence.* New York: Free Press, 1965. Chapter IV.

French, J.R.P. and Raven, B. "The Base of Social Power." Cartwright and Zandler (Eds.), *Group Dynamics Research and Theory.* New York: Harper & Row, 1968. Chapter 20. These categories closely resemble the five developed by French and Raven.

McClelland, D.C. and Burham, D.H. "Power Is the Great Motivator." *HBR* (March-April 1976): 100.

Mintzberg, H. "The Manager's Job: Folklore and Fact." *HBR* (July-August 1975): 49.

Neustadt, R.E. *Presidential Power.* New York: John Wiley, 1960. An excellent discussion of this method.

Reich, C.A. *The Greening of America: How the Youth Revolution Is Trying to Make America Liveable.* New York: Random House, 1970.

Sayles, L.R. *Managerial Behaviors: Administration in Complex Organization.* New York: McGraw-Hill, 1964.

Stewart, R. *Managers and Their Jobs.* London: Macmillan, 1967.

Stewart, R. *Contrasts in Management.* London: McGraw-Hill, 1976.

Weber, M. *The Theory of Social and Economic Organization.* New York: Free Press, 1947. Three of the categories are similar to the types of "authority"-based power described by Weber.

Selection No.

51 "Participative Management: Quality vs. Quantity" (Miles, R.E. and Ritchie, J.B.)

Blankenship, L.V. and Miles, R.E. "Organization Structure and Management Decision Behavior." *Administrative Science Quarterly* (June 1968): 106.

Likert, R. *New Patterns of Management.* New York: McGraw-Hill, 1961.

Likert, R. *The Human Organization.* New York: McGraw-Hill, 1967.

McGregor, D. *The Human Side of Enterprise.* New York: McGraw-Hill, 1960.

McGregor, D. *The Professional Manager.* New York: McGraw-Hill, 1967.

Miles, R.E. "Human Relations or Human Resources?" *HBR* (July-August 1965): 149.

Miles, R.E. "The Affluent Organization." *HBR* (May-June 1966): 106.

Miles, R.E., Porter, L.W. and Craft, J.A. "Leadership Attitudes Among Public Health Officials." *American Journal of Public Health* (December 1966): 1990.

Ritchie, J.B. and Miles, R.E. "An Analysis of Quantity and Quality of Participation as Mediating Variables in the Participative Decision-Making Process." *Personnel Psychology* (Autumn 1970): 347. A more detailed analysis of these data.

Roberts, R.L., Blankenship, V. and Miles, R.E. "Organizational Leadership, Satisfaction, and Productivity: A Comparative Analysis." *Academy of Management Journal* (December 1968): 401.

Selection No.

52 "How to Choose a Leadership Pattern" (Tannenbaum, R. and Schmidt, W.H.)

Argyris, C. "Top Management Dilemma: Company Needs vs. Individual Development." *Personnel* (September 1955): 123-134.

McWhinney, W. "Phenomenarchy: A Suggestion for Social Redesign." *Journal of*

Applied Behavioral Science (May 1973). A description of phenomenarchy.

Moore, C. "Too Much Management, Too Little Change." *HBR* (January-February 1956): 41. A fuller explanation of this approach.

Schmidt, W.H. and Buchanan, P.C. *Techniques That Produce Teamwork.* New London, Conn.: Arthur C. Croft Publications, 1954.

Tannenbaum, R. and Massarik, F. "Participation by Subordinates in the Managerial Decision-Making Process." *Canadian Journal of Economics and Political Science* (August 1950): 413.

Viteles, M.S. *Motivation and Morale in Industry.* New York: W. W. Norton & Company, Inc., 1953.

Section 5
Selection No.

65 "Planned Change"(Dyer, W.)

Bennis, W.G., Benne, K. and Chin, R. *Planning and Change.* New York: Holt, Rinehart and Winston, Inc., 1969.

Coch, L. and French, J.R.P. "Overcoming Resistance to Change." *Human Relations* (1948): 512-532.

Dalton, G., Lawrence, P. and Greiner, L. *Organizational Changes and Development.* Homewood, Ill.: Irwin-Dorsey, 1970.

Lewin, K. "Group Decision and Social Change." In Macoby, Newcomb, and Hartly (Eds.), *Readings in Social Psychology.* New York: Henry Holt and Company, 1958. Pp. 197-212.

Lippitt, R., Watson, J. and Westley, B. *Dynamics of Planned Change.* New York: Harcourt Brace and World, Inc., 1958.

Selection No.

66 "Choosing Strategies for Change" (Kotter, J.B. and Schlesinger, L.A.).

Allen, S.A. "Organizational Choice and General Influence Networks for Diversified Companies." *Academy of Management Journal* (September 1978):

341. Recent evidence on the frequency of changes.

Argyrus, C. *Intervention Theory and Method.* Reading, Mass.: Addison-Wesley, 1970). P. 70.

Beer, M. *Organization Change and Development: A Systems View.* Pacific Palisades, Calif.: Goodyear, 1979.

Bower, M. and Walton, C.L., Jr. "Gearing a Business to the Future." In *Challenge to Leadership.* New York: The Conference Board, 1973. P. 126.

Drucker, P.F. *The Practice of Management.* New York: Harper & Row, 1954.

Greiner, L.E. "Patterns of Organization Change." *HBR* (May-June 1967): 119.

Greiner, L.E. and Barnes, L.B. "Organization Change and Development." In Dalton and Lawrence (Eds.), *Organizational Change and Development.* Homewood, Ill.: Irwin, 1970. P. 3.

Kotter, J.P. "Power, Dependence, and Effective Management." *HBR* (July-August 1977): 125, 135.

Lawrence, P.R. "How to Deal with Resistance to Change." *HBR* (May-June 1954): 49. Reprinted as *HBR* Classic (January-February 1969): 4.

Lorsch, J.W. "Managing Change." In Lawrence, Barnes, and Lorsch (Eds.), *Organizational Behavior and Administration.* Homewood, Ill.: Irwin, 1976. P. 676.

Luke, Robert A., Jr. "A Structural Approach to Organizational Change." *Journal of Applied Behavioral Science* (September-October 1973): 611.

Machiavelli, N. *The Prince*

Marrow, A.J., Bowers, D.F. and Seashore, S.E. *Management by Participation.* New York: Harper & Row, 1967.

Miles, R.H. *Macro Organizational Behavior.* Pacific Palisades, Calif.: Goodyear, 1978. Chapter 4. A discussion of power and politics in corporations.

Nierenberg, G.I. *The Art of Negotiating.* Birmingham, Ala.: Cornerstone, 1968.

An excellent discussion of negotiation.

Schein, E.H. *Organizational Psychology.* Englewood Cliffs, N.J.: Prentice-Hall, 1965). P. 44.

Tagiuri, R. "Notes on the Management of Change: Implication of Postulating a Need for Competence." In Kotter, Sathe, and Schlesinger (Eds.), *Organization.* Homewood, Ill.: Irwin, 1979. A good discussion of an approach that attempts to minimize resistance.

Watson, G. "Resistance to Change." In Bennis, Benne and Chin (Eds.), *The Planning of Change.* New York: Holt, Rinehart, and Winston, 1969. P. 489. A discussion of resistance that is personality based.

Zaleznik, A., deVries, K. and Manfred, F.R. *Power and the Corporate Mind.* Boston: Houghton-Mifflin, 1975. Chapter 6. A discussion of power and politics in corporations.

Zaltman, G. and Duncan, R. *Strategies for Planned Change.* New York: John Wiley, 1977. Chapters 3 and 4.

Selection No.

68   "Hard   Hats   in   the   Boardroom"(Woodworth, W.P.)

Coates, K. and Topham, T. "Participation of Control?" In K. Coates (Ed.), *Can the Workers Run Industry?* London: Sphere Books, 1968. Pp. 227–240.

Donahue, T. International Conference on Industrial and Labor Relations. Montreal, May 26, 1976.

Dujmovic, I. "Modern Management and Workers' Self-Management in Yugoslavia." Paper presented at the Second International Conference on the Economics of Workers' Self-Management, Istanbul, July 16–19, 1980 (mimeo).

Eide, R. and Ohman, B. *Economic Democracy Through Wage Earner Funds.* Stockholm: Arbetslivscentrum, 1980.

IDE (International Research Group.) "The Role of Formal Norms in the Introduction of Industrial Democracy." *Economic Analysis and Workers' Management.* Vol. 15, No. 3, 1981. Pp. 353–364.

Jenkins, D. "Beyond Job Enrichment: Workplace Democratization in Europe." *Working Papers for a New Society.* Vol. 2, No. 1, 1975. Pp. 51–57.

Johnson, A.G. and Whyte, W.F. "The Mondragon System of Worker Production Cooperatives." *Industrial and Labor Relations Review.* Vol. 31, No. 1, 1977. Pp. 18–30.

Kissler, L. and Sattel, U. "Codetermination in the Course of Time." Paper presented at the Tenth World Congress, International Sociological Association, Mexico City, August 16–21, 1982.

"The New Industrial Relations." *Business Week.* May 11, 1981, pp. 84–98.

Stokes, B. *Worker Participation — Productivity and the Quality of Working Life.* Washington, D.C.: Worldwatch Institute, 1978.

Terkel, S. *Working.* New York: Pantheon, 1974.

Woodworth, W.P. "Towards A Labor-Owned Economy in the United States." *Labour and Society.* Vol. G, No. 1, 1981. Pp 41–56.

Zwerdling, D. *Democracy at Work.* Washington, D.C.: Association for Workplace Democracy, 1978.

Selection No.

70   "Beyond Tokenism: Women as True Corporate Peers" (Schwertz, E.B. and Rago, J.J., Jr.).

Block, J.H. "Conceptions of Sex Role: Some Cross-Cultural and Longitudinal Perspectives." Bernard Moses Memorial Lecture, University of California at Berkeley, January, 1972. P. 28.

Connell, D.M. and Johnson, J.E. "Relationship Between Sex-Role Indentification and Self-Esteem in Early Adolescents. *Developmental Psychology* 3 (September 1970): 268.

Douvan, E. and Adelson, J. *The Ado-*

lescence Experience. New York: John Wiley & Sons, Inc., 1966.

Gray-Shelberg, L. et al. "Resolution of Career Conflicts: The Double Standard in Action." Paper presented at the Eightieth Annual Convention of the American Psychological Association, September, 1972. P. 3.

Hollender, J. "Sex Differences in Sources of Self-Esteem." *Journal of Consulting and Clinical Psychology* 38 (June 1972): 343–347.

Horner, M.S. "Fail: Bright Women." *Psychology Today* 3 (November 1969): 36–38.

Janov, A. *The Primal Scream.* New York: Dell Publishing Company, Inc., 1970.

Mead, M. *Male and Female: A Study of the Sexes in a Changing World.* New York: Dell Publishing Company, Inc., 1971.

Rokeach, M. *The Open and Closed Mind.* New York: Basic Books, Inc., 1960.

Schwarts, E.B. "Psychological Barriers to Increased Employment of Women." *Issues in Industrial Society* 2, No. 1 (1970): 60–73.

Subject Index

Name Index

497

†